♛ McKay Chess Library

Basic
Chess
Endings

Reuben Fine

Revised by Pal Benko

Random House
Puzzles & Games

Typeset and printed in the United States of America.

Library of Congress Cataloging-in-Publication data is available.

0 9 8 7 6 5 4 3 2 1

ISBN: 0-8129-3493-8

New York   Toronto   London   Sydney   Auckland

Dedicated

to the Memory of

Dr. Emanuel Lasker

FOREWORD

In the enormous sea of chess literature there are comparatively few books about the endgame, the third and final phase of the game. Among these books only several can be named as real chess classics. And outstanding among these classics is *Basic Chess Endings*, written in 1941 by Reuben Fine, one of the all-time chess greats.

The task of revising this valuable work for the next generations of players has been brilliantly accomplished by Pal Benko, an experienced grandmaster who twice qualified for the candidates' competitions for the world championship. It is important to add that Pal Benko is not only a noted expert in the field of endgames; he is also a famous chess composer who has contributed to the development of endgame theory. His own endgames visibly adorn this book and complement Reuben Fine's analysis.

Reuben Fine (1914–1993) was for a long time one of the top players in the world. Especially remarkable were his tournament successes from 1935 to 1938. He won or shared first place in the following international tournaments: Hastings 1935–36, Zaandvoort 1936, Oslo 1936, Amsterdam 1936, Stockholm 1937, Ostende 1937, and Margate 1937. In the strongest tournament held up to that time, AVRO 1938, he shared first place with Paul Keres.

Fine is the owner of a unique record. In 1937 he won two tournaments in a row in the USSR (Moscow and Leningrad), where, except for Botvinnik, all the best Soviet players competed. So far this result has not been surpassed by any foreign grandmaster.

As an author, Fine showed himself to be a brilliant analyst who understood the depth and all the particulars of the endgame. It is no exaggeration to say that *Basic Chess Endings* was the first systematic textbook on this phase of the game. Fine chose standard positions of various types and in many cases gave useful rules for practical play.

In this book, as in his other works, he revealed himself to be a natural teacher who, using skillfully selected examples, was able to acquaint the reader with all the basic ideas of the endgame. It is no accident that copies of *Basic Chess Endings* are owned by many generations of players, and not only in the English-speaking countries. Mikhail Botvinnik, for example, considered Fine's work the best book on the subject. My own research in this field was based on Fine's book.

Although as a textbook meant for the general chess public Fine's work has never become obsolete, it required deep revision. Pal Benko corrected or replaced some examples with more typical or more instructive ones. It was necessary to add new examples that took into account the latest achievements in chess theory and practice.

Since the original publication of *Basic Chess Endings*, chess theory and practice, including the endgame, have made gigantic progress. Thousands of interesting and instructive endings have been played. A number of monumental works have appeared in different languages, including English, concerning both the endgame on the whole and some particular types. New ideas have appeared and new ways of playing have been described.

But chess programs using computers made a genuine revolution. For instance, despite the opinion of theoreticians, it was established with the help of a computer that two bishops win against knight (no pawns). Some analyses of endings with queen and pawn versus queen were defined more precisely, and so on.

In 1954, when the match USA-USSR was held in New York, I had the pleasure of making the acquaintance of Reuben Fine. Naturally, our talk touched upon *Basic Chess Endings*. He told me that he found the work so fascinating that he completed it in four months—surely a record worthy of inclusion in the *Guinness Book of World Records*. From my own experience I know that to write such a book would take *years*.

Early in the 1990s, I gave an exhibition in the Manhattan Chess Club in New York City. There I met Reuben Fine for the last time. His hair had turned gray; he had grown old. True, we had not seen each other for about half a century. During our talk I asked him if he intended to prepare a new edition of *Basic Chess Endings*.

"Yes, it is my dream," he answered, "but I don't know if I have enough time."

I would like to congratulate the McKay Chess Library for making Fine's dream come true.

Grandmaster Yuri Averbakh

REVISER'S PREFACE

It is impossible to overemphasize the importance of the endgame. This is especially true in today's competitive chess with its faster time controls. A player who is not well equipped with basic endgame knowledge is liable to lose the fruit of even a well-played game.

Grandmaster Reuben Fine's classic book on the endgame was my compass when I started to play chess and continued to guide me after I became a master. Indeed, entire generations of chess players grew up on this great book. No wonder it has been called the bible of the endgame. This very practical and useful one-volume textbook, with its great many examples, explains the mysteries of the final phase of the game in plain language that can be read and enjoyed with profit by amateurs and masters alike.

I was honored to be asked to revise Fine's tremendous work, which had been first published in 1941 and had never been revised. For the most part I have left this great body of knowledge untouched, except to correct errors (unavoidable in such an enormous work) and to delete redundant and out-dated material. I have brought the book up to date as regards endgame theory and added new examples. Fortunately, basic endgame theory, unlike opening theory, has not changed much in the last half century, except in certain technical areas.

Converting the original chess notation from descriptive to algebraic, now the universally accepted system, has enabled a much clearer and more compact presentation of the text while preserving its authenticity. The conversion was professionally accomplished by Laszlo Lovass of Hungary.

Thanks to Burt Hochberg, who initiated and supervised this project and edited the manuscript.

I hope all new readers will learn from and enjoy this book as much as I have.

International Grandmaster Pal Benko
New York, March 2003

EDITOR'S PREFACE

A dozen or so years ago, in the performance of my duties as chess adviser to David McKay Company, I had the chutzpah to suggest that they publish a revised edition of Reuben Fine's massive masterwork *Basic Chess Endings*. Not surprisingly, given the project's projected costs in time and money, the proposal was turned down.

The present generation of McKay editors, to whom, despite my advancing years and decrepitude, I once again proposed a revision of *BCE*—this time with conversion of the old-fashioned descriptive notation to the modern algebraic system—leapt on the idea with alacrity. They were especially encouraged when I told them that one of the world's leading endgame experts, Grandmaster Pal Benko, was available to do the revision.

Grandmaster Benko and I met a few times in New York to discuss technical aspects of the project, and then he was off to Budapest, his original home town, where he lives part of the year. Six months later he reemerged in New York armed with the new manuscript, electronically encoded on a computer disc. For my use as backup, he gave me his densely annotated and well worn original hardcover copy of *Basic Chess Endings*, his constant companion throughout his chess career spanning more than half a century.

Editing such a work was a daunting challenge, not only because of its size and complexity (the original book ran to 573 jam-packed pages) but also because of its stature as one of the foundation-stones of chess literature. Who would dare to edit Beethoven's Ninth Symphony? Nevertheless, as readers familiar with the original edition are well aware, Fine's book was by no means error-free. Aside from various technical mistakes (hardly surprising in a such an ambitious undertaking and considering that Fine did not have access to the modern chess writer's best friend, the computer), the typography and the layout of the pages, designed to keep the book to a reasonable size, made great demands on the reader. The chess moves were rendered in an old-fashioned form of descriptive notation (e.g., Kt—B3, using Kt instead of N for knight and an em-dash instead of a hyphen) and in several fonts, including **boldface,** *italics,* and ***bold italics,*** all smushed together in interminable paragraphs laced with parentheses, brackets within parentheses, and parentheses within brackets. Diagrams were relatively few and you had to look hard to find the relevant analysis, which was sometimes on another page entirely.

Like Grandmaster Benko and most doctors, I have tried first of all to "do no harm." Thanks to his judicious pruning, I have been able to paragraph the text more sensibly, avoiding the need for too many fonts and parentheses while maintaining a reasonable page count. I have also placed each diagram where it belongs; that is, adjacent to the text it illustrates. For the most part, boldface type is used for the main line of an analysis or the actual moves of a game.

The editors at David McKay, which has published most of the major chess works in this country for a century, deserve the gratitude of chess players everywhere for deciding to publish this revision of a major classic. I thank, in particular, Sheryl Stebbins, Beth Levy, Jena Pincott, and Sandy Fein for putting up with delays and other obstacles in their steadfast determination to get the job done. Grandmaster Arthur Bisguier's help in checking for errors was invaluable. Mike Klein copyedited this enormous manuscript with enthusiasm and dedication and with full awareness of the book's importance.

To you, dear reader: May all your games end well.

Burt Hochberg
New York, March 2003

INTRODUCTION

Reuben Fine (1941)[1]

The great importance of the ending has often been recognized, especially in recent years. Yet even masters have had to learn practically everything from bitter experience because the standard material available has been scattered in a thousand different, and often inaccessible, places.

Because of the lack of similar material, I have tried to do two things in this work. In the first place the standard positions which come up time and again have been given at great length. Every experienced player simply must know these: they are as indispensable to further proficiency in the endings as a knowledge of the scales is to the performance of a symphony in music, or the mastery of the alphabet to the reading of novels. In the second place I have at the same time tried to make this a useful book of instruction for the more advanced phases of the ending. With this in mind I have given a large number of rules which are at times incorrect from a strictly mathematical point of view, but are nevertheless true by and large and are of the greatest practical value.

The diagrams and their discussion form the bulk of the book. To facilitate reading and reference the solutions have been printed in bold face type, thus setting them off from the rest of the text. Examples and illustrations which are not diagrammed will be of value chiefly to the student who wishes to perfect his knowledge of any branch of the endgame.

While it is manifestly impossible to present more than a small portion of the endings which come up in practical play, I have tried to solve this problem by the use of *typical positions*. Illustrations taken from master games have been selected only because they are representative of large numbers of similar endings.

Consequently, to use the material given here in the analysis of any particular ending, one must first examine that ending to see what category it will fit into and then compare it with the appropriate position or positions. The endings have been classified first according to the kind of material on the board, then according to the amount, and finally according to the nature of the Pawn position. However, in endings with more than three Pawns on each side, the amount of material is usually irrelevant and has not been consid-

---

[1] This is Grandmaster Fine's original introduction, exactly as it appeared in the first edition.

ered. Thus, to find an ending with Rook and two Pawns vs. Rook and one Pawn, one must consult the appropriate part of the chapter on Rook and Pawn endings, where cases with exactly the same number of Pawns are given. But in an ending with Rook and seven Pawns vs. Rook and six Pawns, one must turn to the part on material advantage in Rook and Pawn endings, and then to the section where that particular type of Pawn position is discussed. While space limitations have unfortunately made it impossible to present more complicated cases where both sides have many pieces, the principles and rules given are equally applicable to all endings.

Only two special symbols have been used. "White" and "Black," where they do not refer to any specific players, denote the superior and inferior sides, respectively. E.g., in endings with R vs. Kt, the side with the Rook is always "White," the side with the Knight always "Black." This facilitates general discussion. The "=" sign has been used to denote a drawn position, rather than mere general equality.

TABLE OF CONTENTS

Chapter I

THE ELEMENTARY MATES

In this chapter we shall consider pieces checkmating a lone king.

The minimum material required in general is either a) one queen; b) one rook; c) two bishops; d) bishop and knight. With two knights a mating position is possible but cannot be forced. Against one knight or one bishop the defender cannot lose even if he tries.

In most cases, however, two knights can force checkmate when the defender has one or more pawns (see Chapter III). Similarly, in certain special positions bishop or knight vs. pawn or pawns can mate.

To checkmate, White must drive the Black king to the edge of the board. A queen or rook can then administer the coup de grace anywhere along the last rank or file, but with bishop and knight or two bishops or three knights, the king must be chased into the corner.

1. THE QUEEN

Before proceeding with the exact moves in this and the other cases, we will identify the final mating positions we are trying to obtain. With the queen, there are basically two types of mate: **White king at d6; Black king at d8, a) Qd7, b) Qa8 (or b8, f8, g8, or h8).** The mate can be forced in at most ten moves from any position, but it usually requires fewer.

White to play mates in 9

In **No. 1**, nine moves are needed. **1. Kb2! Kd5 2. Kc3 Ke5** (or 2. ... Ke6 3. Kd4 Kf6 4. Qe4 Kf7 5. Ke5! Kg7 6. Kf5 Kf7 7. Qb7+ Ke8 8. Ke6 Kf8 9. Qf7+ mate) **3. Qg6 Kf4** (or 3. ... Kd5 4. Qe8 Kd6 5. Kc4 Kc7 6. Kc5 Kb7 7. Qd7+ Ka6 8. Qe7! Ka5 9. Qa7+ mate, but here not 8. Qc7?? stalemate!) **4. Kd4 Kf3 5. Qg5 Kf2** (or 5. ... Ke2 6. Qg2+) **6. Qg4 Ke1 7. Ke3 Kf1 8. Qg7** (again not 8. Qg3?? stalemate) **8. ... Ke1 9. Qg1+,** or **9. Qa1+** mate.

There are two types of stalemate to watch for (Black to play in both cases):

1. Black king at a8, White king at a6, queen at c7 or b6 (and similarly for the other three corners);

2. Black king at a6, White king at c5, queen at c7.

2. THE ROOK

There is only one type of mating position with the rook, although it may occur on any square on the edge of the board. The mate position is: **White king at b6, rook at h8 (or g8, f8, e8, d8); Black king at b8.** The mate requires no more than 16 moves, although in most cases it can be done much more quickly.

No. 2

White to play mates in 15

This position corresponds to the previous one: **1. Kb2 (or 1. Re1) Kd4 2. Kb3 (or 2 Re1) Kd5 3. Re1! Kd4! 4. Kb4! Kd5 5. Kc3! Kc5 6.Rd1! Kb5 7. Rd5+ Kc6 8. Kc4! Kb6 9. Rd6+ Kc7 10. Kc5! Kb7! 11. Rd7+ Kc8 12. Kc6! Kb8 13. Re7 Ka8 14. Kb6 Kb8 15. Re8+ mate.** Again, with the White rook at b2 in the diagram, one more move is necessary.

The most common stalemate is: **White king at c6, rook at b7; Black king at a8**. The only other possibility is: **White king at c8, rook at h7 (or anywhere else along the seventh rank); Black king at a8.**

3. TWO BISHOPS

This mate requires driving the king into a corner. The final position will then be: **White king at c7, bishops at b6, e4 (h1, g2, f3, d5, c6, b7); Black king at a8**. Or **White king at c7, bishops at b7, c5 (b6, d4, e3, f2, g1); Black king at a7**. Checkmate requires at most 18 moves.

No. 3

White to play mates in 18

In **No. 3** the maximum number of moves is needed. **1. Bc8** (1. Bh3 is also good) **Ke5 2. Kb2! Kd4 3. Bb7** (Bf2+ is also good) **Ke5 4. Kc3! Kf4 5. Kd4! Kg4 6. Bd8 Kf5 7. Bc8+! Kf4 8. Bc7+! Kg5 9. Ke5! Kg6 10. Ke6! Kg5 11. Kf7! Kh4 12. Kf6 Kh5 13. Bg3! Kh6 14. Bg4! Kh7 15. Kf7! Kh8 16. Bh5** (or Bf4) **Kh7 17. Bg6+ Kh6 18. Bf4+** mate.

4. BISHOP AND KNIGHT

This is the most difficult case. The king must be driven into a corner the same color as the bishop. The mating position is: **White king at b6, knight at a6, bishop at e4: Black king at a8;** or **White king at b6, bishop at b7, knight at a6 (d7); Black king at b8.** Two other mating positions are possible but cannot be forced. In an unfavorable position the mate may require over 30 moves.

No. 4

White to play mates in 19

No. 4 is the basic position, where the first problem is to chase the king to the other side.

1. Bf5 Kf8 2. Bh7! Ke8 3. Ne5 Kd8

Better than 3. ... Kf8 4. Nd7+ Ke8 5. Ke6 Kd8 6. Kd6 Ke8 7. Bg6+ Kd8 8. Nc5 Kc8 9. Bd3 Kd8 10. Bb5 Kc8 11. Bd7+ Kb8 12. Kc6 Ka7 13. Kc7 Ka8 14. Kb6 Kb8 15. Na6+ Ka8 16. Bc6+ mate.

4. Ke6

4. Be4 is also good and leads to similar variations: 4. Be4 Kc7 5. Nc4 Kd7 6. Kf7 Kd8 7. Bc6 Kc7 8. Bb5 Kd8 9. Ke6 Kc8 10. Kd6 Kd8 11. Na5 Kc8 12. Bd7+ Kb8 13. Kc6 Ka7 14. Nb7 Ka6 15. Kc7 Ka7 16. Bb5 Ka8 17. Nd6 Ka7 18. Nc8+ Ka8 19. Bc6+ mate.

4. ... Kc7

Or 4. ... Kc8 5. Nd7 Kb7 6. Bd3 Kc8 7. Bb5 Kd8 8. Nc5 and continues as in the note to Black's 3rd move.

5. Nd7 Kb7

Or 5. ... Kc6 6. Bd3! and now:

a) 6. ... Kc7 7. Bb5 Kc8 8. Kd6 Kd8 9. Nc5 Kc8 10. Bd7+ and this is familiar from the note to Black's 3rd move.

b) 6. ... Kb7 7. Kd6 Kc8 8. Nc5 Kb8 (or 8. ... Kd8 9. Bb5 as above) 9. Kd7 Ka7 10. Kc7 Ka8 11. Kb6 Kb8 12. Ba6 and mates in two: 12. ... Ka8 13. Bb7+ Kb8 14. Nd7+.

6. Bd3 Kc6 7. Ba6 Kc7 8. Bb5 Kd8 9. Nb6 Kc7 10. Nd5+ Kd8 11. Kd6 Kc8 12. Ke7 Kb7 13. Kd7 Kb8 14. Ba6 Ka7 15. Bc8 Kb8 16. Ne7 Ka7 (or 16. ... Ka8 17. Kc7 Ka7 18. Nc6+ Ka8 19. Bb7+ mate) **17. Kc7 Ka8 18. Bb7+** (not 18. Nc6?? stalemate!) **18. ... Ka7 19. Nc6 (c8)+** mate.

5. TWO KNIGHTS

Either side to play draws

Mate cannot be forced if Black is unwilling; e.g., a) **1. ... Kh8 2. Nf7+ Kg8 3. Nh6+ Kh8 4. Ng5** stalemate; b) **1. Nc4 Kh8 2. Ne5 Kg8 3. Nd7** (or 3. Nf7 stalemate) **3. ... Kh8 4. Ng5 Kg8 5. Nf6+ Kf8!** etc. (not 5. ... Kh8?? 6. Nf7+ mate).

Chapter II

KING AND PAWN ENDINGS

The pawn, as Philidor put it, is the soul of chess, and we can add that in the ending it is also nine-tenths of the body. All endgame play revolves around pawns: how to evaluate their placement, how to maneuver with them, when to exchange them. Positions without pawns occur very rarely, and when they do they are usually of a simple character. Endings with pieces not only require a knowledge of correct pawn play, but also demand an evaluation of the corresponding pawn ending in order to be able to answer the question of whether to exchange or not.

In view of this, the present chapter is in every way fundamental. Fortunately, a good deal of work has been done on the subject, allowing you to acquire a grasp of everything you need for practical play. Remember, too, that 95 percent of the endings that come up are subject to exact calculation. We have classified the endings in this chapter quantitatively; i.e., according to the number of pawns for each player. Always keep in mind that, in materially even positions, unusual circumstances must prevail in order to win, or to draw (or win) when a pawn behind.

There are three basic concepts that we will refer to time and again: opposition, triangulation, and gaining a tempo. Readers who are unfamiliar with these should first turn to Parts IX and X of this chapter.

I. KING AND PAWN VS. KING

The problem in **No. 6** is whether the pawn can queen or not. If the Black king cannot catch the pawn, it can queen and we have an elementary win. There's a simple way to determine whether the Black king can reach the queening file.

Rule of the Square: Mentally draw a square on the board, using the distance from the pawn to the eighth rank as the side of the square. If the pawn is on the second rank, draw the square from the third rank, as shown, assuming a two-square first move by the White pawn.

If the Black king is inside this square with White to move, or can reach it with Black to move, then he can stop the pawn. If not, the pawn promotes and Black loses, as in **No. 8**.

No. 6

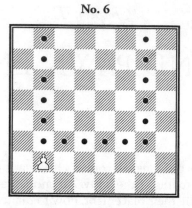

Draw if Black can move inside the square.
White wins if Black cannot move inside the square.

When the Black king is on the queening file or can reach it, the win depends on whether or not White can drive the Black king off the file. This in turn depends on who has the opposition.

There are two basic positional types here: one with the White king behind his pawn, the other with the White king in front of it. In the first case, **No. 7**, the game is always a draw because Black never has to relinquish the opposition.

No. 7

White to play. Draw

Thus: **1. d5+ Kd6 2. Kd4 Kd7 3. Ke5 Ke7 4. d6+ Kd7 5. Kd5 Kd8!** (essential)
6. Ke6 Ke8 7. d7+ Kd8 8. Kd6 stalemate. Note that Black can never lose if he

always moves straight back (keeping the opposition). For instance, if he plays 5. ... Ke8?? (diagonally instead of vertically or straight back), he will be forced to abandon the queening square after 6. Ke6 Kd8 7. d7 Kc7 8. Ke7, when White's long-thwarted pawn realizes all its ambitions.

In the second case (White king in front of the pawn) the result depends on the relative king positions. In **No. 8**, White wins with or without the move:

No. 8

White wins

1. e3 (now he has the opposition) **1. ... Kd6 2. Kf5 Kd7 3. Kf6 Kd8 4. e4 Kd7 5. e5 Ke8 6. Ke6** (again securing the opposition; 6. e6?? Kf8 only draws) **6. ... Kd8 7. Kf7** and the pawn queens. Or **1. ... Kf6 2. Kd5 Ke7 3. Ke5,** etc., as above.

The rule is that if the White king is two or more squares in front of its pawn White always wins; if it is one square in front of it, White wins only if he has the opposition. Thus in **No. 9: White king at e4, pawn at e3; Black king at e6.** White to play draws, but Black to play loses. One important exception must be noted: when the White king is on the sixth rank White always wins regardless of whose move it is.

The above discussion does not apply to the rook-pawn, which is always a draw if the Black king can reach c8/f8, b8/g8, or a8/h8. In **No. 10A** the Black king can never be driven out of the corner, while in **No. 10B** the White king has the pleasant choice of stalemating either himself or his opponent.

No. 10

A Draw B

For instance, **No. 10B: 1. h6 Kf7 2. Kh8 Kf8 3. h7 Kf7** stalemate; or **1. Kg6 Kg8 1. h6 Kh8 2. h7** stalemate. A simple rule to remember in rook-pawn endings is that if Black's king can reach b8/g8 Black draws, but if White's king can reach b7/g7 he wins.

II. KING AND PAWN VS. KING AND PAWN

Although all wins here are special cases, some are also of vital practical importance. There are four reasons White may be able to win: 1. White queens first but one of the drawn queen vs. pawn endings (rook-pawn or bishop-pawn) does not ensue. 2. White queens with check. 3. Both sides queen but White mates or wins the queen. 4. White wins the pawn and the Black king cannot get back in time, or the Black king can reach the queening file but White retains the opposition.

1. White Queens First

Ordinarily this is quite simple. The White pawn promotes and captures the Black pawn fairly quickly. A Black rook pawn or bishop pawn on the seventh rank can usually draw, however. For a full discussion see Chapter VIII.

The task can be quite complicated when Black's pawn is far advanced. In **No. 11**, if Black's king can reach e2, which it might do by gaining a tempo with an attack on the White pawn, a draw would result.

No. 11, H. Rinck 1922

White to play wins

The solution is **1. a4 Kb3 2. a5 Kc3** (if 2. ... Kc4 3. a6 Kd3 4. a7 f2 5. a8=Q f1=Q 6. Qa6+) **3. Kg1!!** (but not 3. a6? Kd2!! 4. a7 f2 5. Kg2 Ke2 =, or 3. Kg3? Kd4!! 4. a6 Ke3 5. a7 f2 =) **3. ... Kd4 4. a6 Ke3 5. Kf1!** and the White pawn queens while the Black one is blockaded.

Note that the White king must be able to actually occupy the queening square in time; with the White king originally at h3 the ending would have been drawn. An example is **No. 12** (Réti 1922): **White king at h8, pawn at c6; Black king at a6, pawn at h5.** White to play. Draw. The solution: **1. Kg7 h4 2. Kf6 Kb6** (or 2. ... h3 3. Ke7 h2 4. c7 =) **3. Ke5!! h3 4. Kd6** and both pawns promote. With Black's king originally on a7 (compare the Rinck study), Black reaches c8 in time and wins.

2. White Queens With Check

Generally, this requires no special elaboration; it merely reduces to a queen vs. pawn ending. But sometimes it is necessary for White to maneuver the Black king into a position where it will be checked by the new queen.

No. 13, P. Benko 1973

White to play wins

1. a4! (1. Kd5? Kf4 2. Ke6 Ke4 3. a4 Kd4 =; or 1. Kd4? Kf4 2. a4 e5+ 3. Kc3 e4 4. a5 e3 5. a6 Kg3! =) **1. ... e5 2. a5 e4 3. Kd4! Kf4 4. a6 e3 5. Kd3! Kf3 6. a7 e2 7. a8=Q+ wins.**

No. 14 (Ljubojevic-Browne, 1972): **White king at a5, pawn at b3; Black king at c6, pawn at f7.** Black to play. **1. ... f5? 2. Kb4! f4 3. Kc4, =,** as in the game, but Black can win by **1. ... Kd5! 2. b4** (if 2. Kb4 Kd4 3. Ka3 f5 4. Kb2 f4 5. Kc2 Ke3 wins) **2. ... f5 3. b5 f4 4. b6 Kc6 5. Ka6 f3** and wins.

3. Both Sides Queen; White Mates or Wins the Queen

We have already seen examples of this, where the Black queen is born but to die. There is one important ending where both sides queen and White can then mate.

No. 15, P. Benko 2000

White to play wins

1. Ke5! (if 1. e4? Kf2! 2. Ke5 Kg3!, =) **1. ... Kf2 2. Kf4! h5 3. e4 Kg2 4. e5** (4. Kg5? Kg3 5. Kxh5 Kf4, =) **4. ... h4 5. e6 h3 6. e7 h2 7. e8=Q h1=Q 8. Qe2+ Kg1 9. Kg3** wins.

Less common is **No. 16** (P. Benko 1998): **White king at e8, pawns at b4, e7; Black king at a7, pawn at b3**. White to play wins. **1. Kd8! b2 2. e8=Q b1=Q 3. Qa4+ Kb6 4. Qa5+ Kc6 5. Qc5+ Kb7 6. Qb5+ Ka7 7. Kc8!** (threatening 8. Qb7 or Qa5 mate) **7. ... Qc2+ 8. Qc5+** wins.

4. White Captures the Pawn

This is a win, of course, but only if the Black king, after capturing the pawn, is too far away, or if the White king retains the opposition. An example of the first is **No. 17: White king at f7, pawn at a6; Black king at b2, pawn at a7.** White to play wins. **1. Ke6 Kc3 2. Kd5!!** (but not 2. Kd6 Kd4 3. Kc6 Ke5 4. Kb7 Kd6 5. Kxa7 Kc7 =) **2. ... Kb4** (2. ... Kd3 3. Kc6 Ke4 4. Kb7 Kd5 5. Kxa7 Kc6 6. Kb8) **3. Kc6 Ka5 4. Kb7 Kb5 5. Kxa7 Kc6 6. Kb8** and wins.

Or a similar example, **No. 18** (Dobias 1926): **White king at e4, pawn at f2; Black king at b5, pawn at g6.** White to play wins. **1. Kd4!! Kc6 2. Ke5! Kc5 3. f4! Kc4 4. Kf6 Kd4 5. Kxg6,** etc. But here if 1. Kd5? Kb4! 2. Kd4 Kb3! 3. f4 Kc2, =, or 1. Kf4? Kc4 2. Kg5 Kd5 3. Kxg6 Ke4! 4. Kg5 Kf3, =.

Another example is **No. 19** (Grigoriev 1925): **White king at g8, pawn at a2; Black king at g6, pawn at a3.** White to play. Draw. **1. Kh8!!** (but not 1. Kf8?, Kf6! and the White king does not get back to c2) **1. ... Kf5 2. Kg7 Ke4 3. Kf6 Kd3 4. Ke5 Kc2 5. Kd4 Kb2 6. Kd3 Kxa2 7. Kc2.**

No. 20 shows the most common cases where both kings are near the pawns.

No. 20

A: White-wins B: Draw

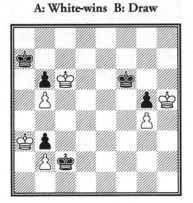

C: Whoever moves loses

In **20A**, Black to play has to abandon the pawn at once; White to play must first play **1. Kc7.** Then after **1. ... Ka8 2. Kxb6** we are back to No. 8. In **20B**, the game is drawn because Black can keep the opposition: **1. Kh6 Kf7 2. Kxg5 Kg7** and nothing can be done.

The same type of draw works if we move all the pieces and pawns back one or two ranks, but not if we move them up one rank, since that gives No. 20A. In **20C**, whoever moves must lose his pawn, after which he cannot even get to the queening file. For example: 1. ... **Kd3 2. Kxb3 Kd4 3. Kb4 Kd5 4. Kb5 Kd6 5. Kb6 Kd7 6. Kb7 Kd6 7. b4 Kd5 8. b5**, etc.

Various applications of these ideas occur time and again. In **No. 21**, for example (see No. 20C): **White king at g4, pawn at e3; Black king at c3, pawn at e4.** Whoever moves wins. **1. Kf5!** (but not 1. Kf4?? Kd3! and Black wins) **1. ... Kd3 2. Kf4.**

Or **No. 22**: **White king at b7, pawn at e4; Black king at h7, pawn at e6.** White to play wins. **1. e5!** (but not 1. Kc6 Kg6 2. Kd7? Kf6 3. Kd6 e5 4. Kd5 Kf7!, =, see No. 20B) **1. ... Kg6 2. Kc6 Kg5! 3. Kd7! Kf5 4. Kd6** and wins; see No. 20C.

Or **No. 23** (see 20A): **White king at b2, pawn at e3; Black king at a4, pawn at e4.** Black to play wins. **1. ... Kb4** (with the opposition) **2. Kc2 Kc4 3. Kd2 Kb3 4. Ke2 Kc2 5. Kf2 Kd2**, etc.

Or, finally, **No. 24** (Kling and Horwitz 1851): **White king at e6, pawn at e2; Black king at e8, pawn at e7.** White to play. Draw. **1. e3** (or 1. e4 Kd8 2. Kf7 e5! =, see 20B) **1. ... Kd8 2. e4** (2. Kf7 Kd7! 3. e4 Kd6 =) **2. ... Ke8 3. e5 Kd8 4. Kf7 Kd7** and now **5. Kf8** draws, but **5. e6+?? Kd6!** loses (see 20C).

Where the pawns are on adjoining files a sacrificial drawing combination is sometimes available.

No. 25, P. Benko

White to play draws

1. Kf2 Ke6 2. c6! bxc6 3. Ke2! Kd6 4. Kd2 Kd5 5. Kd3, draw by opposition.

No. 26 (Dedrle 1921): **White king at c2, pawn at b2; Black king at f6, pawn at a4.** White to play wins. **1. Kb1! a3! 2. b3!** (not 2. b4) **Ke6 3. Ka2 Kd5 4. Kxa3 Kc5 5. Ka4 Kb6 6. Kb4**, and White has the opposition.

III. KING AND TWO PAWNS VS. KING

This is a win unless the Black king can capture both pawns or can capture one and stop the other (a defense that is rarely possible). It is important to consider the following points in play with two pawns.

1. *Connected passed pawns* should be kept one rank apart until the enemy king approaches. If the back pawn is captured, the front one queens. If neither pawn is captured, one of them will be escorted by its king to the eighth rank. There is only one special case that presents any difficulty:

No. 27

White to play wins ·

Here the win can be achieved only by sacrificing the a-pawn at the proper moment; i.e., when it will permit the White king to occupy a6 or c6. **1. Kd5 Ka8 2. Kc5 Kb7 3. a8=Q+ Kxa8 4. Kc6 Kb8 5. b7 Ka7 6. Kc7** and mates in three.

2. *Doubled passed pawns* should not both be advanced. The extra pawn is decisive only because it furnishes a vital tempo at the critical moment.

No. 28

White to play wins

1. Kd2 Kb6 2. Kd3! Kc6 3. Kc4 Kb6 4. b5 Ka5 5. b6! Kxb6 6. Kb4 and wins.

When the pawns are on the fifth and sixth ranks, a win cannot be forced. An example is **No. 29: White king at f5, pawns at e5, e6; Black king at e7.** Black to play. Draw. **1. ... Ke8! 2. Kf6 Kf8 3. e7+ Ke8,** and now the only tempo move, **4. e6,** stalemates.

Two (or more) rook-pawns always draw.

3. *Unconnected passed pawns*, unless they are very far apart, must be supported by the king as soon as convenient. Also, unless one can queen by force they should be kept on the same rank.

No. 30

A	B
Black to play,	If the White
White wins	king is not near,
	both pawns can
	be captured

Pawns that are one file apart, as in **No. 30A,** can mutually defend one another. After **1. ... Ka5 2. c5!** or **1. ... Kc5 2. a5!,** White's king can approach and escort one pawn to the eighth. With White's pawn at a2 instead of a4, **1. ... Kc5** draws. Again, with both pawns on the fourth rank, Black moves **1. ... Kb7,** and if then **2. a5? Ka6** or **2. c5? Kc6!,** and a pawn is lost. The pawns must be kept on the same rank.

Pawns two files apart, as in **No. 30B,** win unaided if they are on the fifth (White to move), sixth, or seventh rank (either side to move), and can mutually defend one another if they are both on the second. To win, they require the support of the king if they are on the third, fourth, or fifth (Black to play attacks one of the pawns). In **No. 30B,** if the White king is at a1 and cannot move away, the game is drawn: **1. h5 Kf6! 2. h6 Kg6,** or **2. e5+ Kxe5** and Black has time to capture both pawns. The same is true when the pawns are on the third rank. But when they are on the second rank, neither can be captured because the other one could then advance two squares and be beyond the reach of the enemy king. However, it would be fatal for either pawn to move before the White king has come to assist. When the pawns are on the fifth rank (White to play), one must queen.

For example, in No. 30B move everything up one rank to get **No. 31: White pawns at e5, h5; Black king at e6.** White to play wins. **1. h6 Kf7 2. e6+ Kg6 3. e7,** etc. But Black to play could afford to capture the e-pawn and still get to the other pawn in time. Obviously, when the pawns are on the sixth or seventh rank, one of them queens by force even if Black has time to capture the other one.

Pawns that are three files apart queen by force unless they are both on the third or fourth rank and Black to move can capture one of them. But again, if they are not on the same rank this may not hold. For example, **No. 32: White pawns at d4, h2; Black king at d6.** Black to play. Draw. **1. ... Kd5** enables Black to capture the d-pawn and still stay in the square of the h-pawn.

Pawns that are four or more files apart promote in any position without the aid of the king; assuming they are kept on the same rank.

IV. KING AND TWO PAWNS VS. KING AND PAWN

This is generally a win, but there are quite a few exceptions. We classify the cases according to the nature of White's pawns.

Case 1. Two Connected Passed Pawns

The White pawns defend each other at, for instance, e4 and d5 (or in any similar diagonal position), while the White king has time to gobble up the remaining Black pawn. But if the Black pawn is beyond the reach of the White king the outcome depends on how soon White can force a queen.

No. 33

White to play wins

1. Ke6 h2 2. d7+ Kc7 (if 2. ... Kd8 3. Kd6 h1=Q 4. c7+ mates) **3. Ke7 h1=Q 4. d8=Q+ Kxc6 5. Qa8+** wins.

Case 2. Two Unconnected Passed Pawns

This is essentially the same as king and two pawns vs. king (see No. 30 and discussion) unless White's king must lose valuable time to stop the Black pawn, or unless the White king cannot catch the Black pawn at all, in which case the outcome depends on who queens first. Sometimes Black can afford to get out of the square of a passed pawn in order to help his own pawn promote. For example:

No. 34

Black to play. Draw

Black draws by **1. ... Kg4! 2. d6** (this would win if there were no Black pawn) **2. ... Kg3! 3. d7 f2 4. Ke2 Kg2 5. d8=Q f1=Q+.** Had White been able to bring his king to f1 he would have won.

In the above two cases White wins without any trouble except for a few problem positions. This is not so in the remaining cases, which are therefore more interesting.

Case 3. One Passed Pawn

A. Pawns Are Separated

Normally this is a simple win. White uses his passed pawns as a decoy to lure the Black king away from the other side and captures Black's pawn. The ensuing ending with king and pawn vs. king is routine. This illustrates the well-known "outside passed pawn."

The more complicated examples in this case occur only when the pawns are one file apart, so the White king must do considerable maneuvering.

No. 35, Berger

Whit to play wins

In **No. 35**, the correct continuation is **1. Ka3! Kb6! 2. Kb2! Ka5 3. Kb3 Kb6 4. Kc3 Ka5 5. Kd2! Ka4 6. Ke3 Ka3 7. Ke4 Ka4 8. Kd5 Kb4 9. a3+**. Note that after 1. Kb3 Ka5 2. Kc3? Ka4 White can only draw, for if 3. Kb2 Kb4, or if 3. Kd3 Kb4! 4. a3+ Kxa3 5. Ke4 Kb3! 6. Kd3 (but 6. Kd5? Kb4! Black wins) 6. ... Kb4, etc.

With center pawns White can sometimes win only by choosing the right moment to sacrifice his pawn.

No. 36, Berger

White to play wins

In **No. 36** the main variation is **1. Ke4** (faster is 1. Kc4 Ke5 2. d4+ Kxf5 3. d5, etc.) **1. ... Kc5 2. d4+ Kd6 3. Ke3** (White wants to play 3. Kd3 only when the Black king is at d5, for otherwise Black could reach e4) **3. ... Kc6 4. Kd2 Kd6 5. Kc3 Kc6 6. Kc4 Kd6 7. d5 Kd7** (or 7. ... Ke5 8. Kc5 Kxf5 9. d6 Ke6 10. Kc6) **8. Kc5 Kc7 9. d6+ Kd8! 10. d7!! Kxd7 11. Kd5,** and White has the opposition, which is decisive here since he captures the pawn on the sixth rank.

In **No. 37** (Berger): **White king at d5, pawns at d3, f6; Black king at d7, pawn at f7.** White to play draws. White's lack of elbow room saves the day for Black. The d-pawn can only be sacrificed on the seventh, when White's having the opposition is useless. But with the pawn at d2 instead of d3, White has an extra tempo and wins by attacking the f-pawn: **1. Ke5 Kc6 2. Kf5 Kd6 3. Kg5 Ke5 4. d3! Ke6 5. d4 Kd5 6. Kh6 Kxd4 7. Kg7,** etc.

Again, in some cases a draw is possible when the king is behind the passed pawn. An example is **No. 38** (Rabinovich): **White king at e2, pawns at c4, e3; Black king at f5, pawn at c5.** White to play. Draw. **1. Kf3 Ke5 2. e4** (or 2. Ke2 Ke4 3. Kd2 Ke5 4. Kd3 Kf5 5. e4+ Kf4!) **2. ... Kd4!!** (not 2. ... Ke6?? 3. Kf4 Kf6 4. e5+ Ke6 5. Ke4, etc.) **3. Kf4 Kxc4 4. e5 Kb3!!** (again not 4. ... Kd5? 5. Kf5 c4 6. e6 c3 7. e7 c2 8. e8=Q c1=Q 9. Qd7+ Kc5 10. Qc7+) **5. e6 c4 6. e7 c3 7. e8=Q c2,** and the c-pawn draws (See No. 1026).

The next example is the only other important exception to the general rule that an outside passed pawn with one remaining set of pawns always wins.

No. 39

White to play. Draw.
Win with White pawn at h5, Black pawn at h6

The Black king has time to capture the a-pawn and return to f8, when the draw is clear: **1. Kc4 Ka5 2. Kd5 Kxa4 3. Ke5 Kb5 4. Kf5 Kc6 5. Kg5 Kd7 6. Kxh5 Ke8 7. Kg6 Kf8**. With the White pawn at h5 or h6 White wins, since his king can occupy g7; with the Black pawn at h4 or h3 the game is still a draw.

In **No. 40** (P. Benko): **White king at b1, pawns at a2, h6; Black king at a3, pawn at h7**. White to play wins: **1. Ka1 Ka4 2. Kb2 Kb4 3. a3+ Ka4 4. Ka2 Ka5 5. Kb3 Kb5 6. Kc3** wins because Black cannot get back in time.

No. 41, Bayer 1911

White wins

Although there is a set of a-pawns White can force the win: **1. Kd4 Kd6 2. c5+ Kc6 3. Kc4 Kc7 4. Kd5 Kd7 5. c6+ Kc7 6. Kc5 Kc8 7. Kd6 Kd8 8. c7+ Kc8 9. Kc6 a5 10. Kb6 a4 11. a3** and Black must abandon the queening square. If Black had played a5, White would have countered with a4 and then won the pawn: **1. Kd4 a5 2. a4 Kd6 3. c5+ Kc7 4. Kd5 Kd7 5. c6+ Kc8 6. Kc5 Kb8** (or 6. ... Kc7 7. Kb5 Kd6 8. Kb6) **7. Kb6**.

Two other variants of this ending are **No. 42** (Grigoriev) and **No. 43** (from a game Fahrni-Alapin).

No. 42

Black to play. Draw.
White to play wins

Black forces his opponent to waste a priceless pawn tempo: **1. ... Kf7! 2. Kg5 Ke6! 3. h3** (or 3. h4 Kf7 4. Kf5 Kf8! 5. Ke6 Ke8 6. h5 Kf8 7. f7 h6, draw.) **3. ... Kf7 4. Kf5 Ke8! 5. Ke6 Kf8 6. h4** (or 6. f7 h6 7. Kf6 h5! 8. Kg6 h4 =) **6. ... Ke8** (Black must not move the pawn) **7. h5 Kf8 8. Ke5 Kf7 9. Kf5 Ke8! 10. Ke6 Kf8 11. f7 h6**, draw.

No. 43

White to play wins

White wins with a triangulation maneuver by which he is able to reach the diagram position with Black to move: **1. Kd5 Kc8 2. Kc4 Kb8** (or 2. ... Kd8) **3. Kd4!** (the key move) **3. ... Kc8 4. Kd5 Kc7** (or 4. ... Kd8 5. Kd6 and White has the opposition) **5. Kc5 K any 6. Kb6**, winning the a-pawn.

In fact, this ending always wins, except for the special case mentioned in No. 39. For example, even with the Black king relatively well placed, a conclusive sacrifice will still be available: **No. 44: White king at c2, pawns at a4, c3; Black king at c4, pawn at a5**. White to play wins. **1. Kb2 Kc5 2. Kc1! Kd5** (2. ... Kc4 3. Kc2 and proceeds as in the main variation. Note that White triangulates in order to get to the original position with Black to play) **3. Kd2 Ke4** (3. ... Kc5 4. Kd3 Kd5 5. c4+ Kc5 6. Kc3, etc., as in No. 41) **4. Ke2 Kd5 5. Kd3 Kc5 6. c4!! Kb4 7. Kd4 Kxa4 8. Kc3!! Ka3 9. c5 a4 10. c6 Ka2 11. c7 a3** (11. ... Kb1 12. Kb4) **12. c8=Q Kb1 13. Kb3** and it's all over.

B. Pawns Are United

This is ordinarily a quite simple win. **No. 45** is the model position:

No. 45

White to play wins

White has only to try to attack the d-pawn by going around to the other side. Black will eventually be unable to keep up because he has to stay inside the square of the passed e-pawn. **1. Ke3 Ke6 2. Kd3 Kd7 3. Kc3 Kc6 4. Kb4 Kb6 5. Ka4** and now **5. ... Ka6** allows the pawn to queen, while after **5. ... Kc6 6. Ka5 Kc7 7. Kb5 Kd7 8. Kc5 Ke6 9. Kc6** the pawn cannot be held.

This model reveals the circumstances under which the player who is a pawn behind has drawing chances. When the White king attacks the pawn, Black must have sufficient leeway to move his king. When the Black pawn is on the second rank and the passed White pawn is on the seventh, the game is drawn if Black's pawn is on the rook or knight files, but lost otherwise.

No. 46

White to play. Draw. Draw with position moved one file to the left

1. Ke5 Kg8 2. Kf6 is stalemate but ...

No. 47

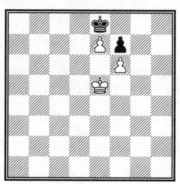

White to play wins. Also with White pawns at e6
/d7, d6/c7, c6/d7, or c6/d7

After **1. Kf5 Kd7 2. Kg5 Ke8 3. Kh6 Kd7 4. Kg7 Ke8 5. Kg8** Black has to move his king and loses.

No. 48

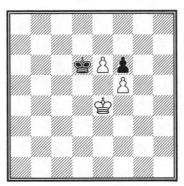

White to play wins. This pawn configuration wins anywhere except on the
a- or h-file

In **No. 48** there are two winning methods, one as in the previous example
and another by sacrificing the pawn at the proper moment: **1. Kd4 Ke7 2. Kc4
Kd6 3. e7! Kxe7 4. Kc5 Kd7 5. Kd5** (now he has the opposition) **5. ... Ke7 6.
Kc6**, etc.

It is only when neither of these winning methods (squeezing out the Black
king or sacrificing the pawn to get the opposition) is available that Black can
draw. With an h-pawn here Black draws because White's choices are either to
try to force the Black king off the board or to give up the passed pawn only
to reach an ending of king and h-pawn vs. king.

We have already seen (No. 45) that with the Black pawn on the fourth rank
White always wins. If the Black pawn is a rook-pawn, White captures it, if
necessary, by advancing his own at the right moment.

There is, however, a trap to be avoided. **No. 49: White king at c5, pawns at
a4, b5; Black king at b7, pawn at a5**. White to play wins. **1. b6?? Ka6!** only
draws (**2. Kc6** stalemate), but **1. Kd5 Kc7 2. Ke6** still wins: **2. ... Kb7 3. Kd7
Kb6 4. Kc8** (or **4. Kd6**) **Ka7 5. Kc7 Ka8 6. Kb6**, etc.

With the Black pawn on the fifth rank there is nothing to gain by sacrificing the passed pawn, for with the pawns on the fourth or third rank Black
can always keep the opposition after his pawn has been captured. However,
the first method (as in No. 45) is applicable except for some special positions.
These occur when Black has the opposition and can prevent the White king
from approaching his pawn, or when Black can afford to let the White pawn
queen because the resulting position is drawn.

The general rule is exemplified in **No. 50**, where White to play wins even
though Black has the opposition:

No. 50

White to play wins. Also all similar
positions except No. 51

1. Kc2 Kc5 2. Kd2 Kd6 3. Ke2 Ke6 4. Kf3 Ke5 5. Kg3 Kf6 6. Kf4 Ke6 7. e5,
etc.

An exception due to the presence of the g-pawn is seen in **No. 51**.

No. 51

Black to play. Draw

1. ... Kd4 2. Kd2 (if 2. Kf2 Ke5 3. Kg2 Kf6 4. Kh2 Kg6! 5. Kh3 Kg5 draw) **2.
... Kc4 3. Kc2 Kd4 4. Kb3 Kd5!** (but not 4. ... Ke3? 5. g5 Kxf3 6. g6 Ke2 7. g7 f3
8. g8=Q f2 9. Qg2! Ke1 10. Kc3! f1=Q 11. Qd2+ mate) **5. Kb4 Kd4! 6. Kb5 Ke3
7. g5 Kxf3 8. g6 Ke2 9. g7 f3 10. g8=Q f2,** draw. See Chapter VIII, No. 1026.

Finally, we come to those positions where Black's pawn is on the sixth
rank. If Black ever has a chance to capture the back White pawn he draws
easily. But in the general case, this is not possible:

No. 52

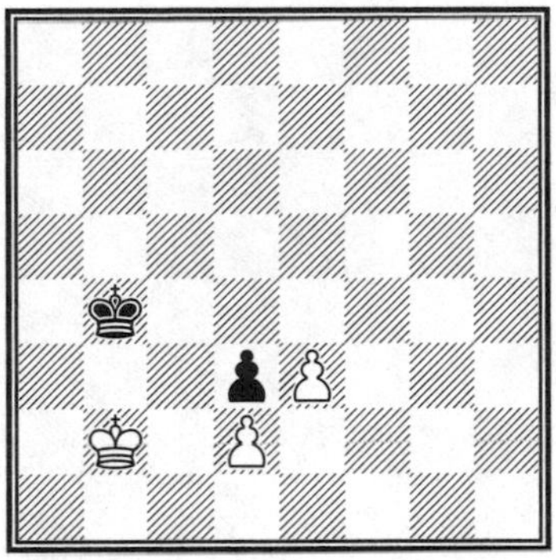

White to play wins

After **1. Kc1 Kc4** (or **1. ... Kb3 2. Kd1 Kb2 3. e4** and the king is outside the square) **2. Kd1 Kd5 3. Ke1 Ke5 4. Kf2 Ke4 5. Kg3 Ke5 6. Kf3,** the Black pawn is lost.

A draw is possible only in such special cases as **No. 53: White king at f1, pawns at g2, h3; Black king at f4, pawn at g3.** Black to play. Draw. **1. ... Ke3 2. Ke1** (if **2. Kg1, Kf4!**) **2. ... Kd3 3. Kd1 Ke3! 4. Kc2 Kf2,** etc.

Or **No. 54: White king at c1, pawns at a2, b3; Black king at c3, pawn at a3.** Black to play. Draw. Black plays **Kd3-c3** and if White's king goes off to the right, ... **Kb2** draws

C. White's Pawns Are Doubled

This is a draw whenever Black's king is in front of the pawns, for White must give one up to be able to capture the Black pawn.

Case 4. White Has No Passed Pawn

Black has drawing chances only when the position is blocked, or when the White pawns have advanced too hastily, or when the White king is in a backward position.

We can divide these endings into those with blocked pawn positions and those with fluid pawn positions. The latter generally present fewer difficulties and are often reducible to a blocked type, so we shall consider the blocked type first.

With the Black pawn on the second rank, White always wins easily unless there is an a- or h-pawn on the board.

No. 55

White to play wins. Also any similar position without a- or h-pawn

In view of Black's limited mobility in **No. 55**, White can get the opposition and win Black's pawn: **1. Kb5** (or 1. d6+ exd6+ 2. Kd5 Kc8 3. Kc6! Kd8 4. Kxd6 wins) 1. … **Kd6** (1. … Kb7? 2. d6) **2. Kc4 Kc7 3. Kc5 Kd8 4. Kb6** (4. Kc6 is also good) **4. ... Kc8 5. Kc6 Kd8 6. Kb7 Ke8 7. Kc7 Kf8 8. Kd7** (or 8. d6 exd6 9. Kd7 d5 10 e7+), etc.

Note that there are two ways for White to win: either by capturing Black's pawn or by queening his own advanced pawn. If Black has an a- or h-pawn, neither of these is possible and so a draw results.

When Black has a knight-pawn and White a rook-pawn, the draw can be held. **No. 56: White king at f5, pawns at g6, h5; Black king at e7, pawn at g7.** White to play. Draw. **1. Ke5 Kf8 2. Ke6 Kg8 3. Ke7 Kh8 4. h6 Kg8!!** (but not 4, ... gxh6 5. Kf7) **5. h7+ Kh8 6. K any,** stalemate.

With Black's pawn on the third rank White can generally win only if he has the opposition, while with rook-pawns he cannot win at all.

No. 57

White to play. Draw.
Black to play loses, but draw with rook-pawns

One can try **1. Kf4 Kf6 2. Kg4,** when 2. ... Kg6? 3. d5! wins for White, but
2. ... Ke6! 3. Kf4 Kf6!, draw (not 3. ... Kd5? 4. Ke3 Ke6 5. Ke4, when White has
the opposition). Black to move must allow the pawn advance or lose his own
pawn **1. ... Kf6 2. d5!** or **1. ... Kd7 2. Kf5! Ke7 3. Ke5,** and now that he has
yielded the opposition Black must ultimately lose his pawn.

But if Black has an a-pawn, **No. 58: White king at c4, pawns at a5, b4;
Black king at c6, pawn at a6,** the opposition is useless, for after **1. ... Kd6 2.
b5 axb5+ 3. Kxb5 Kc7** Black can lose only if lightning strikes.

The same holds when Black's pawn is on the fourth or fifth rank. In general White can win only if he has the opposition, while with rook-pawns on
the board he cannot win at all.

The concept of distant opposition (i.e. where more than one square sepa-
rates the two kings) plays an important role in endings of this type. In **No. 57,**
on **1. Ke3,** Black can only draw by either **1. ... Ke7!** or **1. ... Kf7,** but not **1. ...
Kf6? 2. Kf4 Ke6 3. Ke4,** or **1. ... Kd5 2. Kd3 Ke6 3. Ke4.**

Why the pawn position should be kept elastic is now abundantly clear.
Whenever the pawns are blocked White's winning chances diminish, and at
times even vanish. One seemingly insignificant tempo often makes all the difference. The well-known composer Kling illustrated this principle graphically:

No. 59

White to play wins. Draw with pawn at h3

With White's pawn at h3 the game is drawn regardless of whose turn it, but
in the diagram position White can win. There are two threats that Black must
guard against: one is White's getting the opposition; the other is the exchange
of the rook-pawn for the knight-pawn while Black's king is on the e-file. White
decides the game by using both possibilities: **1. Kf2! Ke6 2. Kg2! Kf6 3. Kg3
Kg6** (3. ... Ke5 4. h4) **4. Kf3 Kf6 5. Ke4 Ke6 6. h3** wins. White has the opposition.

Turning to the general position where White's pawns have plenty of living
and moving space, we find that the win is routine only if such pawn moves
as are essential to White's plan are made.

The dangers of a premature pawn advance is seen in **No. 60.**

Black to move. Draw. White to play wins

1. ... e5+! 2. dxe5+ Ke6. White to move must resort to the maneuver **1. Ke3 Ke7 2. Kd3 Kd6 3. Kc4 Kc6 4. e5!** to win.

Again, in **No. 61: White king at e4, pawns at f4, g4; Black king at e6, pawn at f6**. White to play. Draw. Even having the move does White no good: **1. Kd4 Kd6 2. Kc4** (or 2. f5 Kc6 3. Kc4 Kd6! =) **2. ... Kc6** and if **3. Kb4 Kd5**. This is also true when the pawns are on the second or third rank, but not when they are on the fifth, for then f6+ wins (No. 55).

On the other hand, with White's pawn on g2 instead of g4, the position is a win because of the extra tempo: **No. 62: White pawn at g2,** other pieces as in **No. 61**. White to play wins. **1. Kd4 Kf5** (if 1. ... Kd6 2. g4! Ke6 3. Kc5 Ke7 4. Kd5 Kd7 5. f5 Ke7 6. Kc6 Kf7 7. Kd6, etc.) **2. Ke3 Kg4** (2. ... Ke6 3. Ke4 f5+ 4. Kd4 Kd6 5. g3! is hopeless for Black) **3. Ke4 Kh4!** (not 3. ... Kg3 4. Kf5!) **4. Kf3!** (but not 4. Kf5? Kg3!! 5. Kxf6 Kxf4 =) **4. ... f5! 5. Kf2!!** (but not 5. g3+? Kh3! 6. Kf2 Kh2!, =) **5. ... Kg4 6. g3 Kh5** (6. ... Kh3 7. Kf3 Kh2 8. g4) **7. Kf3! Kg6 8. Ke3 Kf6** (8. ... Kh5 9. Kd4 Kg4 10. Ke5) **9. Kd4** and White wins because he has the diagonal opposition.

Now we can see that there are only two types of positions where White has any difficulty: when he has only one pawn move at his disposal, and when there are rook-pawns on the board. But since neither of these conditions leads to a forced draw, further distinctions must be made.

Where White has only one pawn move, assuming normal king positions, he can win with at least one center pawn but can often only draw when he has no pawn on the e- or d-files. It is always better for Black to have his pawn as far advanced as possible.

The crucial positions are **Nos. 63** and **64**.

No. 63

White to play wins

White must reserve his pawn advance (d5) until it gives him the opposition: **1. Kc3** (or 1. Ke3) **1. ... Kd7 2. Kb4 Kc6 3. Ka5 Kb7 4. Kb5 Kc7 5. Ka6 Kc6 6. d5+! Kc7** (or 6. ... Kc5 7. Kb7 Kd4 8. Kc6 Ke5 9. Kc7) **7. Ka7 Kc8 8. Kb6 Kd7 9. Kb7**. A premature advance of the d-pawn would have ruined White's winning chances; e.g., **1. Kc3 Kd7 2. d5 Kc7!**, and Black draws (See No. 57).

When White's pawns are on the f- and g-files with only one pawn move, Black can usually draw if his pawn is on the f-file, but if it's on the g-file he will as a rule lose.

The variations with the f-pawn are illustrated in **No. 61**. With a g-pawn Black loses because the threat of a pawn sacrifice, which hamstrings the White king in No. 61, does not exist here.

No. 64

White to play wins.
Draw with Black's pawn at f4

White wins with **1. g3**, for if **1. ... Kf5 2. Kd3** or if **1. ... Kd4 2. f3**, while with Black to play, **1. ... Kf4** (if 1. ... Kd4 2. f4! wins) **2. Kd3 g3 3. f3 Kf5 4. Ke3 Ke5**

5. f4+, etc., decides. With the pawns further advanced the winning idea is exactly the same.

Where one or both sides have rook-pawns, the results are exceptions to the general rule. When there are two rook-pawns, White can win only if his king is advantageously placed and he has an adequate reserve of pawn moves.

No. 65

White to move

The win in this position is highly instructive: **1. Kb4 Kb6 2. b3**, and now:

a) **2. ... a6 3. a3!**

a1) **3. ... Kc6 4. Kc4 Kb6 5. Kd5 Kb5 6. Kd6 Kb6 7. a4** (7. Kd7 is also good, but not 7. b4?? a5 =) **7. ... Ka5** (or 7. ... a5 8. Kd5 followed by capture of the a-pawn, or 8. ... Kb7 and again the pawn is lost) **8. Kc6 Kb4 9. Kb6 Kxb3 10. a5!** and the White pawn will queen.

a2) **3. ... a5+ 4. Kc4 Kc6 5. a4 Kb6 6. Kd5**

b) **2. ... Ka6 3. Kc5**

b1) **3. ... Ka5 4. a4! Ka6** (or 4. ... a6 5. Kc6, as in variation a1) **5. Kc6 Ka5 6. Kb7 a6 7. Ka7.**

b2) **3. ... Kb7 4. Kb5 Ka8! 5. Ka6 Kb8 6. b4 Ka8 7. b5 Kb8 8. a3!** (8. a4 draws: White must play his pawn to b6 only when Black's king is at a8).

Now we can also see why it is essential for the side with the extra pawn to have a number of pawn tempi at his disposal.

No. 66, Prins-Benko, Budapest 1949

White to play. Black wins

1. Kg2 Kg4 2. Kf2 (if 2. h3+ Kf4! 3. Kf2 h5 4. Kg2 h4 5. Kf2 g6 6. Kg2 Ke3 wins the h-pawn and the game) **2. ... Kh3 3. Kg1 h5 4. Kh1 h4 5. Kg1 g6!** (an important loss of a tempo) **6. Kh1 g5 7. Kg1 g4 8. Kh1 g3 9. Kg1 g2 wins.**

With g- and h-pawns the ending is almost always lost for Black.

No. 67

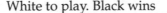

Black to play. White wins

On **1. ... Kf4 2. Ke2 Ke4 3. g3 g5 4. h3 Kf5 5. Kd3!** White has the opposition (5. ... Ke5 6. Ke3 Kf5 7. Kd4!), and after **1. ... g5 2. Kg3 Kf6 3. Kg4 Kg6 4. h3,** again the opposition is decisive.

Even here White must be careful not to exhaust his pawn moves too early. In **No. 68: White king at f5, pawns at g5, h5; Black king at f7, pawn at g7** Black to play. Draw. **1. ... g6+!,** whereas White to play can at best chase Black's king into the corner, where it can safely go to sleep: **1. Ke5 Ke7 2. Kf5 Kf7 3. g6+ Kg8 4. Ke6 Kh8,** etc. (No. 61).

Ordinarily, if the Black king is far from its pawn, White can simply advance his pawns and queen. **No. 69** is an exception that presents some difficulty.

No. 69, Rabinovich

White to play wins

With Black to move, he would either have to abandon the pressure on White's f-pawn (. ... Kh5), when Kf6 would decide, or desert the g-pawn, when f5 would force a queen. So White to play must maneuver to lose a move. This can easily be done, for if Black goes to the sixth rank, f5 queens a pawn.

Thus White wins by **1. Ke4 Kh4** (if 1. ... Kh5 2. Kf5) **2. Kd5!! Kh5** (2. ... Kg4 3. Ke5) **3. Kd6! Kg6** (3. ... Kh4 4. Ke7) **4. Ke7 Kg7 5. f5 Kg8 6. f6**.

We come now to endings where White's pawns are neither connected nor passed. Again, White can win if his king is in a favorable position and he has enough pawn tempi. The idea is as usual - either the capture or the advantageous exchange of Black's pawn.

In general, White can win such endings only if he can attack Black's pawn from the side (i.e., Black pawn at d7, White king at e7 or f7). This in turn is possible only if he can occupy the square in front of the Black pawn, it is his move, and if he has at least one tempo to spare. If his pawn moves are exhausted, or if his king is disadvantageously placed, the draw is inevitable.

No. 70

White to play wins. Black to move draws

In **No. 70** Black draws by **1. ... Kd5!** for if **2. c4+ Kc5 3. e4** (3. Kc3 d5) **Kb6!**
4. Kd4 Kc6 and White can get no nearer. But White to move wins by **1. Kd4!**
Kc7 (1. ... d5 2. c4 dxc4 3. Kxc4. See No. 6) **2. Kd5 Kd7 3. c4 Ke7 4. Kc6 Ke6 5.**
Kc7 Ke7 6. e4! (if this tempo were not available, the game would be drawn,
e.g., 6. Kb6 Kf6! or Kb8, Kf8 or Kb7, Kf7. Black can always hold the distant
opposition on the rank) **6. ... Ke6 7. Kd8 Ke5 8. Kd7.**

Or **No. 71: White king at d2, pawns at c2, e2; Black king at c5, pawn at d7.**
Black to play. Draw. **1. ... Kd4.** White to play wins. **1. Kc3! Kd5 2. Kd3 Kc5 3.**
e4! d5 (3. ... Kc6 4. Kd4 Kd6 5 e5+ wins) **4. e5, or 3. ... d6 4. Kc3 d5** (4. ... Kc6 5.
Kd4 is the same as the previous one; White has two tempi with his c-pawn)
5. exd5 Kxd5 6. Kb4.

As is to be expected, when White has a rook-pawn this type of ending is
drawn.

No. 72

Black to play. Draw

The most favorable position White can possibly force is **No. 72**. Then **1. ... Kc8!** (but not 1. ... Ka8? 2. Kc7 Ka7 3. Kc8 Ka8 4. a6!) **2. Ka7 Kc7** and to carry out the winning maneuver White must either move his king to the "zero" file or suspend it in midair.

Finally, we come to the case where White has doubled pawns.

No. 73

Black to play. White wins

When all the pawns are on the same file, as in **No. 73**, White wins both with and without the move.

a) **1. ... Kc6 2. Ke5 Kc5 3. d4+ Kc4** (3. ... Kc6 4. d3) **4. d5 Kc5 5. d3** followed by Kd6.

b) **1. Kc4 Kc6 2. d4 Kd6** (or 2. ... d6 3. d5+ Kb6 4. Kd4 Kb5 5. d3! Kb4 6. Ke3!! Kc5 7. Ke4 Kb6 8. Kf5 Kb5 9. Ke6 Kc5 10. d4+) **3. d5 Ke5** (if 3. ... Kc7 4. Kc5 d6+ 5. Kb5 Kb7 6. d3) **4. Kc5 Ke4 5. d6** (or 5. Kd6 Kd4 6. d3) **5. ... Ke5 6. d3! Ke6 7. d4**, K any **8. Kb6 Ke6 9. Kc7**.

It is clear that a win is possible only if White can force the position in variation B after his seventh move, with Black to play, or the corresponding position at some other point on the file.

This is the crucial test, whether White or Black moves first in **No. 74: White king at e5, pawns at d6, d4; Black king at c6, pawn at d7.** But with all the pawns on the knight file, the lack of elbow room for Black's king makes the draw inevitable. Applying this test gives a simple solution to almost all such endings with doubled pawns.

In **No. 75: White king at d3, pawns at d4, d5; Black king at d8, pawn at d7.** White to play. **1. d6!** leads after 1. ... Kc8 2. Ke4 Kb7 3. Kf5! Kc6 (or 3. ... Kb6 4. Kf6) 4. Ke5 to No. 74.

No. 76, Grigoriev 1935

White to play wins. Black to play draws.

In **No. 76**, Black to play draws by **1. ... Ke6 2. Kg5 Ke5! 3. f4+ Ke6** (No. 74 again, this time White to move). But White to play wins by an elegant maneuver: **1. Kf5** (not 1. Kg5 Ke5!) **1. ... Kd6 2. f4 Kd7 3. Kg4! Ke8 4. Kh5 Kf8 5. Kg5!!** (now Black is forced to pick one side, when White goes to the other) **5. ... Kg8 6. Kf5 Kh7 7. Ke4! Kh6 8. Kd5 Kg6 9. Ke5**, etc.

When the White and Black pawns are on adjoining files a new type of threat arises.

No. 77. Flohr-Ragozin, Moscow 1935

Black to move

Strange as it seems, the presence of the rook-pawn makes no difference; the above analysis holds no matter what files the pawns are on. Black plays **1. ... Ke4! 2. Kg5 Ke3!! 3. Kh6 Kf4! 4. g5 Kf5!!** (4. ... Kg4 5. g3! Kf5 6. Kh5) **5. g3 Kg4** or **5. Kh5 Kf4**, with an easy draw in either event.

This concludes our consideration of endings with two pawns against one. Disregarding the many special cases, we may sum up our discussion with the rule that *the side that is a pawn ahead wins unless the pawn position is blocked, or almost blocked, and he does not have the opposition.* Exceptions to this rule occur most often when there are rook-pawns, occasionally with knight-pawns, almost never with bishop- or center-pawns.

V. KING AND TWO PAWNS VS. KING AND TWO PAWNS

Other things being equal, this ending is a draw. But because "other things" covers a multitude of chess sins, it is worth our while to subject this type of position to a more careful analysis, especially since the possibilities that these endings exhibit are typical of all king-and-pawn endings with even pawns. Thus the conclusions may be extended to more general cases.

As above, we can classify the possible endings according to the number and kind of passed pawns. Remember that doubled pawns are in effect no better than a single pawn.

1. White Has Two Connected Passed Pawns

A. Black also has two connected passed pawns. This ending is like a horse race – whoever gets there first wins. Normally, however, both kings can stop the advance of the opposing pawns, which then cannot advance without further support.

No. 78

Draw

Neither side can make any progress here. The kings shuttle between a5-b6 and h2-g3, and draw either by agreement or exhaustion. Trivial though it seems, the salient fact this example illustrates is fundamental: *Two connected passed pawns, unsupported by their king, can make no headway against the opposing king.*

It follows that such endings can be won only when White can bring up his king and force a queen ahead of his opponent.

To carry through this winning maneuver when Black also has passed pawns, White's pawns must be relatively far advanced – at least to the fifth rank while Black's pawns are still on their second, third, or fourth – and he must be able to get his king near his pawns without allowing the Black pawns to get out of bounds.

First we must determine how long it takes to promote two pawns with the help of the king.

No. 79

White to play queens after at most three Black pawn moves
or mates after at most four Black pawn moves

In this position, which we may consider typical, **1. d6+** will force a queen in at most six moves with White to play: **1. ... Kd8** (1. ... Kd7 and 1. ... Ke8 lead to similar variations, while 1. ... Kf7 and 1. ... Kf8 shorten Black's agony) **2. e6** (or 2. Ke6 a4 3. d7 a3 4. Kd6 a2 5. e6 a1=Q 6. e7+ mate) **2. ... a4 3. Kf6 a3 4. Kf7 a2 5. e7+ Kd7 6. e8=Q+.**

This analysis shows us that if White's pawns and king are all on the fifth rank, it will take him at least six moves to queen; if they're on the fourth rank, nine moves. Since an unimpeded pawn can promote in five moves (from the second rank), we may conclude that in general White cannot win if his pawns have not passed the fourth rank, but that he *can* win if a) his king is well placed, b) his pawns are on the fifth rank, and c) if Black cannot queen in fewer than four moves.

With these points in mind it is relatively easy to determine when to abandon the square of an opponent's pawn. Two simple rules will be useful in this and similar endings:

1. Always advance your pawns as far as possible.
2. Always try to block your opponent's pawns.

No. 80, Behting 1900

White to play wins

In **No. 80**, we see the effectiveness of advanced pawns. White wins by **1. Kf3!** (to lose a tempo; the point will be obvious in a moment) **1. ... Ke8** (or 1. ... c6 2. Kf4!!) **2. Ke4 c5 3. Kd5!!** (threatening mate in two beginning with Ke6; we see now why White had to lose a tempo and force the Black king back to e8) **3. ... Kd7 4. Kc4 Ke8 5. Kxc5!! d3 6. Kd6** (again intending Ke6) **6. ... Kf7 7. Kd7** and Black is one move too late.

No. 81 (Horwitz 1879): **White king at f3, pawns at d4, e5; Black king at g5, pawns at f5, g6.** Black to play. White wins. This example shows why block-aded pawns are such a serious handicap **1. ... Kh6** (if f4 2. d5 Kf5 3. d6 and wins the f-pawn) **2. Kf4! Kg7 3. d5 Kf7 4. Kg5 Ke7 5. e6** (White has made two pawn moves, Black none) **5. ... Ke8** (or 5. ... Kd6 6. Kf6!) **6. d6 Kf8 7. Kf6** and concludes quickly.

B. Black has two unconnected passed pawns. The result depends on the relative positions of the pawns and kings. We have seen (No. 30) that if two pawns are one file apart, they can defend one another, if they are two files apart they are usually lost unless they are on the fifth or sixth rank. If they are three files apart, one of them cannot be prevented from queening.

These considerations determine the outcome of the endings now under discussion: if the White king can merely hold the Black pawns (one file apart), the game is a draw; if he can capture one of them (two files apart and on third or fourth rank), he wins; if he cannot catch up with them (three or four files apart), he loses. Remember, too, that it is sometimes possible let the enemy pawn run away while coming to the aid of one's own pawns.

No. 82

Draw

No. 82 is a draw. White moves Kd4-d5, Black Kh4-g5.

If the pawn position is more favorable, as in **No. 83: White king at c4, pawns at f6, g6; Black king at f8, pawns at b6, d6,** White wins by 1. Kd5 b5 2. Ke6! b4 3. g7+ (or 3. f7) Kg8 4. Ke7 b3 5. f7+.

In **No. 84: White king at f4, pawns at e4, d4; Black king at e7, pawns at b4, h4,** the Black pawns are too well placed, so White must lose.

Conversely, in **No. 85: White king at f3, pawns at b5, c6; Black king at c7, pawns at d6, h6,** White to play wins by **1. Kf4! Kb6** (if either pawn moves it will be captured) **2. Kf5! Kc7 3. Kf6!! Kb6 4. Ke6 Kc7 5. Kd5 h5 6. b6+ Kxb6 7. Kxd6 h4 8. c7.**

2. White Has One Passed Pawn

If Black also has a passed pawn the outcome depends on which pawn is farthest from the other set of pawns. In other words, whoever has the outside passed pawn wins.

No. 86

White to play wins

In **No. 86**, the White a-pawn advances until it forces Black's king to desert his c-pawn, whereupon White wins the Black pawns. **1. a4 Kc6 2. a5 f6** (2. ... Kd6 3. Kb5) **3. a6 Kb6 4. a7 Kxa7 5. Kxc5 Kb7 6. Kd6 Kc8 7. Ke7,** etc. As in the case of king and two pawns vs. king and pawn, if there is a set of rook-pawns Black's drawing chances are considerably enhanced.

The outside passed pawn is an advantage, however, only when the other pawns are subject to capture. In **No. 87**, Black loses because White has a *protected passed pawn*, which the Black king must watch.

No. 87

White wins

White can capture the Black g-pawn at his leisure and then win on the other side. If his pawn were nearer home, e.g. at d5, Black could draw without trouble, since he could defend his pawn and stay in the square of White's g-pawn at the same time. An exception to this rule occurs when either the White or Black pawns are too far advanced.

In **No. 88: White king at g4, pawns at f5, g6; Black king at f8, pawns at f6, h6,** White can afford to abandon the square of the h-pawn by a very ingenious stratagem: **1. Kf4 Ke8** (if the h-pawn ever moves while the White king can still catch it, the pawn will be lost) **2. Ke4 Ke7 3. Kd5 Kf8 4. Kd6! Kg8 5. Ke7!! h5** (or 5. ... Kg7 6. Ke6!) **6. Kxf6 h4 7. g7 h3 8. Kg6** and mates in two.

Where Black does not have a passed pawn, he loses if his two pawns are blocked by White's one but draws if they are not.

No. 89

White to play wins.
Draw with Black pawns at b6, c6

Here **1. h5 Kg5 2. Ke4** followed by the capture of both Black's pawns decides quickly.

But in **No. 90,** with the **Black pawns at b6 and c6,** the result is a draw, since on **1. h5 Kg5 2. Ke4 Kxh5 3. Ke5 Kg4 4. Kd6 c5!** forces the exchange of the last pawn.

We can draw two important conclusions from the above:

1. An outside passed pawn wins when the opponent's pawns are capturable;

2. A protected passed pawn almost always wins.

In general, subject to inevitable problem exceptions, these rules hold for all king-and-pawn endings.

3. Neither Side Has a Passed Pawn

Here there are only two winning possibilities: either a sacrifice to force a passed pawn, or an advantageous king position. The first is seen here:

No. 90

White to play wins.
Black to play draws

White to play forces a passed b-pawn by **1. d5.** Black to play prevents this by **1. ... d5,** which draws.

The second possibility, advantageous king position, is far more important. This advantage can be of two kinds: either the White king is closer to the pawns, or White has the opposition.

If there is a great deal of difference in the relative positions of the two Kings; e.g., if the White king in **No. 91** were at e6, then White would simply capture all Black's pawns.

The ending is especially interesting only if the kings are close to one other. Where feasible, the winning method is reduction to a simpler ending, either by capturing a pawn or by securing a passed pawn that is well ahead of its rival.

No. 92

White to move

No. 92 is one of the more difficult cases: **1. Kxa5 Kc5 2. Ka6 Kc6** and now **3. a5! g6 4. Ka7 Kc7 5. a6** forces Black either to allow White's king to escape to the other side or to permit the pawn to queen.

No. 93, from a game between two of the celebrated "Seven Pleiades," 1853, is another type of problem.

No. 93, von der Lasa-Mayet 1853

Black to play

Here when White captures a pawn, Black also captures one, so the question becomes one of leading to a won ending with king and pawn vs. king and pawn. With this in view White proceeds as follows: **1. ... Kf1** (White to move wins by either 1. d5 or 1. Kf3, but not 1. b5) **2. Kf3 Ke1 3. Ke3 Kd1 4. Kd3 Ke1 5. Kc4 Kd2 6. Kb5 Kc3 7. d5 Kd4 8. Kc6 b5 9. Kxc7 Kxd5 10. Kb6 Kc4 11. Ka5.** It is an interesting commentary on the state of chess a century and a half ago that this game, conducted by two of the foremost experts of the time, was drawn.

We come now to the most difficult case, where both kings are near their pawns but White has only the advantage of the opposition or a slightly more favorable position.

No. 94

White to play wins.
Black to play draws

This position shows the effectiveness of the opposition. White plays **1. Ke4** and poor Black is saddled with a dilemma. If he tries **1. ... d5+**, then **2. Kf4 Ke7** (or 2. ... f5 3. d4 Kf6 4. f3!) **3. Kf5 Kf7 4. d4 Ke7 5. Kg6 Ke6 6. f4 Ke7 7. f5** costs him the f-pawn. And if he adopts a do-nothing policy with **1. ... Ke7**, then **2. Kf5 Kf7 3. d4 Ke7 4. d5 Kf7 5. f3 Ke7 6. Kg6** again offers him no consolation. Note that if the White pawn were at f3 instead of f2, the opposition would do him no good.

No. 95, Judit Polgar 1998

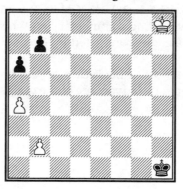

White to play and win

1. Kg7 Kg2 2. Kf6 Kf3 3. Ke5 Ke3 (The first moves were compulsory. If 3. ... a5 then 4. Kd6 Ke4 5. Kc7 Kd4 6. Kxb7 Kc5 7. Ka6 Kb4 8. b3 wins. But 4. Kd5? a5! draws) **4. a5! Kd3 5. Kd5! Kc2 6. Kd6! Kb3 7. Kc5!** (if 7. Kc7?, then 7. ... Kb4! 8. Kb6 Ka4 9. b3+ Kb4 draws, as in the game from which this study is derived) **7. ... Ka4 8. Kb6 Kb4 9. b3** wins.

A few more illustrations show the proper method of exploiting the opposition under different circumstances.

No. 96: White king at f2, pawns at e2, g4; Black king at f7, pawns at e7, g5. White wins. **1. Ke3 Kf6 2. Kd4 Ke6 3. Ke4 Kf6 4. Kd5 e6+** (or 4. ... Kf7 5. Ke5) **5. Kd6 Kf7 6. e4 Kf6 7. e5+ Kf7 8. Kd7** wins the e-pawn.

No. 97

White to play draws. Black to play loses

No. 97 is a fairly common case. Black to play loses, since he must allow either Ke5 or Kc5, while White to play draws by **1. Ke4** (but not 1. Kd3?? Kd5) **1. ... Ke6 2. Kd4 Kd6!**, etc.

A curious use of the opposition is seen in **No. 98: White king at f7, pawns at g4, h3; Black king at h7, pawns at g5, h6.** Black to move is forced to try **1. ... h5** (1. ... Kh8 2. Kg6 is hopeless), but is bowled over by the surprise rejoinder **2. h4!! 2. gxh5** (or 2. ... hxg4 3. hxg5) **3. g5 h3 4. g6+ Kh6 5. g7 h2 6. g8=Q** and mates next move.

But this is only an exception to the more general case **No. 99: White king at e7, pawns at g3, h3; Black king at h6, pawns at g7, h7,** where White can win a pawn but not the game. After **1. Kf7 g5 2. Kf6 g4! 3. h4** (3. hxg4 stalemate) **3. ... Kh5 4. Kf5 h6 5. Kf4 Kg6 6. Kxg4 h5+** we have our old friend No. 57.

A doubled pawn is a serious handicap for Black but it is only fatal if White has an adequate reserve of pawn moves or has the opposition.

In **No. 100: White king at c3, pawns at b2, d2; Black king at b5, pawns at c6, c5,** White to play wins by **1. b3 Ka6 2. Kc4 Kb6 3. d3** (two pawn tempi were necessary), while Black to play draws by **1. ... c4!** (now there are no pawn tempi) **2. Kd4 Kb4 3. Ke5 Kb3 4. Kd4,** etc.

VI. KING AND THREE PAWNS VS. KING AND TWO PAWNS

With any normal and most abnormal pawn positions it is easier to win with three pawns vs. two than with two pawns vs. one. **No. 101** is the general case. It is highly instructive that such endings are usually won by reducing them to simpler cases.

No 101.

White wins

With Black to move, if **1. ... Kf7 2. g6+ Kg8** (2. ... hxg6 3. hxg6+ gives us No. 55) **3. Ke6 Kh8 4. f6 gxf6 5. Kf7.**

With White to move, **1. g6 hxg6 2. hxg6** (see above), or here **1. ... h6 2. Ke4 Kf6 3. Kf4 Ke7 4. Ke5 Ke8 5. Ke6 Kf8 6. Kd7 Kg8 7. Ke7 Kh8 8. f6 gxf6 9. Kf7** and mates in two. If White's f-pawn and Black's g-pawn were missing, the ending would be a draw.

Where White has an outside or protected passed pawn the win is even easier.

Black has drawing chances in such endings only in four cases:

1. He can block the pawn position permanently;
2. He can exchange enough pawns to force one of the more elementary draws;
3. He has a protected passed pawn;
4. He can bring about stalemate.

The blockade of the pawns must go hand in hand with a superior or at least equal king position.

With both kings in the center and no reserve pawn moves, we get **No. 102: White king at d3, pawns at b4, h4; Black king at d5, pawns at a6, b5, h5.** With Black to move, White has the opposition and can draw despite Black's extra pawn; e.g., **1. ... Kc6 2. Kc3 Kb6 3. Kb3 a5 4. bxa5+ Kxa5 5. Ka3** (No. 39), or **1. ... Kd6 2. Kd2!!** and White maintains the distant opposition.

Where the extra pawns are badly isolated but not passed it is often impossible to rectify the unfortunate placement by exchanges. For example, **No. 103 (Lolli): White king at h3, pawns at b3, d3, f3; Black king at h5, pawns at c5, e5. Draw. 1. Kg3 Kg5 2. Kf2 Kf4, or Black to play 1. ... Kg5 2. Kg3 Kf5 3. Kf2 Kf4 4. Ke2 Kg5 5. Ke3 Kf5 6. Kd2 Kf4 7. Kc3 Kxf3 8. Kc4 Ke3, =.**

No. 104, P. Benko 1987

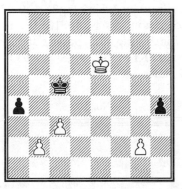

White to play. Draw

No. 104 is a curious example. White is a pawn up, but he has to play for a draw because Black is closer to queening.

A tempting move is 1. Kf5? Kc4 2. Kg4 Kb3 3. c4 Kxc4 4. Kxh4 Kb3 5. g4 Kxb2 6. g5 a3 7. g6 a2 8. g7 a1=Q 9. g8=Q Qh1+ and 10. Qg1+ wins the new queen.

Therefore: **1. Kd7! Kc4 2. Kc7 Kb3 3. Kb8! Kxb2 4. c4 a3 5. c5 a2 6. c6 a1=Q 7. c7 Qg1** (Black cannot check) **8. c8=Q Qxg2 9. Qh8+ and 10. Qxh4 draws.**

No. 105 illustrates the second kind of drawing chance.

No. 105

Black to play draws

1. ... Kf3!

But not 1. ... f4 2. Kg2 f3+ (or 2. ... fxg3 3. Kxg3 Ke5 4. f3 Kf5 5. Kg2 Ke5 6. Kf1! Kf5 7. Ke2 Kf4 8. Kf2 Ke5 9. Ke3 Kf5 10. f4 Kg4 11. Ke4 Kxh4 12. Kf3! (or 12. f5) 12. ... Kh3 13. f5 h4 14. f6 Kh2 15. f7 h3 16. Kf2! and mates in three) 3. Kh3! Kf5 4. g4+!! hxg4+ 5. Kg3, etc.

2. Kg1 (or 2. Ke1 f4 3. gxf4 Kxf4 4. Ke2 Kg4 5. Ke3 Kxh4 6. Kf4 Kh3 and draws) **2. ... f4** White can either lose a pawn by **3. gxf4 Kxf4 4. K any Kg4** or reduce to a well-known draw by **3. Kh2 fxg3+ 4. fxg3 Kg4.**

A simpler but more common case is **No. 106** (Walker 1841). **White king at c1, pawns at f3, g3, h3; Black king at f5, pawns at g5, h5.** Black to play draws. **1. ... h4! 2. gxh4 gxh4 3. Kd2 Kf4 4. Ke2 Kg3! 5. Ke3 Kxh3 6. Kf2! Kh2 7. f4 h3 8. f5 Kh1 9. f6 h2 10. f7** stalemate.

No. 107

Draw. White wins with Black's protected passed pawn on the c-file

No. 107 is an example of the third type of drawing possibility. White's passed pawns do him no good since he cannot afford to leave the square of the Black b-pawn.

But with Black's protected passed pawn on the c-file or further east, White can do better than draw. **No. 108: White king at c3, pawns at b4, g3, h2; Black king at h3, pawns at b5, c4.** By skillful maneuvering White can force one pawn to the sixth and can then afford to leave the square because he mates soon after queening: **1. Kd4 Kg4 2. h4 Kh5 3. Ke3 Kg4 4. Ke4 Kh5 5. Kf4!** (still in the square) **5. ... Kg6 6. g4 Kg7 7. h5! Kh6 8. Ke4! Kg5 9. Kf3** (triangulation) **9. ... Kh6 10. Kf4 Kg7 11. g5 Kf7 12. g6+ Kg7** and now **13. Kg5 c3 14. h6+ Kg8** (or 14. ... Kf8 15. Kf6 c2 16. h7) **15. Kf6 c2 16. h7+ Kh8 17. Kf7** and mates in a few.

The crucial question in all such positions is what happens if White leaves the square of Black's protected passed pawn. It is worth noting that No. 108 is a win only because of the mating threats, which are not usually available if one of the passed pawns is not on the rook file. An example is **No. 109: White king at b3, pawns at a4, f3, g4; Black king at f4, pawns at a5, b4**, is drawn.

In general, the mobility of the pawns is more important than their number. Two connected passed pawns are more valuable than "sextuplets" (six pawns on one file). This is why White can win in a blocked position only if he can get his pawns moving, which is usually possible only if he has the opposition.

When White's extra pawn is doubled, he can win only if he can reduce to a won ending with two pawns vs. one pawn by an appropriate exchange, or if he has the opposition.

No. 110

White to play wins. Black to play draws

White to play wins because the exchange by **1. d5+** is favorable for him **1. ... cxd5+** (or 1. ... Kd7 2. dxc6+ Kxc6 3. Kd4) **2. cxd5+ Kf6** (or 2. ... Ke7 3. Kf5 Kf7 4. c4, see No. 78) **3. Kd4!** (now Black must hurry back to the d-file, for 3. ... Kf5 4. c4 Kf6 5. c5 would be immediately decisive) **3. ... Ke7 4. Kc4 Kd7 5. Kb5 Kc7 6. Ka6** and will soon win the d-pawn.

On the other hand Black to play can force a draw by **1. ... d5+ 2. cxd5+**

Or 2. Kd3 Kd6 (not 2. ... dxc4+ 3. Kxc4 Kd6 4. Kd3!! Kd5 [if 4. ... c5 5. Kc4!! wins] 5. c4+, No. 63) 3. c5+ Ke6 4. Ke3 Ke7! 5. Kf4 Kf6 6. Kg4 Kg6 7. Kh4 Kh6. White can make no headway here because the exchange of his c-pawn for Black's d-pawn results in a draw, see No. 57.

2. ... cxd5+ 3. Kf4 Kf6 and draws because he has the opposition.

A lone king can hold three connected passed pawns, but Black then has no tempo, so if he is forced to move, the pawns advance. This is why three such pawns, even though unsupported by the king, win against two.

No. 111

White wins

After **1. a4 h5 2. b4 g5 3. c4 h4 4. Kh3** (now Black's king must move) **4. ... Kb6 5. a5+ Ka6 6. c5 Kb5 7. Kg4** (the key move) **7. ... Ka6 8. c6 Ka7 9. b5 Kb8 10. b6** and queens shortly, for with two pawns on the seventh he can sacrifice one and promote the other.

An exception to this general tale is seen in **No. 112: White king at g3, pawns at a6, c6; Black king at b8, pawns at f7, g4, h5.** White to play wins. Black loses because he cannot afford to move his king. **1. Kf4 f6 2. Kg3 f5 3. Kg2 h4 4. Kh2 f4 5. Kg1!! f3 6. Kf2 h3 7. Kg3,** and Black has fought nobly but in vain.

Similarly, three connected passed pawns, two of which are doubled, usually win against two. An example is **No. 113: White king at c3, pawns at g5, h4, g3; Black: king at g6, pawns at b5, c4.** Black to play. White wins. **1. ... Kf5 2. Kd4 Kg6 3. g4 Kg7 4. h5 Kh7 5. g6+ Kh6 6. Kc3! Kg7 7. g5 Kg8 8. h6 Kh8 9. g7+ Kh7 10. g6+ Kg8 11. Kd4! c3 12. h7+ (or 12. Ke5) 12. ... Kxg7 13. Kxc3** followed by taking the b-pawn, after which the two passed pawns decide.

Stalemate occurs chiefly in problems, but on rare occasions comes up in practice. Even so, one must be alert to this possible escape.

No. 114, Chigorin-Tarrasch 1896

White to play

White resigned here. But after **1. Kg4 Ke4 2. g6! h6 3. Kh5! Kxf5.** stalemate. If 2. ... hxg6 3. fxg6 f5+ 4. Kg5 f4 5. h5 also draws.

P. Benko version. **No. 115: White king at b1, pawn at f4; Black king at a3, pawns at g6, g7. Draw. 1. Kc2 Kb4 2. Kd3 Kc5 3. Ke4 Kd6 4. f5! g5 5. Kf3 Ke5 6. Kg4 Kf6 7. Kh5! Kxf5,** stalemate.

VII. KING AND THREE PAWNS VS. KING AND THREE PAWNS

As mentioned above, endings with even pawns are drawn unless one side has a clear positional advantage. In the case of two pawns vs. two pawns we were able to enumerate exhaustively all the possible combinations in which such a superiority occurs. Here, however, to attempt a comprehensive classification would lead to an enormously complicated table of little practical value. It is more instructive to group the various types of positional advantage under seven headings:

1. White can force a passed pawn and queen it;
2. White has an outside passed pawn;
3. White has a protected passed pawn;
4. White has qualitative pawn superiority;
5. White's passed pawn or set of passed pawns is qualitatively superior;
6. White's king is closer to the pawns;
7. White has the opposition.

1. Queen by Force

There are of course many positions where the Black king is simply not near enough to stop the passed pawn. What we are chiefly interested in here is the more complicated case in which there is no passed pawn yet. The type of position that most often occurs in practice is seen in **Nos. 116** and **117.**

No. 116

White wins

White to move queens by **1. c6 bxc6 2. b6! axb6 3. a6.** If Black begins, White wins the same way.

Another position that sometimes comes up is **No. 117.**

No. 117

White to play wins. Black to play draws

The solution is **1. b6!! cxb6 2. a6!! bxa6 3. c6.** (or 1. ... axb6 2. c6! bxc6 3. a6). Black to move can prevent the break by **1. ... b6,** but both **1. ... a6 2. c6!** and **1. ... c6 2. a6!** are disastrous.

2. Outside Passed Pawn

Where each side has only two pawns, this is a win if the Black pawns are blocked. This is because when the Black pawns are mobile he can liquidate all the material on the board. It is clear, however, that this drawing resource fails when there are more pawns on the board, since at best only one pair of pawns can be exchanged. Even when the pawns are close together and the Black king well placed, White experiences little difficulty.

No 118 (Breyer-Nyholm, Baden 1914): **White king at d2, pawns at c2, g2, h3; Black king at d4, pawns at e6, g7, h6,** shows this plainly. **1. ... h5 2. h4 e5 3. c3+ Ke4?** (or 3. ... Kc4! 4. Kc2 e4 5. Kd2 Kb3! 6. Ke3 [6. g3 Kc4 =] 6. ... Kxc3 7. Kxe4 Kd2 8. Kf5 Ke3 9. Kg6 Kf2! 10. Kxg7 Kg3 =) **4. Ke2 g6 5. Kd2 Kf4 6. Kd3 g5 7. hxg5 Kxg5 8. Ke4 Kf6 9. Kd5! Kf5 10. c4,** and now if 10. ... e4 11. Kd4! Kf4 12. c5 e3 13. Kd3 Ke5 14. Kxe3 Kd5 15. Kf4 Kxc5 16. Kg5 wins.

Black has drawing chances against an outside passed pawn only when he can secure a pawn position in which he is always threatening to force a passed pawn of his own. White is thus either prevented from attacking the pawns with his king or is forced to a disadvantageous simplification. How this works out in practice may be seen in **No. 119.**

No. 119, Bogolyubov-Fine, Zandvoort 1936

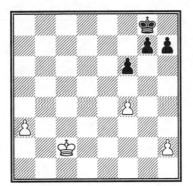

Black to play. Draw

At first sight, White's win looks like child's play, but a little analysis shows what difficulties White is up against. The game continued **1. ... Kf7 2. Kd3 Ke6 3. Ke4 g6! 4. Kd4**

The direct advance 4. a4 Kd6 5. a5 Kc5 6. a6 Kb6 leads to a draw after 7. Kd5 g5! 8. f5 (8. fxg5 transposes to the game) 8. ... h5 9. Ke6 h4 10. Kxf6 g4 11. Ke6 g3 and the pawns queen simultaneously.

4. ... Kd6 5. Kc4 h6 (5. ... Kc6 is also good, but Black is now threatening to put an end to White's hopes by 6. ... g5 and if 7. fxg5 hxg5 8 Kd4, f5-f4) **6. Kd4 Kc6** (now 6. ... g5? 7. Ke4! loses) **7. Ke4 Kb5 8. Kd5 g5!!** (the drawing maneuver) **9. fxg5 fxg5 10. Ke5 Ka4 11. Kf5 Kxa3 12. Kg6 Kb4 13. Kxh6 g4!!,** draw, since the Black king can get back to f8. White could not have won by the preparatory **14. h3** at some earlier stage, since Black would then have exchanged everything by ... g5, ... h5, and ... g4. Again we see that if Black had had blocked pawns he could have resigned immediately.

Sometimes a potential outside passed pawn is more dangerous than one actually on the board. This is seen in **No. 120** (Troitzky): **White king at g2, pawns at a4, c4, f2; Black king at f5, pawns at b7, g4, h5.** After **1. a5!** (threatening 1. c5-c6) **1. ... Ke5** is forced, when **2. Kg3 Kd4 3. Kh4 Kxc4 4. Kxh5 Kb5**

5. Kxg4 Kxa5 6. f4 b5 7. f5 b4 8. f6 b3 9. f7 b2 10. f8=Q b1=Q 11. Qa8+ ~~kingK~~ any 12. Qb8+ wins Black's queen.

For endings with an outside pawn vs. a protected passed pawn, see the next section.

3. Protected Passed Pawn

This is much stronger than even an outside passed pawn because it can draw against two connected passed pawns in most positions. Black can save himself only by preventing the White king from attacking his pawns, which in turn is possible only if he can oppose the enemy king and at the same time remain in the square of the pawn. Such a defense, however, is not often available.

It is worth reemphasizing that an outside passed pawn is a handicap against a protected passed pawn.

No. 121

White wins

Black is hopelessly lost, for White can first win his h-pawn and then queen. **1. ... Ke5 2. Kf3 Kf5 3. Kg3 Ke5** (he must not leave the square of the c-pawn) **4. Kh4 Kd5 5. Kxh5.**

If the Black pawn is on any other file Black can draw, since his king has enough maneuverability to keep the White king out. For example, **No. 122: Black pawn at g5,** other pieces as in No. 121. Black to play draws: **1. ... Ke5 2. Kf3 Kf5 3. Kg3 Ke5 4. Kg4 Kf6 5. c6** (there is nothing else) **5. ... Ke6 6. Kxg5 Kd6 7. Kf6 Kxc6 8. Ke6 a5!, =,** or **8. ... Kb6 9. Kd6 a5, =,** since Black's pawn is on the fifth rank. This is the sole type of exception to the rule that a protected passed pawn wins.

A position similar to No. 121 that is rather difficult to force is **No. 123** (Berg-Petrov, Kemeri 1937): **White king at b2, pawns at a4, g2, h4; Black king at h8, pawns at a5, b4, g7.** Black wins. Black to play would decide immediately by **1. ... g5! 2. hxg5** (2. h5 g4 and wins both kingside pawns) **2. ...**

Kg7 3. Kb3 Kg6. After the capture of both knight-pawns we have reduced to No. 45.

White to play must therefore begin with **1. g4** (to answer 1. ... g5! with 2. h5, =), when Black can win only by getting the distant opposition **1. g4 Kg8 2. Kc2 Kf7 3. Kd3 Ke7! 4. Ke3 Kd7 5. Kd3 Kc7! 6. Ke4** (6. h5 Kd6 7. Ke4 Ke7! 8. g5 Ke6) **6. ... Kc6! 7. Kd4 Kd6 8. Ke4 Kc5 9. Kd3 Kd5** wins. After liquidating the kingside pawns, Black wins easily with his protected passed pawn.

4. Qualitative Pawn Superiority

This occurs when Black's pawns are blocked (or doubled), so that two pawns are held by one. In effect, White has a potential outside passed pawn, and since Black's pawns are blocked White can force a quick decision. How this works out is seen in **No. 124.**

No. 124

Black to play. White wins

On **1. ... Kf7 2. Kf4 Kf6 3. h4 Kf7 4. Ke5 Ke7 5. g5** White gives up his g-pawn to capture both e- and d-pawns. On 1. ... e5 2. dxe5 Kf7 3. Kf4 Ke6 4. h4 d4 5. Ke4 d3 6. Kxd3 Kxe5 7. Ke3, White wins, having the opposition (No. 59).

A doubled pawn is a serious liability, but when all the pawns are on one side it need not be fatal, for in that case there can be no question of two pawns being held by one. **No. 125** (Flohr-Capablanca, Moscow 1935): **White king at d3, pawns at e3, g3, h2; Black king at e6, pawns at f6, f5, h5. After 1. ... Ke5 2. Ke2 Ke4 3. Kf2 h4! 4. gxh4 f4!! 5. exf4 Kxf4** the draw is obvious. White can win only if he can force his king to f4 with at least one tempo to spare.

5. Passed Pawns or Set of Passed Pawns Is Qualitatively Superior

By this we mean that White's pawns are either more mobile (e.g., Black's pawns are doubled or disadvantageously isolated) or farther advanced.

This usually works out in exactly the same way as the analogous case with king and two pawns vs. king and two pawns. **No. 126** is an example from tournament practice.

No. 126, Stoltz-Nimzovich, Berlin 1928

Black to play

Nimzovich won with the break **1. ... f4! 2. gxf4+ Kd6!! 3. a5 g3 4. a6 Kc7!! 5. Ke2 d3+** and queens first.

6. King Is Closer to the Pawns

This is important but not difficult. Sometimes, however, such positions present unusual difficulties, since the Black king is never too far away.

No. 127, H. Mattison

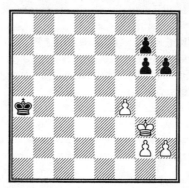

White to play wins

In **No. 127**, after **1. f5!** (not 1. Kf3 Kb5 2. Ke4 Kc6 =) **1. ... Kb5! 2. Kf4!!** (2. fxg6 only draws) **2. ... Kc6** (2. ... gxf5 dooms his remaining pawns) **3. Ke5 Kd7**

4. f6!! Kc8!! 5. fxg7 (5. Ke6 Kf8 6. f7 also wins) **Kf7 6. g8=Q+! Kxg8 7. Kf6 Kh7 8. g4 g5 9. Kf7! h5 10. h4!!** and wins (see No. 98).

Where the pawn position is not yet blocked, it is essential for the inferior side to block it in such a way that he will queen no later than his opponent. This is normally simply a question of counting.

No. 128, Grigoriev

White to play and draw

In **No. 128, 1. h4?** loses, but **1. g4** draws. This result may be calculated as follows. After fixing the pawns on the kingside White must play his king to a5. Then ... b3 exchanges the a- and b-pawns. Now we must count to see who gets to the other side first. With the Black pawns at g4 and h5 (after 1 h4 g4), it will take White's king, now at a5, seven moves to capture the h-pawn, one to get his king off the file, and four to queen, a total of eleven. The Black king, now at b3, will capture the White g-pawn in five moves, and queen in four more, a total of nine (the fact that he will queen with check is unimportant here). But if White had played **1. g4** and fixed the Black pawns at g5 and h4, it would now take him six moves to capture the pawn, and five more to queen, while Black needs six moves to capture the pawn and four to queen, a total of ten. Since White begins the race, the two pawns promote simultaneously, and a draw results.

7. White Has the Opposition

No. 129, Dr. A. Neustadtl

White to play wins

In the simpler cases this is no different from king and two pawns vs. king and two pawns (Nos. 94, 95). **No. 129** is an elegant illustration of the central idea: **1. b4! c5 2. d4!! cxd4** (or 2. ... cxb4 3. Kf6) **3. Kf6 d3** (or 3. ... Kd7 4. Ke5 Kc6 5. Ke6) **4. cxd3 d4 5. Kf5 Kd5 6. Kf4 Kd6 7. Ke4**, etc.

Where the distant opposition is involved, the play is often exceedingly complicated. To illustrate the idea when each side has three pawns we cite two more "natural" problems. The first is **No. 130** (K. Ebersz 1935): **White king at e1, pawns at a4, g5, h6; Black king at e8, pawns at b6, f7, h7.** White wins. The solution is **1. Kd2! Kd8** (1. ... Kd7 2. Kd3) **2. Ke2!! Kc8!** (if 2. ... Kd7 3. Kf3, or 2. ... Ke7 3. Ke3) **3. Kf3 Kd7 4. Ke3 Kc8** (or 4. ... Kd8 5. Kd4, or 4. ... Ke8 5. Ke4, or 4. ... Ke7 5. Ke4 Ke6 6. Kf4) **5. Kd4 Kd8 6. Ke4!! Kd7** (Black is in zugzwang: on 6. ... Ke8 7. Kf5 Ke7 8. Ke5 or 7. ... Kf8 8. Kf6 wins, and on 6. ... Ke7 7. Ke5 is decisive) **7. Kd5** and White has the opposition.

Another interesting example is **No. 131** (Locock): **White king at a1, pawns at d5, e4, g3; Black king at h8, pawns at d7, d6, g4.** White to play wins. After **1. Kb2 Kg7 2. Kc3 Kf7! 3. Kd2!! Kf6 4. Ke2!! Kg6 5. Kd3!** (the key position – Black must now allow either the advance of White's e-pawn or the loss of his g-pawn) **5. ... Kf6** (5. ... Kg5 6. Ke3) **6. Kd4 Kf7 7. e5 dxe5+ 8. Kxe5 Ke7 9. d6+ Ke8 10. Kf6! Kf8 11. Kg5 Kf7 12. Kf5 Kg7 13. Kxg4 Kf6 14. Kh5 Ke6 15. g4 Kxd6 16. g5 Ke7 17. Kh6 d5 18. g6** and promotes one move sooner than Black.

A good deal of attention has been devoted to the next example and its innumerable offshoots.

No. 132

Whoever plays wins

In **No. 132**, whoever moves wins. The main variation is **1. Ke2 Kd7 2. Kf3 Kc6 3. a4 h5 4. c4 f5 5. Kg3! Kb6 6. b4 g5**

Or 6. ... g6 7. a5+ Ka6 8. c5 Kb5 9. Kg2 g5 (or 9. ... h4 10. Kh2! f4 11. Kg1!! g5 12. Kg2 g4 13. Kg1, etc.) 10. Kg3 g4 11. Kf2! f4 12. Kg2 h4 13. Kg1!! f3 14. Kf2 h3 15. Kg3, and now the Black king must move, allowing a White pawn to queen.

7. a5+ Ka6 (7. ... Kb7 8. c5) **8. c5 h4+ 9. Kh3 f4** (or 9. ... Kb5 10. Kh2, as in the variation above) **10. c6 f3 11. b5+ Ka7 12. c7! g4+** (or 12. ... Kb7 13. b6 g4+ 14. Kh2 g3+ 15. Kg1 h3 16. a6+ Kc8 17. a7) **13. Kxg4 f2 14. c8=Q f1=Q 15. b6+** mate.

VIII. FOUR OR MORE PAWNS ON EITHER SIDE

It would be pointless to work out elaborate analyses of these more complicated endings, since we have already considered the principles they exemplify at sufficient length. Instead, we will try to answer some of the more important questions that continually crop up in play.

A. One Side Is a Pawn Ahead

As indicated above, the win with material superiority becomes progressively easier the more pawns there are. The ending with king and two pawns vs. king and one pawn is less difficult than king and one pawn vs. king. King and three pawns vs. king and two pawns is won more quickly and simply than king and two pawns vs. king and pawn. The reason for this is that the extra pawn is used as a decoy to divert the attention of the enemy king, so the greater the number of remaining pawns, the more material White can capture.

We have seen that with two pawns against three Black can hope to draw only under certain special circumstances. With three against four Black's situation is even worse. **No. 133** is the standard position:

No. 133, Berger

White to play wins

White always proceeds by reducing the position to a well-known win. Black has five main defenses:

a) 1. ... Kf4 2. Kd3 Kf5 3. c4 Kf4 4. a4 a6 5. b4 Kf5 6. a5 bxa5 7. bxa5 Kf4 8. d5 cxd5 9. cxd5 Ke5 10. Kc4 Kd6 11. Kd4 (Nos. 65 and 67);

b) 1. ... c5 2. dxc5 bxc5 3. b3 a6 4. a3 a5 5. a4 Ke5 6. Ke3 Kd5 7. Kd3 c4+ (or 7. ... Kd6 8. Ke4) 8. bxc4+ Kc5 9. Kd2! Kxc4 10. Kc2 (No. 44);

c) 1. ... b5 2. b4 a6 3. a3 Kf4 4. Kd3 Kf5 5. c4 Ke6 6. c5 Kd5 7. Ke3 Ke6 8. Ke4 Ke7 9. d5 cxd5+ 10. Kxd5;

d) 1. ... a6 2. b4 a5 3. bxa5 bxa5 4. a4 Kf4 5. Kd3 Kf5 6. Ke3 Ke6 7. Ke4 Kd6 8. c4 Ke6 9. c5 and d5 (No. 41);

e) 1. ... a5 2. a4 b5 3. axb5 cxb5 4. Ke2 b4 5. Kd2 b3 6. Ke2 a4 7. Kd2 Kd5 8. Kd3 Kd6 9. Kc4 Kc6 10. Kb4.

With five vs. four, or six vs. five, the win is child's play.

We can summarize the winning process in endings with one side a pawn ahead as follows:

1. Force a passed pawn;
2. Sacrifice the pawn at the right moment to get either
a) a pawn that queens by force;
b) a sufficient preponderance of material;
c) a win in one of the standard basic positions.

In most cases these rules are easily applied. But chess would not be the game it is if there were not numerous exceptions. Almost all of these are due to irregular pawn structures. Even here, however, Black can seldom avert loss when White has more than three pawns.

We can group the possible difficulties that White may encounter (assuming more or less normal king positions) under two headings: blocked pawns (including doubled pawns), and stalemate.

1. Blocked Pawns

With the pawns interlocked and offering no possibility of exchange, the problem becomes one of forcing the entry of the king. The opposing king is always the obstacle here, so the solution depends on the proper use of the opposition. This applies to what we may call a complete pawn blockade.

If White has the opposition in such cases, he simply waits for Black to get his king out of the way and then marches in. The position requires thought and analysis only when direct and obvious methods fail. In such cases the weapon to be used is the *distant opposition*.

We see how this works in **No. 134.**

No. 134, Lasker and Reichhelm 1901

White to play wins;
Black to move draws

White wants to get his king either to b5 or to g5. On the direct try **1. Kb2 Kb7 2. Kc3 Kc7 3. Kc4 Kb6 4. Kd3 Kc7 5. Ke3 Kd7 6. Kf3 Ke7 7. Kg3 Kf6 8. Kh4 Kg6**, he gets nowhere fast. Obviously, a little finesse is needed. In the above variation we can make two observations:

1. Black must remain no more than one file to the left of White's on his march to the queenside; e.g., if the White king is on the e-file, the Black king must be no farther left than the d-file.

2. Consequently, with the Black king at b6 and the White king at c4, Black to play loses, for 4. ... Ka6 is forced.

Let's carry the analysis one step further. With the White king at d3 and Black's at c7, Black to play loses, since he must go to the b-file to prevent Kc4-b5.

Again, one general point must be remembered. To have the opposition the kings must be one square apart. And to have the distant opposition the kings must be an odd number of squares apart.

Now the solution is clear. **1. Kb1! Kb7 2. Kc1 Kc7 3. Kd1 Kd7** (3. ... Kc8 4. Kd2 Kd7 5. Kc3 Kc7 6. Kd3) **4. Kc2 Kd8 5. Kc3 Kc7 6. Kd3** and Black is lost because he cannot keep the opposition by **6. ... Kd7 7. Kc4**, etc.

Black to move can draw by **1. ... Kb7!! 2. Kb1 Ka7!!**. If then **3. Kb2 Ka8!**, or **3. Kc1 Kb7**, or **3. Kc2 Kb8**, and each time Black's king can remain at a distance of five, three, or one squares, and with White to move, so that Black always retains the opposition.

A winning method closely allied to the opposition is triangulation. Here the struggle is for a certain vital point, and because of the pawn configuration one side has access to one more square than his opponent.

No. 135, Neustadtl-Porges

White to play

In **No. 135**, White wants to occupy the square d4. To do so he must first occupy e4, with the Black king at c5. He has two squares (e3 and f3) from which he can approach e4, while Black has only one. Thus he can reach his goal by **1. Kf3 Kc6 2. Ke2!** (if 2. Ke4 Kc5 3. h4? Kb6! 4. Kd4 Kb5, the game is drawn – White must reserve his pawn tempo) **2. ... Kc5** (2. ... Kd5 3. Ke3 Kc5 4. Ke4) **3. Kf2 Kc6 4. Kf3 Kd5 5. Ke3 Kc5 6. Ke4 h4** (6. ... Kb6 7. Kd4 Kb5 8. h4) **7. Kf3! Kd5 8. h3! Kc6 9. Kg4 Kd5 10. Kxh4 Ke4 11. Kg4 Ke3 12. h4 Ke4 13. Kg3 Ke3 14. h5! gxh5 15. f5! exf5 16. g6** wins (J. Faucher).

A complete pawn blockade is less usual in actual play than positions where some pawn exchanges are possible. Here the problem usually boils down to that of choosing the proper moment to exchange, where the "proper moment" means that in the ensuing position one will have the opposition or some other tangible advantage.

No. 136: White king at g2, pawns at a3, c3, f3, g3; Black king at f5, pawns at a4, c4, c6, g5, h5. Black to play wins. 1. ... h4 2. Kh3 Ke5!! 3. f4+ (if 3. Kg4 hxg3 4. Kxg3 Kf5 5. Kg2 Kf4 6. Kf2 c5 7. Ke2 Kg3 8. Ke3 Kh3! wins; 3. gxh4 gxh4 4. Kg4 c5 5. f4+ Ke4 6. f5 h3!, etc., wins) **3. ... gxf4 4. gxh4 Ke4 5. Kg2** (5. h5 f3 6. h6 Ke3 wins) **5. ... Kd3 6. Kf3 Kxc3 7. h5 Kb3**, etc ,wins.

Another stratagem occasionally used to win with an extra pawn is the sacrifice of one or two pawns, which leads to a forced promotion.

No. 137, Berger-Bauer, correspondence 1889-91

White to play

This is done by **1. c4! bxc3** (1. ... Kg5 2. Kg3 is hopeless) **2. Ke3 Kg5 3. a4!! Kxg4 4. b4 axb4 5. Kd3!!** (the only winning move; if instead 5. a5 b3 6. Kd3 b2 7. Kc2 Kf3 8. a6 Ke2 9. a7 b1=Q+! 10. Kxb1 Kd1 and both sides queen) **5. ... h5 6. a5 h4 7. a6 h3 8. a7 h2 9. a8=Q**, followed by Qh1, and a simple win.

A variant of this idea is **No. 138: White king at b3, pawns at a4, e4, f3, g4, h5; Black king at c5, pawns at b6, f6, g5, h6**. Black to play. White wins. Here the win is achieved by **1. ... Kc6** (on 1. ... Kd4 2. Kb4 White queens first) **2. Kb4 Kd6 3. Kc4 Kc6 4. f4!! gxf4 5. e5! fxe5 6. g5 f3 7. Kd3**.

A similar position, which also involves the exchange of queens after both pawns promote, is **No. 139** (Colle-Grünfeld, Carlsbad 1929): **White king at g3, pawns at a4, f4, g5, h4; Black king at e3, pawns at a5, g6, h5**. White to play won by **1. f5 gxf5 2. g6 f4+ 3. Kg2!!** (on any other move Black draws the ensuing queen-and-pawn ending) **3. ... Ke2 4. g7 f3+ 5. Kg3 f2 6. g8=Q f1=Q 7. Qc4+ Ke1 8. Qxf1+ Kxf1 9. Kf4**. The Black king had to be forced to the same diagonal as the future queen.

A relatively simple device, yet one that is often necessary, is to sacrifice one or more pawns to remove the blockade in order to penetrate to the other side of the board with the king.

No. 140

White to play. Black wins

This is done by **1. h4 c5 2. Kf2 a5! 3. Ke3 axb4** (3. ... cxb4 4. axb4 a4?? is a hopeless draw, since the position is completely blocked) **4. axb4 cxb4 5. Kd2 Kc7 6. Kc2 Kc6 7. Kb2 Kc5 8. Kb3 Kd4.**

When the defending side has a protected passed pawn, the win is exceedingly difficult and sometimes impossible. If the pawn defending the passed pawn cannot be induced to get out of the way then the only winning possibility is leaving the square to guide one's own pawns to queen (compare No. 108).

No. 141

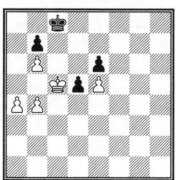

White to play wins

This is done by **1. b5 Kb8 2. a5 Kc8 3. a6 Kb8.** Now White must lose a move, so that when he plays Kd6 he will be threatening Kc7. **4. Kd4 Ka8 5. Kc3 Kb8 6. Kd3 Ka8 7. Kd4 Kb8 8. Kc5 Ka8 9. Kd6 Kb8** (else 10 Kc7 mates) **10. Kxe6 d4 11. Kf7 d3 12. e6** and queens with mate.

Where the extra pawn is doubled, the win is usually long and difficult. Sometimes it is possible to sacrifice the pawn to get the opposition or an otherwise won ending.

No. 142, Spicss-Bürger

White to play wins.
Black to play draws

The only way White can make any progress is by **1. f4! gxf4+ 2. Kh4! Ke4**, and then **3. Kg4!! f3** (or 3. ... h5+ 4. Kxh5 Kf3 5. Kg5) **4. h4 h5+** (4. ... Kd3 5. Kxf3 is equally hopeless) **5. Kxh5 Kf4 6. Kg6** is decisive.

A similar idea is seen in **No. 143** (Von Scheve-Walbrodt, Berlin 1891): **White king at g3, pawns at b4, b2, f3, f2, h2; Black king at g5, pawns at b6, e5, f7, g6**. White to play wins. The main value of the doubled b-pawn is that it gives White two extra tempi. Walbrodt won by **1. b5 f5 2. f4+! Kf6 3. fxe5+ Kxe5 4. Kf3 g5 5. Ke3 Kd5 6. h3! Kc5 7. f4!**, and Black resigned, for if 7. ... g4 **8. hxg4 fxg4 9. f5 Kd5 10. Kf4**.

No. 144

White to play wins

Where no such sacrifice is feasible, as in this example (this could have occurred in Reshevsky-Fine, Nottingham, 1936, see No. 1079), the superior side must jockey for a vantage point from which he can liquidate his unfortunate twin, using the extra tempi his pawn plus assures him. In this position the first advantage the extra pawn confers is that Black cannot sit back and do nothing, for if he allows White's king to reach d6, the advance e4, f4, g4, and f5 will force Black to exchange and undouble White's pawns. So Black must play his king to the center.

On the other hand, White cannot make any direct progress by playing his king to the center. Nor can he penetrate the Black position via f4 and g5, since Black can play his pawn to h6. Therefore, White must force a further weakness in the Black position.

After **1. ... Kf8** this can be done by **2. h4 Ke7 3. Kg2 Kd7 4. h5! Kc6**

Or 4. ... gxh5 5. Kh3 Kc6 6. Kh4 Kd5 7. f4, or 4. ... g5 5. g4 Kc6 6. f4! Kd5 7. Kf3 Kd4 8. h6 Kd5 9. e3 gxf4 10. Kxf4 K any 11. Kg5 K any 12. Kf6.

5. hxg6 fxg6

There is small choice in rotten captures; if 5. ... hxg6 6. f4 Kd5 7. Kf3 followed by Kg4-g5 and either Kf6 or e4-g5, depending on the position of Black's king, is decisive. The rest is easier:

6. f4 Kd5 7. Kf3 Kd4 8. g4 g5

If Black does nothing, then Ke3-d3 followed by e4 and g5 will decide; while if 8. ... h6 9. e3+ Kd5 10. Ke2!! Ke4 11. Kf2 g5 12. Kg3!! wins.

9. fxg5

Now 9. e3+ Kd5 10. Kf2 Ke4 11. Kg3 h6! only draws; e.g., 12. f5 Kxe5 13. fxe6 Kxe6 14. Kf3 Ke5!, etc.

9. ... Kxe5 10. Ke3 Kd5

Or 10. ... Kd6 11. Kf4 Ke7 12. g6! hxg6 13. Kg5 Kf7 14. e4 Kg7 15. e5 Kf7 16. Kh6.

11. g6! hxg6 12. Kf4 Kd4 13. Kg5 Ke3 14. Kxg6 Kxe2 15. Kf6 Kf3 16. g5 Kf4 17. g6 with a simple win.

The possibility of stalemate very rarely occurs in practical play, but it is still wise to be on guard against it. The most usual way to avoid it is by underpromotion, usually to a rook. Sometimes, however, this is insufficient, and it is necessary to change the entire character of the position.

No. 145

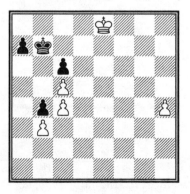

White plays and wins

The obvious 1. h5? only draws after 1. ... Ka6! 2. h6 Ka5!! 3. h7 a6!! and stalemate. Instead, **1. Kd7** wins, even though Black queens: **1. Kd7 a5** (if 1. ... Ka6 2. Kxc6 Ka5 3. Kd7 a6 4. c6) **2. h5 a4 3. h6 axb3 4. h7 b2 5. h8=Q b1=Q 6. Qc8+ Ka7 7. Qc7+ Ka8 8. Kxc6 Qg6+** (8. ... Qe4+ 9. Kb6 Qe6+ 10. c6 Qe3+ 11. c5) **9. Kb5 Qe8+ 10. c6 Qb8+** (10. ... Qh5+ 11. Kb6) **11. Qxb8+ Kxb8 12. Kxb4,** and we have No. 28.

The circumstances under which Black can draw when he is a pawn down have already been discussed in the case of three pawns vs. two pawns; the conclusions reached there are also applicable to all other pawn endings.

The most important points to remember are that doubled or immobile pawns are the most serious handicap for the side who is trying to win, while a protected passed pawn is an almost certain guarantee of a draw for the inferior side.

2. Stalemate

Stalemate defenses are a monopoly of problemists, and problems with this theme are often very stimulating.

No. 146, F. Lazard

White to play. Draw

1. h5! gxh5 2. g6 fxg6 3. e6 dxe6 4. c5 dxc5 5. a6 bxa6 6. b6 axb6 stalemate!

A single change, such as shifting the position one file or rank, can make all the difference! The following "twin" problems demonstrate.

No. 147, P. Benko

White to play. Draw

1. Kf4! (avoiding 1. Ke5? Kc7 2. c5 d5 3. cxd6+ Kd7 and Black wins.) **1. ... Kc7 2. Ke5!** (on 2. Kg5 Kd6 3. Kg6 Ke5 Black wins.) **2. ... Kc8!?** (if 2. ... Kd8 3. Kd6 Ke8 4. c5 Kd8 5. f6! gxf6 stalemate!) **3. Kf4!** (wrong is 3. Kd6? Kd8 4. c5 Ke8 5. Kc7 Ke7 6. Kb6 d6 7. Kxc6 dxc5 8. Kxc5 Kf6 and Black wins) **3. ... Kd8 4. Kg5 Ke7 5. Kg6 Kf8 6. c5** (the try 6. f6? gxf6 7. Kxf6 c5! also wins for Black.) **6. ... Kg8 7. Kh5! Kf7 8. Kg5 Ke7 9. Kg6 Kf8 10. Kh5!** draw, as Black cannot make progress. And now the twin.

No. 148, P. Benko

White to play. Draw

1. Kg4! Kd7 2. Kf5! Kd8 (the try 2. ... Ke8 3. Ke6 Kf8 4. d5 Ke8 5. g6! hxg6 achieves stalemate again) **3. Ke6!** (from here on, the solution is different; the other try 3. Kg4 Ke8 4. Kh5 Kf7 5. Kh6 Kg8 6. d5 Kh8 gives only an illusion of a draw as there is one less file available) **3. ... Ke8 4. d5 Kf8 5. Kd7 Kf7 6. Kc6!** (the saving idea; 6. ... e6 doesn't win, because after 7. Kxd6 exd5 8. Kxd5 Kg6 9. Ke4 draws, as the h-pawn, in this twin, is not enough to win.) **6. ... e5 7. Kxd6 e4 8. Kc6!** (if 8. Kc7 e3 9. d6 e2 10. d7 e1=Q 11. d8=Q Qa5+ Black wins) **8. ... e3 9. d6 e2 10. d7 e1=Q 11. d8=Q** draw.

B. Materially Even Positions

The types of positional advantage in endings with an even number of pawns have been enumerated in Part VI (king and three pawns vs. king and three pawns) and they generally also sum up all the cases where a win is possible despite numerical equality. Here we illustrate these principles in more complicated positions.

1) A Queen Is Forced

Endings where one side can force a passed pawn and queen it usually involve pawns on both sides of the board, which are freed by a sacrifice (compare Nos. 91 and 137).

No. 149, Gossip-Mason, Manchester 1890

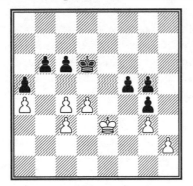

Black to play

Black has two potential passed pawns, on the a-file and the f-file, one of which is bound to queen: **1. ... b5 2. cxb5 cxb5 3. axb5 a4 4. Kd3 a3 5. Kc2 f4**, etc.

An example from an offhand game Stahlberg-Tartakower is more complicated. **No. 150: White king at e2, pawns at d4, g6, h2; Black king at e6, pawns at a7, b7, c4, g7.** White to play forces a queen by **1. h4 a5 2. h5 a4 3. Kd2!** (discretion is the better part of a pawn ending) **3. ... b5 4. d5+ Kd7 5. h6 a3 6. Kc2! b4 7. hxg7 b3+ 8. Kb1! a2+ 9. Ka1! c3 10. g8=Q.** Just in time!

In **No. 151** (Zubarev-Grigoriev, Leningrad 1925): Black queens because the White king is too far away: **White king at f7, pawns at a4, b3, c2, f3; Black king at a6, pawns at a5, b6, c5, d4.** Black to play. **1. ... b5 2. axb5+ Kb6!!** (to save an all-important tempo) **3. Ke6 a4! 4. bxa4 c4 5. f4 d3** and queens when White's pawn is on the sixth.

2) The Outside Passed Pawn

The outside passed pawn is practically certain to win when there are more than three pawns on each side (unless of course the defender has a protected passed pawn).

No. 152, Lasker-Allies, Moscow 1899

White to play wins

No. 152 is typical of thousands of such endings. After **1. h4 a5 2. g4 a4 3. Kf2 a3 4. Ke3 Ke6 5. Ke4 Kf6 6. c4 b6 7. c3 Ke6 8. h5 gxh5 9. gxh5 Kf6 10. h6 Kg6 11. Kxe5** White can either queen in time or capture all of Black's pawns.

Where both sides have outside passed pawns or are threatening to acquire them, careful calculation is required to see who gets there first in what is often a photo-finish.

No. 153, Muller-Rohde, correspondence

Whoever plays wins

Black's potential passed pawn on the kingside is a strong weapon, but his first job must be to block the White pawns. For this purpose both 1. ... a6 and 1. ... b6 come into consideration. Offhand, 1. ... b6 looks better, but there seems to be nothing wrong with the other move. Only after an exact calculation of all the possible consequences can we see which is better.

On **1. ... a6 2. h4!!** (best; if 2. c5 axb5 3. c6 Kd6 4. cxb7 Kc7 5. a6 f3 6. gxf3 gxf3 7. Ke3 b4 and queens first) **2. ... gxh3**

On 2. ... h5?, 3. b6! turns the tables: 3. ... f3 4. gxf3 gxf3 5. Ke3 f2 6. Kxf2 Kd4 7. Kf3 Kxc4 8. Ke4!! Kb5 9. Kd5 Kxa5 10. Kc5!! Ka4 11. Kd6 Kb5 12. Kc7 a5 13. Kxb7 a4 14. Ka7 a3 15. b7 a2 16. b8=Q+.

3. gxh3 f3 4. bxa6 bxa6 5. Ke3 f2 6. Kxf2 Kd4 7. Kf3 Kxc4 8. Kg4. White captures the h-pawn, Black the a-pawn. Although Black queens first, White's pawn reaches the seventh, so no win is possible (see No. 1027).

Since White just manages to escape by the varnish of his pieces in the above variation, 1. ... b6 must also be calculated with great care: **1. ... b6 2. axb6** (2. a6 Kd6) **axb6 3. c5** (the only chance) **3. ... bxc5 4. b6 Kd6 5. b7 Kc7 6. b8=Q+ 6. Kxb8 7. Ke4 Kc7 8. Kxf4 h5 9. h3 c4!** and White can resign.

On the other hand, if it's White's move in the diagram he can force a win by **1. c5!**, for if **1. ... Kd5 2. c6! bxc6 3. b6 axb6 4. a6!** and queens by force.

3) The Protected Passed Pawn.

Endings with a protected passed pawn are exceptions to the rule that the more pawns there are on the board the easier it is to win. The additional pawns either block the position or give the defender tactical counterchances.

4) Qualitatively Better Pawn Position

The general pawn configuration is an essential factor in all endings. Where there are not more than three pawns on each side, one pawn position is better than another only if there is some qualitative pawn majority (e.g., one pawn holding two). In more complicated endings, such advantages are equally decisive, but other questions, such as the relative king positions and the number of reserve pawn moves available, are more important.

Qualitative majorities are due either to doubled pawns or a blockade.

No. 154, Löwenthal-Williams, London, 1851

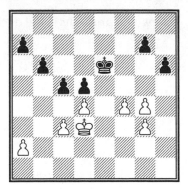

White to play

In **No. 154** we see the fatal weakness of doubled pawns: Black forces an outside passed pawn on the queenside and then sacrifices it to capture the pawns on the other wing. Meanwhile, the White majority is useless. The game continued: **1. Ke3 Kd6 2. f5 Ke7 3. Kf3 cxd4 4. cxd4 b5 5. g5 hxg5 6. g4 Kd6 7. Ke3 Kc6 8. Kd3 Kb6 9. Kc3 Ka5 10. Kb3 b4** and White soon resigned.

Weak pawns are exploited by attacking them with the king. But the success of such an attack depends on whether the king can penetrate the defense, which in turn brings us back to the problem of the opposition. And the effectiveness of the opposition is in large measure determined by who has the extra tempo.

No. 155

Black to play wins

The entrance of the Black king is made possible by the inferior (too far advanced) position of the White pawns.

After **1. ... Kf6 2. Ke3 Ke5 3. c4** it is clear that if the White king can be forced to move Black will mop up either on the queenside or on the kingside. The tempo move **3. ... b4** is for this reason decisive. On **4. Ke2 Ke4** keeps the opposition.

Very often, handling the pawns properly is the decisive factor. **No. 156** is an instructive example.

No. 156, Taubenhaus-Pollock, Bradford 1888

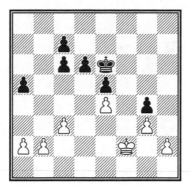

Black to play

White's problem is how to stop the entry of the Black king because his prospective passed pawn (h2) is blocked. **1. ... d5** (if 1. ... a4?! 2. Kg2! d5 3. h4, etc., =) **2. a4! Kd6** (2. ... dxe4 3. Ke3 Kd5 4. b3 or 2. ... c5 3. c4, =) **3. Ke3 Kc5 4. b3,** etc., draws.

One significant difference from the basic endings is that the presence of more than three pawns increases the value of center pawns. In the more elementary cases, a center pawn is often a serious handicap because the opponent then has potential or actual outside passed pawns. When there is more material on the board this is much less important, since usually neither king can get through to the enemy pawns. In view of this, we can see why center pawns are an advantage in the complicated cases.

In **No. 156,** for example, the White king was tied down because of the powerful center phalanx. But when there is a passed pawn it is preferable not to have it in the center. The strength of a passed pawn is that it lures the opponent's king away from the other pawns; the farther away it is the stronger the pawn becomes.

No. 157, Pirc-Alatortsev, Moscow 1935

Black to play

No. 157 is a draw precisely because the center pawn merely gets in White's way and does not hamper Black in the least. The game continued **1. ... Kd5 2. a4 a6 3. b3 f6 4. h4 h6 5. g3 g5 6. Ke3 gxh4 7. gxh4 h5 8. Kd3 b5!** and White can do nothing; e.g., **9. axb5 axb5 10. Ke3** (10. Kc3? Ke4! gives Black winning chances after 11. Kb4, but 11. d5 Kxd5 12. Kd3 still draws) **10. ... Kd6 11. Kd2 b4! 12. Kd3 Kd5**, etc. =.

Although weak pawns are a serious danger, they are not necessarily fatal unless they are combined with an inferior king position.

No. 158, Reinfeld-Fine, New York 1940

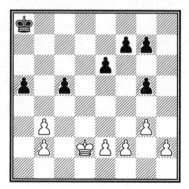

Black to play. Draw

His king is not badly placed, so White could have held the draw. After **1. ... Kb7 2. Kc3 Kb6 3. Kc4 g4 4. f3 f5 5. f4** (now Black does not have an extra tempo) **5. ... Kc6 6. Kd3 Kd5**

6. ... Kb5 7. Kc3 is useless. Black will first try to get a pawn to e4 to deprive White's king of the square d3.

7. Kc3 e5 8. Kd3 (not 8. fxe5 g5 9. e3 Kxe5 10. Kc4 Ke4 with a simple win)
8. ... e4+ 9. Kc3 Kd6 (but 9. ... Kc6 10. Kc4 Kb6 11. Kd5 Kb5 12. Ke6 Kb4 13. Kxf5 Kxb3 14. Kg6 Kxb2 15. Kxg7 a4! 16. f5 a3 17. f6 a2 18. f7 a1=Q, and Black, with his passed pawn, should win the queen ending. White's pawns are only obstacles for perpetual check.) **10. Kd2 Kc6 11. Kc2?**

This inaccuracy in time pressure loses. Clearly, Black needs two pawn tempi to win: one to drive the king from c3, the other to drive it from c2. After 11. e3! Black would only have one tempo and so could only draw. Attempts such as 11. ... c4 or. ... a4 lead to nothing.

11. ... Kb5! 12. Kd2 (or 12. e3 Kb4; or 12. Kc3 e3! 13. Kd3 Kb4 14. Kc2 g6)
12. ... Kb4 13. Kc2 e3! (not 13. ... g6 14. e3!, for if 14. ... c4 15. bxc4 Kxc4 16. b3+ Kb4 17. Kb2, =). Here White resigned, for if he goes after the e-pawn, the Black a-pawn will queen in at most six moves.

Most weak pawn positions are not permanently inferior unless there is an indissoluble doubled pawn or a succession of isolated pawns. Usually, pawn inferiority is relative to the amount of time available to straighten out the pawns and bring up the king. This is quite obvious in a number of examples cited (Nos. 142, 153, etc.).

No. 159, Böök-Fine. Warsaw 1935

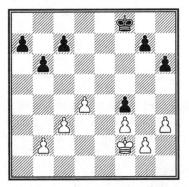

Black to play

Another case in point. If White were an obliging fellow and went to sleep for a while, Black could set up his pawns at c6, b5 and a4, and his king at d5, when White would be hopelessly lost. But Black, able to make only one move at a time, must both defend his f-pawn and prevent the entry of the king on the queenside, an impossible task.

After **1. ... Kf7 2. Ke2 Kf6**

Or 2. ... Ke6 3. Kd3 b5 4. Ke4 g5 5. d5+ Kd6 6. b4 c6 7. dxc6 Kxc6 8. h4 Kb6 9. h5! a5 10. bxa5+ Kxa5 11. Kf5 and White queens while Black's pawn is only on the sixth.

3. Kd3 Kf5 4. Kc4 c6 5. d5 cxd5+ 6. Kxd5 Kg5. Here there is a routine win by **7. c4 Kh4 8. b4,** but White is bedazzled by his ability to win a pawn. The interesting continuation was **7. Ke5? b5! 8. b4 g6!!** (this draws; the point will soon be seen) **9. Ke4 Kh4! 10. Kxf4 h5!!** (it is essential to have this pawn protected) **11. Ke5 Kg3 12. Kf6 Kxg2 13. Kxg6 Kxh3 14. f4** (on 14. Kxh5 Kg3 White loses) **14. ... h4** and White can do nothing in the queen-and-pawn ending.

Where one passed pawn or set of passed pawns is better placed than the opponent's, the winning process (as in the case of three vs. three) consists of blocking the enemy's counterchances and advancing one's own pawns as far as they will go.

No. 160, Euwe-Alekhine, 24th match game 1935

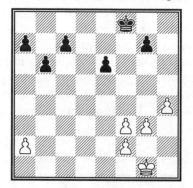

Black to play

White's only hope lies in maneuvering his kingside pawns into a position where the Black king dare not go to further his queenside pawns. For instance, if White could get a passed pawn or set up his pawns at f4, g5, and h5, the constant threat of h6 would confine the Black king to his bed. Black can avoid this only by exchanging his e-pawn for White's f-pawn or by preventing f4.

Alekhine therefore played **1. ... e5!**. If now 2. f4 exf4 3. gxf4 Kf7 and Black can pick up all the White pawns at his leisure. Again, if 2. g4 Ke7 3. h5, and Black can maneuver his king to f4, break with 3. ... e4, and capture the g-pawn and h-pawn, followed later by a similar liquidation of White's e-pawn and f-pawn.

So White is lost unless he can exchange his f-pawn for Black's e-pawn without breaking up his own pawn structure; that is, if he can play 4. f4 and recapture with his king. But since the White king at f4 would be outside the square of a Black b-pawn at b4, Black has only to advance his b-pawn and a-pawn.

2. Kf1 b5 3. Ke2 a5.

In the game Alekhine unaccountably played 3. ... c5, when Euwe drew with 4. Ke3.

4. Kd3 a4 5. Kc3 c5 6. g4 Ke7 7. Kd3 Kd6 8. Kc3 Kd5 9. a3 Ke6 10. Kb2 b4 11. axb4 cxb4 12. Kc2 Kd5 13. h5 Kc4 14. Kb2 a3+ 15. Ka2 Kc3 16. g5 b3+ with mate in a few moves.

A protected passed pawn is qualitatively superior to an outside passed pawn and is generally a sufficient advantage to win.

No. 161

White to play

This position is relatively difficult only because the Black pawn is so far back. Still, White, by making proper use of the greater mobility of his king (the Black king must not venture past the b-file) and the advanced position of his pawn, can manage to score. **1. Kb4 Kb6 2. Ka4 a6** (or 2. ... Kb7 3. Kb5 Kc7 4. Ka6 Kb8 5. h5 gxh5 6. e6 Kc7 7. Kxa7 Kd6 8. Kb6 Kxe6 9. Kc6, etc., wins) **3. Kb4 Kc6 4. Kc4 Kb6 5. Kd5! Kb7** (if 5. ... a5 6. Kd6! a4 7. e6 both pawns promote but White captures Black's queen by 11 Qb8+ and 12 Qa8+) **6. Kd6 Kc8** (or 6. ... a5 7. e6) **7. Kc6** (7. Ke7 is also good) **7. ... K any 8. Kb6,** after which the rest is routine.

An outside passed pawn can draw against a protected passed pawn under certain circumstances (see three vs. three). This can be done by blockade, if the blockader can remain in the square of the outside passed pawn and if the base of the protected passed pawn can be undermined.

No. 162 (Tarrasch-Schiffers, Nuremberg 1896) is an example of this last stratagem: **White: king at c5, pawns at d6, e3, f4, h2; Black: king at d8, pawns at a7, e4, g6, h7.** White to play. **1. Kc6 Kc8** (in the game Schiffers played 1. ... h6?? 2. h4 h5; when 3. Kd5 Kd7 4. Kxe4 Kxd6 5. Kd4 Kc6 6. e4 Kd6 7. Kc4 Kc6 8. Kb4, as in No. 152, is decisive) **2. Kd5 Kd7 3. Kxe4 Kxd6 4. Kd4 Ke6 5. e4 a5 6. Kc5 g5! 7. f5+** (7. fxg5 Ke5 8. h4 is also a draw) **7. ... Ke5 8. f6 Kxf6 9. Kd6** and the pawns promote simultaneously.

Where there are two connected passed pawns against two widely separated passed pawns (or potential passed pawns), the outcome always depends on who can get there first. The principles with more than three pawns on the board remain exactly the same as in the simpler case, but sometimes one must resort to certain finesses to get the pawns through.

No. 163, Pillsbury-Tarrasch, Nuremberg 1896

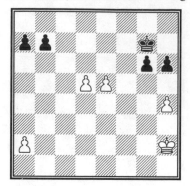

Black to play

No. 163 is of historical interest. Pillsbury was severely criticized for exchanging queens to get into this ending, although it should be a draw with best play. Black must either try to mobilize his own pawns (1. ... b5) or blockade his opponent's (1. ... Kf7). It makes no difference as far as the eventual result is concerned, but on general principles Black should play 1. ... Kf7 to prevent a White pawn from reaching the seventh.

That the game is a draw in either case is shown by the following variations: **1. ... b5 2. h5!**

But not 2. d6? Kf7 3. d7 Ke7 4. e6 a5 5. h5 g5 6. Kg3 b4 7. Kg4 a4 8. Kf5 b3 9. axb3 axb3 10. Kg6 b2 11. d8=Q+ Kxd8 12. Kf7 b1=Q 13. e7+ Kc7 14. e8=Q Qf5+! and Black wins by forcing the exchange of queens.

2. ... gxh5 (if 2. ... g5? 3. Kg3 a5 4. Kg4 b4 5. d6 decides for White) **3. Kg3 a5 4. Kh4 b4 5. d6 Kf7 6. d7 Ke7 7. e6 a4 8. Kxh5 b3 9. axb3 axb3 10. Kg6 b2 11. d8=Q+ Kxd8 12. Kf7,** and the queen-and-pawn ending cannot be won.

If **1. ... Kf7, 2. h5!** at the right moment forces a drawn queen-and-pawn ending.

Tarrasch actually made an incredible blunder in the game: **1. ... b5 2. Kg3 b4 3. Kf4 g5+?? 4. hxg5 hxg5+ 5. Kxg5,** and after 5. ... a5 6. d6 Kf7 7. Kf5 it took White only two moves to queen while it took Black four.

No. 164, Pillsbury-Gunsberg, Hastings 1895

White to play

In **No. 164**, White does not have time to bring his king to the aid of his pawns, but the threat of doing so forces Black to allow White an extra passed pawn. **1. e4! dxe4 2. d5+ Kd6 3. Ke3 b4 4. Kxe4 a4 5. Kd4 Ke7** (5. ... f5 6. gxf5 g4 7. f6 is much easier) **6. Kc4 b3 7. axb3 a3 8. Kc3 f5 9. gxf5 g4**. Now it seems that Black will queen right after his opponent, but because White's pawns are already so far advanced he can manage to queen with check: **10. b4 h5 11. b5 a2 12. Kb2 a1=Q+ 13. Kxa1 h4 14. b6 g3 15. d6+ Kxd6** (or 15. ... Kf6 16. d7 Ke7 17. b7 g2 18. d8=Q+ Kxd8 19. b8=Q+) **16. b7 Kc7 17. e7 g2 18. b8=Q+ Kxb8 19. e8=Q+**.

5) Better King Position and Opposition

The better king position goes hand in hand with the opposition. If one king is placed so that the other has little or no mobility, the opponent must move pawns, and once these have been exhausted either an extra tempo or the opposition will decide.

No. 165, Horwitz

Black to play. White wins

Sometimes it is necessary to exchange a number of pawns before the opposition is of any significance. In **No. 165**, first the c-pawn is blockaded, then the d-pawn is exchanged, and finally Black's c-pawn must fall, because with White's pawn at c4 and Black's at c5 and White's king on the fifth, White always has the opposition. **1. ... Kd7 2. c4 bxc3 3. bxc3 a3 4. c4 Kc7 5. e4 Kd7 6. e5 dxe5 7. Kxe5 Kc6 8. Ke6 Kc7 9. Kd5 Kb6 10. Kd6**, etc.

The same exchange maneuver is decisive when the opposing king has been shunted off to some deserted part of the board and cannot get back in time to challenge the opposition.

An example is **No. 166** (Mason-Englisch, London 1883): **White king at e3, pawns at b4, c4, f3, g3, h2; Black king at a6, pawns at c6, e5, f6, f5, h7.** White to play. On **1. g4** Black does not get back in time after **1. ... f4+**, but does after **1. ... fxg4** (1. ... f4+? 2. Ke4 h6 3. h4 Kb6 4. g5 fxg5 5. hxg5 hxg5 6. Kxe5 g4 7. Kxf4 gxf3 8. Kxf3 Kc7 9. Ke4 Kd6 10. Kf5 and wins, see No. 63) **2. fxg4 h6 3. h4 Kb6 4. Ke4 Kc7 5. g5 fxg5 6. hxg5 hxg5 7. Kxe5 g4 8. Kf4 Kd6 9. Kxg4 Ke5**, =.

A variant on this idea is the sacrifice of a pawn to cramp the opponent's game and secure the opposition. This is seen in **No. 167** (Horwitz): **White king at h6, pawns at c3, d4, e5, f4; Black king at d8, pawns at d5, e7, f7, f5.** Black to play can draw at once by **1. ... e6**. But White to play wins with **1. Kg7** (not 1. e6 fxe6 2. Kg7 Kc7! and Black has the distant opposition) **1. ... Ke8 2. e6! fxe6 3. Kg8** (now White has the opposition) **3. ... Kd8 4. Kf8 Kd7 5. Kf7 Kd6 6. Ke8 e5 7. dxe5+ Ke6 8. Kd8 Kf7 9. Kd7** (White still has the opposition) **9. ... Kf8 10. e6** or **10. Ke6**.

The value of any king position is relative to the pawn skeleton. One king is almost always nearer a certain set of pawns than the other, but it is only when we view the situation as a whole that we can determine which one is better placed. We must also consider whether a given advantageous post can be maintained, which of course again brings up the opposition.

A pawn configuration is relatively static, but a king position is mobile.

No. 168, Loyd-Winawer, Paris 1867

Black to play

There seems to be nothing wrong with White's game, yet after **1. ... g5+! 2. hxg5 hxg5+ 3. Kxg5** (on 3. Kf3 Ke5 4. Ke3 f6! decides) **3. ... Ke5 4. Kh6 Kxe4 5. Kg7?**

White can draw with 5. Kg5! Ke5 6. Kh6 Kf7 7. Kh5 f6 8. Kh4 Kf3 9. Kh3 Ke4 10. Kh4 Kd4 11. Kh5; if 5. g5 Kf4! (diagonal opposition) 6. Kg7 Kxg5 7. Kxf7 Kf5; or 6. Kh5 Kg3 7. g6 fxg6+ 8. Kxg6 Kf4.

5. ... f5!! 6. g5 f4 and Black either queens with check (if the king goes to the f-file) or exchanges queens (if the king goes to the h-file). So White resigned.

When the superior side does not have the opposition but would have it if his opponent were forced to move, this can be obtained using pawn moves to get a position having an extra tempo. Of course, if the position is completely blocked nothing can be done. Keep in mind that the opposition is effective only when the opponent would lose if his king could move to *either* side, not just to one side. Thus with king and rook-pawn vs. king, although White does get the opposition, it is useless because Black can move in only one direction and so cannot be driven away from the queening file. Similarly, in many cases with king and two pawns vs. king and pawn, with a rook-pawn on the board, it doesn't matter whether White has the opposition or not.

In general, then, to be able to exploit the opposition, one must have a winning continuation against all possible enemy king moves.

No. 169, Berger

White to play wins

1. Kd5

Both 1. e5 fxe5 2. fxe5 Kd7 3. Kd5 g5 4. e6+ Ke7 5. Ke5 h5 6. Kf5 g4 7. Kg5 Kxe6 8. Kxh5 Kf5, =, and 1. h4 g6! 2. Kd5 Kd7 3. e5 fxe5 4. Kxe5 Ke7, =, are inadequate.

1. ... Kd7 2. e5 fxe5

What else? If 2. ... Ke7 3. exf6+! gxf6 (3. ... Kxf6 transposes to the main line) 4. Kc6 Ke6 5. Kb6 Kf5 6. Kxa6 Kxf4 7. Kxb5 Ke3, and if 2. ... f5 3. e6+ Ke7 4. Ke5 g6 5. h3! h6! 6. h4 h5 7. Kd5 Ke8 8. Kd6 Kd8 9. e7+ Ke8 10. Ke6 forces mate after 10. ... g5 11. hxg5 h4 12. g6, etc.

3. Kxe5 Ke7

Again no choice: both 3. ... g6 4. Kf6 and 3. ... h6 4. Kf5 Ke7 5. Kg6 Kf8 6. f5 Kg8 7. h4 Kf8 8. h5 Kg8 9. f6 gxf6 10. Kxf6 are equally useless.

4. Kd5 Kd7

Or 4. ... Kf6 5. Kc6 Kf5 6. Kb6 Kxf4 7. Kxa6 g5 8. Kxb5 g4 9. Kc6 h5 10. b5 and again White queens with check.

5. Kc5 Kc7

We have now returned to the starting position with the sole difference that two pawns are missing.

6. f5!! (this gives him the needed extra tempo) **6. ... h6** (if 6. ... g6 7. fxg6 hxg6 8. h4) **7. h3! h5 8. h4 Kd7 9. Kb6 Ke7!! 10. Kxa6 Kf6 11. Kxb5 Kxf5 12. a4** (12. Kc4 g5! 13. Kd4 g4 only draws [see No. 107]) **12. ... g5 13. a5 g4 14. a6 g3 15. a7 g2 16. a8=Q g1=Q 17. Qd5+ Kf6 18. Qxh5 Qf1+ 19. Kb6 Qf2+ 20. Ka6!** with a fairly easy win (for instance, 20. ... Qa2+ 21. Kb5! and Black has no check).

Where the pawns are far apart and there is a constant threat of creating a passed pawn (as in No. 169), the win is neither easy nor certain. In **No. 170: White king at d5, pawns at a4, b3, c5, g4, h3; Black king at e7, pawns at a5, b7, f7, g7, h6**. Black to play. Draw. The dominating position of the White king does him no good. With **1. ... g6** followed by f5 at the proper moment (after White has played c6) Black is assured of equality.

Again, when the defending side has more reserve pawn tempi and the win depends on exploiting the opposition, the result is usually a draw. In this connection, one of the few recorded Morphy endings is pertinent.

No. 171, Morphy-Löwenthal, London 1858

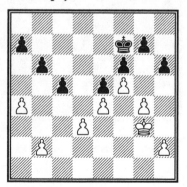

White to play

White's only chance to penetrate Black's position is on the kingside. But first **1. Kh3!** saves a tempo, and after **1. ... g5 2. fxg6+ Kxg6 3. Kh4,** etc., White wins.

The game continuation was **1. Kh4? Kf8?** (the right plan is 1. ... g5+ 2. fxg6+ Kxg6, and Black has enough pawn tempi to keep the White king out) **2. Kh5 Kf7 3. b3?**

This gives away the necessary tempo and the win, as we will see. The correct move is 3. h3!, using the same maneuver as in the game but this time in order to win. The *Encyclopedia of Chess Endings* assesses the position as a draw. It is hard to believe that in more than a century no one had discovered this winning method.

3. ... Kf8! 4. Kg6 Kg8 5. h3 (now this tempo is meaningless because Black can answer with further king tempi) **5. ... Kf8 6. h4 Kg8 7. g5 hxg5 8. hxg5 fxg5 9. Kxg5 Kf7 10. Kh4 Ke7 11. Kg4!?** (White is mirroring the same triangulation method as in the last example, but unfortunately Black has an extra tempo here) **11. ... Kf6 12. Kh5 a6**

Imagine for a moment that the b-pawn remained on b2, as I recommended on move 3. In that case, now 13. b3! b5 14. a5! b4 15. Kh4 g6 (or 15. ... Ke7 16. Kg4!, etc.) 16. fxg6 Kxg6 17. Kg4 wins because this time the e-pawn will fall.

13. Kh4 g6! 14. a5?! bxa5!? (nothing has changed; White is still missing one move to win. Here 14. ... b5 is also good.) **15. fxg6 Kxg6 16. Kg4 a4! 17. bxa4 a5.** Black has the opposition and the draw. If White tries to break in via the c4 square, the Black king arrives at c6 in time to stop it.

No. 172, Bernstein–Fine, New York 1940

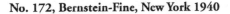

Black to play

The complexity of converting a better king position into a position where one has the opposition is illustrated in **No. 172**. The first winning plan that comes to mind consists of maneuvering against the weak kingside pawns. For instance, 1. ... Kf4 2. Kf2 g4 3. fxg4 Kxg4 4. Kg2 h5 5. Kf2 Kh3 6. Kg1 h4 7. Kh1, but now Black has reached a dead end. However, instead of 2. ... g4, 2. ... h5 might have been tried: 3. Ke2 g4 4. fxg4 hxg4 5. Kf2 Kg5 6. Kg3 b6 7. Kf2 Kh4 8. Kg2 b5 9. Kg1 Kh3 10. Kh1 g3 11. hxg3 Kxg3 12. Kg1.

This variation would also result in a draw, but it furnishes a valuable hint for a winning scheme: if White's pawns on the queenside were weakened—i.e., if his c-pawn were at c3—the king could march over (after 12. Kg1) and gobble up a pawn. So Black's first effort is to induce a pawn advance on the queenside.

1. ... Kd4 2. Kd2 a5

Clearly Black can only force White to push up his c-pawn at the point of a gun, so the reverse of the first plan will be tried: weaken White's queenside pawns, force the White king to stand guard over them, exchange pawns, and finally shift over to the other wing. Why the a-pawn had to move up will soon be seen.

3. Ke2 b5 4. Kd2 c4 (if the Black pawn were still at a6, 5. dxc4 bxc4 6. b4 would draw) **5. bxc4**

With this a draw can just be squeezed out. How the alternatives lose is highly instructive:

a) 5. c3+ Kd5 6. bxc4+ bxc4 7. d4 (7. dxc4+ Kxc4 8. Kc2 a4) Ke6 8. Ke3 Kf5 9. Kf2 Kf4 10. Ke2 h5 11. Kf2 g4 12. fxg4 hxg4 13. Ke2 Kg5 14. Kf2 Kh4 15. Kg2 a4 16. Kh1 Kh3 17. Kg1 g3 18. hxg3 Kxg3 19. Kf1 Kf3 20. Ke1 Ke3 21. Kd1 Kd3 22. Kc1 a3! 23. bxa3 Kxc3 24. a4 (24. Kb1 Kd2 or 24. Kd1 Kb2) 24. ... Kb4 25. Kc2 Kxa4 26. Kc3 Kb5;

b) 5. c3+ Kd5 6. dxc4+ bxc4 7. Kc2 c5 (7. ... cxb3+ only draws) 8. bxc4+ Kxc4 9. b3+ (or 9. Kd2 Kb3 10. Kc1 c4 11. Kb1 a4 12. Kc1 a3 13. bxa3 Kxa3) 9. ... Kd5 10. Kd3 c4+! 11. Kc2 Kc5 12. Kb2 cxb3 13. Kxb3 a4+ 14. Kxa4 Kc4 15. Ka5 Kxc3 16. Kb6 Kd3, and Black gets there first;

c) 5. Ke2 c3!! (the simplest) 6. bxc3+ Kxc3 7. Kd1 a4, and again White will have to give up two pawns to stop the a-pawn.

5. ... bxc4 6. dxc4 (again best: on 6. c3+ Kc5 7. d4+ Kb5 8. Kc1 Ka4 9. Kc2 h5, and Black penetrates to b3) **6. ... Kxc4 7. Ke3 a4 8. f4!!** (8. Ke4? c5 9. f4 gxf4 10. Kxf4 Kd4 11. h4 c4 is hopeless) **8. ... gxf4+** (or 8. ... c5 9. b3+!, =) **9. Kxf4 Kd4 10. Kf3!! h5!!** (the only chance: if 10. ... c5 11. Ke2 c4 12. Kd2 c3+ 13. Kc1! =) **11. Ke2 Ke4 12. Kf2 Kf4 13. Ke2** (White must not move any pawns) **13. ... Kg4 14. Kf2! Kh3 15. Kg1 h4**

The critical position: if it were now Black's move he would win by 16. ... c5 17. Kh1 c4 18. c3 Kg4 19. Kg2 h3+ 20. Kf2 Kf4 21. Ke2 Ke4 22. Ke1 Ke3 23. Kd1 Kd3 24. Kc1 a3!

16. Kh1 c5 17. Kg1 c4 18. c3 Kg4 19. Kf2 Kf4 20. h3, draw. White now has the opposition.

Where one side already has the opposition, other things being equal, it is usually fairly simple to convert it into the gain of material. **No. 173** shows a winning method that can often be applied.

No. 173, Brinckmann-Rubinstein, Budapest 1929

Black to play

Rubinstein chose a less complicated but equally effective line: **1. ... Ke4 2. Ke2 g5 3. Kf2** (if now 3. Kd2 Kf4 4. Ke2 Kg3 5. Kf1 Kh2 6. Kf2 g4 7. Kf1 g3) **3. ... d4 4. cxd4 Kxd4 5. Ke2 b4! 6. Kd2 b3 7. c3+ Ke4 8. Ke2 Kf4 9. Kf2 Kg4 10. Kf1 Kg3 11. Kg1 g4 12. Kf1** (or 12. Kh1 Kf2 13. Kh2 Kf1 14. Kh1 Ke2 15. Kh2 Kd2 16. Kg3 Kc2, etc.) **12. ... Kh2 13. Kf2 Kh1 14. Kg3 Kg1 15. Kxg4 Kxg2** and White resigned, since his pawn will be only on the sixth when Black queens.

Often a game is a draw or a win depending on who has the move and when pawn moves cannot change the situation either way. In **No. 174** (Ed. Lasker-Maroczy, New York 1924): **White king at e4, pawns at a4, b3, c2, d5, h3, h5; Black king at f6, pawns at a5, b4, c5, d6, g5, h6,** White loses if he has to move, for after **1. Kd3 Ke5 2. Kc4 Ke4 3. Kb5 Kxd5 4. Kxa5 Kc6! 5. Ka6 d5 6. a5 c4 7. Ka7 Kc7 8. a6 cxb3 9. cxb3 d4 10. Ka8 d3 11. a7 d2 12. h4 d1=Q** and mates next move. But Black to play can hold the draw with **1. ... Ke7!** (not 1. ... Kf7 2. Kf5, when White has the opposition) **2. Kd3** (or 2. Kf5 Kf7 White has no extra tempo) **2. ... Kf6! 3. Ke4,** for **3. Kc4?? Ke5!** loses as above.

When one side has the opposition, but needs several extra tempi to exploit it properly, it is all-important to maneuver the pawns properly. The consequences of neglecting a timely clarification of the pawn position is seen in **No. 175.**

No. 175, Lissitzin-Alatortsev, Moscow 1935

Draw only if White fixes the pawns on the kingside

1. Kc3 a5 2. h4 h5 3. Kd3? (this should not yet lose, but it deserves a question mark because 3. g4 removes all danger: 3. ... hxg4 [3. ... g6 4. g5] 4. fxg4 f6 5. h5 b6 6. e4 e5 7. Kd3!, etc.) **3. ... Kb4 4. Kc2 b5** (he must exchange first, since 4. ... Ka3 5. Kc3 Ka2 6. Kc4! is bad) **5. axb5 Kxb5 6. Kc3 Kc5 7. Kd3??**

Now this is fatal. Both 7. g4 as above and 7. e4! hold the position:

a) 7. e4! e5 8. f4 f6 9. Kd3 Kb4 10. Kc2 a4 (or 10. ... Ka3 11. Kc3 g6 12. Kc4 Kb2 13. b4! a4 14. b5 and the pawns promote at the same time) 11. bxa4 Kxa4 12. Kc3 Kb5 13. Kb3 Kc5 14. Kc3 g6 15. Kd3 Kb4 16. Ke3, and Black must take the draw with 16. ... Kc5, for if 16. ... Kc4?? 17. f5!! gxf5 18. exf5 Kd5 19. g4! Kd6 20. g5! wins for White.

b) 7. e4! Kb5 8. f4 Kc5 9. e5! Kb5 10. Kd3 Kb4 11. Kc2 a4 12. bxa4 Kxa4 13. Kc3 Kb5 14. Kb3 =.

7. ... Kb4 8. Kc2 Ka3 9. Kc3 Ka2 10. Kc2

Now 10. b4 loses after 10. ... axb4+ 11. Kxb4 Kb2 12. Kc4 Kc2 13. Kd4 Kd2 14. Ke4 Ke2 15. Kf4 f6! 16. g4 g6! 17. gxh5 (17. g5 e5+ 18. Ke4 fxg5) gxh5 18. Ke4 Kf2 19. Kf4 Kg2.

10. ... f5 (now it is perfectly clear why White's do-nothingness was fatal: Black has the requisite pawn tempo) **11. Kc3 Kb1 12. e4 fxe4 13. fxe4 e5! 14. Kd3 Kb2 15. Kc4 Kc2 16. Kd5** (the condemned man dines on a pawn) **16. ... Kxb3 17. Kxe5 a4** and White soon resigned.

IX. MANEUVERING FOR A TEMPO

As most of the above examples indicate, maintaining as large a reserve of pawn moves as possible is often vital. While there is no rule that covers all positions, the elementary cases will suffice for a large percentage of the endings that do occur.

To gain a tempo it is disadvantageous to have to move first. Starting from the symmetrical position in **No. 176**, the player not on the move always retains an extra tempo by simply copying his opponent's moves.

No. 176

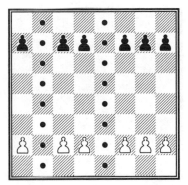

Whoever moves loses the tempo

a) 1. a3 a6 2 a4 a5;

b) 1. c3 c6 2. d3 d6 3. c4 c5 or 3. d4 d5,

c) 1. f3 f6 2. g3 f5! 3. f4 (3. g4 fxg4 4. fxg4 g5 or 3. h3 g5) 3. ... h6 4. h3 h5 5. h4 g6.

From this last variation we can draw the all-important conclusion that an *exchange loses the tempo.*

Where the pawns are not in a symmetrical position, one must generally determine who has the tempo by trial and error, always remembering, however, that in a symmetrical position whoever moves loses the tempo.

X. THE OPPOSITION

One of the most important considerations in pawn endings is how to occupy certain squares with the king, or how to drive the enemy king from a vital square. Because the kings cannot approach each other directly but must always be separated by a *cordon sanitaire*, the occupation of squares is determined by the position of the pawns and the other king. When no relevant pawn moves are available, such occupation depends solely on the relative positions of the kings. Of all such possible relative positions, those involving the opposition are the most interesting.

No. 177

Whoever is not on the move has the opposition

Here is the simplest case, where whoever plays has to cede one of the two (presumably vital) squares he is holding. Thus **1. ... Kf6 2. Kd5**, or **1. ... Kd6 2. Kf5**, or **1. Kd4 Kf5**, or **1. Kf4 Kd5**. If we imagine pawns on the d- and g-files we can see why these squares are ordinarily vital.

No. 178: White king at e4, pawns at c4, g4; Black king at e6, pawns at c5, g5. If it's Black to move, White has the opposition and wins, for on **1. ... Kf6 2. Kd5** captures the c-pawn and similarly on the other side. But if it's White to move the game is only a draw. For on **1. Kd3**, both Kf5 and Kd5 are impossible, so it does Black no good to have the opposition. Only if White makes the blunder **1. Ke3?** is Black able to do anything, for he then replies **1. ... Ke5!** and now he has the opposition where it means something.

Direct opposition may be vertical (as in the No. 177) or horizontal (White king at c6 or g6) or diagonal (White king at g4 or c4). All of these are equally effective as far as capturing squares is concerned, but whether they are a winning advantage or not depends on the pawn position.

Thus **No. 179: White king at g4, pawns at d3, e4; Black king at e6, pawns at d4, e5.** Black to play. White has the opposition and wins because the occupation of f5 is decisive. **1. ... Kf6 2. Kh5 Kf7 3. Kg5 Ke6 4. Kg6** (horizontal opposition) **4. ... Kd6 5. Kf6**, etc.

But in **No. 180: White king at g4, pawns at c4, d3, e4; Black king at e6, pawns at c5, d6, e5,** Black to play, the opposition is useless because occupation of f5 leads to nothing **1. ... Kf6 2. Kh5 Kf7 3. Kg5 Kg7 4. Kf5 Kf7,** =.

No. 181

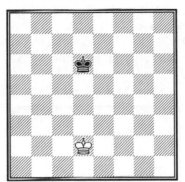

Whoever is not on the move has the distant opposition

The distant opposition is an extension of the same principle. When two kings are on the same file and an *odd number of squares* apart, then whoever is *not* on the move has the distant opposition.

The distant opposition is usually a potent weapon when the pawn position is badly blocked or complex. Its effectiveness depends not only on the occupation of certain squares but also on forcing the enemy king to go to or keep off certain files.

No. 182, Folbys 1931

White to play wins

In **No. 182**, 1. Kf1 gives White the distant opposition (five squares separate the kings). But in order to win he clearly must occupy either f4 or a6, and not merely a5, for then Black's king could prevent further invasion. This means that when the White king gets to a5, the Black king must be no nearer than c7. In other words, White must contrive to force Black to stay two files to his right.

The solution is **1. Kf1! Ke7 2. Ke1! Kf7 3. Kd1 Ke7 4. Kc2 Ke6**

If 4. ... Kd7 5. Kc3 Kc7 6. Kd2 Kb7 7. Ke3 Ka6 8. Kf4 Ka5 9. Ke5!! b4 10. axb4+ Kxb4 11. Kd6 Ka3 12. Kxc6 Kxa2 13. Kxd5 Kb3 14. c6 a3 15. c7 a2 16. c8=Q a1=Q 17. Qxg4 and wins.

    5. Kd2 Kf6 (or 5. ... Kd7 6. Ke3 Kc7 7. Kf4, etc.) **6. Kc3 Ke7 7. Kb4 Kd7 8. Ka5 Kc7 9. Ka6 Kd8 10. Kb7 Kd7 11. Kb6** and wins.

No. 183, L'Hermet 1914

White to play has the opposition and must reach a8 or c8
in at most 17 moves

    This problem sums up all the advantages of the opposition. The solution is **1. Kh2** (distant opposition) **1. ... Kg8 2. Kg2 Kf8 3. Kf2 Ke8 4. Ke2 Kd8 5. Kd2 Kc8 6. Kc2 Kb8 7. Kb2 Ka8 8. Kc3** (a triangulation maneuver; White can now keep the distant opposition at a distance of only three squares) **8. ... Kb7 9. Kb3 Ka7** (if 9. ... Kc7 10. Ka4 and reaches a8) **10. Kc4 Kb6 11. Kb4 Ka7 12. Kc5** (diagonal opposition) **12. ... Kb7 13. Kb5 Ka7 14. Kc6 Kb8 15. Kb6 Ka8 16. Kc7 Ka7 17. Kc8.**

    Other examples of the uses of the distant opposition may be found in Nos. 134, 130, 131, and others.

    Remember the principle that with kings on the same file, rank, or diagonal and an odd number of squares apart, whoever does not play has the opposition. Maneuvering in such positions becomes automatic.

    For example, **No. 184: White king at c6, pawns at c4, e4; Black king at e6, pawn at d6.** White to play. Draw. **1. Kc7 Ke7 2. Kc8 Ke8,** or **1. Kb7 Kf7!!** (but not 1. ... Ke5? 2. Kc7, or 1. ... Kf6 2. Kc8!!, or 1. ... Ke7 2. Kc7) **2. Kb6 Kf6!** (again not 2. ... Kf8? 3. Kc6 Ke7 4. Kc7) and White's extra pawn is worthless.

    Other examples of the opposition are almost everywhere in this chapter.

Chapter III

KNIGHT
AND PAWN ENDINGS

I. THE KNIGHTS ALONE VS. PAWNS

A lone knight can win against pawns only in certain problem positions where the enemy king is blocked by its pawns. What White usually faces is whether his knight can draw against one or two or more pawns. This question can be answered definitively in practically every case.

Knight against one pawn is a draw whenever the knight can reach any square on the queening file ahead of the pawn (except a1 with the a-pawn). Here is the crucial position:

No. 185

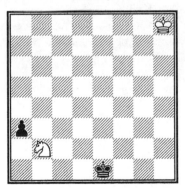

Draw

1. Nd3+ Kd2 2. Nb4 Kc3 3. Na2+ Kb2 4. Nb4 Kb3 5. Nd3 Kc3 6. Nc1, etc., =. If the Black king is at f1, Black wins: **1. Nc4 a2 2. Nd2+ Ke2 3. Nb3 Kd1! 4. Kg7 Kc2 5. Na1+ Kb2** wins.

Only when the pawn is at a2 does White lose, for when Black plays ... Kb2 the only moves that don't put the knight en prise are off the board. The worst place for the knight is one square diagonally in front of the pawn. When the knight is at some distance from the pawn, or for some other reason cannot get to a square on the queening file directly, he can very often get back in time by checking or threatening to check.

No. 186, Grigoriev

White to play. Draw

This is the saving idea in **No. 186**: **1. Nf7!!** (1. Ng6 loses: 1. ... h3 2. Nf4 h2 3. Ne2+ Kd2 4. Ng3 Ke1!) **1. ... h3 2. Ng5 h2 3. Ne4+ Kc2**

Or 3. ... Kd4 4. Nf2!! and Black must retreat to be able to approach the knight, which gives White a breathing space to bring up his king: 4. ... Kc3 5. Kd6 Kd2 6. Ke5 Ke2 7. Nh1! Kf3 8. Kd4 Kg2 9. Ke3 Kxh1 10. Kf2 stalemate.

4. Ng3 Kd1 5. Kd6 Ke1 6. Ke5 Kf2 7. Kf4, =.

When the pawn is on the seventh with the king nearby, a knight-pawn or rook-pawn offers good winning chances, but a center pawn or bishop-pawn does not.

No. 187

White wins. Draw if the pawn is on c, d, e, or f file. Win if the pawn is on a, b, g, or h file

Here Black to play is lost, for on **1. ... Nd7+ 2. Kc8!** (not 2. Kc7? Nc5! =) **2. ... Nb6+ 3. Kd8** and queens. But in **No. 188: White king at c8, pawn at c7; Black king at h1, knight at f5**, after **1. ... Ne7+** (1. ... Nd6+? 2. Kd7 Nc4 3. Kc6 Ne5+ 4. Kc5 Nd7+ 5. Kb5) **2. Kd8 Nc6+ 3. Ke8 Na7!** we are back to **No. 185**.

Knight vs. two pawns is also generally a draw because a knight can blockade two connected passed pawns.

No. 189, P. Benko

White to play. Draw

In **No. 189** the blockade is achieved by_**1. Ne7 c3** (if 1. ... Kg3 2. Nd5 b3 3. Kc7 Kf3 4. Kd6 b2 5. Nc3 Ke3 6. Kc5 draws, but not 6. Nd1+ Kd4 7. Nxb2 c3 and Black wins) **2. Nf5+ Kg4 3. Nd4! Kf4 4. Nc2 b3 5. Nd4 b2 6. Ne2+ Ke3 7. Nxc3,** draw.

For example, **No. 190 (P. Benko): White king at c6, knight at b4; Black king at g5, pawns at e3, f4**. White to play draws. **1. Nc2 e2 2. Nd4! Kg4** (if 2. ... e1=N 3. Ne6+ Kg4 4. Nxf4) **3. Nxe2 f3 4. Nc3! f2 5. Nd1 f1=Q 6. Ne3+** draws.

When the king is supporting the two pawns, the side with the knight can hold the game only if his king is also on the scene.

If the king is off in some far corner, Black can clearly force a queen even if his pawns are only on the fourth or fifth rank.

There is a mate possibility with two pawns:

No. 191

White wins

If White begins, **1. Nf6 Kh1 2. Ng4 h2 3. Kf1 g5 4. Nf2+** mate. If Black begins, **1. ... Kh1** (or 1. ... g5 2. Nf6 g4 3. Nxg4+ Kh1 4. Kf1) **2. Nf6 Kh2 3. Ng4+ Kh1 4. Kf1 g5 5. Kf2 h2 6. Ne3 g4 7. Nf1 g3+ 8. Nxg3+** mate.

When the pawns are disconnected they can be stopped by the knight only if they are one, two, or three files apart. The outcome then depends on the relative king positions.

No. 192, P. Benko 1980

White wins

Most players would think "a passed pawn must be pushed." However, after 1. b6 Ng4! 2. b7 Ne5 3. Kb6 Nd7+ 4. Kc7 Nc5, and now 5. b8=Q Na6+,

Black can trade the knight for the new queen, after which no one would object to a draw.

With **1. Kb6!** White paradoxically blocks his own pawn, but this is the only way to try locking out the knight. Now after 1. ... Kxf5 2. Kc7!, Black has no way to stop the b-pawn.

1. ... Ng4 2. Kc7! Ne3

The best approach may be 2. ... Nf6, but White still wins with 3. Kd6! (3. Kc6? Kxf5 4. b6 Ke6 and 5. ... Nd7) 3. ... Ne4+ 4. Kc6 Nd2 5. Kd5 Nb3 6. b6 Na5 7. Ke6.

3. Kd7! Nd5 (or 3. ... Nxf5 4. Ke6) **4. Kd6 Nb6 5. Ke6!**

Suddenly, White has protected his f-pawn and can now work with that, too. **5. ... Kh6 6. f6 Kg6!** Despite all his efforts, White appears to be stuck. The obvious 7. f7 Kg7 8. Ke7 Nd5+ 9. Ke8 Nf6+ 10. Kd8 Nd5 leads to a draw by repetition.

7. Ke7! Nd5+ 8. Kd6! Nb6 9. Ke6! Kh7.

Again, how to make progress? After 10. f7? Kg7, there is the same draw as before starting with 11. Ke7 Nd5+. But a similar king maneuver helps again.

10. Ke7! Nd5+ 11. Kd6! Nb6 12. Kc6!! The only way. The knight is too good on b6! **12. ... Nc4 13. Kd7 Kg6 14. Ke7!** The rest is easy after either **14. ... Nb6 15. f7** or **14. ... Nc5 15. b6** (or 15. Ke6). Black can't hold back the two pawns any longer.

No. 193: White king at e2, knight at h7; Black king at e7, pawns at b4, h6. White to move, Draw. The king takes care of one pawn while the knight takes care of the other: **1. Kd3 Kf7 2. Kc4 Kg6! 3. Nf8+ Kf5 4. Nd7 h5** (4. ... b3 5. Kc3!) **5. Nc5! h4 6. Nb3! h3 7. Nd2 h2 8. Nf1 h1=Q 9. Ng3+**, draw.

Knight vs. three pawns. Here is the critical position with three connected passed pawns.

No. 194

White to play wins; Black to play draws.
White wins if pawns are on fifth or sixth rank

White to play wins by **1. f5+!** (not 1. g5 Nd5! 2. Ke4 Ne7! 3. Ke5 Kh5!! 4. f5 Kxh4 5. Kf6 [5. g6 Kg5! 6. g7 Ng8 7. Ke6 Nf6] 5. ... Nd5+ 6. Ke6 Kxg5 7. Kxd5 Kxf5) **1. ... Kg7 2. g5 Nd5 3. h5 Nc3** (for 3. ... Kf7 4. h6 Nc3 5. h7 Kg7 6. g6 Nd5, see No. 196) **4. Kf4 Ne2+ 5. Ke5 Ng3 6. f6+ Kg8 7. h6! Nh5 8. g6 Ng3 9. h7+ Kh8 10. f7.**

From this we may infer that if the White pawns are anywhere beyond the fourth rank, unless they are completely blockaded they will be able to promote.

This is borne out by two subvariations: **No. 195: White king at g4, pawns at h5, g5, f4; Black king at e6, knight at f7.** White wins. **1. ... Nd6 2. h6 Kf7 3. Kh5 Ne8** (or 3. ... Kg8 4. g6 Ne4 5. f5 Nf6+ 6. Kg5 Ne4+ 7. Kf4 Nf6 8. h7+ Kg7 transposing into the next example) **4. f5 Nd6 5. g6+ Kf6 6. h7 Kg7 7. f6+ Kh8 8. f7.**

No. 196: White king at e5, pawns at f5, g6, h7; Black king at h8, knight at f6. Black to play. White wins. **1. ... Nh5** (or 1. ... Ng4+ 2. Ke6 Kg7 3. f6+ Nxf6 4. h8=Q+ Kxh8 5. Kxf6 and White has the opposition. Or 1. ... Nd7+ 2. Ke6 Nf8+ 3. Ke7 Nxh7 4. gxh7 Kxh7 5. f6) **2. Ke6 Kg7** (or 2. ... Nf4+ 3. Ke7 [White must avoid stalemate possibilities] 3. ... Nh5 4. Kf7) **3. Ke7 Nf4 4. f6+ Kh8 5. g7+!** (not 5. Kf7? Nxg6) **Kxh7 6. Kf7.**

But with Black to move in **No. 194**, he can draw with **1. ... Nd5 2. h5+** (2. f5+ Kf6 3. Ke4 Nc3+ 4. Kd4 Ne2+! 5. Ke3 Ng3, =) **2. ... Kh6!** (the most advanced pawn must be blockaded; if 2. ... Kf6 3. h6! Kg6 4. g5 Ne7 5. Kg4 and wins, for 5. ... Nf5 6. h7! costs Black his knight) **3. Ke4 Nf6+ 4. Kf5 Nd5 5. Ke5 Ne3 6. g5+ Kxh5 7. Kf6 Nd5+, =.**

To sum up: The three pawns win if and only if at least two can reach the fifth rank. Black should always keep his king in front of the pawns.

Where the three pawns are unconnected (two connected), it is clear that the knight cannot hold them back. Either the knight must be sacrificed to stop one isolated pawn, or it must blockade the two connected pawns until White, after advancing his isolated pawn to drive the Black king to the other side of the board, brings his king to the support of his two passed pawns.

Against three isolated pawns the chances of holding the game are somewhat better because the king can usually capture one, while the knight holds the other two. However, even here the three pawns should win as a rule.

Although **two knights against a lone king** cannot mate, in certain positions **two knights vs. a pawn** can. This is because the knights can only mate by stalemating the king first and letting the pawn make two or three more moves, depending on where it is.

The winning idea consists of three steps:

1. Blocking the pawn;

2. Confining the king to a corner where it must move back and forth between two squares;

3. Lifting the blockade at the right moment, when the win is possible by briefly stalemating the Black king.

There is a vast literature on this ending, but since most of it has little or no relation to practical play we shall give only the main results here.

No. 197

White wins

Once the king is in the corner, as here, mate can be given in six moves (White to play) or eleven moves (Black to play). **1. Nc4! a3 2. Ne5 a2 3. Ng6+ Kh7 4. Nf8+ Kh8 5. Ne7 a1=Q 6. Neg6+** mate. We can see why a b-pawn may not be beyond the fourth rank, for if it queens at b1, White can't play Ng6+ because of Qxg6. With Black to move, on **1. ... Kh7** White must first maneuver to get the diagram position: **2. Kf6 Kg8 3. Ke7! Kh8 4. Kf8 Kh7 5. Kf7 Kh8 6. Nc4** and continue as above.

All this is relatively simple. Complications arise when the king is in the center.

No. 198

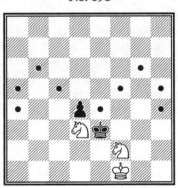

Black to play. White wins if the pawn cannot cross the line

With best play it takes 79 moves to mate after **1. ... Kd2**. The process of driving the Black king into a corner is so long and involved that it requires an extension of the normal 50-move rule.

This ending actually occurred in a tournament game. Although Black was the well-known Hungarian grandmaster A. Lilienthal, the game resulted in a draw. The position reached was **No. 199** (Norman-Lilienthal, Hastings 1934-35): **White king at e8, pawn at b3; Black king at e6, knights at e5, b4.** Black to play. The road to victory (not found by Lilienthal) is **1. ... Nf7 2. Kf8 Nd6 3. Kg7 Kf5 4. Kh6 Ne8! 5. Kh5! Ng7+ 6. Kh4 Kf4 7. Kh3 Nf5 8. Kg2 Ke3 9. Kf1! Nh4! 10. Ke1 Ng2+ 11. Kd1 Kd3 12. Kc1 Ne3 13. Kb2 Nec2! 14. Kc1 Ke2 15. Kb1 Kd1 16. Kb2 Kd2 17. Kb1 Na3+ 18. Kb2 Nb5! 19. Kb1 Nd3 20. b4 Nc3+ 21. Ka1 Kc2 22. b5 Nc1 23. b6 Nb3+** mate. It can sometimes take over 100 moves!

No. 200, Benko-Tan, U.S. Open 1990

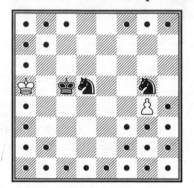

Black to play

Even if one knight stops the pawn only on g4, this doesn't mean an automatic draw. In **No. 200,** the board is divided into two zones. The inside zone (not dotted) is where the White king should be able to draw. The other zone (dotted, including White king), made up of 29 squares around the edge of the board, represents danger. If the White king is trapped in this area it does not necessary lose, but there are a number of losing positions that can arise, most of them involving zugzwang. If the pawn is farther advanced, say on g5 with a Black knight at g6, the losing zone shrinks to 24 squares around the edge. Now let's see how theory works in practice.

We can see that White's king is in the danger zone. In fact, White is already lost.

1. ... Nb6! 2. Ka6 Nc4 3. Kb7 Kd6 4. Ka6?

This makes things easy for Black, who can still win, though with more difficulty, after 4. Kc8 Ne6! (not 4. ... Na5? 5. Kd8!, and the White king reaches the safe zone) 5. g5 (or 5. Kb7 Kd7 6. g5 Nc5+ 7. Kb8 Ne5 8. g6 Nc6+ 9. Ka8 Kc7 10. g7 Nd7 11. g8=Q Nb6+ mate) 5. ... Kc6 6. g6 Nd6+ 7. Kb8 Ng7! 8. Ka8 Kb5 9. Ka7 Ka5 10. Ka8 Ka6 11. Kb8 Kb6 12. Ka8 Ne6 13. g7 Nc7+ 14. Kb8 Na6+ 15. Ka8 Nb5 16. g8=Q Nbc7+ mate.

4. ... Kc6 5. Ka7 Nd6 6. Ka6 Nb7 7. Ka7 Nc5 8. Kb8 Kd7 9. Ka8 Kc7 (closing the box) **10. Ka7 Nge6.**

White resigned, seeing 11. g5 Nd4 12. g6 Nc6+ 13. Ka8 Nd7 14. g7 Nb6+ mate.

When Black has more than one pawn, the two knights win if they can reduce to a position like **No. 198**. The first step is to blockade the pawns, the next to capture all but one.

No. 201

White to plays wins

This is done by **1. Ka3!** (diagonal opposition) **1. ... Kb5 2. Kb3 Ka5 3. Kc2!! Kb5 4. Kd1! Kc5 5. Ke1 Kd6 6. Kf2 Ke6 7. Kg3 Kf5 8. Kh4! Kf6 9. Kg4 Kg6 10. Nf3 Kf6 11. Ng3 Ke6 12. Kg5 Kd6 13. Kf5 Kc5** (13. ... d4 14. Ke4!) **14. Nxe5 d4 15. Nd3+ Kc4 16. Ke4** and we have No. 198.

Against four connected passed pawns the knights cannot set up an effective blockade, so the result is a draw. More than four pawns win against two knights unless a reduction to a simpler draw is available.

II. KNIGHTS AND PAWNS VS. PAWNS

One knight alone is not a sufficient advantage to win, but if there is a pawn on the board, it is. Naturally, Black can draw only if he can capture the pawn. For this reason the pawn should always be defended from the rear by the knight, which will gladly sacrifice itself to let the pawn achieve its ambition. With the knight in front of the pawn a win is possible only if the king is so close that the knight can be sacrificed to give the king the opposition.

No. 202: White king at h1, pawn at b3, knight at c7; Black king at e2. Black to move. Draw: **1. ... Kd3 2. Nd5 Kd4 3. Nf4 Kc3; or 2. b4 Kc4 3. b5 Kc5 4. Kg2 Kb6.**

But **No. 203: White king at h1, knight at d7, pawn at c3; Black king at f3** is a win for White: **1. Nc5 Ke3 2. Na4 Kd3 3. Kg2 Kc4 4. Kf3 Kb3 5. Ke4! Kxa4 6. Kd5.**

One must be careful not to advance a rook pawn to the seventh too hastily.

No. 204

Draw

Black simply moves his king back and forth. The knight cannot move without abandoning the pawn; the king cannot approach without creating stalemate.

A knight cannot win a tempo (as a bishop can). This is strikingly illustrated in **No. 205**.

No. 205

White to play draws. Black to play loses. A knight cannot gain a tempo

White to move can never drive the king from c7-c8, since the knight can approach either square only by giving check. With Black to move, however, **1. ... Kc7 2. Ng7 Kc8 3. Ne6 Kd7 4. Kb7** is immediately decisive.

Knight and pawn against pawn is generally a win, but if the Black king is too near the enemy pawn and the White king too far away, a draw may sometimes be unavoidable. If White has a passed pawn he can defend it with his knight and take care of his opponent's pawn with his king, or vice versa. If there is no passed pawn (that is, the two pawns are facing each other) and the White king is near the pawns, he can always capture the enemy pawn with the help of his knight. Difficulties crop up only when the king cannot approach the pawns in time, and when the knight cannot prevent either the exchange or the capture of the last pawn.

When the pawns are on the same file, the knight can defend its pawn without being subject to attack.

No. 206

White to move wins

In **No. 206**, White gains time for the king to approach by **1. b4 Kd5 2. Nc5 Kc4 3. Na6 Kd5 4. Kg7**, etc.

With Black to play, after **1. ... Kd5 2. Kg7 Kd4 3. Nc1! Ke3 4. Nb3!! Kd3 5. Na5 Kc2 6. b4 Kc3 7. Nc6 Kc4 8. Kf6 Kd5 9. Na5** (or 9. Nb8 Kc4 10. Na6) is decisive.

The above diagram makes it clear that it is useless to leave the knight at d3. But even when the White king is right near the scene of action it is best to defend the pawn with the knight at a more advanced post.

It is never advisable to allow a simultaneous attack on knight and pawn. The danger is that a knight cannot gain a tempo. In **No. 207** (Blackburne-Zuckertort, 1881): **White king at e2, knight at e3, pawn at g4; Black king at f4, pawn at g6**, Black to play draws. **1. ... Kg3 2. Kd1 Kf3 3. Kd2 Kf2** (Black maintains the opposition) **4. Kd3** (if 4. Nf5 Kf3 5. Nh6 Kf4) **4. ... Kf3 5. Kd4 Kf4**. Now **6. Kd5** would still lead to nothing after 6. ... Kxe3 7. Ke5 Kf3 8. Kf6 (8. g5?? loses: 8. ... Kg4 9. Kf6 Kh5). With White to move in the initial position, he wins with **1. Kf2 g5** (or 1. ... Ke4 2. Ng2) **2. Ke2 Kg3 3. Kd3 Kf3 4. Kd4 Kf4**; and now the sacrifice **5. Kd5 Kxe3 6. Ke5 Kf3 7. Kf5**.

With the pawns on adjoining files the problem of gaining time for the approach of the king is often more involved. In **No. 208: White king at h8; knight at b5, pawn at b2; Black king at d7, pawn at a5**, White to move wins. White can reach his goal only by **1. Nd4!** (if 1. Kg7 Kc6 2. Nd4+ Kc5 3. Nb3+ Kc4! 4. Nxa5+ Kb4, =) **1. ... Kd6 2. Nb3! a4** (if now 2. ... Kd5 3. Nxa5 Kc5 4. Nb3+ Kc4 5. Nc1) **3. Na1! Kd5 4. Kg7 Kd4 5. Kf6 Kd3 6. Ke5 Kd2 7. Kd4 Kc1 8. Kc3**, and the rest is simple.

No. 209 is deceptively simple. Isn't the White knight trapped?

No. 209, P. Benko 1989

White to play wins

1. Kc8! But not the more obvious 1. Kc7? Ke7! 2. Kc6 Ke6, and White soon loses his pawn. **1. ... Kf8** But now 1. ... Ke7 fails to 2. Kc7 Ke6 3. Kd8! Kf5 4. Nf7 Kg6 5. Ke8 Kg7 6. Ke7 and wins. **2. Ng6+!!** The point! The knight escapes, since 2. ... hxg6 leads to a won king-and-pawn endgame for White. Instead of 2. Ng6+, tempting is 2. Kd7 Kg7 3. Ke6 Kxh8? 4. Kf7 winning. But correct is 3. ... h6 4. g6 h5, with a draw.

2. ... Kf7 3. Nf4!!

We can appreciate this move only by examining the plausible alternative 3. Nh4. White wins easily after 3. ... Ke6 4. Kd8 Ke5 5. Ke7 Kf4 6. Kf6, but Black has the resource 3. ... Ke8!!. This position deserves careful study. White has no time to correct his error with 4. Ng2 Ke7 5. Nf4, as 5. ... Kd6 6. Nh5 Ke6 holds the draw.

3. ... h6! 4. g6+ (of course not 4. gxh6? Kg8, followed by Kg8-h7xh6, drawing; now the race begins) **4. ... Kf6 5. Kd7 h5 6. Ke8 Kg7** (or 6. ... h4 7. Kf8 h3 8. g7 h2 9. Nh5+ and 10 Ng3, winning) **7. Ke7 h4 8. Ke6 h3 9. Kf5 h2 10. Nh5+ Kf8 11. Ng3** Just in time! Now the win is clear after **11. ... Kg8 12. Kf6 Kf8 13. g7+ Kg8 14. Nh1** (14. Nf5 also works).

No. 210, Reti-Marshall, Baden-Baden 1925

White wins

When Black has two pawns against knight and pawn, White should have no trouble. Two winning ideas are open to him: he can either maneuver to capture one pawn or give up his knight to win both opposing pawns.

The first is seen in **No. 210.** Black to move would have to give up one of this pawns, for on **1. ... Kg6 2. d6** the pawn queens. The real problem is how to win with White to play. The idea is clearly to lose a move and get back to the diagram position with Black to play. This can be done by a triangulation maneuver: Black may not move his king away from the f-file but White may. **1. Kg3 Kf5 2. Kf3 Kf6 3. Kg4**.

No. 211, Reti and Mandler 1924

White to play wins

The other idea is seen in **No. 211.** White can force the entry of his king only by offering to sacrifice his knight: **1. Ng1 Kd2 2. Nf3+ Kd3 3. Ke1 Ke3 4. Ne5 Ke4 5. Nc4! Kd3 6. Nd2 Ke3 7. Nf3 Kd3 8. Kf1 Ke3 9. Ne1 Kd2 10. Nc2!! Kd1** (if 10. ... Kxc2 11. Ke2 followed by Kf3, etc.) **11. Nb4 Kd2 12. Nd5.**

The win is not always smooth sailing for White. Difficulties arise when the opponent's pawns are too far apart or too far advanced or when White's king is too far away. In practice, however, such obstacles are rarely insurmountable, and one of the two winning ideas will be found applicable, so long as the White pawn can be defended by either the king or the knight.

A rare kind of winning possibility is seen in **No. 212**.

No. 212, P. Benko 1999

White to play wins

1. b5! a3 (1. ... Kd5 2. b6 a3 3. Nd4!) **2. b6 a4 3. Nd4! Kd3** (3. ... Kxd4 4. b7 a2 5. b8=Q a1=Q 6. Qh8+ wins) **4. Nc6 Kc4 5. Nb4! Kxb4 6. b7 a2 7. b8=Q+ Ka3 8. Qe5** wins. If 2. ... a2 3. Nc5+ Kd4 4. Nb3+ Kc3 5. Na1! Kb2 6. b7 Kxa1 7. b8=Q a4 8. Ka7! a3 9. Kb6 Kb2 10. Kc5+ wins.

No. 213

Black to play. Draw

Knight plus pawn wins against three pawns only if the opposing pawns can be blockaded or isolated and subsequently captured. In any normal position such as **No. 213**, this cannot be done, for Black forces the exchange of the last pawn: **1. ... h4+ 2. Kf2 f5 3. N any g4.**

Even if the Black pawns were isolated he could still hold the draw. For instance, **No. 214: White king at g3, knight at e3, pawn at h3; Black king at g6, pawns at e6, g5, h5.** Black to play. **1. ... Kf6 2. Kf2 Ke5 3. Ng2** (3. Kf3 g4+) **3. ... Ke4**, no progress can be made.

No. 215, P. Benko 1983

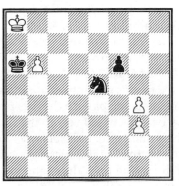

White to move wins

After **1. b7** Black has three ways to stop the pawn:

a) **1. ... Nd7 2. b8=N+!** (only this underpromotion works because 2. b8=Q? Nb6+ 3. Qxb6+ Kxb6 brings Black's king closer to the pawns, ensuring a draw: 4. Kb8 Kc6 5. Kc8 Kd5!) **2. ... Nxb8 3. Kxb8 Kb6 4. Kc8 Kc6 5. Kd8 Kd6 6. Ke8 Ke6 7. Kf8 f5 8. g5,** and White wins. One tempo can make a big difference!

b) **1. ... Nc6 2. b8=Q** (but not 2. b8=N+? this time, because 2. ... Kb6 allows Black to hold a draw) **2. ... Nxb8 3. Kxb8** and White wins the same as before. Note the interesting reversal of the pawn promotions. That was easy enough, but we are still left with an indirect defense.

c) **1. ... Nc4!** Which promotion is good this time—queen or knight? Neither! **2. g5! fxg5 3. g4!** solves the problem. Black is in zugzwang! **3. ... Nb6+ 4. Kb8 Nd5 5. Kc8 Nb6+ 6. Kc7 Nd5+ 7. Kd6 Kxb7 8. Kxd5 Kc7 9. Ke6 Kd8 10. Kf5 Ke7 11. Kxg5 Kf7 12. Kh6!** and wins.

When White can win a pawn and secure a passed pawn, it is better to blockade the opposing pawns with the knight than with the king. The reason is that the knight alone cannot force the promotion of the pawn, but the king alone can if it can rely on tempi gained by the knight .

The best White an do with knight plus pawn against more than three pawns is a draw. When Black has three connected passed pawns and the knight manages to blockade them (e.g., pawns at a5, b6, c5; knight at b5) and prevent the king from coming to the aid of the pawns, White can hold the game. Ordinarily this is too much to expect, so we may set the rule that three passed pawns in an ending with nothing but knight and pawns are worth more than a knight. Even with a bad structure (doubled, isolated) the pawns may be successful.

No. 216 (Levenfish-Fine, Leningrad 1937): **White king at f2, knight at e2, pawn at e3; Black king at d6, pawns at b4, b3, e5, e4.** White to move. Black wins. This example illustrates the helplessness of a knight against an army of pawns: **1. Ng3 Kd5 2. Nf1 Kc4 3. Ke2** (or 3. Nd2+ Kc3 4. Nxe4+ Kc2) **3. ... Kc3 4. Nd2 b2 5. Kd1 Kd3 6. Nb1 Kxe3 7. Kc2 Kf2** and White resigned.

Exceptions to this rule occur only when all the pawns are blockaded, as in **No. 217** (Ponziani 1782): **White king at c4, knight at e3, pawn at b3; Black king at b6, pawns at a5, b4, c5, f5.** White to play. **1. Nxf5 a4! 2. bxa4 Ka5 3. Kb3 c4+** only draws, but White can win with **1. Nd5+ Ka6 2. Nc7+ Kb6 3. Ne6 a4 4. bxa4 Ka5 5. Nxc5 f4 6. Kb3 f3 7. Ne4 Kb6 8. Kxb4.**

Against more than three pawns a knight is totally helpless.

With a knight and more than one pawn a draw is possible only if a number of pawns are captured or exchanged, or if the Black pawns are so far advanced that the knight is immobile. If the enemy king can run loose among the pawns defended only by the knight, it can generally manage to capture or exchange all of them. By luring the White king away from his pawns and entering with his own king, Black then gets excellent drawing chances. With pawns on the sixth or seventh rank he may even have winning chances.

A blockaded position can only postpone the win or make it more complicated but cannot guarantee a draw.

NO. 217

White to move wins

It seem that Black can hold the draw by playing Kg8 and Kh8, but White can force the Black pawn out of the way by sacrificing his knight. **1. Nd6 Kg8 2. Ne4 Kh8 3. Nf6! gxf6 4. Kf7.**

No. 219, Troitzky 1898

White to play. Draw

In **No. 219** we see a pretty drawing maneuver in which the king can attack the enemy pawns. **1. f3! Ne5 2. Kg7 Nxf3 3. Kxf6 g4 4. Kf5 g3 5. Kg4 g2 6. Kh3!!** and whatever Black promotes to does him no good. For instance, 6. ... g1=R 7. b7+ Kxc7 8. b8=Q+ Kxb8 stalemate, or 6. ... g1=N+ 7. Kg2 and neither knight can move.

No. 220 shows how a knight wins against pawns in an ordinary over-the-board position.

No. 220, Nimzovich-Alekhine, New York 1927

White to play

1. Ke3 c5 (if 1. ... b5 2. Nd2 h4 3. g4! h3 4. Kf3 c5 5. Ne4 c4 6. b4! [to keep as many pawns as possible] 6. ... Kb6 7. Kg3 Kc6 8. Nxg5 c3 9. Nf3! Kd5 10. Ne1 and the passed pawn is decisive) **2. a4 b5 3. axb5 axb5 4. Nd2 Kb6 5. Ne4 h4 6. g4! h3! 7. Kf3 b4** (or 7. ... c4 8. b4! Kc6 9. Kg3 Kd5 10. Nc3+ Kd4 11. Nxb5+ Kd3 12. Na3 c3 13. b5, etc.) **8. Nxg5 c4! 9. Ne4!!** cxb3 (9. ... c3 10. Nf2) **10. g5 b2 11. Nd2 Kc5 12. g6 h2 13. Kg2 Kd4 14. g7 Kd3 15. g8=Q Kxd2 16. Qa2 Kc2 17. Qc4+**, resigns.

From this example we can see that the winning method in such endings consists of three steps:

1. Weaken the enemy pawns either by blockading theme or forcing a disadvantageous advance;

2. Force a passed pawn in order to divert the enemy king;

3. Either queen the passed pawn or establish a decisive material superiority in pawns.

No. 221, Zukertort

Draw

No. 221 shows how Black can normally draw when his king is able to attack the enemy pawns. In fact, White can just draw by **1. Kg4 Kxa3 2. Nd3!** (if 2. Kxg5 Kxb4 3. Kxg6 Kc3! 4. h4 b4 Black queens with check, gives up his queen for the rook-pawn, and his remaining two pawns decide) **2. ... Kb3 3. Kxg5 Kc3 4. Kxg6 Kxd3 5. h4 c5 6. bxc5 b4 7. h5** and both players queen.

Where no such counterattack can be carried through, the winning method outlined above is normally quite simple to execute. In a blockaded position, if Black can't force a passed pawn White can capture material.

We have already pointed out that two pawns are not sufficient compensation for a knight, other things being equal.

No. 222, Botvinnik-Thomas, Nottingham 1936

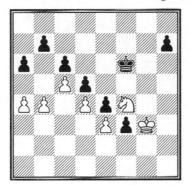

White to play

Even a strong protected passed pawn cannot save Black. Botvinnik scored by **1. b5 axb5 2. axb5 Ke7**

Or 2. ... cxb5 3. Nxd5+ Kf5! 4. Nb4! h5 5. d5 h4+ 6. Kf2 Kg4 (or 6. ... Ke5 7. d6 Ke6 8. Nd5! Kd7 9. Nc3 b4 10. Nxe4 Kc6 11. Kxf3 b3 12. Kg4 b2 13. Nd2 b6 14. cxb6 Kxd6 15. Kxh4 Kc6 16. Kg4 Kxb6 17. Kf3 Kb5 18. e4 Kb4 19. Ke3) 7. d6 h3 8. d7 h2 9. d8=Q h1=Q 10. Qg8+ Kf5 11. Qf7+ Ke5 12. Qf4+ Ke6 13. Qxe4+ Kd7 14. Qxb7+, etc.

3. b6 (threatening 3. Nxd5+ cxd5 4. c6 and queens) **3. ... Kd7 4. Nh5 Kd8 5. Nf6 h6 6. Ng4 h5 7. Nf2 Kd7 8. Kh4 Kd8 9. Kxh5 Ke7 10. Kg4 Ke6 11. Kg3 Kd7 12. Nh3 Kd8 13. Nf4 Kd7 14. Nh5 Ke6 15. Ng7+ Kd7 16. Nf5 Kc8 17. Kf4! Kb8 18. Ke5 Kc8 19. Kd6 Kb8 20. Kd7 Ka8 21. Ng3! Kb8 22. Nf1 Ka8 23. Kc8,** resigns. For now he must play **23. ... f2**, when the White king comes all the way back and captures the f-pawn, and the rest is elementary.

Two pawns draw against a knight only when the pawn structure is such that the enemy king is not in a position to attack the pawns. A knight, as we have seen, can defend pawns but cannot help one to queen without the aid of the king. So when there are one or two passed pawns that cannot be adequately blockaded by the knight, a draw is very often the result.

No. 223, Charousek/Fahndrich-Halprin/Marco, Vienna 1897

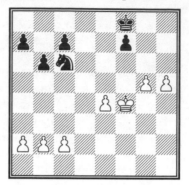

Black to play

The game continued **1. ... Kg7**

After the very tempting 1. ... Nb4, White cold-bloodedly replies 2. h6! Nxc2 3. Kf5 Nd4+ 4. Kf6 Kg8 5. e5 c5 6. h7+! Kxh7 7. Kxf7 Nf3 8. g6+ Kh6 9. g7 Nxe5+ 10. Kf8 Ng6+ 11. Kf7 Ne7! 12. Kxe7 Kxg7 13. Kd6 Kf6 14. a4! Kf5 15. a5, and the ending is drawn.

2. c3 (now 2. ... Nb4 is a serious threat) **2. ... Ne7 3. e5 c6 4. Ke4 c5 5. e6!** (the decisive break, after which the draw becomes clear; now the Black king must stay on the kingside and the White king can mop up on the other wing) **5. ... fxe6 6. Ke5 Nd5 7. c4** (hoping for a win; 7. Kxe6 Nf4+ 8. Kd6 of course draws without any trouble) **7. ... Ne3 8. b3 Kf7 9. g6+ Ke7 10. Kf4 Nf5 11. Kg5 Nd4 12. a3**

On 12. h6, Black has the forced draw 12. ... Nf3+ 13. Kg4 Ne5+ 14. Kg5 Nf3+, =, or if 12. Kh6? Kf6 13. Kh7 Nf5 14. h6 Ne7 15. g7 Kf7! 16. Kh8 e5! and Black wins, for 17. h7 allows 17. ... Ng6+ mate!.

12. ... a6 13. b4 a5 14. bxa5 bxa5 15. a4 Nf3+ 16. Kh6 Kf8 17. g7+ Kg8 18. Kg6 e5 19. h6 Nh4+ 20. Kf6 Nf3; and the players agreed to a draw.

Two connected passed pawns that are far advanced may often win against a knight, regardless of the total material strength.

An advantage of two knights when both sides have pawns is so overwhelming that drawing chances are found only in problems.

III. ONE KNIGHT AND PAWNS VS. ONE KNIGHT AND PAWNS

A. Positions With Material Advantage

Winning with an extra pawn with knights on the board is by no means as simple as in pure pawn endings. Nevertheless, the principles established in pawn endings, such as the value of outside and protected passed pawns, the need to preserve the mobility of the pawns, and many others are equally applicable here. In fact, the outlines of the general winning process are exactly the same as for the corresponding pawn ending: force an outside passed pawn, drive the king toward it, and establish a decisive material superiority. Where there are pawns on both sides of the board, there is little difference in the conduct of the two types of ending. It is only when all the pawns are on one side of the board that we find new problems.

Knight and pawn vs. knight is generally a draw because the knight can be sacrificed for the pawn. To effect this sacrifice, however, Black must have both king and knight in favorable positions; i.e., covering the squares on the queening file. When this is not the case, White can usually win. The most favorable files for the pawn are the knight and rook files.

If the pawn manages to reach the seventh rank and is supported by both king and knight, it can almost always queen.

No. 224, Kling 1867

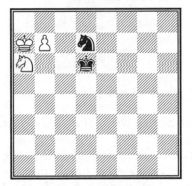

White to play wins

White need only keep the Black knight out of c6 and d7. If the Black king were off in some other part of the board, 1. Nc5 Ne5 2. Kb6 would decide at once. Here some more manipulation is required. **1. Nb4 Ke5** (or 1. ... Kc7 2. Nd5+ K any 3. Nb6 and queens) **2. Nd3+ Kd5** (or 2. ... Ke4 3. Nc5+, or 2. ... Kf5 3. Nc5 Ne5 4. Kb6) **3. Nf4+ Kc6 4. Ng6 Kd5** (or 4. ... Kc5 5. Nf8 Ne5 6. Ka8 Nc6 7. Ne6+ K any 8. Nd8) **5. Nf8 Ne5 6. Kb6 Nc6! 7. Nd7 Kd6 8. Ne5 Nb8 9. Ka7 Kc7 10. Nc4 Nc6+** (if 10. ... Nd7 11. Nb6 Nb8 12. Nd5+) **11. Ka8 Nb8! 12. Nb6 Na6 13. Nd5+ K any 14. Ka7** or **14. Nb4** and the knight finally has to quit the neighborhood of the queening square.

The same idea is effective in the similar ending **No. 225** (Von Scheve-Estorch, 1905): **White king at b6, knight at c7, pawn at a6; Black king at d7, knight at c6.** White to play. **1. Nb5 Ne7 2. Kb7 Nc6** (or 2. ... Nc8 3. Na3 Nd6+ 4. Kb8 Nc8 5. Nc4 Kd8 6. Kb7 Kd7 7. Nb6+) **3. Nd4 Na5+ 4. Kb8 Nc4 5. a7 Nb6 6. Kb7 Na8! 7. Ne6!!** and Black resigned gracefully.

Another such position is **No. 226** (Reti 1929): **White: king at b7, knight at e4, pawn at a6; Black king at a5, knight at b5.** White to play wins. **1. Nc5 Kb4**

2. Kb6 Nd6 3. Ne4 Nc8+ 4. Kc7 Kb5! 5. Kb7! Ka5 6. Nc5 Nd6+ 7. Kc7 Nb5+ 8. Kc6 Na7+ 9. Kb7! Nb5 10. Ne4 Kb4 11. Kb6 Ka4 12. Nc3+. Care must always be exercised in this type of ending, since the slightest misstep will allow the sacrifice of the knight for the pawn.

Compare **No. 227** (Reti 1929): **White king at g5, knight at e3; Black king at h2, knight at f2, pawn at h3.** White to move. Draw. **1. Kh4 Kg1 2. Ng4 Kg2 3. Ne3+ Kh2 4. Nc2 Nd3 5. Kg4 Ne5+ 6. Kh4 Nf3+ 7. Kg4 Ng5! 8. Ne1! Kg1 9. Nf3+! Kg2! 10. Nh4+! Kf2! 11. Nf3!** and Black can make no headway.

No. 228

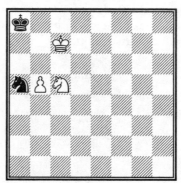

White to play wins. Black to play draws

When the king is in front of the pawn, a win is possible only in certain positions. In **No. 228** we've set up a kind of knight opposition: **1. b6 Nb7! 2. Ne6! Na5** (or c5 or d8, If 2. ... Nd6 3. Kxd6) **3. Kc8! N any 4. Nc7+** mate (or 4. b7-b8=Q). Black to move can hold the draw by **1. ... Nc4** for the same old reason: White cannot gain a tempo: **2. Nd3 Ka7 3. Nb4 Ka8 4. Nd5 Ka7 5. Ne7 Ka8** (if it were now Black's move he would lose) **6. Nc6 Nb6!!**.

It's easier to defend versus center pawns.

No. 229, Benko-Bronstein, Moscow 1949

White to play. Draw

1. Kd2 Ne5 2. Ke3 Nc4+ 3. Kd4 (3. Kd3? Nd6!) **3. ... Na3 4. Kd3 Nb5 5. Kd2** (5. Ke3? Nc3!) **5. ... Nd4 6. Kd3 Ne6 7. Ke3 Nc7 8. Kd3 Nd5 9. Kc2 Ne3+ 10. Kc3 Nf5 11. Kd2 Ng3 12. Nf6 f2 13. Ng4 f1=N+ 14. Kc3 Kf3 15. Nh2+ Nxh2** draw.

With two connected passed pawns the win is simple, since the knight cannot even threaten to sacrifice; e.g., **No. 230: White king at g4, knight at f4, pawns at g5, h5; Black king at g7, knight at f7.** White to play wins. **1. Ne6+ Kg8 2. g6 Ne5+ 3. Kf5 Nf3 4. h6 Nh4+** (spite check) **5. Kf6 Nf3 6. Ng5 Nd4 7. h7+**, etc.

No. 231, Mason-Reggio, Monte Carlo 1903

White to play

With knight and two pawns versus knight and pawn the game is won if the enemy's outside passed pawn is blockaded by a knight or the side with the extra pawn has an advanced protected passed pawn, but drawn otherwise.

In **No. 231**, the finish was **1. Nf6 Kh4** (or 1. ... Nd3+ 2. Kd4 Nxf2 3. Ne4+) **2. b6 Kh3 3. Kf5 Kg2 4. Ne4 Nd7 5. b7 Kf3 6. Nf6 Nb8 7. Nxg4 Na6 8. Nf6**

Kxf2 9. Ke5 Ke3 10. Kd5 Kd3 11. Nd7 Kc3 12. Kc6, Black resigns. There is no defense against 12. ... Kb6.

The really decisive factor here is the far more favorable position of the White king. If the passed pawn is stopped by the king (e.g., Black king at b7) White can do nothing, for Black attacks the f-pawn with his knight, and if the White knight moves, 1. ... Kb6 wins the pawn. A similar idea is **No. 232** (Botvinnik-Lisitsin, Moscow 1935): **White king at b3, knight at c2, pawn at f3; Black king at d5, knight at d6, pawns at b6, f4.** White to move. **1. Ne1 Kd4 2. Ng2 Ke5 3. Kb4 Kf5 4. Ka4!** the draw is obvious.

When there is a protected passed pawn an equally simple win is available only in special cases. **No. 233** (Horwitz 1880): **White king at e3, knight at e6, pawns at f7, g6; Black king at h8, knight at f8, pawn at g7.** White to play wins. The solution is **1. Nf4 Ne6 2. Ke4 Nc5+ 3. Kd5 Ne6 4. Kd6 Nf8 5. Ke7 Ne6 6. Nh5 Nf8 7. Ke8 Ne6** (or 7. ... Nxg6 8. Nf4 or 7. ... Nd7 8. Nxg7) **8. Nf6! gxf6 9. f8=Q+** and mates in four. But move all the pieces and pawns back two squares (with the Black knight at f7 instead of f6) and the result is a draw. If the king tries to approach, Black gives up his g-pawn to capture his opponent's.

Similarly, in a position with no passed pawn and all the pawns on one side; for example, **No. 234: White king at e3, knight at f3, pawns at f4, g4; Black king at f6, knight at e6, pawn at g6,** Black's game is perfectly tenable. On **1. Ke4** there could follow **1. ... Nc5+ 2. Kd5 Nd3** or **2. Kd4 Ne6+.**

With knight and three pawns vs. knight and two pawns, again an outside passed pawn is enough to win, and again if all the pawns are on one side the outcome should be a draw. But a greater number of pawns creates other possibilities. Three pawns vs. one on one side, or two connected passed pawns should win.

An example is **No. 235** (Chekhover-Rabinovich, Leningrad 1934): **White king at e5, knight at a3, pawns at f5; g5, h4; Black king at f7, knight at b3, pawns at a4, h7.** Black to play. After **1. ... Nd2 2. h5 Nf3+ 3. Kf4 Nd4 4. h6! Nc6 5. Nc4 Ne7 6. Ke5 Nc6+ 7. Ke4 Ne7 8. Kf4 Nc6**, White could have scored with 9. g6+! Kg8 (or 9. ... hxg6 10. Nd6+ Kf6 11. Ne8+) 10. Kg5, etc.

No. 236, Anderssen-Steinitz, 1866

Black to play

No. 236, from a world championship match game, continued **1. ... Ne6 2. Ne5+ Kf5 3. Nd3** (3. Nc4 is preferable) **3. ... g6 4. Ne1 Nd4+ 5. Kg2 Ke4 6. Kf1 f3 7. Kg1 g5 8. Kh2 h5 9. Kg3 Nf5+** (here Steinitz could have won by force with 9. ... Nc2+ 10. Kh2 h4! 11. Nc2 Nf4 12. Ne3 Kd3, followed by Ke2, when the f-pawn cannot be defended) **10. Kh2 g4? 11. hxg4 hxg4 12. Kg1 Kd4 13. Nc2+ Kd3 14. Na3?** (and here Anderssen could have drawn with 14. Nb4+ Ke2 15. Nd5 g3 16. Nf4+ Ke1 17. Nd3+ Kd2 18. Nf4, etc.) **14. ... g3! 15. Nb5 g2**, followed by Nd4-e2.

The variation played indicates that if Black can set up his pawns at f3 and h4, either the White f-pawn or h-pawn will in the long run be untenable. From this we can infer that White's best drawing chance is advancing his own f-pawn, and analysis reveals no conclusive refutation of such a defense. Thus, **1. ... Ne6 2. Kg2! Kf5 3. f3! g5** (3. ... Kg5 4. Ne5 Kh4 5. Ng6+ leads to nothing) **4. Kf2 Nc5 5. Ne7+ Ke6 6. Nc6 Kd5 7. Ne7+ Kc4 8. Nf5 h5 9. Ng7 h4 10. Ke2** and it's not clear how Black can make progress. If White's pawns were connected instead of isolated Black would have no winning chances at all, unless the position were such that he could force a decisive gain of material.

No. 237

Black to play. White wins

Knight and four pawns probably win against knight and three pawns even when all the pawns are on one side. For example, **1. ... Kf6 2. g3 Ke5 3. Nc6+ Ke6 4. Ke3** and now there are three types of defenses:

a) **4. ... Kd7 5. Nd4 f6 6. f4 Ke7** (Black plays passively) **7. h4 Nf7 8. g4 Kd7 9. Kd3 Ke7 10. Kc4 Kd6 11. g5 fxg5 12. hxg5 Ke7** (if 12. ... h6 13. e5+ Ke7 14. gxh6 Nxh6 15. Kd5 Ng4 16. Nc6+ Ke8 [or 16. ... Kd7 17. e6+ Ke8 18. Kd6 Nf6 19. Nb4 Ne4+ 20. Ke5 Nf2 21. Nd5 Ng4+ 22. Kd6 and wins] 17. Ke6 Ne3 18. Nb4 Ng2 19. Nd5 and White will soon capture Black's last pawn) **13. e5 Nd8 14. Kd5 Nf7 15. Nc6+ Ke8 16. e6 Nh8 17. Ke5 Kf8 18. Kf6 Ke8 19. Kg7**

b) **4. ... g5 5. Nd4+ Kf6 6. f4 gxf4+ 7. gxf4 Nc4+ 8. Kf2! Kg7 9. e5 Kg6 10. Ke2 Nb2 11. Kf3 Nc4 12. Ke4 Nd2+ 13. Kd5 Nf1 14. f5+ Kg5 15. e6 fxe6+ 16. Kxe6 Nxh2 17. f6** and the pawn cannot be stopped.

c) **4. ... f5 5. e5 Nf7 6. f4** is good enough.

One of the chief drawing methods at the disposal of the defender is that of reduction to a more elementary case, often by the sacrifice of the knight to get rid of the remaining pawns.

No. 238, Benko-Reshevsky, New York 1964

White to play

1. h4 b5 2. h5 c4 3. Nd5 Nc2 4. Ke4 a5 5. Ne7 b4 6. Nf5+ Kf8 7. g6 hxg6 8. hxg6 b3 (if 8. ... a4 9. g7+! [9. Nd6? b3 10. axb3 a3!] 9. ... Kg8 10. Ke5! Ne3? [10. ... Kf7 11. Nd6+, =] 11. Nxe3 b3 12. Kf6 and White wins) **9. axb3 cxb3 10. Kd3 a4 11. Kc3 Na3 12. Nd4 Nb1+ 13. Kd3 Kg7 14. Nxb3!** draw, for if 14. ... axb3 15. Kc4 Nd2+ 16. Kc3, etc.

No. 239, Reshevsky-Rellstab, Kemeri 1937

White to play

In more complicated positions a pawn plus should win unless the defender succeeds in setting up a complete blockade.

No. 239, an instructive ending with a potential outside passed pawn, may be considered typical. Black brings about the decision by first tying White's pieces down to watch the queenside pawns and then securing a winning superiority on the other wing. **1. Ke3 Kg6 2. Nd2 Nc5 3. Kd4 Nb7 4. Kd5 Kg5 5. Kc6 Nd8+ 6. Kd7 Kh4!!** (the crux of the winning process: with the king so far away, the knight will not be able to stop both the h-pawn and the potential passed b-pawn) **7. Kxd8 Kxh3 8. Ke7 h5 9. Kf7 h4 10. Kxg7 Kg3** (simpler is 10. ... Kg2) **11. Kf6** (if 11. Ne4+ Kxf3 12. Ng5+ Kg2 13. Kf6 a4!, etc.) **11. ... h3 12. Nf1+ Kf2 13. Nh2 a4! 14. bxa4 b3 15. f4 b2** and White resigned.

The nearer the outside passed pawn is to the main group of pawns the harder it is to win, but of the ultimate outcome there should never be any doubt. The principle is always the same: use the outside pawn to divert the king and then secure a sufficient advantage on the other wing.

No. 240, Keres-Reshevsky, Leningrad-Moscow 1939

Black to play

This "sufficient advantage" must be either in the form of two connected passed pawns, or two connected passed pawns with the king favorably placed, or one passed pawn that can be stopped only by the sacrifice of the knight.

In **No. 240**, it is instructive to see how this transformation of a small material advantage into a larger one takes place. **1. ... Kf8 2. Kf1 Ke7 3. Ke2 Kd6 4. Nc2 Ke5 5. Ne3 Nb2 6. Nd1 Na4** (Black naturally cannot afford to exchange pieces) **7. Kd3 Kd5 8. Ne3+ Kc5 9. Nf5** (forcing weaknesses in the opponent's pawn structure) **9. ... g6 10. Nh6 f5 11. Nf7 Kd5 12. Ng5 Nc5+ 13. Ke3 h6 14. Nf3 g5 15. g3 Ne4 16. Nd4 Nxc3 17. Nxf5 h5 18. f4!**

The pawns must first be fixed; in the game Keres continued 18. Ng7 h4 19. gxh4 gxh4 20. f4 h3! 21. Nf5 Ke6 22. Ng3 Kd5 and the favorable position of the Black king made it impossible for White to do better than draw.

18. ... g4 (or 18. ... gxf4+ 19. Kxf4 Ne4 20. h4! Nf6 21. Ng7 Kd6 22. Kf5 Ke7 23. Kg6; or 18. ... Ne4 19. Ne7+) **19. Ng7 Kd6** (19. ... h4 20. gxh4 is hopeless) **20. Nxh5 Ke6 21. Ng7+ Kf6 22. Ne8+** and wins without much trouble.

When no immediate outside passed pawn can be forced, the winning process must begin with forcing weaknesses in the pawn structure, which are then exploited by the king. In **No. 241** (Fajans-Fine, New York 1940): **White king at f2, knight at c2, pawns at a2, b2, f3, g2, h2; Black king at f8, knight at d5, pawns at a7, b6, e6, f7, g6, h7.** White to play. Black wins. **1. a3** (if 1. Nd4 Nb4 2. a3 Nd3+ wins a pawn) **1. ... e5** (to immobilize the White knight) **2. a4** (to get out via a3 and b5) **2. ... Ke7 3. Na3 f6 4. g3 Ke6 5. Ke2 Nb4 6. Nb5 a6 7. Nc3 f5 8. Kd2 Kd6 9. Ne2 Kc5 10. Kc3 Nd5+ 11. Kb3** (11. Kd3

Kb4) **g5 12. h3** (White is in zugzwang: if 12. Kc2 Kb4 13. b3 Ne3+ 14. Kb2 Nf1 15. h3 Nd2, winning a pawn) **12. ... h5 13. h4 gxh4 14. gxh4 f4 15. Kc2** (15. Ka3 Kc4) **Ne3+ 16. Kd3 Ng2 17. Ke4 Kd6 18. Nc1 Nxh4 19. Nd3 Ng6 20. Kf5 Ne7+ 21. Kg5 Kd5 22. Kxh5 Kd4,** etc.

Because the knight is effective only at short distances it is often advisable to sacrifice it to divert the enemy king (see No. 239). Thus in **No. 242** (Marco-Maroczy, Vienna 1899): **White king at c2, knight at c1, pawns at b4, c3, d4; Black king at e3, knight at b2, pawns at a3, b5, c6, d5.** Black to move wins. The coup de grace is delivered by **1. ... Nd3!! 2. Nb3 Ne1+ 3. Kd1 Kd3!! 4. Kxe1 Kxc3 5. Na1! Kxd4** (5. ... Kb2? 6. Kd2 Kxa1 7. Kc1! a2 8. Kc2 c5 9. dxc5 d4 10. c6, =) **6. Nc2+ Kc3 7. Kd1 a2 8. Kc1 d4 9. Na1 d3 10. Nc2 c5** and White resigned.

If he cannot force a favorable reduction by pawn exchanges, the defender's best bet is a blockade. This is much more effective than in the corresponding king-and-pawn ending because there is no possibility here of gaining the opposition by a pawn sacrifice.

No. 243, Botvinnik-Lisitsin, Moscow 1935

White to move

The blockade is so strong here that despite his protected passed pawn Black can make no headway. Of course, if he exchanged knights his king could enter via b4 or g3 by sacrificing his d-pawn. But without the trade of knights this sacrifice leads to nothing. After **1. Kd2 Ng6** (1. ... Kc5 2. Nd3+) **2. Kd3 Nf8 3. Kc4 Ne6 4. Nd3 Ng5**

On 4. ... Nc5 5. Nxc5! bxc5 6. a5 draws, for after 6. ... Kd7 7. Kd3 c4+ 8. Kxc4 Kd6 9. Kb4 d3 10. Kc3 Kc5 11. b6 axb6 12. axb6 Kxb6 13. Kxd3 Kb5 the diagonal opposition does Black no good: 14. Kc3 Kc5 15. Kd3 Kb4 16. Kd2!, etc.

5. Ne1 Ke6 6. Kb4

The game continued 6. Kd3 Kd6 7. Kc4 Nh3 8. Nd3 Ng1 9. Ne1 Ke6 10. Kd3 (10. Kb4 draws as above) 10. ... Nh3 11. Kd2 Kf6 12. Kd3 Ke7 13. Ke2 Kd6 14. Nd3 Ng5 15. Nb2 Nf7 16. Nd3 Nd8 17. Nb2 Nb7 18. Kd2 Nc5 19. Kc2 Ke6 20. Kd1 Kf6, but even here Black could find nothing decisive.

6. ... Nh3 7. Nd3 Ng1 8. Ne1 Kf6 (or 8. ... Ne2 9. Kb3 Ng3 10. Nd3 Nf1 11. Kc2 and Black's king must not abandon the defense of the e-pawn) **9. Kc4 Kg5 10. Kd5 Kh4 11. Kxe5 Kg3 12. Kxd4 Nxf3+ 13. Nxf3 Kxf3 14. e5, =.**

B. Positions With Even Material

Such positions are normally drawn, but there is a wide variety of possible advantages that must be considered. These may be conveniently grouped as follows:

1. Better pawn position;
2. Better king position;
3. Better knight position.

The last two groups are not completely independent of the first, since the value of any piece depends to a large extent on the pawn structure. Often one can speak of an advantage only when two or three of these factors occur together.

1. Better pawn Position

In practical play this type of advantage consists of one or more of four factors.

a) Outside Passed Pawn

When there are pieces on the board such a superiority is usually overwhelming. It is even greater than in the corresponding endings without pieces, for there, as we have seen, one protected passed pawn can often draw against two outside passed pawns, while with one outside passed pawn reduced material frequently gives Black excellent drawing chances.

The principles for exploiting an outside passed pawn remain exactly the same no matter how many pieces are on the board. The pawn is advanced as far as possible. The opponent must stop it either with a piece or the king. In either case, the other side is weakened, the king enters the breach, and a sufficient material superiority is established. If the pawn is not adequately blockaded its advance and support will win a piece. Sometimes two passed pawns on opposite sides of the board are just as good as a considerable material advantage.

No. 244, Lasker-Nimzovich, Zurich 1934

Black to move

No. 244 is a classical illustration. There are four parts to Black's winning plan: 1. fixing the queenside pawns; 2. blockading the e-pawn with his knight and not his king; 3. maneuvering his king to the queenside; 4. finally, going back to the kingside and forcing the promotion of his h-pawn.

1. ... Kf7 2. Kc1 Kf6 3. Kd2 Ke5 4. Ke3 h5 5. a3 a5 6. Nh3 Nc2+ 7. Kd3? (7. Kd2) 7. ... Ne1+ 8. Ke2 Ng2 9. Kf3 Nh4+ 10. Ke3 Ng6 11. Ng5 Kf6 12. Nh7+ Ke7 13. Ng5 Ne5 14. Kd4 Kd6 15. Nh3 a4 16. Nf4 h4 17. Nh3 b6!! (to gain a tempo) 18. Nf4 b5 19. Nh3 Nc6+ 20. Ke3 Kc5 21. Kd3 b4! (pawn exchanges are as a rule inadvisable in such endings, but Nimzovich had carefully calculated that this would win) 22. axb4+ Kxb4 23. Kc2 Nd4+ 24. Kb1 Ne6 25. Ka2 (25. Kc2 Kc4) Kc4! 26. Ka3 Kd4!! 27. Kxa4 Kxe4 28. b4 Kf3 29. b5 Kg2 and Lasker resigned.

No. 245 (Botvinnik-Lilienthal, Moscow 1936) shows how the outside pawn is used to create a decisive material superiority: **White king at f2, knight at c8, pawns at a5, e4, f3, g3, h4; Black king at g8, knight at f6, pawns at d6, e6, f7, g6, h7**. Black to play. White o play. 1. ... Ne8 (or 1. ... d5 2. a6) 2. a6 Nc7 3. a7 Na8 4. Nxd6 Kf8 5. e5 Ke7 6. Ke3 f6 7. Kf4 h6 8. Nc8+ Kf7 (8. ... Kd7 9. exf6) 9. Ke4 Kg7 10. Kd4 Nc7 11. Kc5 and the Black knight will soon be lost.

b) Protected Passed Pawn

A protected passed pawn is not quite as strong here as an outside pawn, unlike king-and-pawn endings. The reason is that the knight is a natural blockader; that is, it loses little or no mobility by stopping such a pawn, so the king is free to scare up effective counterchances elsewhere (compare No. 240). Nevertheless, where the base of the pawn is securely defended, a protected passed pawn is inevitably a powerful threat and will, other things being equal, be enough to win.

No. 246, Pillsbury-Gunsberg, Hastings 1895

White to play

The cramped positions of the Black pieces, forced by White's threat to advance his c-pawn, make it possible for White to reduce to a simpler ending. **1. f5!** (to win the d-pawn and thus have two connected passed pawns in the center) **1. ... g5** (1. ... gxf5 2. gxf5 exf5 3. Nf4) **2. Nb4!! a5 3. c6!! Kd6 4. fxe6!! Nxc6** (if 4. ... axb4 5. e7 Kxe7 6. c7 and queens) **5. Nxc6 Kxc6 6. e4!** and wins (No. 164).

c) Qualitative Pawn Majority

Here two cases must be distinguished: doubled and blocked pawns. Where one side has two doubled pawns held by one, or three held by two, without any chance to dissolve them, the other side's winning procedure is exactly the same as though he were a pawn ahead. But when the pawns are blocked, this is a minor advantage with knights on the board because the threat to free the pawns compels the blockade to be maintained with either knight or king so that the opponent's pieces are in no way constricted.

d) Qualitatively Superior Pawns

A better pawn position is of value here only when the knight and king are in advantageous positions. Examples of this will be found under other headings but could just as well have been included here (see in particular No. 244).

No. 247, Maroczy-Salve, Vienna 1908

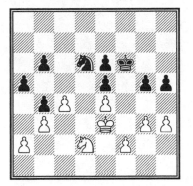

White to play

The position looks closed but White makes a hole. **1. c5! bxc5 2. Kd3 g4** (if 2. ... Ke7 3. Nc4 Nxc4 4. Kxc4 Kd6 5. Kb5 the pawn ending is just as bad) **3. hxg4 hxg4 4. Nc4 Nb7 5. Ke3! Nd8** (Black is in zugzwang) **6. Nxa5 Ke7 7. Kd3 Kd7 8. Kc4 Nf7 9. Nb7 Ng5 10. Nxc5+ Kd6 11. Kxb4 Nh3 12. Kb5 Nxf2 13. a4 Nd1 14. a5 Kc7 15. a6 Kb8 16. Kb6 Nc3 17. Nxe6,** Black resigned.

2. Better King Position

We need not consider in detail those cases where one king is so far ahead of its rival that it can simply knock down all the pawns like a bowling ball among ninepins. Of more interest are positions where one king is only somewhat better placed and some skill is required to exploit this minimal superiority.

A characteristic feature of complicated endings that plays a minor role in pawn endings is the value of a centrally posted king. When one king is at e4 or d4 and the other at e2 or d2 or even e3 or d3 with only pawns on the board, this in itself makes little differences, but with knights or other pieces on the board it is frequently the decisive factor.

No. 248, Keres-Rabinovich, Leningrad-Moscow 1939

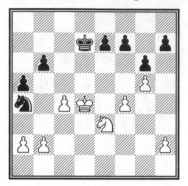

White to play

The strong position of White's king makes it impossible for Black to avoid the loss of a pawn. **1. b3 Nc5 2. Nd5 Kd6 3. Nxb6 Ne6+ 4. Ke3 Nc7 5. Nc8+! Kd7 6. Na7 f6 7. gxf6** (Keres actually played 7. h4 fxg5 8. hxg5 e5! 9. fxe5 Ne6 10. Nb5 Nxg5 11. Nd4 h5 12. Kf4 Ne6+! and could only draw) **7. ... exf6 8. Nb5 Ne6** (8. ... Nxb5 9. cxb5 Kd6 10. Kd4 Ke6 11. Kc5 Kd7 12. Kd5 is hopeless) **9. a3 Nc5 10. Nd4 g5 11. f5** (pawn exchanges should be avoided wherever possible) **11. ... Kd6 12. b4 axb4 13. axb4 Na6 14. c5+ Kd5 15. c6!** and the passed pawns decide.

No. 249 (Belavenetz-Kan, Leningrad-Moscow 1939) is another instance where a king on a central square dominates the board. **White king at c4, knight at c1, pawns at a3, b4, e3, f2, g2, h3; Black king at e5, knight at d5, pawns at a6, b6, e4, f5, g5, h5.** White to play. The game continued **1. Ne2 f4! 2. exf4+ Nxf4 3. Nc3** (if 3. Nxf4 gxf4 4. h4 [else 4. ... h4] 4. ... f3 5. gxf3 exf3 6. Kd3 Kf4 7. Kd4 Kg4 8. Ke4 Kxh4 9. Kxf3 Kh3 10. Kf4 Kg2 11. Kg5 Kxf2 and Black wins the race) **3. ... Nxg2 4. b5.** Here a simple conclusion was possible by **4. ... axb5+!** (instead of the complicated 4. ... a5 as played) **5. Kxb5 h4 6. Kxb6 g4 7. hxg4 Nf4! 8. g5** (or 8. a4) **8. ... h3** and the pawn cannot be stopped).

Another example where centralization of the king is the decisive factor is **No. 250** (Salvioli): **White king at d3, knight at d6, pawns at a2, b3, c2, f3, g4, h3; Black king at a7, knight at g2, pawns at a6, b7, c5, d4, g7, h6.** White to move wins. **1. Ke4! Ne1** (1. ... Nh4 2. f4 b5 3. f5, followed by Ne8) **2. Nf5 Nxc2 3. Nxg7 Nb4 4. Nf5** and White's pawns on the kingside cannot be stopped.

3. Better Knight Position

No. 251, Alekhine-Andersen, Folkestone 1933

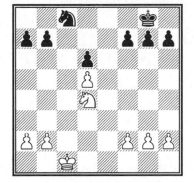

White to play

Unlike the bishop, the knight is at home in any pawn structure; advantages of this type must be utilized immediately or they will dissipate into thin air. The superior knight is always the one that is nearer the pawns and can either force the gain of material or a serious positional weakness (e.g., blocked pawns).

In **No. 251,** the decisive maneuver began with **1. Nb3!! Kf8**

Black has no choice because his king is too far from the queenside; if 1. ... Ne7 2. Na5 Nxd5 3. Nxb7 Nf4 4. Nxd6 Nd3+ 5. Kc2 Nxf2 6. b4! Kf8 7. a4, and if 7. ... Ke7 8 Nc8+, or if 7. ... Ng4 8. b5 Nxh2 9. a5, and the a-pawn cannot be stopped.

2. Na5 b6 3. Nc6 Ke8 (Black is in an uncomfortable bind) **4. Kd2 Ne7** (if the White king gets too near, it will be all over) **5. Nxa7 Nxd5 6. Nb5** (Alekhine has thus transformed his original superior knight position into the more lasting advantage of a potential outside passed pawn) **6. ... Kd7 7. Nd4 g6 8. a4 Nc7 9. Kc3 g5 10. Kb4 d5 11. Nf3 f6 12. Nd4 Kd6** (hastens the end, but even after 12. ... Ke7 13. a5 bxa5+ 14. Kxa5 Kd7 15. b4 Kc8 16. Kb6 Black is hopelessly lost) **13. Nb5+ Nxb5 14. Kxb5 Ke5 15. b4 d4 16. Kc4** and Black resigned.

Very often there is a choice between giving up a center pawn or a wing pawn. The great strength of the outside passed pawn has been repeatedly demonstrated, so the center pawn should always be the victim when there's a choice.

Passive defense in knight-and-pawn endings is rarely successful. The most effective way of saving an apparently lost position is a vigorous counterattack. Here, as in pawn endings, lengthy and precise calculations are sometimes required. In **No. 252** (Berger-Maroczy, Barmen 1905): **White king at g1, knight at e5, pawns at a2, b3, d4, h3; Black king at g7, knight at c3, pawns at a7, b7, d5, h6.** White to play. White clearly must lose a pawn. **1. Ng4** (1. a4 Ne2+ 2. Kf2 Nxd4 3. b4 Ne6 is no improvement) **1. ... Nxa2 2. Ne3 Nc1?** (2. ... Nc3 wins) **3. b4 Ne2+ 4. Kf2 Nxd4 5. Nxd5 Kg6 6. Ke3 Ne6,** and now **7. Ke4!** draws by one tempo: **7. ... Ng5+ 8. Ke5 Nxh3 9. Kd6 Kg5 10. Kc7 b6 11. Kb7 Nf4 12. Ne3! a5?**

Black should still play 12. ... h5! 13. Kxa7 h4 14. Kxb6 (or 14. b5 h3 15. Nf1 Nd5 16. Kb7 Kf4 17. Kc6 Ne3 wins) 14. ... Nd5+! 15. Nxd5 (15. Kc5 Nxe3 16. b5 Nd5! wins) 15. ... h3 16. Nc3 h2 17. Ne4+ Kf4, etc., wins.

13. b5! Ne6 14. Kxb6 a4 15. Nc4 h5 16. Ka5 h4 17. Kxa4 h3 18. Nd2 Kf4 19. Nf1, =.

IV. TWO KNIGHTS AND PAWNS

The presence of the extra knights practically never requires any change in the rules and principles that have already been established. On rare occasions it is possible to get a bind on the opponent's position with two knights that cannot be had with one. Here is such a case:

No. 253, Marco-Maroczy, Vienna 1899

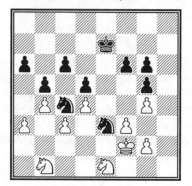

Black to play

With either Black knight off the board, the White king would be free to roam wherever it pleased, since the constant threat against his pawns would be absent.

As it is, he is completely tied up and condemned to a useless career of royal dawdling. Maroczy won by first advancing his pawn to a4 (so that if and when he captures the a-pawn he will have a protected passed pawn nearer to queening) and then forcing an entry on the kingside.

The winning procedure is highly original. **1. ... Kd6 2. Ke2?** (2. Nd3 Nc2 3. Nc5 N2xa3 4. Nxa3 Nxa3 5. Ke2! and 5. Nxa6 =) **2. ... Kc7 3. Kf2 Kb6 4. Ke2 a5 5. Kf2** (5. bxa5+ Kxa5 is worse) **5. ... a4 6. Ke2 Kc7 7. Kf2 Kd6 8. Ke2 Ke7 9. Kf2 Kf7 10. Ke2 Kg7 11. Kf2 Kh7 12. g3** (this makes no difference) **12. ... Kh6 13. Ke2 f5 14. gxf5 gxf5 15. Kf2 Kh5 16. Ke2 f4 17. gxf4 gxf4 18. Kf2 Kg5 19. Ke2 Kh4 20. Kf2 Kh3! 21. Nd3** (there is no alternative; on 21. Ke2 Kg3 forces a knight move, for if then 22. Kd3 Kf2) **21. ... Nc2 22. Nxf4+ Kh4 23. Nd3** (if 23. Ng6+ Kg5 24. Ne5 N4xa3 25. Nxa3 Nxa3 26. Nxc6 Nc4 and the pawn queens) **23. ... N2xa3 24. Nxa3 Nxa3 25. Nc1 Nb1 26. Na2 Kh3 27. Ke3 Kg3 28. f4 Kg4 29. f5** (White is in zugzwang) **29. ... Kxf5** and the outside passed pawn decides.

Chapter IV

BISHOP AND PAWN ENDINGS

I. BISHOP VS. PAWNS

The results here are pretty much the same as in knight endings. Bishop vs. one or two pawns is a draw (unless the pawns are so far advanced that they can no longer be stopped); bishop vs. three pawns is a draw or a win for the pawns, depending on the relative positions of the pawns.

Except for some unusual cases, the bishop draws against one pawn if it can cover any square on the queening file that the pawn must cross. A win for the pawn is possible only when the bishop is blocked by its own king or when the pawn can gain a move by checking. **No. 254** (Kling and Horwitz 1853): **White king at a5, pawn at b6; Black king at c6, bishop at g6.** White to play. Draw. White has no check, so Black can get back in time. **1. Ka6 Be4! 2. b7 Kc7 3. Ka7 Bxb7** stalemate!

Two pawns have a better chance to win against a bishop. If the pawns are not beyond the fourth rank, Black should have no difficulty drawing, but if they are, the outcome depends on whether Black's king can stop one pawn while the bishop takes care of the other one. An exception:

No. 255, H. Otten

White to play

No. 255 shows how a king can get in the way of his own piece. The solution is **1. a5 Bf8 2. Kd5 Bh6 3. g5+!! Bxg5** (or 3. ... Kxg5 4. a6) **4. Ke4 Bh4 5. Kf3!** and the pawn marches on. If the Black king were anywhere else near either pawn the draw would have been obvious.

With two pawns on the fifth the king positions decide. For instance, **No. 256** (Salvioli 1887): **White king at h5, bishop at e2; Black king at g1, pawns at a4, d4.** White to move. Black wins. **1. Bc4 a3 2. Kg4 Kf2!** (2. ... d3 4 Kf3!) **3. Kf4 d3 4. Ke4 d2 5. Bb3 a2,** etc.

Pawns two files apart (as here) cannot be stopped by a bishop in any position once they are on the fifth rank or beyond. If they are one file apart (e.g., a4 and c4), they can be stopped by a bishop at b2 or b4. If they are three files apart (a4, e4), they can be stopped by a bishop at c1 or c5. Thus the most favorable position for the pawns is to be two, four or more files apart.

Two connected passed pawns can be stopped by the bishop unless they are both on the sixth. With connected pawns one must always advance the pawn that is not on the same color as the bishop, else they will be blockaded immediately. **No. 257** (Kling and Horwitz 1853) is a case where blockaded pawns do not win despite the proximity of the king: **White king at d8, bishop at h3; Black king at d6, pawns at g3, f2.** White to play. **1. Bg2! Ke5 2. Ke7 Kd4 3. Ke6 Ke3 4. Ke5 Ke2 5. Kf4** and the kings will have to fight it out alone.

Three connected passed pawns win but only if all three are able to cross the fourth rank (except for certain special cases). The defense always consists of blockading the pawns, but this is not feasible if the pawns are too near the queening square.

The all-important position of the bishop is shown in **No. 258.**

No. 258, Horwitz 1880

Black to play

1. ... Kf5

1. ... f3+ is far inferior: 2. Kg1!!; the only drawing move, for after 2. ... Kf5 [2. ... Kf4 3. Bd2+] 3. Ba5 g4 4. Bd8 h3 5. Bc7 Ke4 6. Kf2 Black can do nothing. The text is decisive because the bishop doesn't have enough freedom to stop the pawns.

2. Ba5 (2. Kh3 Ke4 3. Kg4 Ke3! wins) **2. ... g4 3. Bd8 h3+ 4. Kh2 Ke4 5. Bb6 Kf3 6. Bc7 Ke3 7. Bb8 f3 8. Kg1 Ke2 9. Bg3 h2+ 10. Kxh2 f2 11. Bxf2 Kxf2 12. Kh1 Kg3!** wins.

With White to play, **1. Ba5! Kf5** (1. ... f3+ 2. Kf2) **2. Bd8** draws.

When the pawns are on the sixth or seventh rank the battle is hopeless; e.g., **No. 259** (Kling and Horwitz, 1853): **White king at g1, bishop at e1; Black king at h3, pawns at e2, f3, g2.** Black maneuvers his king to d1, then wins the bishop by promoting his g-pawn and e-pawn and finally queens his f-pawn.

Or **No. 260: White king at g1, bishop at b4; Black king at g3, pawns at f4, g4, h3.** Black to play wins. Here 1. ... f3?? 2. Bd6+ Kh4 3. Kf2 only draws, but **1. ... Kf3 2. Kh2 Ke2,** as in No. 239, is good enough to win.

On the other hand, it is easy to see that with the pawns farther back none of the above methods can be carried out.

No. 261 (Berger 1890): **White king at g2, bishop at d1; Black king at f5, pawns at f4, g5, h5.** Black to play. Draw. 1. ... g4 2. Bc2+ Ke5 3. Kf2 h4 4. Bd1! Kf5 5. Bc2+ Kf6 6. Be4 h3 7. Bc6 g3+ 8. Kf3 Kg5 9. Bd7 h2 10. Kg2 f3+ 11. Kh1 f2 12. Bh3.

No. 262 (Berger 1890): **White king at g3, bishop at e2; Black king at g5, pawns at f5, g6, h5.** Black to play. Draw. 1. ... Kf6 2. Bf3 Ke5 3. Kh4 Kf6 4. Bc6 Ke6 5. Kg5 =.

The essential point in all these examples is that if the pawns can be blockaded before two of them reach the seventh, the ending is a draw; if not it's a win (except for the rook-pawn, which allows certain stalemate possibilities). It makes no real difference whether the pawns are on center or side files.

Three isolated pawns (or two connected and one isolated), unlike the similar knight ending, are not stronger than three connected pawns. They win when one pawn can reach the sixth, but draw otherwise.

No. 263, Handbuch

Black to play. Draw

No. 263 is a draw because the b-pawn is too far back. **1. ... Kf5** (or 1. ... e4 2. Kc4 Kf5 3. Kd4 b5 4. Bd6 b4 5. Bxb4 Kf4 6. Be1 Kf3 7. Bh4 e3 8. Kd3 and Black is at a standstill) **2. Kc4! Ke4 3. Kc5 b5 4. Bh2 b4 5. Kc4 b3 6. Kxb3 Kd4 7. Kc2 e4 8. Kd2 =.**

But consider a position such as **No. 264: White: king at b1, bishop at g3; Black king at f5, pawns at b3, e5, g4.** Black to play wins. White has no time to delay capture of the b-pawn. **1. ... e4 2. Kb2 e3 3. Kxb3 Ke4 4. Kc2 Kf3 5. Bb8 g3 6. Kd1 g2 7. Bh2 Kf2!!** White is in zugzwang and Black wins.

Or again in **No. 265** (problem by Dr. Lewitt): **White king at f3, pawns at b2, b5, h6; Black king at a5, bishop at b6.** White to play wins. The advanced pawns are irresistible. **1. Ke4 Bd8 2. b6!! Ka6!!** (2. ... Kxb6 3. Kf5) **3. Ke5 Bg5 4. h7 Bc1 5. Kd6 Bxb2 6. Kc7 Be5+ 7. Kc6 Bf6 8. b7 Ka7 9. Kc7,** and one pawn will queen.

Four or more pawns clearly win against a bishop, unless they are doubled or so far back that they can be captured at will.

However, two bishops win against four pawns. Berger gives the following position. **No. 266: White king at f3, bishops at b5, f2; Black king at e6, pawns at d5, e5, f5, g5.** White to play wins. The main line is **1. Bc5 e4+ 2. Ke3 f4+ 3. Kd4 g4 4. Bc6 e3 5. Bxd5+ Kf5 6. Kd3 Kg5 7. Be7+ Kf5 8. Be4+ Ke5 9. Bd8 Kd6 10. Bf5 g3 11. Be4 Ke5 12. Bc7+** and White wins all the pawns. Black is defenseless against the plan of first blockading the pawns and then winning them.

II. BISHOP AND PAWNS VS. KING, WITH AND WITHOUT PAWNS

In **No. 267** White can do nothing because he cannot chase the Black king out of the corner.

No. 267

White to play

After **1. Kb5 Kb7 2. a6+ Ka8 3. Kb6 Kb8 4. Be5+ Ka8,** the best White can do is stalemate. On the other hand, with the bishop on light squares—that is, of the "right" color—the win is child's play. Place the bishop on d3 instead of d4, and now **1. Kb5 Kb7 2. Be4+ Ka7 3. a6 Kb8 4. Kb6** and queens in two moves.

To draw against a bishop of the wrong color the Black king must either be actually in the corner or able to reach it. **No. 268** (Troitzky 1896): **White king at e3, bishop at h3, pawn at h5; Black king at e8.** White to play wins by **1. Be6! Ke7 2. h6!! Kf6 3. Bf5!! Kf7 4. Bh7 Kf6 5. Kf4 Kf7 6. Kg5 Kf8 7. Kf6,** etc. Another application of this rule will be seen in No. 274.

There is one position with a knight-pawn that completes the list of cases where bishop and pawn do not win against a lone king. **No. 269** (Mouret 1838): **White king at a4; Black king at b7, pawn at b4, bishop at a2.** Black to play. Draw. After **1. ... b3 2. Ka3 Kc6 3. Kb2 Kc5 4. Ka1,** the bishop can't move and the Black king cannot get too close because of stalemate.

With bishop and pawn vs. pawn we have pretty much the same state of affairs: simple win unless there is a rook-pawn with a bishop of the wrong color and the opposing king can creep into the corner. In general, the extra material is only a handicap for the defender. As we shall see, when he has one knight-pawn against bishop and pawn, the game is usually but not always a draw, but with doubled knight-pawns the game is usually lost.

There are two winning possibilities when extra pawns are added to positions such as **No. 267**: one is to shut the Black king out of the corner; the other to force Black to sacrifice a pawn to the White rook-pawn and thereby transform it into a knight-pawn.

No. 270 (Short-Kasparov, Belgrade 1989): **White king at e1, pawns at b2, b4; Black king at g1, bishop at b5, pawn at a6.** Black to play. **1. ... Kg2 2. Kd1 Kf3 3. Kd2 Ke4 4. Kc3 Ke3 5. Kc2 Ke2 6. Kc1 Bd3 7. b3 Ke1 8. Kb2 Kd2 9. Ka1 Kc2 10. Ka2 Kc1 11. Ka1** (if 11. Ka3 Kb1 12. Ka4 Kb2, etc.) **11. ... Bb1,** White resigned.

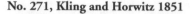

No. 271, Kling and Horwitz 1851

White to play wins

Here's a case of keeping the king out of the corner. If White attacks the Black pawn directly, Black will have time to get to a8 The problem then is to keep the Black king at a respectable distance from the a-file. The solution is **1. Bf4! Kg2 2. Kg4!!** (if 2. Ke4 Kh3 3. Kd5 Kg4 4. Bh2 Kf5 5. Kc6 Ke6 and White is no nearer his goal) **2. ... Kf2 3. Bc1 Ke2** (if 3. ... Kg2 4. Be3 Kf1 5. Kf3 Ke1 6. Bf4 Kd1 7. Ke3 Kc2 8. Kd4 Kb3 9. Bd6) **4. Kf4 Kd1** (or 4. ... Kd3 5. Be3 Kc4 6. Ke5 Kb3 7. Bc5 Kc4 8. Kd6 Kd3 9. Kd5 Kc3 10. Bd6 Kd3 11. Kc5 Ke4 12. Bh2) **5. Be3 Kc2 6. Ke5 Kb3 7. Bc5 Kc4 8. Kd6 Kb5 9. Kd5 Ka5! 10. Kc6 Ka6 11. Be3 Ka5 12. Kb7 Kb5 13. Bb6 Kc4 14. Kc6 Kb3 15. Bc5 Kc4 16. Be3 Kb3 17. Bc1 Kc4 18. Bb2!!** (the point) **18. ... Kb3 19. Kb5!** and wins.

With Black to move White has a much harder time. It was long held that White could only draw, but Rauser demonstrated in 1928 that this opinion was incorrect. White can win by **1. ... Kg3 2. Bf6! Kf3** (if 2. ... Kh3 3. Kf4 Kh2 4. Kf3 Kh3 5. Bg5 Kh2 6. Kg4 Kg2 7. Bf4 as in the main variation) **3. Be5 Ke3 4. Bb2!!** (the only winning move; if 4. Bb8? Kd4! 5. Ke6 Kc5 6. Kd7 Kb6 and draws; e.g., 7. Kc8 Kc5 8. Kc7 Kd5! 9. Kd7 Kc5 10. Bc7 Kb5!, etc.) **4. ... Kd3** (or 4. ... Kf3 5. Bc1 Kg3 6. Bg5 Kf2 7. Kf4 Ke2 8. Ke4 Kf2 9. Bf4) **5. Ke5 Ke3** (if 5. ... Kc4 6. Kd6 Kb5 7. Bd4 Kc4 8. Bc5 Kb5 9. Kd5, again as in the main variation above) **6. Bc1+ Kf3 7. Kf5! Kg3 8. Bg5 Kf3** (or 8. ... Kh3 9. Kf4), and we have come back to the diagram position with White to play **9. Bf4**.

The key to this ending is to be found in **No. 272.** It makes no difference whose move it is, but if the Black king manages to reach any square *behind* the dotted squares (a6-b5-c4-d3-e4-f3-g4-h5) before his pawn is captured (but not more than two files away from the White king), he can draw; if not, he loses.

No. 272, Rauser 1928

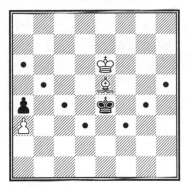

White wins if the Black king is not behind the dotted squares

The solution is **1. Bh2 Kd4 2. Kd6 Kc4** (2. ... Ke4 3. Kc5 Kf5 4. Kb5 Ke6 5. Kxa4 Kd7 6. Kb5 Kc8 7. Kc6 and wins) **3. Kc6 Kb3 4. Bd6 Kc4 5. Bc5 Kb3 6. Kb5.** Black to move: **1. ... Kf3 2. Kf5 Ke3 3. Bb2! Kd3 4. Ke5 Ke3 5. Bc1+ Kf3 6. Kf5 Kg3 7. Bg5 Kf3 8. Bf4** and we have come back to No. 271.

If the Black pawn still has moves, Black loses unless his king is in the corner. **No. 273** (Teichmann): **White king at a6, pawn at a2, bishop at g3; Black king at c8, pawn at a4.** White to play wins. **1. Kb6 Kd7 2. Kb7 Kd8 3. Kc6! Ke7! 4. Bc7 Ke6 5. Bd6 Kf5 6. Kd5 Kf6 7. Bb4 Kf7 8. Kd6 Ke8 9. Ba5 Kf7 10. Bd8 Ke8 11. Bh4 Kf7 12. Kd7 Kg6 13. Ke6 Kh5 14. Be7 Kg6! 15. Bf6 Kh6! 16. Kf5 Kh7 17. Bb2 Kg8 18. Ke6 Kf8 19. Bf6 Kg8 20. Ke7 Kh7 21. Kf7 Kh6 22. Be7 Kh5 23. Kf6 Kh6 24. Bf8+ Kh5 25. a3 Kg4 26. Bh6**, and Black's king cannot get out of the losing zone.

Another illustration is **No. 274** (Duras 1908): **White king at h1, bishop at a3, pawn at a2; Black king at g7, pawn at d7.** White to play wins. **1. Bb4! Kf7**, and after **2. a4 Ke6** (or 2. ... Ke8 3. a5 Kd8 4. Bd6 Kc8 5. a6) **3. a5 Kd5 4. a6 Kc6 5. Ba5!** Black's pawn moves will soon be exhausted and his king will have to abandon the square of White's a-pawn. When the bishop is of the right color, the only point to keep in mind is that the White pawn should be allowed freedom if it is still at its original square.

The trap position to be avoided is **No. 275** (Lolli 1763): **White king at b1, pawn at a2; Black king at d3, bishop at d4, pawn at a3.** This is a draw no matter who begins; e.g., 1. ... Kc3 2. Kc1! Be3+ 3. Kb1 Kd3 4. Ka1 and 4. ... Kc2 is stalemate.

When Black has a knight-pawn, White wins if he can get to the position in **No. 276.**

No. 276, Paulsen-Metger, Nuremberg 1888

White to play

Various traps must be avoided here: 1. Kc5? b6+, = (2. Bxb6+ Kb7, No. 267; or 2. axb6+ Kb7, No. 270), or 1. Kc4? b5+!!. But White wins with **1. Kd4!! Kc6** or:

a) 1. ... b5 (or 1. ... b6) 2. a6 Kc6 3. Kc3 Kd7 4. Kb4 Kc6 5. Ka5.

b) 1. ... Kd7 (or 1. ... Kd8, 1. ... Kc8) 2. Kc5 Kc7 3. Kb5 b6 4. a6!!

2. Bb6! Kd6 (2. ... Kb5 3. Kd5 Ka6 4. Kd6) **3. Kc4 Kc6 4. Kb4 Kd6 5. Kb5 Kd7 6. Kc5 Kc8 7. Ba7 Kc7 8. Kb5 Kd7 9. Bb8 Kc8 10. Bh2 Kd7 11. Kb6**.

With the Black king snugly in the corner the game is a draw regardless of where White's pieces are. In the most favorable case, where Black has an e-pawn, the pawn may be forced to move by stalemating the king, but even that leads to nothing, for if White captures the pawn, Black is stalemated, but if he passes the pawn, Black gives it up and transposes to No. 267.

With two b-pawns we can have a position similar to that with an a-pawn.

No. 277

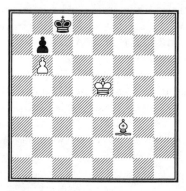

White to play. Draw

No win is possible here because of the constant stalemate threat: **1. Kd6 Kb8 2. Kd7 Ka8**, and now **3. Kc7** is stalemate, while **3. Bc6** is met by the cold-blooded **3. ... Kb8!**. With White's bishop on the dark squares he could not even approach with his king. Black would simply move his king between c8 and d7 and nothing could budge it. A bishop on e3 also draws.

Except for these special cases, a draw is possible with pawn vs. bishop and pawn only if the opponent's pawn can be captured. As a rule, this is out of the question but sometimes it can be managed.

No. 278 (Sarysev 1928) is an astonishing miniature: **White king at d7, pawn at c7; Black king at g3, bishop at h7, pawn at b7**. White to play. Draw. **1. Kc8!! b5 2. Kd7 b4 3. Kd6 Bf5 4. Ke5! Bc8 5. Kd4** draws.

Since a bishop is worth approximately three pawns, bishop-and-pawn generally win against two pawns. But the extra Black material, as expected, creates many more drawing possibilities for the defender.

A rook-pawn with a bishop of the wrong color must be sharply distinguished from the general case. Here, too, if the Black king can reach the corner the game is usually drawn. But if Black has doubled knight-pawns or a knight-pawn and rook-pawn, the extra pawn is a severe handicap because it ruins his stalemate defense and allows White to transform his rook-pawn into a knight-pawn.

No. 279, Kling and Horwitz 1851

White to play wins

In the most difficult position, White proceeds by stalemating the Black king. **1. Bd2** (to answer 1. ... Ka5 with 2. a3) **1. ... Kc7**

Or 1. ... Kb7 2. Kd6 Kb6 3. Be1 Kb7 4. Bh4 Kb6 5. Bd8+ Kb7 6. Bc7 Ka8! 7. Kc6 Ka7 8. Bd8 Ka8! 9. Kb6 Kb8 10. Bc7+ Kc8 11. Kc6 and 11. ... b3 is forced, when 12. axb3 b4 13. Bd6 is decisive.

2. Bg5 Kd7 3. Kc5 Kc7 4. Bh4 Kc8 5. Kb6 Kb8 6. Bg3+ Kc8 (6. ... Ka8 7. Bf4 and 7. ... b3 must come) **7. Bf4 Kd7 8. Kxb5 Kc8 9. Kb6 Kd7 10. Kb7 Ke6 11. Kc6 Ke7 12. Bd6+ Kd8 13. Kb7** and Black cannot get back.

There are many variations on this theme. **No. 280** (Horwitz 1885) is an example: **White king at c5, bishop at f4, pawn at a3; Black king at a7, pawn at a4, b5.** White to move wins. **1. Kc6 Ka8** (on 1. ... Ka6 2. Be3 mates in five: 2. ... Ka5 3. Bc5 b4 4. axb4+ Ka6 5. Bb6 a3 6. b5+ mate) **2. Kb6 b4 3. axb4 a3 4. b5 a2 5. Be5 a1=Q 6. Bxa1,** etc.

But with Black's pawn at a6 instead of a4, he draws: **1. Kc6 a5 2. Be3+ Ka8 3. Bb6 b4 4. a4 Kb8** and now the stalemate idea does White no good because his rook-pawn can never become a knight-pawn.

As we have seen, Black loses when he has a knight-pawn and a rook-pawn only when the rook-pawn is ahead of the knight-pawn, so he cannot offer to exchange without transforming the White rook-pawn. Similarly, Black cannot lose with a pawn on some other file in conjunction with a knight-pawn, provided, as usual, that his king can reach the corner.

In **No. 281** (Kling and Horwitz 1851): **White king at b4, bishop at c5, pawn at a2; Black king at b7, pawns at c6, b5,** the extra bishop-pawn makes no difference at all, for if the White bishop moves it can be sacrificed at once, while if it does not move we have in effect the ending of king, bishop, and rook-pawn vs. king and knight-pawn.

No. 282, P. Benko

White to play wins

1. Kc2! (1. b4? h3 2. Kb2 Kf5 3. Bd5 Ke5 4. Bh1 Kd4 =) **1. ... Kf5 2. Kd3! h3 3. Bb1! Ke5** (3. ... Kf4 4. Kd4 h2 5. Be4) **4. Ke3 h2 5. Be4 Kd6 6. Kd4,** etc., wins.

When there is no rook-pawn Black can draw only under certain special circumstances.

No. 283 (Portisch-Stein 1967): **White king at f2, bishop at d7, pawn at g3, h3; Black king at f6, pawn at f7, g6, h7.** White to play. **1. Be8!** gains an important tempo by delaying the Black king. **1. ... Ke7 2. Bb5 f5 3. Ke3 Kf6 4. Kd4 h5** (if 4. ... Kg5 5. Ke5 h5 6. h4+! Kg4 7. Kf6 Kxg3 8. Kg5! wins) **5. Ke3 h4** (if 5. ... g5 6. Kd4! h4 7. g4, or 6. ... g4 7. h4 wins) **6. g4 Ke5 7. Bf1 Kf6 8. Kf4 g5+ 9. Ke3 Ke5 10. Ba6,** Black resigned. Wrong is 1. Ke3? Ke5 2. Bb5 f5 3. Bd3 g5 4. Kf3 f4 5. g4 h5! 6. Bg6 (6. gxh5 Kf6 7. h6 Kf7 leads to a draw with rook-pawn and wrong bishop) 6. ... hxg4+ 7. hxg4 Kd4 leads only to a new draw position: 8. Ke2 Kc3 9. Bd3 Kd4 10. Kd2 Ke5 11. Kc3 f3! 12. Kd2 Kf4 13. Bf5 Kg3 14. Ke1 Kg2 15. Be4 Kg3, draw (Averbakh).

When the White pawn is not passed, the winning method consists of first blockading the Black pawns (so that no pawn exchange is feasible) and then capturing them with the king.

No. 284

White to play wins

No. 284 is typical. **1. Bf4 d5** (1. ... Kc7 2. c5) **2. c5 Ka6 3. Kb3 Kb5 4. Be3** wins.

A. Bishop and Pawn vs. Two Pawns

Exceptions to the rule that bishop and pawn win against two pawns (in addition to the case of a rook-pawn with a bishop of the wrong color) may be grouped under three headings:

1. The pawns are so far advanced that they divert the bishop or king and enable the king to capture the last pawn.

2. The pawns are so far advanced that one of them queens, winning.

3. The White king cannot approach without allowing an exchange of pawns.

1. Advanced Pawns Draw

No. 285, Reti 1928

White to play draws

No. 285 is a beautiful illustration of this theme. **1. Kc6!!** (1. h7? loses: 1. ... Kg7 2. Ke6 Kxh7) **1. ... Ba5** (if 1. ... Kg6 2. Kd7 Ba5 3. Ke6 Bc3 4. d7 Ba5 5. h7!) **2. Kd5 Bc3 3. h7 f5** (3. ... Kg7 4. Ke6! Kxh7 5. d7) **4. d7 Ke7 5. d8=Q+ Kxd8 6. Ke6!! f4 7. Kd5 f3 8. Kc4! Bh8 9. Kd3** and the pawn cannot be saved.

No. 286 (Alapin-N.N. 1907) is a somewhat analogous case where one passed pawn suffices to draw. **White king at f2, pawns at a5, h2; Black king at f6, bishop at h3, pawn at h7.** White to move. Draw. **1. a6 Bc8 2. a7 Bb7 3. Kg3 Kg5 4. Kh3 Kf4** (4. ... Kh5 5. Kg3; if Black's king does not venture out, White will simply stick to his two squares g3 and h3) **5. Kh4 Kf3 6. Kh5 Kg2 7. Kh6 Be4 8. a8=Q.**

2. Advanced Pawns Win

We have seen that pawns two, four, or more files apart are most dangerous against a bishop.

No. 287, Handbuch, 1st Edition

Whoever plays wins

This is again the case. Black wins by **1. ... f4 2. Bd4** (2. K any c3 3. K any c2) **2. ... f3 3. Kf6 c3 4. Ke5 c2 5. Be3 f2** and one pawn must promote. White to play wins both pawns by **1. Kf6 f4 2. Kf5 f3 3. Kf4 c3 4. Kxf3 c2 5. Be3**.

3. Pawn Exchange Unavoidable

In **No. 288** (Walker 1841): **White king at c3, bishop at e3, pawn at c4; Black king at b7, pawns at b6, c6.** White to play wins. White's only winning chance is **1. Kd4**, when **1. ... Ka6! 2. Ke5 c5 3. Kd5 b5** is sufficient. Black must not play c5 too soon; e.g., 1. Kd4 c5+?? 2. Kd5 Ka6 3. Kc6 Ka5 4. Bxc5, etc. Compare No. 284.

B. Bishop and Pawn vs. Three or More Pawns

The bishop is still theoretically favored but because of the reduced material the pawns offer excellent chances to draw and even at times to win. The result depends largely on the relative positions of the kings and pawns.

When White has a passed pawn and Black has three connected passed pawns on the fourth rank or beyond, Black can draw, while if they are on the third or second they lose.

No. 289

Whoever plays wins

Here is another one of those positions where the outcome is determined by whose move it is. After **1. ... c4** the pawns cannot be stopped; e.g., **2. Bb6 a4 3. Ba5 a3 4. Bc3 a2 5. Kg5 b4 6. Ba1 c3**. On the other hand, **1. Bxc5 b4 2. Bd6 b3 3. Ba3 a4 4. Bb2** blockades the pawns and forces a quick conclusion.

With the pawns on the third rank (at a6, b6, c6, other pieces unmoved), they can be stopped after **1. ... c5** (or **1. ... b5 2. Bc5!! a5 3. Bb6! a4 4. Bc5**) **2. Bf4 c4 3. Bc7 b5** (or **3. ... c3 4. Bxb6 c2 5. Be3 a5 6. Bc1**) **4. Ba5**.

Of course with the White king in No. 289 anywhere near the Black pawns, a draw would be certain.

It is generally easier to win if the White pawn is not passed, for a bishop can easily blockade two pawns. The winning process is then exactly the same as in bishop and pawn vs. two pawns—blockade the enemy pawns, then either capture all of them or the most important one, and queen one's own pawn. White's task is much easier if Black has already blockaded his pawns or is obliging enough to do so.

In **No. 290**, the problem is relatively difficult (Walker gives it as a draw).

No. 290, Walker 1841

White to play wins

1. Ke2 Kh3 2. Bg5 Kg3 3. Ke3 Kg2 4. Bh4! Kh3 5. Be1 g3 (or 5. ... Kh2 6. Kf4 Kh3 7. Bg3 f5 8. exf6 e5+ 9 Kxe5) **6. Kf4! g2 7. Bf2** followed by Kg5-f6.

The classification of the defender's drawing and winning chances given above is also valid here. The only difference is that the extra material increases the number of exceptions to the dictum that White wins. The case of bishop of the wrong color and rook-pawn vs. three or more pawns differs in no essential respect from that of bishop and rook-pawn vs. two pawns, so it need not be considered here.

1. Advanced Pawns Draw

No. 291

White to play. Draw

Black is threatening to queen, so White must begin with **1. Bf6**. Then 1. ... Kb4? 2. g5! Kc4 3. Ka3 loses, but there is an ingenious resource in **1. ... g5!! 2. Bxg5 Kd4 3. Bf6+ Ke4 4. g5 Kf5 5. Kxb3 a1=Q.**

No. 292 (Reti 1929) has a different drawing idea: blocking the bishop. **White king at a8, pawns at c7, d5, g4; Black king at f6, bishop at a6, pawn at h6.** White to play. Draw. **1. d6!** (not 1. Ka7 Bc8 2. ... Bxg4) **1. ... Ke6 2. d7!! Kxd7 3. Ka7 Be2 4. Kb8 Ba6 5. Ka7 Bc8 6. Kb8** and Black cannot gain the needed tempo.

2. Advanced Pawns Win

Unless the pawns are on the sixth or seventh rank they need the support of the king to be able to advance against a bishop. This allows the opponent's king to capture a Black pawn or to come back in time to stop the passed pawns. All this goes to show that such endings cannot be solved by applying *a priori* rules, but always require exact calculation.

No. 293, Flohr-Thomas, Hastings 1935-36

Black to play

Flohr sacrificed a piece to get this position and in fact wins by only one tempo. The game concluded **1. ... d4? 2. Kd6?** (2. Bd2! Kd3 3. Ba5 draws) **2. ... a5 3. g4 a4 4. g5 d3 5. Ke7 a3! 6. Bxa3 d2 7. Kxf7 d1=Q 8. Be7 Kd5 9. g6 Qf3+ 10. Bf6 Qf5! 11. g7 Qe6+** and Black resigned.

No. 294 also illustrates this point: **White king at a8, pawn at h5, bishop at g6; Black king at e7, pawns at h6, g7, e4.** Black to play wins. After **1. ... e3 2. Bd3 g5! 3. hxg6 Kf6** (3. ... h5? 4. g7 Kf7 5. Bg6+! =) **4. Kb7 h5** one pawn must queen. With the Black pawn on f6, the outcome is a draw.

Connected passed pawns must be supported by the king, for they can easily be blockaded by a bishop. With the king, though, they are quite powerful and always win unless the opposing king can approach too quickly.

No. 295, Charousek-Caro, Berlin 1897

White to play wins

Black loses because he cannot approach the dangerous c-pawn, which cramps his bishop's mobility, but White must be careful not to allow a blockade of his pawns. **1. Kc6! Ke7 2. b5 Ke6** (or 2. ... Ke8 3. a4 Ke7 4. a5 Ke8 5. a6 Ke7 6. b6) **3. a4 Ke5 4. a5 Kd4 5. b6** and queens in a few moves. The freedom of the pawns is all-important here. 1. b5 Bb7 2. a4 (2. a3! still wins) only draws after 2. ... a6! 3. b6 (or 3. bxa6 Bxa6 4. a5 Bc8 5. Kc6 Ke7 6. Kb6 Kd6) a5 4. Kc5 Kd7 5. Kb5 Kd6 6. Kxa5 Kc5.

When there is a choice whether to set up connected or unconnected passed pawns, the proximity of the king and the rank the pawns are on always decide. **No. 296** (from Horwitz 1884): **White king at b7, bishop at c2, pawn at a3; Black king at g7, pawns at a5, b5, c4.** The Black king is so far away that connected pawns will be useless. So only unconnected ones come into consideration, and they actually win. **1. ... a4! 2. Kb6 b4! 3. axb4 a3 4. Bb1 c3,** etc. White to play could have won by forcing connected pawns: **1. Kb6 b4 2. a4! b3 3. Bd1! b2 4. Bc2** and the bishop is of the right color.

3. Pawn Exchange Unavoidable

With the pawns doubled or blockaded the side with the bishop should at least draw. But again, advanced pawns are an exception.

No. 297, Reti 1929

White to play wins

White wins by **1. Kd3!! Kg3 2. Ke3 Kh4 3. Kd4 Kg4** (or 3. ... Bd8 4. g6! Kh5 5. f5 Bf6+ 6. Kc5 Kg5 7. Kd6 Bd8 8. Ke6) **4. Ke4 Bd8 5. Ke5 g6 6. d6 Ba5 7. f5 Kxg5 8. f6!! Bc3+** (or 8. ... Kh6 9. Ke6 Bd8 10. Kf7 g5 11. Ke8 Bxf6 12. d8=Q Bxd8 13. Kxd8 g4 14. Ke7 g3 15. d7 g2 16. d8=Q g1=Q 17. Qh8+ and captures the Black queen) **9. Kd5!! Bxf6 10. Ke6 Bd8 11. Kf7 Kf5 12. Ke8 Ba5 13. d8=Q** and the second pawn queens ahead of Black's.

Unusual stalemate combinations occasionally crop up here.

No. 298, P. Benko 1991

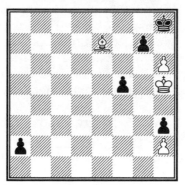

White to play draws

1. Bf8! gxh6 2. Be7 Kg7 (2. ... a1=Q 3. Bf6+!) **3. Bc5 Kf6** (3. ... a1=Q 4. Bd4+! Qxd4 stalemate) **4. Bd4+ Ke6 5. Kh4 Kd5 6. Bb2 Ke4 7. Kg3 Ke3 8. Bc1+ Ke2 9. Bb2,** =

Against two pawns and a bishop, Black must usually have the full equivalent of the bishop (three pawns) to be able to draw; otherwise, White's extra pawn(s) makes a pawn exchange much less meaningful, since White will still retains enough material to win. The method when Black has fewer than five pawns is either to win several pawns or to force an unstoppable passed pawn. Just how this is done in any particular case cannot be described by any general rule, but the outlines of the procedure are always quite clear. Here we'll look at some more difficult cases.

To win enemy pawns once they are blockaded is normally fairly simple, since king and bishop are in effect battling against a king. But where there is danger of losing one's own pawns, complications arise. **In No. 299** (A. Havasi): **White king at c4, bishop at c1, pawns at g2, g3; Black king at f5, pawns at c6, c5, d6, g5.** White to play wins. White's first thought must be to defend his own pawns. He wins by **1. Be3 Kg4 2. Bf2 Kf5 3. Bg1! Kg4** (if 3. ... Ke4 4. g4) **4. Bh2 Kf5 5. g4+ Ke6 6. Bg3 Ke7 7. Be1 Ke6 8. Bd2 Kf6 9. g3!** (the winning tempo) **9. ... Kg6 10. Ba5 Kf6 11. Bd8+ Kg6 12. Be7** and now Black's pawns go the way of all wood.

Positions in which Black can draw when he has fewer than three pawns for the bishop are again similar to those given above: special positions with the rook-pawn, advanced pawns, or forced pawn exchanges. As expected, these stratagems are much less effective when White has two pawns. The exchange of one pawn still does not solve Black's drawing problem, while against advanced pawns White can often sacrifice the bishop and emerge with a won pawn ending.

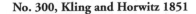

No. 300, Kling and Horwitz 1851

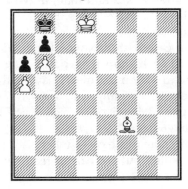

White to play. Draw

No. 300 is a special position with the essential characteristic of rook-pawn with bishop of the wrong color: the king cannot approach without stalemating. And an attempt such as **1. Bxb7 Kxb7**, or **1. Be2 Ka8 2. Bxa6 bxa6** leads to a drawn pawn ending (No. 48). There remains only the idea that worked in the similar knight ending (No. 217), **1. Bg2 Ka8 2. Bc6.** But Black dispels all illusions by coolly replying **2. ... Kb8!** A bishop on e3 (i.e., on the dark squares) also draws.

Occasionally certain unusual drawing possibilities come up that can be overcome with careful play. In **No. 301** the solution is immediately clear once you realize that with the Black g-pawn and f-pawn off the board the game is a draw.

No. 301

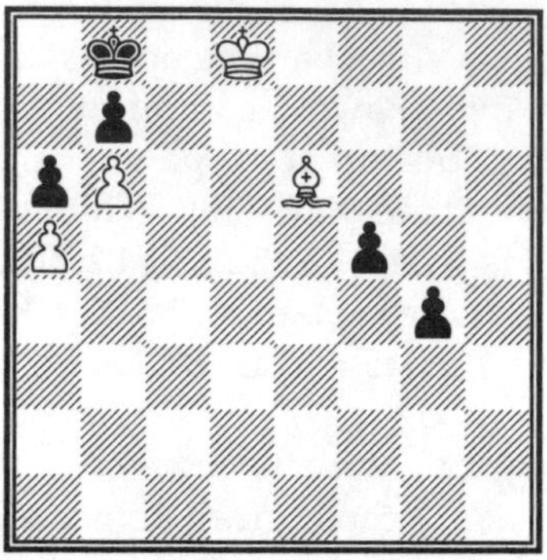

White to play wins

Consequently 1. Bxf5 would be a mistake because of 1. ... g3 2. Be4 g2!. Instead, a win is achieved by **1. Kd7 g3** (or 1. ... f4 2. Bxg4 f3 3. Bh3! f2 4. Bf1) **2. Bd5 f4 3. Bf3 g2** (if 3. ... Ka8 4. Kc7 and mates) **4. Bxg2 f3 5. Bf1 f2 6. Kd8 Ka8 7. Bxa6! Kb8** (7. ... bxa6 8. Kc7 and mate in two) **8. Bf1 Ka8 9. Bg2 Kb8 10. Kd7 Ka8 11. Kc7 f1=Q 12. Bxb7+** mate. For the position without Black's Kingside pawns see No. 300.

No. 302 is a common case with h-pawns (from Alekhine-Tylor, Nottingham 1936): **White king at b1, bishop at a4, pawns at g4, h4; Black king at d5, pawns at g6, h7**. White to play must merely avoid the ending with bishop and rook-pawn; i.e., he must exchange his h-pawn. This is done by **1. Be8!! Ke5 2. h5 Kf6** (or 2. ... gxh5 3. Bxh5; on 2. ... g5 3. Bd7 holds everything until the king gets there) **3. hxg6 hxg6 4. Bd7**, etc.

Finally, we must again note those cases where it is not possible to prevent the opponent from queening but we can instead set up a mating position with queens on the board.

No. 303, P. Benko, version 1984

Black to play. White wins

The main line is **1. ... a5 2. d3!** (surprising, because after this the a-pawn cannot be stopped, but if 2. Bh4? d3! draws) **2. ... a4 3. Bh4 a3 4. Bf6 a2 5. c4+ Kc5 6. Kb7 a1=Q 7. Be7+** mate. Black has other possibilities: 1. ... d3!? 2. c4+! (2. cxd3? or 2. c3? only draw after 2. ... a5) 2. ... Kxc4 3. Bb6! Kb5 4. Bd4 a5 5. Kb7 a4 6. Kc7 Kc4 7. Bc3 a3 8. Kd6 a2 9. Ke5 Kb3 10. Kd4 Kc2 11. Ke3 (just in time to win. Similarly, 1. ... Kc4 2. Kb7 a5 3. Kc6 a4 4. d3+ Kc3 5. Kc5, etc., also wins.

No. 304, P. Benko 1991

White to play wins

1. Bb1 f4 2. Kc5 Kb3 3. g6 f3 4. g7 f2 5. g8=Q f1=Q 6. Qxd5+ Kc3 7. Qd4+ Kb3 8. Qa4+! Kxa4 9. Bc2+ mate.

Advanced pawns draw less often against a bishop when there are a larger number of pawns on the board, and when they do, the play is generally more involved. Some of the added difficulties are seen here:

No. 305, P. Benko, after Reti

White to play and draw

1. e5!, etc. On **1. ... dxe5** we get **2. Kg7 Bd3 3. h6 Bh7!?.** Otherwise, Black can't make progress because he can't push his pawns. **4. Kxh7 Kf7 5. g5! fxg5 6. Kh8 g4 7. h7** stalemating the White king.

An exchange of pawns is a saving maneuver (when there are fewer than three pawns for the bishop) only when the superior side has a doubled pawn. We see this in **No. 306** (Burn-Marco, Vienna 1898): **White king at g3, pawns at a2, c3, g2, h3; Black king at d5, bishop at f5, pawns at h6, h5.** White to play. Draw. After **1. Kh4 Bg6 2. a4 Kc4 3. g4 hxg4 4. hxg4 Be8 5. Kg3 Bxa4 6. g5 hxg5 7. Kg4,** draw agreed. If **5. ... Kc5** (instead of 5. ... Bxa4) the answer would be **6. Kh4 Kb6 7. c4! Bf7 8. Kg3 Bxc4 9. g5 h5 10. g6!** and the Black h-pawn cannot be held.

No. 307, Fine-Kevitz, New York 1936

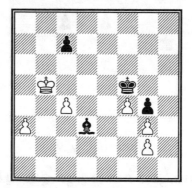

White to play. Draw

No. 307 may be called a normal position in this type of ending: the three pawns draw against the bishop. The continuation was **1. Kc6 Ke4 2. Kxc7 Bxc4 3. a4 Kd5 4. a5 Ke6** (4. ... Kc5 5. Kd7 Kb5? 6. f5 Kxa5 7. f6 Kb4 8. Ke7 loses for

Black) **5. Kb7 Bd5+ 6. Kc7!** (6. Kb6 Kd6 7. a6 Bxg2 8. a7 Bf3 9. Ka5 Kc7 is inferior)
6. ... Bc4, and the game was called a draw. That every pawn played its part here,
even the despised doubled pawn, is shown by the fact that without the pawn at
g2, White loses. After **1. Kc6 Bxc4 2. Kxc7 Ke4 3. a4 Kf3! 4. f5 Kxg3 5. f6 Kf4 6.
a5 Ke5 7. a6 Kxf6 8. a7 Bd5** the pawn is stopped and Black will soon queen.

Clearly the result of such endings depends on the relative positions of the
pawns, kings, and bishop. In practice, it is "normally" a draw even though
the side with the bishop does not win as often as the side with the pawns.

No. 308 (Cochrane-Staunton, London 1842) has some instructive errors in
the handling of both bishop and pawns: **White king at a6, pawns at a4, b6,
c6, g2, h3; Black king at c8, bishop at d2, pawns at a5, h4.** White to play
could have forced a speedy conclusion by **1. b7+ Kb8 2. c7+ Kxc7 3. Ka7** and
the pawn queens. Instead he tried 1. Kb5 Be1 2. Kc4 (2. Ka6 still wins) 2. ... Bf2
3. b7+?? (3. Kb5 was still good enough) 3. ... Kc7 4. Kb5 Ba7 5. Ka6 Bb8 6. Kb5
Kd6 7. Kxa5 Kxc6 8. Kb4 Kxb7 9. Kc4 Kb6 10. Kd3 and here Black could have
won with 10. ... Bg3.

With a large number of pawns on the board (bishop plus three or more),
the bishop almost always wins. Black has only two possible saving chances:
advanced passed pawns, or a complete blockade. Of these only the first
occurs with any frequency in actual play, and the side with the bishop is
often hard pressed to hold the game.

When there is the full equivalent of three pawns for the bishop and the side
with the bishop has a weak pawn position, the bishop is frequently unable to
stem the tide.

No. 309, Capablanca-Lasker, New York 1924

Black to play. White wins

Capablanca won as follows: **1. ... Bd5 2. b4 a6 3. Kg4!** (first the pawns must
get to the fifth; 3. Ke5 Kg6 is inferior) **3. ... Bc4 4. f5 Bb3 5. Kf4 Bc2 6. Ke5 Kf7
7. a4 Kg7** (7. ... Bxa4 8. Kxe4 also leaves Black helpless) **8. d5 Bxa4** (or 8. ...
cxd5 9. Kxd5 Bxa4 10. Kxe4 and the three connected passed pawns cannot be
held) **9. d6 c5 10. bxc5 Bc6 11. Ke6 a5 12. f6+,** Black resigned.

Unless these passed pawns already exist, such a defense is rarely feasible, for even if the king gets to the enemy pawns they can usually be defended by the bishop at a distance (in contrast to the similar case with the knight). Pawns are weakest in blocked positions where they are on the same color as the bishop.

An example is **No. 310: White king at e5, pawns at a5, b4, c5, h4; Black king at h7, pawns at a6, b5, c6, bishop at h5.** White to play wins: **1. Kd6 Kg7 2. Kc7!** (the simplest: it is better to have the bishop cut off from the Pawns than to be deceived by a mess of wood) **2. ... Kf7 3. Kb6 Ke7 4. Kxa6 Kd8 5. Kb7 Bg4 6. a6 Bc8+ 7. Kb6** and wins. Or here **1. Kd6 Bg4 2. Kc7 Kg6 3. Kb7 Kh5 4. Kxa6 Bc8+ 5. Kb6 Kxh4 6. a6** etc.

Where pawns can no longer be stopped, a stalemate defense is the only chance.

III. BISHOP AND PAWNS VS. BISHOP OF THE SAME COLOR, WITH AND WITHOUT PAWNS

A. Positions With Material Advantage

Here we have the same situation noted in knight endings: one pawn ahead in general is enough to win but the fewer pawns there are the harder it is.

1. Bishop and Pawn vs. Bishop

A great deal of work has been done with this endgame, notably by L. Centurini toward the end of the 19th century, and the results are exhaustive.. Centurini summed up his investigations in the two following principles:

1) The game is drawn when the Black king either is on or can occupy any square in front of the pawn from which it cannot be driven away by the bishop.

2) If the Black king is behind the pawn and the White king near the pawn, then Black can draw only if his king is attacking the pawn and has the opposition and only if his bishop can maneuver on two diagonals on each of which it can occupy at least two squares.

These principles will become clearer from the following analysis. The first case is elementary. With his king in front of the pawn Black plays his bishop *ad infinitum* and draws by exhaustion.

If the Black king is on a rank ahead of the pawn but not directly in front of it, the outcome depends on whether he can reach a crucial square. If not, he must either transpose into some case to be considered later or allow White to promote.

An example is **No. 311** (Regence, 1856): **White king at c6, bishop at h2, pawn at e6; Black king at c8, bishop at a5.** Black to play draws at once by **1. ... Kd8 and 2. ... Ke8.** White to play seems to win with **1. e7,** but Black has the ingenious rejoinder **1. ... Bd8!!** and if **2. e8=Q (or R)** stalemate, while **2. e8=N (or B)** both lead to nothing. And if **1. Bc7! Bb4! 2. Bb6 Be7! 3. Ba5 Ba3**

4. Kd5 Kb7 5. Ke5 Be7 6. Kf5 Kc6 7. Kg6 Kd5 8. Kf7 Bc5 9. Bd8 Ke4 10. Be7 Bf2 11. Bb4 Bh4 12. Bc3 Kf5 and we have reached the drawn position.

No. 312 (Berger) is an example where the White pawn queens by force: **White king at c6, bishop at c5, pawn at a6; Black king at c8, bishop at b8.** White to play wins. After **1. Bd4**, Black must either release the pawn by a bishop move or allow 2. Kb7 after 1. ... Kd8, when he again must allow the pawn to queen.

No. 313, Centurini

White wins

If the Black king is not in front of the pawn and not near it, the win is fairly simple. In **No. 313**, where Black's king is only two squares away, **1. Bc6** soon decides: **1. ... Be2 2. Bd5 Bb5 3. Be6 Ke3 4. Bd7 Bf1** (or 4. ... Ba6 5. c6 Kd4 6. c7 Kc4 7. Bh3 Kb4 8. Kc6 Ka5 9. Bg4 Kb4 10. Kb6) **5. c6 Kd4 6. c7 Ba6 7. Kc6 Kc3 8. Kb6** and the pawn promotes.

Even if the White pawn is still on its original square a win is possible.

No. 314, P. Benko, after Grigoriev 1931

White to play wins

In the original endgame the Black bishop is on h5, but after 1. b4 Bd1! the move 2. b5 is no good because of 2. ... Ba4. The study is therefore cooked. My version adds some new variations to the solution: **1. b4 Bf1 2. Bd5 Kg5 3. Bc4 Bh3.** Strangely, this is the best defense. If 3. ... Bg2 4. b5 Kf6 5. Kb4! Ke7 6. Ka5 and the king goes to a7!, securing the win. **4. b5 Kf6 5. b6 Bc8.** If 5. ... Bg2 6. Kd4 Ke7 7. Bd5 wins. **6. Kd4 Ke7 7. Kc5 Kd7 8. Bb5+! Kd8 9. Kc6!.** But 9. Kd6? Bb7 10. Bd7 Bf3 11. Be6 Bb7! with a draw due to zugzwang. **9. ... Bd7+ 10. Kd6 Bc8 11. Bc4! Bb7 12. Be6** and White wins. If 12. ... Ba6 13. Kc6 Bc8 or 13. ... Ke7 14. Bc4 wins.

My added line goes: **1. ... Kg5 2. b5 Kf6 3. b6 Bc8 4. Kb4 Ke7 5. Kb5 Kd6 6. Bf3 Ke7 7. Kc6 Kd8 8. Be2** wins. The White king eventually gets to a7.

When the Black king is near the pawn but behind it, we get a more elaborate series of possibilities. First of all, in accordance with our principle, we consider those positions where Black's bishop has two long diagonals. This is the case when White has either a bishop-pawn (with the bishop not of the same color as the queening square) or a center pawn.

No. 315, Centurini

Draw

In **No. 315,** the only attempt White can make is **1. Bf7 Be2 2. Bg6 Bc4,** but **3. Bh7 Bb3 4. Bg8 Bxg8** destroys White's illusions. On other moves, such as **1. Be6,** Black can always reply 1. ... Be8; or 1. Bb5 Bg6.

From this example we can also see why diagonal opposition is not enough for Black to draw. The Black bishop must have at least two squares available from which it can be driven only when the opposing bishop blocks his pawn.

For example, **No. 316: Black king at e5, other pieces as in No. 315. 1. Bd3 Kf4 2. Bg6** is conclusive.

Another case where a bad king position, though near the pawn, is ruinous is **No. 317 (Horwitz 1880): White king at g5, bishop at d5, pawn at f6; Black king at h7, bishop at g6.** White to play wins by **1. Bg8+! Kh8!** (1. ... Kxg8 2. Kxg6, White has the opposition) **2. Be6 Be8** (if 2. ... Kh7 3. Bf5 and again White has the opposition, while if 2. ... Bd3 3. Kf4 Bb5 4. Ke5 Be8 5. Kd6 Kh7

6. Ke7 Kg6 7. Bd7 Bf7 8. Bf5+) **3. Kf5 Kh7 4. Bd5 Bh5** (or 4. ... Bd7+ 5. Ke5 Kg6
6. f7 Kg7 7. Kd6 Bf5 8. Ke7) **5. Kc6 Kg6 6. Ke7 Kf5** (6. ... Kg5 loses—diagonal
opposition!) **7. Bf7 Bd1 8. Be6+** and **9. f7.**

With a center pawn we get a position such as **No. 318** (Centurini): **White
king at f7, bishop at d8, pawn at e6; Black king at f5, bishop at c5.** White to
play. Draw. **1. Be7 Bf2 2. Bb4 Bh4; or 1. Bf6 Bb4 2. Bg7 Bc5 3. Bf8 Bxf8.**

Here too the diagonal opposition would lose. **No. 319: Black king at d5,
other pieces as in No. 318. 1. Be7 Bf2 2. Bb4 Bh4 3. Bc3 Kd6 4. Bf6** and the
pawn cannot be stopped.

When the Black bishop has only one long diagonal, a knight-pawn always
wins, but a bishop-pawn or rook-pawn wins or draws depending on the king
positions.

No. 320, Centurini

White wins

No. 320 is the typical win with a rook-pawn. **1. Bg7 Bd2 2. Bh6 Bb4** (2. ...
Bxh6 3. Kxh6 Kf5 4. Kg7) **3. Be3 Bf8** (or 3. ... Bc3 4. h6 Ba1 5. h7 Bb2 6. Bh6-g7)
4. Bd4 Kh4 5. Be5! Kg4 6. Bf6 Kf4 7. Bg7 Ba3 8. h6 and queens in two moves.
It is essential to have the square in front of the pawn available for the bishop.

For this reason, if we move everything up two ranks—**No. 321: White king
at g8, bishop at e7, pawn at h7; Black king at g6, bishop at e5**—the result is
a draw, since White's bishop cannot get to h8.

Here again, in **No. 322: White king at g8, bishop at f8, pawn at h7; Black
king at e6, bishop at e5. 1. Bg7** decides at once. Or Black to play, **1. ... Bh8 2.
Bg7!** (just to be fancy, 2. Kxh8 is of course good enough: 2. ... Kf7 3. B any) **2.
... Bxg7 3. Kxg7** and queens.

On the other hand, horizontal instead of vertical opposition draws for
Black because he can then exchange bishops and get back to f7 with his king.
No. 323: Black king at e6, other pieces as in No. 320. Nothing can be done,
for if **1. Bg7 Bd2 2. Bh6 Bxh6 3. Kxh6 Kf7 =.**

No. 324, Centurini

White to play wins

The knight-pawn, as already mentioned, always wins, although in **No. 324** considerable finesse is required. **1. Bh4 Kb6** (if 1. ... Bf4 2. Bf2 Bh2 3. Ba7 Bf4 4. Bb8 Be3 5. Bg3 Ba7 6. Bf2—this is the variation White is trying to force) **2. Bf2+ Ka6! 3. Bc5!!** (to get the Black bishop out of his corner—the point will soon be apparent) **3. ... Bg3** (or any other square) **4. Be7 Kb6 5. Bd8+ Kc6 6. Bh4!** (gaining the decisive tempo; with the bishop at h2 this was impossible) **6. ... Bd6 7. Bf2 Bh2 8. Ba7 Bd6 9. Bb8 Bc5 10. Bh2 Ba7 11. Bg1** and wins.

With the pawn on the sixth, the winning idea is exactly the same but easier to execute. **No. 325** (Centurini): **White king at f5, bishop at e7, pawn at g6; Black king at h5, bishop at g7.** White to play concludes with **1. Bg5 Bf8 2. Kf6! Kg4** (or 2. ... Be7+ 3. Kf7!! Bf8 4. Bd2 and Black cannot maintain his grip on the pawn with both bishop and king) **3. Bd2 Ba3 4. Bc3 Bf8 5. Kf7 Bh6** (5. ... Kh5 6. Bd2) **6. Bd2.**

Or Black to play: **1. ... Kh6** (if 1. ... Bh6 2. Kf6 Bg5+ 3. Kf7 Bh6 4. Bc5 K any 5. Be3) **2. Bf6 Bf8 3. Bd4 Be7** (or 3. ... Bg7 4. Be3+ Kh5 5. Bg5 Bf8 6. Kf6 as in the variation where White begins) **4. g7 Kh7 5. Ke6,** and **6. Kf7.** In the analogous position with a center pawn, Black draws by maintaining vertical or horizontal opposition, but not diagonal.

With a suitable king position, the knight-pawn can win even when it is on the fifth with two squares covered by the opponent's bishop still to be crossed.

No. 326, Berger 1920

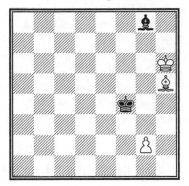

White to play wins

In **No. 326** (Berger 1920), after **1. g4** (Black to play of course draws by 1. ... Kg3) **Be6** (1. ... Bf7 2. g5) **2. g5 Bf5 3. Bg6 Be6 4. Bc2 Bf7 5. Bd1 Kf5 6. Bh5 Bb3 7. g6 Kf6 8. g7 Bg8** (else 9. Kh7) **9. Bg6 Ke7** (if 9. ... Bb3 10. Kh7 Bc4 11. Bc2 Kg5 12. Kh8 Kh6 13. Bh7 Ba2 14. Bg8 Bb1 15. Bb3 Bh7 16. Bc2) **10. Bc2 Kf6 11. Bd3 Ke7 12. Kg6 Ke8 13. Kf6 Kd7 14. Bg6 Kd6 15. Bf7 Bh7 16. Kg5 Ke7 17. Kh6** and wins. The win here is again due to that old rascal, the diagonal opposition.

In **No. 327: Black king at h4, other pieces as in No. 326.** On **1. g4 Bf7** draws at once. But even **1. g4 Bb3 2. g5 Bc2** draws, for after **3. Bg6 Ba4 4. Bd3 Be8 5. Be2 Bf7**; White does not have **6. Bh5** at his disposal. With a g-pawn the win is conditional upon whether or not the White king is on the suitable square, although the position of the Black king this time makes little or no difference.

No. 328, Centurini

White to play wins

In **No. 328**, White always wins because his king covers the square g7. **1. Bc3 Ba3 2. Bg7 Bb4 3. Bf8 Bd2 4. Ba3 Bh6 5. Bc1 Bg7 6. Bd2 Kf6 7. Bc3+.**

But in **No. 329**, with the **White king at e8, other pieces as in No. 327**, nothing can be done because the Black bishop has two long diagonals to maneuver on. **1. Ba5 Kf6 2. Bd8+ Ke6 3. Bg5 Bb4 4. Bh6 Bc5 5. Bf8 Be3 6. Bb4 Bh6 7. Bd2 Bg7 8. Be3 Kd6**, etc.

Applications of this fact are seen in the next two illustrations. **No. 330** (Rabinovich): **White king at d6, bishop at e4, pawn at c7; Black king at b6, bishop at c8**. White to play. Draw. **1. Bc6 Ba6 2. Bd7 Bb7 3. Bh3 Ba6 4. Kd7 Kc5! 5. Kd8 Kd6** and we are back to No. 329.

With the king positions reversed, White of course wins: we get to Centurini's position, No. 328.

No. 331 (J. Crum 1921): **White king at f3, bishop at h5, pawn at c5; Black king at d2, bishop at f1**. White to play wins. **1. c6 Kc3 2. c7 Ba6 3. Ke3! Kb4 4. Be2**, and now:

a) **4. ... Bc8 5. Kd4 Bb7 6. Bf1 Bc8 7. Kd5 Bb7+ 8. Kd6 Ka5 9. Kc5!** (else 9. ... Kb6 transposes into Rabinovich above) **9. ... Bc8 10. Kc6 Bg4 11. Kb7 Bf5 12. Kb8**, and we have Centurini.

b) **4. ... Bb7 5. Kd4 Bc8 6. Kd5 Bb7+ 7. Kd6 Ka5 8. Kc5 Bc8 9. Kc6 Bh3 10. Kb7 Bf5 11. Kb8** and wins as in Centurini.

If the White pawn is still on the sixth rank, and the seventh is covered by the bishop, the game is a draw (No. 315).

Where the pawn is only on the fourth or fifth rank and the Black king is near it, the result is always a draw except for the rook-pawn and some special positions (see No. 326). This will require no elaborate demonstration if we merely recall that with the pawn on the sixth or seventh the win always (except for a rook-pawn) involves a bishop sacrifice to divert the rival from the queening square. Even when the pawn can be forced to the sixth or seventh the resulting position is so disadvantageous that a win is out of the question.

For example, **No. 332** (Berger 1920): **White king at c4, bishop at e7, pawn at b5; Black king at a4, bishop at a7**. White to play. Draw. **1. Bc5 Bb8 2. b6 Ka5 3. Kd5 Kb5 4. b7 Bc7!** but not 4. ... Ka6 5. Kc6 Bh2 6. Be7 Bg3 7. Bd8 Bb8 8. Bb6! Bf4 9. Bc7.

We can sum up all the above results in the general conclusion that when the Black king is behind the pawn, rook-pawn and bishop-pawn win on occasion, knight-pawn always, center pawns never.

2. Bishop and Two Pawns vs. Bishop

Bishop plus two pawns win against bishop as a rule without any trouble. Where the two pawns are connected, White must simply take care to keep them together. In **No. 333** an added precaution is necessary: to prevent the sacrifice of Black's bishop for the White knight-pawn, since the White bishop is the wrong color. Nevertheless, there is no special difficulty in the winning process.

No. 333

Black to play. White wins

1. ... Bh3 2. g3 Kh6 3. Bf1 Bg4 4. h4 Bf5 5. Kf2 Bg4 6. Ke3 Be6 7. Kf4 Bd7 8. Bd3 Bh3 9. Bf5 Bf1 10. g4 Be2 11. g5+ Kh5 (or **11. ... Kg7 12. Bg4** and **13. h5**) **12. Kg3** (not **12. g6? Kh6 13. Ke5 Bh5, =**) **12. ... Bd1 13. Be4 Bb3 14. Bf3+ Kg6 15. Kf4 Bf7 16. h5+ Kg7 17. Ke5 Bb3 18. Be4 Bf7 19. h6+ Kh8 20. Kf6 Bh5 21. Bd5 Kh7 22. Bf7.**

Black can draw against bishop plus two connected passed pawns only if he can effectively blockade the pawns with his king or force an ending with nothing but rook-pawn and bishop of the wrong color. The latter case is seen in a simple transformation. White king at f1, other pieces as in No. 333. Black to play draws by **1. ... Bh3**, since **2. g3** is impossible.

An example of the former is **No. 334: White king at c2, bishop at e1, pawns at b4, c3; Black king at c4, bishop at g5.** White to play. Draw. The attempt **1. Kb2 Bf4 2. Ka3 Bc7 3. Ka4** is met by **3. ... Bd8 4. Bf2 Kxc3 5. Kb5 Kb3 6. Bc5 Kc3 7. Kc6 Kc4 8. b5 Ba5 9. Bb6 Be1** and White can do nothing (compare No. 327). This type of blockade is by no means always unbeatable, however, since White has the threats of both bishop and pawn sacrifices available.

For example, **No. 335: White king at f3, bishop at c1, pawns at f4, g5; Black king at f5, bishop at f8.** White to play wins by **1. Kg3 Bg7 2. Kh4 Bf8 3. Kh5 Bg7 4. g6 Bf8 5. Ba3 Bg7 6. Bd6 Ke6 7. Be5 Bf8 8. g7.**

Two unconnected passed pawns likewise are enough to win. If the pawns are more than two files apart the win is simple: White advances both pawns as far as possible, brings his king to the support of the pawn that is not blockaded by Black's king, meanwhile defending the other pawn with his bishop. Black will then have to give up his bishop for the distant passed pawn, leaving White with bishop and pawn vs. the lone king. Or he can give up one pawn to divert the Black king and then queen the other pawn as in one of the variations Nos. 313-328.

This latter stratagem was used in **No. 336** (Kashdan-Fine, New York 1936): **White king at g2, bishop at d2; Black king at b5, bishop at a5, pawns at a6,**

h4. White to play. Black wins. The continuation was **1. Bg5 Bb6 2. Bxh4 a5 3. Kf3 a4 4. Ke2 a3 5. Bf6** (if 5. Kd3 Bd4!!) **5. ... Kc4 6. Kd2 Kb3 7. Kc1 a2** and White resigned, since there is no defense to Bc5-a3-b2.

No. 337, Goglidze-Kasparian, Tiflis 1929

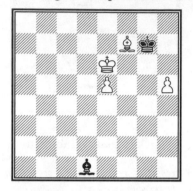

Black to play draws

Black draws only if he can blockade or has a favorable position against rook-pawn and bishop of the wrong color. Such a defense against rook-pawn and bishop can usually be set up if White's other pawn is on the bishop file or rook file. To win, White will surely have to give up his rook-pawn to divert the king, but both bishop and king-pawn vs. bishop and bishop and bishop-pawn vs. bishop are almost always drawn (Nos. 315 and 316).

No. 337 illustrates this point. **1. ... Bg4+ 2. Ke7 Be2 3. Bg6** (if 3. e6 Bg4 or Bc4 followed by Bxe6) **3. ... Bg4 4. Kd8 Kh6 5. Be8 Kg7 6. Ke7 Bd1 7. Bf7 Be2 8. h6+ Kxh6 9. Kf6 Bg4 10. Bg6 Be2 11. e6 Bc4 12. e7 Bb5 13. Kf7 Kg5**, draw.

Bishop and three or more pawns vs. bishop is, of course, an elementary win.

3. Bishop and Two Pawns vs. Bishop and Pawn

With all the pawns on one side, this is a draw (as is the similar knight ending) if the Black king is anywhere in front of the pawns. The best White can do is to exchange one pawn, when we get to bishop plus pawn vs. bishop. But if the Black king is not near its pawn and the White king is, then the win is quite simple: White captures the pawn and remains with bishop and two pawns vs. bishop.

If the Black king is near the pawns, as normally happens, White has winning chances only if he has an outside passed pawn. Whether such a pawn wins or not depends on its distance from the other pawn. If it is far away (e.g., both on knight files), then Black must sacrifice his bishop to stop it, whereupon White wins. But when the pawns are closer (e.g., e- and g-files), then the Black king can blockade the pawns.

No. 338

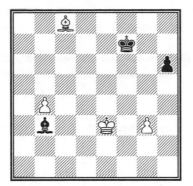

Black to play. White wins

Where one of White's pawns is a rook-pawn and he has the bishop of the wrong color, no general rule is applicable; the position must be judged on its merits.

No. 338 is the general win with the outside passed pawn. After **1. ... Bc4** (or 1. ... h5 2. b5 h4 3. gxh4 Bd5 4. b6 Kg6 5. Kd4, etc.—compare No. 336) **2. Bg4 Ke7** (on 2. ... Kf6 3. Be2 Bd5 4. Kf4 Kg6 5. b5 Bb7 6. Bf3 Bc8 7. b6 h5 8. b7 Bxb7 9. Bxb7 h4 10. g4! is decisive) **3. Be2 Bf7 4. b5 Kd6 5. Kf4 Kc5 6. Kf5 h5** (sooner or later forced) **7. Kg5 Be8 8. Kh6 Kb6 9. Bxh5 Bxb5 10. g4** and wins as in No. 326.

In **No. 339** (Santasiere-Kashdan, Boston 1938), the pawns are closer together and White has a bishop-pawn: **White king at d6, bishop at d5, pawns at b6, f4; Black king at b8, bishop at g4, pawn at f6.** White to play wins.

1. Ke7 f5 2. Kf6 Bh3! 3. Ke5!!

Excellent. If instead 3. Kg5 Kc8 4. Be6+ Kb7 5. Bxf5 Bg2 6. Bd3 Bh3 7. Be2 Kxb6 8. Bg4 Bf1 9. f5 Kc5 10. f6 Bc4 11. Kg6 Kd6 12. Kg7 Ke5 13. Bh5 Kf4 14. Bf7 Be2 15. Bb3 Bh5 16. Bc2 Kg5 and Black has just managed to reach No. 315.

3. ... Kc8 4. Be6+ Kb7 5. Bxf5 Bf1 6. Be6 Kxb6 (Black delays 6. ... Bd3 [played in the game]; he resigned after 7. Kd4) **7. f5 Bd3** (or 7. ... Kc7 8. f6 Kd8 9. Bf7 Bd3 10. Kf4 Kd7 11. Kg5 Kd6 12. Kh6 Ke5 13. Kg7 Bb5 14. Bb3 and Black loses because he has only diagonal opposition) **8. f6 Bg6 9. Kd6 Bh5 10. Ke7 Kc5 11. Bf7** and again Black loses because he cannot get the vertical opposition with his king at e5.

Where the pawns are close together a draw may be expected. **No. 340** (Euwe-Alekhine, third match game 1937): **White king at h4, bishop at f3, pawns at g2, e3; Black king at f6, bishop at f1, pawn at h6.** White to play. Draw. The game continued **1. Kh5 Kg7 2. e4 Bd3 3. e5 Bg6+ 4. Kg4 Kf7 5. Bd5+ Ke7 6. Kf4 Bh7 7. g3 Kf8** (7. ... Kd7 is also good enough; e.g., 8. Be4 Bg8 9. Bf5+ Ke7 10. Bc8 Bh7, etc.) **8. Be4 Bg8 9. Bf3 Ke7 10. Kg4 Ke6 11. Kf4 Ke7 12. Bg4 Bb3 13. Bc8 Kf7** and a draw was agreed.

With a rook-pawn and bishop of the wrong color we naturally expect an exception to the general rules, and we are not disappointed. Everything depends upon where the kings are.

No. 341, Eliskases-Capablanca, Semmering-Baden 1937

White to play wins

No. 341 is a win because Black's king cannot manage to blockade the pawn and maintain control of the long diagonal. Eliskases concluded as follows: **1. Bc8 Bf1 2. Bg4 Bd3** (for 2. ... Kb7 see No. 343) **3. Bf3+ Kd6 4. Bb7 Be2 5. Ba6 Bf3 6. Bf1** (threatening Kh6) **6. ... Bb7 7. Bh3! Ke7 8. Kb5 Kd6 9. Bg4** (now Black is in zugzwang) **9. ... Ke7 10. Kc5 Bg2 11. Bc8 Kd8** (or 11. ... Bf3 12. Ba6 Bg2 13. Bb5 Bb7 14. Bc6 Ba6 15. Bf3 Kd7 16. Bg4+ Kd8 17. Kc6, etc. as in the game) **12. Ba6** (12. Be6 is also good enough) **12. ... Bf3 13. Kd6 Bg2 14. Bc4 Kc8 15. Bd5 Bf1** (on 15. ... Bxd5 16. Kxd5 Kb7 17. Ke6 Black gets back one move too late) **16. Ke6 Be2 17. Kf6 Kd7 18. Kg6 h5 19. Kg5 Kd6 20. Bf7 Kc6 21. Bxh5** and Capablanca resigned; White wins as in No. 320.

Two further points are worth noting here. With the Black king at b8, White draws if his king is at a5 but wins if it's at c5. The difference is seen in **No. 342: Black king at b8, other pieces as in the Eliskases-Capablanca game above.** **1. Kb5 Bf1+ 2. Ka5 Bg2** is the rejoinder; if **1. Kb4 Bb7!! 2. Bc4 Bg2 3. Kc5 Kb7** and White can make no progress. Finally, **1. Kb4 Bb7 2. Kb5!** is met by **2. ... h5!!** when, as you will recall, **3. Bxb7 Kxb7** only draws.

On the other hand, in **No. 343: White king at c5, bishop at a6, pawns at b6, h4; Black king at b8, bishop at g2, pawn at h6.** White to play wins because **1. ... Bb7** can be answered by **2. Bxb7 Kxb7 3. h5!! Kb8 4. Kd6 Kb7 5. Ke6,** and the White king reaches g7 after capturing the Black h-pawn.

When Black's pawn is also passed, the win is not difficult, since White can block the pawn with his bishop or his king and proceed to exploit his own pawns. **No. 344** is a pretty illustration of a win in an unusually difficult position.

No. 344, Reti 1925

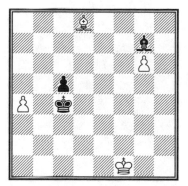

White to play wins

White wins by **1. Ba5! Kb3** (if 1. ... Kd5 2. Ke2 Kc6 3. Kd3 Kb7 4. Bc3 Bh6 5. Kc4 Kb6 6. Kd5 Bf8 7. Be1 Bg7 8. Bd2 Bf8 9. Be3 Ka5 10. Bxc5 Bg7 11. Bd4 Bh6 12. Ke6, and the bishop must soon abandon the diagonal f8-h6) **2. Bc3!! Kxc3 3. a5 Kb2 4. a6 c4 5. a7 c3 6. a8=Q c2 7. Qb7+ Ka2 8. Qf7+ Ka3 9. Qc7 Kb3 10. Ke2 Bc3 11. g7! Bxg7 12. Kd3.**

Two connected passed pawns similarly win against one without any trouble. If necessary, White can even sacrifice his bishop for the Black pawn and queen his own advanced pawns. For example, **No. 345** (Santasiere-Fine, New York, 1938): **White king at c6, bishop at c5, pawns at a4, b3; Black king at e6, bishop at e1, pawn at h7.** Black to play. White wins. After **1. ... h5 2. b4 h4 3. b5 Bg3 4. Bg1 h3 5. a5 Kf5** (or 5. ... h2 6. Bxh2 Bxh2 7. a6 Bg1 8. b6) **6. b6 Ke4 7. a6 Kf3 8. a7 Kg2 9. Bc5!** (9. a8=Q Kxg1 gives Black drawing chances but should also be good enough) **9. ... h2 10. a8=Q h1=Q 11. Kd7+ Kh2 12. Qxh1+ Kxh1 13. Bd6,** and Black resigned.

4. Two or More Pawns on Each Side

Unless all the pawns are on one side, a pawn ahead normally wins. The winning method, which is essentially the same as that for pawn-and-knight endings, should conform to the following pattern:

1. White first gets his king and bishop to the best possible squares (centralization).

2. He then sets up a passed pawn and advances it as far as he can.

3. If this passed pawn is blockaded by the Black bishop, an exchange of bishops is offered. This will either win the bishop or force a queen.

4. If the passed pawn is blockaded by the Black king, the White king goes to the other side (if necessary sacrificing the passed pawn), where a decisive superiority in material is established (two extra pawns or one passed pawn, which will cost Black his bishop).

No. 346

Black to play. White wins

No. 346 is typical. **1. ... g6** (1. ... f6 is no better, since it weakens Black's light squares and makes king entry easier) **2. Kf1 Kf8 3. Ke2 Ke7 4. Kd3 Kd6 5. Kc4** (first phase concluded) **5. ... Kc6 6. b4 Bb6 7. f3 Bc7 8. a4 Bb6 9. Bd4 Bc7 10. b5+ axb5+ 11. axb5+ Kb7** (or 11. ... Kd7 12. b6 Bg3 13. Kd5 Bf4 14. b7 Bb8 15. Be5) **12. Kd5 Bb8** (12. ... Bf4 13. Be5 Be3 14. Kd6) **13. b6 Bh2 14. Be5 Bg1 15. Kd6** (fourth phase) **15. ... Kxb6 16. Ke7 Kc5 17. Kxf7 Kd5 18. Bg7 h5 19. Kxg6**, and White comes out three pawns ahead. Or, if he wishes, he can advance his f-pawn until Black sacrifices his bishop for it.

A similar example is **No. 347** (Weiss-Blackburne, New York 1889): **White king at e1, bishop at d2, pawns at a2, d3, f2, g2; Black king at g8, bishop at b2, pawns at a7, b7, e7, f7, g6.** White to play. Black wins. Blackburne conducted the ending impeccably:

1. Be3 a6 2. Kd2 Kf8 3. Kc2 Be5 4. Kb3 Ke8 5. Kc4 Kd7 6. Kc5 Bc7 7. f3 e6 8. a4 b6+ 9. Kc4 Kc6 10. Bf2 f6 11. Be3 Bd6 12. Bd4 e5 13. Be3 b5+ 14. axb5+ axb5+ 15. Kb3 Kd5 (first and second phases concluded) **16. Bf2 f5 17. Kc3 g5 18. g4** (or 18. Be3 Be7! 19. Kb3 g4!) **18. ... fxg4 19. fxg4 Bc5 20. Be1 e4! 21. dxe4+ Kxe4 22. Bd2 Be3 23. Be1 Kf3 24. Kb4 Kxg4 25. Kxb5 Kf3 26. Kc4 g4 27. Kd3 Bf2 28. Ba5 g3 29. Bc7 g2 30. Bh2 Bb6 31. Kd2 Kg4**, and White resigned.

No. 348 (Fine-Kashdan, New York 1938) is an illustration with a passed pawn already on the board: **White king at g1, bishop at e4, pawns at a3, c5, e5, g3, h2; Black king at e7, bishop at d7, pawns at a6, e6, g7, h7.** White to play wins. The conclusion was **1. ... h6 2. Kf2 Kd8 3. Ke3 Kc7 4. Kd4** (the first and second steps are completed) **4. ... a5 5. Bd3 Be8 6. Bc4 Bd7 7. Bb3 Bc8** (7. ... Kb7 8. c6+!) **8. Ba4 Bb7 9. Kc4 Ba6+ 10. Bb5 Bb7 11. Kb3**, Black resigned, for he must lose a second pawn.

Very often one or more of these steps may be omitted. For instance, when you already have an outside passed pawn and your king is centrally placed, then only one of the last two phases will be required. Again, if you are more than one pawn ahead, the simple advance of passed pawns will usually force a bishop exchange at the expense of a pawn, after which the pawn ending is routine.

The purpose of forcing a passed pawn is to divert the enemy king or bishop from the scene of action where they are most needed. When the king is already diverted, of course, this step is superfluous.

No. 349, Mieses-Schiffers, Breslau 1889

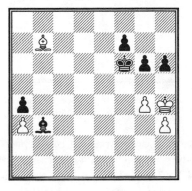

Black wins

In **No. 349,** all Black has to do is go to the queenside and capture the pawn there. The bishop can defend the f-pawn from a distance, which in turn defends the g-pawn, meaning that White can do nothing while Black's king is absent. So a simple win is possible by **1. ... Ke5 2. g5 h5** (pawn exchanges should be avoided whenever possible; if 2. ... hxg5+ 3. Kxg5 Kd4? 4. Kf6 Kc3 5. Bc6 Kb2 6. Bxa4 Bxa4 7. Kxf7 Bc2 8. a4, draw) **3. Kg3 Kd4 4. Kf4 Kc3 5. Ke5 Kb2 6. Kf6 Kxa3 7. Bc6 Kb2** (or 7. ... Kb4) **8. Bxa4 Bxa4 9. Kxf7 Bc2** and Black's king will come back and capture both White pawns.

The more pawns there are the easier the win. But even with three pawns against two the win is not difficult.

For example, **No. 350** (Kashdan-Fine, New York 1936): **White king at f3, bishop at a5, pawns at a4, h3; Black king at f5, bishop at e7, pawns at a6, f7, g5.** Black to play wins. **1. ... Ke6 2. Kg4 f5+ 3. Kf3 Kd5 4. Bc7 Kc5 5. Ba5 Kc4 6. Bc7 Kb4 7. a5 Kc5 8. Bb6+ Kc6 9. Be3 Bd8 10. Bd2 Kb5 11. Kf2 f4 12. Bc3 Kc4** (not 12. ... Bxa5 13. Bf6) **13. Bd2 Be7** (threatening 14. ... Bb4; if 14. Bc1 Kb4 15. Bd2+ Kb3) **14. h4 gxh4 15. Bxf4 Bd8 16. Bd2 Kb5 17. Kg2 Bxa5** and we have No. 336.

The most common difficulty found in these endings is the blockade. The pawns are in such an unfortunate position that no passed pawn can be forced, and the king can always be prevented from piercing the enemy defense. This obstacle may often be overcome by a sacrifice at the proper moment.

No. 351, Lasker-Bogatyrchuk, Moscow 1935

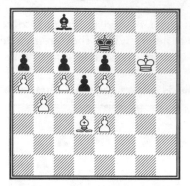

White to play wins

The only way White can force a passed pawn is by exchanging his pawn on e3 for Black's d-pawn. So Lasker played **1. e4?**, but after **1. ... d4!! 2. Bc4 Bb7 3. Kg5 Bc8 4. Kf4 Kd7 5. Kf3 Bb7 6. Ke2 Bc8 7. Kd3 Bb7 8. Kxd4 Bc8 9. Ke3 Bb7.** a draw was agreed because the blockade can only be broken by a bishop sacrifice that will prove insufficient: 10. Kf4 Bc8 11. Kg5 Ke7 12. Kg6 Bb7 13. Kg7 Bc8 14. Kg8 Bb7 15. Bxe6 Kxe6 16. Kf8 Kxe5 17. Ke7 Kxe4 18. Kd7 Kd4 19. Kc7 Ba8! 20. Kb6! Kc4 21. Kxa6 Kxb4 22. Kb6 Kc4 23. a6 Kb4 24. a7 (if 24. Ka7?? Kb5 and Black wins) 24. ... Kc4 25. Kc7 Kxc5 26. Kb8 Kb6 27. Kxa8 Kc7 stalemate!

After the game Grigoriev pointed out the following highly ingenious win **1. Kg5! Kf7 2. Bg6+ Ke7**

White is trying to reach d4 with his king without freeing Black's king; if 2. ... Kg7 3. Be8 Bb7 4. Kg4 Kf8 5. Bh5 Kg7 6. Kf3 Bc8 7. Be8! Bb7 8. Ke2 Kf8 9. Bh5 Kg7 10. Kd3 Bc8 11. Be8 or 10. ... Kh6 11. Bf7 Bc8 12. Be8 Bb7 13. Bd7.

3. Kg4 Bb7 4. Kf3 Kf8 5. Ke2 Kg7 6. Be8! Kf8 (again, if 6. ... Kh6 7. Bd7) **7. Bh5 Kg7 8. Kd3 Kf8** (once more, if 8. ... Kh6 9. Bf7 Bc8 10. Be8 Bb7 11. Bd7) **9. Kd4 Ke7 10. e4** and now:

a) 10. ... dxe4 11. Kxe4 Bc8 12. Kf4 Bb7 13. Kg5 Bc8 14. Kg6 Bb7 15. Kg7 Bc8 16. Bf3 Bb7 17. Be4!! Ba8 18. b5! axb5 19. a6, and with Black's bishop stalemated he must move his king, when his e-pawn falls;

b) 10. ... Kd7 11. Be2 Ke7 12. exd5 exd5 (if 12. ... cxd5 13. b5 axb5 14. Bxb5 Kd8 15. c6 Ba8 16. Kc5 Kc7 17. a6 d4 18. Kxd4 Bxc6 19. Bxc6 Kxc6 20. a7 Kb7 21. Kc5 and wins) 13. Bg4 Kf7 14. Bd7!! Ke7 15. e6 Kf6 (15. ... Ba8 16. Bc8; White now wins by an ingenious triangulation maneuver) 16. Kd3 Ke7 17. Ke3 Kf6 18. Kd4 Ke7 19. Ke5 Ba8 20. Bc8, and Black's position is hopeless.

In general, a sacrifice (such as that in variation "a" above) is the knife that cuts the Gordian knot of a blockade. Two other illustrations follow.

No. 352 (Gunsberg-Berger, Nuremberg 1883): **White king at g3, bishop at c2, pawns at b4, d4, e3; Black king at g5, bishop at d7, pawns at b5, c4, d5, f5.** Black to play wins. **1. ... Be8 2. Kf2 Bh5 3. Ke1** (if 3. Kg3 Be2 4. Kf2 Bd3 5.

Bxd3 cxd3 6. Ke1 f4) **3. ... Bg4 4. Kd2 Kh4 5. Kc3 Kg3 6. Kd2 Kf2 7. Bb1 c3+
8. Kd3 Bf3! 9. Kxc3 Be4! 10. Bd3 Bxd3 11. Kxd3 Ke1 12. Kc3 Ke2**.

Or **No. 353** (Bird-Janowski, Hastings 1895): **White king at a4, bishop at d2,
pawns at a6, b5, c4, f4, h4; Black king at a7, bishop at c7, pawns at c5, f6, f5,
h5.** White to play wins. White can decide at once by **1. b6+! Bxb6** (1. ... Kxb6
2. Ba5+ Kc6 3. a7) **2. Kb5 Bd8 3. Ba5 Be7 4. Bb6+ Ka8 5. Bxc5**, etc. Instead
White tried 1. Be3 Bd6, but could only manage to draw.

Wherever a sacrifice or an exchange is contemplated, it is essential to calculate the resulting pawn vs. bishop ending with great precision. **No. 354** is a
case in point with a blockaded pawn position.

No. 354, Fine-Kevitz, New York 1936

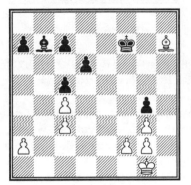

White wins

After **1. ... Ba6 2. Bd3 d5 3. Kf1 Kf6! 4. Ke2 d4!** (4. ... dxc4 leaves Black with
a hopeless tripled pawn, while 4. ... Bxc4 5. Bxc4 dxc4 6. Ke3 Ke5 7. f3 is an
easily won king-and-pawn ending) **5. Kd2 Bb7 6. Be2 Bc8** (the exchange of g-
pawns is clearly inadvisable, since White would then have two connected
passed pawns) **7. f3 Be6 8. a3 Bd7 9. Kc2 Bf5+ 10. Bd3 Be6** (again the
exchange of Bishops leads to a hopeless loss) **11. Kb3 a5 12. cxd4 cxd4**, and
here **13. Ka4** leads to a simple win because of a finesse in the pawn ending:
13. ... c5 (if 13. ... Bf5 14. Bxf5 Kxf5 15. c5! Ke5 16. Kb3 Kd5 17. c6!! Kc5 18. a4
Kd5 19. fxg4 and it is all over) **14. Kxa5 Bf5 16. Be2** and wins.

With weak pawns a bishop sacrifice is often the shortest road to victory.
No. 355 is a beautiful example.

No. 355, Miese-Gunsberg, Hannover 1902

White to play. Draw

Mieses played **1. Bg8!! Bxg8** (else Be6-c8) **2. Kxb7 Bc4 3. c6 Bd5 4. Kb6 Kd8 5. f6! gxf6 6. h6 Be4 7. Kb7!!** (very pretty: Black is in zugzwang) **7. ... Ke7 8. Kxa6 Kf7 9. Kb6** and Black resigned.

When both sides have passed pawns, the usual rule that the one who gets there first wins is again applicable. Of course, when one side has two passed pawns and the other side only one, he needs only to blockade his opponent's pawn and advance his own.

No. 356 (Duras 1906-07) is a position in which this plan can be executed only after some subtle maneuvering: **White king at a7, bishop at c1, pawns at a5, b7, h2; Black king at d3, bishop at c7, pawns at g5, f4**. White to play wins. **1. Ba3 Kc4** (1. ... f3 2. Bc5 is hopeless) **2. Be7 f3 3. Bd8! Bxh2** (3. ... f2 4. Bxc7 f1=Q 5. b8=Q Qf2+ 6. Qb6 gives Black no perpetual check) **4. Bb6 Kb5!** (or 4. ... g4 5. Bf2 Kb5 6. a6, as in the main variation) **5. a6 g4 6. Bf2 Bc7 7. b8=Q+!! Bxb8+ 8. Kb7!! Ka5 9. Bh4 Kb5 10. Be1! g3 11. Bxg3 Bxg3 12. a7 f2 13. a8=Q f1=Q 14. Qa6+** and the Black queen will not live long.

Where there are pawns on both sides of the board, Black can draw only by a blockade (see No. 351) or by setting up dangerous counterplay (No. 354). But it should be remembered that such stratagems are possible only in exceptional cases or when the superior side has made a mistake. These exceptional cases occur usually when the pawn majority is doubled or hopelessly isolated, or when the king is in a terribly cramped position.

When all the pawns are on one side (3 vs. 2, 4 vs. 3), the ending is drawn.

No. 357, Stahlberg-Fine, Kemeri 1937

Black to play. Draw

After **1. ... f6 2. Kc5 Bd7 3. Bg8 h6 4. Kd5 Ba4 5. Kd4 Bd7 6. Bc4 Ba4 7. Bd3 Be8 8. h4 g5,** it is clear that no further progress is possible. The fact that the White bishop is of the wrong color is immaterial. With dark-square bishops Black would merely set up his king at e6 instead of c7.

Even in the most favorable case White can make no headway against skillful defense. For example, **No. 358: White king at e4, bishop at c3, pawns at e5, f4, g3, h2; Black king at e6, bishop at c5, pawns at f7, g6, h7.** White to play. Draw. After **1. g4 Bg1 2. f5+ Kd7 3. h3 Bf2 4. Kd5 Be3 5. e6+ fxe6+ 6. fxe6+ Ke8 7. Ke5 Bg5,** there is no way for White to get to the kingside pawns; e.g., 8. Be1 Be7 9. h4 Bd8 10. h5 Be7, etc. However, 7. ... h5 would be a mistake: after 8. gxh5 gxh5 9. Kf5 Bf2 10. Kg5 h4 11. Kg4 Bc5! 12. Be1! Be7 13. Bxh4 Bxh4 14. Kxh4 Ke7 15. Kg5 Kxe6 16. Kg6, White just manages to win.

Bishop plus three pawns vs. bishop plus two pawns is also a draw unless the Black pawns are isolated. **No. 359: White king at e4, bishop at c3, pawns at f4, g4, h3; Black king at e6, bishop at c5, pawns at g6, h7.** This is a draw.

But **No. 360** is a win for White.

No. 360

White to play wins

1. f5+ (if 1. Kh5? f5!! 2. exf5+ Kxf5 3. Be5 Be3, draw; but not 1. ... f6!? 2. Kh6!! Be3 3. Kxh7 Bxf4 4. Kg6 Bg5 5. e5! and wins) **1. ... Ke7 2. e5** (2. Kh5 Be3) and now Black has two main lines of defense:

a) **2. ... f6 3. e6!** (3. exf6+? Kf7 4. Kh5 Be3 is of course much inferior) **3. ... Be3 4. Bb4+ Ke8 5. Kf3! Bc1 6. Ke4 Bg5** (Black must mark time) **7. Kd5 Bc1 8. e7!! Kd7 9. e8=Q+!! Kxe8 10. Ke6 Bb2 11. Be7 Bc1** (11. ... Ba1 12. Bxf6 Bxf6 13. Kxf6 is obviously hopeless) **12. Bxf6 Ba3 13. Bg7** followed by f6-f7+ winning the bishop;

b) **2. ... Be3 3. Be1! Kd7 4. Bh4 Kc6** (or 4. ... Ke8 5. e6) **5. e6** (the simplest) **5. ... fxe6 6. fxe6 Kd6 7. Kf5** (threatening Kf6) **7. ... Bd4 8. Be1 Ke7 9. Bb4+ Ke8 10. Bd6 Bf2**

If 10. ... Bb6 with the idea of taking the sting out of 11. Bg3 Ke7 12. Bh4+ Kd6 13. Kf6? Bd8+!, White makes the tempo move 11. Bb4! and 11. ... Bf2 is forced; again, if 10. ... Bc3 11. Be5 Be1 12. Bf6; the point is that White cannot be prevented from getting his bishop on the diagonal h4-d8 with the Black king at e8.

11. Bf4 Ke7 12. Bg5+ Ke8 13. Kg4 Bd4 14. Kh5 Kf8 (or 14. ... Bg7 15. h4! Bf8 16. Bf6! Be7! 17. Kg5!! Bf8 18. h5 Ba3 19. Kh6 Bc1+ 20. Kxh7, etc.) **15. e7+ Kf7 16. Kh6 Bc3 17. Kxh7 Bd4 18. h4 Bc3 19. h5 Bb2 20. h6 Bd4 21. e8=Q+!! Kxe8 22. Kg8 Bc3 23. h7 Bd4 24. Bh6** and wins.

With a bishop of the wrong color and the same pawn position—**No. 361: White king at g4, bishop at d3, pawns at e4, f4, h3; Black king at e6, bishop at b3, pawns at f7, h7**—this winning maneuver is not possible, so the result will be a draw: **1. ... Kf6 2. e5+ Kg7 3. Kg5 h6+ 4. Kg4 Bd1+ 5. Kg3 f6 6. e6** (6. Kf2 fxe5 7. fxe5; compare No. 341) **6. ... Bb3 7. f5** (7. Bf5 Kf8) **7. .. Bd1 8. Kf4 Kf8 9. Be4 Be2 10. Bd5 Bd1** and the extra pawn is insufficient. White cannot win this ending even if he gets his pawn to f6.

Bishop plus five pawns vs. bishop plus four pawns, all on one side (i.e. pawns on the d, e, f, g, and h files), is a win. White can set up a passed d-pawn and then proceed exactly as in the general case No. 346.

B. Even Material

Such endings are normally drawn, but the significant point is the circumstances under which a win is possible. As with knight endings, we can group positional advantages under three general headings: pawn, bishop, and king superiority, with the proviso that these groupings are not completely independent.

1. Better Pawn Position

This category can be broken up into many different types. We'll distinguish the same four classes that we used for knight endings.

a) Outside Passed Pawn

In knight endings this was the most important group, mainly because a knight cannot block a pawn at a distance. But since a bishop can, such an advantage is not quite so overwhelming here, although still usually sufficient to win.

The main difficulty in winning with an outside passed pawn is that of penetrating the enemy defenses with the king. For this reason, some pawn exchanges are desirable (as exception to the general rule that pawn exchanges reduce the winning chances of the superior side).

The situation when no straightforward entry with the king is feasible is illustrated by **No. 362** (List-Fine, Ostend 1937): **White king at e2, bishop at d4, pawns at e3, e5, f3, g2, h2; Black king at g8, bishop at a3, pawns at a2, e6, f7, g6, h7.** White to play. Black wins. After **1. Kd3 Bc5! 2. Ba1 Kg7 3. g4** (3. Kc4 Bxe3 4. Kb3 Kh6 5. Kxa2 Kg5 6. Kb3 Bg1 7. Kc4 Bxh2 8. Kd3 Kf5 also loses) **3. ... h5 4. h3 Kf8** (now entry via h6 and g5 is not feasible, since White can play 4. f4) **5. e4 Bf2** (again threatening 5. ... Kg7-h6-g5 if White's king goes after the a-pawn) **6. Ke2 Bg3 7. Ke3 Ke7 8. Kd4?** (a mistake; but on 8. Kd3 Kd7 9. Kc4 Kc6 10. Bc3 Kb6! 11. Kb3 Kc5 12. Kxa2 Kc4 13. Kb2 Kd3 White also loses) **8. ... f6! 9. exf6+ Kxf6 10. g5+** (else Be5) **10. ... Kxg5** and White resigned.

No. 363, Chigorin-Pillsbury, London 1899

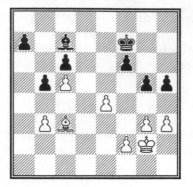

Black to play wins

Sometimes entry with the king is not even necessary until a late stage. This generally happens when the outside passed pawn is blockaded by the bishop.

In **No. 363,** Black decides by **1. ... a5!** (else 2. b4) **2. Kf3 Ke6 3. Ke3 g4!** (all-important; not only are the three kingside pawns now held by Black's two, but the vital square e5 is reserved for the Black bishop or king) **4. hxg4 hxg4 5. Kd3 a4 6. bxa4 bxa4 7. Bb4 Be5** (threatening Bb2) **8. Ba3 Ba1!** (to occupy e5 with the king) **9. Bc1 f5** (9. ... Ke5 10. Bf4+ and Black's king must go right back) **10. Ba3** (or 10. exf5+ Kxf5 11. Kc4 Ke4) **10. ... Ke5 11. exf5 Kxf5 12. Ke3 Ke5 13. f4+ Kd5 14. f5 Be5 15. Kf2 Ke4** and Chigorin abandoned the hopeless struggle.

Ordinarily, the important question you must answer when you have an outside passed pawn is how and when to force an entry with the king. Very often this requires considerable care, since any misstep that reduces the amount of material also increases the opponent's drawing chances. Such calculation is at times rather involved, but is always based on the principle of exchanging as few pawns as possible.

That an outside passed pawn may win when there are as few as two pawns on each side is shown by **No. 364,** a study by Lasker: **White king at e2, bishop at d2, pawns at b2, g2; Black king at g8, bishop at e7, pawns at e5, g7.** White to play wins. The main line is **1. Bc3 Bd6 2. Ke3 Kf7 3. Ke4 Ke6 4. b4 Bc7 5. b5 Kf6 6. g4 Ke6 7. g5 g6 8. Bb2 Bd8 9. Bxe5 Bxg5 10. b6!** and the pawn queens.

Finally, how even one passed pawn may win under certain circumstances is seen in two problems by Troitzky. **No. 365: White king at e5, bishop at g1, pawn at a4; Black king at h3, bishop at g5, pawn at h5.** White to play wins. **1. a5 Bh4** (or 1. ... Kg3 2. Kf5! Bf4 3. Bh2+, or 1. ... Bd8 2. Bb6!) **2. a6 Bg3+ 3. Ke4 Bb8 4. Kf3! Kh4 5. Be3! Kh3 6. Bf2 Kh2 7. Bg3+** and wins.

No. 366: White king at e8, bishop at a8, pawn at a5; Black king at h2, bishop at c2, pawn at c5. White to play wins. **1. a6 c4 2. a7 c3 3. Bh1!!** (the only winning continuation, for if now 3. ... Bg6+ 4. Ke7 c2 5. a8=Q c1=Q 6. Qg2+ mate) **3. ... Ba4+ 4. Kf7!** (in seven moves the point of going to this square with the king will be clear!) **4. ... Bc6! 5. Bxc6 c2 6. a8=Q c1=Q 7. Qa2+ Kg3 8. Qg2+ Kf4** (or 8. ... Kh4 9. Qf2+ Kg4 10. Bd7+ Kh5 11. Qh2+, etc.) **9. Qf3+ Kg5 10. Qg3+ Kf5 11. Qg6+** (now we see why the king had to be at f7) **11. ... Kf4** (11. ... Ke5 12. Qf6+ mate) **12. Qh6+** and wins the Black queen.

b) Protected Passed Pawn

This is a greater advantage here than in the corresponding knight ending because the bishop is not as good at blockading. The protected passed pawn consequently cramps the mobility of the Black pieces. How this is exploited is seen in **No. 367**.

No. 367, Maroczy-Grünfeld, Vienna 1920

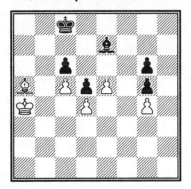

White to play wins

1. Bd2 Bd8 2. e6! Bf6 3. Ka5! Kb7! (if 3. ... Bxd4 4. Kb6) **4. Be1! Bd8+ 5. Ka4 Kc6 6. Bg3 Bf6! 7. Ka5! Bxd4** (White has gained a tempo; if 7. ... Kb7 8. Bd6) **8. Kb6 Bf6 9. Kxc6 d4 10. Be5** and Black resigned, for 10. ... Bxe5 would be followed by 11. e7, while 10. ... Be7 11. Bxd4 is hopeless.

c) Better Quality Passed Pawns

In general, when there are pieces on the board, connected passed pawns are preferable to unconnected ones because they can be more easily advanced. And, of course, the closer the pawns are to the eighth rank, the stronger they are. In such cases it is imperative to push your pawns ahead as quickly as possible, taking only the most essential precautionary measures against the opponent's pawns.

No. 368, Alatortsev-Levenfish, Leningrad 1934

Black to play. White wins

With pawns on the fifth and sixth ranks White has an undeniable advantage, but this will become decisive only if he gets one pawn to the seventh. The best defense for Black is **1. ... e4**

The game continued 1. ... g5 2. Ba6 Kd8 3. Bb5 Ke7 4. c6 Kd6 5. c7 Bb7 6. Bd3 Kc5 (6. ... Bc8 7. Bf5) 7. Bf5 Kxb6 8. c8=Q Bxc8 9. Bxc8 e4 10. Bf5 e3+ 11. Kf3 h6 12. Bd3 and Black resigned, since he loses both pawns after 13 Ke4.

2. Ba6 Kd8 (if 2. ... Kd7 3. Bb5+ Kc8 4. c6 Kb8 5. g5!) **3. Bb5 Kc8** (or 3. ... g5 4. c6 h6 5. h3 e3+ 6. Ke2 Be4 7. c7+ Kc8 8. Ba6+ Bb7 9. Bd3! Bc6 10. Bf5+ Bd7 11. Kd3! and wins) **4. c6! Kb8** (if instead 4. ... d3 5. Ba6+ Kb8 6. c7+) **5. g5! e3+ 6. Ke2 Be4 7. h3 Bg2 8. h4 Be4 9. c7+ Kc8 10. Ba6+ Bb7 11. Bc4 Kd7** (if 11. ... Bc6 12. Kd3! and again Black must move a pawn, since a bishop or king move would be immediately fatal) **12. Kd3 Kd6** (12. ... Bf3 13. Be6+ or even 13. Ba6) **13. Kxd4** and it is all over.

We may set up a rule that is applicable to all types of endings: Advance passed pawns as rapidly and as far as possible, but take care to avoid a blockade that stalls them.

Another illustration of this principle in bishop endings is **No. 369** (Zukertort, from an 1868 game): **White king at h5, bishop at c1, pawns at c4, d3, f5, g6; Black king at h8, bishop at c7, pawns at a3, c5, c2, d4.** White to play wins, but only by **1. f6! Be5!** (or 1. ... a2 2. f7 Bd6 3. Bh6; or 1. ... Kg8 2. Bh6 followed by f7+) **2. f7 Bg7 3. Bxa3 Bf8 4. Bc1 Kg7** (on other moves, such as 4. ... Bg7, 5. Bf4 is conclusive) **5. Kg5! Be7+ 6. Kf5 Bd6 7. Bg5 Bf8 8. Bf4 Be7 9. Be5+ Kh6** (9. ... Kf8 10. Ke6) **10. g7! c1=Q 11. g8=Q Qf1+ 12. Bf4+!** and mates in a few moves.

No. 370 is a twin study that illustrates mating and other possibilities after both sides have queened.

No. 370, P. Benko 1985

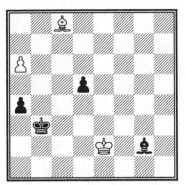

White to play and win

White has to chase the bishop to a bad spot. **1. Kf2!** (the only way) **1. ... Be4 2. Bb7 a3 3. a7 a2 4. a8=Q Kb2 5. Qb8! a1=Q 6. Bxd5+ Kc1 7. Qf4+ Kd1 8. Qg4+ Kc1 9. Qg5+ Kc2 10. Bxe4+ Kc3! 11. Qc5+** (11. Qe5+ Kd2 12. Qxa1? is stalemate) **11. ... Kb3 12. Bd5+ Kb2 13. Qd4+ Kb1 14. Be4+ Ka2 15. Qa4+ Kb2 16. Qb4+ Kc1 17. Ke1!** wins.

Changing the Black king's position from b3 to c1 gives us a different story: **1. Kf2 Bh1 2. Kg1** (2. Bb7? a3 3. a7 a2 4. a8=Q Kb1! =) **2. ... Bf3 3. Bg4 Be4 4. Bf5 Bf3 5. Kf2 Bh1 6. Be4! Bxe4** (6. ... dxe4 7. Ke3) **Ke3 Bg2 8. Kd4** wins.

It must not be assumed that superior passed pawns win automatically in all cases. They confer an advantage, but whether this is sufficient to win cannot be determined beforehand.

No. 371 (from a Morphy-Löwenthal game): **White king at f1, bishop at e5, pawns at a2, f2, h2; Black king at h7, bishop at c5, pawns at a7, b5, c7.** White to play. Draw. Black's connected passed pawns against White's unconnected ones are not quite sufficient. The game was drawn after **1. ... Bd6 2. Bd4!**

The pawn ending after 2. Bxd6 cxd6 would be lost: 3. Ke2 a5 4. Kd3 a4! 5. Kc3 d5 6. Kd4 (on pawn moves Black plays 6. ... Kg6 when both White pawns are on the fourth, so the king must move then anyhow) 6. ... b4!! 7. f4 b3 8. axb3 a3 9. Kc3 d4+ 10. Kc2 d3+ and queens.

2. ... c5 3. Be3 a5 4. Ke2 a4 5. Kd3 a3 (5. ... c4+ 6. Kc3 Bxh2 7. Kb4) **6. Bc1! Kg6 7. Ke4 c4 8. f4 b4 9. Bxa3! bxa3 10. Kd4** and draws, since after all the loose pawns have been disposed of we get to No. 275.

If you already have a winning superiority, you must be careful to avoid traps that give the opponent counterchances. Above all, when there are advanced passed pawns you must be on the lookout for unexpected sacrificial combinations.

No. 372, P. Benko 2000

White to play. Draw

To emphasize once again that special positions may invalidate every rule (Reti's motto is said to have been: "No rule without exceptions"), in **No. 372** White draws even though he cannot stop Black from queening (stalemate theme).

1. f5! e4 2. Kf7! and now:

a) **2. ... h3 3. Bb8 e3 4. Bf4! e2 5. Bg5 e1=Q 6. f6 Qe8+ 7. Kxe8 Bxf6+ 8. Kf7! Bg7 9. Bf4 c4 10. Bd6 c3 11. Bf8 Bf6 12. Be7 Be5 13. Bd6 Bd4 14. Bc5 Bg7 15. Bf8**, drawn by repetition;

b) **2. ... e3 3. Bxc5 e2 4. f6 Bxf6 5. Be7 Be5 6. Bxh4 c5 7. Bg3! Bg7 8. Be1 c4 9. Bb4! Be5** (9. ... c3 10. Bf8 Bxf8 11. Kxf8 e1=Q 12. g7+ Kh7 13. g8=Q+ Kh6 14. Qe6+! [14. Qg7+ Kh5 wins] 14. ... Qxe6 stalemate).

If **1. fxe5? Kg7 2. Bxc5 h3 3. Bg1 Kxg6 4. Kd6 Kf5 5. e6 Bf6 6. Bh2 c5** wins

d) Better Pawn Position

This comprises all cases where the superiority does not consist of a passed pawn or pawns, but is rather due to an inherent weakness in the opponent's pawn structure, such as badly isolated doubled pawns and blockaded pawns.

No. 373, Riumin-Kan, Moscow 1935

Black to play wins

It is often exceedingly difficult to draw the line here and determine whether the advantage comes from the weak pawns or the weak bishop. In fact the two go so closely together that they can frequently be distinguished only for purely theoretical purposes.

No. 373 is a typical instance of pawns blockaded by a bishop. White's majority on the queenside is worthless. Black can regard his kingside majority as a potential outside passed pawn and proceed accordingly.

The game continued **1. ... Ke5 2. Bc6 f5 3. a4 g5 4. h4**

Hastens the end but other moves are equally useless in the long run; e.g., 4. Kf2 h5 5. Ke2 h4 6. Kf2 g4, etc. If 6. Kf3, Bd5+ is conclusive: 7. Bxd5 Kxd5 8. b3 Ke5! 9. b4 Kd5; or 9. Ke2 g4 10. hxg4 fxg4 11. b4 h3 12. Kf2 h2 13. Kg2 g3, etc.

4. ... gxh4+ 5. Kxh4 f4! 6. Kg4 (6. exf4+ Kxf4 and Black gets to the queenside) **6. ... Bd1+! 7. Kh3 fxe3 8. Kg2** (8. Kg3 Bb3! and 9. Kf3 is met by 9. ... Bd5+) **8. ... Kf4 9. b4 Bb3**, White resigned.

When the pawns are absolutely weak (doubled or hopelessly blocked by pawns), the win proceeds in exactly the same way as in No. 373; i.e., you simply ignore the extra pawn (since it has no practical value) and act as though you were a pawn ahead.

For example, **No. 374** (Konstantinopolsky-Alatortsev, Leningrad-Moscow 1939): **White king at h1, bishop at f3, pawns at c2, c3, f4, g4, h3; Black king at d7, bishop at a6, pawns at c4, e6, f7, g7, h7.** White to play. Black wins.

The doubled White c-pawns are held by one Black pawn. The only drawback is the White bishop's color.

1. Kg1 e5! 2. fxe5 (2. f5 g5! 3. Kf2 f6 and White has a further weakness: his pawns are fixed on light squares) **2. ... Ke6 3. Kf2 Kxe5 4. Ke3 Bc8 5. h4 h6 6. Be2 Be6 7. Bf3 g6 8. Be2 Bd5 9. Bf1 g5** (Black prefers to establish a passed g-pawn, but many pawns are exchanged during this process) **10. hxg5 hxg5 11. Be2 f6 12. Bf1 f5 13. gxf5 Kxf5 14. Kd4 Be6 15. Ke3 Kg4 16. Kf2 Bd5 17. Be2+ Kh3 18. Kg1 g4 19. Bf1+ Kg3 20. Be2**

White misses his chance to free his bishop by the tricky 20. Bg2! Be6 (20. ... Bxg2 stalemate) 21. Bb7 Kf4 22. Kf2! g3+ 23. Kg1 and Black can't make progress.

20. ... Be6!! 21. Bd1

If 21. Bf1 Kf3 22. Bg2+ Ke2 23. Kh2 Kd2; while if 21. Kh1 Kf2; and if 21. Kf1, Kh2 is conclusive.

21. ... Kf4 22. Be2 (or 22. Kf2 g3+ 23. Kg1 Bg4! and the pawn ending is easily won) **22. ... Ke3 23. Bf1 Kd2 24. Kf2 Kxc2 25. Kg3 Kxc3** and wins.

An isolated pawn is a serious weakness in bishop endings only if it is subject to direct attack by the king and there are other pawn weaknesses.

No. 375, Santasiere-Fine, New York 1938

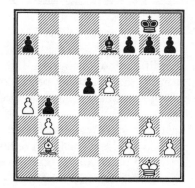

White to play wins

White wins because the Black queenside pawns (including the d-pawn) are weak and because he has a kingside pawn majority. The game continued **1. f4 f6 2. Bd4 a6 3. Kf2 Kf7 4. Ke3 fxe5 5. Bxe5 g6 6. Kd4 Ke6 7. g4** (White simply ignores the Black d-pawn and proceeds as though he had an outside passed pawn) **7. ... Bd8 8. f5+ gxf5 9. gxf5+ Kxf5 10. Kxd5 Kg4 11. Bd6 a5 12. Kc6 Kh3 13. Kd7 Bb6 14. Be7 Kxh2 15. Kc6 Bf2 16. Kb5 Kg3 17. Kxa5** and the two White pawns are too strong.

Under certain circumstances a chain of advanced pawns can become a winning advantage if they go together with a bishop, which by capture or sacrifice can force one through. The most common case is seen in **No. 376** (Amateurs, 1775): **White king at f4, bishop at d2, pawns at a6, b5, c4; Black king at e7, bishop at d4, pawns at a7, b6, c5.** White to play. White can either win two pawns or force a queen with **1. Ba5!!**, for if **1. ... bxa5 2. b6 Kd6 3. bxa7** and queens, while if **1. ... Kd7 2. Bxb6!! Kc8 3. Bxa7** with a decisive superiority. Black to play can draw with **1. ... Kd7 2. Ba5 Kc7!** (but still not 2. ... bxa5? 3. b6 Kc8 4. bxa7 and queens).

2. Better Bishop

This brings us to the well-known topic of "good" and "bad" bishops.

Any piece is good or bad according to its mobility. This is why, for instance, a rook is better than a knight—the rook is able to cover more ground. If a bishop is forced to defend a number of pawns that are on its own color squares, it becomes cramped and is reduced to the status almost of a pawn. This is a "bad" bishop; the opponent's, which is free to roam at will, is a "good" bishop.

This situation is peculiar to bishops because they are perforce confined to squares of only one color, and when those squares are occupied by pawns, the bishop's moves are reduced. Even when the pawn position is not intrinsically weak the bad bishop may be a fatal handicap.

No. 377, Averbakh 1954

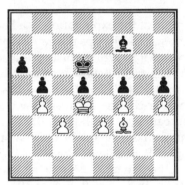

White to play wins

Black's problem is that his bishop has to defend three weak pawns. With Black to play he would have to give up one of them immediately. So White's first task is to lose a move. He can do that because his bishop has more maneuvering room. **1. Be2 Be8** (if 1. ... Bg6 2. Bd3 Bh7 3. Bf1! Bg6 4. Bg2 Bf7 5. Bf3 wins) **2. Bd3 Bg6 3. Bc2! Bh7 4. Bb3! Bg8 5. Bd1! Bf7 6. Bf3.** Black is in zugzwang and most lose.

More often than not, the pawn position is itself intrinsically weak when there is a bad bishop on the board. This is because with all or most of the pawns on one color, the squares of the opposite color are easily occupied.

No. 378, Winawer-Steinitz, Vienna 1882

Black to play wins

No. 378 is a fine example of the exploitation of a bad bishop coupled with weak squares. With dark-square bishops the game would be a draw, possibly even in White's favor. But as it is, White's bishop is a good-for-nothing, while all his pawns are subject to attack. Steinitz won as follows: **1. ... Bf1 2. Kf3 g5!** (not 2. ... Bxh3 3. Bd3! Kf6! 4. Kf4! Bg2 5. g5+ Ke6 6. Bc4+ Ke7 7. Bd3! h3 8. Kg3 Ke6 9. e5! with good counter-chances because now it is Black's bishop that is tied down) **3. Ba2 c6** (threatening 3. ... Bd3) **4. Bf7** (if instead 4. Bb1 a5 5. Bc2 Bc4; and Black wins a pawn because the White bishop has no moves; e.g., 6. Ke3 Bf7 7. Bd1 Bg6 8. Bf3 c5 9. Bg2 Be8, or here 7. Kf3 Bg6 8. Ke3 d5) **4. ... Bd3 5. Kf2** (if 5. Bg6 d5 wins the pawn) **5. ... Kf4 6. a5 Bxe4 7. Bc4 d5 8. Ba6** and the conclusion is not difficult: **8. ... c5 9. Bc8 c4 10. a6 Ke5 11. Bd7** (11. Ke3 Bg2) **11. ... d4 12. cxd4+ Kxd4 13. Ke2 Bd3+ 14. Ke1 c3 15. Bc8 Ke3 16. Kd1 Kf2 17. Bf5 Bxa6 18. Kc2 Bf1 19. Kxc3 Bxh3** and soon queens.

Where the pawns are already weak (even without the bad bishop), a bad bishop is the last straw.

No. 379 is an excellent illustration.

No. 379, Eliskases-Brauer, correspondence 1933

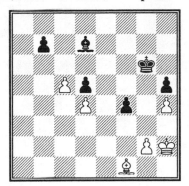

White to play wins

The Black pawns are all isolated and therefore inferior to White's, but the added handicap of a bishop with three pawns fixed on its color is fatal. Eliskases continued **1. g3!** (to exchange Black's only strong pawn) **1. ... Bg4** The alternatives are no better:

a) 1. ... Kf5 2. Bh3+ Ke4 3. Bxd7 fxg3+ 4. Kxg3 Kxd4 5. Kf4! Kxc5 6. Ke5! b5 7. Be8 b4 8. Bxh5 b3 9. Bg6 and the White pawn queens;

b) 1. ... fxg3+ 2. Kxg3 Kf5 3. Bh3+ as above;

c) 1. ... Be6 2. Kg2!! (but not 2. gxf4 Kf5! 3. Bh3+ Kf6! 4. Bxe6 Kxe6 5. Kg3 Kf5 6. Kf3 Kf6! with a drawn pawn ending) 2. ... Kf5 3. Kf3 fxg3 4. Bd3+! Kf6 5. Kxg3 Bf5 6. Bb5 Bg6 7. Kf4, and will win by Bd7-c8 or Be8;

d) 1. ... f3 2. Kg1 Bg4 3. Kf2 Kf5 4. Ke3 (or 4 Bd3+ Kf5 5 Bc2 and 6 Bd1), and Black is in zugzwang and must lose his f-pawn.

2. Bg2! (but not 2. gxf4 Kf5 3. Bg2 Kxf4 4. Bxd5 Bc8 5. Bg2 Ke3 6. d5 Bd7! 7. c6 bxc6!! 8. dxc6 Bxc6!! 9. Bxc6 Kf4 and draws because the king gets back to h8) **2. ... f3** (if 2. ... Be6 3. gxf4 Kf5 4. Kg3 Kf6 5. Kf3, and wins by an eventual Bf3-d1-a4) **3. Bf1 Kf5 4. Bd3+ Ke6 5. Kg1 Kd7** (or 5. ... Bf5 6. Bb5) **6. Kf2 Kc6 7. Bc2!!** (threatening 8. Bd1 and preparing to answer 7. ... Kb5 with 8. Bb3! Be6 9. Ke3!! Kb4 10. Bd1 Kc3 11. Bxf3 Bf7 12. g4!, etc.) **7. ... b6 8. cxb6 Kxb6 9. Bd1 Be6** (9. ... Kb5 10. Bxf3 Bxf3 11. Kxf3 Kc4 12. Ke3 Kc3 13. g4! hxg4 14. h5! and queens first) **10. Bxf3 Bf7 11. Ke3 Kb5 12. Kf4 Kb4! 13. Ke5 Kc4** and now White wins an extra pawn by the typical tempo-losing maneuver we saw in No. 338: **14. Bh1 Bg8 15. Bg2! Bf7 16. Bf3 Kd3 17. Bxd5**, and Black resigned.

Where the superior side has an outside or potential outside passed pawn, the win with the good bishop is quite simple.

No. 380, Eliskases-Capablanca, Semmering-Baden 1937

Black to play. White wins

Black's bishop not only has to stop the pawn but must also defend the a-pawn to enable the king to get back. This is too much to ask of one poor chess piece, so loss is inevitable. After **1. ... Bg4 2. e5 fxe5+ 3. fxe5 h6** (3. ... a5 4. bxa5+ Kxa5 5. Kc5 and wins) **4. h4 Bh5 5. e6 Be8,** White could have brought the game to a speedy conclusion by **6. e7 Kc7 7. Ke5 Kc8 8. Kf6 Kc7 9. Kg7 Kc8 10. Kf8 Kd7 11. Bf7.**

No. 381 (Pillsbury-Billecard, Munich 1900) is another illustration of play with a good bishop and a passed pawn. **White king at f4, bishop at d3, pawns at b4, c3, e5, g4; Black king at e6, bishop at f7, pawns at b5, c6, d5, g6.**White to play wins. After **1. g5!** the Black bishop is hardly better than a chunk of wood **1. ... Be8 2. Bf1 Bf7** (on 2. ... Bd7, as in the game, the pawn ending is easily won after 3. Bh3+ Ke7 4. Bxd7 Kxd7 5. Ke3 Ke7 6. Kd4 Ke6 7. Kc5) **3. Bh3+ Ke7 4. Ke3 Be8 5. e6! Kd6** (or 5. ... c5 6. bxc5 Bc6 7. Kd4) **6. Kd4** and Black's game is hopeless.

Sometimes pawns that are all on the color of their bishop are so weak that the opposing king can come in and just pick them off at will. Such a case is **No. 382** (Van Scheltinga-Fine, Amsterdam 1936): **White king at h2, bishop at c3, pawns at b4, c5, e5, f3, f2, h3; Black king at g8, bishop at g7, pawns at a6, b7, e6, f7, g6, h6.** Black to play wins. After **1. ... Kf8 2. Kg3 Ke8 3. Kf4 Kd7 4. Ke4 Kc6 5. Kd4 Kb5 6. Bd2 h5 7. f4 Bf8 8. f3 a5** White resigned since he must lose at least one pawn to begin with.

Whenever there is a choice of where to place the bishop to defend a weak pawn, the spot that leaves the bishop the most mobility should always be chosen. For example, **No. 383** (Kashdan-Fine, New York 1936): **White king at g1, bishop at g3, pawns at a4, c4, f4, h3; Black king at g8, bishop at d2, pawns at a7, b6, f7, g6.** Black to play. Draw. After **1. ... Kg7 2. Kf2 Kf6 3. Ke2 Bc1** and now **4. Kf3 Kf5 5. Bh2 Ba3 6. Bg1! Bd6 7. Be3 Bf8 8. Bf2!** is the only correct continuation, for if **8. ... Bd6 9. Be3!** defends the pawn and leaves two good reserve squares for the bishop. Instead, White played **4. Kd1? Ba3 5. Ke2 Bd6 6. Kf3 Kf5** and White had to lose a pawn, for if **7. Ke3** or **7. Bh2, g5** and the f-pawn is pinned, while on **7. h4 f6**, and ... g5 is still an unanswerable threat.

3. Better King Position

This is of greater importance here than in any other ending with pieces. The reason is that once the king is firmly secured at some vital point it cannot be driven away. In addition, as in knight endings, once the king manages to attack the enemy pawns it can invariably reap a plentiful harvest.

Those cases where the king is unopposed and can simply capture all the pawns need not be considered in any detail. The interesting examples arise only when there is a race to see who gets there first or when some unusual sacrificial defense is offered.

If White's king succeeds in getting to the bulk of the enemy pawns, the fact that White is a pawn (or even two) behind frequently does not matter.

No. 384, Berger

White to play wins

In **No. 384** two pawns win against three. 1. Bc7? is unsatisfactory because of 1. ... Kg8 2. Bxb6 Bd4 3. Kf3 Kf7 4. Ke4 Ke6 =. Therefore, **1. Kf3 b5** (1. ... Kg8 2. Ke4 Kf7 3. Kd5 Ke7 4. Kc6 is hopeless for Black: he loses all his pawns) **2. cxb5 c4 3. bxc4 b3 4. Bc1**, and now:

a) **4. ... b2 5. Bxb2 Bxb2 6. Ke4 Kg7 7. b6 Ba3** (or 7. ... Kf6 8. Kd5 Be5 9. c5! Bg3 10. Kc6 Ke7 11. Kb7, and c6) **8. Kd5 Bc1 9. Kd6 Bf4+ 10. Kd7 Kf7 11. c5 Be3 12. b7** and queens.

b) **4. ... Kg8 5. Ke4 Kf7 6. b6 Ke6 7. b7 Be5 8. Bb2 Bh2 9. c5 Bg3 10. Kd4 Kd7 11. Kd5 Kc7 12. c6 Bh2** (king moves do not save the game either; e.g., 12. ... Kb6 13. Bd4+ Kc7 14. Ba7 Kd8 15. Bb6+ Ke7 16. c7 b2 17. Bc5+, or 13. ... Ka6 14. Ke6 b2 15. Bxb2 Ka7 16. Bd4+ Kb8 17. Be5+) **13. Kc5 Bg3 14. Kb5 Bh2 15. Bd4** (threatening Bb6+ and Ka6) **15. ... Kb8 16. Bb6 b2** (if 16. ... Bc7 17. Ka6 Bxb6 18. Kxb6 b2 19. c7+ mate) **17. Ka6 b1=Q 18. c7+ Bxc7 19. Ba7+** mate.

Although the king may be ready to gobble up a number of pawns, care must still be taken to make sure that the superiority established is a winning one.

For example, **No. 385** (Alekhine-Bogolyubov, 3rd match game 1929): **White king at f5, bishop at g6, pawns at a5, f3, g2, h3; Black king at e7, bishop at f1, pawns at a7, f4, g5, h4.** White to play. Alekhine played 1. Bh5? Bxg2 2. Bg4 Kd6, but after 3. Kxg5 Ke5 4. Kxh4 Kd4! 5. Kg5 Ke3 6. h4 Bxf3 could only draw. He could have won quickly with **1. Kxg5 Bxg2 2. Kg4! Kf6 3. Be4 Ke5 4. Kxh4 Kd4 5. Kg4 Ke3 6. h4**, etc.

Even when each side has only one pawn (not passed), a favorable king position may be decisive. In **No. 386** (Horwitz 1880): **White king at f6, bishop at c6, pawn at g3; Black king at h5, bishop at g8, pawn at f7.** White to play wins by **1. Bf3+ Kh6 2. g4 Kh7** (2. ... Bh7 3. g5+ mate) **3. g5 Kh8 4. Be4 Bh7 5. Bxh7 Kxh7 6. Kxf7**, etc.

Or a pawn is won and the opposing bishop is prevented from stopping the passed pawn, as in **No. 387** (Teichmann-Marshall, San Sebastian 1911): **White king at e4, bishop at f1, pawn at g2; Black king at g3, bishop at g4, pawn at h4.** Black to play wins. Marshall concluded with **1. ... Bc8 2. Ke3 Bd7!** (not 2. ... Bb7 3. Bc4! Bxg2 4. Be6 =; see No. 232) **3. Ke4** (unfortunately necessary; if 3. Ke2 Bc6 4. Ke1 Bxg2, as played, or if 3. Kd2 Kf2! 4. Bc4 Kxg2 5. Ke1 Kg1! 6. Bf1 Be6! 7. Bb5 h3 8. Bc6 h2 9. Be4 Bh3 and wins) **3. ... Bc6+ 4. Ke3 Bxg2** and Black wins, for after **5. Bc4 h3** the pawn queens.

IV. BISHOPS OF OPPOSITE COLORS

Because such bishops cannot possibly attack the same points or be exchanged, winning is considerably more difficult with a material advantage. In fact, one pawn ahead usually only draws, while even with two pawns there are many positions where winning is impossible.

1. Bishop and Pawn vs. Bishop

The simplest case, bishop and pawn vs. bishop, is almost always a draw: White's "extra" bishop is useless, so we have, in effect, an ending of pawn vs. bishop. The pawn can queen only in certain very special positions.

2. Bishop and Two Pawns vs. Bishop

There is no simple general rule that covers all cases where bishop and two pawns win against bishop.

a) Doubled Pawns

Doubled pawns win only if the Black king cannot reach a square in front of the pawn from which it cannot be driven away.

No. 388

White to play. Draw, also with all pieces one or two files to the left

1. Bg5 Bf5 2. c7! Bh3 3. c6 Kf7 (3. ... Bg4? 4. Kc5 Bh3 5. Kb6 wins) **4. Kc5 Bc8! 5. Kb6 Ke6 6. Ka7 Kd5, =.**

b) Connected Passed Pawns

This is the most complicated case; the result depends on the files and ranks that the pawns are on as well as the locations and colors of the bishops. We classify the positions according to the ranks the pawns are on.

Keep in mind that it is always desirable for the defender to force the enemy pawns onto squares the opposite color of his bishop; he can then blockade them and draw easily. The superior side must therefore play his pawns to squares the same color as the opponent's bishop. If he can do this he wins; if not he draws.

1. Both Pawns on the Sixth Rank

This is usually a win (except for certain positions such as with the rook-pawn).

No. 389

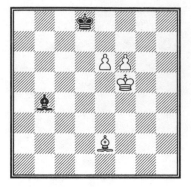

Black to play. White wins. Pawns may be on any file except
a and b or g and h

After **1. ... Ke8 2. Bb5+ Kf8** (or 2. ... Kd8 3. Kg6 Ba3 4. Kf7) **3. Ke4**, the Black bishop must stay on the diagonal f8-a3 to prevent the e-pawn from queening, so White's king is free to march to d7 and support the advance of the e-pawn.

Where there is a rook-pawn with a bishop of the wrong color, the ending is a win if the Black king is confined to the corner, but otherwise a draw.
No. 390: **White king at a5, bishop at d2, pawns at a6, b6; Black king at a8, bishop at f3.** White to play wins by **1. Bf4** (but other moves such as 1. Kb4? lead to a draw after 1. ... Kb8!).

2. One Pawn on the Sixth Rank, the Other on the Fifth

This is an immediate draw if the pawns are blockaded, but otherwise a win, since it transposes into the first case. Sometimes Black has the alternative of getting his king out behind the pawns but this is of no avail.

For example, **No. 391: White king at g4, bishop at f1, pawns at f6, g5; Black king at f7, bishop at e1.** Black to play. **1. ... Ke6** (White to play begins with 1. Kf5, when g6-g7 and Bc4 forces a queen) **2. Kh5 Bb4** (or 2. ... Kf5 3. Bh3+) **3. Bh3+ Ke5 4. Kh6 Bd2** (or 4. ... Kf4 5. g6; or 4. ... Bf8+ 5. Kh7 Bb4 6. f7) **5. f7 Bb4 6. g6 Kf6 7. g7!**.

3. Both Pawns on the Fifth Rank

When the two pawns are on the fifth, the outcome depends on whether or not they can both get to the sixth. This in turn is determined by whether Black's bishop can control the square in front of the pawn and also prevent the White king from covering that square a second time.

No. 392

Draw. Win with Black bishop at a3

In **No. 392**, for instance, the square d6 is covered by the bishop, and the White king cannot leave the pawn at e5 undefended. The position is therefore drawn.

But in **No. 393**, with the **Black bishop at a3**, other pieces unchanged, the White king can get to c6 and support the advance of the d-pawn: **1. Kc4 Ke8** (or 1. ... Bb2 2. d6+ Ke8 3. e6 or 3. Kd5; No. 389) **2. d6 Kd8 3. Kd5 Ke8 4. e6** and wins.

Or **No. 394, Black king at c7,** other pieces as in No. 393. White wins by **1. Ke4 Bf8 2. Kf5 Ba3 3. Ke6 Bb4 4. d6+**, etc.

With White's bishop on the dark squares, the results correspond to those in No. 392; that is, if the Black bishop is at g8, where it stops e5-e6 and prevents the entry of the king, the game is a draw, but if it is at h3, the White king gets to f6 or the pawn advances and White wins.

No. 395: **White bishop at g3, Black bishop at g8**, other pieces as in No. 392, is a draw, while **No. 396**: **White bishop at g3, Black bishop at h3**, other pieces as in No. 392, is a win. Some finesse is required here: On 1. Bh4+ Kd7 2. Ke3 Bg4 3. Kf4 Bh3 4. Kg5?? Bg2!! draws, for if 5. e6+ Kd6! 6. Bg3+ Ke7!! =. But White wins with **1. Be1 Bg4 2. Bb4+ Kd7** (2. ... Kf7 3. Kc5) **3. Ke3-f4-g5-f6**, as in No. 392, for if at any time ... Bg2, then e6+ and d6 is decisive.

If we move the pawns two files over to the left or to the right the color of the bishop, rather than the particular square it is on, is the decisive factor.

No. 397

White to play wins. Draw if the positions of the bishops are reversed

In **No. 397** White wins by **1. Bf3+ Ka7 2. Kd5 Ba5 3. Kc6**, etc. The position that corresponds to No. 392, **No. 398, Black bishop at a7,** other pieces as in No. 397, does Black no good here because he has no reserve square for his bishop. After **1. Bf3+ Kc7 2. Kb4** he cannot prevent **3. b6** in any reasonable manner. With the bishops' colors reversed—i.e., if White's bishop is on dark squares, Black's on light squares—the lack of elbow room is in Black's favor this time.

In **No. 399: White king at c4, bishop at d2, pawns at b5, c5; Black king at c7, bishop at f3.** White to play, after **1. Ba5+, Kd7!** saves the day for Black because White cannot get his king through on the queenside: **2. Kb4 Bg2 3. Bb6 Bf3 4. Ka5 Bb7!** (but not 4. ... Bg2? 5. Ka6 6. Ba5 7. Kb6 and wins) **5. Ba7 Kc7!** and White is at a standstill. Again, it does White no good to play his king to the kingside after 1. Ba5+ Kd7, since it doesn't cover the crucial square c6.

Similarly **1. Bf4+** is met by **1. ... Kb7** (but not 1. ... Kd7 2. Kb4-a5) and if **2. Bg5 Kc7! 3. Kb4 Kb7! 4. Bd8 Kc8! 5. Bb6** (5. Ba5 Kd7! as above) **5. ... Kb7!** and **6. Kc4** is refuted by **6. ... Bh5 7. Kd4 Be8!**, etc.

White could only win here if Black made the mistake **1. Ba5+ Kb7?**, for then the White king gets to d6: **2. Kd4 Bg2 3. Ke5 Bf3 4. Kd6 Bg2 5. c6+**, etc.

No. 400 is again the equivalent of the draw in No. 392: **White king at c4, bishop at a5, pawns at b5, c5; Black king at b7, bishop at e8.** White can do nothing at all.

Rook-pawn and knight-pawn still on the fifth rank draw regardless of the positions and colors of the bishops. Obviously, White has winning chances only in the equivalent of No. 396 – **No. 401: White king at a4, bishop at f3, pawns at a5, b5; Black king at a7, bishop at f2.** White to play—but **1. Kb3** is answered by **1. ... Be1! 2. b6+ Ka6! 3. b7 Ka7!,** or 3. Be2+ Kxa5; or 3. Ka4 Bxa5.

4. One Pawn on the Fifth Rank, the Other on the Fourth.

Ordinarily, this merely transposes into the corresponding position with the pawns on the fifth, but there is one important exception.

No. 402

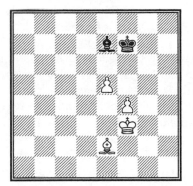

White wins

After **1. ... Bf8 2. Bc4+ Ke7 3. Ke4** (but not 3. f5? Bg7! =) **3. ... Bg7 4. Kf5 Bh6 5. Kg4!!** and Black is in zugzwang, for if 5. ... Bg7 6. Kg5! Kf8 7. Kg6 Bh8 8. Kh7 Bg7 9. Bb3!! and Black's bishop is lost, while if 5. ... Ke8 6. f5 Ke7 7. f6+ is conclusive.

This possibility occurs uniquely with the e- or d-pawns and bishop-pawns. Shifting the corresponding position one file to the right (or three files to the left), we get **No. 403: White king at e4, bishop at e2, pawns at f4, g5; Black king at f7, bishop at a5.** On **1. Bh5+ Ke7!** still draws. For instance, **No. 404: White king at d6, bishop at e2, pawns at a5, b4; Black king at a7, bishop at d8.** Draw, for after **1. Kd7 Bh4 2. b5 Be1!** (but not 2. ... Bf2 3. Kc6) **3. b6+ Kb7 4. Bf3+ Ka6!**, etc., one pawn is lost.

5. Both Pawns on the Fourth Rank

No. 405, Henneberger 1916

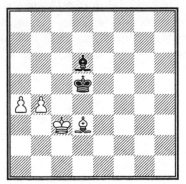

White to play. Draw

Almost all such positions are drawn, since Black has time to set up an adequate defense against White pawns on the fifth.

No. 405 is the unusual possibility of a bishop sacrifice, but Black can stop the pawns in time. **1. Be4+ Kxe4 2. Kc4 Bf4! 3. Kc5 Be3+ 4. Kc6 Kd4 5. b5** (or 5. a5 Kc4 6. b5 Kb4 7. a6 Ka5) **5. ... Kc4 6. b6 Kb4 7. b7 Ba7.** Or here **3. a5 Be3!** (but not 3. ... Bd2, when 4. Kc5 wins, for if 4. ... Be3+ 5. Kc6 Bd2 6. a6!) **4. b5 Ke5 5. b6 Kd6 6. Kb5 Kd7 7. Ka6 Kc6 8. Ka7 Bf2** and the b-pawn is pinned.

With a knight-pawn and bishop-pawn, any reasonable position draws. If his bishop is on the light squares (queenside) or the dark squares (kingside), we get **No. 406: White king at c3, bishop at e3, pawns at b4, c4; Black king at c6, bishop at e6.** White to play. Draw. **1. b5+ Kb7 2. Kd4 Bf7 3. Kc5 Bh5 4. Kd6 Be2;** or **4. Kb4 Be8,** but even the clumsy **3. ... Be8** draws after **4. Kd6 Kc8! 5. Ke7 Bh5 6. c5 Be2 7. b6 Kb7 8. Kd6 Bf3.** If his bishop is on the dark squares (queenside) or the light squares (kingside), Black must prevent the pawns' advance to the fifth to be able to draw (see No. 397).

So we get a situation similar to that in No. 392: if the bishop can attack one pawn and prevent the advance of the other, a draw results; if not he loses.

For example, **No. 407: White king at b3, bishop at e2, pawns at b4, c4; Black king at b6, bishop at f2.** White to play wins. **1. Bh5! Bg1** (1. ... Bg3 2. c5+ Kc6 3. Kc4: No. 397) **2. Be8 Bf2 3. Kc2 Bg1** (if 3. ... Be1 4. c5+ Kc7 5. Kb3!, but not 5. b5? Bf2 6. b6+ Kb7 =) **4. Kd3 Bf2 5. Ke4 Be1** (or 5. ... Bg1 6. Kd5) **6. c5+ Kc7** (6. ... Ka6 is no better; the same continuation is conclusive) **7. b5 Ba5 8. Kd5 Kb7 9. Kd6 Bc7+ 10. Kd7 Ba5 11. Bh5 Bc7 12. Bf3+ Kb8 13. Kc6!** and wins. But again **No. 408: Black bishop at f8,** other pieces as in No. 407, is a clear draw.

With c-pawn and d-pawn similar results ensue. With a dark-square bishop (light-square bishop if e-pawn and f-pawn), any reasonable square draws; e.g., **No. 409: White king at c3, bishop at a4, pawns at c4, d4; Black king at c7, bishop at g1.** White to play. Draw. After **1. c5 Bf2 2. Kc4,** Black has time for **2. ... Bh4 3. d5 Be7.** And again, even so favorable a variation as **3. Kd5 Be7 4. Ke6 Kd8!** (but not now 4. ... Bf8? 5. Kf7 Bh6 6. d5 wins) leads to nothing; e.g., **5. Bb5 Bf8 6. Kf7 Bh6 7. d5 Be3 8. c6 Bf4,** etc.

When White's bishop is on dark squares, again the position of the Black bishop is conclusive. **No. 410: White king at c3, bishop at a3, pawns at c4, d4; Black king at c6, bishop at f7,** is a draw, but **No. 411: Black bishop at g2,** other pieces unchanged, is a win for White.

With center pawns the results are still the same. When White has a dark-square bishop, the game is always a draw. **No. 412** (Tarrasch): **White king at e3, bishop at c1, pawns at d4, e4; Black king at d6, bishop at c2.** Black to play. Draw. **1. ... Bd1! 2. Ba3+ Kd7 3. d5 Bh5 4. Kf4 Bg6 5. Ke5 Bh7 6. Kd4 Bg6 7. e5 Bf7,** etc.

But when White has a light-square bishop, he wins if Black's bishop is at h2, draws if it is at h8. **No. 413: White king at d3, bishop at b3, pawns at d4, e4; Black king at d6, bishop at h2.** White wins by Ke2-f3-g4-f5 and again the attempt ... Bg1 is refuted by e5+ and Kd3 or Ke4, or d5, depending on circumstances.

6. Pawns on the Second or Third Rank

It seems self-evident that such positions must be drawn, since Black has so much time at his disposal to effect one of the defenses described above. This is in fact the case, but there is still one exception. **No 414** (Berger 1889): **White king at g4, bishop at d3, pawns at e2, f2; Black king at f7, bishop at g7.** White wins. **1. f4 Bf8** (there is nothing better: Black must mark time and can only hope to stop the pawns by keeping his bishop on the long diagonal) **2. e4 Bg7 3. e5 Ke6 4. Bc4+ Ke7 5. Kg5.** With the Black bishop at d6 in No. 414, the game is an easy draw; e.g., **1. f4 Kf6 2. e4 Bb8,** etc.

We can sum up with five general rules for bishop and two connected passed pawns against a bishop of the opposite color:

a. Always wins when both pawns are on the sixth rank (except for rook-pawn and bishop of the wrong color);

b. Wins in many positions when both pawns are on the fifth rank; in some cases regardless of where the opponent's bishop is; in others only when the bishop cannot attack one pawn and prevent the advance of the other one at the same time. Rook-pawn always draws;

c. Wins only in a number of special cases when both pawns are on the fourth rank;

d. Wins only in a few problem positions when the pawns are still on the second rank;

e. A light-square bishop with f-pawn and e-pawn, and a dark-square bishop with c-pawn and d-pawn offers the best winning chances.

We have considered only those positions where the Black king is in front of the pawns (except No. 405). If the king is behind the pawns and White's king is supporting them, the bishop cannot hold the position. If the king is near the pawns, but not in front of them, the result can only be determined by considering the position that arises when the Black king finally manages to blockade the pawns. In general, White wins if his pawns are on the fourth rank or beyond, provided he has at least one center pawn. If we shift all the pieces in No. 405 one file to the right, the position is still tenable for Black.

No. 415, White: king at d3, bishop at e3, pawns at b4, c4; Black king at e5, bishop at e6. White to play. Draw. **1. b5 Kd6! 2. c5+ Kc7 3. Bf4+ Kb7**, and 4. c6+ is refuted by 4. ... Kb6, when the b-pawn cannot be defended. The sacrifice 1. Bf4+ is met in exactly the same way as in No. 405: 1. ... Kxf4 2. Kd4 Bg4! 3. b5 Bf3! (3. ... Be2 3. Kd5! again loses) 4. Kc5 (or 4. c5 Be2 5. b6 Bf3) Ke5, etc., =.

But if we go one more file to the right, **No. 416: White king at e3, bishop at f3, pawns at c4, d4; Black king at f5, bishop at f6,** White wins: **1. c5 Bh4 2. Bc6!! Ke6 3. Ke4 Bf2** (or 3. ... Bg3 4. d5+ Ke7 5. Ba4) **4. Ba4!** (not 4. d5+?? Kf7!! =) **4. ... Bg1** (4. ... Ke7 5. Kd5) **5. Kd3 Kd5 6. Bb3+ Kc6 7. Kc4.**

c) Unconnected Passed Pawns

There is a general rule here that applies to most cases: If the pawns are two or more files apart they win; if they are only one file apart they draw. The reason is simple: if the pawns are far apart, the bishop must blockade one while the king stops the other, so the White king can support the pawn held by the bishop and win that piece. But if the pawns are close together, the Black king can stop the advance of both.

No. 417

White to play wins.
Draw with the f-pawn on the e-file

In **No. 417** White wins by **1. Bf3 Bh4 2. Ke6 Kd8 3. f6 Bg5 4. f7 Bh6 5. Kf6 Bf8 6. Kg6 Ke7 7. Kh7! Kd8 8. Kg8 Ke7 9. c7** and one pawn queens. With **White's pawn at e5** (instead of f5), the position is again a draw because in the similar variation, **1. Bf3 Bh4 2. Ke6 Bg5 3. Kf7 Bh4 4. e6,** Black has the defense **4. ... Kd8.** White can then win the bishop, with **5. e7+ Bxe7 6. c7+,** but not the game. However, this fact is in itself significant because it shows that when there are more pawns on the board, two such unconnected pawns, as in No. 418, are sufficient.

A rook-pawn and bishop of the wrong color are, of course, an exception to this rule, since the bishop can be sacrificed for the other pawn, when rook-pawn and bishop draw. For example, **No. 418: White king at b5, bishop at e3, pawns at a5, f6; Black king at a8, bishop at d5.** Draw, since the Black bishop stops the f-pawn and the Black king takes care of the a-pawn.

It is now quite clear that three passed pawns usually win, but again there are exceptions. **No. 419: White king at b2, bishop at e5; Black king at d3, bishop at e6, pawns at a2, b3, c4.** Draw, for if **1. Ka1 c3, etc.**

3. Both Sides Have Pawns

One pawn ahead or a positional superiority that is decisive in other endings is usually insufficient here because White can attack the enemy pawns only with his king. In general, it is necessary to have effective threats on both sides of the board to be able to win.

a) The Defender Draws Despite Material or Positional Inferiority

No. 420, J. Polgar-Kramnik, 2003

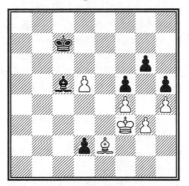

White to play

1. Bd1 Kb6 2. Ke2 Ka5 (Black gives up his passed pawn in order to go after White's kingside pawns. But once the White bishop gets free Black's pawns will also be vulnerable. The more exact move is 2. ... Kb5.) **3. Bc2 Bg1 4. Kxd2 Bh2 5. g4! Bxf4+ 6. Ke2 hxg4 7. h5! gxh5 8. Bxf5 Kb5 9. Bg6 h4 10. Bf5 g3 11. Kf3 Kc4 12. Bh3 Be5 13. Ke4** (the blockade is complete; Black has no more winning chances) **13. ... Bf6 14. Bf1+ Kc3 15. Bg2 Kc4 16. Bf1+**, etc., and the game was drawn.

No. 421, Vidmar-Spielmann, St. Petersburg 1909

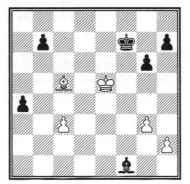

Black to play. Draw

As we have pointed out, this is the most frequent case. The drawing method always consists of blockading the enemy's dangerous pawns with the king and defending one's own pawns with the bishop at a distance.

No. 421 is typical. Spielmann tried **1. ... Bh3** (to block the kingside pawns and get some counterplay there), when White could have drawn most simply by **2. Kd4 g5 3. Kc4 Bd7 4. h4 gxh4** (or 4. ... g4 5. Bd6 and the bishop can hold the two pawns) **5. gxh4 Ke6 6. Kb4** and White can give up the c-pawn and still draw the game, since the queenside pawns are blocked.

Even if White were careless and allowed Black the most favorable position on the kingside—e.g., 2. Kd4 Bd7 3. Kc4 g5 4. Kb4 Ke6 5. c4 Kf5 6. Be7 g4 7. Bh4 Ke4 8. c5 Kf3 9. Bd8 Kg2, losing a pawn—White's disadvantage would be inconclusive. After 10. Bh4 Kxh2 11. Ka3 Kg2 (Black can obviously do nothing on the kingside) 12. Kb4 Kf3 13. Ka3 Ke2 14. Kb4 Kd3 15. Bf6 Kc2 16. Bh4! Kb2 17. Bf6+ Ka2 18. Bh4 a3 19. Bf6 Be8 20. Bh4 Kb2 21. Bf6+ and still no progress is possible.

Black can win this ending only if he is allowed to secure a passed pawn on the kingside; e.g., in the above variation, 13. Ka3 Ke4 14. Be7? Kd4 15. Bd6? h5 16. Kb4? h4! 17. gxh4 Be8! 18. h5 Bxh5 19. Kxa4 Be8+ 20. Kb4 Ke3 21. Kc3 Kf2 and wins White's bishop.

Why it is essential to blockade the Black a-pawn with the king rather than the bishop is seen in the game continuation: **1. ... Bh3 2. Ba3? g5 3. Bb4? Kg6 4. c4 Kh5 5. Kf6?** (5. Kd4 is still good enough) **5. ... Kg4 6. Ba3 Bg2 7. Bd6 Bf1 8. Kg7 Kf5! 9. c5** (9. Kxh7 Bxc4 and Black will have two active passed pawns against White's one; if the positions of the king and bishop are interchanged [king at b4, bishop at g7] White draws) **9. ... a3! 10. c6 a2! 11. g4+ Ke4 12. Be5 bxc6 13. Ba1 c5 14. Kxh7 c4 15. Kg6 Kd3 16. Kxg5 c3** and White resigned.

Examples of such positions where the inferior side draws by blockading one wing with his king and defending the other with his bishop are legion. The drawing method then consists of two steps: forcing as many enemy pawns as possible onto the color of the enemy bishop in order to increase the effectiveness of your own bishop and augment the mobility of the king, and then blockading the side where there is a passed pawn or potential passed pawn with your king, while the wing where there is an even number of pawns is held by the bishop.

No. 422, Walther-Fischer, Zurich 1959

White to play. Draw

1. a4?. Believe or not, this move throws away the win. White must first control the crucial square b6. White should play **1. b4! Kc7 2. Ka5! Kb8 3. b5** Black lands in a losing zugzwang; e.g., **3. ... Bc5 4. b6 Ba3 5. Ka6**, and Black cannot prevent White from promoting one of the queenside pawns. **1. ... Kc7 2. b4 Kb8 3. a5 Ka7 4. Ka4 Bg3 5. b5 Bf2** (the position is a draw, since 6. b6+ is met by 6. ... Bxb6) **6. Be2 Be3 7. Kb3 Bd2 8. b6+ Kb7 9. Ka4 Kc6 10. Bb5+ Kc5**, draw.

No. 423 (Maroczy-Pillsbury, Munich 1900) is a case where the superior side has a rook-pawn and bishop of the wrong color: **White king at e4, bishop at c3, pawns at e5, f5; Black king at g5, bishop at c4, pawns at a4, a3, c5, f7**. White to play. Draw. **1. e6! fxe6 2. fxe6 Bxe6 3. Ke5 Bb3 4. Kd6 c4 5. Kc5 Kf4 6. Kb4 a2 7. Ka3 Ke3 8. Kb2 Kd3 9. Ka1!!**.

Once an effective blockade of the pawns by the king is established, two connected passed pawns are not enough to win. In fact, there is one special case where three connected passed pawns do not win (No. 419). But two blockaded pawns draw even when there are pawns on the other side of the board, while three win.

b) Material or Positional Advantage Is Decisive

Despite common belief, it is not true that bishops of opposite colors always draw. In many cases, one extra pawn is a sufficient advantage, and sometimes even materially equal positions are untenable just *because* the bishops are of different colors.

Once more we must make certain necessary distinctions in addition to the general rule. First of all, we shall consider only those positions where the material is even or where one side is at most a pawn ahead.

We have already seen that there must be significant threats on both sides of the board if the superior side is to have any winning chances. In addition, it is evident that when one side has two connected passed pawns, unblocked, his opponent will have to give up his bishop to stop them.

In discussing endings with bishops of the same color, we showed that having all your pawns on the same color as your bishop is a severe handicap, since that piece is then left without any mobility. Such a situation with opposite-color bishops likewise opens the road for the entrance of the White king.

We can distinguish five cases in which an ending with bishops of opposite colors can be won with an advantage of one pawn or a superior position. In all except the last it is essential to have pawns on both sides of the board.

1. The king is better placed.

2. The passed pawns are qualitatively superior (two passed pawns against one).

3. There is one passed pawn and sufficient play on the other wing.

4. The pawns are better placed (all the defender's pawns are on the same color as his bishop and the attacker has the initiative).

5. Special combinations.

No. 424, Portisch-Besser 1967

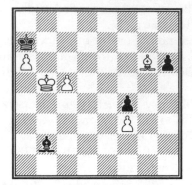

White wins

White has to assist his c-pawn. So he first protects his a-pawn even though this frees Black's passed pawn. **1. Bd3! h5 2. Kc6 h4 3. Kd7 h3 4. c6 h2** (4. ... Be5 5. Bf1 h2 6. Bg2 and 7. c7 wins) **5. c7 h1=Q 6. c8=N+! Kb8 7. a7+ Kb7 8. Be4+** wins.

(1) Better King Position

This usually occurs as a result of previous exchanges.

No. 425, Euwe-Fine, AVRO 1938

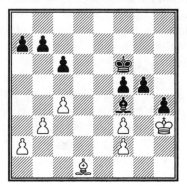

Black to play wins

The rooks have just come off. Black wins by playing his king to the queen-side. **1. ... Bd6** (to prevent b4 and c5 or b5, when White might be able to defend his pawns from a distance) **2. Bc2 Ke5 3. Bd3 a5 4. Kg2 Bc5 5. Bc2 f4** (else this pawn will be lost when Black's king goes to d4) **6. Bg6 Kd4 7. Bf5 Kc3 8. Bc8 Kb2** and White resigned, for after **9. Bxb7 Kxa2 10. Bxc6 Kxb3** the a-pawn decides.

The king position is usually the decisive factor in these endings. To keep your own king mobile and prevent the opponent's from supporting his pawn majority is often worth a pawn; in many cases a pawn sacrifice is required to make sure that the enemy king does not occupy a dominating position.

No. 426 (Pinkus-Fine, New York 1940): **White king at f2, bishop at e3, pawns at a2, b2, e5, f4, g2, h2; Black king at f5, bishop at e4, pawns at b4, c7, d5, f7, g7, h4.** Black to play. Black stands better, but his slight superiority will disappear into thin air unless he gets his king to e4. Accordingly, he tries **1. ... Bb1** but after **2. Kf3!!** the best he can do is win a worthless pawn.

If instead White makes a routine move such as 2. a3? bxa3 3. bxa3 Ke4 is decisive; e.g., 4. a4 d4 5. Bd2 c5 6. a5 Bd3 7. g3 hxg3+ 8. hxg3 Ba6 9. g4 c4 10. Ke1 c3 11. Bc1 d3, etc. But the ingenious **2. Kf3** drew the game: 2. ... Bxa2 3. g4+ hxg3 4. hxg3 Bb3 5. g4+ Ke6 6. Bc5 Bd1+ 7. Ke3! b3 8. g5 Kf5 9. Ba7 g6 10. Bc5 and the pawn is worthless because the dark squares are effectively blocked. After the attempt **10. ... Kg4 11. Ba7 Bc2 12. Bc5 Bf5 13. Ba7 Kg3 14. Bd4 Kg2 15. Ba7 Be6 16. Bd4 Kf1 17. Kd2!** a draw was agreed.

(2) Better Placed Passed Pawns

This and a better king position are the most common advantages for winning endgames with opposite bishops. When White has two connected passed pawns against one, the bishop can both hold the enemy pawn and support the advance of its own.

No. 427, Olland-Pillsbury, Hanover 1902

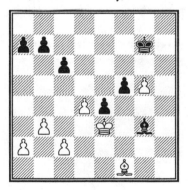

White to play. Black wins

The game continued **1. c4 Kg6 2. a4 Kxg5 3. Bh3 Bh2!** (to get the White king away from e3) **4. Kf2 a5 5. Bf1 Bf4 6. Bh3** (White can do nothing) **6. ... Bc1 7. d5 cxd5 8. cxd5 Ba3 9. Bf1 Bc5+ 10. Ke1 f4 11. Bc4 b6 12. Kd2 f3 13. d6** (else e3+-e2) **13. ... Bxd6 14. Ke3 Kf5 15. Kf2 Kf4 16. Bb5 e3+** and White resigned, for the best he can do is give up his bishop for the two pawns.

From the discussion of bishop and two pawns vs. bishop it is clear that in most cases the presence of a Black passed pawn would not change the result. If we add a pawn at d2 in No. 389, we get **No. 428: White king at f5, bishop**

at e2, pawns at e6, f6; Black king at d8, bishop at b4, pawn at d2. Black to play. White wins. **1. ... Ke8 2. Bb5+ Kf8 3. Ba4 Ba3 4. Ke4 Bb4 5. Kd5 Ba3 6. Kc6 Bb4 7. Kd7**, exactly as in No. 389. The only time the extra pawn makes a difference is when the bishop must get off the right diagonal to block it. In No. 392, for instance, with Black's bishop at b4 he loses, but with his bishop at b4 and a pawn at a4 he draws because the White bishop must abandon the diagonal h3-c8.

An example is **No. 429: White king at d4, bishop at g4, pawns at d5, e5; Black king at e7, bishop at b4, pawn at a4.** White to play. Draw. If **1. Kc4 a3 2. Kb3 Bc5! 3. Bf5 Bb4 4. Bb1 Ba5! 5. Kxa3** (5. d6+ Ke6, =) **5. ... Bc7** and we have No. 392; if **1. Bd1 a3 2. Bb3 Kd7! 3. Kc4 Be7 4. Kb5 Kc7 or 4. Kd4 Bf8 5. Ke4 Bc5 6. Kf5 Ke7 or 4. Kd4 Bf8 5. Ba4+ Kc7** and the White bishop has to go right back.

Two connected passed pawns may sometimes win even without the pawn advantage; for instance, if the enemy pawns are blocked or doubled. **No. 430** (from a game in London 1851): **White king at e2, bishop at d3, pawns at a4, f2, f3; Black king at d4, bishop at f4, pawns at a6, b7, c5.** Black to play wins by **1. ... c4 2. Bf5 b5 3. axb5** (or 3. a5 b4 4. Bc8 b3! 5. Kd1 c3!) **3. ... axb5 4. Kd1 Kc3 5. Bd7 b4 6. Be6 b3 7. Bf7 Kb4 8. Be6 c3**, etc., as in No. 389. A piece or pawn that cannot play is as bad as no piece at all, sometimes even worse.

You might expect that unconnected passed pawns would win more easily than connected ones with a number of pawns on the board, as they do with bishop and two pawns vs. bishop, but this is not the case because the extra pawns complicate the problem of entry for the White king.

No. 431, Berger-Mackenzie,, Frankfurt 1887

Black to play wins

In **No. 431,** if we removed all the pawns except White's d-pawn and Black's b- and h-pawns, the win would be child's play. But as it is Black must work out some rather complicated maneuvering to score. The game continued **1. ... Kf6 2. Bb8 a6 3. Bc7 b5 4. Kf2 Ke6 5. g3 Kd5 6. Ke3 h5 7. h4 Bd1 8. Bd8 Kc4 9. Ba5 Bc2 10. Kd2 Bf5 11. Kc1 Kd3 12. Kb2 Be6 13. Ka3 f6 14. Kb4 g5 15.**

hxg5 fxg5 16. Bd8 g4, draw. Instead, as Berger later demonstrated, **1. ... Bb3!** wins, with the following main variation: **2. Bb8 a5!! 3. Bc7 a4 4. Bxb6 a3 5. d5 Bxd5** (but not 5. ... Bc4? 6. d6!! a2 7. d7 a1=Q+ 8. Kh2! =, since both 8. ... Qa8 9. d8=Q and 8. ... Qxc3 9. d8=Q are inadequate) **6. Bd4+ f6 7. c4 Bxc4 8. Kf2 Kf7 9. Ke3 Ke6 10. g3 g5! 11. h4 gxh4 12. gxh4 f5,** and the passed pawns on both sides of the board decide.

The essential point in all such endings is that two passed pawns are needed to win. For this reason, the inferior side should try to avoid any unbalance in the pawn structure and any weakness that might lead to any such unbalance.

How such a slight weakness is exploited is seen in **No. 432** (Rubinstein-Treybal, Carlsbad 1929): **White king at g1, bishop at d6, pawns at a2, c3, e4, f2, g2, h3; Black king at g8, bishop at e6, pawns at a6, c4, f6, g7, h7.** Black to play cannot hold the position. If the Black pawn were at b5, the game would be a certain draw. But its exposed position at c4 facilitates the creation of two passed pawns. Rubinstein won as follows: **1. ... f5 2. f3! fxe4 3. fxe4 Bd7 4. Kf2 Kf7 5. Ke3 Ke6 6. Bf4** (shuts the Black king out) **6. ... Be8 7. Kd4 Bb5 8. Kc5** (now White will exchange his a-pawn for Black's c-pawn; but first he wants to get his e-pawn to e7) **8. ... Kd7 9. e5 Ke6 10. g4 g6 11. a3 h5 12. gxh5 gxh5 13. h4 Kf5 14. Bg3 Ke6 15. Bh2 Ke7 16. Kd5 Kd7 17. e6+ Ke7 18. Ke5 Kf8 19. Bf4 Kg7 20. Bg5 Kg6 21. Kd5 Kf5 22. e7 Kg6 23. Kc5 Kf7 24. Kb4** (now the time is ripe) **24. ... Ke6 25. a4 Bc6 26. Kxc4 Bxa4 27. Kc5 Kd7 28. c4 Kc7 29. Kd5 Kd7 30. Ke5 Bd1 31. Kf6 Ke8 32. c5 a5,** and Black resigned. The simplest win is 33. c6 a4 34. c7 Bg4 35. Bc1 Bc8 36. Ba3 Bd7 37. Kg6 Bg4 38. Bb4, and Black is in zugzwang.

When the White bishop cannot both prevent the advance of the enemy pawn and support his own, he can still usually win once he has, or will be able to, set up passed pawns on both sides of the board, cramping the Black pieces.

No. 433, Rubinstein-Grünfeld, Carlsbad 1929

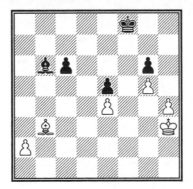

White to play

White's bishop cannot effectively support his eventually passed g-pawn, for Black will advance his c-pawn and exchange it for the White pawn. Nevertheless, since the Black bishop must guard a5 and a7 in view of White's passed a-pawn, and the Black king must guard g7, a fairly simple win is possible.

First, Black's c-pawn must be forced to a dark square to limit the mobility of the bishop. **1. Kg4 Be3 2. Ba4! c5 3. Bb5!**

The game continuation Rubinstein chose is also quite adequate, but less direct: 3. Bb3 Bd2 4. Bc4! (blocking the diagonal g1-a7 so that the Black bishop may never relax its watch of a5) 4. ... Kg7 5. a4 Kf8 6. Kf3 (6. h5 transposes to the above variation after 6. ... gxh5+ 7. Kxh5 Kg7 8. Bb5) 6. ... Ke7 (not 6. ... Be1? 7. Ke2! and if 7. ... Bxh4? 8. a5! queening) 7. Ke2 Ba5 8. Kd1, etc., = (8. Bd5 looks better but is not, for after the best reply, 8. ... Bb4 9. Kd3 c4+!! 10. Bxc4 Be1, etc., it's a draw).

3. ... Kg7 4. a4 Bd2 5. h5! gxh5+ 6. Kxh5 Ba5 (or 6. ... Kf7 7. Kg4 Ke6 8. Bc4+, and White's king still gets to f5) **7. Kg4 Kg6 8. Be8+ Kg7 9. Kf5 c4 10. Bb5 c3 11. Bd3 Bc7 12. Bc2 Kf7 13. Bd1!** (Black is in zugzwang) **13. ... Kg7** (if 13. ... Ba5 14. Kxe5 Kg6 15. Kd6 Kxg5 16. e5 Bb4+ 17. Kd7 Kf5 18. e6 Kf6 19. a5 and wins) **14. Bb3 Kh7 15. Kf6 Bd8+** (now forced) **16. Kxe5 Bxg5 17. a5 Be3 18. a6 Kg7 19. Kd6** and the bishop cannot hold both pawns.

In a similar position with fewer pawns there's nothing to it. For instance, **No. 434** (Reti-Tartakower, Semmering 1926): **White king at f3, bishop at c4, pawns at b3, g3, h2; Black king at f8, bishop at c5, pawns at e3, h5.** White to play wins. **1. Ke4 h4** (or 1. ... Kg7 2. h3! Bd6 3. g4 hxg4 4. hxg4 Bc5 5. Kd5 Ba7 6. b4 Kg6 7. b5 Kg5 8. Be2, etc.) **2. g4!** (not 2. gxh4? Kg7, =, since the bishop is the wrong color) **2. ... Ke7 3. Kd5! Ba7 4. h3 Kd7 5. b4 Bb8 6. Ke4 Bd6 7. b5 Bc5 8. Kf4 Bb6 9. g5.** and Black soon resigned.

No. 435, Kotov-Botvinnik, USSR Championship 1955

Black to play

It seems as though White has sufficient control of the dark squares (if 1. ... Kg3, 2. Be7 holds), Botvinnik finds a way to force a win. **1. ... g5!! 2. fxg5** (if 2.

hxg5 h4 3. Bd6 Bf5 4. g6 Bxg6 5. Kxb3 Kg2 wins) **2. ... d4+!** (safeguarding his b-pawn) **3. exd4 Kg3 4. Ba3 Kxh4 5. Kd3 Kxg5 6. Ke4 h4 7. Kf3 Bd5+,** White resigned. There is no defense against the entry of Black's king. He forces the trade of his b-pawn for the bishop and wins with his h-pawn and right-color bishop.

(3) One Passed Pawn (Actual or Potential) and Play on the Other Wing

The classical illustration of this type of superiority is **No. 436**.

No. 436, Nimzovich-Capablanca, Riga 1913

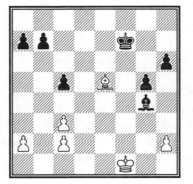

White to play. Black wins

If White's pawn were at b2 instead of c3 Black would have no winning hopes at all. As it is, Capablanca worked out the following magnificent conclusion: **1. a4 Ke6!! 2. Bb8 a5** (much better than 2. ... a6; the point will soon be clear) **3. Ke1** (if 3. Bc7 b5! 4. axb5 a4 5. c4 a3 6. Ba5 a2 7. Bc3 Kd6! and 8. ... Be6 and both pawns go the way of all wood; so Black is left with passed pawns on both sides) **3. ... Kd5! 4. Kd2** (or 4. Bc7 Kc6! 5. Bxa5 b6) **Bd7 5. Bc7 Kc6! 6. Bd8 b6 7. c4 Kb7 8. Kc3 Bxa4** (the rest is not difficult) **9. Kb2 Bd7 10. Kb3 Be6 11. Kc3 a4 12. Kd3 Kc6 13. Kc3 g4 14. Bh4 h5 15. Bg3 a3 16. Kb3 Bxc4+!! 17. Kxa3** (if 17. Kxc4 a2 18. Be5 h4 19. Kb3 g3! 20. hxg3 h3! or 20. Kxa2 g2! and Black queens) **17. ... b5,** etc. The two pawns win easily.

If White had not started with 1. a4 but with some other play, such as 1. Ke1, Black would still have won but not so easily.

(4) Better-Placed Pawns

This has any real meaning only when all or most of the pawns are on the same color as the defender's bishop. This not only weakens the pawns and cramps the bishop but also allows the White king to roam freely. Because the pawns are not easily defended the king has to come to their rescue and, as we have seen, this may be fatal because passed pawns have to be blockaded by a king rather than a bishop.

No. 437, Nimzovich-Tarrasch, Bad Kissingen 1928

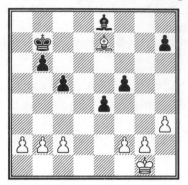

White to play

In this example, **1. Kh2 c4?** (if 1. ... f4 2. Bg5 f3 3. g4! with potential passed pawns on both wings; but 1. ... Bb5! 2. Kg3 Bf1 3. h4 h5 could save the game) **2. Kg3 Kc8 3. Kf4 Kd7 4. Bb4 Ke6 5. Bc3 Bd7 6. g3 b5 7. Kg5 Kf7 8. h4 Bc8 9. Kh6 Kg8 10. b3!** (forcing the decisive passed pawn on the queenside) **10. ... cxb3 11. cxb3 f4** (desperation; if 11. ... Bd7 12. Be5! Black is in zugzwang, for if 12. ... Bc8 13. a4, or if 12. ... Be8 13. Kg5 Bd7 14. Kf6 Kf8 15. Bd6+ Kg8 16. Ke7 Bc6 17. Ke6, winning a pawn; or here 16. ... Bc8 17. a4 and wins) **12. gxf4 Bd7 13. Kg5 Kf7 14. f5 Bc6 15. Kf4 Ke7 16. Ke5** and the unconnected pawns decide. The remaining moves were **16. ... Be8 17. Kxe4 Bc6+ 18. Ke5 Be8 19. Kd5 Bf7+ 20. Kc5 Be8 21. Be5 Bd7 22. Kb6 Kf7 23. f6 Be8 24. f4 Ke6 25. Ka6! Kf7 26. b4 Ke6 27. a4! bxa4 28. b5,** Black resigns.

With two connected passed pawns or two passed pawns on both sides of the board the win is fairly simple even in blocked positions. Two illustrations follow.

Unconnected pawns: **No. 438** (Bardeleben-Mackenzie, Bradford 1888): **White king at f2, bishop at a7, pawns at a2, b3, d4, e5, f4, g2, g3; Black king at e6, bishop at e8, pawns at b5, c6, d5, f5, g7, h5.** Black to play; White wins **1. ... Bd7 2. Ke3 Bc8 3. Kd3 Kd7 4. Bb6!** (this is important, else the Black king gets to c7 and impedes the progress of the White king) **4. ... b4** (or 4. ... Ba6 5. Kc3 Bc8 6. Kb4 Bb7 7. Kc5 Ba6 8. Ba5 Bc8 9. Kb6 and wins; note how Black's pawns get in the way because they are all on light squares) **5. Bc5 Ba6+ 6. Kc2 Bf1 7. Bxb4 Bxg2 8. Be1** (else Black might have counterchances with 8. ... g5, ... g4 and ... h4) **8. ... Bf1 9. Kc3 Ba6 10. Kb4 g6 11. Kc5 Bd3 12. Kb6 Bc2 13. a4 Kc8** (13. ... Bxb3 transposes into the main variation) **14. a5 Bxb3 15. a6 Kb8 16. e6 c5** (desperation) **17. dxc5 d4 18. e7** and Black resigned.

No. 439 (Makarychev-Averbakh, 1937): **White king at e2, bishop at f5, pawns at f3, g2, h3; Black king at d4, bishop at g3, pawns at c3, c7, f6, g5, h6.** Black to play. At first glance, Black doubled extra c-pawns seem meaningless in view of White's control of the light squares. But Averbakh shows that he can create a passed pawn on the kingside, though at the moment that possibility is quite hidden. **1. ... Ke5 2. Bc2 Kf4 3. Bb1 Bh2 4. Kf2 Bg1+ 5. Ke2** (of course, 5. Kxg1 Ke3, etc., wins for Black) **5. ... Kg3 6. Kf1 Bf2! 7. Bc2 f5! 8. Bb1** (if 8. Bxf5 Kf4 9. Bg6 Ke3, etc., wins) **8. ... f4 9. Bg6 Be3 10. Bc2 h5 11. Bf5 c5 12. Bg6 h4 13. Bf5 g4! 14. hxg4** (if 14. fxg4 f3 15. gxf3 Kxh3 wins) **14. ... h3 15. gxh3 Kxf3 16. g5 Kg3 17. g6 Bd4 18. h4 f3 19. h5 Bg7 20. Ke1 f2+,** White resigned (if 21. Kf1 Kf3-Ke3-Kd2 wins). A classical, instructive endgame.

We have repeatedly emphasized that mobility is the decisive factor in all phases of chess. Nowhere is this more clearly demonstrated than in endings with bishops of opposite colors. At times the defender can draw when he is two pawns down because his opponent's pawns are blocked. And with weak pawns the defender can lose when material is even.

No. 440, Rabinovich-Romanovsky, Leningrad 1934

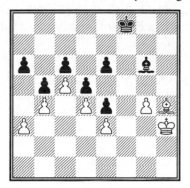

White to play wins

After **1. Bg3!** Black is lost (other moves are inferior because Black could get counterchances by sacrificing his e6 pawn) **1. ... Kg7** (the game continuation, 1. ... e5 2. Bxe5 Kf7 3. Kh4 Ke6 4. Kg5 Be8 5. Kh6 Bf7 6. Kg7 Be8 7. g5 Kf5 8. Kf8!, was equally hopeless) **2. Be5+ Kh7 3. Kg3 Be8** (or 3. ... Kg8 4. Kf4 Kf8 5. Kg5 Kf7 6. Kh6! and the bishop is lost) **4. Kf4 Kg6 5. Bc7 Kf6 6. Bd8+ Kf7 7. Ke5 Bd7 8. Kd6 Be8 9. Bg5! Kf8 10. Kxe6 Bf7+ 11. Kd7 Be8+ 12. Kd8 Bf7 13. Bh6+ Kg8 14. Kd7,** and after the capture of the c-pawn the win is routine.

(5) Special Combinations

These usually arise when the defender's bishop must stay at some vulnerable point to protect a vital pawn.

No. 441 (Horwitz 1880): **White king at c7, bishop at f2, pawns at a3, b3; Black king at a5, bishop at a6, pawn at b7.** White to play wins. **1. Be1+ Kb5 2. Bb4!** (if 2. a4+? Kc5 3. b4+ Kc4 4. Kb6 Kb3! 5. a5 Ka4! 6. Bd2 Be2!! 7. Kxb7 Kb5! 8. a6 Bf3+, = because the pawns are blocked) **2. ... b6 3. Be1 Kc5 4. Bf2+ Kd5** (or 4. ... Kb5 5. Bxb6 Bb7 6. a4+ wins) **5. Kxb6 Be2 6. b4 Kc4 7. Ka5 Kb3 8. a4 Bf1 9. b5 Be2 10. b6 Bf3 11. Kb5 Be2+ 12. Kc5 Ba6 13. a5 Ka4 14. Be1 Bb7 15. Bd2 Ba6 16. Kc6** and wins, for the bishop is lost and Black's king cannot get to the corner.

No. 442 (Topalov-Shirov, Linares 1998): **White king at g1, bishop at c3, pawns at g2, h4; Black king at e6, bishop at f5, pawns at a4, d5, f6, g6.** Black to play wins. With an advantage of two pawns the win is relatively simple, unless of course we have one of the positions Nos. 397-405 or a position that reduces to them. But the general case presents no real difficulty provided care is taken not to blockade the pawns.

Despite his two extra pawns, the game still looks drawish. If 1. ... Kd6 2. Kf2 Kc5 3. Ke3, and Black gets nowhere because White controls the dark squares.

1. ... Bh3!! (this looks like the worst move on the board, but it clears the way for the Black king and frees the f-pawn. Furthermore, White gets nowhere declining the sacrifice, since 48. Kf2 Kf5 49. Kf3 Bxg2+ wins.) **48. gxh3 Kf5 49. Kf2 Ke4! 50. Bxf6** (on 50. Ke2 a3, the three passed pawns are too much to handle) **50. ... d4 51. Be7 Kd3 52. Bc5 Kc4 53. Be7 Kb3!** White resigns. If **54. Ke1**, then **54. ... Kc2**, followed by ... d4-d3 and ... a4-a3 wins.

Chapter V

MINOR PIECE ENDINGS

In this chapter we consider all possible combinations of minor pieces, except those with only knights (Chapter III) and only bishops (Chapter IV) .

I. BISHOP VS. KNIGHT

For many years there has been a theoretical controversy, at times heated, about the respective merits of these two pieces. In the latter part of the nineteenth century most experts, apparently intrigued by the romantic and unpredictable powers of the knight, preferred that piece on the ground that it can get to every square on the board, which a bishop cannot do. So great a master as Chigorin openly maintained that to exchange a bishop for a knight conferred a definite, even if perhaps intangible, advantage, while a player who kept on struggling with two bishops against two knights was just being plain pigheaded.

Then along came Steinitz who reversed the entire theory: a bishop is in every respect superior to a knight. This advantage, he claimed, is so great that when one has a bishop vs. a knight one may be said to have the "minor exchange." This view, systematized by Dr. Tarrasch, was prevalent for a while but was eventually seen to be much too radical. After the First World War the pendulum swung the other way, when the hypermodern school, with its penchant for exotic chess, showed a marked preference for the knight. And finally, with the decline of the hypermoderns (from 1930 on) the bishop again came into its own, but this time the peculiar virtues of the knight were also given their due.

As far as the endgame is concerned, we may summarize the contemporary views on this topic in four conclusions.

1. The bishop is in general better than the knight.

2. Where there is material advantage the values of the two pieces are of minor importance. Nevertheless, a bishop usually wins more easily than a knight in such cases.

3. Materially even positions should normally be drawn, but if there is a slight positional advantage the bishop will be able to exploit it more effectively.

4. When all or most of the pawns are on the same color as the bishop, the knight is preferable.

We will now consider the question more systematically.

A. The Basic Positions

1. Bishop and Pawn vs. Knight

This is a draw if the Black king is in front of or reasonably near the pawn, but a win if the king is far away or behind the pawn. In the simplest case, **No. 443: White king at d4, bishop at f4, pawn at e4; Black king at d7, knight at g4,** after **1. Bg5** (1. Kd5 Nf6+ and 2. ... Nxe4) **1. ... Ke6** White can do nothing to budge the rock at e6. The knight cannot be stalemated unless it is on the edge of the board. If the Black king were at g6 in this example, the result would still be a draw.

No. 444, Horwitz 1880

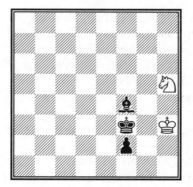

White to play. Draw

If the pawn is far advanced it is essential for the defending king to be directly in front of it. If it is not, the only defense is stalemate.

On **1. Ng3!! Be5** (or 1. ... Bxg3 stalemate) **2. Nf1 Ke2 3. Kg2 Bf4! 4. Kh1!! Kf3** (4. ... Kxf1 stalemate) **5. Ng3! Be3 6. Kh2 Bf4 7. Kh1** and Black can only wring his hands in despair because White is so eager to give away his piece. But if we move the position one file to the left, it is clear that there is no stalemate and that the Black pawn will queen.

When the Black king is behind the pawn, White should generally win if his pawn is on the sixth rank and if his king can attack the knight directly. By skillful manipulation of his pieces White can force the knight away from the pawn.

No. 445, Chess Players Chronicle 1856

White to play wins

The pawn is freed as follows: **1. Bc3!** (better than 1. Be5? Kb6 2. Bd4+ Kb5! and White has no good waiting move) **1. ... Kb6** (if 1. ... Kd5 or 1. ... Kb5 2. Bd4!! wins) **2. Ba5+ Kb5 3. Bd8 Kc5 4. Bh4 Kb5 5. Bg5 Kc5 6. Be3+ Kd5 7. Bd4! Nd6 8. c7!** and wins.

A similar stratagem is seen in **No. 446** (from a game of Dr. Lasker's): **White king at d5, bishop at f6, pawn at c6; Black king at f7, knight at e6**. White to play wins **1. Be5! Ke7 2. Bg3!** (to answer Ng5 by Bh4) **2. ... Kf6** (2. ... Kf7 3. Bh2! Ke7 4. Be5! Kf7 5. Kd6, etc.) **3. Kd6 Nd4** (or 3. ... Kf7 4. Be5) **4. Be5+**.

But if the Black knight were at b5 in No. 445, the game would be drawn. **No. 447: Black knight at b5**, other pieces as in No. 445. **1. Bg7 Kd5 2. Bh6 Kc5 3. Be3+ Kd5 4. Bg1 Ke5! 5. Kc8 Kd5! 6. Kb7 Nd6+ 7. Kc7 Ne8+** (but not 7. ... Nb5+? 8. Kb6 Nd6 9. c7 Nc8+ 10. Kb7 Ne7 11. Bf2 and 12. Bh4) **8. Kb6** (8. Kd7 Nf6+) **8. ... Kd6 9. Bh2+ Kd5** and White is no nearer his goal.

Again, if the White king can attack the knight, the ending is won. **No. 448: White king at b7, Black knight at b5**, other pieces as in No. 445. **1. Be5 Kc4 2. Kb6 Kb4 3. Bg3 Kc4 4. Be1 Nd6 5. c7 Kd5 6. Bb4 Nc8+ 7. Kb7**, etc.

The rook-pawn wins more easily than any of its colleagues when the king is behind it, chiefly because the bishop can so often be sacrificed.

No. 449, Handbuch 1843

White to play wins

After **1. Kg5!** the pawn cannot be stopped: **1. ... Nf2 2. h4 Ne4+** (or 2. ... Ng4 3. h5 and the knight must move) **3. Kg6 Nxd6 4. h5 Nc4 5. h6 Ne5+ 6. Kg7 Kf4 7. h7** and Black is one move too late.

Or a similar case, **No. 450** (Englisch-Wittek, Vienna 1882): **White king at b7, bishop at d8, pawn at a5; Black king at a4, knight at h6**. White wins. **1. ... Nf7 2. a6 Nd6+** (2. ... Nxd8+ 3. Kb6) **3. Kc6 Nc8** (3. ... Nb5 4. Be7 Na7+ 5. Kb7 Nb5 6. Kb6) **4. Bb6 Kb4 5. Kb7! Nd6+ 6. Kc7! Nb5+ 7. Kc6 Ka4 8. Bc5 Ka5 9. Kb7 Ka4 10. Kb6** and again the knight must move.

However, when the rook-pawn is on the seventh with the king stalemated, the defender can draw and sometimes even win. Even when the king is not completely stalemated there are good drawing chances. **No. 451** (Schindlbeck 1911): **White king at e2, knight at f1; Black king at g2, bishop at f2, pawn at h3**. White to play. Draw. **1. Nh2! Bc5** (1. ... Kxh2 2. Kxf2 draws because of the rook-pawn) **2. Nf3!** (but not 2. Nf1? Bd4! 3. Ke1 Bc3+ 4. Ke2 Bd2!! and wins) **2. ... Bb4 3. Nh4+ Kg3 4. Nf3 Bc3 5. Kf1! Kxf3 6. Kg1** =.

Finally, when the Black knight is stalemated a win is possible even with the king in front of the pawn.

No. 452, Calvi 1847

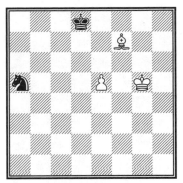

White to play wins

1. Bd5! is decisive. **1. ... Ke7 2. Kf5 Kd7 3. Kf6 Ke8 4. e6 Kf8 5. e7+ Ke8 6. Ke6** (or 6. Bf7+) **6. ... Nc6** (or N any) **7. Bxc6+ mate.**

2. Knight and Pawn vs. Bishop

With the king in front of, or near, the pawn, this is also an elementary draw. The bishop remains on the diagonal that the pawn has to cross and it is impossible for the knight to block the diagonal and also chase the king away.

When the king is not in front of the pawn there is a win only if the enemy king is far away, except that with a center pawn a draw is forced. To win, the knight must block the diagonal of the bishop and allow the pawn to advance.

With a rook-pawn, any winning hope vanishes. **No. 453** (Sam Loyd 1860): **White king at e1, bishop at a4; Black king at g2, pawn at h3, knight at h4.** White to play, Draw. **1. Bd7!! h2 2. Bc6+ Kg1 3. Bh1!!** (the point of White's first move) **3. ... Kxh1** (if 3. ... Ng2+ 4. Ke2!! Nf4+ 5. Ke1, etc.) **4. Kf2! =**, since the knight cannot gain a tempo (see No. 205).

No. 454 (Jakimcik 1958): **White king at b5, knight g6, pawn b6; Black king at d6, bishop at b3.** White to play wins. **1. Ne7!** (wrong is 1. Nf4? Bd1 2. Nd5 Be2+ 3. Ka5 Kc6, =) **1. ... Bd1** (or 1. ... Bc2 2. Nd5! Bd3+ 3. Ka5 Kc6 4. Nb4+ wins) **2. Nf5+ Kd7 3. Nd4 Bg4** (if 3. ... Kc8 4. Ka6 Ba4 5. Ka7 wins) **4. Ka6 Kd8 5. Nc6+** wins.

When the Black king is at a distance from the pawn, the bishop may be blocked by the knight and the pawn will then queen.

No. 455, Kosek 1911

White to play wins

The general case is **No. 455**. The solution is **1. Nd6 Bg1 2. c6 Bb6 3. Ke6 Bc7** (the threat was 4. Kd7 followed by Nc4) **4. Kd7 Bb8 5. Nb5 Kg2 6. Nc7 Kf3 7. Kc8 Ba7 8. Nb5 Bb6** (if 8. ... Be3 9. Nd6 Bb6 10. Nc4 Bf2 11. Kd7 Bg3 12. Nd6) **9. Nd6!** (but not 9. Kb7? Bd8 10. Na3 Ke4 11. Nc4 Kd5 =) **9. ... Kf4 10. Nc4** wins as the pawn can no longer be stopped.

Or the similar case with the knight-pawn, **No. 456** (Kosek 1910): **White king at c5, knight at d4, pawn at b5; Black king at g1, bishop at g2.** White to play wins. **1. Nc6 Bf1 2. b6 Ba6 3. Kd6 Bb7** (else 4. Kc7 and 5. Nb4) **4. Kc7 Ba8 5. Na5 Kf2** (5. ... Bf3 6. Nc6) **6. Nb7! Ke3 7. Kb8,** etc. The difference between this and the similar bishop and pawn vs. knight ending is that here if the defender's king is anywhere near the pawn (barring certain special stalemate possibilities), the game is hopelessly drawn, while with bishop and pawn vs. knight there are winning chances as long as the defender's king is not directly in front of the pawn.

It is evident that White can win only if he can shut the Black bishop out of either diagonal from which the pawn can be held. With a center pawn on the sixth this is not possible, but with one on the seventh it is.

No. 457

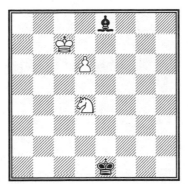

White to play. Draw. Win if the bishop is on dark squares

No. 457 is a draw, for after **1. Kd8 Ba4 2. Kc7 Be8**, or **1. Nc6 Kd2 2. Ne5 Ke3 3. Nd7 Kd4 4. Kd8 Bg6 5. Nf6** (or 5. Nf8 Bf5 6. Ke7 Bc8!) **5. ... Bf5** the bishop is still covering the vital square.

Of course, it may happen that as a result of previous exchanges the knight can block the bishop. Or the Black king may be in such a bad position that it facilitates this kind of blockade.

On the other hand, with the pawn on the seventh there is too little leeway for the bishop. **No. 458: White king at c7, knight at d4, pawn at d7; Black king at f1, bishop at h4**. White wins: **1. Nc6 Ke2 2. Kd6 Ke3 3. Ne7**. But, as we have seen, if the Black king is near the pawn this case is likewise a draw.

No. 459: Black king at f7, other pieces unchanged. Nothing can be done, since the square e7, where the knight blocked the bishop in No. 457, is now doubly guarded.

With a rook-pawn, a win may be possible even though the king is relatively near. **No. 460** (Horwitz 1885) is an ingenious problem: **White king at c7, knight at b8, pawn at a7; Black king at b4, bishop at a8**. White to play wins. **1. Kb6!! Kc4 2. Na6 Kd4 3. Nc7 Bg2 4. Ne6+ Ke5 5. Nd8 Ba8 6. Kc7 Kd5!! 7. Nb7** (not 7. Kb8? Kd6! 8. Kxa8 Kc7 =) **7. ... Ke6 8. Na5 Ke7 9. Kc8 Ke8 10. Nc4! Ke7 11. Kb8 Kd8 12. Na5 Kd7 13. Nb7! Kc6 14. Kxa8 Kc7 15. Nd6!** and the White king gets out of the corner.

But if the Black king is favorably placed this is a win or a draw depending on who has the tempo.

No. 461, P. Benko 1998

White to play. Draw

1. Be4 (if 1. Kf2?, Black wins with 1. ... Nc5) **1. ... Nc5!?** (if 1. ... a4, White draws with 2. Kf2 a3 3. Bb1 Kc5 4. Ke2 Kc4 5. Kd2 Kb3 6. Kc1, and the king arrives just in time) **2. Bg6!** (The obvious 2. Bc2 loses after 2. ... Kd5 3. Kf2 Kc4 4. Ke2 Nb3! 5. Bd3+ [or 5. Kd1 a4] 5. ... Kc3 6. Bb5 Nd4+; the same goes for 2. Bb1.) **2. ... a4** (now on 2. ... Kd5, White draws with 3. Be8) **3. Kf2 a3 4. Bb1 Ne4+!?** (again the best try; if 4. ... Kd5, then 5. Ke3 Kc4 6. Kd2 Kb3 7. Kc1 Nd3+ 8. Bxd3 a2 9. Bc4+ draws) **5. Ke3 Nc3 6. Ba2!** (but not 6. Kd2? Nxb1+ 7. Kc2, when 7. ... Nd2! wins) **6. ... Nxa2 7. Kd4!** (after this centralization, which keeps out the Black king, White will force the pawn to a2 and stop it there, thus reaching a theoretical draw.) **7. ... Kc6 8. Kc4 Nc1 9. Kc3 Kb5 10. Kc2 a2 11. Kb2,** draw. Black can't get the White king out of the corner but can only stalemate it.

3. Bishop and Two or More Pawns vs. Knight

Two extra pawns are generally a sufficient winning advantage and this case is no exception. The model positions present no difficulties whatsoever—the pawns are advanced and either queen or cost the defender his piece.

No. 462, analysis by W. Ward

White to play. Black wins

No. 462 is one of the most involved wins with two connected passed pawns, and it's further complicated by the bishop of the wrong color. The solution is **1. Nf4!** (or 1. Nh4! Bg5! 2. Ng2 Ke2!) **1. ... Bg5!** (but not 1. ... Kf3?, which only draws after 2. Nd3 g2+ 3. Kxh2 Bd6+ 4. Kg1 Kg3 5. Nf2! Bf4 6. Ng4!! Kf3 7. Ne5+!, etc.) **2. Nd3+** (again, if 2. Ng2 Ke2, or 2. Nh3+ Kf1 3. Nxg5 g2+ 4. Kxh2 g1=Q+ and mates in two) **2. ... Ke2 3. Ne5 Kf1! 4. Nf3 g2+ 5. Kxh2 Kf2 6. Ng1 Bf4+.** But if we move this position up two ranks, the knight has more room and the blockade of the pawns ensures a draw.

For the sake of completeness, here is the model win when the pawns are not blocked. **No. 463: White king at d3, bishop at c3, pawns at d4, e4; Black king at e6, knight at b6.** White to play wins. **1. Ba5 Nd7 2. d5+ Kd6** (or 2. ... Ke5 3. Bc7+, or 2. ... Ke7 3. Kd4) **3. Kd4 Ke7 4. e5 Ke8 5. e6 Nf6 6. d6 Kf8 7. d7,** etc.

The general case with two unconnected passed pawns is again an elementary win. In a typical position such as **No. 464: White king at d4, bishop at d3, pawns at b4, e4; Black king at d6, knight at d7,** White to move wins. A model continuation is **1. b5 Ne5 2. Be2 Nd7 3. Bg4 Ne5 4. Bf5 Nf3+ 5. Kc4 Ne5+ 6. Kb4 Nd3+** (6. ... Kc7 7. Kc5) **7. Ka5 Kc7 8. b6+ Kb7 9. Be6 Ne5 10. Bd5+ Kb8 11. Kb5 Nd7 12. Kc6 Ne5+ 13. Kd6 Nd3 14. e5,** and the knight has to be sacrificed for the e-pawn.

Black draws with a knight against bishop and two pawns in one of two cases: 1. blockade; 2. rook-pawn and bishop of the wrong color. Neither of these, however, is foolproof. A case where the bishop gets in the way of the pawns is **No. 465** (H. W. Butler 1889): **White king at b5, bishop at c7, pawns at c6, d6; Black king at e6, knight at e5.** Black to play draws. **1. ... Kd5 2. d7 Nxc6 3. Kb6 Nd8! 4. Bxd8** (or 4. Bg3 Nf7 =, see No. 447) **4. ... Kd6, =.**

With rook-pawn and wrong bishop the game is drawn only if the knight is in a position to be sacrificed for the extra pawn, which generally happens only if the pawns are connected. For if they are separated White can sacrifice the rook-pawn to divert the king and then win with the other pawn as in No.

445 or 449. But even when they are connected, if the knight-pawn is ahead of the rook-pawn a win should be possible.

No. 466: White king at h2, bishop at e2, pawns at g3, h3; Black king at g6, knight at e5. White to play. **1. g4 Nc6** (if 1. ... Kg5 2. Kg3 Ng6 3. Bd3 Nh4 4. Be4!) **2. Kg3 Nd4 3. Bd3+ Kf6 4. h4 Ne6 5. Bc4 Nc5 6. Kf4 Nd7 7. Bd3 Kg7 8. g5 Nf6! 9. Be4 Nh5+ 10. Kg4 Nf6+ 11. Kf5 Nh5 12. Bf3 Ng3+ 13. Kf4 Nf1 14. h5**, etc.

But with the rook-pawn too far advanced the sacrifice of the knight is a serious and often unavoidable drawing threat. **No. 467: White pawns at h4, g3**, other pieces unchanged, is drawn after **1. ... Kh6 2. Kg2 Kg7 3. Kf2 Ng6! 4. h5** (else . ... Nxh4) **4. ... Ne5 5. Ke3 Kh6 6. Kf4 Nf7 7. Bc4 Ng5** = (No. 447).

An example that combines the motifs of blockade and the disadvantage of the rook-pawn is **No. 468** (Stein 1789, solution by Walker): **White king at e6, bishop at c8, pawns at a6, d7; Black king at d8, knight at b5**. White to play. Draw. **1. Kd5** (if 1. Bb7 Nc7+ 2. Kd6 Nxa6) **1. ... Na7 2. Kd6 Nxc8+ 3. Kc6! Na7+! 4. Kb7 Kxd7 5. Kxa7 Kc7,** =.

A doubled pawn wins unless the defending king is in front of it. Of course, bishop and three pawns vs. knight is routine, what annotators love to call "simple technique."

4. Knight and Two Pawns vs. Bishop

In general this is a fairly simple win. The exceptions come up only with a blockade. Sometimes it is necessary to sacrifice one pawn and win with the other.

No. 469, Horwitz 1885

White to play wins

The solution is **1. Nb8+ Kb5** (if 1. ... Ka7 2. b5) **2. a6 Ba8** (or 2. ... Kxb4 3. Kb6 Ba8 4. Nc6+ Kc4 5. Nd8 Kb4 6. Nb7 Kc4 7. Kc6! Kd4 8. Kc7 Kd5 9. Kb8 Kc6 10. Kxa8 Kb6 11. Nc5) **3. a7 Bg2** (3. ... Kxb4 4. Kb6! transposes to No. 460) **4. Nd7 Kxb4 5. Kb6 Kc4 6. Nc5 Ba8 7. Na6**, etc., as in No. 460.

The general case is illustrated in **No. 470** (Lasker-Pillsbury, Paris 1900): **White king at a5, knight at c7, pawns at a2, b3; Black king at e5, bishop at d3.** White to play wins. The conclusion was **1. Kb4 Kd6 2. Nb5+ Kc6 3. a4 Kb6 4. Na3 Be2 5. Nc4+ Ka6 6. Kc3 Bd1 7. Nb2 Bh5 8. b4 Be8 9. Kb3 Bc6 10. Kc4 Bd7 11. Kc5 Bg4 12. Nc4 Bd1 13. b5+ Ka7 14. a5 Bf3 15. Ne5 Bb7 16. Nc6+ Ka8 17. Kb6 Ba6! 18. Nb4! Bb7 19. Na6 Bf3 20. Nc7+ Kb8 21. a6,** resigns.

The blockade is, as we know, the only drawing weapon at Black's disposal. It is usually quite effective even though the knight, unlike the bishop, can cover every square.

No. 471, Fine-Reshevsky, Semmering-Baden 1937

Black to play. Draw

In **No. 471,** White's win seems at first to be a simple technical problem. But even though the White king can roam at will all over the board, White can never manage to advance his pawns. The ending can be won only if White gets his king to f3 or h4, but Black is able to prevent this. The conclusion was **1. ... Bb6 2. Kd3** (if 2. Kf1 Kf3! 3. g5 Bd8 4. g6 Bf6 5. g7 Bxg7 6. Nxg7 Kg3 and the rook-pawn goes) **2. ... Bd8 3. Kd4 Bf6+ 4. Kd5 Bh8 5. Kd6 Be5+ 6. Ke6 Ba1 7. Ke7 Bb2 8. Kf7 Kg5!** and a draw was agreed.

That No. 469 is won only because of the favorable position of White's pieces is clear when you compare it to **No. 472** (Horwitz 1880), where the blockade cannot be broken. **White king at h3, bishop at e8; Black king at f4, knight at e5, pawns at g5, h4.** White to play. Draw. **1. Bb5! Ng4!** (or 1. ... Nf3 2. Bd7 Nd4 3. Bg4 Nf5 4. Be2. Alternatives are 1. ... Ng6 2. Be2 Ke3 3. Ba6 Kf2 4. Kg4 Ne5+ 5. Kxg5 Kg3 6. Bc8 =; or 1. ... g4+ 2. Kxh4 Nf3+ 3. Kh5 g3 4. Bf1 Ke3 5. Kg4 Kf2 6. Bh3 Ng1 7. Bf1! and again Black is at a standstill) **2. Ba6!!** (but not 2. Bd7? Nf2+ 3. Kg2 Nd3).

A blockade cannot be set up with unconnected passed pawns, so exceptions to the general rule that such pawns win are to be found only in problems.

No. 473, Dr. Neuastadtl 1894

White to play wins

No. 473 is typical of the winning strategy employed in this kind of ending. **1. Nf8** (the simplest; 1. Kc8 is good enough but is more complicated) **1. ... Kf5** (if 1. ... Kg3 2. Ne6 Kxg2 3. Nc7 Kf3 4. Kc8 transposes to No. 455) **2. Ne6 Bg3 3. Nd4+ Ke4 4. Ne2 Be5 5. c7 Bxc7 6. Kxc7** and the knight holds the fort until the king gets back.

A doubled pawn (unless it is a rook-pawn) usually wins even when the enemy king is directly in front of it. This is because there is no safe haven for the king, no square from which it cannot be chased. For instance, **No. 474: White king at c4, knight at d4, pawns at c3, c5; Black king at c7, bishop at h3.** White wins. **1. Kb5 Bf1+** (else c6 followed by Kc5 or Kb6) **2. c4 Bd3 3. Ne6+** (better than 3. c6 Kd6! 4. Kb6? Bxc4 5. c7 Kd7 6. Kb7 Ba6+! =) **3. ... Kd7 4. Nf4 Bf1 5. Nd5 Bd3 6. c6+ Kc8** (6. ... Kd6 7. Kb6 Bxc4 8. c7) **7. Kc5 Be2 8. Kd6! Bf1** (8. ... Bxc4 9. Nb6+) **9. Ne7+** followed by 10. c7+ and 11. c8=Q.

No. 475, Averbakh 1980

Black to play draws

1. ... Bg1+ 2. Kc4 Bb6! 3. Nc5+ Kd6 4. d4 Ba7! 5. Ne4+ Kd7 6. Nc3 Bb6 7. Nb5 Ke7 8. Kd3 (8. d6+ Ke6, =) 8. ... Ba5! 9. Ke4 Be1 10. Ke5 Bg3+ 11. Ke4 Kd7 12. Kd3 Bh4 13. Kc4 Be7, =. White to play wins just as before: 1. Kc5 Bg1+ 2. d4, etc.

5. Bishop and Two Pawns vs. Knight and Pawn

The results here are about the same as similar cases with other minor-piece endings. An outside passed pawn usually wins: the pawn either wins a piece or decoys the king when the decision comes on the other wing.

An example is **No. 476: White king at d3, bishop at d4, pawns at b5, g4; Black king at d6, knight at d7, pawn at g6.** Black to play. White wins. 1. ... Kd5 2. b6 Kc6 (if 2. ... Nb8 3. b7 Kc6 4. Be5 Kxb7 5. Bxb8 Kxb8 6. Ke4 Kc7 7. Ke5, etc.) 3. Ke4 Kb7 4. Kf4 Nf8 5. Ke5 Nd7+ 6. Ke6 Nf8+ 7. Kf7 Nd7 8. Kxg6, etc. Of course, if the pawns are closer together or if there is a rook-pawn with wrong-color bishop, all winning efforts will be in vain.

Two connected passed pawns should likewise win because the bishop can hold the Black pawn from a distance and at the same time support its own pawns.

But when all the pawns are together (with or without a passed pawn), no win is possible if the defending king can place itself in front of the pawns. Similarly, if the king cannot do this but is too far from "home" to get back in time, the knight cannot hold the fort alone.

No. 477, Monke-Heinrich, Westphalia Hauptturnier 1926

Black wins

No. 477 is an example of a complicated win with an h-pawn and the king in front of it. The analogous case with the g-pawn would offer no trouble at all: Black would merely get his king out of the way and advance his pawn. But here the king is stalemated and the problem is how to break this deadlock. **1. Ne2 Be3!** 2. Ng3 (if 2. Kxe3 Kg2 and the pawn marches triumphantly on) **2. ... Bd2! 3. Ne2** (or 3. Nf1+ Kg1 4. Nxd2 h2 and wins, or 3. Kf2 Be1+!) **3. ... Be1 4. Nd4 Kh1 5. Ne2 h2 6. Nd4 Kg1 7. Ne2+ Kf1 8. Ng3+ Bxg3 9. Kxg3**

h1=R! (not h1=Q, stalemate), and the rest is simple. Of course, if the White king were at h1 in the original position, the game would be a fairly certain draw.

Under certain circumstances, the path of an advanced passed pawn may be smoothed by a judicious sacrifice. In **No. 478** (Kubbel 1910): **White king at g1, knight at g6, pawn at a6; Black: king at g4, bishop at b3, pawns at d7, e6,** White wins by **1. Ne7! Bc2** (or 1. ... Bd1 2. Nc6! Bf3 3. Ne5+) **2. Nd5! Be4 3. Nf6+.**

6. Knight and Two Pawns vs. Bishop and Pawn

Surprisingly, the results here are somewhat different from the analogous cases above. This is because the knight is useless at a distance.

In general, an outside passed pawn does not win, because the knight cannot both defend the extra pawn and attack the enemy pawn. In addition, if the king wins the bishop for one pawn, it is very often unable to defend the other pawn. The outcome therefore depends on the corresponding knight and pawn vs. bishop ending.

Even in a case like **No. 479**, where one wee check would do the trick, the bishop foils its agile adversary.

No. 479, O. Hey 1913

White to play. Draw

White's knight can try to reach f7 by various paths, such as Ne6 (via g5 or d8) Nf5 (via d6, h6) Nf3 (via e5, g5), etc. But by posting his bishop on the proper diagonal Black prevents the realization of any of these plans. For example, **1. Ne6 Bh4 2. Nc5 Bd8!** (not 2. ... Be7? 3. Nb7! and wins) **3. Nb7 Bc7 4. Nc5 Bd8 5. Ne4 Be7 6. Nd2** (if 6. Ng5 Bxg5) **6. ... Bd6 7. Nf3 Bf4 8. Nh4 Be5 9. Nf5 Bf4**, etc. Obviously going over to the queenside would offer no chance.

Two connected passed pawns, again unlike the similar case with bishop and two pawns vs. knight and pawn, are as a rule not a sufficient winning advantage. The knight must guard the enemy passed pawn, and because the knight's field of action is so limited, it can do nothing to aid its own pawns. Clearly, the nearer the defender's pawn is to his rival's, the greater the winning chances.

A type of winning possibility that is uniquely seen in knight vs. bishop endings is that of advancing a passed pawn to trap a bishop, despite the bishop's great number of available moves.

No. 480 is the most striking and beautiful illustration of this theme that we have ever come across.

No. 480, Reti 1922

White to play and win

After **1. Nd4+ Kc5 2. Kh1!!** Black cannot move his bishop without losing it (e.g., 2. ... Bf4 3. Ne6+, or 2. ... Bd2 3. Nb3+), and he has only two moves with his king to stay within the square of the a-pawn. But on 2. ... Kd5 3. a6, the square c6 is taboo, while 2. ... Kd6 3. Nf5+ again costs him his Bishop. So he must try 1. ... Kb7 in reply to 1 Nd4+, and this loses by exactly one tempo.

The solution is **1. Nd4+! Kb7** (1. ... Kc5 2. Kh1!!) **2. Kxh2 Ka6 3. Nb3 Bf4+ 4. Kh3 Kb5 5. Kg4 Bb8 6. f4 Kb4 7. f5 Kxb3 8. f6 Kb4 9. f7 Bd6 10. a6** and the bishop cannot stop both pawns.

We see a similar idea in **No. 481** (Kubbel 1909): **White king at d1, knight at d4, pawns at b3, d5; Black king at a7, bishop at b1, pawn at b7.** White to play and win. **1. d6 Kb8** (or b6) **2. Kc1! Bd3** (2. ... Be4 amounts to the same thing; 2. ... Bg6 or h7 is met by 3. d7 Kc7 4. Ne6+ Kxd5 5. Nf8+) **3. d7 Kc7 4. Ne6+ Kxd7 5. Nc5+** and the bishop goes.

Curiously, with knight and two pawns vs. bishop and pawn, the winning chances are greatest when all the pawns are on one side. This is for the same reason that knight and pawn vs. knight or bishop is sometimes won even when the enemy king is in front of the pawn – the knight can cover all squares. But ordinarily a decision is forced not by queening a pawn but only by capturing Black's last stalwart. Where this is not possible the ending is drawn.

No. 482, Romanovsky-Verlinsky, Moscow 1925

White to play wins

The most favorable type of case is seen in **No. 482**. The position suggests a clear winning plan: to attack the f-pawn with the king going to e5 (or g5) and the knight to d6 or e7 and then to force Black either by check or zugzwang to abandon the pawn. This is indeed possible, as shown by the game continuation.

1. Ke3 Kg5 2. g3 Ba4 (if 2. ... Kg4 3. Kf2 Be4 4. h3+ Kg5 5. Ke3 Bc6 6. Ne6+ Kf6 7. Nd4! Bg2 8. h4 Ke5 9. Nf3+ Kf6 10. Kf4 transposes to the game) **3. Nh3+ Kg4 4. Nf2+ Kg5 5. h3** (5. h4+ at once is simpler) **5. ... Bc6 6. h4+ Kf6 7. Kf4! Be8 8. Nd1 Bd7 9. Ne3 Be6 10. Nc2** (not 10. h5 Bd7 11. h6 Be6!, =) **10. ... Bf7**

Or 10. ... Bc8 11. Nd4 Bd7 12. Nb3 Bc8! (or 12. ... Be6 13. Nc5 Bd5 14. Nd7+ Ke7 15. Ke5, etc.) 13. Nc5 Kg6! 14. Ke5 Kh5 15. Nd3! Kg4 16. Nf4 Bb7 17. Kf6 Kxg3 18. h5 Kxf4 19. h6, and the ending with queen vs. bishop-pawn is hopeless for Black.

11. Na3! Bd5 12. Nb5 Be6

If 12. ... Ba2 13. Nd6 Bb1 14. Ne8+ Kf7 15. Nc7 and now:

a) 15. ... Kg6 16. Nd5 Bc2 17. Ke5 Kh5 18. Nf4+! Kh6 19. Kf6 Bb1 20. Ne6 Kh5 21. Kg7! Kg4 22. Nf4 Kxg3 23. h5 and the pawn cannot be stopped;

b) 15. ... Kf6 16. Nd5+ Ke6 17. h5! Be4 18. Nc3 followed by 19 Kg5, etc.

13. Nd6 Bd7 14. h5 Be6 15. Ne8+ Kf7 16. Nc7 Bc8 17. Kg5 Bd7 18. Nd5 Kg7 19. Ne3 Kh7 20. Nxf5, resigns.

If the superior side's pawns are far advanced, the possibility of an exchange or sacrifice may be just as dangerous as that of a capture. For example, **No. 483** (Horwitz 1885): **White king at f8, knight at b1, pawns at e6, f5; Black king at d8, bishop at b4, pawn at e7**. White wins. 1. Kf7 Kc7 (or 1. ... Be1 2. Na3 Bc3 3. Nc4 Bd4 4. Nd6! Be5 [or 4. ... Bf6 5. Ne4 Bh4 6. f6! and Black is in zugzwang] 5. Nc8 Bf6 6. Nxe7, etc., as in the main variation) **2. Nd2 Kd8** (2. ... Bxd2 3. f6) **3. Nf3 Bd6 4. Nh4 Ba3 5. Ng6 Bb4 6. Nxe7 Bxe7 7. f6 Bxf6 8. Kxf6 Ke8 9. e7** and White has the opposition.

But without the possibility of a capture or sacrifice the game is normally a draw. For example, **No. 484** (Capablanca-Fine, Semmering-Baden, 1937):

White king at h2, knight at e1, pawns at f4, g4; Black king at g7, bishop at d5, pawn at h7. Draw. Capablanca tried 1. Kg3 Kf6 2. Nf3 Be4 3. Ne5 Bc2 4. Kh4 h6 5. Nd7+ Kg7 6. f5 Ba4, but after 7. Nc5 Bd1 8. Kg3 Kf7 9. Kf4 Be2 10. Ne4 Bd1 11. Nc3 Bb3 12. Ke5 Bc4 agreed to a draw.

If the enemy king can attack the pawn directly and win it, then of course the game is lost. In such cases the defender's only hope lies in simplification. For example, **No. 485** (Judd-Mackenzie, 1888): **White king at f2, bishop at d6, pawn at h5; Black king at e4, knight at e3, pawns at g7, g4.** White to play draws at once by **1. Bf8 Nf5 2. Bxg7**, for if 2. ... Nxg7 3. h6. Black to play tried **1. ... Nf5**, when **2. Bc7** and if 2. ... Nd4 3. Bd6 Kf5 (or 3. ... Ne6 4. Kg3 Kf5 5. Kh4, =) 4. Bf8 Ne6 5. h6 was the best defense. Instead White played **2. Bf8?** (2. Bc7 was correct) and lost after 2. ... g3+ 3. Kg1 Kf3! 4. Bxg7 Nxg7! 5. h6 Ne6 6. h7 Nf4 7. h8=Q Ne2+ 8. Kf1 g2+ 9. Ke1 g1=Q+ 10. Kd2 Qc1+ 11. Kd3 Nf4+ 12. Kd4 Qb2+ and wins the queen.

B. More Complicated Ending

We come now to the great mass of endings that are met in practical play but are not immediately reducible to one of the more elementary cases (A1-6). We'll confine ourselves here to certain all-important general rules that will serve as a guide through the maze.

1. Material Advantage

As we have seen, the advantage of a pawn is enough to win. We have also noted that the general winning idea is either to force a queen or to gain more material. With two pawns or a piece up, of course, the technical problem requires merely a judicious advance of the pawns.

The winning process in the case of bishop and knight endings may be conveniently divided into these five steps:

1. Place all your pieces in the most favorable positions available.
2. Weaken the opponent's pawns as much as possible.
3. Create an outside passed pawn.
4. If a piece is diverted to stop the pawn, capture it.
5. If the king is used to block the pawn, maneuver your own king to the other wing and establish a decisive superiority there.

In many cases, one or more of these steps has already been carried out. Sometimes one or two steps are superfluous; e.g., in endings where the superior side has a knight, the threat of an outside passed pawn is just as strong, possibly stronger, than its fulfillment.

The best position for the pieces is the center. A bishop, however, is just as effective from some other point on a long diagonal (h1-a8, a1-h8). Pawns are weakened by forcing them to advance too hastily or by forcing them to squares of the same color as their bishop. The side with the bishop, however, should try to force the pawns off the bishop's color.

No. 486, Godai-Becker, Vienna 1926

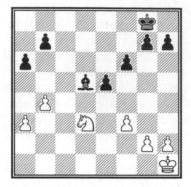

White to play. Black wins

No. 486 is a model case with a bishop.

The first step requires bringing the king to the center (the bishop is already well posted at d5).

1. Kg1 Kf7 2. Kf2 (2. Nc5 is no help; Black simply replies 2. ... Ke7 and 3. ... Kd6) **2. ... Ke6 3. Ke3 Kd6**.

Next the White pawns must be weakened. Since Black has the bishop, he wants the White pawns on dark squares, for then both bishop and king will have attained maximum mobility.

4. g3

Saving his opponent a lot of hard work, but, of course, there is no really adequate defense. If White tries to stave off defeat by keeping Black's king out, the win would be achieved by weakening the pawns on the queenside; e.g., 4. Nc5 Kc6 5. Na4 Kb5 6. Nb2 g5 7. Kf2 h5 8. Ke3 b6 9. Kf2 a5 10. bxa5 bxa5 11. Ke3 Bc4 12. Kf2 Kc5 13. Ke3 Bb5, and White is in zugzwang. Clearly, the side on which the final blow falls will vary according to circumstances; it will usually be the side that happens to be most vulnerable.

4. ... b6 5. Nf2

The *threat* of a passed pawn is sufficient here. If White offers Black a passed pawn in the center he will still be unable to prevent the entry of the Black king to one side or the other; for example, 5. f4 Bc4 6. fxe5+ fxe5 7. Nb2 Bb5 8. Ke4 g6 9. h4 Bc6+ 10. Ke3 Kd5 11. Nd3 Bb5 12. Nb2 h5 and Black's king must penetrate either via c4 or d4.

5. ... Kc6 6. Nd1 Kb5 7. Nb2 g5

White has in effect stopped the passed pawn with his king. Now if he does nothing he will allow his rival to gain a decisive material advantage on the queenside. Instead he plays for a phantom counter-chance and permits Black a passed pawn on the h-file.

8. f4 (or 8. Ke2 a5 9. bxa5 bxa5 10. Ke3 h5 11. Ke2 Kc5 12. Ke3 Bc6 and again Black cannot be kept out) **8. ... exf4+**

To create a protected passed pawn here by 8. ... e4?? would be a serious strategic error, not only because the knight is a born blockader but also because it places a vital pawn on the same color as the bishop.

9. gxf4 g4 10. f5 h5 (threatening to win at once by ... h4, ... g3, ... h3, and ... h2) **11. Kd4** (desperation; if 11. Kf4 a5 12. bxa5 bxa5 13. Kg3 Kc5 14. Kh4 Bf7! followed by capturing the a-pawn or f-pawn; e.g., 15. Nd3+ Kd4 16. Nf4 Ke4, or 16. Nc1 Kc3) **11. ... Bf3 12. Ke3 h4 13. h3**

Preferring the shorter and less painful way out. This move leads to the fourth step: loss of a piece. 13. Kf4 would be an example of the fifth step: 13. Kf4 a5 14. bxa5 bxa5 15. Ke3 Bc6 16. Kf2 Kc5, etc.

13. ... Bc6! 14. hxg4 h3 15. Nd3 h2 and White resigned. After **16. Nf2 h1=Q** all the romance goes out of White's life.

When the superior side has a knight, it is usually not desirable to create an outside passed pawn right away. The reason is that the defender's bishop could hold it at a distance and so the pawn would not deprive it of mobility. Instead, the weakening of the opponent's pawns and the threat of a potential outside passed pawn, which would tie down the bishop but allow the knight to move freely, are the most important of the three preliminary steps.

No. 487, Walbrodt-Charousek, Nuremberg 1896

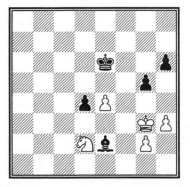

Black to play wins

The e-pawn must fall. Charousek played **1. ... Ke5**, and after **2. Kf2 Bd3 3. Kf3 h5 4. g3** (4. g4 h4) **4. ... Bxe4+!** won quickly, for if 5. Nxe4 g4+ 6. hxg4 hxg4+ 7. Kxg4 Kxe4 8. Kh4 d3. The conclusion was **5. Ke2 h4!** (fixing the h-pawn) **6. gxh4 gxh4 7. Kf2 Kf4 8. Nb3 d3 9. Nd2 Bd5 10. Nf1 Be6 11. Nd2 Bxh3 12. Nf3 Bg4 13. Nxh4 d2** and it's all over.

Where there already is an outside passed pawn, having the bishop presents no difficulty for the superior side: the idea is the same as that in endings with bishops of the same color. Either the knight tries to stop the pawn and is captured, or the enemy king comes to the rescue and leaves the pawns on the other wing exposed.

No. 488 (Rubinstein-Nimzovich, Carlsbad 1907): **White king at g1, knight at c3, pawns at f4, g3, g2; Black king at f8, bishop at c4, pawns at a5, f7, g7, h7**. Black to play wins. The continuation was **1. ... Ke7** (going to the queenside. 1. ... Bb3 2. Nb5 a4 3. Na3 would require a little forceful persuasion by the king to dislodge the recalcitrant cavalier) **2. Kf2 Kd6 3. Ke3 Kc5 4. g4 Kb4 5. Kd4 Bb3 6. g5 a4 7. Nb1** (now Nimzovich could have won prosaically by 7. ... a3 when 8. Nxa3 would be necessary. He prefers instead to force the desolate knight to abandon the Black pawn and allow it to promote) **7. ... Be6 8. g3 Kb3 9. Nc3 a3 10. Kd3 g6 11. Kd4 Kc2** and White resigned. The knight cannot be maintained at c3.

No. 489 (Nimzovich-Janowski, Carlsbad 1907) is strikingly similar to No. 346: **White king at g3, bishop at b3, pawns at b5, f4, g2, h3; Black king at f6, knight at d7, pawns at f7, g6, h6**. White wins. First: centralization (first step in our schema). **1. Kf3 Ke7 2. Ke3 f6 3. Kd4 Kd6 4. Bd1 Nb6 5. Bf3 Nc8 6. h4** (further softening the kingside) **6. ... Ne7** (if 6. ... Nb6 7. Be4 g5 8. fxg5 fxg5 9. h5 Nd7 10. Bf3 Nb6 11. Ke4 Ke6 12. Bg4+ Kf6 13. Kd4 and it's all over: the knight is lost) **7. Be4 g5**

Neither the knight nor the king can budge; alternative pawn moves are likewise useless; e.g., 7. ... f5 8. Bf3 Nc8 9. Bd5 Ne7 10. b6! Kd7 11. Ke5, etc.; or 7. ... h5 8. b6 Nc6+ 9. Bxc6 Kxc6 10. b7 Kxb7 11. Kd5 Kc7 12. Ke6 and Black has breathed his last.

8. fxg5 fxg5 9. hxg5 (the simplest) **9. ... hxg5 10. b6 g4** (if 10. ... Nc6+ 11. Bxc6 Kxc6 12. Ke5 is conclusive) **11. b7 Kc7 12. Ke5** (now White captures the other pawn, which will cost Black his knight) **12. ... g3 13. Kf4 Ng8 14. Kxg3 Nf6 15. Bf3 Nd7 16. Kf4 Kd6 17. Kf5 Ke7 18. Bc6 Nb8 19. Bb5,** resigns. With the knight "on ice" White will soon queen.

Sometimes a piece has to be sacrificed to succeed, as in **No. 490**.

No. 490, Sandor-Benko, Budapest 1949

Black to play wins

1. ... Kb5! (1. ... Bc5? 2. Nb8 a5 3. Nc6 and Nxa5, =) **2. Nxa7+ Kc5! 3. Nc8 a5 4. Ne7 a4 5. Nf5 a3 6. Ne3 a2 7. Nc2 Kc4,** White resigned.

With a knight, an outside passed pawn is somewhat more difficult to exploit. Usually the most essential step is to weaken the enemy pawns by forcing them to squares of the same color as their bishop.

No. 491, Fine-Reshevsky, Semmering-Baden 1937

White to play wins

No. 491 is typical of the problems involved. White clearly cannot get his king to an any more advantageous post than e2, and his b-pawn is hard to support. On the other hand, Black's pieces are or will be better placed because his king can occupy a more central square and his bishop can both stop the b-pawn and keep an eye on the f-pawn. The only way White can win is by diverting the Black king to the queenside and capturing two pawns on the kingside. To do this he must not only get his b-pawn to b5 (to make the threat of an advance more real) but must also soften up his quarry on the kingside.

1. b3 Bd4 2. Nc6 Bb6 3. Nb4

The knight would be too exposed at c6; e.g., 3. b4 Kf6 4. b5 Ke6 5. Kf1 Kd6 with excellent counterchances.

3. ... Kf7 4. Nd5 Bd4 5. Kf1 Ke6 6. Ne3 Bc5 7. Ke2 h5

To keep the knight out of an important square. On 7. ... Ke5 8. Nc2 Kd5 9. b4 Bf8 10. b5 Bc5 (or 10. ... Kc5 11. Ke3 Kxb5 12. Kxe4 Kc6 13. Ke5 Kd7 14. Kf6 Ke8 15. Ne3 and wins another pawn. Black is gambling on the possibility of exchanging one or more pawns) 11. Ne3+ Kd4 12. h4 Bb6 13. Ng4 Kc5 14. Nf6 Kxb5 15. Nxh7 Bd8 16. g3 Kc4 17. Nf8 g5 18. h5, the bishop is doomed.

8. Nc2 g5 9. b4 Bd6 10. g3 Ke5 11. b5 Bc5 12. Ne3 Kd4 13. Nf5+ Ke5

After 13. ... Kc4 he would inevitably lose two pawns on the kingside: 14. Ng7 Kxb5 15. Nxh5 Kc4 16. Nf6 Kd4 17. f3! exf3+ 18. Kxf3 Be7 19. Ng8! Bd8 20. Nh6! Bf6 21. Kg4 Kd5 22. Nf7.

14. Ng7 h4 15. g4

Now all the preliminary spadework is completed.

15. ... Bb6 16. Nf5 Bc5 17. Ne3 Kd4 18. f3!

In the game, White made the mistake of postponing this essential freeing move too long: 18. Nf5+ Kc4 19. Nh6 Kxb5 20. Nf7 Kc4!! 21. Nxg5 Kd5 22. f3 exf3+ 23. Nxf3 Ke4!! 24. Nxh4 Kf4 25. Nf5 Bb6, and the result is a draw because White's king is only an innocent bystander.

18. ... Bb6

Or 18. ... exf3+ 19. Kxf3 Ke5 20. b6!.

19. Nf1! Ke5

If 19. ... exf3+ 20. Kxf3 Kc4 21. Ke4 Kxb5 22. Kf5 Bd8 23. Nd2 is conclusive.

20. Nd2 exf3+ 21. Kxf3 Kf6 22. Nc4 Bc7 23. b6 Bf4 24. b7 Ke6

Or 24. ... Bc7 25. Na5-c6, the fourth step.

25. Ke4 Kd7 26. Kf5 and both Black pawns are lost.

The lesson that No. 491 teaches us is that before sacrificing an outside passed pawn, be sure that there's enough material to win the ensuing ending with all the pawns on one side.

With a potential outside passed pawn the procedure is essentially the same. Nimzovich's maxim that the threat is stronger than its fulfillment is quite appropriate here, though one is inclined to qualify it a bit.

No. 492, Bernstein-Reshevsky, New York 1940

Black to play wins

No. 492 seems to be relatively unfavorable for the bishop, since the potential passed pawn is blocked. But this makes no difference here because the pawns are stuck on dark squares and the bishop can always help them advance later. So g5-g4 is inevitable. The fact that most White pawns are on light squares is no problem for Black, since they are exposed to attack. In general, it is always a serious disadvantage if the pawns of the side with the bishop are on the same color as the bishop, but the other side's pawns should be placed on that color only if they will not be subject to attack.

Reshevsky wound up as follows: **1. ... Kf7 2. Nb5** (if 2. Ne6 Bxc2 3. Nxf4 Bb3 4. Ne6 Bxc4 5. Nxc7 b5 and wins) **2. ... Bxc2 3. Nxc7 Bd3 4. Na8 b5** (4. ... Bxc4 5. Nxb6 Ba6 transposes to the game) **5. cxb5 Bxb5 6. Kf2 Kf6 7. Nb6** (7. Kf3 Kf5 8. Nb6 Bd3 or a6) **7. ... Ba6 8. Kf3 Kf5 9. Na8 Bd3 10. Nb6 g5 11. a4 Ba6** (more accurate than 11. ... Be4+ 12. Kf2 Ke5 13. Nc4+) **12. Na8 Bc4 13. Nb6 Bb3! 14. Kf2 Ke4** and White resigns. He must lose at least one more pawn.

Another illustration is **No. 493** (Vidmar-Marshall, Carlsbad 1929): **White king at g1, bishop at d1, pawns at a2, b2, f2, g2, h3; Black king at g8, knight at f6, pawns at a7, b7, f7, g7.** White to play and win. **1. Bf3 b6 2. Kf1 Kf8 3. Ke2 Ke7 4. Kd3 Kd6 5. Kd4 Nd7 6. Bd5 Ne5 7. f4 Ng6 8. g3** (the preliminaries are over; now the main bout begins) **8. ... f6 9. Be4 Nf8 10. Bf5** (freezing the knight. It is usually good policy to force enemy pawns to be placed on the same color as the bishop because the pawns will then be subject to attack) **10. ... g6 11. Bc8 b5** (a desperate gamble: players like Marshall do not like to be choked to death without saying a word) **12. h4** (12. Bg4 is safer but not quite as accurate) **12. ... f5 13. h5 Kc7 14. Bxf5** (decisive, but also satisfactory is 14. h6! Kxc8 15. Ke5 Kd7 16. Kf6 Ke8 17. b4!) **14. ... gxf5 15. Ke5 Kd7 16. Kxf5** (in the game, Vidmar played 16. Kf6 but after 16. ... Ke8 retreated by 17. Kxf5 because of the trap 17. Kg7 a5 18. h6? Nh7 19. Kxh7? [19. Kg6 still wins] 19. ... Kf7, =) **16. ... Ke7 17. g4** and the three connected passed pawns are too much for one poor mortal.

Where the passed pawn is in the center the technical difficulties are greatest, especially with a bishop. This is because very skillful maneuvering is required to force an entry with the king or an adequate material advantage. Such positions, particularly when coupled with other weaknesses, can frequently be held to a draw by the defender.

No. 494, Euwe-Botvinnik, Nottingham 1936

Black to play. Draw

No. 494 is one of the most involved cases of this type ever to occur in tournament play.

1. ... Nb8 2. Kf3 Nc6 3. Bc3 (to prevent Na5) **3. ... g6** (to be able to play his king to e6) **4. Kf4 a6 5. a4 Ke6 6. h4 Nb4 7. Kf3**

The reason White cannot win is that, despite his extra pawn, the exchange of pieces does him no good. If, for instance, 7. Bg7 Nd3+ 8. Kf3 Ne5+ 9. Bxe5 Kxe5 10. g4 g5 11. h5 a5 the ending is hopelessly drawn.

7. ... Nd3 8. Bg7 Ne5+!

But not 8. ... h5? 9. Ke2 Ne5?? 10. Bxe5 Kxe5 11. Kf3 a5 12. g4 hxg4+ 13. Kxg4 Kxe4 14. Kg5 and White gets there first.

9. Ke2 (now 9. Bxe5 only draws, as in the note to White's seventh move) **9. ... Nxc4 10. Bxh6 b5**

This is the simplest drawing line. The game continued 10. ... Nb2, when White could have forced a favorable decision by 11. Bg7 Nxa4 12. g4 b5 13. h5 gxh5 14. gxh5 Kf7 15. Ba1 Nb6 16. Kf3 b4? 17. e5 Nd7 18. Ke4 Ke6 19. h6 Nf8 20. Kd3 Kd5 21. e4+ Kc6 22. Kc4 a5 23. Kb3!! Kb5 24. e6 a4+ 25. Ka2 Ng6 26. Bf6 Kc6 27. e7 Kd7 28. e5 c4 29. e6+ Ke8 30. Kb1 c3 31. Kc2 a3 32. Kb3 Nf4 33. h7 Ng6 34. Bg5 Nh8 35. Bh4 Ng6 36. Bf6 and Black is in zugzwang.

11. axb5 axb5 12. Bf8 Nd6! 13. Bxd6 Kxd6 14. g4, but the king and pawn ending is only a draw despite White's extra pawn – the doubled e-pawns are no better than a single pawn.

But if there are no weaknesses, a central passed pawn wins just as surely, though often not quite as quickly, as one on the outside files.

No. 495, Euwe-Spielmann, match 1922

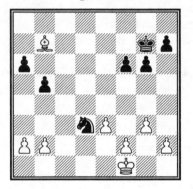

Black to play. White wins

No. 495 is an excellent example. The first phase is centralization.
1. ... Nc5

1. ... Nxb2 2. Bxa6 b4 3. Ke2 Na4 4. Bc4 Nc3+ 5. Kd3 Nd1 6. f4 is inferior.
2. Bd5 a5

To prevent 3. b4, which would leave Black's pawns hopelessly weak. 2. ... Nd3 is refuted by 3. Ke2 Nxb2 4. Bb3! a5 5. Kd2 a4 6. Bd5! a3 7. Kc2 f5 8. Bf3 Nc4 9. Be2 Nd6 10. Kb3, and both the a-pawn and the b-pawn will be captured.

3. e4 Kf8 4. Ke2 Ke7 5. Ke3 Kd6

Or 5. ... Na4 6. Kd4 Nxb2 7. Kc5 Nd3+ 8. Kxb5 Nxf2 9. Kxa5 and wins.
6. Kd4 g5 7. f4 gxf4 8. gxf4 Nd7 9. Bf7!

White will now force a passed pawn in the center, which will function in exactly the same way as an outside pawn; that is, to tie down the Black king and make it possible for White to switch over to the queenside.

9. ... h6

Euwe gives the following alternatives:

a) 9. ... Nc5 10. e5+ fxe5+ 11. fxe5+ Kc6 12. Bd5+ Kb6 13. e6 Na6 14. e7 Nc7 15. Bf7;

b) 9. ... Nb6 10. e5+ fxe5+ 11. fxe5+ Ke7 12. Bg8 h6 13. b3 Nd7 14. Kd5 b4 15. Bh7 Nf8 16. Bf5 h5 17. h4, with a simple win in both cases.

10. Be8 Nf8 11. e5+ fxe5+ 12. fxe5+ Kc7 13. Bxb5 Ne6+ 14. Kd5 Ng5 15. e6 Kd8 16. h4, Black resigns.

A center pawn is even stronger with a knight than it is with a bishop, mainly because the function of the passed pawn is to constrict the mobility of the enemy king and force the entry of one's own king on one of the flanks.

An apt illustration of the model winning procedure (weakening the pawns, forcing an entry with the king) is **No. 496** (Botvinnik-Riumin, 1936): **White king at f2, knight at a4, pawns at a2, b3, e2, g3, h2; Black king at e6, bishop at e7, pawns at a7, c5, g7, h7.** White wins. **1. Ke3 Kf5 2. Kf3 Ke5 3. e3 Bd6 4. Nb2 Kd5 5. Nc4 Bc7 6. Ke2** (threatening to break through on the queenside with Kd3, e4+, and Ne3 or Nd2) **6. ... Ke4 7. Nd2+ Kf5 8. Kf3 Ke5 9. g4** (it is more important right now to limit the mobility of Black's king than that of his bishop) **9. ... Kd5 10. h3 Bd8 11. Ke2 Bc7 12. Kd3** (now that the kingside pawns are safe, White is going to get his king to c4) **12. ... Bg3 13. Ne4** (to weaken the Black pawns first; there is no hurry) **13. ... Be1 14. Ng5! h6 15. Ne4 Bh4 16. Nc3+ Ke5** (or, as in the game, 16. ... Kc6 17. Ke4 Bf6 18. Nb1 Kd6 19. Na3 Ke6 20. Nb5! a5 21. Nc7+ Kd7 22. Nd5 Bb2 23. Nb6+, and Black resigned, for he must lose a second pawn after 23. ... Ke6 24. Kd3 Ba3 25. Kc4 Ke5 26. Kb5 Bb4 27. Nc4+, etc.) **17. Kc4 Bf2** (or 17. ... Be7 18. Kb5 and the a-pawn is the victim) **18. Nd1 Bg1 19. Kxc5**, with a simple win.

With only a few pawns (three vs. two), a center pawn still wins when the superior side has a knight, but there will often be difficulty with a bishop.

For example, **No. 497** (Euwe-Fine, Bergen aan Zee 1938): **White king at d3, knight at e4, pawns at a2, b3, d4; Black king at g4, bishop at c1, pawns at a7, b6.** Black to play. White wins. **1. ... Bf4 2. Kc4 Kf3 3. Nc3 Bh2 4. b4 Bc7 5. b5 Bd6 6. Nd5 Ke4 7. Nf6+ Ke3 8. Kd5 Be7 9. Ng4+ Kd3 10. Ne5+ Kc3 11. Nc6 Bf6 12. a4 Bg7 13. Kd6** and Black resigned.

Now consider a similar case with a bishop.

No. 498 (Foltys-Benko, Budapest 1948): **White king at f3, knight at b4, pawns at c2, h2; Black king at g8, bishop at b2, pawns at f7, g7, h7. Black to play.** Besides the extra pawn, the pawn formation favors Black because he has a chance to create connected passed pawns. **1. ... Be5 2. h3 f5 3. Nc6 Bd6 4. c4 Kf7 5. Nd4 Kf6 6. Nb3 g5 7. c5 Be5** (against Nd4-b5) **8. c6 Ke6 9. Nc5+ Kd5!** (if 9. ... Kd6? 10. c7! Kxc7 11. Ne6+ draws) **10. Nd7 Bd6 11. c7!** (after 11. Nf6+ Kxc6 12. Nxh7 Be7, the knight is trapped) **11. ... Bxc7 12. Nf6+ Ke5!** (12. ... Kd6? 13. Ne8+ Kd7 14. Ng7 f4 15. h4 draws) **13. Nxh7 Bd8 14. Nf8 Kd6 15. Ke3**

White should try 15. Ng6 Bf6 16. h4!? (because it's the wrong-corner bishop, but the knight remains in danger after 16. ... g4+! 17. Kf4 Ke6 18. Nf8+ Kf7 19. Nd7 Bd4 20. h5 Ke8 21. Nb8 Be5+! 22, Kxe5 g3 23. h6 Kf7 wins.

15. ... Bf6 16. Kf3 Ke7 17. Nh7 Kf7 18. Nxf6 Kxf6 19. Kf2 Kg6 20. Kg2 Kh5 21. Kg3 f4+, White resigned (if 22. Kh2 Kh4 23, Kg2 f3+ wins).

So far so good. But if we juggle the pieces around a bit we see that though the bishop often wins, the simplicity of the last example is only apparent.

No. 499

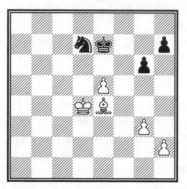

White to play wins

No. 499 is more typical and requires considerable maneuvering before the point is scored.

The first step is to force the pawns to advance, which leads back to the easier case. This is made possible by the threat of an effective sacrifice.

1. Bd5 Nb8

If 1. ... Nb6 2. Bg8 Kf8 3. Bxh7 Kg7 4. Kc5 Nc8 5. Kc6! Kxh7 6. Kd7 Nb6+ 7. Kd8 Nd5 8. e6 is sufficient.

2. Bg8! h6

Again, if 2. ... Kf8 3. Bxh7 Kg7 4. Kd5! Kxh7 5. Kd6 Kg7 6. e6 Kf8 7. Kc7! Ke7 8. Kxb8 Kxe6 9. Kc7 Kf5 10. Kd6 Kg4 11. Ke6 Kh3 12. Kf6 Kxh2 13. g4 Kg3 14. g5 and wins.

3. Bd5 Nd7 4. Be4 Nf8

4. ... g5 5. Bd5 transposes into No. 498, while 4. ... Kf7 is met by 5. Kd5 Nb6+ 6. Kc6! Nc8 7. Kc7! Ne7 8. Kd7 Kf8 9. Ke6. If here 7. ... Na7 8. Bd5+ Ke7 9. Bc4! wins the knight.

5. Kd5 Kd7 6. h4! and now:

a) **6. ... Ke7 7. h5! gxh5 8. Bf5!** (the point: the knight is stalemated) **8. ... h4** (if 8. ... Nd7 9. Bxd7 Kxd7 10. e6+ Ke7 11. Ke5 h4 12. gxh4 h5 13. Kf5 is decisive, while if 8. ... Kd8 9. Kd6 Ke8 10. e6 h4 11. e7!! hxg3 12. Be4 is the refutation) **9. gxh4 Kd8** (or 9. ... h5 10. Kd4 Kf7 11. Kc5! [triangulation] 11. ... Ke7 12. Kd5 and Black's king must give way) **10. Kd6 Ke8 11. h5** (not 11. e6?? Nxe6!, =) **11. ... Kf7** (11. ... Kd8 12. Bg6!) **12. Bc2! Kg8** (12. ... Ke8 13. Bg6+! Nxg6 14. hxg6 h5 15. e6 h4 16. g7 or here 13. ... Kd8 14. e6) **13. Ke7 Kg7 14. Bf5! Kg8 15. Kf6 Kh8 16. Kf7** and if Black could only skip a move he might be able to defend himself, but he can't, so his game is hopeless; e.g., 16. ... Nh7 17. Bxh7, or 16. ... Ng6 17. hxg6.

b) **6. ... h5 7. Bc2! Ke7 8. Bb1! Kd7** (he has no choice) **9. Ke4 Ke7** (if 9. ... Ne6 10. Ba2 Nc5+ 11. Kd4 Na4 12. Bf7) **10. Ba2 Nd7 11. Kf4 Kf8** (11. ... Nc5 12. Kg5! Ne4+ 13. Kxg6 Nxg3 14. Bc4 Kf8 15. Kg5 Ne4+ [else the knight is lost] 16. Kxh5 Nc5 17. Bb5! Ke7 18. Kg6 Ke6 19. h5 Kxe5 20. h6 Ne6 21. Bc4 Nf8+ 22. Kg7 and wins) **12. Bb1 Kf7 13. Bc2! Nf8** (13. ... Kg7 14. e6 Nc5 15. Ke5) **14. Bb3+ Kg7 14. Ke4 Nd7 15. Kd5 Kf8 16. Kd6 Nb6 17. Kc7 Na8+ 18. Kb7** and wins.

On the other hand, if the Black pawns were on their original squares here White could do nothing. **No. 500: White king at d4, bishop at d5, pawns at e5, g3, h2; Black king at e7, knight at d7, pawns at g7, h7.** White to play. Draw.

1. Bc4 h6! (the point) **2. Bf5 Nb6 3. Bc2 Nd7 4. Bb3 Nb6 5. Ke4 Kf8! 6. Kf5 Nc8 7. Ke6** (or 7. Kg6 Ne7+ 8. Kh7 Nc6 9. e6 Ne7; the knight cannot be stalemated by the bishop so can always cover the square e7 and prevent the only pawn sacrifice that might give White winning chances) **7. ... Ne7 8. Kd6 Ng6 9. e6 Ne7 10. Bc2 Nc8+ 11. Kd7 Ne7 12. h4 Ng8**, etc. Again, the knight cannot be stalemated and White cannot get through.

A protected passed pawn is not as strong in conjunction with a bishop as it is with a knight. The bishop is at home in open positions, while the knight is most effective when the pawns are blockaded.

No. 501 illustrates the type of ending where the bishop is effective.

No. 501, Petrov-Reshevsky, Semmering-Baden 1937

Black to play. White wins. Draw with the White bishop at d3 instead of d8

The knight is practically stalemated by the bishop; as a result, the decisive entry of the White king cannot be prevented.

The conclusion was **1. ... Nf8 2. Bg5 Kc7 3. Kb3 Nd7 4. Be7 Kb6 5. Bd8+ Kb7 6. Kc3** (6. Ka4 Ka6) **6. ... Kc8 7. Be7 Kc7 8. Kd3** (White has reached the position he was striving for; any knight move costs Black a pawn) **8. ... Kc8 9. Ke3 Kc7 10. Kf3 Kc8 11. Kg4 Nb6** (desperation) **12. Bxc5 Nxc4 13. Bb4!** (or 13. Bf8 Nd2 14. Bxg7 Nxe4 15. Bxe5, when White will still win, though perhaps with some technical difficulties; the text is simpler) **13. ... Nb2 14. Kg5 Nd3**

15. Kg6!, and Black resigned, for after 15. ... Nxb4 16. Kxg7 the pawn cannot be stopped.

But if the bishop were on the light squares in No. 501, the knight could not be stalemated and no entry with the king could be forced.

For example, **No. 502, White bishop at d3,** other pieces unchanged. White to play. Draw. First, the queenside: **1. Kb3 Kc7 2. Ka4 Kb6 3. Be2 Nf6 4. Bf3 Ne8 5. Be2 Nd6 6. Bd3 Ne8** and White is at a standstill. Similarly on the kingside: **7. Kb3 Kc7 8. Kc2 Kd7 9. Kd2 Nf6 10. Ke3 Nh5 11. Kf3 Nf4 12. Bc2 Kd6 13. Kg4 Ke7 14. Kg5 Kd6 15. f6 gxf6+ 16. Kxf6** and now all Black needs to do is move back and forth until White gets tired.

If the pawn position is not blocked, a protected passed pawn is just as great an advantage as an outside pawn. For example, **No. 503** (Spielmann-Tarrasch, Gothenburg 1920): **White king at d1, knight at e2, pawns at a2, b2, c3, g2, h2; Black king at g8, bishop at a6, pawns at a7, c5, c4, d5, g5, h7.** Black wins. The d-pawn is a potential protected passed pawn. **1. ... Kf7 2. Ng1 Bc8 3. Kd2 Bg4** (stalemating the knight temporarily; to get out of the straitjacket White has to set up new targets for Black to aim at) **4. h3 Bh5 5. g4 Bg6 6. Nf3 Kf6 7. Ke3 Bb1 8. a3 Be4 9. Nd2 Ke5** (not 9. ... Bg2 10. Kf2! Bxh3 11. Kg3! and the bishop is lost) **10. Kf2 Kf4 11. Nf1 Bb1** (to gain time) **12. Nd2 Bc2 13. Nf3 Bd1 14. Nd2 h6 15. Ke1 Ba4 16. Kf2 Bc2 17. Nf1 a5** (to block the queenside completely before the decisive break on the other wing) **18. Nd2 Bg6 19. Nf3 a4 20. Nd2 h5 21. gxh5 Bxh5** (now the h-pawn is White's Achilles' heel) **22. Nf1 Bf7 23. Ng3 Bg6 24. Nf1 Bf5** and White soon resigned.

If the superior side has a knight instead of a bishop, no such difficulties arise; the enemy bishop is deprived of mobility by having to guard the passed pawn. The defender can draw with a pawn down or put up a rousing good fight mainly in cases of blockade and weak pawn structure (the two are not completely independent).

As we have seen, an advantage of one pawn wins only because it can be increased to two pawns or a piece by attacking the enemy pawns with the king. If the position is blocked, this attack is out of the question, while if one's own pawns are weak, they must be guarded before venturing out to harass the opponent's.

The blockade is usually most effective when the inferior side has a knight. Nevertheless the superiority of the bishop is such that, unless the position is completely blockaded, an entry with the king can usually be forced.

No. 504, Winawer-Blackburne, Nuremberg 1883

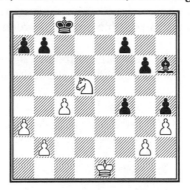

Black to play wins

In **No. 504**, offhand one would say that Black's majority of four vs. two on the kingside is counterbalanced by White's three vs. two on the queenside because the f-pawns are doubled, and therefore the game should be a draw. But with the long diagonal still at Black's disposal, he can win. **1. ... Kd7 2. Ke2 f5 3. Kf3 g5** (tying the king down) **4. Nb4 Bg7 5. Nd3 Kd6** (now the knight must not move) **6. b3 Bd4 7. Ke2 Be3 8. Kf3** (the threat was 8. ... g4+) **b6 9. b4 a6 10. a4 Bd4** (White's pawn moves are finally exhausted) **11. Ke2 Bc3 12. b5 a5 13. Kf2 Bd4+ 14. Kc2 Bg1! 15. Kf3 Be3!**

He has finally reached his goal. If the knight moves, a pawn on the queenside is lost, or if the king moves, the advance 15. ... g4 is conclusive) **16. g4** (desperation; if 16. Ke2 g4 17. Kf1 f3! 18. gxf3 gxh3 19. f4 Bd4 and the knight must move) **16. ... hxg3 17. Kg2 Bd2 18. c5+** (or 18. Kf3 g4+ 19. hxg4 fxg4+ 20. Kg2 Be3 21. Kf1 f3) **18. ... bxc5 19. b6 c4 20. Ne5 c3** (20. ... Kxe5! is also playable: 21. b7 Ke4 22. b8=Q f3+ 23. Kf1 g2+ 24. Kf2 Be3+ and mate next move) **21. Nc4+ Kc6 22. Na3 Kxb6** and White will soon have to lose his knight.

A similar case where it was very difficult to penetrate enemy lines is **No. 505** (Spielmann-Krejcik, Vienna 1930): **White king at g3, bishop at d3, pawns at a3, c2, c4, d5, h3; Black king at f6, knight at e5, pawns at a7, b7, c5, d6.** White to play wins. White's problem is how to get his king to the queenside, for a direct attempt by Kf2-e2-d2-c3-b3-a4 would be frustrated by ... Nxd3 and . ... Kg6-h5. Spielmann solved the problem as follows: **1. Kf4 a6 2. Be2 b6 3. h4 Nf7 4. h5 Nh6** (now White can make progress by successively stalemating the Black knight) **5. Bg4 Nf7 6. a4 Ne5 7. Be2 Nf7 8. Bd3 a5 9. Be2 Ne5** (if 9. ... Nh6 10. Bf1 Nf7 11. Bd3 Nh6 12. Bg6 Ng8 13. Bf5 Nh6 14. Be6) **10. h6 Ng6+ 11. Kg4 Ne5+ 12. Kh5 Nf7 13. h7 Kg7 14. Bd3 Kf6 15. Kg4 Ne5+ 16. Kf4 Nf7 17. Be2 Kg6 18. Bf3 Nh8 19. Bg4 Nf7 20. Be6 Nh8 21. Bd7! Kxh7 22. Kf5 Kg7 23. Be8** (to keep the knight tied down: the king-and-pawn ending is always won because White has an extra tempo) **23. ... Kf8 24. Bh5 Ke7 25. Kg5 Nf7+ 26. Bxf7 Kxf7 27. Kf5** and Black resigned.

The method of defeating a blockade is to maneuvering into a position where the opponent has no good moves: zugzwang. This is accomplished by advancing the king as far as possible and then stalemating the knight with the bishop.

Another type of difficulty that comes up often is weak or blocked pawns. No. 494 is an example. The pawns were so weak that Black could draw with best play.

No. 506, Balogh-Eliskases, Budapest 1934

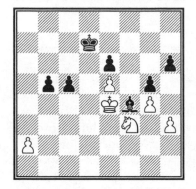

Black to play wins

Barring such extreme cases, a blocked position is annoying and requires technical ingenuity, but there should never be any doubt as to the ultimate outcome.

In **No. 506,** Black's passed pawn is so near the enemy king that it implies no real threat, his bishop is almost wholly ineffective, and his e-pawn is a potential target that makes it dangerous for his king to take any long trips. Nevertheless, he wins because of the possibilities on the queenside.

1. ... Kc6 2. Ne1 (pinning his hopes on passive defense; the more active 2. h4!? is met by 2. ... b4 3. h5 Kb5 4. Nh4!? c4! 5. Ng6 b3! 6. axb3 cxb3 7. Kd3 Kb4 8. Nxf4 gxf4 9. g5 f3 10. g6 f2 11. Ke2 f1=Q+! 12. Kxf1 b2 13. g7 b1=Q+) **2. ... b4** (not 2. ... c4 3. Nc2! Bd2 4. Nd4+ Kd7 and Black is nowhere) **3. Nd3 Bh2 4. Ne1** (4. Nb2 Kb5 5. Kd3? leaves the e-pawn en prise) **4. ... Kb5 5. Nf3 Bg3 6. Kd3 c4+ 7. Ke4 Bf2** (7. ... b3 8. axb3 cxb3 9. Kd3 Kc5 10. Kc3 Kd5 11. Kxb3 Ke4 is also good enough; if here 8. Nd4+ Ka4 9. axb3+ cxb3 10. Kd3 Bxe5 11. Nxe6 Ka3 is conclusive) **8. Nd2 c3 9. Nb3 Ka4** (this inroad is decisive) **10. Kd3 Ka3 11. Kc4 Kxa2 12. Kxb4 Kb2! 13. Nc1 Kxc1 14. Kxc3 Bg3 15. Kd4 Kd2** and resigns.

Endings with all the pawns on one side (four vs. three, or three vs. two) are not easy to judge. With three vs. two, if there is no passed pawn (e.g., f-, g-, h-pawns vs. g- and h-pawns), the game is surely a draw (see No. 484). With a passed pawn (e.g., e-, g-, h-pawns vs. g-, h-pawns), if the superior side has a knight he should win, but if he has a bishop he wins only if he can force a weakness in the enemy's pawn structure (No. 500). With four vs. three (e-, f-, g-, h-pawns vs. f-, g-, h-pawns), if the superior side has a knight he should usually win, since he can convert his e-pawn and f-pawn into an outside passed pawn by exchanging the enemy f-pawn. But with a bishop, although he has better prospects than with three vs. two, a draw will frequently result because of the bishop's inability to cover all squares.

2. Positional Advantage

All chess theory is based on the concept of mobility: one piece is stronger than another if it can cover more squares; one position is preferable to another if the pieces act together more harmoniously and do not get in one another's way. This consideration is the key to questions of positional advantage in general, but is especially applicable in the case of bishop vs. knight. A knight in the center covers eight squares; a bishop thirteen. It is only because the knight can cover squares that the bishop cannot reach that the discrepancy is not more marked.

We can distinguish four different types of superiority here, of which the first two are the most important: better bishop, better knight, better king position, better pawn position. By examining all these cases in detail we'll get a clearer picture of why the bishop is generally superior, even though the knight is quite often just as strong or stronger.

a) The Bishop Is Superior

It stands to reason that the bishop needs wide open spaces to show its talents: it can control h8 from c3, but if there are enemy pawns at g7, f6, and e5 this control is only potential and does him no good. Similarly, if its own pawns are at d4 and e5 the bishop is almost as useless as a pawn.

The first type of position where we can note the power of the bishop is one in which the pawns are balanced and unblocked. That is, there are as many Black pawns as White ones on the queenside (and similarly on the other wing) and these pawns are free to move. In such cases, the bishop may be exploited in one of three ways:

1. By forcing a direct entry with the king.

2. By creating weaknesses in the enemy pawn position, which will permit the king entry.

3. By capturing one or more pawns.

The first of these is the central idea, for a positional advantage is useless if it cannot be converted into a material advantage.

The third is also important but usually occurs only in special positions. The second is of course subsidiary to either the first or, less frequently, the third; it almost always goes hand in hand with them.

Even with the knight solidly entrenched in the center, the power of the bishop may make itself felt. The only conditions are that there should be pawns on both sides of the board and that they should be mobile.

No. 507, Stoltz-Kashdan, The Hague 1928

Black to play wins

In **No. 507,** the greater scope of the bishop is the reason Black's king cannot be prevented from attacking the pawns on either side. The first step is centralization: **1. ... Kf8 2. Kf1 Ke7 3. Ke2 Kd6 4. Kd3 Kd5** (the White king must be driven away from d3) **5. h4** (to avoid losing a pawn) **5. ... Bc8! 6. Nf3 Ba6+ 7. Kc3** (or 7. Ke3 Kc5 8. Ng5 Kb4 9. Nxf7, and the knight will soon give its life for the passed pawn) **7. ... h6 8. Nd4 g6** (first the pawns must be immunized against attack) **9. Nc2 Ke4** (at last! the first point is scored) **10. Ne3 f5 11. Kd2 f4 12. Ng4 h5 13. Nf6+ Kf5 14. Nd7** (he has little choice; if 14. Nd5 Bb7 15. Ne7+ Kf6 16. Ng8+ Kf7 17. Nh6+ Kg7 is decisive) **14. ... Bc8! 15. Nf8 g5 16. g3** (16. hxg5 Kxg5 costs the knight) **16. ... gxh4 17. gxh4 Kg4** (finally Black is ready to pluck the ripened fruit) **18. Ng6 Bf5 19. Ne7 Be6 20. b4 Kxh4 21. Kd3 Kg4 22. Ke4 h4 23. Nc6 Bf5+ 24. Kd5 f3!** (else Ne5+ followed by Nf3; now the pawn queens by force) **25. b5 h3 26. Nxa7 h2 27. b6 h1=Q 28. Nc6 Qb1 29. Kc5 Be4** and White resigned.

Often it is essential to weaken the enemy pawn position or open the game before the king can enter for the decisive break. **No. 508** is a simple case of this type.

No. 509, Chekhover-Lasker, Moscow 1935

White to play. Black wins

1. Kf1 (if 1. a4 Kb6 2. b4 Bd6 3. b5 Ka5 4. Nc3 Be5 is conclusive) **1. ... b5!** (Lasker conducts the ending with mathematical precision; after 1. ... Bb2 2. a4 Kb6 3. Ke1 Ka5 4. Kd2 Kb4 5. Kc2 it is doubtful whether Black can win) **2. Kc1 Bb2 3. a4 bxa4 4. bxa4 Kc6!!** (again admirably calculated; on 4. ... Kb6 5. Kd2 Ka5? 6. Kc2! Be5 7. f4 Bd6 8. Kb3, White's position is tenable) **5. Kd2 Kc5! 6. Nc3** (a sad necessity; if 6. Kc2 Bd4! 7. f3 Kc4! is conclusive: 8. Nxd4 Kxd4 9. Kb3 a5! and the ending is easy; or 8. Nc1 Be5 9. h3 Kb4 and wins a vital pawn) **6. ... Kb4 7. Nb5 a5!**

Now a pawn is lost without any compensation. The rest involves nothing new: **8. Nd6 Kxa4 9. Kc2** (if 9. Nxf7 Kb3 10. Nd8 a4 11. Nxe6 a3 12. Nc5+ Kc4 and the knight must be given up at once to stop the pawn) **9. ... Be5 10. Nxf7 Bxh2 11. Nd8 e5 12. Nc6 Bg1 13. f3 Bc5 14. Nb8 Kb5 15. g4 Be7 16. g5** (the knight was endangered) **16. ... fxg5 17. Nd7 Bd6 18. Nf6 Kc4!**, resigns. For after **19. Nxh7 Be7** White will lose both pawns and knight.

Even when the position is more complicated, this scheme of weakening the pawns to open a path for the king is feasible. While it would be an exaggeration to say that the bishop wins by force in all such balanced pawn positions, it is true that the slightest unfavorable deviation from the normal will usually cost the side with the knight the game.

No. 509, Reti-Rubinstein, Gothenburg 1920

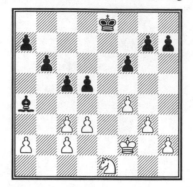

Black to play

Here the doubled pawns are fatal. **1. ... Ke7 2. Ke3 Ke6** (to weaken the kingside pawns; the threat is Kf5-g4-h3) **3. g4?** (3. d4! Kd6 [3. ... Kf5 4. Kf3 and 5. Ng2] 4. Kd2 Kc6 5. Ng2 Kb5 6. Ne3 saves the game) **3. ... Kd6** (to answer 4. Kd2 with 4. ... Bd7) **4. h3 g6 5. Kd2** (the changing of the guard; but the weak kingside pawns require the attention of the king) **5. ... Bd7 6. Nf3 Ke7!**

Threatening 7. ... h5! 8. gxh5 gxh5 9. h4 Ke6; if at once 6. ... h5? 7. g5! Bxh3 8. gxf6 Bf5 (not 8. ... Ke6 9. Ng5+) 9. Ne5 h4 10. Ke3 and should draw.

7. Ke3 h5! 8. Nh2 (or 8. g5 Bxh3, or 8. gxh5 gxh5 9. h4 Ke6 10. Ne1 Kf5 11. Kf3 d4!, etc.) **8. ... Kd6!**

The king has done a good day's work on the kingside and now shifts to the other wing. The weak c-pawn keeps White's king tied down.

9. Ke2

On 9. Kf3 Ba4! wins a pawn: 9. d4 is refuted by 9. ... Kc6 10. Kd2 Kb5 11. Kd3 Bc8 12. Kd2 Kc4 13. dxc5 bxc5 14. Nf1 d4 15. cxd4 Kxd4 16. Ne3 Ke4.

9. ... d4 (fixing the queenside pawns) **10. cxd4?**

This loses much more quickly than the alternative 10. c4!, when Black's best line is 10. ... hxg4 11. hxg4 (11. Nxg4 Ke6 12. Nh6 f5) 11. ... Ke7 (11. ... g5? 12. fxg5 fxg5 13. Kf2!! Ba4 [or 13. ... Ke5 14. Kg3 Ba4 15. Nf3+ Kf6 16. Ne1, =] 14. Nf3 Bxc2 15. Ke2!!, =) 12. Kd2 g5 13. f5 (13. fxg5 fxg5 14. Ke2 Kf6! 15. Kd2 Ke5 and wins. Or 15. Kf2 Ba4) 13. ... Kd6 14. Nf3 Bc6 15. Ke2 a6 16. Kf2 Bxf3 17. Kxf3 b5!! and the king-and-pawn ending is won: 18. Ke4 Kc6 19. Kf3 Kd7! 20. Ke4 Kd6 21. Kf3 Ke5 22. cxb5 (22. Kg3 bxc4 23. dxc4 d3! 24. cxd3 Kd4, or 22. a3 Kd6 23. Ke4 Kc6 24. Kf3 Kd7!, etc., as above.) 22. ... axb5 23. a3 Kd5 24. Kg3 c4 25. Kf3 c3! 26. Kg3 Kc5 27. Kf3 b4 28. axb4+ Kxb4 29. Ke4 Ka3 30. Kxd4 Kb2 31. Ke4 Kxc2 32. d4 Kb2 33. d5 c2 and gets there just in time.

10. ... cxd4 11. Kd2 (he must do something against the march of the Black king to the queenside; if 11. gxh5 gxh5 12. h4 Kc5 13. Nf3 Bg4 14. Kf2 Bxf3 15. Kxf3 f5! decides) **11. ... hxg4 12. hxg4** (again 12. Nxg4 Bxg4 leads to a lost pawn ending) **12. ... Bc6 13. Ke2** (if 13. c3 dxc3+ 14. Kxc3 Bg2! and the knight is stalemated) **13. ... Bd5 14. a3 b5** (in effect, Black has a pawn majority on the queenside and by advancing them will secure an outside passed pawn) **15. Nf1 a5 16. Nd2 a4! 17. Ne4+** (desperation; if 17. Nb1 Be6! 18. Kf3 Ba2! 19. Nd2 b4! 20. axb4 a3 and the pawn can no longer be stopped) **17. ... Bxe4 18. dxe4 b4! 19. Kd2** (19. axb4 a3 and the pawn queens) **19. ... bxa3 20. Kc1 g5,** White resigned, for after **21. fxg5 fxg5 22. Kb1** both **22. ... Ke5** and **22. ... Kc5** are sufficient for Black.

Putting all your pawns on your bishop's color is a serious positional handicap (because your own pieces then obstruct one another); the opponent should place them on that color only if he has the initiative and if they are not subject to attack. We have seen several examples (Nos. 492 and 509) where exposed pawns enhance the value of the bishop. In No. 509 White's pieces were tied down to the defense of the pawn, which made possible a decision on another part of the board. Sometimes this situation is so bad that a pawn is lost by force.

No. 510, Maroczy-Teichmann, Nuremberg 1896

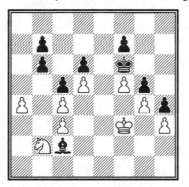

Black to play wins

In **No. 510** Black can win a pawn in various ways, but he must make sure that the resulting ending will not be drawn because of his weak b-pawns. For instance, 1. ... Ke5 2. Ke3 Be4 3. Nd1 Bg2 4. Nf2 Bf1, but then White holds the game by 5. Ne4! Bxc4 (or 5. ... f6 6. Nd2 Bg2 7. Nf3+!) 6. Nxg5 Bxd5 7. Nf3+!! and the king-and-pawn ending is drawn.

But in view of the fact that White's knight is stalemated and six of his seven pawns are potential targets, White's position is untenable in the long run.

1. ... Ke7 2. Ke3 Kd7 (going to the queenside) **3. Kf3** (if 3. Kd2 Be4 4. Nd3 Bg2 5. Nf2 Bf1 6. Ne4 Bxh3 7. Nxg5 Bxg4 8. Nxf7 Bxf5 and wins) **3. ... Kc7 4. Ke3 Kb8 5. Kf3**

If 5. Kd2 Be4 6. Nd3 Bg2 7. Nf2 Bf1 8. Ne4 Bxh3 9. Nxg5 Bxg4, and the king must lose valuable time to get back to the h-pawn, so Black comes out a clear pawn ahead: 10. Ke3 Bxf5 11. Nxf7 Kc7, etc., or here 9. Nxd6 f6! 10. Ne4 Bxg4 11. Nxf6 Bxf5, and the two connected passed pawns decide.

5. ... Ka7 6. Ke3 Ka6 7. Kd2

If 7. f6 Ka5 8. Kf3 Bxa4 9. Nxa4 Kxa4 10. Ke4 Kb3 11. Kf5 Kxc3 12. Kxg5 b5! 13. cxb5 c4 14. Kh6 Kd4 15. Kg7 c3 16. Kxf7 c2 17. Kg7 c1=Q 18. f7 Qg5+ and wins.

7. ... Be4 8. Nd1 Ka5, and White's pawns will fall like ripe apples: **9. Nf2 Bg2 10. Ke3 Kxa4 11. Kd2 Kb3 12. Kd3 Bf1+ 13. Ke3 Kxc4 14. Ne4 Bxh3 15. Nxd6+ Kxd5 16. Nxf7 Bxg4 17. Nxg5 Bxf5,** and Black is three pawns ahead.

Even if the defender just manages to hold all his material in positions like this with exposed pawns, he is at a definite disadvantage because of his constricted pieces.

When the superior side has no tempo with which to exploit his control of more terrain, a sacrifice will sometimes do the trick. Remember that it is harder for a knight to stop pawns than it is for a bishop, and that a knight is especially weak against a passed rook-pawn.

This fact is utilized in **No. 511** (Marco and Faehndrich vs. Charousek and Schlechter, Vienna 1897): **White king at d2, knight at e2, pawns at a3, b3, e4, f3, g3, g2; Black king at d6, bishop at c6, pawns at a5, b6, e5, f6, g6, h5.** Black won: **1. ... Kc5 2. Kc3 Bb5 3. Nc1 Bf1 4. Nd3+ Kb5! 5. Ne1 g5 6. f4 gxf4 7. gxf4 h4 8. fxe5 fxe5 9. Nf3** (else the sacrifice 9. ... Bxg2 anyway: 9. Kd2 Bxg2 10. Nxg2 h3, and the pawn queens) **9. ... Bxg2 10. Nxe5 h3 11. Ng4 Bxe4 12. Kd4 Bc2** and the rest is simple: **13. Kc3 Bf5 14. Nh2 Kc5 15. Kd2 Kd4 16. Nf1 Be6,** White resigned.

If the superiority of the bishop is manifest in a balanced pawn position, it is even more so when the pawns are not in equilibrium; i.e., when there is a pawn majority on one side. The bishop can support his potential passed pawn at a distance, which means that he can both support the advance of his own pawns and prevent the march of his opponent's.

Even in positions where the material is greatly reduced, this power of the bishop to combine offense and defense is evident.

No. 512, Dubois-Steinitz, match 1862

White to play. Black wins

In **No. 512,** the bishop stops the White kingside pawns while keeping an eye on the square c1, where the c-pawn will queen, and meanwhile the knight will be exhausted by the task of watching the c-pawn. **1. Nd4+ Kb2 2. g6 Bh6 3. h4 a5 4. h5 a4 5. Nc2** (now we see the problem: the knight cannot come to the aid of his pawns) **5. ... a3 6. Nd4 a2 7. Nc2** (hoping for 7. ... a1=Q+?? 8. Nxa1 Kxa1 9. Kc2 Bg7 10. h6! =) **7. ... Bg7!!** (now White is in zugzwang) **8. Na1 Kxa1 9. Kc2 Bh6 10. g7 Bxg7 11. Kc1 c2!!** (the coup de grace) **12. Kxc2 Bh6,** and White resigned since he can no longer keep the Black king from coming out of the corner.

Clearly, the more material there is, the easier it is to make the bishop's superiority count. In No. 512, if there were more pawns White would not have had the slightest chance of confining Black's king to the corner. In general, where both sides have passed pawns (or potential passed pawns) and there are five or six pawns apiece, the bishop is clearly better.

No. 513 Golombek-Keres, Margate 1939

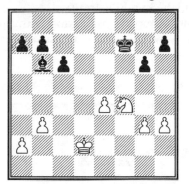

Black wins

No. 513 may be considered typical. The bishop in conjunction with the pawn majority on the queenside make it possible for the Black king to force an entry. The winning process is exactly the same as though Black were a pawn ahead, for since the e-pawn is almost automatically blocked, Black can ignore it and mobilize his own pawn majority.

Keres continued **1. ... Bf2!** (first step: weaken the enemy pawns) **2. g4** (or 2. Nc2 Kf6 3. Kd3 Ke5 and both White's pieces are tied down) **2. ... Kf6 3. Ke2 Bd4 4. Kf3** (hoping to hold the other wing with his knight. If 4. Kd3 Bb6 5. a4 Ke5 6. Ne2 a5 and the Black king enters via f4) **4. ... a5 5. g5+ Ke5** (not 5. ... Kxg5? 6. Ne6+) **6. Nd3+ Kd6 7. h4 b5 8. Ne1** (on king moves, 8. ... c5-c4 will force the knight away) **8. ... Bc5 9. Nd3 Bb6 10. Nf4 Bd4 11. Nd3 c5**

Now White is faced by exactly the same dilemma as in the case where he is a pawn down: either he stops the pawn with the king and loses the kingside pawns, or he stops the pawn with his knight and loses that piece or transposes into a lost king-and-pawn ending. He chooses the latter.

12. Nf4 (or 12. Ke2 c4 13. bxc4 bxc4 14. Nf4 Ke5 15. Nd5 Kxe4 16. Nf6+ Kf5 17. Nxh7 Bg7! 18. Kd2 Kg4 19. Nf6+ Kxh4 20. Ne4 Kg4 21. Ke3 Be5, and the extra pawn is decisive) **12. ... c4 13. bxc4 bxc4 14. Nd5 Ke5 15. Nf6 h5 16. Nd5 c3 17. Nf4 c2 18. Nd3+ Kd6 19. Ke2 Bb2!!** and White resigned, for after **20. Kd2 c1=Q+ 21. Nxc1 Bxc1+ 22. Kxc1 Ke5 23. Kb2 Kxe4 24. Ka3 Kf4 25. Ka4 Kg4 26. Kxa5 Kxh4 27. Kb5 Kxg5 28. a4 h4,** Black queens first.

If in addition to the unbalanced pawn structure the defender has further weaknesses, the game is as good as lost. For example, **No. 514** (Jeney-Benko, Budapest 1950): **White king at d3, knight at e2, pawns at a3 b3, c4, f4, g3, h3; Black king at c5, bishop at e1, pawns at a5, b6, e6, f5, f7, h5.** Black to play. Black has a substantial advantage, but how to proceed? 1. ... f6 2. Nd4 Kd6 3. Ke3 Bxg3 4. b4 and c5 gives White counterplay. But if White is to move he must yield, so Black tries triangulation: **1. ... Kc6! 2. Ke3 Kd6 3. Nd4** (if 3. Kd3 Kc5 and now with White on move, 4. Ke3 f6 5. Nd4 Bf2+, etc.) **3. ... Bxg3 4. b4 Be1 5. Ke2 Bh4 6. Nb5+ Kd7 7. Kd3 axb4 8. axb4 Bg3 9. Ke3 Be1 10. c5 Bxb4 11. cxb6 Kc6 12. Nc7 Bc5+ 13. Kf3 Bxb6,** White resigned, since after 14. Ne8 Bd4 or 14. Na6 Ba5 the knight is trapped.

In No. 514 we saw the bishop in conjunction with a passed pawn (or potential passed pawn) that is on the outside because of the relative positions of the kings.

No. 515, Rubinstein-Johner, Carlsbad 1929

White wins

When the passed pawn is on the rook or knight file, so that it is outside no matter where the kings are, the speedier maneuverability and greater range of the bishop becomes even more effective.

We see this in **No. 515**, where the bishop decides despite the unfavorably blocked position of White's pawns. Rubinstein won as follows:

1. a4

The first step is to advance the a-pawn as far as feasible in order to constrict the Black pieces. The direct attempt 1. Kc5 is refuted by 1. ... Nd7+.

1. ... Nd7 2. a5 h6 3. Bd3 Kb7 4. g4!!

He can make no further progress on the queenside and must first weaken the other wing. The test threatens to secure a decisive passed pawn by 4. h4, h5, and g5!

4. ... Kc7 5. h4 Nf8 6. Bf1 Nd7 7. Bh3!! Nf8 8. h5! f6

The point of White's maneuvering has become clear: he has made this weakening unavoidable. For if 8. ... Nd7 9. g5! hxg5 10. h6 Nf8 11. Bg4! Nh7 12. Bh5 f6 13. Bf7! Nf8 14. Bxe6! Ng6 15. h7 Nh8 16. Bf5 Nf7 17. Bg6 Nh8 18. Bh5, and now the entry of the White king is conclusive, while if 8. ... Nh7 9. Kc5 Ng5 10. Bg2 Nh7 11. a6! Nf8 12. g5!! Nd7+ 13. Kb4 Kb6 14. g6 fxg6 15. hxg6 h5 16. g7 Nf6 17. Bh3 h4 18. Bxe6 Kxa6 19. Kc5 with a simple win.

Now the knight is further hampered by the necessity of defending the f-pawn, and this straw is too much for his already overburdened back.

9. Bf1 Nd7 10. Bc4 Nf8 11. Bb3 Nh7! 12. Kc5!! (not 12. Bxe6 Ng5! followed by Nxf3) **12. ... Nf8 13. Ba2 Nd7+ 14. Kb4 Nf8 15. a6! Kb6 16. a7 Kxa7 17. Kc5 Kb7** (just too late) **18. Kd6** (decisive) **18. ... Kb6 19. Ke7 Nh7 20. Bxe6 Kc7** (or 20. ... Ng5 21. Bb3 Nxf3 22. Kxf6 Kc5 23. Kg6 Kd4 24. Kxh6 Kxe4 25. g5 and wins. If here 22. ... Nh2 23. Bd1! is sufficient) **21. Bc4!** (not 21. Bf5? Ng5 22. Kxf6 Kd6! 23. Kg6 c5!! and the bishop cannot get back) **21. ... Ng5 22. Kxf6 Kd6 23. Kg6 Ke7,** Black resigned. The conclusion might have been 24. Kxh6 Nxf3 25. g5, etc., or 24. Kxh6 Kf6 25. f4 Nxe4 26. g5+ Kf5 27. Bd3! Kxf4 28. Bxe4, etc.

The power of a bishop together with passed pawns is so great that sometimes it can even compensate for the loss of a pawn. In **No. 516** (Lasker-Lipke, Breslau 1889): **White king at g4, bishop at d2, pawns at b2, f4, g3, h4; Black king at d7, knight at d5, pawns at a6, b7, c7, d6, h6.** Black to play. White wins. The bishop can easily hold the queenside pawns as long as necessary, while the knight cannot effectively blockade the kingside pawns. Lasker wound up as follows: **1. ... Nf6+ 2. Kf5 Ke7 3. g4 d5 4. g5 hxg5 5. fxg5** (keeping the passed pawns as far outside as possible) **5. ... Nd7** (or 5. ... Ne4 6. Bc1 Nc5 7. h5 Nb3 8. Bf4 d4 9. h6 Kf7 10. g6+) **6. g6 Kf8 7. h5 d4 8. h6 Kg8 9. h7+ Kh8 10. Ke6 Nf8+ 11. Kf7,** and Black resigned.

One of the most important conclusions we can draw from this discussion is that the bishop is at its best with pawns on both sides of the board, preferably as far apart as possible.

The third kind of position where the bishop is superior is when all the pawns are on one side; the only winning chance for the bishop, even when a pawn ahead, is based on stalemating the knight. We have already seen examples of this with pawns on both sides, when the object of the stalemate was to divert the enemy king and effect an entry with one's own. But when such an entry is pointless because there are no pawns to be captured, the stalemate must result in capture of the knight. It is rather surprising to find that when the knight strays to the edge of the board (often as a result of exchanges), the danger of its being lost is quite real.

No. 517 is a classic illustration. The knight can get out only at the cost of a lost king-and-pawn ending.

No. 517, Marshall-Nimzovich, Berlin 1928

Black to play wins

After **1. ... Kd5!** there are three main variations:

a) **2. Nd8 Kd6 3. Nb7+ Kc6!! 4. Na5+ Kd5!! 5. Nxc4** (for 5. Nb7 see the next variation) **5. ... Kxc4 6. Kf1** (or 6. f3 e3! 7. Kf1 Kd3 8. Ke1 f5 9. g4 f4! 10. Kd1 e2+ 11. Ke1 Ke3 12. g3 fxg3 and mates in two) **6. ... Kd3 7. Ke1 h5 8. Kd1 e3!! 9. fxe3** (if 9. f3 f5! 10. f4 e2+ 11. Ke1 Ke3, etc.) **9. ... Kxe3 10. Ke1 Ke4 11. Ke2 Kf5 12. Kf3 Kg5 13. Ke3 Kg4 14. Kf2 f6 15. Kf1 Kxg3 16. Kg1 h4 17. Kf1 h3 18. Kg1! Kg4 19. gxh3+ Kxh3 20. Kf2 Kg4,** and wins because his king is two squares in front of the pawn, so he has the opposition;

b) **2. Nd8 Kd6 3. Nb7+ Kc6! 4. Na5+ Kd5 5. Kh2** (or 5. Nb7 Ba2! 6. Nd8 Kd6 7. Nb7+ Kc6 8. Na5+ Kb6, and the knight is lost) **5. ... Ba2! 6. Kh3 Kc5 7. Nb7+ Kc6! 8. Na5+ Kb6,** and again the knight has no escape;

c) **2. Kh2** (the game continuation) **2. ... Ba2! 3. g4 f6!** (the simplest) **4. Kg3 Kc6 5. Na5+ Kb6 6. Kf4 Kxa5 7. Kxe4** (if instead 7. Kf5 Kb4! 8. Kxf6 Kc3 9. g5 hxg5 10. Kxg5 Kd2 11. Kf4 Bb1! 12. g4 Ke2 13. Kg3 Ba2! 14. g5 Bf7 15. Kg2 Bg6 16. Kg1 Kf3 17. Kf1 Kf4 18. Ke2 Bh5+ and wins) **7. ... Be6! 8. Kf4 Kb4 9. Kg3 Kc5 10. Kh4 Bf7! 11. f4! Kd6 12. g5 hxg5+ 13. fxg5 f5 14. g6! Be6! 15. Kg5 Ke5 16. Kh6 Kf6! 17. g3 Bd7 18. Kh5 Kg7** (simpler is 18. ... Be8) **19. Kg5 Be6 20. Kh5 Bc8! 21. Kg5 Bd7 22. Kh5 Kf6! 23. Kh6 Be8! 24. g7 Bf7!** and White resigned, for after **25. Kh7 Kg5 26. g8=Q+ Bxg8+ 27. Kxg8 Kg4** he cannot catch the f-pawn.

The complete stalemate of the knight without the help of pawns occurs only when the knight is on the edge of the board and the bishop is in or near the center; e.g., knight at d1, bishop at d4, or knight at a1, bishop at d1. When this happens, the game is naturally untenable for the knight's side unless he can free his knight or exchange enough pawns.

But such a stalemate may win even when each side has only one pawn, as in **No. 518** (Berger-Chigorin, Barmen 1905): **White king at d6, bishop at f4, pawn at c5; Black king at f7, knight at h5, pawn at c6.** White to play won by **1. Be5! Ke8 2. Kxc6 Ke7 3. Kb7 Ke6** (too late) **4. c6 Kxe5 5. c7** and wins (Compare No. 452).

However, with one pawn the win is always uncertain. In **No. 519: White king at e2, knight at h8, pawn at h2; Black king at e8, bishop at c2, pawn at h7.** White to play and draw. **1. h4! h5** (if 1. ... Kf8 2. h5 and Ng6, =) **2. Kd2 Bb1 3. Ke3 Ke7 4. Kf4 Kf6 5. Nf7! Kxf7 6. Kg5 Bg6 7. Kh6 Kf6** stalemate.

To sum up: The bishop is better than the knight when the pawns are not blocked because it then controls more terrain. This advantage is exploited by forcing the enemy king to one side and penetrating to a group of pawns with one's own king. The bishop is most effective when there are pawns on both sides of the board. In an unbalanced pawn position, the superiority of the bishop is more marked than in a balanced one. Above all, one should avoid placing one's pawns on the same color as one's bishop.

b) The Knight Is Superior

The type of position occurs, as we have seen, when the pawns are fixed (immobile) on the color of the bishop. This solidification results in a loss of mobility for the bishop, especially when it is blocked by its own pawns, which must be defended while the knight hops about as carefree as ever. Remember that although the bishop is handicapped when the opponent's pawns are on the same color, this is usually not serious, but to have its own pawns fixed on the same color is usually disastrous. Other illustrations of this are found in Chapter IV (Bishop endings), Parts III B, IV B (4).

The manner in which the knight makes use of this kind of advantage (bad pawn position, bad bishop) may be deduced from our general principles. A positional superiority must be converted into a gain of material. Normally, this is done by attacking a group of pawns with the king. To break through with the king, both enemy pieces (king and bishop) must be diverted either by checks or by a direct attack on pawns. Sometimes the pawns are so weak that they cannot be defended even when threatened only by the knight.

This leads us to a threefold classification of the types of positional advantage that a knight may enjoy against a bishop:

1. A weak color complex (opposite to the bishop), which makes it impossible to put up any effective barrier to the march of the enemy king.

2. The pawns are subject to direct attack by the knight. This immobilizes the bishop and again facilitates the entry of the king.

3. The pawns are weak, but not because they are on the same color as the bishop but because they are doubled or isolated. Since the knight can reach all squares, this means that the pawns may be attacked by two pieces (king and knight) but defended only by one (the king). Loss of material cannot be postponed for long.

The first two almost always go together, the chief difference is that in the first case the bishop has much more scope.

b1) Weak Color Complexes

The bishop can cover only half the squares on the board; the other half must be taken care of by the pawns and the king. But when the pawns are all on

the same color squares as the bishop, the other squares are governed by whoever is able to govern them. In such cases we speak of a *weak color complex*.

No. 520, Zubarev-Alexandrov, Moscow 1915

White to play wins

No. 520 illustrates all the drawbacks of such a pawn configuration. White
can get his king to c5, and the best Black can do is oppose it at c7. The next
step is to force the Black king out of the way. This can be done only by checking the king or stalemating the bishop. The first is not feasible, for all the
squares from which the knight could check are guarded. So we must get the
bishop to a position where it has no good moves. This is accomplished by
attacking two pawns on light squares, both of which must be defended by
the bishop, which will then be unable to leave its post. Finally, a tempo move
with a pawn (there are at least four extra tempo moves on the queenside) and
Black will have to give way. The conclusion capture of pawns and exploitation of one or more passed pawns is already familiar.

With this general outline in mind, the game continuation is naturally broken up into six phases.

i) Advance the king as far as it can go. **1. Kf2 Ke7** (it would be even worse for
Black to go to the kingside, since it gets nowhere there and will then not be
able to keep the White king out; e.g., 1. ... Kf7 2. Ke2! Kg6 3. Ne3! Kg5 4. g3!
h5 5. Kd3! h4 6. Kd4!, etc.) **2. Ke3 Kd8 3. Kd4 Kc7 4. Kc5 Bc8.**

The next step is to attack two pawns, both of which must be defended by
the bishop. There are no such pawns available at the moment, so they must
be created. We know that they must be on light squares and that they must
be immobile. The knight must therefore start snooping around the kingside,
which brings us to the second phase.

*ii) Weaken the enemy pawns by fixing as many as possible on the color of the
bishop.* **5. Nb4 Bb7** (forced: if 5. ... a5 6. Nc2 Bd7 7. a3 Be8 8. Nd4, and wins a
pawn) **6. g3** (Black was threatening to get some air by 6. ... d4 and 7. ... Bxg2)
6. ... Bc8 7. Nd3 Bd7 8. Nf4 g6 (he has little choice; if 8. ... Bc8 9. Nh5 g6 10.
Nf6 h5 11. h4 Bb7 12. Ne8+ Kd7 13. Nd6 is immediately conclusive) **9. Nh3!**

h6 (else 10. Ng5 h6 11. Nf7 h5 12. h4, etc.) **10. Nf4 g5 11. Nh5 Be8 12. Nf6 Bf7** (if 12. ... Bc6 13. h4 gxh4 14. gxh4 Bb7 15. Ng8 h5 16. Nf6, and wins a pawn) **13. Ng4!** (he wants the pawns on light squares) **13. ... h5 14. Ne3** (good enough, but 14. Nf2 followed by Nh3 was simpler) **14. ... Bg6** (Black's inability to undertake any counteraction is striking; if 14. ... h4 15. gxh4 gxh4 16. Ng2, winning a pawn) **15. h4!** (finally fixing the pawns) **15. ... gxh4** (15. ... g4 16. Ng2 is even worse) **16. gxh4 Be4**. Now that the situation on the kingside has been cleared up, we come to the third phase:

iii) Attack two pawns with the knight, both of which must be defended by the bishop. The bishop will thus be immobilized. Here the two pawns are the e-pawn and the h-pawn, so the knight must get to either f4 or g7. The most practical, of course, is f4. **17. Nf1 Bf3** (if 17. ... Bg6 18. Ng3 Bf7 19. Ne2-f4) **18. Nd2 Be2** (or 18. ... Bd1 19. a3 Be2 20. Nb3 Bf3 21. Nd4 Bg4 22. b3 Bh3 23. Ne2, etc.) **19. Nb3 Bg4 20. Nd4 Bh3 21. Ne2 Bf5 22. Nf4 Bg4**. Now the bishop is chained to its post, and any tempo will give Black the choice of losing a pawn on the kingside or the queenside.

iv) Now that the bishop is immobilized, make any pawn tempo. This will force either the bishop or the king to play with consequent loss of material. **23. b4 Kd7**.

v) Gain of material with either the king or the knight (depending on Black's choice). **24. Kb6 Bf3 25. Kxa6 Kc6 26. Nxe6**. Here Black resigned. The final stage would be:

vi. Advance the passed pawns until a piece is won.

The *double attack* is the key to the ending in weak color complexes. Where there are no reserve pawn moves a tempo must be gained by the king; if this is not possible the defender will be able to hold the game.

Where the weak color complex is accompanied by an unfavorable pawn position (isolated, doubled, blocked pawns), the win is practically certain. A common case is that of the isolated d-pawn. Such an isolated pawn is not in itself fatal (see No. 527) but in conjunction with another weakness it is too much for one poor chess player.

A weak color complex is often accompanied by a virtual or qualitative pawn minority on one side—all the pawns, being on one color, are blocked and a majority is useless. In that event, the opponent has a real or potential outside passed pawn with which to force the win.

This is illustrated in **No. 521**, where White has three-to-two on the queenside, while the Black d-pawn is blocked and practically worthless.

No. 521, Thomas-Landau, Amsterdam 1937

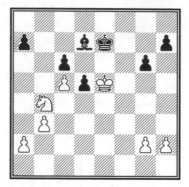

White to play wins

White forced the entry of his king as follows: **1. Nc2 Be8 2. b4 Bd7 3. Nd4** (an ideal position for the knight) **3. ... Be8 4. a4 a6 5. a5!!** (an unusual move; he does not wish to exchange the a-pawn) **5. ... Bd7 6. b5 cxb5** (if 6. ... axb5 7. a6 Bc8 8. Nxc6+ Kd7 9. Kxd5) **7. Kxd5**. White is now one step nearer his goal. The Black b-pawn is, like its erstwhile colleague on the d-file, blocked and worthless **7. ... Be8 8. Nc2 Bd7 9. Nb4 Bc8 10. Kc6 Kd8 11. Kd6! Bb7 12. c6 Bc8 13. c7+ Ke8 14. Kc6 Kf7 15. Kb6 Ke7 16. Nxa6 Kd6 17. Nb4** and Black gave up.

Even with White's bishop free to roam, it is always kept in check by its weak pawns and the threat of a king entry. An example where a potential passed pawn decides in such a case is **No. 522** (Michell -v. Scheltinga, Amsterdam 1937): **White king at e2, bishop at f8, pawns at a2, c3, e3, f3, h2; Black king at e6, knight at e5, pawns at a6, c7, f5, g5, h7**. Black to play wins. **1. ... g4! 2. fxg4** (forced: if 2. f4 Nf3 3. h3 Ng1+) **2. ... fxg4 3. Bh6 Kd5 4. Kf2 Ke4 5. Kg3 c5!** (to fix the c-pawn) **6. Bf8 c4 7. Bc5 Kf5 8. Bd4 Nf3 9. h3 h5 10. hxg4+ hxg4 11. Bb6 Ng5 12. Bd4 Ne4+ 13. Kh4 Nf2!!** (prepares the decisive king break) **14. Kg3 Nd1 15. a3 Ke4! 16. Kxg4 Nxe3+ 17. Kg5 Nc2! 18. Bc5 Kd3 19. Kf5 Kxc3 20. Ke4 Kb3 21. Kd5 c3 22. Ke4 Nxa3 23. Kd3 Nc4 24. Bf8 a5 25. Bg7 Nb2+ 26. Ke2 a4**, and White gave up the hopeless struggle. Note that in No. 522 White's passed center pawn was useless.

b2. The Bad Bishop

We have seen examples of this in the pure bishop endings (see Nos. 379 and 440). Against a knight, a bad bishop – one with all or most of its pawns on the same color – is even worse. The winning idea is the same as that in weak color complexes: the two, as already mentioned, go hand in hand. The main difference is that in these examples the bishop is much worse off.

No. 523, Henneberger-Nimzovich, Winterthus 1931

Black to play wins

Here is the knight at its best. With a bishop, Black would not be able to exploit his advantage. The win is achieved by stalemating the bishop and then forcing an entry with the king. The first step then is to cramp the bishop by compelling it to defend the c-pawn and g-pawn.

1. ... Ne4 2. Ke2 Kd5 3. Ke3.

What next? Black can stalemate the bishop completely only by getting his knight to b1. When he gets there, if the White bishop is at d2, White to play can draw by Be1, a3, Bd2, for after the exchange of pieces Black does not have the opposition. He must therefore manage to get his knight to b1 only when the bishop is at e1, for then Bd2 can be met by ... Nxd2, Kxd2, Ke4, Ke2, a3!, securing the opposition. So he must lose a move with his king.

3. ... Kd6! 4. Ke2 Kc6 5. Ke3 Kd5 6. Ke2 (now the knight maneuver can begin) **6. ... Nd6 7. Ke3 Nb5 8. Bd2 Na3 9. Bc1** (as indicated above, if 9. Be1 Nb1 10. Bd2 Nxd2 decides, or simply 9. ...Nc2+, with a transposition) **9. ... Nb1 10. Bb2 a3 11. Ba1**

Now the bishop has no moves at all and Black only needs to lose a tempo to get in with his king. Of course, the knight is lost if White goes after it, but as the sequel shows, Nimzovich has calculated that he will then win on the kingside.

11. ... Kd6 12. Ke2 Kc6 13. Kd1 (13. Ke3 Kd5 14. Kf2! Nd2! 15. Kg2 Ke4 or 15. Ke2 Ne4 is much worse) **13. ... Kd5 14. Kc2 Ke4 15. Kxb1 Kf3 16. Bb2! axb2!!** (not 16. ... Kxg3 17. Bxa3 Kf3 18. Bc5! g3 19. a4 g2 20. d5!, and White wins) **17. a4 Kxg3 18. a5 Kh2 19. a6 g3 20. a7 g2 21. a8=Q g1=Q+ 22. Kxb2 Qg2+!!** (obviously Nimzovich has foreseen this) **23. Qxg2+ Kxg2 24. Ka3 Kf3 25. Kb4 Kxf4 26. Kxc4 Ke3 27. d5 exd5+ 28. Kxd5 f4,** and White resigned since his pawn will be only on the sixth when White queens. A masterful example of precise calculation.

The bishop hemmed in by the enemy pawns is almost as bad. The only difference is that the possibility of a sacrifice comes up, though such a threat is rarely serious. For example, **No. 524** (Riemann-Blackburne, Hamburg 1885):

White king at f2, bishop at c1, pawns at a2, c3, d4, f3, g4, h4; Black king at f6, knight at c4, pawns at a7, b7, d5, f4, g5, h6. Black to play wins. **1. ... a5 2. h5** (Clearly, Black can win only by playing his king to the queenside; in that event, White wants to have the threat of 2. Bxf4 followed by g5 in reserve) **2. ... Ke6 3. Ke2 Kd7 4. Kd3 Kc6 5. Kc2 Kb5 6. Kb3** (the "threat" turns out to be a bluff; if 6. Bxf4 gxf4 7. g5 hxg5 8. h6 Nd6 9. h7 Nf7) **6. ... Kb6!** (intending to lose a move) **7. Kc2 Kc6! 8. Kb3 Kb5 9. a4+** (forced) **9. ... Kc6 10. Kc2 b5** (setting up an outside passed pawn) **11. axb5+ Kxb5 12. Kb3 Kb6!** (another triangulation maneuver to lose a move) **13. Ka4 Ka6 14. Kb3 Kb5 15. Kc2 Ka4 16. Kb1 Kb3** and White cannot save his bishop: if **17. Ka1 Kc2** (of course 17. ... Kxc3 also wins without any trouble).

In this example, the winning method consisted of taking advantage of the knight's blockade of the c-pawn and d-pawn by setting up an outside passed pawn. The bishop's inability to undertake any counteraction and the power of the knight to constrict both the bishop and the king were equally striking.

A bishop is a bad defensive piece, and when it is glued to the defense of a pawn it is just as badly off as when it is blocked by its own or enemy pawns. In **No. 525** (Charousek-Marco, Nuremberg 1896): **White king at e3, bishop at g4, pawns at a3, b3, c4, e4, f5, h3; Black king at c6, knight at g5, pawns at a7, b6, c5, e5, f6, h4.** Black to play wins. The bishop is chained to the h-pawn while the knight is able to attack two points. As a result, Black can do as he pleases with his king, while White can only mark time. The simplest win is **1. ... a6 2. Kd3** (if 2. a4 b5 3. cxb5+ axb5 4. axb5+ Kxb5 5. Be2+ Kb4) **2. ... b5 3. cxb5+** (or 3. Ke3 bxc4 4. bxc4 Kb6 5. Kd3 Ka5, etc.) **3. ... axb5 4. Ke3 c4 5. bxc4 bxc4 6. a4 Kc5 7. a5 Kb5 8. Be2 Nxh3 9. Bxc4+ Kxa5 10. Bf1 Nf4,** and the pawn plus is sufficient.

We see then that a bishop's mobility may be limited either by his own pawns or the enemy's. The former is worse because there is no resource available to break out of the straitjacket. It is exploited by attacking the enemy pawns from an unassailable position and then coming in with the king. With the bishop stalemated, the opponent is virtually a piece ahead.

Where the bishop is blocked by enemy pawns, the possibility of a sacrifice must be taken into account. The operating procedure is essentially the same as that in the first case: proper manipulation of the king, setting up an outside passed pawn, and then continuing in the routine manner with such a pawn; i.e., decoying the enemy king and bringing about a decision on the other wing.

Remember that the knight is effective against a bishop only if it is able to set up a double attack; unlike the opposite case, where a simple threat is too easily parried. As a result, the side with the knight is interested in fixing the pawns on the color of the bishop in order to set up additional targets. This theoretical point is the clue to the defense in a good many endings.

No. 526, Alekhine-Yates, Hastings 1925-26

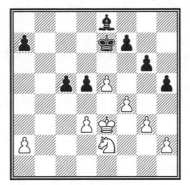

White to play

White can win only by fixing a sufficient number of Black pawns on squares where they can be threatened.

1. d4! c4

Not 1. ... cxd4+ 2. Kxd4 Ke6 when we have an isolated d-pawn in conjunction with a weak color complex. The win is then accomplished by 3. Nc3 Bc6 4. Kc5 Bb7 5. Nb5 a6 6. Nd4+, etc.

2. f5!

Now Black must make a crucial decision: should he play ... gxf5 or ... g5? It is by no means easy to answer such a question over the board, but the double target principle is quite helpful. If 2. ... gxf5 3. Nf4 (else 3. ... f6) Bc6! 4. Nxh5, he is left with weak pawns (unavoidable in any case), but White has no easy double attack.

On the other hand, if 2. ... g5, White will reply 3. h4 to make the square f4 available for his knight, and then d5 and h5 will be obvious and simple points of attack.

On purely theoretical grounds, Yates should have replied 2. ... gxf5 (see below). Not having read this book, he chose 2. ... g5, when Alekhine secured an overwhelming position in the following convincing manner 3. h4 f6 (3. ... gxh4 4. gxh4 f6 5. Nf4 is much worse: 5. ... fxe5 6. dxe5 Bf7 7. Kd4 Kd8 8. e6, and it's all over) 4. hxg5 fxg5 5. Ng1! Bd7 6. f6+ Ke8 7. Nf3 g4 8. Nh4, and the conclusion is similar to that in other examples—after a double attack the bishop will be in zugzwang: 8. ... Be6 9. Ng6 Bf7 10. Nf4 Kd7 11. Ke2 a5 12. Ke3 (voilà!) 12. ... Bg8 (on a king move, 13. e6 is conclusive) 13. Nxh5 Bf7 14. Nf4 Bg8 15. Ne2. Now that there is only one target left (d4); the knight can do no more and the king is brought up. 15. ... Be6 16. Kf4 Ke8 17. Kg5 Kf7 18. Nc3 (forcing the king to move) 18. ... Kf8 19. Kg6 Kg8 20. f7+!! Kf8 21. Kf6 Bxf7 22. e6 Bh5 23. Nxd5 Be8 24. Nc3 and Black resigned.

Returning to the critical point above, there is no guarantee that the theoretical reply would have saved the game, but analysis bears out the feeling that it would have offered White a much harder nut to crack.

2. ... gxf5 3. Nf4 (if 3. Kf4 f6!! 4. Nc3 Bc6 5. Kxf5 Bd7+! 6. Kf4 Be6, and Black is out of the woods) **3. ... Bc6** (he must not abandon the support of his protected passed pawn) **4. Nxh5 Kf8 5. Nf6**

5. Nf4 Kg7 6. Ne2 Kg6 7. Kf4 is no better: after 7. ... a6 8. a3 Bb7 9. h4 Bc6 10. h5+ Kxh5 11. Kxf5 Bd7+ 12. Kf6 Be6!, Black has all the winning chances, while if 5. Kf4 Kg8 6. Kxf5 c3 7. Nf4 Bb5!! and wins.

5. ... Kg7 6. Kf4 Kf8!! (relying on his passed pawn) **7. h4 Kg7 8. h5 Kh6 9. Ng8+ Kxh5 10. Ne7 Ba8! 11. Nxf5 Kg6 12. Nd6 a6**, and there is still no clear win in sight.

In the above variation. the double targets d5 and f5 could have been attacked only from e7, which White could not reach, or from e3, which would have involved playing the king away from f4, thereby easing Black's defense.

Where there is only one target the game is normally drawn. The isolated d-pawn with no other weaknesses is not fatal.

No. 527, Flohr-Capablanca, Moscow 1935

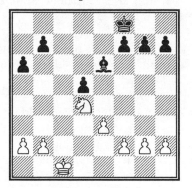

Black to play. Draw

1. ... Ke7 2. Kd2 Kd6 3. Kc3 b6! 4. f4 Bd7 5. Nf3 f6! (keeping his pawns on dark squares) **6. Kd4 a5! 7. Nd2 Bc8 8. Nb1 Be6 9. Nc3 Kc6**

This is the best White can do. His only winning hope now lies in creating a second threat (besides the d-pawn). This might be done by 10. Nb1-d2-f3-h4, f5, g4, Ng2-f4. Then Black's bishop at f7 would be tied down to the defense of two points, for if . ... Bg8, Nh5 wins a pawn, while his king would be unable to leave d6, since Ne6!, Bxe6, fxe6, Kd6, e7! would then decide. So Black would have to weaken his kingside pawns. This would not necessarily be fatal, but it would give White something to aim at. However, Capablanca sees through this plan and it dies against his careful defense.

10. a3 h6 (this makes no difference) **11. g3 h5** (he is going to block the kingside) **12. b4 axb4 13. axb4 Kd6 14. b5 g6** (now the plan sketched above is impossible and a speedy draw may be expected) **15. f5!** (a sacrifice to get his knight to f4) **15. ... gxf5 16. Ne2 Bd7! 17. Nf4 Be8!!** (the point: he does not mind losing the worthless d-pawn, but the h-pawn is vital) **18. Nxd5 Bxb5 19.**

Nxb6 (19. Nxf6 Be2) **Bc6 20. Nc4+ Ke6,** and it is clear that there is no longer any real danger. This ending should be compared with No. 526, where the presence of an extra weakness provides the needed additional threat.

b3. Weak Pawns

Weak pawns are often more effectively exploited by the knight than by the bishop. Such cases occur mainly when a pawn majority is blocked and when pawns are exposed on squares not covered by the bishop. A bishop can capture pawns only when they are on its color, obviously, but a knight can snare them anywhere.

No. 528, Rubinstein-Alekhine, London 1922

Black to play wins

No. 528 is typical of the first case – a blocked pawn majority. The bishop cannot break the blockade, while Black's knight and pawn keep the White king out. Black wins by simply marching his king over to support of his passed pawn. **1. ... Kf8 2. Kg2 Ke7 3. Bg8 Kd6 4. Bf7 Kc5 5. Bxh5 Nxb3 6. Kf3** (if 6. g4 Nd4 7. g5 fxg5 8. fxg5 Nxf5 is sufficient) **6. ... Kd4 7. Bf7 Kd3 8. Bxb3 Kd2 9. Bc4 b3 10. Bxb3 e2,** and White resigned.

Instances where the bishop is unable to defend exposed pawns are more common. **No. 529** may be taken as a model.

No. 529, Gilg-Spielmann, Carlsbad 1929

Black to play wins

White's e-pawn is exposed and can be defended only by the f-pawn. This is prevented by **1. ... g5!**, after which the pawn is lost. **2. Kg2 Nd7 3. h4 h6 4. hxg5 hxg5 5. f4 gxf4 6. Kf3 Nxe5+ 7. Kxf4 f6**, when the two connected passed pawns win. **8. Ke4 Kf7 9. Kd4 Nc6+ 10. Kc3 Ke7 11. b4 axb4+ 12. axb4 Kd6 13. Bd1 e5 14. Bg4 Ne7 15. Bf3 f5 16. Bg2 e4 17. Bh3 Ke5 18. c5 b5!** (to preserve an extra pawn against the possibility of a sacrifice) **19. Bf1 Nd5+ 20. Kd2 Nc7 21. Bh3 f4 22. Ke2 f3+ 23. Kf2 Kf4 24. Bd7 e3+ 25. Kf1 Kg3 26. Bc6 e2+ 27. Ke1 Ne6,** and White resigned.

No. 530 (Dake-Fine, Chicago 1934) is somewhat more complicated: **White king at e4, knight at b6, pawns at a2, b2, c2, g4, h3; Black king at e7, bishop at e8, pawns at a6, c6, c5, g6, h7.** Black to play, White wins. After **1. ... Bf7 2. Ke5! Bxa2 3. g5! Bb1 4. c3 Bc2 5. Nc4 Kd7 6. Ne3 Bd3 7. Ng4 Kc7 8. Nf6 Kb6 9. Nxh7**, the White kingside pawns won. Here White was able to sacrifice a pawn on the queenside because with Black's c-pawns doubled the extra pawn was meaningless.

To sum up: The knight is preferable to the bishop in positions where the pawns are blocked. It is especially bad for the player with the bishop to have all or most of his pawns on the bishop's color. Weak color complexes and a bad bishop go together. The key to the winning method in both cases is the double attack, thus placing the bishop in zugzwang. The knight then either captures a pawn or allows the entry of the king. If the pawns are weak or exposed, the knight is in a better position to take advantage of the inferiority.

c) Better Pawn Position.

Not all bishop vs. knight endings are determined by the superiority of one of the minor pieces. On the contrary: very often other factors loom just as large and it makes no difference whatsoever which piece one has. This is what distinguishes these last two sections from the first two: the positional advantage can be exploited with equal success by either piece.

The outside passed pawn is again the principal kind of superiority. Ordinarily, a bishop is somewhat more effective here than a knight, but the strength of such a pawn is so great that either piece will usually win with ease. Remember how the pawn is used: to decoy the enemy king so that one's own king may penetrate.

No. 531, Levenfish-Ragozin, Leningrad-Moscow 1939

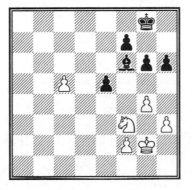

Black to play. White wins

No. 531 is an example with a knight. **1. ... Kf8** (if 1. ... e4 2. Nd2 wins a pawn) **2. Nd2 Ke8** (the White king cannot be kept out; if 2. ... Be7 3. c6 Ke8 4. Kf3 f5 5. gxf5 gxf5 6. Nc4 Bf6 7. Nd6+ Kd8 8. c7+ and wins) **3. Kf3 Be7 4. c6 Kd8 5. Ke4 Kc7 6. Kd5 f5** (hoping to create a diversion on the kingside; 6. ... f6 7. Ne4 is hopeless) **7. gxf5 gxf5 8. Kxe5** (the simplest) **8. ... Kxc6 9. Nb3 Bd6+ 10. Ke6 Bh2 11. Nd4+ Kc5 12. Nxf5 h5 13. Ng3 Kd4 14. Kf5 h4 15. Nh5 Bg1 16. f3 Bf2 17. Nf4 Be1 18. Ng6 Kd5 19. Kg4,** and the rest is routine (see No. 473).

With two outside passed pawns (one for each side) one must get going as fast as one can, sit tight, and hope for the best. In **No. 532** (Pillsbury-Lasker, St. Petersburg 1895-96): **White king at d4, knight at b6, pawns at a4, b3, g2, h3; Black king at f4, bishop at f5, pawns at c6, f7, g6, h4.** Black ignored this rule and had to pay the penalty. He could have drawn by **1. ... g5! 2. a5** (or 2. Kc5 Bxh3 3. gxh3 g4 4. a5 g3 =) **2. ... Bxh3 3. gxh3 g4 4. a6 g3 5. a7 g2 6. a8=Q g1=Q+ 7. Kc3 Qe3+ 8. Kb2 Qxb6,** with an even position. Instead Lasker played **1. ... Be4?,** when **2. a5 c5+ 3. Kxc5 Bxg2 4. a6 g5 5. Nd5+! Ke5 6. Ne3!! Bf3 7. b4 Ke6 8. b5 Be2 9. Nd5** forced him to resign.

No. 533, Naegeli-Colin, Berne 1932

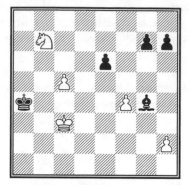

White to play wins

Advanced passed pawns, when not blocked by the king, almost invariably cost the defender a piece, especially with knight vs. bishop.

In **No. 533,**. White to play can win by **1. c6! Kb5** (if 1. ... Bf3 2. Nc5+! Kb5 3. c7 and queens) **2. c7 e5 3. f5!!** (3. Nd6+ Kc6 4. c8=Q+? Bxc8 5. Nxc8 exf4 only draws) **3. ... Bxf5 4. Nd6+ Kc6 5. Nxf5 Kxc7 6. Nxg7,** and the rest is routine.

With the knight such combinations occur much more frequently than with the bishop. **No. 534** (Berger): **White king at g1, knight at c7, pawns at b6, c4; Black king at f3, bishop at a2, pawns at b7, f7**. White to play wins. **1. f5 Bb1** (forced: c6 must be met) **2. Ne6!! fxe6** (2. ... Be4 3. Ng5+) **3. c6** and will queen, for if **3. ... Be4 4. c7,** and if **3. ... Bf5 4. cxb7**.

Exposed pawns often cannot be defended, especially when attacked by a bishop and defended by a knight.

No. 535, Spielmann-Maroczy, Carlsbad 1929

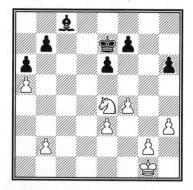

White to play wins

No. 535 is a model case with a knight.

Black's queenside pawns are irretrievably on squares of the wrong color, so the pawns on the other wing are the only ones that White needs to consider. It is clear that if Black does nothing, White will march his king to b6 or c7 and capture a pawn there (playing Nc5 if necessary). Black must therefore do something against this threat. But all he can do is drive the knight away, which can only be done by fixing more of his pawns on light squares.

The game continued **1. Kf2 f5**

If 1. ... Bd7 2. g3 Bc6 3. Nc3 Kd6 4. b4 Ke7 5. e4 Kd6 6. e5+ Kc7 7. Ke3 Kd7 8. Ne4 Ke7 9. Nd6 Kf8 10. Kd4, followed by annihilation of the queenside.

2. Nc3!

Somewhat surprising. But it is important to keep the Black king out and to preserve the square d4 for the White king. On 2. Nc5? Kd6 3. b4 Kd5, Black has excellent counterchances.

2. ... e5

Pawn exchanges are usually advisable for the defender; the fewer the pawns the greater the drawing chances.

3. Ke2 exf4 4. exf4 Kd6 5. b4 Bd7

Why doesn't Black try to exchange his weak queenside pawns? Because that would permit the entry of the White king to the kingside; for example, 5. ... Kc6 6. Kd3 b6 7. axb6 Kxb6 8. Kd4 a5 9. bxa5+ Kxa5 10. Ke5 with a simple win.

6. Ke3 Bc6 7. g3 Bd7 8. Kd4

The first two steps have been completed. It would be pointless for White to now try to set up a passed pawn on the kingside, since that would require moving his knight to e3, and even then he would not succeed, because Black could counter with ... h5. But the constant threat of a passed pawn brings about Black's downfall, first because he can never dare to exchange his bishop for the knight, and second, because his bishop must not stray too far afield but must always keep an eye on the kingside, while the knight may do as it pleases. The immediate winning idea consists of chasing the Black king away from d6 so that White may enter via either e5 or c5.

8. ... Be6

8. ... Bc6 makes no difference. After 9. Nd1 Be4 (9. ... Bd7 transposes back to the game) 10. Ne3 Bb1 11. g4 gives White his long-coveted passed pawn, which is conclusive here. For example, 11. ... fxg4 12. Nxg4 h5 13. Nf6 h4 14. Ne4+ Kc6 15. f5 Ba2 16. f6 Kd7 17. Ke5 and wins.

9. Na4 h5 10. Nc5 Bd5 11. Nd7! (very pretty, but of course 11. Nd3 is just as good) **11. ... Bb3 12. Ne5 Bc2 13. Nc4+ Kc6 14. Ne3 Bb1 15. Nd1! Kd6! 16. Nc3 Bc2 17. Kc4! Kc6 18. h4! Kd6 19. b5! axb5+ 20. Nxb5+ Ke7 21. Kc5 Be4 22. Nd6** and Maroczy resigned.

Doubled pawns that are isolated are born but to die. Even if not captured they are no better than one pawn, so the enemy is virtually one pawn ahead. Usually, however, they cannot even be defended. No. 536 (Hanauer-Fine, New York 1938) is an example: **White king at b1, knight at d5, pawns at c6, f6, g5; Black king at f7, bishop at e5, pawns at a6, a4, h7.** Black must lose both his a-pawns. The game went: **1. ... Bh2 2. Kb2 Bd6 3. Ka2 Kg6 4. Ne7+ Kf7 5. Nf5 Bc7 6. Ka3 Kg6 7. Kxa4 Kf7 8. Kb3 a5 9. Ka4 Bd8 10. Kb5 Ke6 11. Kc4 Kf7 12. Kd5 Bb6 13. Nd6+ Kf8 14. Ke6 a4 15. Nc4 Bc7 16. Ne5,** resigns.

d) Better King Position

Here again we may omit the obvious case where one king is so near that it can simply take a lot of pawns. A more refined method is required when the king is near enough only to threaten the pawns and cramp his rival's pieces. This, too, will normally result in material gain but only after considerable maneuvering.

No. 537, Chigorin-Charousek, 4th match game, Pest 1896

Black to play. White wins

No. 537 is typical. The White king can get to a6 or c6 but, but although it cannot win anything directly, the strong post at c6 is sufficient to win. Chigorin concluded **1. ... Be7 2. Kc4 Kf8 3. Kb5 Ke8 4. Ka6 Bc5 5. Kb5** (5. Nc3 is also good) **5. ... Be3 6. Kc6 Kd8 7. b4 h5 8. a4 Bd2 9. b5 h4 10. Nd4 g5 11. Nf5 Be1 12. Nh6 f6 13. Nf5 Bb4 14. Nd4 Kc8 15. Ne6 Bd6 16. a5 Bg3 17. b6 axb6 18. axb6 cxb6 19. d6,** and Black had to give up his bishop and soon resigned.

II. BISHOP, KNIGHT, AND PAWNS VS. BISHOP, KNIGHT, AND PAWNS

Almost all such endings are governed by the same principles as those that apply to simple bishop or simple knight endings, or a combination of the two. There are only two questions that need to be considered – bishops of opposite colors and reduction (exchange).

A. Bishops of Opposite Colors

There are many cases in which an extra pawn does not win with only opposite-color bishops on the board. These are all positions where the superior side can take the initiative on only one side of the board. In such positions it is essential to avoid exchanging knights, although the exchange of bishop for knight, or knight for bishop are both all right.

Except for some very unusual cases, it is not possible to win materially even positions. Where one side is a pawn ahead the winning method differs in no essential respect from that in pure knight or pure bishop endings—place your pieces as well as possible, secure a passed pawn, tie up the enemy pieces, divert the king, switch over to the other side of the board, and establish a decisive superiority there. A pawn down, the defender's other pawns are exposed and often lost. Most of the time, a suitable exchange (knight for bishop, or bishop for knight) is feasible.

No. 538, Marshall-Nimzovich, New York 1927

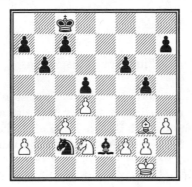

White to play. Black wins

No. 538 is a model for the superior side. **1. f4** (the defender as usual tries to exchange as many pawns as possible) **1. ... Na3!** (holding the a-pawn and threatening 2. ... Nb5 3. Nb1 Bd3) **2. fxg5 fxg5 3. Kf2 Bh5 4. Be5 g4** (to clear up the situation on the kingside. If 4. ... Nb5 5. g4 Bg6 6. c4 dxc4 7. Nxc4 Bf7 8. a4 Bxc4 9. axb5 Bxb5 10. Bf6 and wins a pawn on the kingside, after which it's doubtful whether Black can win) **5. hxg4 Bxg4 6. Ke3 Bf5 7. Bg7 Be6** (threatening 7. ... Nb5 8. Nb1 Bf5) **8. Bf8** (loses a pawn, but even after 8. Kd3 Kd7 9. Bf8 Nb5 10. c4 dxc4+ 11. Nxc4 a5 12. a3 Bf5+ 13. Ke3 Kc6 14. Ne5+ Kd5 15. Nf3 a4! 16. Be7 c5, White must lose another pawn) **8. ... Nb5 9. Nb1 a5 10. Kd2** (if 10. a4 Na7 followed by Bd7) **10. ... Bf5 11. Na3 Nxa3 12. Bxa3 Bb1 13. Bf8 Bxa2** and the rest is not difficult: **14. Bg7 Bc4 15. Ke3 Kb7 16. Bh6 Ka6 17. Kd2 Bf1 18. g3 Kb5 19. Kc1 Kc4 20. Kb2 c5 21. Be3 cxd4 22. Bxd4 b5 23. Bb6 a4 24. Ba5 d4! 25. cxd4 b4 26. Bb6 a3+ 27. Ka2 Kb5 28. Bc5 Ka4,** White resigned.

The winning chances are greatest when the pawns are unevenly distributed; i.e., three to one on one side, three to two on the other. In such unbalanced pawn positions, a pawn ahead normally wins despite the opposite-color bishops.

No. 539, Kan-Flohr, Leningrad-Moscow 1939

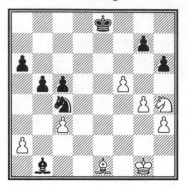

White to play. Black wins

No. 539 is typical. The weakness of White's position is not so much that he must lose a pawn but rather in the danger of the remote passed pawn that Black will obtain. **1. Ng6 Bxa2 2. Bg3** (if 2. Bf2 a5 3. Bxc5 a4 4. Nf4 a3 5. Nd3 Bb1 and wins a piece) **2. ... Bb1 3. Ne5 Nd2** (Black must of course avoid the exchange of knights) **4. Nc6 Be4 5. Na5 Bd5!** (White's knight is stalemated and we have in effect an ending of knight vs. bishop) **6. Bd6 c4 7. Bb4 Ne4 8. Kh2 Kf7 9. Kg1 h5!** (Black has a winning advantage on the other wing, so he wants to rid himself of the danger on the kingside) **10. gxh5 Ng3 11. Kf2 Nxf5 12. Ba3 Kf6 13. Bc1 Ke6 14. Bf4 Be4 15. Bc7 Kd5 16. Bb8 Kc5 17. Ba7+ Kd6 18. Bb8+ Ke6 19. Bf4 Ba8 20. Bc7 Ne7 21. Bb6 Nd5 22. Bd4 Nf6** (decisive) **23. Ke3 Nxh5 24. h4 Ng3 25. Kd2 g6 26. Bb6 Nf5 27. Bd8 Kd5 28. Ke2 Ke4 29. Kd2 Kf3 30. Kc2 Kg4 31. Kb2 Nxh4 32. Ka3 Nf5 33. Kb4 Ng7!**, and White soon resigned, for if **34. Kc5 Ne6+.**

Again, the fewer pawns there are, the greater the likelihood of a draw. For example, **No. 540** (Winawer-Pillsbury, Nuremberg 1896): **White king at f2, bishop at a1, knight at g5, pawns at g2, h4; Black king at e7, bishop at a2, knight at c6, pawns at a7, b4, g6.** White to play draws. **1. g4!** (1. Ke2 was actually played, and lost after 1. ... a5 2. Nf3 a4 3. Nd4 Nxd4+ 4. Bxd4 Kd6 because the kingside pawns had not yet been exchanged) **1. ... a5** (or 1. ... Bf7 2. h5 gxh5 3. Nxf7 Kxf7 4. gxh5 Kg8 5. Ke2 Kh7 6. Kd3, and Black cannot win with his king so far away) **2. h5 gxh5 3. gxh5 a4 4. h6 Bb1 5. h7 Bxh7 6. Nxh7 a3 7. Ke2 b3 8. Kd2, =.**

B. Bishops of the Same Color

These endings ordinarily differ in no essential respect from the corresponding simple cases of bishop vs. bishop, knight vs. knight, or bishop vs. knight. It is important to exchange the right piece. If all the opponent's pawns are on the color of his bishop, do not exchange the bishop; otherwise, do exchange it. The rule to follow is: *exchange the opponent's most active piece.*

No. 541, Eliskases-Capablanca, Semmering-Baden 1937

White to play wins. White should not exchange his opponent's bishop

In **No. 541,** it is all right to exchange Black's knight but not his bishop; even the exchange of knights should be permitted only at the proper moment; i.e., when it will not facilitate Black's break on the queenside. Eliskases won after **1. Bf1!** (preventing the freeing move 1. ... a5) **1. ... Ne6** (1. ... a5 2. Na4+) **2. Na4+!** (no exchange yet! After 2. Nxe6 Bxe6, either 3. ... a5 or 3. ... c5 will get Black out of the woods) **2. ... Kc7 3. Kf2 g5 4. Ke3 gxf4+ 5. gxf4 Ng7 6. Nc5! Ne6 7. Nxe6+!** (now it is all right because White's king is centralized) **7. ... Bxe6 8. Kd4! Kb6 9. Bc4!**, etc. For the continuation see No. 380.

To sum up: When each side has a bishop and a knight the basic principles remain the same as for the corresponding simpler endings. If the bishops are of opposite colors, the superior side should be careful not to exchange knights. If the bishops are the same color, the superior side should try to exchange his opponent's most active piece. As a rule, it is to the superior side's advantage to exchange pieces, but disadvantageous to exchange pawns; conversely, the inferior side should avoid the exchange of pieces but should try to reduce the number of pawns.

III. THE TWO BISHOPS

The superiority of the two bishops in any more or less normal pawn position is now universally recognized. Steinitz was the first to point it out and since his day countless tournament games have repeatedly demonstrated it. Here we analyze the nature of this advantage and lay down some general rules for its proper exploitation.

In the case of bishop vs. knight we saw that the bishop helped the king penetrate enemy lines. With an additional piece on the board this penetration is often not feasible.

We also saw how a bishop can limit the mobility of a knight, and it is this constriction idea that is the key to endings with two bishops against bishop and knight or two knights. The bishops must be made to work together and cramp the enemy position; wherever possible, they then facilitate the entry of the king; otherwise they create weaknesses and hammer away at them until some more tangible advantage (king entry, material gain) turns up.

The strength of an outside passed pawn with one bishop is clear enough; with two bishops it is almost a winning advantage. The bishops in unison can control every square on the queening file.

There are two main reasons the two bishops are so strong: 1. They can cramp the enemy position; 2. they can provide a perfect escort for an outside passed pawn.

In order to examine the winning process in greater detail, we consider unbalanced and balanced pawn positions separately. We are interested only in positional advantage here; material advantage is exploited according to the principles explained in Chapter IV and Chapter V, Part I.

A. The Pawn Structure Is Unbalanced

By this we mean that the pawns are not distributed on the same files; i.e., that there is at least one file on which there are more pawns (either two to one, or one to zero) for one side or the other. For example, White has one pawn on each of the b-, c-, g-, and h-files; Black has one pawn on each of the a-, b-, g-, and h-files. In such cases the power of the two bishops is tremendous; very often this alone is sufficient to win.

The winning process in these endings may be divided into four steps.

1. Place the pieces in the best possible positions. These will be squares from which they cramp the mobility of the enemy pieces.

2. Set up an outside passed pawn or a potential outside passed pawn. In other words, advance the pawns as far as you can. Black will stop them.

3. If Black goes to the threatened sector with his king, turn your attention to the other wing, where you will be able either to capture material with the bishops or force an entry with the king.

4. If Black does not try to stop the pawn with his king, the advance of the passed pawn will cost him a piece.

Notice that this method differs in no essential respect from that of bishop vs. knight. In actual play, however, it will be found that it works much more smoothly and easily.

No. 542, Leonhardt-Bernstein, Barmen 1905

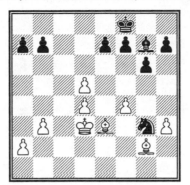

White to play wins

No. 542 illustrates the great strength of the outside passed pawn. The first step has been completed. White now tries to set up a two versus one majority on the queenside. **1. d6! exd6** (forced: if 1. ... b6 2. d7!) **2. Bxb7 Nf5 3. Bf2 Bh6 4. Ke4 Ne7 5. d5!** (cramping the enemy pieces and at the same time threatening to win the a-pawn) **5. ... f5+ 6. Kf3 a6** (if 6. ... a5 7. Bb6) **7. a4** (threatening 7. b4-b5, and if then axb5, a5!-a6-a7-a8=Q. Once the pawn gets to a5 it will be impossible to stop) **7. ... Bg7 8. Ke2** (not 8. b4? Bc3 9. b5 axb5 10. axb5 Ke8 11. Ba7 Kd7 12. b6? Bd4, and Black still has some fight left) **8. ... Bc3** (if 8. ... Ke8 9. Kd3 Kd7 10. Kc4, wins a pawn)

The second step is done. Now we jump to the fourth. **9. Kd3 Bb4 10. Bxa6 h6** (if 10. ... Nxd5 11. Kc4 Nc7 12. Kxb4 Nxa6+ 13. Kb5 Nc7+ 14. Kb6 Nd5+ 15. Kb7, and the advance of the a-pawn will decide) **11. Bb7 g5 12. fxg5 hxg5 13. Kc4 Bd2 14. b4,** and soon won. The advance of the b- and a-pawns will cost Black at least a piece, while Black's g-pawn is easily stopped.

Sometimes a passed pawn cannot be obtained by simple advances and exchanges. In such cases a cramped enemy position can often be exploited by means of a sacrifice to create a passed pawn.

No. 543 (Perlis-Baird, Barmen 1905) is an example: **White king at d2, bishops at c2, b6, pawns at a3, b4, e4, f3, g3, h2; Black king at e8, bishop at e6, knight at d8, pawns at b7, c6, e5, f6, g7, h7.** White won as follows: **1. f4 exf4 2. gxf4 Ba2 3. Kc3 Ne6 4. Be3 Nf8 5. a4 Nd7 6. Bd3 Kd8 7. Kd4 Nf8 8. f5! Nd7 9. Bf4 Ke7 10. h4 Bb3 11. a5 h6 12. Be2 Ba2 13. Bd1 Bf7 14. Bc7! Ba2 15. Ba4 Bf7.** The critical position. White cannot improve his position, so he breaks through with a sacrifice. **16. Bxc6 bxc6 17. a6 c5+,** and now the simplest win is 18. bxc5 Nb8 19. Bxb8 Be8 20. Kd5, although **18. Ke3 Nb6 19. Bxb6 Be8 20. Bxc5+,** as played in the game, is of course also good enough.

Against doubled pawns the two bishops will generally be able to force the gain of material or the creation of an outside passed pawn.

No. 544, Soultanbieff-Flohr, Folkestone 1933

Black to play wins

In **No. 544**, the weakness of White's b-pawn is the key to Black's winning plan. First he will force the pawn to b4. Then he will play his king to the queenside. To prevent the entry of Black's king White will have to play his knight to c3, for his king is kept impotent by the iron grip of the two bishops. And finally Black will capture the b-pawn and establish an outside passed pawn. In the absence of White's king, such a pawn is sure to cost White a piece.

Flohr worked out his plan as follows: **1. ... Kg6 2. Kg2** (2. Kf1 Bb5+ and poor White has to go right back) **2. ... Bd5 3. b4 Kf7** (first and second steps are now in progress) **4. Ng3 Ke8 5. Ne2 Kd7 6. Nc3 Kc6 7. Kh2** (last chance for 7. b5+!, and if 7. ... axb5 8. b4 closes the queenside) **7. ... Bb3** (a few moves to gain time on the clock; 7. ... Be7 at once is perfectly all right) **8. Kg2 Bc4 9. Kg1 Bd3 10. Kg2 Bc4 11. Nb1 b6 12. Kg1 Bd3 13. Nc3** (if 13. Na3 b5! 14. Kg2 Be7 15. Kf2 a5! 16. bxa5 b4 wins the knight) **13. ... Be7 14. Kf2 Bxb4 15. Nxe4 Be7 16. Nc3 Bh4+** (confining the king to the kingside) **17. Kg1 Bc4 18. Kg2 a5 19. Kg1 b5 20. Kg2 h5 21. Kg1** (the impotence of the king illustrates the fourth step in our schema) **21. ... Bb3 22. Kg2 b4 23. Ne2 Bd5+ 24. Kf1 Bc4 25. Be1** (desperation; 25. Bc1 a4 26. Bd2 a3 is also hopeless) **25. ... Bxe1 26. Kxe1 Bxe2 27. Kxe2 a4** and White resigned. For if **28. Kd3 Kd5 29. Kd2 a3 30. bxa3 bxa3 31. Kc3 Ke4** he loses three pawns on the kingside.

Against an isolated d-pawn, a single knight is more effective than a single bishop, although with no extra weaknesses the game should be a draw in either case. But with two bishops an isolated d-pawn may be serious enough to lose, although this cannot be demonstrate with any degree of certainty.

In **No. 545** (Rubinstein-Gajdos, Barmen 1905) Rubinstein worked out a win but was helped by some inferior play by his opponent. **White king at g1, bishops at d4, e2, pawns at a2, b2, e3, f3, g2, h2; Black king at f7, bishop at c8, knight at d6, pawns at a6, b7, d5, f6, g7, h7.** White to play wins. **1. Kf2 Bd7 2. Ke1 Nb5** (better is 2. ... Bb5) **3. Bc5 Ke6 4. Kd2 f5??** (a horrible positional blunder, immobilizing his own bishop and strengthening his opponent's bishop on the dark squares) **5. b3 Nd6 6. a4 Nc8 7. Kc3 Ne7 8. Bd4 g6 9. Kb4 Bc6 10. Kc5 Kd7 11. a5 Nc8 12. Bd1 Na7 13. h4 Nb5 14. Bc2 Nc7 15. g3 Ne8 16. Be5! Ke6 17. f4 Kd7 18. b4 Nc7 19. Bxc7 Kxc7 20. Bb3 h5 21. Ba2 Kd7 22. Bxd5 Bxd5 23. Kxd5 Kc7 24. Ke5,** Black resigned.

Where there is a weak color complex the two bishops can usually clear a path for the king by stalemating or constricting the enemy pieces. In **No. 546** (Hasenfuss-Fine, Kemeri 1937): **White king at g1, bishop at e3, knight at c2, pawns at a4, b3, d4, e5, f4, g3, h2; Black king at g8, bishops at d7, e7, pawns at a7, b7, d5, f7, g7, g4, h5.** Black won as follows: **1. ... Bf5 2. Ne1 Bb1! 3. Bd2 Kh7 4. Kf2 Kg6 5. Ke3 Kf5 6. a5 g5!** (setting up a potential outside passed pawn) **7. Nd3 Bc2 8. Nc5 gxf4+ 9. gxf4 b6 10. axb6 axb6 11. Nd7 b5 12. b4 h4! 13. Nc5 g3 14. hxg3 hxg3 15. Kf3 Bh4 16. Be3 Bd1+ 17. Kg2 Kg4 18. Bd2 Bf3+ 19. Kg1 Kf5 20. Be3 Be4 21. Bd2 g2 22. Nxe4 Kxe4 23. Kxg2 Kxd4 24. Kh3 Be7 25. Kg4 Kd3,** and the d-pawn decides.

The possibility of stalemating or cramping the mobility of knights is one of the most important stratagems available to the bishops. This is the reason why the knights may never stray far afield.

No. 547, Walbrodt-Charousek, Nuremberg 1896

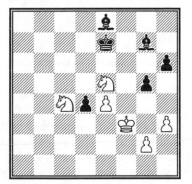

Black to move wins

In **No. 547,** Charousek won by **1. ... Bb5!** (threatening 2. ... Ba6! and 3. ... Ke6) **2. Na3** (if 2. Kg4 Ke6 3. Na3 Be2+ 4. Nf3 d3! 5. Nb1 Be5 6. Kh5 Bf4 and wins) **2. ... Bf1! 3. Nec4** (if 3. Kf2 Bxg2, while if 3. Nac4 Ke6 4. Nd2 Bxg2+) **3. ... Ke6 4. Nd2 Bd3 5. Nac4 Bf8 6. Nb2 Ba6 7. Nbc4** (the knights cannot find a haven; if 7. Ndc4 Bg7 8. Ke2 d3+! 9. Kd2! Bd4! 10. Kd1 Bxb2 11. Nxb2 Ke5 and wins) **7. ... Bb4 8. Kg4 Bxd2!** (the decisive exchange) **9. Nxd2 Be2+ 10. Kg3 Ke5,** and Black won (see No. 487).

While there is no precise analogy with two bishops against bishop and knight, if the pawns are on the color of the lone bishop an exchange of bishop for knight would leave one with a better bishop ending.

For instance, **No. 548** (Scheltinga-Fine, Amsterdam 1936): **White king at h2, bishop at d2, knight at f3, pawns at b4, c5, e4, f2, g2, h3; Black king at**

g8, bishops at d3, g7, pawns at a6, b7, e6, f7, g6, h6. White to play. Black wins. After **1. e5** (forced) **1. ... Be4! 2. Bc3 Bxf3 3. gxf3 Kf8**, White has the bad bishop and his game is untenable (No. 382).

B. The Pawn Structure Is Balanced

Here the defender's drawing chances are much greater than with an unbalanced pawn structure. Even so he often finds it impossible to hold the game, for the bishops working together can usually weaken the enemy pawns and cramp the enemy pieces. Once this is done the rest is not too difficult.

No. 549, Berger-Chigorin, Carlsbad 1907

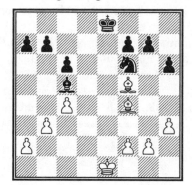

Black to play. White wins

No. 549 is a model case. The winning process consists of five steps.

1. Weakening the opponent's pawns. This is the most important of all—on it hinges the outcome of the game. In this example the weakening took place voluntarily, although it could have been forced. **1. ... Ke7 2. Be5** (correct is 2. Bc8) **Ne8 3. Ke2 Bd6 4. Bc3 b6?** (4. ... Kd8 is better. Whether Black could hold the game in that event is not certain, but it would have offered better chances than the text) **5. g3 f6?** (better 5. ... g6). From here on we may take it that White has a forced win. The next step is:

2. Cramping the opponent's pieces. **6. f4 Bc5 7. Be4 Kd7** (now the king is tied down to the defense of the c-pawn) **8. b4 Be7 9. Kf3 Nd6 10. Bd3 Ke6 11. g4 g5.**

This move is so obviously weakening that one is forced to inquire how a player of Chigorin's strength chose it. The reason is that he wanted to prevent the entry of the White king; e.g., if 11. ... Kd7 12. Kg3 Kc7 13. Kh4 f5+ 14. Kh5 and wins. On the other hand, if 11. ... Kf7 12. Bd4 Ke6 13. a3 Kf7 14. c5 bxc5 15. Bxc5 Nc8 16. Bf5! Bxc5 17. bxc5 Ne7 18. Bd7, Black is in zugzwang and has no defense against the march of the White king to the queenside. In other words, the cramping effect of the bishops, which can attack both sides of the board simultaneously, has already made itself felt. The next step is:

3. Clearing a path for the entrance of the king. **12. a3 Nb7 13. Bf5+** (not 13. Ke4 Nd6+) **13. ... Kd6 14. Bg6 Nd8 15. fxg5 hxg5** (forced, for if 15. ... fxg5 16. Bg7 wins the h-pawn) **16. Ke4**.

The game is approaching a climax. To keep the White king out, Black must stalemate his knight. **16. ... Ne6 17. Bf7! Ng7** (17. ... Nd8? 18. Bg8!, or 17. ... Nf4 18. Kf5 Nxh3 19. Bxf6 Bxf6 20. Kxf6 and the g-pawn cannot be held) **18. Be1 Kd7 19. Bc3 Bd8 20. b5!** (opening the way on the queenside as well) **20. ... Ke7 21. Bg8 Kf8 22. Bh7 cxb5 23. cxb5 Ke7**.

Black has kept the White king out but he has had to submit to a terrific battering and now gets into zugzwang. This brings us to the fourth step.

4. After the White king has penetrated as far as possible, forcing the exchange of the piece that is holding him back. **24. Bb4+ Ke6 25. Bg8+ Kd7 26. Kd5!** Now he is in zugzwang. **26. ... Be7** (forced, for if 26. ... Kc7 27. Bf8 Ne8 28. Be6 Kb7 29. Bd7! Nc7+ 30. Ke4 a6 31. a4 axb5 32. axb5 Kb8 33. Bd6 Kb7 34. Bc6+ Kc8 35. Kf5 and Black must lose his kingside pawns) **27. Bxe7 Kxe7**.

And now the fifth and final phase.

5. Penetrating with the king and capturing material. **28. Kc6 Ne8 29. a4** (29. Kb7 Nd6+ 30. Ka6! is also good enough) **29. ... Nd6 30. Kc7 Ne4 31. Bb3 Nc5 32. Bc2 Ke6 33. Kb8** (the game continued 33. Kc6? Ke5 34. a5 Ne6 35. axb6 Nd4+ 36. Kb7 axb6 37. Bd3, when 37. ... f5! 38. gxf5 Nxb5! would have drawn) **33. ... Kd6** (if 33. ... a6 34. Kc7 axb5 35. axb5 Ke7 36. Kxb6 Kd6 37. Ka7 Kc7 38. b6+ Kc6 39. Be4+ wins) **34. Kxa7 Kc7 35. a5! bxa5 36. b6+ Kc6 37. Be4+ Nxe4 38. b7** and wins.

No. 550, Tarrasch-Rubinstein, San Sebastian 1912

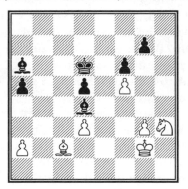

Black to play wins

The idea of *stalemating the knight* is central in these endings.

No. 550 is a classic illustration. The first three steps above have been completed. Rubinstein concludes as follows: **1. ... Ke5 2. g4 Be3! 3. Kf3** (if 3. Nf2 Bxf2 4. Kxf2 Kf4) **3. ... Kd4 4. Bb3 Bb7** (4. ... Bxd3 5. Bxd5 Bf1 is simpler; if then 6. Bb7! Bxh3 7. Ba6!! Kc3!! 8. Kg3! Kb2 9. Bc4 Bf1 10. Bxf1 Kxa2 11. Kf3 Bh6 12. Bb5 Kb3 13. Ke4 a4 14. Kd4 a3 wins) **5. Ke2 Ba6 6. Bc2** (6. Bxd5 Bxd3+

7. Kf3 Bf1 transposes into the note to Black's fourth move) **6. ... Bb5** (to provoke a4. 6. ... Kc3 7. Kxe3 d4+ is also good enough) **7. a4 Bd7 8. Kf3 Kc3 9. Kxe3 d4+ 10. Ke2 Kxc2 11. Nf4 Bxa4**, and it's all over. The last moves were **12. Ne6 Bb3! 13. Nxd4+ Kb2 14. Nb5 a4 15. Ke3 a3 16. Nxa3 Kxa3 17. Kd4 Kb4**, White resigned.

The bishops are at their worst in blocked positions and where all the pawns are on one side. With these two disadvantages combined, even a pawn up may not be enough to win.

No. 551, Euwe-Alekhine, 3rd match game, 1937

Black to play. Draw

After **1. ... Kf7 2. h4 g5!** (essential to prevent Bf4 and h5, which would free the king) **3. Bh5+ Ke7!** (not 3. ... Kf6? 4. Bd8+ Kf5 5. g4+, winning a pawn, or 3. ... Kg7? 4. Bd8! gxh4 5. Bxh4 followed by Bg3-f4 and marching the king to the queenside) **4. Bg4 Bb7** (White can make no further progress with his bishops, so he offers to exchange a bishop for the strong knight, but his winning hopes are soon dissipated) **5. Be5 Nxe5 6. dxe5 gxh4 7. Kg1 Ba6 8. Kh2 Kf7**, and the game was eventually drawn (No. 340).

Endings with all the pawns on one side are almost always drawn if the superior side has three pawns or fewer and usually drawn if he has four pawns.

An example where two bishops and two pawns hold bishop and knight and three pawns is **No. 552** (Gygli-Alekhine, Berne 1932): **White king at h3, bishops at c8, f8, pawns at f3, h2; Black king at h8, bishop at d4, knight at d1, pawns at h7, g7, f5.** Black to play. Draw. **1. ... Ne3 2. Be6 f4 3. Ba3 Be5 4. Bc1 Nc2 5. Bb3 Ne1 6. Bd5 Nd3 7. Bd2 g6 8. Bc4 Nb2 9. Be2 h5 10. Bc1 Na4 11. Bd2 Kg7 12. Bb4 Kf6 13. Ba5 Nc5 14. Bd8+ Kf5 15. Be7 Nd7 16. Bd3+ Ke6 17. Bd8 Kf7 18. Bg5**, and Alekhine soon admitted that he could make no headway against White's stubborn defense.

To sum up: Two bishops are better than two knights or bishop and knight in most normal pawn positions. If the pawns are unbalanced so that the side with the two bishops can set up an outside passed pawn, the game is practically a forced win. If the pawns are balanced, the slightest weakness in the pawn structure may prove fatal. The three ideas that are the key to all such endings are:

1) Limiting the opponent's mobility.

2) Stalemating the knight (or knights).

3) Exchanging one set of pieces to transpose into a favorable simple ending (especially a bishop ending where the opponent's pawns are on the same color as his bishop).

IV. TWO PIECES VS. ONE

The advantage of a piece generally wins only if there are pawns on the board and the inferior side has fewer than three pawns for the piece.

A. No Pawns

Just as one minor piece cannot mate a lone king, two minor pieces against one usually cannot win. But there are a number of exceptions .

It is always bad for the defender's king to be in the corner. Such positions give rise to most of the exceptions to the general rule that two pieces only draw against one. The reason, of course, is the threat of checkmate.

No. 553, Berger

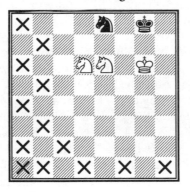

White to play wins. The Black knight may be on any square marked X

No. 553 is an example with two knights vs. one. The solution is **1. Nf7!** (1. Nxe8? of course only draws) **1. ... Nd6** (any other knight move amounts to the same thing: the point is that Black cannot give check in fewer than three moves) **2. Nh6+ Kh8 3. Ng5!** Now we see what difference the extra Black piece makes: if it were not on the board Black would be stalemated. **3. ... Nc4 4. Ngf7+** mate.

An analogous case with two bishops vs. one is **No. 554** (Berger): **White king at g5, bishops at e4, f8; Black king at h8, bishop at e8.** White to play wins. **1. Kh6** (threatening 1. Bh7!) **1. ... Kg8 2. Ba3 Bb5** (there is nothing to be done; if 2. ... Kf7 3. Bg6+ and 4. Bxe8; if 2. ... Kh8 3. Bh7! any 4. Bb2+ mate, and if 2. ... Bf7 3. Bh7+ Kh8 4. Bb2+ mate) **3. Bd5+ Kh8 4. Bb2+** mate.

No. 555 illustrates the mating possibilities with bishop and knight vs. bishop.

No. 555, Kling and Horwitz 1851

White to play wins

The solution is **1. Be5+ Kg8 2. Bg7! Bh4! 3. Nf4 Be7 4. Nd5 Bg5** (if 4. ... Bd8 5. Bh6 Bh4 6. Ne3 Be7 7. Nf5 Bd8 8. Bg7 and wins) **5. Bc3 Bh4** (or 5. ... Bc1 6. Nf6+ Kh8 7. Ne4+ Kg8 8. Bg7 Bg5 9. Nd6 Be7 10. Nf5; or 5. ... Bd8 6. Bb4 Bh4 7. Ne3 Bg3 8. Nf5 Bf4 9. Ne7+ Kf8 10. Nd5+, winning the bishop) **6. Bb4 Bf2** (he must prevent Ne3) **7. Nf6+ Kh8 8. Bf8 B any 9. Bg7+** mate.

With bishop and knight vs. knight another kind of winning threat appears: trapping the knight. For example, **No. 556** (Berger): **White king at e5, bishop at c4, knight at f5; Black king at h8, knight at e8.** White to play wins. **1. Bf7! Nc7** (if 1. ... Ng7 2. Nh6! Kh7 3. Ng4! Kh8 4. Nf6! and the knight is lost) **2. Kd4 Na6** (if 2. ... Nb5+ 3. Kc4 Na3+ 4. Kb4 Nc2+ 5. Kc3 Na3 6. Be8 Nb1+ 7. Kd3 Na3 8. Ne3 Kg8 9. Kc3 Kf8 10. Ba4 Ke7 11. Kb2) **3. Kc4 Nb8 4. Be8 Kg8 5. Kd5 Na6 6. Kd6 Nb4 7. Bb5 Nc2 8. Bd3 Ne1 9. Be4 Kf7 10. Ke5 Kg6 11. Kf4 Kf6 12. Nd4 Ke7 13. Nf5+ Ke6 14. Ng3 Kf6 15. Ke3 Kg5 16. Ne2 Kg4 17. Kf2** and the knight will finally pay the penalty for not being a bishop.

No. 557 (Amelung 1896) is a mating attack with bishop and knight vs. knight: **White king at g6, bishop at h6, knight at f6; Black king at h8, knight at d4.** Black to play. **1. ... Nf5 2. Bf8 Nh4+ 3. Kf7 Nf5 4. Ne4 Kh7 5. Ng5+ Kh8 6. Bc5 Nd6+ 7. Kf8 Nf5 8. Bb6 Ng7 9. Ba5 Nf5 10. Bc3+ Ng7 11. Bxg7+** mate. However, the knight can draw if it's on one of a number of other squares: c6, c4, d3, and, of course, any square from which a capture is possible.

No. 558, Kling and Horwitz 1851

White to play wins

No. 558 differs from the other examples in that there is no immediate threat of mate or of capturing the knight.

The solution is **1. Bb4 Nh7**

If 1. ... Nd7 2. Bd5+ Kg7 3. Bc4 Nf8 4. Bc3+ Kh6 5. Bf7 Nh7 6. Be8 Nf8 7. Bb2 Nh7 8. Bd4 Nf8 9. Kf6 Nh7+ 10. Kf7 Ng5+ 11. Kg8 Nf3 12. Be3+ Ng5 13. Kf8 and wins the knight; or 1. ... Ng8 2. Bd5+ Kg7 3. Kg5! Kh7 4. Bf8! Kh8 5. Be4 N any 6. K or BxN; or, finally, 1. ... Ne8 2. Bh5+.

2. Bc3 Ke8

If 2. ... Kf8 3. Kg6, while if 2. ... Kg8 3. Bd5+ Kf8 4. Kg6; a knight move also does not help: 2. ... Nf8 3. Bh5+ Kg8 4. Be8 Kh7 5. Kf6 Kh6 6. Bd2+ Kh7 7. Bb4 Kg8 8. Bf7+ K any 9. Bxf8.

3. Bh5+ Kf8 (or 3. ... Kd8 4. Bb4 followed by Bg6) **4. Kg6 Kg8 5. Bg4 Nf8+ 6. Kf6 Nh7+** (if 6. ... Kh7 7. Kf7 Ng6 8. Bf5, etc.) **7. Ke7 Ng5** (on 7. ... Nf8 8. Bh5 Ng6+ 9. Kf6 Nh8 10. Be2 Kh7 11. Bc4 Kh6 12. Bd3 Kh5 13. Kg7 decides) **8. Bf6** (8. Bf5 Ne4! is harder) **8. ... Ne4! 9. Be6+ Kh7 10. Bf5+ Kg8 11. Bh4!** (not 11. Bxe4? stalemate) **11. ... Nc3** (or 11. ... Nc5 12. Bf2 Na6 13. Kd6; or 11. ... Nd2 12. Kf6 Kf8 13. Bd3 Nb3 14. Bf2 and the knight is trapped in both cases) **12. Ke6 Nb5 13. Bf2 Nc7+ 14. Kd7 Nb5 15. Bd3** and again the cavalry must make its last stand.

To sum up: Without pawns, two pieces win against one only in certain special positions. These occur chiefly when the defender's king is in the corner. The win is accomplished by checkmate. When the lone piece is a knight, there is the added possibility of trapping it. Two bishops vs. knight is a theoretical win but sometimes takes more than 50 moves.

B. With Pawns

1. White Has One Pawn

a) If Black has no pawns the win is routine.

Difficulties arise for one of three reasons: 1. The superior side has two knights. 2. The pawn is on the seventh. 3. There is a rook-pawn plus wrong-color bishop. These may make the win more complex, but prevent it only in problem positions.

No. 559, Berger

White to play wins

The first difficulty (two knights) is shown in **No. 559**, the solution to which is **1. h6 Bb3! 2. Nd6!!** (not 2. h7+ Kh8 3. Nd6? Bc2+ 4. Kh6 Bxh7) **2. ... Bc2+ 3. Nf5! Bb3 4. h7+ Kh8 5. Ne7! Bc2+ 6. Kh6 Bxh7 7. Nf7+** mate.

Two knights and pawn also win against a knight. **No. 560** (Berger): **White king at f6, knights at e4, f5, pawn at h5; Black king at g8, knight at h3.** White to play wins. **1. Ng5! Nf2** (if 1. ... Nf4 2. Ne7+ K any 3 Ng6+, while if 1. ... Ng1 2. Ne7+ Kh8 3. Kg6) **2. Nh6+ Kf8** (or 2. ... Kh8 3. Kg6 any 4. Ngf7+ mate) **3. Ne6+ Ke8 4. Ng8 Kd7 5. Kg7! Kxe6 6. h6** and wins.

In the second case (pawn on the seventh), the danger of stalemate is always present. Nevertheless, with accurate play this can normally be avoided.

One example will suffice **No. 561** (Horwitz 1880): **White king at f5, bishop at f8, knight at f6, pawn at h7; Black king at h8, knight at c6.** White to play wins. The main variation is **1. Bd6! Kg7 2. Kg5 Nd4 3. Bf8+ Kh8 4. Kg6 Ne6 5. Bh6 Nf8+ 6. Kf7 Ne6! 7. Ng4!! Nd8+ 8. Kg6 Ne6 9. Bg7+!! Nxg7 10. Ne5 any 11. Nf7+** mate.

In the third case (rook-pawn and wrong bishop), take care not to exchange the wrong piece or push the pawn too hastily.

For example, **No. 562** (Alekhine-v. Scheltinga, Amsterdam 1936): **White king at h6, bishop at d3, knight at h5, pawn at h3; Black king at h8, knight at e3.** White wins. **1. ... Nd5 2. Kg5 Ne7 3. h4 Nd5 4. Ng3 Ne7 5. Bc4 Kg7 6.**

Nh5+ Kh8 7. Nf4 Kg7 8. h5, Black resigned, for if 8. ... Kh8 9. Ng6+ Nxg6 10. hxg6, etc.

The ending with two bishops and pawn vs. bishop is not quite so easy. Be careful not to advance the rook-pawn to the seventh rank too early. **No. 563** (Berger): **White king at f5, bishops at a2, a3, pawn at h5; Black king at h6, bishop at c3.** White to play wins. **1. Bc1+! Kh7** (1. ... Kxh5 2. Bg5! any 3. Bf7+ mate) **2. h6 Ba5 3. Kg5 Bd8+ 4. Kh5 Bf6 5. Bb1+ Kh8 6. Kg6** (now 6. h7?? only draws, for Black plays his bishop back and forth along the long diagonal and refuses to budge his king) **6. ... Bc3 7. Ba3 Bd4 8. Ba2 Bc3 9. Bf8 Bd4 10. Bg7+ Bxg7 11. hxg7+** mate.

b) If Black has one pawn the win is achieved by first capturing that pawn (which brings us back to the previous case).

No. 564 (Alekhine–v. Scheltinga, Amsterdam 1936) is a model. **White king at f2, bishop at c2, knight at g5, pawn at h3; Black king at g7, knight at a6, pawn at h7.** Black to play, White wins. Alekhine won as follows: **1. ... h6 2. Ne4 Nb4 3. Bb1 Nd5 4. Kf3 Nf6 5. Nd6 Ng8 6. Nf5+ Kg6 7. Kf4 Nf6 8. Ng3+ Kg7 9. Kf5 Kf7 10. Ba2+ Kg7 11. Bb3!** (a tempo move) **11. ... Ne8 12. Nh5+ Kh7 13. Bc2 Nc7 14. Kf6+ Kh8 15. Kg6 Nd5 16. Kxh6.** For the rest of the game see No. 562.

The most difficulty is offered by rook-pawn and wrong bishop with bishops of opposite colors. If Black defends his pawn, White can capture it only at the cost of exchanging a piece, which would leave him with a drawn ending. Similar variations occur in the analogous case with two knight-pawns. For instance, **No. 565** (Horwitz 1885): **White king at d7, bishops at a5, f1, pawn at b6; Black king at b8, bishop at c5, pawn at b7.** White wins. **1. Bh3 Bg1 2. Kd6 Bh2+ 3. Kc5 Bg1+ 4. Kb5 Bh2 5. Bd2 Bg3 6. Bg5 Bh2 7. Bd8 Bg3 8. Kc5 Bh2 9. Kd5 Bg3 10. Ke6 Bf2 11. Kd7 Be3 12. Bg2 Bf2 13. Bc7+ Ka8 14. Kc8 Bxb6 15. Bb8 any 16. Bxb7+** mate.

c) If Black has two pawns, the winning method is still to capture them (unless the White pawn is passed).

This can very often be done by means of mate threats. For instance, **No. 566** (Alekhine–v. Scheltinga, Amsterdam, 1936): **White king at f2, bishop at b3, knight at f3, pawn at h3; Black king at h5, knight at b4, pawns at g5, h7.** White wins. **1. Ne5! Na6** (if 1. ... Kh4 2. Kg2 Na6 3. Bf7! threatening mate and forcing 3. ... g4) **2. Bc2! Kh6** (if 2. ... h6 3. Kg3 mates in a few) **3. Nf7+ Kg7 4. Nxg5,** etc. (No. 564). It stands to reason, however, that with two pawns there will be many positions where Black can exchange the last pawn and draw.

d) If Black has three pawns, he should usually be able to draw unless his pawns are badly blockaded.

No. 567 (Fine–Keres, Semmering–Baden, 1937): **White king at f1, bishop at g3, pawns at f4, g2, h2; Black king at e6, bishop at b2, knight at g4, pawn at f5.** White to play. Draw. **1. h3 Nf6 2. Bf2 Nd5 3. g4** and Black cannot win.

e) If Black has four pawns or more, he should at least draw. Usually, as in the analogous case with bishop (or knight) and pawn vs. four pawns, he will win.

2. White Has Two or More Pawns

The same rule applies here as in the analogous cases with one piece: three pawns for the piece draw, any fewer lose, any more win.

The win with a piece for two pawns often presents some difficulty. The general idea is first to blockade the pawns, then attack them. Eventually, more material must be lost because the defender simply does not have enough pieces to hold off his opponent.

No. 568, Schwann-Fahrni, Barmen 1905

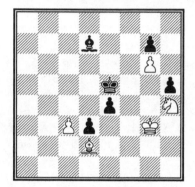

White to play wins

Where no direct attack is successful, zugzwang will often do the trick. **No. 568** is a good example. White wins by **1. Kf2 Kd5 2. Ke3 Bc8 3. Kf4 Bg4 4. Ng2 Bf3** (if 4. ... Kc4 5. Ne3+ Kb3 6. c4, or 6. Ke4) **5. Ne3+ Ke6 6. Kg5 Ke7 7. Nf5+ Kf8 8. c4 Bg4 9. Bb4+ Kg8 10. Ne3 Bf3 11. c5 Kf8 12. c6+ Ke8 13. Bc3 Kd8 14. Bxg7 d2 15. Bf6+ Ke8 16. c7 Bg4 17. Nxg4** and wins.

To sum up: If there are fewer than three pawns for the piece, the superior side wins. The method consists of capturing as many pawns as possible, always being careful to keep one's own.

Chapter VI

ROOK AND PAWN ENDINGS

I. ROOK VS. PAWNS

The results here are quite different from those for bishop and knight endings because the rook is a sufficient mating force. Therefore, if it manages to capture all enemy pawns it will win. In general, if the White king is near the pawns, one and two pawns lose, three or four draw; if the White king is not near the pawns but the Black king is, one pawn draws, two or more pawns win.

A. Rook vs. One Pawn

To have any prospects at all, Black's king must be near the pawn and must be able to stay near it. For this reason, Black's king and pawn must both be at least on the fourth rank.

No. 569

White to play wins

What happens if the king is only on the third rank is seen in **No. 569: 1. Rb5 h4 2. Kb7 h3 3. Rb3 h2 4. Rh3** wins.

But when the Black king and pawn are both on the fourth rank or beyond, the outcome depends on the position of the White king. Of course, if the White king manages to occupy some square directly in front of the pawn, the game is over, since he can attack the pawn with both pieces and capture it. Problems arise only when the White king cannot reach the queening file. This gives us our basic *Rule 1: White wins with rook vs. pawn if and only if both king and rook can cover some square that the pawn must still cross.* It is difficult if not impossible to set up exact subsidiary rules, but those given here hold in the great majority of cases.

Rule 2. If the White king is in front of the pawn but to one side, the game is won if it is two files from the square of the pawn (White to play).

No. 570

White to play wins.
Black to play draws

No. 570 is the general case. Black to play draws by **1. ... h5 2. Kb2 h4 3. Kc2** (if 3. Rg1+ Kf3 4. Rh1 Kg3 does not alter matters) **3. ... h3 4. Kd2 h2 5. Ke2 Kg3** =. But with White to play he can impede the advance of the pawn and gain time to get his king to the h-file. **1. Rg1+ Kf4 2. Rh1 Kg5 3. Kb2 h5 4. Kc2 h4 5. Kd2 Kg4 6. Ke2 h3 7. Rg1+** wins.

The crucial question here is whether or not the White king can reach e2 before the pawn gets to the seventh.

With the White rook behind the pawn, the king can be one square farther away because White gains time by attacking the pawn. **No. 571: White rook at b8,** other pieces as in No. 570, is a win: **1. ... h5 2. Rg8+ Kf3** (or 2. ... Kh3 3. Kb2 h4 4. Kc2 Kh2 5. Kd2 h3 6. Ke2 Kh1 7. Kf3, as in the main variation) **3. Rh8 Kg4 4. Kb2 h4 5. Kc2 h3 6. Kd2 Kg3 7. Ke2!** (not 7. Ke3 Kg2!! 8. Rg8+ Kf1!! =, or 8. Ke2 h2 =) **7. ... Kg2** (if 7. ... h2 8. Kf1! and the king must abandon the pawn to its fate) **8. Rg8+ Kh1 9. Kf3!** (not 9. Kf1? h2! =) **9. ... h2 10. Kg3!! Kg1 11. Kh3+ Kh1 12. Ra8**, etc.

When the White king is behind the pawn, there are various cases. With a rook-pawn or knight-pawn it is better to have the rook behind the pawn (on the eighth rank). We then have:

Rule 3. If the White rook and king are both behind the pawn (rook-pawn or knight-pawn), White wins if his king is two ranks from the square of the pawn. More precisely, it should be added that the king does not need to lose a tempo to stay within two ranks of the square.

No. 572, Euwe 1934

White to play wins. Draw with White rook at d6 or a3

No. 572 illustrates this rule. There are two ways to win:

a) **1. Kd6 g4** (or 1. ... Ke4 2. Rg8 Kf4 3. Kd5, etc.) **2. Kd5 Kf4 3. Kd4 Kf3** (if 3. ... g3 4. Rf8+ Kg4 5. Ke3, etc.) **4. Kd3 g3** (or 4. ... Kf2 5. Rf8+ Kg2 6. Ke2 Kh2 7. Rg8 g3 8. Kf3) **5. Rf8+ Kg2 6. Ke2 Kg1** (or 6. ... Kh2 7. Rg8 g2 8. Kf2 Kh1 9. Rh8+ mate) **7. Kf3** (or 7. Rg8) **g2 8. Rg8 Kh1 9. Kf2!** (but not 9. Rxg2? stalemate), and White mates in at most three moves.

b) **1. Rf8+ Ke4** (or 1. ... Kg4 2. Kf6 Kf4 3. Kg6+ Kg4 4. Rf5) **2. Kf6 g4 3. Kg5 g3 4. Kh4 g2 5. Rg8 Kf3 6. Kh3** and wins the pawn.

In both variations, it is essential that the White king does not lose a tempo on its way back; i.e., it must stay near the square without loss of tempo. This is why **No. 573: White rook at d6**, other pieces as in No. 572, is drawn. On 1. Rf6+ Ke4 2. Ke6 g4 3. Rg6 Kf3! 4. Kf5 g3, White has no good tempo move: if 5. Kg5 g2 6. Kh4 Kf2 and he is one move too late, for if 7. Rf6+ Ke2 8. Rg6 Kf2!, etc. The best try for White is **1. Rd5+ Kf4 2. Kf6 g4 3. Rd4+ Kf3 4. Kf5 g3 5. Rd3+ Kf2 6. Kf4 g2 7. Rd2+ Kf1 8. Kf3 g1=N+!! 9. Ke3 Nh3!! =** (No. 966).

No. 574, with the **White rook at a3**, other pieces as in No. 572, the previous diagram, the trouble is that time is lost with the rook: after **1. Kd6** (or 1. Kf7 g4! and White must mark time with 2. Kg7 Kf4 3. Kg6 g3 4. Kh5 g2 5. Ra1 Kg3, etc.) **1. ... g4 2. Kd5 Kf4 3. Ra8** is the only chance, but then **3. ... g3 4. Rf8+ Ke3 5. Rg8 Kf2 6. Ke4 g2** makes the draw clear.

All of these endings are *critical positions*, in the sense that if White is any nearer he wins easily; if he is not as well placed, the draw is certain. An example is **No. 575: White king at f7,** other pieces as in No. 573, White wins: **1. Rf6+ Ke4** (or 1. ... Kg4 2. Kg6 Kh4 3. Kf5) **2. Kg6 g4 3. Kh5! g3 4. Kh4 g2 5. Rg6 Kf3 6. Kh3 Kf2 7. Rxg2+,** etc.

Similarly in **No. 576: White king at f7,** other pieces as in No. 574, the win is clear after **1. Ra5+ Kf4 2. Kg6 g4 3. Kh5 g3 4. Kh4 g2 5. Rg5 Kf3 6. Kh3.**

No. 577 is an instance of a distant king but where a tempo-losing rook move lets the king approach.

No. 577, P. Benko 1987

White to play wins

1. Kb7 Kg4!? (this paradoxical move is the best defense) **2. Rf6!!** (the only winning maneuver. Though it costs a tempo, it keeps the Black king off the f-file and aids the approach of the White king. The move 2. Kc6 doesn't work here because of 2. ... Kf3! 3. Kd5 g4 4. Ra3+ Kf4!, avoiding 4. ... Kf2 5. Ke4 g3 6. Ra2+) **2. ... Kh3 3. Kc6 g4 4. Kd5 g3 5. Ke4!** (5. Rh6+ is a subtle mistake that lets Black off the hook after 5. ... Kg2! 6. Ke4 Kf2 7. Rf6+ Ke2 8. Ra6 g2 9. Ra2+ Kf1 10. Kf3 g1=N+!) **5. ... g2 6. Kf3! g1=N+ 7. Kf2** wins.

A rook-pawn is an exception, as usual. In **No. 578,** analogous to previous examples: **White king at f7, rook at e6; Black king at g5, pawn at h5,** White wins by the checking sequence: **1. Re5+ Kg4 2. Kg6 h4 3. Re4+ Kg3 4. Kg5 h3 5. Re3+ Kg2 6. Kg4 h2 7. Re2+ Kg1 8. Kg3!! h1=N+ 9. Kf3 Kf1 10. Rg2!!** and wins the knight.

With a bishop-pawn or center pawn the play is somewhat different. Here we have *Rule 4.*

If the Black king is on the same rank as the pawn and the White rook is on the first rank, White to play always wins when the pawn is on its second, third, or fourth rank, wins if and only if his king is three ranks behind the pawn on its fifth rank, two ranks behind the pawn on its sixth, and on the same rank as the pawn on its seventh. In addition, if the kings are on the same side of the pawn, White must never move into a position in which the Black king has the opposition.

When the kings are on opposite sides of the pawn, the win is simpler.

579, Euwe 1934

White to play wins. Black to play draws

No. 579 is the critical position. **1. Kc6 d3 2. Kc5 Ke3 3. Kc4 d2 4. Kc3 Ke2 5. Kc2 or Ra2**. Or Black to play, **1. ... d3 2. Kc6 d2 3. Kc5 Ke3 4. Kc4 Ke2 5. Ra2 Ke1**, draw. With the pawn on its second, third, or fourth ranks we really have a trivial case, since the White king can be at most three ranks behind. With the pawn on its sixth rank the White king must be closer because his rival has gained an extra move.

The critical position here is **No. 580: White king at b5, rook at a1; Black king at e3, pawn at d3**. White to play wins; Black to play draws. **1. Kc4 d2 2. Kc3 Ke2 3. Kc2**. Or **1. ... d2 2. Kc4 Ke2**. In addition, when the pawn is on the sixth, White's king must not be more than two files from the square of the pawn (Rule 2). If the Black king is at g3, pawn at f3, White king at b5, rook at a1 wins, but king at a6 only draws.

When the kings are on the same side of the pawn there is the added difficulty of giving Black the opposition and having to lose a valuable tempo. The critical position is **No. 581:**

No. 581, Euwe 1934

White to play wins. Black to play draws. Draw with white king at b7

The solution is **1. Kd6 e3** (or 1. ... Kd4 2. Ke6 e3 3. Kf5: No. 579) **2. Ke5 Kd3 3. Kf4 e2 4. Kf3 Kd2 5. Kf2.** Or **1. ... e3 2. Kd6 e2 3. Ke5 Kd3 4. Kf4 Kd2 5. Ra2+ Kd3!** or even **5. ... Kd1.**

But **No. 582, White king at b7**, other pieces unchanged, is drawn because after **1. Kc6 e3** Black has the opposition and White must waste a move.

Similarly, with the pawn on its fourth rank, **No. 583: White king at a8, rook at a1; Black king at e5, pawn at f5,** White to play can only draw because after **1. Kb7 f4 2. Kc6 f3 3. Kc5 Ke4 4. Kc4 f2** Black has the opposition. Gaining the opposition is of the utmost importance in such endings.

For instance, **No. 584: White king at b5, rook at a1; Black king at e5, pawn at f4.** Black to play. According to the rule, White wins unless his opponent holds him off with the opposition. This is in fact what happens. **1. ... Kd4! 2. Rd1+** (2. Kb4 f3) **2. ... Ke3 3. Re1+ Kd2!, or 3. Kc4 f3 4. Kc3 f2** and again the king cannot approach.

With the pawn on any one of the four central files, having the White rook on the eighth is equivalent to the loss of a move. For instance, with the **rook at a8** in No. 581, the game is a draw. For **1. Re8 Kd4 2. Kd6 e3 3. Ke6 e2** (or even 3. ... Ke4!) **4. Kf5 Kd3 5. Kf4 Kd2** gets there one move too late.

When the kings are on the same file, the win is achieved by going to the opposite side. This of course requires gaining the opposition as a preliminary step.

No. 585, Reti 1928

White to play wins

White has the opposition and must hold it while his rook is on the first rank. So the solution is **1. Rd2! d4 2. Rd1!!**. Now Black must lose, according to Rule 4, because White has the opposition. All White needs is to go to the opposite side of the pawn. **2. ... Kd5 3. Kd7!!** (but not 3. Kf6? Ke4 4. Ke6 d3 and Black has the opposition!) **3. ... Kc4** (or 3. ... Ke4 4. Kc6) **4. Ke6:** No. 579.

No. 586, Averbakh 1981

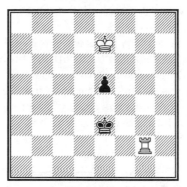

White to play wins

For **No. 586,** the solution is **1. Ke6! e4 2. Rg5! Kf3** (2. ... Kd3 3. Rd5+! Kc2 4. Re5 Kd3 5. Kf5, etc.) **3. Rf5+! Kg3 4. Re5 Kf3 5. Kd5 e3 6. Kd4 e2 7. Kd3** catches the pawn.

In certain rare cases the rook cannot stop the pawn on the seventh. A classic problem with this idea is **No. 587** (Saavedra 1895): **White king at b6, pawn at c6; Black king at a1, rook at d5.** White to play wins by **1. c7 Rd6+ 2. Kb5** (not 2. Kb7 Rd7, or 2. Kc5 Rd1) **2. ... Rd5+ 3. Kb4 Rd4+ 4. Kb3 Rd3+ 5. Kc2 Rd4!! 6. c8=R!!** (if 6. c8=Q Rc4+ 7. Qxc4 stalemate) **6. ... Ra4** (necessary to stop mate) **7. Kb3!** and either mates or captures the rook.

B. Rook vs. Two Pawns

As usual, three different types must be distinguished.

Two connected passed pawns, in the absence of the kings, win if they are both on the sixth, but otherwise lose.

No. 588

White to play wins

This is shown in **No. 588**. With White to play, **1. g7 Rg4 2. h7** forces a queen (for the ending queen vs. rook see No. 1101). Or Black to play **1. ... Rb8 2. g7 Rg8 3. h7**, etc.

If the enemy king can reach any square in front of the pawns, he wins. This is to be expected, since the rook can then capture both pawns.

Such endings normally arise as a result of a sacrifice that draws the enemy king away from the pawns and allows one's own king to approach them. The crucial question then is how near the enemy king must be to the pawns to be able to stop them. The critical position is **No. 589**.

No. 589

Whoever plays wins. Draw with Black king at e5, f5, or g5

White to play queens the e-pawn, captures the rook, and then queens his f-pawn. **1. e8=Q Rxe8 2. Kxe8 Ke6 3. f7**, etc. Black to play blockades the pawns and then captures them. **1. ... Kd7 2. Kg6 Ke6! 3. Kg7 Rb8 4. Kg6** (if 4. e8=Q+ Rxe8 5. f7 Re7) **4. ... Rg8+ 5. Kh7 Kf7 6. Kh6 Kxf6**.

Black does not win, however, when White has bishop-pawn and knight-pawn because of a stalemate possibility. **No. 590, White king at g7, pawns at g6, f7; Black: king at e6, rook at a8**. Black to play can only draw. **1. ... Ke7 2. Kh6 Kf6 3. Kh7 Rb8 4. f8=Q+!! Rxf8 5. g7 Rf7 6. Kh8!! Rxg7**, stalemate.

The same holds true for bishop-pawn and rook-pawn. **No. 591: White king at h7, pawns at g7, h6; Black king at f6, rook at a8**. Black to play, draw. **1. ... Kf7 2. g8=Q+ Rxg8**, stalemate.

If Black's rook is behind the pawn in No. 589; i.e., on the e-file, he can only draw at best. **No. 592: Black rook at e1**, other pieces as in No. 589. White to play wins as before. Black to play can only draw by **1. ... Kd7 2. Kf8! Re6 3. Kf7**, or even **3. f7! Rxe7 4. Kg8**. Or **2. Kg7**, in the hope of provoking 2. ... Ke8?? 3. f7+, is met instead by **2. ... Rf1 3. Kf7 Re1**, or **3. ... Rxf6+ 4. Kxf6 Ke8**.

To decide the outcome of any ordinary ending with king and two pawns vs. king and rook, we compare it with previous diagrams.

No. 593, Tarrasch-Janowski, Ostend 1907

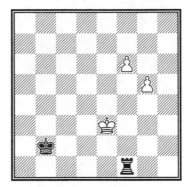

White to play wins

In **No. 593**, White wins because he forces both pawns to the sixth. **1. Kd4 Kb3** (if 1. ... Rf5 2. Ke4!! Rxg5 3. f7 and queens after 3. ... Rg4+ 4. Ke3 Rg3+ 5. Kf2) **2. Ke5 Kc4 3. g6 Re1+ 4. Kd6 Rg1** (the game continuation was 4. ... Rd1+ 5. Ke7 Re1+ 6. Kf7, Black resigned resigns) **5. g7!!** (but not 5. f7? Rxg6+ 6. Ke5 Rg5+ =, for if 7. Ke4 Rg1! 8. f8=Q?? Re1+ 9. Kf5 Rf1+) **5. ... Kd4! 6. Kc6!!** (6. f7 is refuted by 6. ... Rg6+! 7. Ke7 Rxg7 and the f-pawn is pinned) **6. ... Kc4!** (the only move: if 6. ... Ke5 7. f7 Rg6+ 8. Kb5, while if 6. ... Rg6 7. Kb5 is again the answer) **7. Kd7!!** (the point: White will reach e8) **7. ... Kd5 8. Ke8 Ke6 9. f7 Ra1 10. f8=N+!! K any 11. g8=Q**.

Two pawns on the fifth cannot win if the enemy king is close. **No. 594** (Kling and Horwitz 1851): **White king at d5, rook at h5; Black king at c3, pawns at a4, b4.** Draw. **1. Rh3+ Kb2 2. Kc4 b3 3. Rh2+** (or 3. Kb4 Ka2 4. Kxa4 b2 5. Ra3+ Kb1 6. Rb3 Ka1, =) **3. ... Ka3!** (but not 3. ... Kc1? 4. Kc3! Kb1 5. Re2 Ka1 6. Re4! b2 7. Rxa4+ Kb1 8. Rb4 Ka1 9. Kc2! and wins) **4. Kc3 b2! 5. Kc2 Ka2 6. Rh1 a3**.

Or **No. 595** (Keidanski 1914): **White king at b5, rook at c2; Black king at d5, pawns at e3, f4.** White to play draws. **1. Rc8!! e2 2. Rd8+ Ke4 3. Kc4 Ke3** (or 3. ... Kf3 4. Re8 Kf2 5. Kd3, No. 589) **4. Re8+ Kd2** (or 4. ... Kf2 5. Kd3 f3 6. Kd2, =) **5. Rd8+ Kc2 6. Re8 f3 7. Re3!!** and Black can do no better than wear White out by allowing perpetual check.

When the king with the pawns is on or near the edge of the board, the threat of checkmate may often be an adequate defense against two pawns on the sixth and seventh, while if both pawns are on the sixth, or one is on the seventh and the other on the fifth, the rook may even win.

No. 596, Keres-Eliskases, Nordwijk 1938

Black to play draws

No. 596 is the typical drawing case. 1. ... Kc3! 2. Kb1 Ra6! 3. b7 Rb6+ 4. Kc1 (the only way to escape the checks: if 4. Ka1 Ra6+) 4. ... Rh6!!, and here a draw was agreed. If 5. Kd1 Kd3 6. Ke1 Ke3 7. Kf1 Kf3 8. Kg1 Rg6+, and the best White can do is try again on the other side, since 9. Kf1 Rh6! 10. Ke1 Ke3!, etc., is the only way to avoid perpetual check.

There are innumerable variations on this theme. One where the mate threat is used to allow the king to approach the pawns is No. 597 (Kling and Horwitz 1851): **White king at f6, rook at b1; Black king at h5, pawns at a3, b2. White to play draws. 1. Kf5 Kh4** (the only chance: if 1. ... Kh6 2. Kf6) **2. Kf4 Kh3 3. Kf3 Kh2 4. Ke3!! Kg2** (the win is a mirage: on 4. ... Kg3 5. Rg1+! Kh3 6. Kf3 Kh2? 7. Rb1 wins for White, while 4. ... a2?? is likewise answered by 5. Rxb2+, destroying Black's hopes) **5. Kd3!!** (the point) **5. ... Kf3 6. Kc2 a2 7. Kxb2** (or 7. Rf1+ Kg2), draw.

In No. 598 (Freeborough 1898), the mate threat almost wins but Black just manages to escape by underpromoting. **White king at c3, rook at f1; Black king at a3, pawns at a2, b3. Draw. 1. ... b2 2. Rf8! b1=N+! 3. Kc2 a1=Q 4. Ra8+ Kb4 5. Rxa1 Na3+ 6. Kd3 Nb5, =** (see No. 496).

When the pawns are still on the sixth or disunited (one on fifth, other on seventh) the rook usually wins.

No. 599, Shapiro 1914

White to play wins

For **No. 599**, the solution is **1. Rd2+ Kb1** (if 1. ... Ka1 2. Kb3 and mate next move) **2. Kc3! Kc1** (or 2. ... g2 3. Rd1+ Ka2 4. Rg1!! and wins, as in No. 597) **3. Ra2 Kd1** (3. ... Kb1 4. Re2 g2 5. Re1+ Ka2 6. Rg1) **4. Kd3 Kc1 5. Ke3! h2** (if 5. ... g2; 6. Kf2) **6. Ra1+ Kb2 7. Rh1! Kc3 8. Kf3** and wins.

No. 600 (Sackmann 1920) is a more complicated instance: **White: king at d6, rook at f1; Black king at g6, pawns at g7, h4.** White wins. The main variation is **1. ... Kh5 2. Ke5 Kg4! 3. Ke4! Kg3 4. Ke3 Kg2 5. Ke2 h3 6. Rf2+ Kg3 7. Rf7! g5 8. Kf1 Kh2 9. Kf2 g4 10. Rg7 Kh1 11. Kg3 Kg1 12. Rxg4 h2 13. Kh3+ Kh1 14. Rd4** and the last pawn falls.

Two unconnected passed pawns, in the absence of the kings, have a chance against a rook only if both are at least on the sixth. In that case they hold the rook if it is on the eighth rank, but win against the rook if one pawn is on the seventh and the rook is stopping it on the file.

No. 601, P. Benko 1997

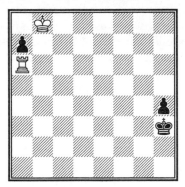

White to play wins

1. Rg6! a5 2. Kc7 a4 3. Kd6 a3 4. Ke5 a2 5. Ra6 Kg4 6. Ra4+ Kg5 (6. ... Kg3 7. Kf5 h3 8. Ra3+ Kg2 9. Rxa2+ Kg1 10. Kg4 h2 11. Kg3 wins) **7. Ke4! Kg4 8. Ra7!!** mutual zugzwang. Black has to move, therefore loses, but with White to play it's a draw. **8. ... h3 9. Rg7+ Kh5 10. Kf5! Kh4 11. Kf4 Kh5 12. Rg1** White wins.

If the king with the pawns is near enough and the enemy king is not, two pawns on the sixth, or on the fifth and sixth, may win against a rook.

However, where the pawns are far apart, if the rook reaches the first rank the pawns cannot win. **No. 602** (Szabo-Portisch 1959): **White king at c5, pawns at b7, g7; Black king at d1, rook at d8.** Draw. For if **1. Kc6 Rg8! 2. Kb6 Ke2** and the White king cannot approach without allowing the capture of one pawn either with check or with a pin on the other pawn.

Where the pawns are not yet on the sixth, it is always better to attack the pawn that is farther advanced. In rook-vs.-pawn endings, the nearer the pawn is to the eighth rank, the better the drawing chances.

No. 603, P. Benko 1986

White to play wins. Twin: No. 604

1. Kf8 Kg5 2. Kf7! (White must preserve the e-pawn so that Black later will not have stalemate possibilities) **2. ... h4 3. Ke6 Kg4 4. Ke5 h3 5. Ke4 Kg3 6. Ke3 Kg2 7. Ke2! h2 8. Rg8+ Kh3 9. Kf2! h1=N+ 10. Kf3 Kh2 11. Rg2+ Kh3 12. Rg7 Kh2 13. Rxe7.**

In the twin, **No. 604**, a small change in the position makes a big difference in the solution.

No. 604, P. Benko 1986

White to play wins

1. Rg7+! The move 1. Rh8 produces No. 603 but with Black to play, who can reach a theoretically draw after 1. ... e5 (the try 1. ... Kg5? permits 2. Kf7, when White wins as above) 2. Kf8 Kg5 3. Kf7 h4 4. Ke6 Kg4 5. Kd5!? h3 6. Ke4 Kg3 7. Kc3 Kg2 8. Ke2 h2 9. Rg8+ Kh3 10. Kf2!? h1=N+ 11. Kf3 e4+! 12. Kxe4 Ng3+ 13. Kf3 Nh5!) **1. ... Kf5 2. Kh7! h4 3. Kh6 h3 4. Kh5 Kf4 5. Kh4 h2 6. Rf7+ Ke3 7. Rf1 e5 8. Kg3 e4 9. Kxh2 Kd2 10. Kg2 e3 11. Kf3 e2 12. Rf2.**

Doubled pawns cannot defend themselves in the absence of the kings. With their king nearby and the enemy king not directly in front of them, they normally draw. But even if the enemy king is far away they can rarely win.

No. 605

White to play draws. White king at h3 loses, White rook at f6 loses.

No. 605 is the general case. White draws by **1. Rc7+ Kb2 2. Rb7+ Ka2** (not 2. ... Ka3? 3. Rb1!) **3. Ra7+ Kb3 4. Rb7+ Kc4 5. Rc7+** (not 5. Rb1 Kc3) **5. ... Kd4 6. Rd7+ Ke3 7. Re7+ Kf3 8. Rf7+,** etc. Neither side can do better than perpetual check. But if the White king is at h3 (or any square on the fourth-seventh rank except f4 or e4), the Black king can escape to h1, and when White runs out of checks he must resign.

In **No. 606**: **White king at h3,** other pieces as in No. 605. Black wins. **1. Rc7+ Kd4 2. Rd7+ Ke3 3. Re7+ Kf2 4. Rf7+ Kg1 5. Rg7+ Kh1** and the pawn queens.

Similarly, if the rook is on the sixth rank (or fifth or nearer), the checks are soon exhausted. **No. 607: White rook at f6,** other pieces as in No. 605. Black wins. **1. Rc6+ Kd4 2. Rd6+ Ke4 3. Re6+ Kd5** and White has no checks.

To sum up: In the absence of the kings, two connected passed pawns on the sixth or beyond win against the rook; two unconnected passed pawns on the sixth or beyond hold the rook, but neither side can make any progress. Two doubled pawns lose. Pawns that are not yet on the sixth always lose. If the king with the pawns is supporting them but the other king is far away, two connected pawns win, unconnected and doubled pawns only draw. If the enemy king is directly in front of the pawns, connected and doubled pawns lose, but unconnected pawns may draw. Finally, if both kings are near the pawns but the enemy king is not directly in front of them, the result is normally a draw. It is always best to have the rook on the first rank.

C. Rook vs. Three Pawns

1. All Pawns Are Connected

Three pawns on the fifth or beyond win against the rook in the absence of the kings.

No. 608

Black to play. White wins

In **No. 608**, after **1. ... Rh5** (on 1. ... Rb7 2. b6 is murder: 2. ... Kg7 3. c6 Rb8 4. c7, and White should not be satisfied with anything less than two queens) **2. b6 Rxc5 3. a6** is No. 588. If the king with the pawns is supporting them while the other king is away on vacation, three pawns on the fourth may also win. But without the aid of the king, three pawns that are not all on the fifth lose.

No. 609, Rosetto-Benko, Portoroz 1958

White to play

1. c5 Ke4 2. a4 Kd5 3. a5 Rg8 4. a6 Rb8+ 5. Ka4 Kc6 6. a7 Rg8 7. Ka5 Ra8 8. b5+ Kxc5, =. If 1. a4 Rg8 2. a5 Rb8+ 3. Kc5 Rc8+ 4. Kd6 (4. Kd5 Rd8+) 4. ... Rxc4 5. b5 Ra4 6. a6 Ra5! 7. Kc6 Ke4, etc., draw.

With the enemy king directly in front of the pawns, the critical position is **No. 610**. Move everything back one rank and the rook wins.

No. 610, Handbuch

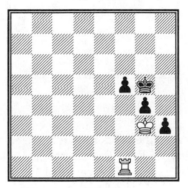

Draw. Pawns on sixth, fifth, fourth lose. Pawns on fourth, third, second win

Best play for both sides is **1. Rf2 Kg6 2. Kf4 Kf6** (but not 2. ... Kh5 3. Rd2 Kh4?? 4. Rd6 Kh5 5. Re6 h2 6. Re8 and wins) **3. Re2 Kf7 4. Re5** (4. Kxf5 g3! and Black wins) **4. ... Kg6.** (Black needs only to keep away from h5 and h7, and prevent the capture of the f-pawn with check) **5. Re6+** (if 5. Rxf5 h2! 6. Rg5+ Kh6, and the h-pawn promotes) **5. ... Kg7** (not 5. ... Kh5 6. Rd6!, as in the note to Black's second move, or 5. ... Kh7 6. Kg5! Kg7 7. Rg6+ Kh7 8. Rh6+ Kg7 9. Rh5 followed by Kxf5; if 9. ... g3 10. Rxh3 g2 11. Rg3) **6. Rd6 Kf7 7. Rh6 Kg7 8. Rh5** (if 8. Kg5 f4! 9. Kxg4 Kxh6 10. Kxh3 leads to an elementary draw)

8. ... Kg6 9. Rg5+ Kh6! 10. Rg8 (on either 10. Kxf5 or 10. Rxf5 h2 wins for Black) **10. ... Kh7 11. Rd8 Kg7,** and White is moving in circles.

If the pawns are not yet advanced to the position in No. 610: e.g., **No. 611: White king at g4, rook at f1; Black king at g6, pawns at f6, g5, h4,** White wins because he can afford to capture the f-pawn. **1. Rf2 Kg7 2. Kf5 Kf7 3. Re2 Kg7 4. Re6 Kh7 5. Rxf6 h3 6. Kxg5 h2 7. Rf1.**

The following trap must be noted. **No. 612** (Berger): **White king at f2, rook at g8; Black king at h6, pawns at f5, g4, h4.** White wins. The solution is **1. Ke2!! h3 2. Ke3 Kh5** (2. ... h2 3. Rh8+, or 2. ... Kh7 3. Rg5) **3. Kf4 Kh6 4. Kxf5** and wins. If Black replies **1. ... g3** (instead of 1. ... h3) **2. Kf3 Kh5 3. Kf4** decides.

When the enemy king is blocking the pawns and the other king is absent, the rook of course wins if it can capture at least one pawn to begin with. An exception is when two pawns are on the seventh.

No. 613, Rinck 1914

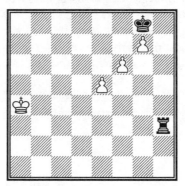

White to play draws

No. 613 is drawn because the Black rook cannot get to the first rank quickly enough. The solution is **1. e6 Rc3** (Black must get to the first rank. If 1. ... Re3 2. e7 Kf7 3. Kb5, Kxf6? is impossible because of 4. g8=Q, while 3. ... Re6 4. Kc5 is also useless, since 4. ... Rxf6? is refuted by 5. e8=Q+ Kxe8 6. g8=Q+) **2. Kb5 Rc8 3. Kb6!** (not 3. e7? Re8 4. Kc6 Kf7 5. Kd7 Ra8! and wins) **3. ... Kh7** (threatening 4. ... Re8) **4. Kb7 Re8 5. g8=Q+!!** (but not 5. e7? Kg8 6. Kc7 Kf7, or 5. f7 Re7+ 6. Kc6 Kxg7 and Black wins in both cases) **5. ... Rxg8** (or 5. ... Kxg8 6. f7+) **6. f7 Rf8 7. Kc6! Kg7 8. e7 Kxf7 =.**

No. 614 is the critical position where the enemy king is to one side of the pawns.

No. 614, Meyer 1890

White to play draws. Pawns on fifth, fourth, third win.

In **No. 614**, after **1. Ke5 Rd8 2. d5 Re8+** nothing can be done. **3. Kf6 Kf3 4. d6 Kxf2 5. d7 Rf8+! 6. Ke7 Ra8 7. e4 Ke3 8. e5 Kd4 9. Kd6** (9. e6 Ke5 is No. 589) **9. ... Ra6+ 10. Kc7** (10. Ke7 Ra8) **10. ... Ra7+ 11. Kc8 Kxe5 12. d8=Q Ra8+.**

On the other hand, in, **No. 615: White king at e5, pawns at d5, e4, f3; Black king at g5, rook at d7,** White to play wins. After **1. Ke6 Rd8 2. d6 Kf4 3. Kd5 Kxf3 4. e5**, the two pawns decide.

2. Only Two Pawns Are Connected

It is practically impossible to set up any explicit rules or even critical positions here. With the king far away, the rook normally cannot hope to stop the pawns, while with the king nearby, the pawns draw only if the king can bring about one of the earlier positions with rook vs. two pawns. **No. 616** is an interesting example of the strategy involved.

No. 616, Reti 1929

White to play draws

The only correct solution is **1. Rg8! g3!** (1. ... f3 2. Rxg4 b4 3. Rf4 offers no hope) **2. Rg4 b4 3. Rxf4 b3 4. Rf1! g2 5. Rg1 b2 6. Kg7 Kd4 7. Kf6 Ke3 8. Rb1! Kd3 9. Rg1!** and both sides must keep repeating moves.

3. Isolated Pawns

The results are the same as usual: the pawns must be far advanced. If the king is near its pawns but the other king is not, the pawns win; if the other king is nearby, the rook wins. In all cases it is essential to have the rook on the first rank.

No. 617 (Reti 1928): **White king at g1, rook at c1; Black king at f5, pawns at c2, e2, g2.** White to play wins. The main variation is **1. Kf2! Ke4 2. Kxe2** (White has the opposition) **2. ... Kd4 3. Rg1 Ke4 4. Re1!! Kd4** (4. ... Kf4 5. Kf2 or 4. ... Ke5 5. Ke3!!) **5. Kd2** and wins.

No. 618, P. Benko 2001

White to play wins

1. Rc8! Kb2 2. Rb8+ Kc2 3. Rh8! d5+ 4. Kb4 a2 5. Rh2+ Kb1 6. Ka3! a1=Q+ 7. Kb3 wins. The try 6. Kb3? a1=N+! 7. Kc3 d4+ leads only to a draw.

To sum up: Three connected passed pawns, in the absence of the king, win against the rook if they are on the fifth rank or beyond. When the enemy king is in front of them they draw if they are on the fourth, fifth, and sixth ranks, respectively; win on the fifth, sixth, and seventh; lose on the third, fourth, and fifth. Where only two pawns are connected, the result depends entirely on the relative positions of the kings and pawns. When all the pawns are isolated, the rook is on the first rank and the king is stopping the pawns, the side with the rook will generally win.

D. Rook vs. Four or More Pawns

As is to be expected, four pawns normally win against the rook. However, when they are not far advanced, the rook will be able to stem the tide.

No. 619 is a case in point.

No. 619, Euwe-Capablanca, Carlsbad 1929

Black to play. Draw

After **1. ... Ra6+ 2. Kf5 Kd4 3. e5 Kd5 4. g3** (4. g4 Ra8 5. h4 Rf8+ 6. Kg5 Rb8 does not win either) **4. ... Ra8 5. Kf6 Ra6+ 6. Kf5 Ra8** a draw was agreed. A possible continuation, given by Tartakower, is **7. h4** (7. g4 Rf8+ 8. Kg5 Rg8+ 9. Kh4?? Ke4 10. Kg3 Ra8! and Black will win) **7. ... Rg8 8. Kf6** (8. g4 Rf8+ and draw by perpetual check) **8. ... Rxg3 9. e6** (9. h5? Rh3 10. Kg5 Ke6 is worse) **9. ... Rg4 10. f5 Rxh4 11. e7 Re4 12. Kf7 Kd6! 13. f6** (13. e8=Q Rxe8 14. Kxe8 Ke5) **13. ... Kd7 =** (No. 598).

More than four pawns should win without any trouble.

E. Rook and Pawns vs. Pawns

The rook has no real equivalent here for a certain number of pawns because a passed pawn supported by the rook will become a queen. **No. 620** illustrates.

No. 620, P. Benko

White to play wins

Here w see some tactic to create a passed pawn. **1 a4! Kb2** (if 1. ... b4 2. Kf7 b3 3. Ke6, etc., wins) **2. Ra3! Kxa3 3. axb5 a4 4. b6,** etc., wins.

II. ROOK AND PAWN VS. ROOK

General rule: *If the Black king can reach the queening square, the game is drawn; if not the game is lost.* While this is true in most cases, it must be regarded as only a convenient rule of thumb. In particular, the rook-pawn is an exception to the second part.

Since it is difficult to grasp the essence of this ending without knowing a number of specific examples, and since this ending is so basic to all rook-and-pawn play, we shall analyze it fairly exhaustively. To begin, we'll give the ideal drawing position, according to our general rule. Some complicated wins require over sixty moves!

A. The Black King on the Queening Square

If the pawn is not far advanced, the king cannot be driven away. This has been known since the time of Philidor.

No. 622

White to play. Draw

This is the standard position. Black keeps his rook on the third rank until the pawn reaches the sixth, and then goes to the eighth. When the square e6 is no longer available to the White king, it will not be able to occupy d6 or f6 and will be unable to drive the Black king out. The moves in **No. 622** might be **1. e5 Ra6 2. e6 Ra1** (2. ... Rb6?? is a blunder: 3. Kf6 Kd8 4. Rh8+ Kc7 5. Kf7 wins) **3. Kf6 Rf1+ 4. Ke5 Re1+ 5. Kd6 Rd1+,** etc.

There are three traps that the defender must avoid — immobilizing his rook unnecessarily, allowing his king to be driven away from the queening square, and, when he must leave, going to the wrong square. *These are the only three cases where you can lose with the king on the queening square.*

1. Immobilizing the Rook

The idea of the defense in the previous example was not to allow the White king to reach the sixth rank unmolested. This can only be prevented by keeping the rook mobile, playing it to the eighth rank. What happens if it is kept on the first rank is shown in **No. 623**.

No. 623

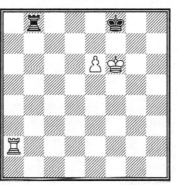

White wins. Win in analogous positions with d-pawn, bishop-pawn, draw with knight-pawn and rook-pawn

Black to play can only mark time, since he must keep his rook on the first rank to prevent mate. White then wins as follows **1. ... Rc8** (or 1. ... Kg8 2. Rg2+ Kf8 3. e7+ Ke8 4. Rg8+ Kd7 5. Rxb8) **2. Rh2 Kg8 3. Rg2+ Kh8** (or 3. ... Kf8 4. e7+, etc.) **4. Kf7 Rc7+ 5. e7,** and the rook must be sacrificed for the pawn.

With the bishop-pawn there is no mating threat at a distance because there is not enough elbow room, but there is an alternative that is good enough.

No. 624, White king at g6, rook at a2, pawn at f6; Black king at g8, rook at b8. White wins. **1. ... Rc8** (again he can only twiddle his thumbs) **2. Ra7 Rb8 3. Rg7+ Kf8** (or 3. ... Kh8 4. Rh7+ Kg8 5. f7+ Kf8 6. Rh8+) **4. Rh7 Kg8 5. f7+ Kf8 6. Rh8+ Ke7 7. Rxb8.**

With a knight-pawn or rook-pawn no effective mating threat is possible, so the game is a draw even when the Black rook is on the first rank.

No. 625: White king at h6, rook at a2, pawn at g6; Black king at g8, rook at b8. Draw. For if **1. Ra7 Rc8 2. Rg7+ Kh8 3. Rh7+ Kg8,** the advance 4. g7?? boomerangs because of the crushing reply 4. ... Rc6+. With a rook-pawn you can't make even an unsound combination.

2. Allowing the King to Be Driven From the Queening Square

With proper play this should never be permitted. **No. 626** shows what happens if it is.

No. 626, Dr. Emanuel Lasker

Black to play loses. Draw with Black rook anywhere else
on the first rank except e1

The mate threat forces Black's king to move. **1. ... Kc8** (or 1. ... Ke8 2. Rh8+
Kf7 3. Kd7 Ra1 4. d6 Ra7+ 5. Kc6 Ra6+ 6. Kc7 Ra7+ 7. Kb6! Rd7 8. Kc6 and
wins) **2. Rh8+ Kb7 3. Kd7 Rg1 4. d6 Rg7+ 5. Ke6 Rg6+ 6. Ke7 Rg7+** (or 6. ...
Kc6 7. Rc8+ Kb7 8. d7) **7. Kf6! Rd7 8. Ke6 Rg7 9. d7** and wins the rook for the
pawn. With the Black rook on d1 in the diagram, **1. ... Kc8 2. Rh8+ Kb7** draws
(No. 664). With the rook on a1, b1, f1 or g1, a check on the third rank transposes into No. 622.

Finally, note that a win is not possible if the White rook is at g7 or on the
queenside. For example, **No. 627: White rook at g7,** other pieces as in No.
626. Black to play draws. **1. ... Kc8 2. Rg8+ Kb7 3. Kd7 Rh1! 4. Rg7** (if now 4.
d6 Rh7+ 5. Ke6 Rh6+ 6. Ke7 Rh7+ 7. Kf6 Kc6 =) **4. ... Rh8!! 5. d6 Kb6!!** and
draws (No. 661).

Or **No. 628: White rook at a7,** other pieces as in No. 626. **1. ... Kc8 2. Ra8+
Kb7 3. Rh8 Rd1!** and draws (No. 664). But not **1. ... Ke8? 2. Ra8+ Kf7 3. Kd7**
and wins as in the original position. The difference is that White's king must
guard the pawn.

No. 629 (Salve-Burn, St. Petersburg 1909) shows a series of elementary
blunders that are easier to prevent than to cure. **White king at d5, rook at f6,
pawn at d4; Black king at d7, rook at e3.** The game went **1. Rf7+ Ke8 2. Rh7
Rd3?** (2. ... Ra3 3. Ke6 Ra6+ is No. 622) **3. Ke6! Re3+?** (3. ... Kd8 4. d5 Rd1 is
simpler) **4. Kd6 Ra3 5. Rh8+ Kf7 6. Rc8** and now 6. ... **Rd3!** was the move to
draw.

With a rook-pawn, two drawing methods are feasible. **No. 630: White king
at a6, rook at h7, pawn at a5; Black king at a8, rook at b1.** Draw. If Black
keeps his rook on the knight file White can obviously do nothing; for
instance, **1. ... Rb7!** (why not be fancy?) **2. Rh8+ Rb8 3. Rh3 Rb3!,** etc. But
even **1. ... Kb8** is good enough: **2. Rh8+ Kc7 3. Ka7 Rb5 4. a6 Rb2 5. Ka8 Rb3
6. a7 Rb1 7. Rh2 Rc1!.** The Black king will always stay at either c7 or c8.

3. Playing the King to the Wrong Side

One example of this is No. 628. The most common case, however, is that with the bishop-pawn.

No. 631

White to play. Draw

Although it is fairly frequent, even masters go astray: in 1931 Capablanca won two games with a bishop-pawn although a "book" draw had been reached.

The trap is (analysis by Kashdan in *Chess Review* 1933), after **1. Kb6 Rc1!** (the alternatives 1. ... Rg6+??? 2. c6 Rg8 is No. 624, but 1. ... Rb1+ 2. Kc6 Kb8! 3. Rh8+ Ka7 =) **2. Kc6** (on 2. Rh8+ Kd7 3. c6+? is met by 3. ... Rxc6+) **2. ... Kb8!!** (this is the critical point, where the error is most likely to be made: 2. ... Kd8 3. Rh8+ Ke7 4. Rc8!! wins. No. 665) **3. Rh8+ Ka7 4. Rc8 Rh1!** (now we see the difference: the Black king is on the rook file and does not block the check) **5. Rd8 Rc1! 6. Rd5 Kb8 7. Kd7 Kb7** =. White has made no progress.

B. The King Is Cut Off From the Queening File

By this we mean that the White rook occupies the file between the pawn and its king so that the Black king is unable to blockade the pawn. There are three questions to be considered here: the ideal position (known as the Lucena position); when it can be reached; and what are the exceptions.

1. The Lucena Position

This is the key to all these endings.

No. 623, The Lucena Position

White wins and in all analogous positions except with rook-pawn

The solution is **1. ... Rh3 2. Rf4!** ("building a bridge" is an apt description of the winning method) **2. ... Rh1 3. Re4+ Kd7 4. Kf7 Rf1+ 5. Kg6 Rg1+ 6. Kf6 Rf1+** (if 6. ... Rg2 7. Re5 followed by 7. ... Rg4, while if 6. ... Kd6 7. Rd4+ Kc6 8. Rd8 Rf1+ 9. Ke5 Re1+ 10. Kf4, etc.) **7. Kg5 Rg1+ 8. Rg4** and wins.

If the Black rook leaves the rook file, say **1. ... Re2**, then **2. Rh1** allows the White king to exit to h8 or h7, freeing the pawn. If the Black king goes to e7 and f6, the White king gets to f8; e.g., **1. ... Ke7 2. Re1+ Kf6** (2. ... Kd6 3. Re4 as above) **3. Kf8**.

These lines clearly don't apply to a rook-pawn, since there the White king's exit to the knight-file is blocked by both king and rook. The case of the rook-pawn will be discussed in Nos. 649-654.

2. When the Lucena Position Can Be Reached

In general, if the White pawn is on the fifth and the Black king is cut off, White always wins, but if the White pawn is on the fourth, White always wins only if the Black king is kept at a distance of at least three files from the pawn. Thus if the pawn is on the b-file, the king must be on the f-file. There are, however, a number of cases where White wins even though the king is much nearer. These occur when there is a distance of two or more ranks between the king and the pawn.

Rule 5: White wins if the pawn is on the fifth rank with its king near it and the Black king cut off from the queening file. **No. 633** illustrates.

No. 633

White wins

It makes no difference whose move it is. The win proceeds: **1. Ka5 Ra8+** (or 1. ... Kd7 2. b6) **2. Kb6 Rb8+ 3. Ka6 Ra8+** (if 3. ... Kd7 4. b6 Rh8 5. b7 followed by 6. Ka7, winning the rook) **4. Kb7 Ra2 5. b6 Rb2 6. Ka7 Ra2+ 7. Kb8 Rb2 8. b7**, and we have the Lucena position.

An exception to this rule occurs when Black has time to oppose rooks. **No. 634: Black king at d7**, other pieces as in No. 633, is a draw, for after **1. ... Rc8!** White cannot afford to exchange, and on **2. Re1 Kc7 3. Ka5 Ra8+ 4. Kb4 Kb6** is No. 622.

The only other exception occurs when the White king is cut off from the pawn by the Black rook on the intermediate rank. **No. 635: White king at b3, rook at c2, pawn at b5; Black king at d8, rook at f4.** Draw. **1. Ka3 Rh4 2. b6 Rh6 3. b7** (or 3. Rb2 Kc8) **Ra6+! 4. Kb4 Rb6+, =.**

With the e-pawn or f-pawn, if the Black king is on or near the edge of the board, it must be kept at least two files away from the pawn. **No. 636** is the critical position.

No. 636

White to play wins. Black to play draws

White to play decides by **1. Rg2! Re8 2. Kf5 Rf8+ 3. Ke6**, etc., as above. But Black to play draws by **1. ... Kg7!! 2. Rf2 Ra4+ 3. Kd5 Ra5+ 4. Kd6 Ra6+ 5. Ke7 Ra7+ 6. Ke6 Ra6+**, etc. If **7. Kf5 Kf7**. The point is that the White king cannot escape perpetual check unless he plays his rook to the queenside, in which case the Black king goes in front of the pawn. The proviso that the Black king must be at a distance of two files from the pawn holds even when the pawn is on the sixth.

As long as the White king is not more than one square away from its pawn, it makes no difference whether the Black rook is on the rank or the file. For example, **No. 637: White king at e3, rook at g1, pawn at e5; Black king at h6, rook at a4.** White wins. **1. Kd3 Rb4 2. e6 Rb6 3. Re1 Rb8 4. e7 Re8 5. Kd4 Kg7 6. Kd5 Kf7 7. Kd6 Ra8 8. Rf1+ Kg7 9. Ra1!** and wins.

Rule 6: If the pawn is on the third or fourth rank and its king is near it, White can always force a win if and only if the Black king is cut off at a distance of three files from the pawn (knight-pawn) or two files from the pawn (bishop-pawn, d-pawn, or e-pawn). If the pawn is on the second rank, and Black's king on the fourth or fifth, White wins if and only if the king is cut off at a distance of five files from the pawn.

It seems surprising that the same distance holds true even though the pawn is farther back. The reason will become clear from the examples. However, at times it is essential for the Black king to attack the rook.

No. 638

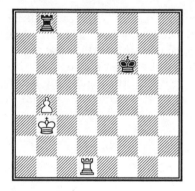

White to play wins. Black to play draws

No. 638 is the critical position for Rule 6 with the pawn on the fourth rank.
The win is **1. Re1! Kf5** (or 1. ... Kf7 2. Re5! Kf6 3. Rc5 Ke6 4. b5 Kd7 5. Kb4 Rc8 6. b6! and wins: No. 633) **2. Kc4 Rc8+ 3. Kd5 Rb8** (3. ... Rd8+ 4. Kc6 Rc8+ 5. Kb7) **4. Rb1 Kf6 5. b5 Ke7 6. Kc6! Kd8 7. b6 Kc8 8. Rh1** and wins.

On the other hand, with Black to play, we get **1. ... Ke6! 2. Rd4 Ke5! 3. Rd7** (3. Rc4 Kd5) **Ke6! 4. Rd4** (4. Rc7 Kd6) **Ke5 5. Kc3 Rh8** (5. ... Ra8 is also good: 6. Rc4 Rb8 7. Rc6 Kd5 8. Ra6 Rc8+ 9. Kb3 Rc6! =) **6. b5** (6. Rd7 Ke6! 7. Ra7 Kd5) **6. ... Rb8 7. Rh4** (7. Rb4 Kd5 =) **7. ... Kd6! 8. Kb4 Kc7**, which is the standard draw of No. 622.

No. 638 is very delicate, and the slightest misstep can be fatal. For example, if Black retreats to e7, he loses. **No. 639: Black king at e7,** other pieces as in No. 638. White to play wins. **1. Rd4! Ke6** (or 1. ... Rd8 2. Rxd8 Kxd8 3. Ka4! Kc8 4. Ka5) **2. Kc4! Rc8+** (if 2. ... Ke5 3. Rd5+ Ke6 4. b5 Rc8+ 5. Rc5 Kd7 6. b6!) **3. Kb5 Rb8+ 4. Kc6 Rc8+ 5. Kb7 Rc1 6. b5** and wins.

The point that is most essential for the defense is that the Black king must be able to attack the rook whenever the rook threatens to let the pawn advance or free the king. Thus we get another critical position.

No. 640, Grigoriev 1937

White to play wins.
Black to play draws

White to play wins by **1. Ka4! Ra8+** (1. ... Kd6 2. b5, or 1. ... Rc8 2. Rxc8 Kxc8 3. Ka5, or 1. ... Rb7 2. Ka5!! Rb8 3. b5) **2. Kb5 Rb8+ 3. Ka6! Kd6** (3. ... Ra8+ 4. Kb7) **4. b5** and again we have No. 633. On the other hand, Black to play can attack the rook and prevent the advance. **1. ... Rc8 =.**

Again, if the Black king is too far down (on the same rank as the pawn), White's rook can penetrate to the sixth and cut off the Black king on a rank, which is another winning stratagem. **No. 641** is the critical position.

No. 641, Grigoriev 1937

White to play wins. Black to play draws

White to play wins by **1. Rd6! Ke5 2. Ra6 Kd5 3. Ka4 Rh8** (or 3. ... Rb7 4. b5, or 3. ... Kc4 4. Rc6+ Kd5 5. b5) **4. b5 Rh1 5. Rc6** and we have No. 633.

The rule does not hold unchanged when the Black rook cuts off the White king from the pawn by occupying the third rank. In that case the Black king must be four files from the pawn.

No. 642, Grigoriev 1937

White to play wins.
Black to play draws

The critical position is **No. 642.** The win is possible only because the sixth rank is available to the rook. **1. Kc2!! Kf5**

1. ... Rg3 2. b5 Rg5 3. b6 Rc5+ 4. Kd3 Rb5 5. Re6 is just as bad: 5. ... Kf5 6. Rc6 Ke5 7. Kc4 Rb1 8. Kc5 Rb2 9. Rc7 Ke6 10. b7 Rc2+ 11. Kb6 Rb2+ 12. Ka7 Ra2+ 13. Kb8, etc., the Lucena position.

2. b5 Kf6

If 2. ... Rg3 3. b6 Rg7 4. Kc3 Rb7 5. Rb1 Ke6 6. Kc4 Kd7 7. Kb5! Kc8 8. Rh1! Rd7 9. Ka6 Rd8 10. Ka7 Rd7+ 11. Ka8 and wins: 11. ... Rg7 12. b7+ Rxb7 13. Rh8+, etc.

3. b6 Kf7 (or 3. ... Rh8 4. Kc3 Rb8 5. Rb1 Ke6 6. Kc4 Kd7 7. Kb5!! Kc8 8. Rc1+! Kd7 [8. ... Kb7 9. Rc7+ Ka8 10. Ra7+ mate] 9. Ka6 and wins) **4. Rb1! Rh8 5. Kc3 Ke6 6. Kb4! Kd7 7. Rc1! Rc8 8. Rc5!! Rc6** (8. ... Rxc5 9. Kxc5 Kc8 10. Kc6, and White has the opposition) **9. Kb5 Rxc5+ 10. Kxc5 Kd8 11. Kd6!** and wins.

But with Black to play in No. 642, he can prevent the winning stratagem in which, as in the above variations, White always noses in by exactly one move. **1. ... Kf5! 2. b5** (if 2. Kc2 Kf6! 3. b5 Rh5! 4. b6 Rc5+! 5. Kd3 Rb5) **2. ... Rd3!!** (the only reply: if 2. ... Rg3 3. Kc2, while if 2. ... Kf6 3. b6, both transposing into the above variations) **3. Rb1!!** (or 3. Kc2 Rd5 4. Rb1 Rc5+ 5. Kd3 Ke5 6. b6 Rc8 7. b7 Rb8 8. Kc4 Kd6 =) **3. ... Ke6! 4. b6 Rd8!!** (but not 4. ... Kd7?? 5. b7 Kc7 6. b8=Q+ Kxb8 7. Kc2+) **5. Ka3 Kd7 6. Rd1+ Ke8!!** (6. ... Kc8?? 7. b7+ Kc7 8. Rxd8. Ke7 is equally good) **7. Rc1 Rd6 8. Rb1 Kd7!!** (the saving clause; 8. ... Rd8? 9. Kb4 Kd7 10. Rd1+ or simply 10. Rc1 Rc8 11. Rc5 would be a blunder) **9. Ka4** (such is life on a chessboard; 9. b7 looks good but is refuted by 9. ... Ra6+ 10. Kb2 Rb6+ 11. Kc2 Rxb1 12. Kxb1 Kc7) **9. ... Kc8 10. Ka5 Kb7,** =.

The winning maneuver with the pawn on the fourth involves playing the rook behind the pawn and advancing the king. With a knight-pawn there is not enough room to get near the pawn, but with a more central pawn there is. This fact accounts for the second part of the rule.

With a center pawn we have the same situation as before — if Black's king is on or near the edge of the board he draws; if not he loses.

No. 643

Black to play, White wins

This example, which applies equally to a bishop-pawn, illustrates this point. Unlike the analogous cases in Nos. 638 and 641, White can get his king to the sixth. The solution is **1. ... Kg6 2. Kc4 Rc8+ 3. Kb5 Rd8 4. Kc5 Rc8+ 5. Kb6 Rd8 6. Rd1 Kf7 7. Kc7!!** (the point; 7. d5? Ke7 8. Kc7 Rd7+ only draws) **7. ... Rd5** (or 7. ... Ra8 8. Re1 Ra7+ 9. Kc6 Ra6+ 10. Kb5, etc.) **8. Kc6 Rd8** (8. ... Ra5 9. Re1 Ra6+ 10. Kb5 Rd6 11. Kc5, or 10. ... Re6 11. Rxe6 Kxe6 12. Kc6) **9. d5 Ra8** (9. ... Ke8 10. Re1+) **10. Re1 Ra6+ 11. Kb5 Ra2 12. d6** and wins (No. 633). The win here is possible because the checks on the rank are soon exhausted.

With a bishop-pawn, once Black's king is on the edge of the board, the game is a hopeless draw, but with the king on the other side it works in exactly the same way as a center pawn.

When the pawn is on the third rank, the rule still holds, but there are fewer exceptions. The reason the Black king doesn't need to be one file farther from the pawn is that a new winning method is available: defending the pawn on the rank.

The difficulty with the pawn on the third rank is that it is not enough to merely get the king to the fifth or the sixth, for Black can then still prevent the advance of the pawn. But it turns out that in the best defensive position Black is in zugzwang, so the stratagem of losing a tempo always provides a solution.

It is essential to keep the pieces integrated until a clear win is in sight. If White plays his king out too early, he may get into the critical position.

No. 644, Grigoriev 1937

White to play wins

The win is achieved by **1. Kc5 Kf4** (if 1. ... Rc8+ 2. Kd4 Rb8 3. Kc3 Rc8+ 4. Kb2, etc.) **2. Rh3 Ke5 3. Rh5+!** (not 3. b4? Rc8+ 4. Kb5 Rb8+; the king is forced back to b3, when ... Kd6 draws) **3. ... Ke6 4. Rh6+ Kd7 5. Rh7+ Ke6 6. b4 Rc8+ 7. Kb6 Rb8+ 8. Rb7 Rh8 9. b5** and wins.

With a center pawn or a bishop-pawn, White can win only if the Black king is at the required distance of three files. This means that when White has an e-pawn, if Black's king is on the h-file he draws, if it is on the a-file file he loses.

When the pawn is on the second rank, if the Black king is properly placed — i.e., in a position to attack the White rook on the third — White can win only if the king is cut off at a distance of five files from the pawn. **No. 645** is the critical position.

No. 645

White to play wins. With Black king at g7 wins no matter who moves

White to play wins by **1. Rg1 Kh5 2. Kc2 Rc8+ 3. Kd3 Rb8 4. Kc3 Rc8+ 5. Kd4 Rb8 6. Rb1 Kg6 7. b4 Kf7 8. Kc5! Ke7 9. Kc6** and wins. But since White wins by only one tempo, Black would obviously save the game if his king were one file nearer.

If the Black king is on the second rank (with White to play), White can win even though the king is only three files away, for he can play his rook to the third rank, his pawn to the third, and his king to the second.

3. Exceptions

There are two main types of exceptions to the general theory: one is when the pawn has already reached the seventh, and the other is with a rook-pawn.

a) The Lucena Position.

Exceptions here occur when the pawn is on the four center files when the kings are on opposite sides of the pawn. White must use his rook to cut off the Black king, and this allows perpetual check on the other side. **No. 646** is the case with the e-pawn.

No. 646

White to play wins. Black to play draws.
Always wins with Black king at g8 or Black rook at b2

Black to play forces the king to the b-file and then attacks and captures the pawn. **1. ... Ra8+ 2. Kd7 Ra7+ 3. Ke6 Ra6+ 4. Ke5 Ra5+ 5. Kd4 Ra4+ 6. Kc5 Ra5+ 7. Kb6** (7. Kd6 Ra6+) **7. ... Re5** =. White to play wins quite simply by **1. Rg1+ Kh7** (1. ... Kf6 2. Kf8) **2. Re1 Rd2 3. Kf7 Rf2+ 4. Ke6**, etc.

In **No. 647: Black king at g8,** other pieces unchanged, the check at f8 decides. **1. ... Ra8+ 2. Kd7 Ra7+ 3. Kd6 Ra6+ 4. Kc5 Re6 5. Rf8+ Kg7 6. e8=Q**.

Similarly, if the Black rook is at b2, the checks are exhausted too soon. **No. 648: Black rook at b2,** other pieces as in No. 646. White wins. **1. ... Rb8+ 2. Kd7 Rb7+ 3. Kd8 Rb8+ 4. Kc7 Ra8** (4. ... Re8 5. Kd7) **5. Ra1!! Re8 6. Kd7** and wins, for if **6. ... Kf7 7. Rf1+**.

b) The Rook-Pawn.

This case presents the unusual problem of extricating the White king once the pawn has reached the seventh. It is to be expected that the Black rook will occupy the knight file; the White rook will then have to oppose its rival in order to free the king. When the Black king is on the first or second rank it will normally take the White rook three moves to get to b8. This accounts for:

Rule 7. With a rook-pawn on the seventh, White wins if and only if the Black king is no nearer than the f-file (a-pawn), or c-file (h-pawn).

This is illustrated in **No. 649.**

No. 649

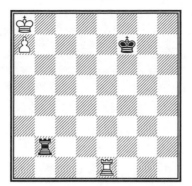

White wins. Draw with Black king closer to the pawn

The win here hangs by a thread: **1. Rh1** (tempo moves are meaningless) **1. ... Ke7 2. Rh8** (2. Rh7+? Kd6 3. Rb7 is a mistake because of 3. ... Rh2!, for if then 4. Kb8?? Rh8+ mate!) **2. ... Kd6** (if 2. ... Kd7 3. Rb8 Rh2 4. Kb7 Rb2+ 5. Ka6 Ra2+ 6. Kb6 Rb2+ 7. Kc5, etc.; the checks are soon exhausted) **3. Rb8 Ra2 4. Kb7 Rb2+ 5. Kc8** (5. Ka6 does not get the king out: 5. ... Ra2+ 6. Kb6 Rb2+ 7. Ka5 Ra2+ and 8. Kb6 is necessary) **5. ... Rc2+ 6. Kd8 Rh2!** (with a rather annoying threat) **7. Rb6+ Kc5** (7. ... Ke5 8. Kc7) **8. Rc6+!** (the quickest, though 8. Rb2! is also good enough; e.g., 8. ... Rh8+ 9. Kc7 Rh7+ 10. Kb8, and the White king escapes to a6) **8. ... Kb5** (or 8. ... Kxc6 9. a8=Q+, or 8. ... Kd5 9. Ra6 Rh8+ 10. Kc7 Rh7+ 11. Kb6 Rh6+ 12. Kb5) **9. Rc8 Rh8+ 10. Kc7 Rh7+ 11. Kb8** and wins.

If the Black king is any closer in No. 649, the White king can never get out of the corner. **No. 650: White king at a8, rook at d1, pawn at a7; Black king at e7, rook at b2. Draw. 1. Rh1 Kd7 2. Rh8 Kc7 3. Rb8 Rh2 4. Rb7+ Kc8! 5. Rb1 Rc2 6. Rb8+ Kc7**, etc.

With the pawn on the sixth rank, White's prospects are somewhat better because his king is not completely stalemated. Nevertheless, the rule holds. This may be seen from the critical position, **No. 651.**

NO. 651

White to play wins. Black to play draws

The win is **1. Rb8! Rc1 2. Kb7 Rb1+** (2. ... Kd7 3. a7 and 2. ... Kd6 3. a7 both transpose into No. 649 and notes) **3. Ka8 Ra1 4. a7 Kd6 5. Kb7**, etc., is the main variation of No. 649. But Black to play: **1. ... Kd7 2. Rb8 Ra1 3. Kb7 Rb1+ 4. Ka8 Ra1 5. a7 Kc7** =, No. 650.

If the White rook has command of the knight file, the critical position occurs one file closer; i.e., Black's king must be on the d-file (a-pawn) or e-file (h-pawn) to draw.

No. 652, Rabinovich

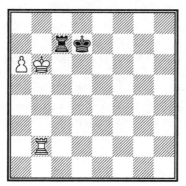

White to play wins. Black to play draws

In **No. 652,** White to play plays **1. a7**, and Black can resign. Black to play can save himself by **1. ... Rc6+ 2. Ka5** (2. Kb5 Kc7!! 3. a7 Rb6+ 4. Kc5 Rh6 =. If 4. Ka5?? Rxb2 5. a8=Q Ra2+ wins for Black. If 2. Kb7 Rc7+ 3. Kb8 Rc8+ 4. Ka7 Rc1! =, see No. 651) **2. ... Rc5+** (not 2. ... Rc8? 3. a7! Ra8 4. Ka6 and wins) **3. Ka4 Rc6!!** (3. ... Rc8? is a mistake: 4. Rb7+ Kc6 5. Ka5 Rh8 6. Rb6+ Kc7 7. a7 Rh5+ 8. Ka6 Rh1 9. Rc6+! Kd7 10. Rc5 and wins, Again, 3. ... Rc4+? also loses: 4. Kb5! Rc7 5. Rh2 Rc1 6. a7 Ra1 7. Rh8!!, etc.) **4. Rb7+ Kc8 5. Kb5 Rc1** (5. ... Rh6

6. Ka5 Rg6 7. Rb1 Rg7 8. Kb6 Kb8 is also good enough) 6. **Kb6 Rb1+ 7. Ka7 Rc1** =.

Once more it is clear that with Black's pieces one file farther away, the game is won in any case. **No. 653: White king at b6, rook at b2, pawn at a6; Black king at e7, rook at d7.** White wins. 1. **... Rd6+ 2. Ka5 Rd5+ 3. Rb5! Rd1 4. a7 Kd7 5. Ka6! Ra1+ 6. Ra5** and wins.

With the pawn on the fifth or fourth rank, White has winning chances only if Black is unable to oppose rooks. This means that with the pawn on the fifth the White rook must be on the e-file, while if it is on the fourth the White rook must be on the f-file. In the best possible position for the Black pieces — rook on the first rank, king on the first or second — the rule holds as above.

No. 654, Cheron 1926

Draw. Black king at e6 or rook at a7 loses

In **No. 654,** after **1. Kb5 Rd8!!** (not 1. ... Rb8+? 2. Kc6 Rb1 3. a6 Ra1 4. Kb6 Rb1+ 5. Ka5!! Ra1+ 6. Ra4 and wins) **2. Rc4** (2. Rxd8 obviously leads to nothing but a draw, while 2. Ra4 Kd7 3. Kb6 Rb8+ 4. Ka7 Rb1 5. Rc4 Rb2 is also insufficient: Nos. 651 and 652) **2. ... Rb8+!** (tempting but erroneous is 2. ... Kd7 3. a6 Rc8 4. a7!! and wins) **3. Ka4** (3. Ka6 Kd7 transposes back into the well-known draws) **3. ... Kd7 4. a6 Rc8!** (or 4. ... Rb1 5. Ka5 Ra1+ 6. Kb6 Rb1+, =) **5. Rb4 Rh8!** (inferior is 5. ... Kc7? 6. Rb7+ Kc6 7. Ka5) **6. Ka5 Kc7 7. a7** (if now 7. Rb7+ Kc8! 8. Kb6 Rh6+ 9. Ka7 Rf6 or 9. ... Rh1 =) **7. ... Rh5+ 8. Ka6 Rh6+ 9. Ka5 Rh5+ 10. Ka4 Rh8** =.

If the Black king is on the f-file and the White rook on the e-file, opposing rooks is impossible because after the exchange the Black king is outside the square of the pawn. So White wins by advancing his pawn to the seventh and continuing as in No. 651.

Again, if the Black pieces are not on the best squares in the last diagram, he loses. **No. 655: Black rook at a7,** other pieces as in No. 654. White to play wins. **1. Kb5 Rd7 2. Ra4! Kd8** (or 2. ... Rd8 3. a6 Ra8 4. a7 Kd7 5. Kb6 Kc8 6. Rh4) **3. a6 Ra7 4. Kb6 Ra8 5. a7** and wins the rook.

Or **No. 656: Black king at c6,** other pieces as in No. 654. White to play wins. **1. Kb5 Rb8+ 2. Kc6 Ke5** (if 2. ... Ra8 3. Re4+ Kf5 4. Ra4 Rc8+ 5. Kb7 Rc1 6. Rb4! and wins) **3. Ra4 Rc8+! 4. Kb7! Rc1 5. a6 Rb1+ 6. Kc6 Rc1+ 7. Kb5 Rb1+ 8. Ka5 Rb8 9. a7 Ra8 10. Kb6** and wins.

With the pawn on the fourth rank, when the Black pieces are on the best possible squares, White wins only if the Black king is on the g-file (a-pawn) or the b-file (h-pawn) for otherwise Black can oppose rooks.

B1. The Black King Is Not on the Queening File But Is Not Directly Cut Off

This is complementary to section B, since transpositions are obviously possible in many cases. What we are interested in are those positions where no such simple transposition is available; chiefly, where the Black king is one file from the pawn. In order to win, White's king must be in front of his pawn, which must be on the fifth rank or beyond.

With an e-pawn or d-pawn, it is always better for the defense to have his king on the short side of the pawn; i.e., with an e-pawn, the king should be on the kingside, with a d-pawn, on the queenside.

When the e-pawn is on the sixth, Black draws only if his king is at g7. **No. 657** is the ideal defensive position for Black.

No. 657, Grigoriev 1937

Black to play draws. White rook at a8 or e1 wins

The defense is **1. ... Rb7+ 2. Kd6 Rb6+!** (but not 2. ... Kf8? 3. Ra8+ Kg7 4. e7 and wins) **3. Kd7 Rb7+!** (king and pawn must part) **4. Kd8** (if 4. Kc6 Rb2!! 5. Rf1 [else Kf8] 5. ... Re2! 6. Kd7 Ra2!! 7. e7 Ra7+ 8. Ke6 Ra6+, =, No. 646) **4. ... Rb8+! 5. Kc7 Rb2 6. Rf1** (else 6. ... Kf8) **6. ... Ra2 7. e7 Ra7+** = (No. 646).

With the White rook on the eighth, Black's rook checks are not sufficient, for in **No. 658: White rook at a8,** other pieces as in No. 657, after **1. ... Rb7+ 2. Kd6 Rb6+** (2. ... Kf6 3. Rf8+ Kg7 4. e7) **3. Kd7 Rb7+ 4. Kc6! Re7** (or 4. ... Rb1 5. e7) **5. Kd6 Rb7 6. e7** is decisive.

No. 659 (Grigoriev 1937): **Black king at g6,** other pieces as in No. 657. White wins. **1. ... Rb7+ 2. Kd8 Rb8+ 3. Kc7 Rb2 4. Re1! Rc2+ 5. Kd7 Rd2+ 6. Ke8 Ra2 7. e7,** and the king can get out.

Note, however, that with the positions of the rooks reversed Black always draws, even when the White rook is on one of the ideal squares.

No. 660, Tarrasch 1906

Black to play, White wins. White rook may be anywhere
on b-, c-, d-, or h-file. Draw with Black king at g7 or g6

On **1. ... Kg7 2. Rg2+** wins at once (No. 636). Likewise, after **1. ... Ra7+ 2. Kf6 Ra8** (forced) **3. Rg2+** is decisive. If the White rook is on the e- or f-file, Ra7+ forces the king away from the pawn and allows the approach of either the rook or the king. With the king at g7 or g6, the situation is different (compare No. 659). For then on 1. ... Ra7+ White cannot easily escape the checks but must go to the queenside, when ... Kf6 will draw.

No. 661, Tarrasch 1906

White to play wins.
Black to play draws

With the Black rook attacking the pawn, **No. 661** is the critical position. White to play wins by **1. Rc8 Ra1** (1. ... Re2 2. Kd7 Rd2+ 3. Ke8) **2. Ke8! Kf6 3. e7 Ke6** (3. ... Ra7 4. Rc6+) **4. Rc6+ Kd5 5. Kd7** and wins. Black can draw by

1. ... Ra1! 2. Rd8 Ra7+ 3. Rd7 (3. Ke8 Kf6) **3. ... Ra8** (but not 3. ... Ra6? 4. Ke8+ Kf6 5. e7 Ra8+ 6. Rd8 Ra7 7. Rd6+ and wins, No. 646) **4. Rb7 Kg6!** (not 4. ... Kg8? 5. Kf6, No. 660) **5. Kd7** (or 5. Rc7 Kg7! 6. Rd7 Kg6 7. Rd1 Ra7+ 8. Kd6 Ra6+, etc. Or 5. Rb1 Ra7+ 6. Kf8 Ra8+, =) **5. ... Kf6! 6. Rc7** (6. e7 Kf7 7. Rc7 Re8 8. Kd6 Ra8! =, but not 8. ... Rh8? 9. e8=Q+! Kxe8 10. Rc8+) **6. ... Kg7!** (a mistake is 6. ... Ra1? 7. e7 Rd1+ 8. Ke8!) **7. Kd6+ Kf8 8. Rh7 Ra6+, =.**

But with the Black king on the long side of the pawn, the rook does not have enough room for checks and consequently always loses.

No. 662

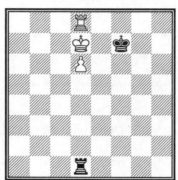

White wins

For after **1. ... Ra1 2. Rh8 Ra7+ 3. Kc6 Ra6+ 4. Kc7 Ra7+ 5. Kb6,** both Black and the checks are exhausted. **5. ... Rd7 6. Kc6 Ke6 7. Rh6+.** Or **6. ... Ra7 7. d7.** Of course, if Black could give check in the diagram position he would be able to draw.

No. 663: Black rook at a1, other pieces as in the last diagram. Black to play draws. **1. ... Ra7+ 2. Kc6 Ra6+ 3. Kc7 Ra7+ 4. Kb6 Ra1! 5. d7 Ke7, =.**

With the pawn on the fifth, Black may have his king on the long side and still draw, but he must be able to prevent an advantageous advance to the sixth. **No. 664** is the critical position.

No. 664

White to play wins; Black to play draws. Black king at b7 draws

The win is rather unusual. **1. Kc7 Ra1** (or 1. ... Rc1+ 2. Kd7 Ra1 3. Rc8! Ra7+ 4. Rc7 Ra8 5. d6, etc., as in the main variation) **2. Rb8!** (the only move: if 2. d6? Ra7+ 3. Kb6 Ra1, =) **2. ... Ra7+** (2. ... Ke7 3. d6+ Ke6 4. Rc8+, or 3. ... Kf7 4. d7 Rc1+ 5. Kd8!) **3. Rb7 Ra8 4. Kd7** (4. d6?? is a mistake, for the reply 4. ... Ke6! draws: 5. d7 Ke7!, or 5. Rb1 Ra7+ 6. Kb6 Rd7) **4. ... Kf6! 5. d6 Kf7!** (so that if now 6. Kc6+ Ke8! 7. Rh7 Ra6+!, =, and if 6. Kc7 Ke6 7. d7 Ke7, =) **6. Rc7!!** (now we see why the short side is so bad for Black: the rook cannot maintain the position) **6. ... Rb8 7. Rc1! Rb7+ 8. Kc6 Rb2 9. Re1!** and we have No. 633. Black must check on the short side and cannot prevent the Lucena position.

Black to play has time to obstruct the advance of the pawn: **1. ... Ra1! 2. Rc8** (if 2. Kc7 Ra7+ 3. Kb6 Ra1 4. d6 Ke6, =) **2. ... Rd1!** (but not 2. ... Ra6+ 3. Kd7! Ra7+ 4. Rc7 Ra8 5. d6, etc., as above) **3. Rc2** (3. Kc6 Ke7) **Ke8 4. Rh2 Rd3 5. Rh8+ Kf7 6. Rd8 Ra3!**, etc. White's king cannot leave d6 without allowing the Black king to approach.

With the Black king at b7 — i.e., on the short side — the game is always drawn because the Black rook then has plenty of room to maneuver. Even if White gets his pawn to the sixth in a relatively favorable position such as No. 661, Black will always be able to retain the move and draw. In practice, it is essential to keep the Black rook active.

With the bishop-pawn, it makes no difference whether the pawn is on the fifth or the sixth: if Black's king is on the short side he draws, if not he loses.

No. 665

White wins. Draw with Black king at h7

No. 665 illustrates. The continuation might be **1. ... Rh1 2. Kg7 Rg1+ 3. Kf7 Rf1 4. f6 Rh1** (4. ... Rg1 5. Re8) **5. Ra8 Rf1** (5. ... Rh7+ 6. Kg8 Rh1 7. f7, etc.) **6. Ra2 Re1 7. Rd2+**, etc.

But if the Black king is on the h-file, the rook has checks galore and can draw. **No. 666: Black king at h7**, other pieces as in last diagram. **1. Re8 Rb1 2. Kf7 Rb7+ 3. Re7 Rb8 4. f6 Ra8 5. Re8** (now there is no question of stalemating the Black rook) **5. ... Ra7+ 6. Kf8** (or 6. Ke6 Ra6+ 7. Kf5 Ra5+ 8. Re5 Ra6, etc.) **6. ... Kg6 7. Re6 Ra8+, =**.

If the pawn is on the sixth, there is one winning position that must be noted: **No. 667: White king at f7, rook at f8, pawn at f6; Black king at h7, rook at f1.** White to play wins. **1. Re8! Ra1 2. Kf8! Kg6 3. f7 Kf6 4. Rb8 Ra6 5. Kg8.**

Cases with the rook-pawn and the knight-pawn are essentially the same as those where the Black king is cut off. All the difference is due to the position of the Black king on the long or short side of the pawn, and there is no such thing with the pawn on the edge files.

C. The Black King Is Cut Off on a Rank

Here the Black king is behind the pawn. As in the positions where the Black king is to one side of the pawn, if the pawn is on the fifth or beyond, the king can escort it to the eighth, but if not, the Black rook can impede its forward march. So the general rule that a pawn on the fifth wins, but on the fourth only draws, holds true here, too.

No. 668 is the critical position:

No. 668

White to play wins.
Black to play draws

1. f5 Rf8 2. Ke5 Re8+ 3. Kf6 Rb8 (or 3. ... Rf8+ 4. Kg6 Rg8+ 5. Kf7, etc.) **4. Kg6 Rb6+ 5. f6 Rc6** (Black can do nothing) **6. Kg7 Rc7+ 7. f7 Rb7 8. Kg8.** Black to play checks until the White king is forced back and then attacks the pawn: **1. ... Re8+ 2. Kd3** (2. Kf5 Rf8+ 3. Kg5 Rg8+ 4. Kh6 Rf8 5. Ra4 Kf3 is no better) **2. ... Rd8+ 3. Kc2 Rf8 4. Ra4 Kf3,** =. Again, if the rook is nearer, or if the king is farther away, White wins.

No. 669, Black rook at b7, other pieces as in No. 668. White wins. **1. ... Re7+ 2. Kd5 Rf7 3. Ke5 Re7+ 4. Kf6,** etc.

And **No. 670: Black king at g1,** other pieces as in No. 668. White wins. **1. ... Re8+ 2. Kd5 Rf8 3. Ke5 Re8+ 4. Kd6 Rf8 5. Ra4 Kf2 6. Ke7! Rf5 7. Ke6 Rf8 8. f5,** etc.

These variations do not work with a rook-pawn because the White king cannot escape checks by hiding behind the pawn. To have winning chances, White's pawn must be on the sixth and the rook must be on the knight file.

No. 671

White to play wins.
Black to play draws

No. 671 is a critical position. The simplest win is **1. a7 Ra8** (if 1. ... Rg1 2. Ka5! Ra1+ 3. Ra4, or 2. ... Rg5+ 3. Rb5 Rg1 4. Ka6) **2. Rb7 Kc4 3. Ka5 Kc5 4. Ka6 Kc6 5. Rb8.** Black to play draws by **1. ... Rg6 2. Rb3+** (2. Ka5 Rxa6+) **2. ... Kc4 3. Rb4+ Kc3 4. Kb5 Rxa6**.

A common case is where the White rook is on the seventh rank, the Black king on the sixth (i.e., cut off from the eighth), and the White king not confined to the rook file.

This is normally a draw if the Black king is on the king file or nearer, unless the pawn is on the seventh or can reach there without the rook abandoning control of the rank.

No. 672, Euwe-Alekhine, 16th match game, 1935

White to play wins.
Black to play draws

No. 672 is from the 16th game of the 1935 Euwe-Alekhine match (with colors reversed). Analysis showed that despite the apparent simplicity of this critical position, the ending was bungled by both sides. Alekhine played **1. Rh7?**, when 1. ... Ra1! 2. Kb6 Kd6! 3. a6 Rb1+ 4. Ka7 Kc6 would have drawn. Euwe actually replied **1. ... Rc1+?**, when after **2. Kb7! Rb1+ 3. Kc8 Rc1+ 4. Kb8! Rb1+ 5. Rb7 Ra1 6. Rb6+ Kd5 7. a6 Kc5 8. Kb7 Rh1 9. Rc6+,** Black resigned.

The correct play (Grigoriev) is **1. a6! Rc1+** (if 1. ... Ra1 2. Ra8 wins: 2. ... Rc1+ 3. Kb5 Rb1+ 4. Kc4 Rc1+ 5. Kb3 Ra1 6. a7 Kd7 7. Rh8!, or 2. ... Kf7 3. Kb6 Rb1+ 4. Ka7 Ke7 5. Rb8, etc. No. 651) **2. Kb7** with the following possibilities:

a) 2. ... Rb1+ 3. Kc8 Ra1 4. Rh7 Kd6 5. a7 Kc6 6. Rc7+ (an amusing alternative, which occurred in a problem by Ponziani 200 years ago, is 6. Rh6+ Kc5 7. Kb7 Rb1+ 8. Kc7 Ra1 9. Rh5+ Kc4 10. Kb7 Rb1+ 11. Kc6 Ra1 12. Rh4+ Kc3 13. Kb6 Rb1+ 14. Kc5 Ra1 15. Rh3+ Kc2 16. Rh7 Kc3 17. Kb6 Kc4 18. Rh8) 6. ... Kb6 7. Kb8;

b) 2. ... Kd6 3. Kb8 Ra1 4. Rh7 Rb1+ 5. Rb7 Ra1 6. a7;

c) 2. ... Kd5 3. Kb8 Ra1 4. Rd7+ Ke6 5. Rh7 Rb1+ 6. Rb7, etc.;

d) 2. ... Kd7 3. Kb8+ Kd8! 4. Rh7 Rb1+ 5. Rb7 Rc1 6. Rb2 Rc8+ 7. Kb7 Rc7+ 8. Kb6 Kc8 9. Rh2 Kb8 10. Rh8+ Rc8 11. a7+;

e) 2. ... Rh1 3. Ra8 Kd7 4. a7 Rb1+ 5. Ka6 Ra1+ 6. Kb6! Rb1+ 7. Kc5! Rc1+ 8. Kd4 Rd1+ 9. Ke3 Re1+ 10. Kf2 Ra1 11. Rh8!;

f) 2. ... Ra1 3. Ra8 Kd6 4. Rd8+! Ke7 5. Rd5 Rb1+ 6. Kc6 Ra1 7. Kb6 Ke6 8. Ra5 Rb1+ 9. Rb5.

Black to play draws by the odd tempo: **1. ... Rc1+ 2. Kb7 Kd7! 3. Kb8+ Kd8 4. Rh7** (or 4. a6 Rc8+ 5. Kb7 Rc7+ 6. Kb6 Rxa7 7. Kxa7 Kc7) **4. ... Ra1! 5. Rh5 Rb1+ 6. Ka7 Kc7,** = (No. 651).

As a rule, it is worse for the defense to be cut off on a rank than on a file. If the Black king cannot get in front of the pawn, a win may be possible even with the pawn on the third rank. **No. 673** is the critical position with the knight-pawn.

No. 673, Grigoriev 1937

White to play wins.
Black to play draws. Always wins with Black king at d3

The win is **1. Ka3 Ra8+** (1. ... Kc3 2. Rc5+ Kd4 3. b4) **2. Kb4 Rb8+** (or 2. ... Kd3 3. Ra5 Rb8+ 4. Ka4) **3. Ka4 Ra8+ 4. Ra5 Rc8 5. b4 Kc4** (if 5. ... Rc1 6. Rh5 Ra1+ 7. Kb5 Ra8 8. Kc6) **6. Ra7 Kd5 7. b5 Kc5 8. Ka5 Kd6 9. b6 Kc6 10. Ka6 Kd6 11. Rh7 Ra8+ 12. Kb7 Ra1 13. Rc7,** with a standard win (No. 633). Black to play holds everything with **1. ... Ra8 2. Rb5** (2. b4 Kc4) **2. ... Ra7 3. Rb8 Kc5!,** etc.

C1. The Black King Is Behind the Pawn But Not Directly Cut Off

This is the analogue of B1, but the results are different. There is nothing resembling cases of the long and short sides of the pawn, but there are certain other special features to be considered.

When the pawn is on the seventh, watch for the trap shown in **No. 674.**

No. 674

Black to play, White wins

The threat, of course, is g8=Q (the fact that the pawn queens with check is of no real importance, since queen vs. rook is a theoretical win). Against the only plausible defense, **1. ... Ra6+** (1. ... Ra8 2. Rh8), White continues **2. Kd5!! Rg6 3. Ke5!!**, when Black is in zugzwang. **3. ... Kg4 4. Rh1! Kg5 5. Rg1+ Kh6 6. Rxg6+.** It is always bad to try to stop a passed pawn from the side.

With the pawn on the sixth, the trap pointed out by Kling and Horwitz in 1851 **(No. 675)** must be noted.

No. 675, Kling and Horwitz 1885

Black to play draws.
White wins with pawn on the d-file

The saving clause is **1. ... Rb6!! 2. e7** (if 2. Rh8 Rxe6 3. Rh5+ Kg4, while on 2. Re7 Black merely tempos on the rank) **2. ... Rf6+ 3. Kg7 Rg6+ 4. Kh7** (4. Kh8 Rh6+) **4. ... Kf6!!** (the point) **5. Rf8+** (else 5. ... Rg7+ and 6. ... Rxe7) **5. ... Kxe7**.

When the pawn is on the d-file, or farther west, this combination does not work, because the White rook has more room.

No. 676: White king at e7, rook at d8, pawn at d6; Black king at e5, rook at a5. White wins. **1. ... Ra6 2. Rh8!!** (but not 2. d7? Re6+ 3. Kf7 Rf6+ 4. Kg7 Ke6, =) **2. ... Rxd6** (2. ... Ra7+ 3. d7 is hopeless: there follows simply 4. Ke8) **3. Rh5+ K any 4. Kxd6.**

With the pawn on the fifth, there is a different type of trap, shown in **No. 677.**

No. 677

Black to play draws.
White wins with pawn on bishop or center files

Here the catch comes after **1. ... Kh5! 2. g6+** (or 2. Kf6 Rg2 3. Rd1 Rf2+) **2. ... Kh6 3. Rd6** (again, if 3. Rd2 Rf1+, while 3. Rf5 is of course answered by 3. ... Rxg6) **3. ... Rg2 4. Rf6.** Now Black is faced with the apparently irresistible attack beginning with 4. Rf1, but he has something up his sleeve **4. ... Rg5! 5. Rf1 Rf5+!! 6. Rxf5,** stalemate!!

With the pawn on the fourth, Black can draw only if his rook is on the first rank, where it can drive the White king away.

No. 678, Rabinovich

White wins

This, as we have seen (No. 668), would be a draw with the Black rook at b8. Now White wins as follows: **1. ... Rb8** (or 1. ... Rb4 2. Kh5! Rb8 3. g5) **2. Ra3+ Ke4 3. Kh6! Kf4 4. g5 Rh8+ 5. Kg7** and wins. With the pawn on the third Black can get to No. 668.

No. 679, Salvioli 1887

White to play wins.
Black to play draws

Where the White king is not immediately near the pawn, the problem is always one of transposing into the standard positions. **No. 679** is the critical position.

White wins by **1. Kg4! Rc8** (if 1. ... Rc1 2. Rd5 Kc4 3. Rd8 Rf1 4. f5, etc., or 1. ... Re2 2. Kf5 Kc5 3. Ke6+ Kd4 4. e5 Kc5 5. Ke7, No. 668; or 1. ... Rd2 2. Kf5 Kc5 3. Ke6+ Kc6 4. Rd5! Rh2 5. Rd1 Rh6+ 6. Kf5 Rh5+ 7. Kf6 Rh6+ 8. Kg5 Re6 9. Kf5 Re8 10. e5 and wins, No. 636) **2. Rd5! Kc4 3. Rd6! Rg8+ 4. Kf5 Rf8+ 5. Rf6! Rd8 6. Rf7! Kd4 7. e5 Kd5 8. e6 Kd6 9. Kf6 Ra8 10. Rd7+ Kc6 11. Rd1** and wins, No. 636. The variation is essentially the same as that of No. 673.

D. The White Rook Is in Front of the Pawn

This type of position normally occurs when both kings are at a distance, so the pawn has to be defended by the rook. The best place for the Black rook then is behind the pawn because this preserves its freedom of action.

When the pawn is on the seventh, White can win only in the special case where he can move his rook with check or the threat of check. This is illustrated in **No. 680.**

No. 680

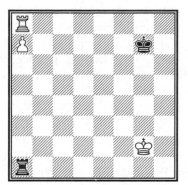

Draw. Black to play loses only if his king is outside the border

White to play can do nothing, for if he gets his king to b7 the Black rook checks him until he leaves the neighborhood of the pawn. But if the Black king is not on a safe square, White's rook will be able to leave a8 with check and then queen the pawn. Or, with the Black king at e7, **1. Rh8** follows, when **1. ... Rxa7 2. Rh7+** wins the rook. The fact that we have an a-pawn here makes no difference. On the contrary, any other pawn would be much less promising because the Black king would be so much nearer.

Unlike the similar ending with more pawns on the board, the Black king cannot hide behind his rival here. For example, **No. 681** (Troitzky 1896): **White king at g4, rook at a8, pawn at a7; Black king at g2, rook at a1.** White wins. **1. Kf4** (threatening Rg8+) **1. ... Kf2** (hide-and-go-seek on the chessboard) **2. Ke4 Ke2 3. Kd4 Kd2 4. Kc5 Kc3** (if 4. ... Rc1+ 5. Kb4 Rb1+ 6. Ka3 Ra1+ 7. Kb2 and wins) **5. Rc8!! Rxa7 6. Kb6+.**

With the pawn farther back, we have either a horserace to see who gets there first or a transposition into some other case.

No. 682

White to play wins. Black to play draws

No. 682 is a critical position. White to play continues **1. Kf4 Kg6 2. Ke5 Kf7 3. Kd6 Rb2 4. Kc6 Ke7 5. Rh8 Rc2+ 6. Kb7 Kd7 7. Rh1 Rd2 8. Rc1** (No. 636). It's a fatal mistake to advance the pawn here: 3. b7?? (instead of 3. Kd6) 3. ... Kg7!! (not 3. ... Ke7? 4. Rh8) and draws as in the previous diagram.

Black to play can get to the pawn in time: **1. ... Kg6 2. Kf4 Kf6 3. Ke4** (3. b7 Kg7, and the White king can never approach) **3. ... Ke6 4. b7** (or 4. Kd4 Kd6 5. Kc4 Kc6, or 4. Rh8 Kd6! 5. Rh6+ Kc5, or even 4. ... Kd7 5. Kd5 Rb2 6. Kc5 Rb1 7. Rh8 Rb2, and White still cannot win) **4. ... Kd7!** (of course not 4. ... Kf7 5. Rh8) **5. Kd5** (or 5. Rh8 Rxb7 6. Rh7+ Kc6) **5. ... Kc7** =.

Things are somewhat different with a rook-pawn, again because of the threat of a series of checks. The critical position, **No. 683**, at first sight seems much more favorable for White than the corresponding case with the knight-pawn because the Black king is confined to its first rank.

No. 683

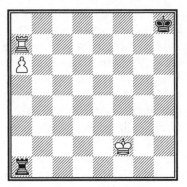

White to play wins Black to play draws

White to play wins in this unusual manner: **1. Ke2!** (not 1. Ke3? Re1+ 2. Kd4 Re6, =) **1. ... Kg8** (or 1. ... Ra3 2. Kd2 Kg8 3. Kc2 Kf8 4. Kb2 Ra5 5. Ra8+ Kg7 6. Kb3 Rf5 7. Rb8 Ra5 8. Rb6 Kf7 9. Kb4 Ra1 10. Kb5 Ke7 11. Kc6 and wins. Or 1. ... Ra5 2. Kd3 Rd5+ 3. Kc4 Rd6 4. Kb5, or, finally, 1. ... Rh1 2. Rb7 Ra1 3. a7 Ra3 4. Rb8+) **2. Kd3 Kf8** (2. ... Rd1+ 3. Kc4 Rc1+ 4. Kb5 Rb1+ 5. Kc6 Rc1+ 6. Kb6 Rb1+ 7. Kc7 Rc1+ 8. Kb8 Ra1 9. Ra8! Kg7 10. Kb7 Rb1+ 11. Ka7 and wins [No. 320]) **3. Ra8+ Kg7 4. Kc4 Rf1 5. Re8! Ra1 6. Kb5 Kf7 7. Re4**, transposing to No. 651.

Black to play can draw in a variety of ways; the simplest is **1. ... Ra5! 2. Ke3 Re5+ 3. Kd4 Re6 4. Kd5 Rf6 5. Kc5 Kg8 6. Kb5 Rf5+ 7. Kc6 Rf6+ 8. Kc7 Rf7+ 9. Kb8 Rf8+**, etc. White's king must leave the neighborhood of the pawn.

The best position for the Black rook is behind the pawn. Guarding the pawn from the side is bad because the rook does not cover the queening square. The threat of getting the White rook out with check is then so strong that both Black pieces are tied up and the White king can approach.

No. 684, Grigoriev 1934

White wins

In **No. 684**, the threat of Rd8+ is decisive. **1. ... Rf7+** (1. ... Rd7 2. Ke4 Re7+ 3. Kd4 Rd7 4. Kc4 Rc7+ 5. Kb5) **2. Ke3!** (but not 2. Ke4? Rd7!, when Black can draw!!: 3. Kc3 Kd5! 4. Kf4 Rf7+, etc., or 3. Kf4 Kd5 4. Kf5 Rf7+ 5. Kg6 Rd7! 6. Kf6 Kd6!, etc.) **2. ... Rd7 3. Ke4** (now Black is in zugzwang again) **3. ... Re7+ 4. Kd4 Rd7** (4. ... Ke6 5. Kc5 Ke5 6. Kc6 Ke6 7. Kb6) **5. Kc4 Rc7+ 6. Kb5! Rd7 7. Kb6,** and Black is defenseless against the move of the White rook.

E. The White Rook Is Behind the Pawn

There are winning chances here, of course, only when the Black rook is blockading the pawn. There are few finesses: the win or draw depends on who gets there first.

No. 685, Seyburth 1889

White to play wins.
Black to play draws

No. 685 is a critical position. After **1. Kd6 Kb5 2. Kc7 Kc5 3. Kb7,** it's all over. Black to play holds everything by an ingenious defense **1. ... Kc5! 2. Kd7 Kb6 3. Rb1+! Kc5!!** (not 3. ... Kxa7 4. Kc7 when White wins. Or 3. ... Ka6? 4. Kc7! Rxa7+ 5. Kc6! and again the threat of mate is fatal) **4. Rb7 Rh8!!** (the Black defense is not easy: if 4. ... Kd5? 5. Rb5+ Kc4 6. Ra5 Kb4 7. Ra1 Kb5 8. Kc7 wins) **5. Kc7 Ra8!** (if 5. ... Rh7+ 6. Kc8 Rh8+ 7. Kd7 Rh7+! 8. Ke6 Rh6+, =) **6. Kd7 Rh8!,** draw.

III. ROOK AND TWO PAWNS VS. ROOK

Just as in the simpler cases with bishops and knights, this is normally a win, but, as usual, there are a number of exceptions. We distinguish the three possible pawn combinations.

A. *Connected Pawns*

Connected pawns always win unless they are blockaded. The only case that presents any real difficulty is the knight-pawn plus rook-pawn, partly because of the absence of hideouts for the White king, and partly because of the threat of stalemate when the pawns reach the seventh.

No. 686, Zukertort-Steinitz, London 1883

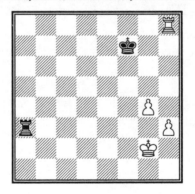

White wins.

The model win is shown in **No. 686**. White must advance his pawns cautiously in order to avoid either an unpleasant blockade or an annoying series of checks. **1. Rb8 Kg6** (on rook checks the White king gets to h4) **2. Rb5 Rc3 3. Re5!** (not 3. h4 at once because of the checks, when White has no good flight square) **3. ... Ra3 4. h4** (if 4. ... Ra2+ 5. Kf3 Ra3+ 6. Re3) **4. ... Rb3 5. h5+ Kh6 6. Rf5** (preparing the entry of his king) **6. ... Ra3 7. Rf3 Ra1 8. Kg3 Rg1+** (the best chance: if the rook stays on the rook file, the pawns advance more easily; e.g., 8. ... Ra2 9. Rf6+ Kg7 10. g5 Ra4 11. h6+ Kh7 12. Rf4 Ra5 13. Kg4, etc.) **9. Kh4 Rh1+ 10. Rh3 Rg1 11. Rh2!** (Black is in zugzwang) **11. ... Ra1 12. g5+ Kg7 13. Rf2! Rh1+ 14. Kg4 Rg1+ 15. Kf5 Rh1 16. h6+ Kh7 17. Rf4!** (the most systematic; an alternative is 17. g6+ Kxh6 18. Kf6 Kh5 19. g7 Rg1 20. Rh2+, but 17. ... Kg8 gets back to the main variation) **17. ... Rg1 18. Re4! Rf1+ 19. Kg4 Rg1+ 20. Kh5 Rh1+ 21. Rh4 Rg1 22. Rh2** (again Black is in zugzwang) **22. ... Rg3 23. Re2 Rh3+ 24. Kg4 Ra3 25. Re7+ Kg8 26. g6 Ra4+ 27. Kf5 Ra5+ 28. Re5 Ra8**.

This position can be won in various ways, of which the safest is to leave the pawns intact and to exchange rooks: **29. Kf6 Ra6+ 30. Re6 Ra8 31. Rd6 Re8 32. Rd5 Ra8 33. Ke7 Ra7+ 34. Rd7 Ra8 35. Rd8+,** and the rest is simple.

As long as you remember the two principles that the pawns must not be blockaded and that the king must always have a safety square (or a way of avoiding checks), you cannot go wrong here.

A variant that often arises is when the king is far away and the rook must defend the pawns. This can be done only with the rook on the rook file, so there may be some difficulty extricating it. But the win is always possible. For example, **No. 687: White king at b3, rook at h6, pawns at g6, h5; Black king at g7, rook at g4.** White to play wins. **1. Rh7+ Kg8** (for 1. ... Kf6 see No. 689) **2. Kc3 Rh4 3. Kd3 Rg4 4. Ke3 Rh4 5. Kf3 Rb4 6. Kg3 Ra4 7. Re7 Ra3+ 8. Kg4 Ra4+ 9. Kg5 Ra5+ 10. Kf6 Ra8 11. h6** and we have No. 686.

Another type of problem that may occur is when the White king cannot find a haven without blocking his pawns. Sometimes this problem is insoluble (No. 696) and White cannot win. Usually, however, if the pawns are not blocked, a way out can be found. For example, **No. 688** (Chess Players' Chronicle 1872-73): **White king at c7, rook at d5, pawns at a5, b5; Black king at a7, rook at b1.** Black to play. White wins. The trouble here is not only that any pawn advance is bad but also that the king cannot easily get out of the way to let the rook hold the pawns (as in No. 687). The only solution is **1. ... Rc1+ 2. Kd6! Kb7** (if 2. ... Ra1 3. Kc6!! Rxa5 4. b6+ wins, while 3. ... Rc1+ is refuted by 4. Rc5 Rh1 5. Rc4! followed by Kc5-b4) **3. Rd4 Ra1 4. Kc5!! Rxa5** (else 5. Rd7+) **5. Rd7+ Kc8 6. Rh7 Ra1 7. Kb6 Rb1 8. Rh8+ Kd7 9. Rb8!** and wins.

Still another difficulty is when the pawns are stopped by the combined efforts of the enemy king and rook. Again, the win involves holding the pawns with the rook and approaching with the king. An example is **No. 689** (Thomas-Alekhine, Hastings 1922): **White king at f3, rook at g7; Black king at c6, rook at h2, pawns at g3, h4.** White to play. Black wins. For the time being, Black cannot push either pawn, nor is it immediately clear just how the king can approach. Still, the method chosen by Alekhine is a forced win. **1. Rg6+ Kd5 2. Rg7 Kd4 3. Rg8 Kd3 4. Rd8+ Kc3 5. Rg8 Kd2 6. Ra8! Rf2+! 7. Kg4 g2 8. Ra1! Ke3!** (8. ... Rf1?? 9. Ra2+ and 10. Rxg2, =) **9. Kh3 Re2! 10. Rg1** (10. Ra3+ Kf2; if 10. Kh2 Kf2 11. Rg1 h3, as in the game) **10. ... Kf3 11. Kh2 h3 12. Ra1.** White resigned here. On 12. Kxh3 Re8! 13. Kh4 Rh8+ 14. Kg5 Rh1 forces the win. The game might have continued **12. ... Kf2 13. Rb1 Re1 14. Rb2+** (14. Rxe1 Kxe1 15. Kg1 Ke2, etc.) **14. ... Ke3 15. Rb3+ Kd4 16. Rb4+ Kc5 17. Rg4 Rh1+** and wins.

When the pawns are blocked by the king, the game is usually a draw. An exception occurs when one pawn is on the seventh.

No. 690, Kling and Horwitz 1851

White wins.
Draw with Pawns on 5th and 6th

No. 690 is a win, but with the pawns on the fifth and sixth it would be a draw. The win is **1. Ka5 Rh5+ 2. Rb5 Rh8 3. Rb6!** (the rook must not leave the knight file yet; if 3. Rc5? Rh6!, draws) **3. ... Rh5+ 4. Kb4 Rh4+ 5. Kc5 Rh5+ 6. Kd4 Rh4+ 7. Ke5 Rh5+ 8. Kf4 Rh4+ 9. Kg5 Rh8 10. Rc6!!** (the winning move) **10. ... Kb8** (the threat was 11. Rc8) **11. Kg6 Rf8 12. Kg7 Rd8 13. Kf7 Rh8 14. Ke7 Rh7+ 15. Kd6 Rh6+ 16. Kc5 Rh5+ 17. Kb6 Rh8 18. a7+** mate.

Black may draw with rook vs. rook and two pawns for one of three reasons: blockade, stalemate, or bad position of the White rook.

a) Blockade

If neither pawn has reached the sixth, this is always a draw; but if one is on the sixth and the other on the fifth, a win is usually possible provided there are no rook-pawns.

The two main cases are shown in **No. 691** and **No. 692**.

No. 691, Cheron 1926

Black to play draws

1. ... Ra8! 2. Ke4 Ra4+ 3. Kd3 Ra3+ 4. Kc4 Ra4+! 5. Kb3 Ra8 6. Kb4 Ra1! 7. Ra5 Rb1+ 8. Kc3 Rc1+! 9. Kd2 Rh1 10. Ra8 Rh7 11. Rd8+ Kc7 12. Rf8 Kd6 13. Rf5 Rh3, =.

No. 692, Cheron 1926

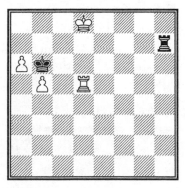

Draw

A win is not possible with a rook-pawn because in the rook and pawn vs. rook ending, a rook-pawn is an exception to the general rules.

In **No. 692**, after **1. Kc8 Rg7 2. Rd7 Rg8+ 3. Rd8 Rg7 4. Kb8!** (4. Rd6+ Kxb5 5. Kb8 Rg8+, =) **4. ... Rh7 5. Rd6+!** (or 5. Re8 Rg7 6. Re6+ Kxb5 7. a7 Rg8+, =. If now 5. ... Kxb5 6. a7 Rh8+ 7. Kc7 Rh7+ 8. Rd7 wins) **5. ... Kc5!! 6. b6** (if 6. Re6 Kxb5 7. a7 Rh8+ 8. Kc7 Rh7+ 9. Kb8 Rh8+, =, while if 6. a7 then simply 6. ... Kxd6 7. a8=Q Rh8+ 8. Kb7 Rxa8 9. Kxa8 Kc5) **6. ... Kxd6 7. Ka8 Rh8+! 8. Ka7 Kc6 9. b7 Kc7 10. b8=Q+ Rxb8** stalemate!

In other cases it is essential to prevent the main winning attempt: the sacrifice of one pawn to force a won rook and pawn vs. rook ending.

No. 693

Draw. Win with White king at c6

No. 693 is drawn by keeping the rook on the d-file and shutting the White king out of the kingside. The only possibility is **1. Rh8 Kxc3 2. b5 Kc4! 3. b6 Rd5+ 4. Ke6 Rb5,** etc., =.

With the White king at c6, the advance of the knight-pawn is secured by a sacrifice. **No. 694: White king at c6,** other pieces unchanged. White wins. **1. ... Rg1 2. Rh4+ Kxc3 3. b5,** etc.

b) Stalemate

This defense is seen mainly with the rook-pawn and is one of the reasons that this ending is so much more difficult than the corresponding one with center pawns. All the important points are seen in the **No. 695.**

No. 695. Horwitz 1881

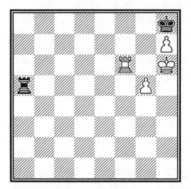

Black to play draws

In **No. 695** the draw is held by **1. ... Ra6!! 2. Kg6** (2. Rxa6 stalemate) **2. ... Rb6! 3. Kh5 Rb5 4. Rh6** (if 4. Rf7 Rxg5+! 5. Kh6 Rg6+!) **4. ... Ra5 5. Kg4 Ra4+ 6. Kf3 Ra3+ 7. Ke4 Ra4+ 8. Kd3 Rg4 9. g6 Rg1,** and White cannot win because there is no haven in the neighborhood of the pawns.

c) The White rook is badly placed

This occurs only in conjunction with pawns on the same rank; that is, not defending one another. The main type is **No. 696**.

No. 696

White to play. Draw

1. Rb6+ Ka7 does White no good because the king still cannot approach. As soon as it gets near the pawns it is checked away. The similar case with center pawns is won because the White king can escape to either side.

B. Unconnected Pawns

This is generally a fairly simple win. The idea is the same as that in the similar cases with bishops and knights discussed earlier: one pawn is sacrificed to force one of the winning positions with rook and pawn vs. rook.

No. 697

Black plays, White wins

No. 697 may be taken as the general case. The most difficult continuation for White is **1. ... Rg8 2. Rf4+ Kd5 3. g4 Kc5 4. Kd3 Kd5 5. c4+ Ke5 6. Re4+ Kd6** (if the king goes to the kingside, Kc3 wins) **7. Ke3 Kc6 8. Kf4 Rf8+ 9. Kg3 Rg8 10. Re5 Kd6 11. Rf5 Ke6 12. c5 Rg7 13. Kf4 Ra7 14. Re5+ Kd7 15. g5 Kc6 16. Kf5,** and now that the pawns are on the fifth, the c-pawn is not important. White sacrifices it and wins by advancing his g-pawn (No. 636).

No. 698, P. Benko

White to play wins

In **No. 698,** the solution is **1. Re1 Kd8 2. e7+ Ke8 3. a4 Rb3+ 4. Kg2 Rb2+ 5. Kh1!! Rb4 6. a5 Rb5 7. a6 Rb6 8. a7 Ra6 9. Rg1!** wins. There are some tries, too: 1. e7? Rb3+ 2. Kf2 (if 2. Kf4 Kd7 3. Re1 Ke8 4. a4 Rb4+ draws) 2. ... Rb2+ 3. Kf1 Kd7 draws, or 1. Rd1? Rb6! 2. Re1 Kd8 draws.

Black can draw against two rook-pawns and against rook-pawn and bishop-pawn. With other pawns he can draw only in special cases, mainly when the White rook is immobilized.

a) Rook-pawn and bishop-pawn

This ending has been notorious ever since the famous game Marshall-Rubin-stein, San Sebastian 1911, although it had already occurred in a game Steinitz-Blackburne, Vienna 1898. The drawing idea is simply this: White cannot hold both pawns if he wants to try to win, but must sacrifice one of them to divert the Black king. It stands to reason that he will sacrifice the rook-pawn. But we have seen that rook and bishop-pawn vs. rook is a draw when the Black king is on the edge of the board (No. 666) except for one special position. So Black needs only to avoid this special position (No. 667) to draw.

The best continuation for both sides may begin from **No. 699.**

No. 699, Schlechter-Tarrasch, Cologne 1911

White to play wins

1. Re3 (threatening to exchange rooks) **1. ... Kf6 2. Rg3 Ra1 3. Kg4 Ra8 4. Rb3** (or 4. h4) **4. ... Rg8+ 5. Kf3 Rg1 6. Rb8 Rf1+ 7. Kg4 Rg1+ 8. Kh5 Kf7!** (in the game, Tarrasch played the inferior 8. ... Rg7; when 9. Rf8+ Ke7 10. Rf5 Ke6 11. Rg5 Rh7+?? 12. Kg6 Rxh3 13. Rc5† won [No. 665]. 11. ... Rf7! would still have saved everything: 12. Kg4 Ra7 13. h4 Ra1 14. Rg6+ Kf7 15. Rb6 Kg7! 16. Kf5 Ra5+ 17. Kg4 Ra1 18. Kg5 Rg1+ 19. Kh5 Rf1, etc., as in the main variation) **9. Rb6 Kg7 10. h4 Kf7** (Black must take care to keep the White pawns and king as far back as possible.) **11. Rb5 Kf6 12. Rg5 Rf1 13. Rg6+ Kf7!** (if 13. ... Kf5 14. Rg8 and the king will be driven to the wrong side of the pawn) **14. Rg4 Ra1**

We are now following the Marshall-Rubinstein game with colors reversed. If 14. ... Kf6 15. Kh6 Kf5? 16. Rg8! drives Black's king away from the all-important squares c7 and c6. **15. Kg5** (if 15. Kh6 Ra6+!! 16. Kh7 Rf6!! 17. h5 Kf8 18. h6 Kf7 19. Rh4 Kf8 20. Kh8 Kf7 21. h7 Kf8, etc., =).

The bishop-pawn plays no significant part in these proceedings, since it hampers White's rook as well as Black's.

15. ... Ra8!

Obstructing the threatened advance of the bishop-pawn. However, 15. ... Ra5+ is a good alternative: 16. f5 Ra1! 17. h5 Kg7! 18. h6+ Kh7 19. Re4 Rg1+ 20. Kf6 Ra1! 21. Re8 Ra2! (not 21. ... Ra6+? 22. Kg5 Ra7 23. Re5! Rb7 24. f6 Kg8 25. Kg6 Rb8 26. Re7 and wins) 22. Kf7 Kxh6 23. f6 Ra7+ 24. Re7 Ra8, = (No. 666).

16. h5 Kg7 17. Kh4+! Rubinstein tried 17. h6+, but after 17. ... Kh7! 18. Kh5 Rf8!! 19. Rh4 (or 19. Rg7+ Kh8 20. Kg5 Rf5+! 21. Kg6 Rf6+, etc., =) 19. ... Rg8! 20. f5 Rg1 21. Rf4 Rh1+ 22. Kg5 Rxh6 23. f6 Rg6+ 24. Kf5 Rg1, a draw was agreed.

17. ... Kh7 (17. ... Kf6 18. h6 Ra1 19. Kh5 Ra5+ 20. Rg5 Ra1 21. Rg6+ Kf7 22. Rg4 wins) **18. f5 Ra1 19. f6 Kh6 20. Rf4 Ra8 21. Kg4 Rb8 22. Re4 Ra8 23. Kf5 Rb8 24. Re7 Ra8 25. f7 Kg7 26. h6+ Kxh6** (26. ... Kf8 27. Re8+ wins) **27. Re8 Rb5+ 28. Ke4,** etc. wins.

Another trap with the two pawns that cannot come out of the main variation is nevertheless worth noting. **No. 700** (Reshevsky-Apscheneek, Kemeri 1937): **White king at f3, rook at d4, pawns at f5, h5; Black king at h8, rook at g5.** White to play wins. **1. f6!! Ra5** (1. ... Rxh5 2. Rd8+? [but 2. Kg4 wins] 2. ... Kh7 3. Kg4! Rh1? [3. ... Rg5+!] 4. f7, or 1. ... Rf5+ 2. Rf4, or 1. ... Kg8 2. Rb4) **2. Rd8+ Kh7 3. Kg4 Ra4+ 4. Kf5 Ra5+ 5. Ke6 Ra6+ 6. Ke7 Ra7+ 7. Rd7 Ra1 8. Ke8+ Kh8 9. f7 Re1+ 10. Re7 Rf1 11. Re6!** and Black resigned.

b) The two rook-pawns

This depends on the transposition into the corresponding rook and rook-pawn vs. rook ending. If the pawns are not beyond the middle of the board a draw will normally result.

No. 701, Gothenburg-Stockholm

Draw

No. 701 illustrates the possibilities. The draw was achieved by **1. ... Ra4! 2. Rf3+** (or 2. h5 Kg5) **2. ... Kg6 3. Kf2 Rxh4 4. Ke2 Ra4 5. Kd2 Ra6 6. Kc2 Rf6 7. Rd3 Kf7 8. Kb3 Ke7 9. Kb4 Rd6** and a draw was agreed.

Or **No. 702** (Chigorin-Salve, Carlsbad 1907): **White king at h6, rook at d3, pawns at a4, h5; Black king at e5, rook at a2.** Draw. The conclusion was **1. Rf3 Rxa4 2. Kg7?** (2. Kg5! Ra1 3. h6 Rg1+ 4. Kh5 Rh1+ 5. Kg6 Rg1+ 6. Kf7 Rh1 7. Rf6 wins) **2. ... Rg4+ 3. Kf7 Rh4 4. Ra3 Rf4+ 5. Ke7 Rb4 6. Ra5+ Kf4 7. h6 Kg4 8. Ra7 Kg5 9. h7 Rb8 10. Kf7 Kh6**, drawn.

c) The immobilized rook

We have seen that it is not advisable to have the rook in front of the pawn.

No. 703

Draw. Win with pawn at b6 instead of b7

The lack of mobility here makes it impossible to win. The Black king remains at g7, from which square it can be driven away only by an earthquake, while the rook plods patiently to and fro along the b-file. The White king, of course, cannot approach the b-pawn; as soon as it gets to c7, checks will drive it away again. With pawn on h3 instead of g2, the game is still a draw.

With the pawn at b6, however, White wins by marching his king in. If Black's king goes over to the queenside, White's g-pawn advances and calls it back. **No. 704: White pawn at b6,** other pieces unchanged. White wins. **1. Kg3 Kf7 2. Kf4 Kg7** (if 2. ... Ke7 3. b7! Kd7 4. Rh8 Rxb7 5. Rh7+ and the g-pawn wins) **3. Ke5 Kf7 4. Kd6**, etc.

C. Doubled Pawns

Doubled pawns are not much better than a single pawn in rook-and-pawn endings. With a few exceptions, exactly the same rules apply, whether the Black king is in front of the pawn or cut off from it. The main exception occurs with a knight-pawn on the sixth with the Black rook confined to the first rank.

No. 705

White to play wins:

Without the extra pawn this is a draw, but here White can force the exchange of rooks. **1. Ra6!** (but not 1. g4 Rc8 2. g5? Rb8 3. g7?? Rb6+! 4. g6 Rxg6+! 5. Kxg6 stalemate) **1. ... Rf8 2. g4!** (or a rook tempo along the rank; 2. g7? at once allows the unpleasant rejoinder 2. ... Rf6+!! 3. Rxf6 stalemate) **2. ... Re8 3. g7 Rd8 4. Rf6 Rb8 5. Rf8+ Rxf8 6. gxf8=Q+ Kxf8 7. Kh7** and wins.

A pawn on one of the four center files that reaches the sixth and confines the Black rook to the first rank wins even if it is single, so the rules remain the same. Note that this winning position with the pawn on the sixth cannot be forced from any normal beginning; the extra pawn makes no difference.

In the Lucena position the extra pawn may even be in the way! **No. 706** (Duras 1903): **White king at b8, rook at g2, pawns at b6, b7; Black king at d7, rook at a3.** White has to resort to the problem continuation **1. Rd2+ Ke7! 2. Rd6!!** (normally 2. Rd4 would decide, but not here, for after 2. ... Ra1 3. Kc7 Rc1+ the king has to go back to his cubbyhole) **2. ... Rc3** (or 2. ... Kxd6 3. Kc8 Rc3+ 4. Kd8 Rh3 5. b8=Q+) **3. Rc6!! Rxc6 4. Ka7** and wins.

IV. ROOK AND TWO PAWNS VS. ROOK AND PAWN

As usual, the extra pawns create more and different winning possibilities. Roughly speaking, rook and two pawns always win against rook and pawn when White has two passed pawns, win most of the time when White has one passed pawn, but always draw when there is no passed pawn. Exactly the same situation holds in minor piece endings.

The various combinations of pawn positions give us three cases.

A. White Has Two Passed Pawns

1. Only *connected passed pawns* win here with any regularity. In practice, two connected pawns on one side of the board vs. one on the other side occur

most often. The winning idea is to get the rook behind the enemy pawn to be able to stop it while supporting one's own.

First we consider the most usual case, when the Black rook is in front of its pawn, the White rook behind it. **No. 707** is the critical position.

The point is that the White king must be able to ensconce itself behind its pawns without allowing Black to exchange his a-pawn for either of White's pawns. White just manages to do that.

No. 707

White to play wins. Black to play draws

1. Kh5 a2 (1. ... Rg1 2. g4 Rg3 3. g5 is worse) **2. g4 Kh7** (to get the king out is no better: 2. ... Kf6 3. g5+ Ke6 4. Kg6 Kd6 5. h5 Kc6 6. h6 Kb6 7. Ra8 Kb5 8. h7 Rh1 9. Rxa2 and wins) **3. g5 Kg7 4. Ra7+ Kf8** (4. ... Kg8 5. Kg6, threatening mate) **5. g6!** (the simplest; 5. Kg6 is also good) **5. ... Kg8** (5. ... Rb1 6. Rxa2 Kg7 7. Ra7+ Kf6 8. Rf7+, or 5. ... Ke8 6. g7 Rg1 7. Kh6! a1=Q 8. Rxa1, etc.) **6. Kh6! Rf1 7. Rxa2** and it's all over.

Black to play can prevent White from advancing his pawns side by side. **1. ... a2! 2. Ra7+ Kg6 3. h5+ Kh6 4. Ra8 Kg7 5. Ra3 Kf6!** (but not 5. ... Kh6?? 6. Ra7!, and the rook must move) **6. h6** (there is no way to make progress: if 6. Ra6+ Kg7 7. Kg5 Rg1! 8. Rxa2 Rxg3+, =, or 6. Ra7 Ke6 7. h6 Kf6 8. h7 Rh1, etc.) **6. ... Kg6 7. Ra6+ Kh7 8. Kg5 Rg1 9. Ra7+ Kg8 10. Rxa2 Rxg3+**, draw.

With bishop-pawn and knight-pawn we have the same critical position, for rook and knight-pawn vs. rook does not win even when the Black rook is confined to the first rank, while rook and bishop-pawn vs. rook does not win if the Black king is on the side of the board. Even the most favorable case, with two center pawns, is only a draw with correct defense. A rook and e-pawn (or d-pawn) ending will result, where Black has a simple draw if he moves his king to the short side of the pawn (Nos. 660-664).

With his rook defending the pawn from the side (e.g., on the seventh rank), Black has no threat of a check, so pawns even on the second rank may win. The only resource for the defense is then to come to the aid of the pawn with his king (see No. 711). The result in such cases depends on how far advanced the pawns are: normally the two pawns will win unless the enemy pawn is on the sixth or beyond and supported by the king.

If the two pawns are supported by the rook and stopped by the enemy king and rook, it may sometimes be difficult for the king to approach. As a rule, however, Black will get into zugzwang, allowing either the enemy king to get close or the pawns to advance.

For example, **No. 708** (Thomas-Alekhine, Hastings 1922, with colors reversed): **White king at g2, rook at a7, pawns at a5, b6; Black king at c6, rook at b3, pawn at g4.** White to play wins. First note that Black is in zugzwang: if his king leaves c6, or if his rook leaves the b-file, White wins immediately with b7. So White only needs to tempo with his king. The win is **1. Kf2 Rb1 2. Kg3 Rb4 3. Kh4!** and now Black must give up his g-pawn. For the resulting ending see No. 689.

The ending is far more difficult when the Black rook is behind the pawn, the White rook in front of it.

No. 709, Marshall-Euwe, Bad Kissingen 1928

Black to play, White wins

A model case from practical play is seen in **No. 709** (Marshall-Euwe, Bad Kissingen 1928, with colors reversed). To determine whether this position is won, we must compare it with No. 707. Thus 1. ... Rb1 2. Ra6 Ra1 3. Kg4 a4 4. f4 a3 5. e4 a2 6. Kf5, and now we see that White wins. So Black feels compelled to offer a different defense. The winning method may then be divided into four phases:

1. White guards the Black passed pawn by placing his rook behind it.

2. With the help of both king and rook he advances his own pawns as far as possible, taking care to avoid a blockade.

3. If Black prevents the further advance by manipulating his rook, White will either capture Black's pawn or rook.

4. If the Black rook does not try to stop the pawns, a queen will be forced by their steady advance.

The game continued **1. ... Kg7 2. Kg3 Kf7 3. f4 Ke7 4. e4 Kd7** (an example of the third phase: the Black king tries to drive the rook away from the a-file, speculating on the strength of his own pawn. This is the only defense that gives him any chance whatsoever, but he is much too late.) **5. Ra6 Kc7 6. f5 Kb7 7. Rh6 a4 8. f6! Kc7** (now the king has to come back, else the rook is lost) **9. Rh7+ Kd6 10. Re7!!** (a vital move; otherwise, his pawns will be blockaded) **10. ... Rb1!** (there is a cute tactical refutation of 10. ... a3 11. e5+ Rxe5 12. Rxe5 Kxe5 13. f7 a2 14. f8=Q a1=Q 15. Qh8+ and wins) **11. Kf2** (to keep the Black rook out of f1) **11. ... Rb2+ 12. Ke3 Rb3+** (or 12. ... Rb1 13. Kd4! Rd1+ 14. Kc4, etc., as in the main variation) **13. Kd4 a3 14. e5+ Kc6 15. Ra7 Rb4+ 16. Kc3 Rf4 17. Kb3!** (better than 17. Rxa3 Kd5!) **17. ... Kd5 18. Re7 Rf3+ 19. Ka2 Kc4 20. f7 Kb4 21. Rb7+ Ka4 22. Ra7+ Kb4 23. e6 Rf2+ 24. Kb1 Kb3 25. Rb7+ Ka4 26. Rb8,** Black resigned.

Note that when the Black king left the White pawns, their advance was secured by the rook while the White king held the Black pawn. This is a subsidiary phase that is seen often. If Black's rook and king together stop the pawns, White must bring up his king, since the rook alone cannot force any progress; but if only one of the two pieces tries to stop the pawns, either a queen will be forced or the rook will be lost.

If the defender's rook is in front of the pawn, as in No. 707, so that he threatens to advance to the seventh and queen, it is essential for the superior side to keep his king in front of one of his pawns in order to make sure that the other rook cannot get out with check.

For example, **No. 710** (Janowski-Yates, New York 1924): **White king at h5, rook at e8, pawn at a4; Black king at f6, rook, pawns at f5, e4.** White to play, Black wins. Janowski chose the line **1. Kh4 Ra3 2. Ra8 Ke5 3. Kg5 Rg3+ 4. Kh5 e3 5. a5 Kf4! 6. a6 Rg1 7. a7 Ra1** (now White has no check) **8. Kg6 Ra6+ 9. Kh5 e2! 10. Re8 Kf3!!,** and White resigned, for if 11. a8=Q+ Rxa8 12. Rxa8 e1=Q.

Black can draw this ending only if he is able to make his own pawn a threat, or if he can blockade the two pawns.

The lone pawn becomes a threat when it is advanced to the seventh and is supported by its king. If it is aided merely by the rook, the White rook preserves its freedom of action; the only conceivable threat, a rook check, is easily warded off (see the previous example). But if the king comes up too, White may run the risk of losing his rook. Such a defense is feasible, of course, only when the White pawns are not far advanced, for if they are, White can sacrifice his rook and win with two pawns vs. rook.

No. 711 is an example.

No. 711, Reshevsky-Alekhine, AVRO 1938

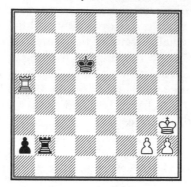

White to play. Draw

After **1. g4, Kc6!** saved the day (1. ... Ke6?? 2. Kg3 Kf6 3. h3 Kg6 4. Kh4 is hopeless: No. 709) **2. Kg3** (on 2. g5 Rb5! 3. Ra6+ Kb7 4. Rxa2 Rxg5 5. Rc2 Rg8 is the simplest drawing line) **2. ... Kb6 3. Ra8 Kb5 4. h3** (if 4. g5 Kb4 threatens 5. ... Rb3+ and 6. ... Ra3, so the White king must leave the third rank and lose his h-pawn) **4. ... Kb4 5. Kf4 Rc2!** (threatening 6. ... Rc4+ followed by either 7. ... Rc3+ and 8. ... Ra3, or 7. ... Rc5+ and 8. ... Ra5. Since there is no defense to this threat, White is compelled to take a draw by perpetual check.) **6. Rb8+ Kc3! 7. Ra8 Kb4!,** drawn.

If the king is blockading the pawn, a similar type of drawing stratagem is available: Black advances the pawn to the seventh and threatens either to mate or to queen, which compels White to accept perpetual check. For example, **No. 712** (Reshevsky-Capablanca, AVRO 1938): **White king at c2, rook at b5, pawns at a3, b2; Black king at g3, rook at h1, pawn at e3.** Draw. **1. Kd3 Kf4! 2. Rb8 Rd1+ 3. Ke2 Rd2+ 4. Ke1 Kf3 5. Rf8+ Ke4 6. b4 Ra2 7. Ra8** (or, as in the game, 7. Re8+ Kf3 8. Rf8+ Ke4, draw agreed) **7. ... Kd3** (or even 7. ... e2 8. b5 Ke3 9. Re8+ Kf3 10. Rf8+, etc.) **8. Rd8+ Ke4 9. Ra8 Kd3,** =.

The blockade is of course an effective weapon even with rook and two pawns vs. rook. But there are many cases (especially with one pawn on the sixth) where White may still win. When Black has an extra pawn the added counterplay may neutralize even those advanced pawn positions that would otherwise be won.

No. 713, Steinitz-Lasker, match 1894

White to play. Draw

In **No. 713**, without the g-pawn Black would be lost despite the blockade (see No. 691), but as it is, Black can draw.

1. Kd4

The normal 1. Rb1 is not good because White cannot afford to exchange rooks: 1. ... Ra4+ 2. Rb4?? Rxb4+ 3. Kxb4 g4, and the White king is outside the square. So in answer to 1. ... Ra4+, 2. Kb5 is forced, but then 2. ... Rd4 3. Re1 Rxd5+ 4. Kc4 Rc5+ 5. Kd4 Rc7 destroys all of White's winning hopes.

1. ... Ra4+!

Best; if 1. ... Rf8 2. Re5!! g4 3. Rg5 Ra8 4. Ke3 Ra3+ 5. Kf4 Ra4+ 6. Kg3!, White has excellent winning chances. White's second move here is based on a pretty trap: 2. ... Rf4+? 3. Kd3!! Kxe5 4. e7 Rd4+ 5. Kc3, and the pawn queens.

2. Kd3 Ra8!!

In the game, Lasker played 2. ... Ra3+? and resigned after 3. Ke4 g4 4. Kf5 Ra8 5. e7 Re8 6. Kf6 g3 7. Kf7 Kd7 8. d6! g2 9. Rg1. **3. Ke4 Rf8!! 4. Kd4!** (or 4. Rg1 Rf4+ 5. Ke3 Rf5!, =; if now 6. Rd1 Rf8 7. Ke4 Rf4+, etc.) **4. ... g4!** (not 4. ... Rf4+? 5. Re4 Rf8 6. Re5! g4 7. Rg5, etc., as above) **5. Rg1** (or 5. Ra1 Rf4+ 6. Ke3 Rf8! 7. Ra5 g3; or 5. Ke4 g3 6. Rc1 g2 7. Rg1 Rg8 8. Kf3 Kxd5) **5. ... Rf4+ 6. Ke3 Rf5**, draw.

Another game from a world championship match that uses the weapon of the blockade is **No. 714** (Alekhine-Euwe, 13th match game, 1935): **White king at d4, rook at c7, pawn at a7; Black king at g6, rook at a1, pawns at f7, g4.** Draw. The simplest drawing line here is **1. Ke3! f5** (1. ... Ra4 2. Rc4!) **2. Kf4 Ra4+ 3. Kg3 Kf6 4. Rb7! Ke5 5. Rb5+ Ke6 6. Rb6+ Kd5 7. Rb5+**, etc. Instead, the game continued **1. Ke5? f6+??** (correct is 1. ... Ra4! and if then 2. Rc4 f6+ 3. Kd6 Ra6+ 4. Kd5 Kg5 and wins: the blockade is lifted) **2. Kf4 Ra4+** (too late) **3. Kg3 f5** (or 3. ... Kg5 4. Rg7+ Kf5 5. Kh4!) **4. Kh4! Kf6 5. Rb7!** and a draw was agreed, for if 5. ... Ke5 6. Rb5+ Ke6 7. Rb6+, etc., since if the Black king goes to the queenside the f-pawn falls.

We see that two connected passed pawns win against one pawn unless

either the single pawn is far advanced and supported by both king and rook
or the two pawns are blockaded.

2. *Unconnected passed pawns* win only if a transposition to a simpler case
with rook and pawn vs. rook is feasible. In other words, normally the rooks
will capture one pawn each. Often, of course, one passed pawn or set of
pawns will be much more dangerous than the rival set. In such cases, one
pawn may even win against two.

No. 715, Leonhardt-Spielmann, San Sebastian 1912

Black to play wins. White to play draws

No. 715 is typical of many such endings. In the game, it was White's move,
and after **1. g6! Kd3 2. Rd7!** (not 2. Rg8 d4 3. g7 b3 4. Rb8 Rg1+! 5. Kb2 Rxg7
6. Rxb3+ Kd2 7. Rh3 Rb7+ and wins. It is imperative for White to preserve his
rook's freedom of action.) **2. ... d4 3. g7 Rg6** (Black can find no really satisfactory solution because the White king is too near the pawns. If, for instance,.
3. ... Rg1+ 4. Kb2 Ke3 5. Kb3 d3 6. Kxb4 d2 7. Kc3! Ke2 8. Re7+ Kd1 9. Ra7
Rg3+ 10. Kb2 Ke2 11. Re7+, etc. The trouble is that Black must give up one
pawn to get the White king out of the way.) **4. Kb2 Rg1 5. Kb3**, and a draw
was agreed, for if **5. ... Rb1+ 6. Ka4,** and the Black rook has to return.

But the result in such cases obviously depends on the positions of the
pawns. For this reason, Black to play wins because he can advance his pawns
more quickly. For example, **1. ... Kc3 2. Rc7+ Kb3 3. Rg7 d4 4. g6** (4. Rd7 Rxg5
5. Rxd4 Rg1+ 6. Kd2 Ka3 is lost: No. 636) **4. ... d3 5. Rg8 d2+ 6. Kd1 Kb2 7. g7
b3 8. Rd8 Rxg7 9. Rxd2+ Kb1 and wins.**

The defending side must choose the moment for the pawn exchange carefully. **No. 716** (Spielmann-Landau, 3rd match game, 1936) illustrates some of
the traps that occur. **White king at f1, rook at a6, pawn at h6; Black king at
e5, rook at b4, pawns at b5, d5.** Draw. The game continued **1. ... Rf4+ 2. Ke2
Kd4 3. Rb6 Kc5 4. Rb8** (keeping the rook on the seventh rank, as in the previous diagram, is also good) **4. ... Rh4 5. Rh8 Kd4 6. h7 Rh2+ 7. Kd1!** (but not
7. Kf3 Kd3! and Black wins, for if 8. Rd8 Rxh7 9. Rxd5+ Kc4, White's king is
too far away) **7. ... Kd3 8. Kc1 d4 9. Kb1 b4** (9. ... Kd2 is met by 10. Rd8) **10.**

Ka1! (the simplest: if 10. Kc1? Rc2+ 11. Kb1 Rc7! and wins) **10. ... Kd2 11. Kb2!** (again the safest. if 11. Rd8? Rxh7 12. Rxd4+ Kc3! 13. Rd8 Rh1+ 14. Ka2 b3+ 15. Ka3 Ra1+ mate, or 13. Rd1 Kc2!) **11. ... d3 12. Kb3 Rh4 13. Ka4! Kd1 14. Rd8 Rxh7 15. Rxd3+,** draw.

Where the pawns are far apart, the king should take care of one and the rook the other, always, of course, with an eye on the resulting rook and pawn vs. rook ending. **No. 717** (Spielmann-Capablanca, Moscow 1925): **White king at e2, rook at c5, pawn at d4; Black king at g6, rook at g3, pawns at g4, c3. Draw. 1. Kf2! Rh3 2. Kg2 Rd3 3. Kh2 Kf6 4. Kg2 Ke6 5. Kh2 Kd6 6. Kg2 Rd2+ 7. Kg3 c2 8. Kh4!** (of course not 8. Kxg4? Rxd4+; similarly, 8. Rc3? Kd5 9. Kxg4 Kxd4 is bad) **8. ... Rg2 9. Kg5!!** (the Black king must be kept out at all costs) **9. ... Rg1 10. Rxc2 Kd5 11. Kf4 Kxd4 12. Rd2+,** draw.

In the above examples the defender's king is always directly in front of one of the pawns. But even when this is not the case, a draw may be secured by exploiting the counterchances offered by the single passed pawn. In **No. 718,** the pawn at c5 guarantees the draw.

No. 718, Bogolyubov-Thomas, Hastings 1922

Black to play. Draw

After **1. ... Ra6** (on 1. ... g4 2. c6 g3 3. Rxg3 a3 4. Rg1 a2 5. Ra1 draws easily, but even 4. Rxa3 Rxa3 5. c7 Rc3 6. Kd6 is sufficient) **2. c6 Ke7 3. Kc5 Kd8 4. Kd6 g4 5. Rg3 a3 6. Rxg4.** Black's advantage is dissipated and a draw is the natural result.

If the passed pawn is blocked by the rook (instead of the king as above), the superior side is in effect fighting with one active piece against two, so a win is out of the question.

For example, **No. 719** (Levenfish-Pirc, Moscow 1935): **White king at c6, rook at f1, pawns at b4, d4; Black king at f7, rook at f4, pawn at f2. Black to play draws. 1. ... Ke8!** (it would take much too long, of course, for the king to come to the aid of the pawn, while 1. ... Rxd4 2. Rxf2+ Ke8 3. b5 transposes to a loss) **2. b5 Rf6+! 3. Kc7 Rf7+ 4. Kc8 Ke7!** (the only move; if now 5. b6 Kd6! 6. d5 Rf8+ 7. Kb7 Kxd5, etc.) **5. Kc7 Ke8+ 6. Kc6** (6. Kb8 Rf6) **6. ... Rf6+ 7. Kb7**

Rf7+ 8. Ka6 Kd7 9. b6 (or 9. d5 Kd6 10. b6 Rf3! 11. b7 Ra3+ 12. Kb6 Rb3+ 13. Ka7 Ra3+ 14. Kb8 Rf3, =) **9. ... Kc8 10. d5 Rf3!**, and White can only wring his hands in despair.

The single pawn may even win against the two pawns if it is supported by both king and rook and if the superior side's forces are disorganized. **No. 720** (Tarrasch-Schlechter, 8th match game, 1911): **White king at d6, rook at a8, pawn at e6; Black king at h7, rook at f5, pawns at a3, g7.** White wins. **1. ... Rf6** (or 1. ... Rf1 2. e7) **2. Kd7! Kg6 3. e7 Rf7 4. Kd6 Rxe7 5. Kxe7 Kf5 6. Kd6! g5 7. Kd5 Kf4 8. Kd4 g4 9. Rf8+!! Kg3 10. Ke3 a2 11. Ra8 Kh3 12. Rxa2 g3 13. Kf3**, Black resigned.

3. *Doubled pawns* practically never win. If the Black king is near them, even without Black's extra pawn the game would be drawn, while if the Black king is supporting his own pawn, the likely result is a rook vs. two pawns ending, which is a draw in this case.

To sum up: Rook and two passed pawns vs. rook and pawn is normally a win when the pawns are connected, but a draw when they are unconnected or doubled.

B. White Has One Passed Pawn

Unlike the similar cases with minor pieces, the extra pawn here is normally not enough. The theoretical reason is that the rook is so strong that it doesn't need to permit the enemy king to cross over and capture the last pawn (this was the winning method with bishops). Still, it is worthwhile to examine the major possibilities.

Though the passed pawn may be blocked by either the king or the rook, it is far better to block it with the king because the rook is immobilized in front of a pawn. *The basic rule of all rook endings is that rooks belong behind pawns.*

When the pawn is blocked by the king a draw is to be expected.

No. 721, Lasker-Steinitz, 14th match game, 1896

Draw

No. 721 may be taken as the general case. The simplest drawing line is **1. ... Re3 2. Rd4+** (if 2. Rf2 Rxb3 3. Rf4+ Ka3 4. Rf3 Rxf3 5. gxf3 Kb4 6. Kd3 Kc5, =, or 3. Rxf5 Rg3 4. Rf2 Kc4, =) **2. ... Kc5** (2. ... Ka3 3. Ra4+ mate) **3. Rd3 Re2+ 4. Rd2 Re3 5. Rf2 f4! 6. Kb2 Rg3 7. Ka3 Kb5 8. Kb2 Kc5! 9. Kc2 Kb5 10. Kd1 Rxb3 11. Rxf4 Rg3 12. Rf2 Kc5 13. Ke1 Kd6 14. Kf1 Ke7,** and White cannot win.

An alternative defense is **1. ... Re4 2. Rf2 Rg4 3. Kb2 f4!** (the game went 3. ... Re4?? 4. g3! Re5 5. Rf4+, and now Lasker could have won with 5. ... Kb5 6. Ka3 Rd5 7. Rf3 Ka5 8. b4+ Kb5 9. Kb3 Kb6 10. Kc4 Kc6 11. Rb3! Re5 12. b5+ Kb6 13. Kd4 Re4+ 14. Kd5 Re8 15. Kd6 Re1 16. Rf3 Kxb5 17. Rxf5+ Kc4 18. g4, and Steinitz soon resigned) **4. Kc2 Kc5! 5. Kd3 Rg3+ 6. Ke4 Rxb3 7. Kxf4 Kd6 8. Re2 Rb8,** = (No. 638).

It is clear that if he wants to win, White must rely on the possibility of giving up his passed pawn to capture the enemy pawn and secure a won rook and pawn vs. rook ending. The outcome then depends on whether this plan can actually be carried out. As usual, the rook-pawn is harder to capitalize on than other pawns, and if the Black king is in any reasonable position, a draw is unavoidable.

An example is **No. 722** (Gracs-Benko, Budapest 1950): **White king at h1, rook at a6, pawns at a5, g2, h4; Black king at g4, rook at b2, pawns at b4 f4. Black to play. 1. ... b3 2. Rb6?** (White doesn't realize that his own pawn will help Black. Necessary is 2. Rg6+ Kxh4 3. Rb6) **2. ... f3! 3. Rg6+** (too late; but on 3. gxf3+ Kg3! 4. Rg6+ Kh3, the h-pawn covers the Black king: 5. Kg1 Ra2 6. Rb6 b2 7. a6 Ra1+ wins) **3. ... Kh5! 4. Rb6** (if 4. Rf6 fxg2+ 5. Kh2 Ra2 5 Rb6 b2 7. a6 Ra1 wins) **4. ... Rb1+ 5. Kh2 f2,** White resigned.

To block the pawn with the rook is less favorable. It is relatively best to have the rook behind the pawn. In that event, the defender draws if his king can find a haven behind the pawns, but loses if he cannot. As a rule, the king can find a safe spot only if the two remaining pawns are on the same file.

No. 723, Steinitz-Gunsberg, 9th match game, 1890

White to play. Black wins

No. 723 is typical. White is defenseless against Black's threat to move his rook out of the pawn's way with check, for on 1. Kh6 g5! forces him to expose his king. His only hope, therefore, lies in driving the Black king as far from the kingside as possible, giving up his rook for the a-pawn and taking his chances on the ensuing rook vs. pawn ending. This stratagem is bound to fail here because the Black king is too near. Black wins as follows: **1. Ra4+ Kd5** (the game continued 1. ... Kf3? 2. Ra3+ Kf2?? 3. Kxg6 Rg1+ 4. Kf7 a1=Q 5. Rxa1 Rxa1 6. h5, and drew because the Black king is too far behind the pawn) **2. Ra5+ Kc6 3. Ra6+** (if 3. Kh6 g5 4. hxg5 Rh1+ 5. Kg7 a1=Q+ 6. Rxa1 Rxa1 7. g6 Kd7 8. Kf6 Rf1+ 9. Kg5 Ke7 and wins, while 3. Kxg6 Rg1+ is essentially the same as the main variation) **3. ... Kb7 4. Rxa2 Rxa2 5. Kxg6 Kc6 6. h5 Kd7 7. h6 Ke7 8. h7 Rg2+ 9. Kh6 Kf7 and wins.**

If the pawns are on the same file here, the check can be prevented. **No. 724: White pawn at g4**, other pieces unchanged, is drawn. After **1. Kxg6** the only sensible continuation is **1. ... Rg1 2. Rxa2 Rxg4+** followed by a handshake.

It is far worse for the defense to have his rook in front of the pawn. He then has no moves with it, and his opponent can capture either the rook or the last pawn. **No. 725: White king at f4, rook at a1, pawns at a7, h4; Black king at f6, rook at a8, pawn at g6.** White wins. **1. ... Kf7 2. Ke5 Ke7 3. Ra2!** (tempo) **3. ... Kf7** (or 3. ... Kd7 4. Kf6 Kc6 5. Kxg6 Kb7 6. h5, etc.) **4. Kd6 Kf6 5. Kd7 Kf5 6. Kc7 Kg4 7. Ra4+ Kg3 8. Kb7 and wins.**

When the superior side has any choice in the matter, he should naturally try to force the rook to block the pawn. If he can cut off the king, as is likely, the ending may not differ in any essential respect from rook and pawn vs. rook.

The historic ending Morphy-Riviere, Paris 1863, is an example. **No. 726: White king at f3, rook at c3, pawn at a3; Black king at d6, rook at a4, pawns at b5, d5.** Black to play wins. The shortest and most logical road to victory is **1. ... Re4!** and now:

a) 2. Rc8 Re6 3. Rd8+ Kc5 4. Rc8+ Kd4 5. Rb8 Kc4 6. Rc8+ Kd3 7. Rb8 d4! 8. Rxb5 Rf6+ 9. Kg2 Kc4! 10. Rb8 d3 11. Rd8 Kc3 12. Rc8+ Kb3 13. Rd8 Kc2! 14. Rc8+ Kd1 15. a4 Rf5! 16. Rc7 d2 17. Rc8 Ke2 18. Re8+ Kd3 19. Rd8+ Kc3 20. Rc8+ Kd4 21. Rd8+ Rd5.

b) 2. Rb3 Kc5 3. Rc3+ Kd4 4. Rb3 Re6 5. Rxb5 Kc4 6. Rb8 d4 7. a4 d3 8. a5 d2 9. Rd8 Kc3 10. Kf2 Kc2 11. Rc8+ Kd1 12. Kf1 (if 12. Ra8 Rc6 followed by ... Kc2) 12. ... Rf6+ 13. Kg2 Ra6 14. Rc5 Ke2 15. Re5+ Kd3 16. Rd5+ Ke3 17. Re5+ (else simply ... Rxa5) 17. ... Kd4 18. Re8 Rd6, and the pawn queens.

When the pawns are close to one another (as in the analogous case with bishops), the game is tenable. The Black king will necessarily stay nearby so there can be no question of forcing a won rook and pawn vs. rook ending.

No. 727, Reti-Breyer, Baden 1914

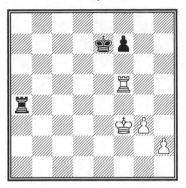

Draw

No. 727 is a relatively favorable case, yet even here White can do nothing. The game continued **1. Rf4 Ra2 2. h4 Ra5 3. Kg4 Kf8 4. Rf5 Ra4+ 5. Kg5 Ra3 6. g4 Kg7 7. h5 Ra6 8. Rd5 Rb6 9. Kf4 Rb1 10. g5 Rf1+ 11. Ke4 Rh1 12. h6+ Kg6,** draw.

Or **No. 728** (Reshevsky-Apscheneek, Kemeri 1937): **White king at f4, rook at e5, pawns at f3, g4; Black king at f6, rook at a3, pawn at h6.** Draw. White tried **1. Re4 Rb3 2. Ra4 Rb6 3. Kg3 Rb3 4. Ra6+ Kg5 5. Ra5+ Kf6 6. Rf5+ Kg6 7. Rc5 Ra3 8. Rd5 Kf6 9. Kf4 Ra4+,** etc., but no real progress could be made. Black later lost by making an incorrect sacrifice at the wrong time.

To win, the superior side must capture the last pawn. As a rule, this cannot be done without the opponent's help; e.g., **No. 729** (Grünfeld-Wagner, Breslau 1925): **White king at g4, rook at a7, pawn at h4; Black king at h6, rook at f1, pawns at f7, g6.** White to play. **1. Ra8** draws quite simply, for if **1. ... f5+ 2. Kg3 Rg1+ 3. Kh3 Rb1 4. Rh8+!,** the Black king cannot get through. Instead, there occurred **1. Rb7? f5+ 2. Kg3 Rg1+ 3. Kh3 Ra1 4. Rb8 Ra3+ 5. Kh2 Kh5 6. Rh8+ Kg4 7. Rh6 Ra6! 8. Kg2 f4 9. Kf2 f3 10. Ke3 Kg3,** White resigned.

C. No Passed Pawn

In view of No. 727, this must inevitably be a draw with any normal king position. Still, the superior side may win if his king manages to penetrate to the enemy pawn. But starting from scratch this can never be forced.

So this is the main winning chance in such endings: capturing the last pawn. The only other type of win occurs in a position such as **No. 730.**

No. 730

Black to play, White wins

If it were White's move, 1. Kf6 Rb6+ 2. e6, threatening both 3. Ra8+ and 3. Rxf7+, would decide at once. The best defense is **1. ... Rb6** (if 1. ... Kg7 2. e6 Rf8 3. f6+ Kg8 4. e7 Re8 5. Rd7) **2. Ra8+ Ke7** (or 2. ... Kg7 3. f6+ Kh7 4. Ra7! Kg8 5. Kh6 Rb8 6. e6!! fxe6 7. Kg6 e5 8. Rg7+ Kf8 9. Rh7 Kg8 10. f7+) **3. f6+ Ke6** (or 3. ... Kd7 4. Rf8) **4. Re8+ Kd5 5. Kh6 Rb1** (5. ... Re6 6. Rxe6 Kxe6 7. Kg7) **6. Kg7 Rb7 7. Re7**. Of course, such a position can be reached only through extremely passive play on the defender's part.

With the pawns on the rook and knight files, even this chance does not exist. **No. 731: White king at f5, rook at a7, pawns at g5, h5; Black king at g8, rook at b8, pawn at h7.** Draw. The rook cannot be driven off the first rank. Exchanging pawns leads to nothing, and a move such as **1. h6** is similarly fruitless.

V. MATERIAL ADVANTAGE (IN GENERAL)

There is no ending in which more mistakes are made transforming a won position into a point than rook endings. Even the games of the greatest masters are often chock full of inaccuracies and sometimes outright blunders. And yet there is no more common and more important type of ending.

We follow our usual system of classification according to material and position. Unfortunately, it is hardly possible to set up one general winning schema (as in bishop endings) that would apply to all varieties of material advantage; we'll have to be content with one for each of the specific classes.

In all of the following cases we refer to positions where one side is one pawn ahead.

A. Outside Passed Pawn

Even here there is such a variety of possibilities that one general winning plan is still impossible.

In the first place, we must consider those cases where the pawns are otherwise evenly balanced. This means that the only passed pawn (or potential passed pawn) is the one that confers the advantage. This pawn must be stopped by the defender. So we have a second division, depending on whether the rook or the king is watching the pawn.

In most cases the pawn is held by the rook. Such games are drawn if the defender's rook is behind the pawn, but lost if it is in front of the pawn. An exception occurs when the Black king is cut off and White can move his king to the support of the passed pawn, a situation that differs in no essential respect from rook and pawn vs. rook.

When the Black rook is behind the pawn and the White rook in front of it, we get the typical draw in **No. 732.** The idea of the draw is this: To win, White will have to keep his pawn at a6 and march his king to the queenside. He will thereby expose his kingside and will have to lose at least one pawn. Once Black has captured a pawn, White will advance his king and win Black's rook for the a-pawn. White will emerge with a rook vs. pawn ending in which his king is too far away to effect a win. If White gets too frisky and sacrifices more than one pawn, Black may even win.

No. 732

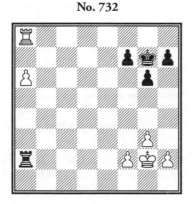

Draw

The model continuation is **1. Kf3 h5 2. h4** (2. Ke4 Rxf2 3. Rc8 Ra2 4. Rc6 Rxh2 5. Kd5 Ra2 6. Kc5 g5 7. Kb6 h4 8. gxh4 gxh4 9. a7 h3 10. Kb7 h2 11. Rc1 Rb2+ 12. Ka6 Ra2+ 13. Kb7, etc., =. But if here 4. Ra8? Rxh2 5. a7 Ra2, Black wins) **2. ... Kf6** (Black may move his king out only if, as in this position, he is not exposed to a check. See No. 680.) **3. Ke3** (if now 3. Ke4 Rxf2 4. Rc8 Re2+! 5. Kd5?? Ra2 6. Rc6+ Kf5 7. Kc5 Kg4 8. Kb6 Kxg3, and Black has all the winning chances) **3. ... Kf5 4. f3 Ra3+ 5. Kd4 Rxf3 6. Rf8 Ra3 7. Rxf7+ Kg4 8. Rf6 Kxg3 9. Rxg6+ Kxh4 10. Kc5 Kh3 11. Kb6 h4 12. a7 Kh2 13. Kb7 Rxa7+** (even 13. ... h3 draws now: queen vs. this advanced rook-pawn cannot be won) **14. Kxa7 h3 15. Kb6 Kh1,** etc., =.

If the White king is stalemated, he has no winning possibilities at all. **No. 733: White king at h3, rook at a8, pawns at a6, f4, g3, h2; Black king at g7,** rook at a2, pawns at f5, g6, h7. Draw. The only chance is **1. g4**, but then **1. ... fxg4+ 2. Kxg4 Rxh2 3. a7 Ra2**, etc., is all right. The White king cannot approach his pawn because of the strong h-pawn, but even if he could, it would do him no good (No. 680).

White has winning chances in positions analogous to No. 732 in two cases: when the Black pawns are too far advanced or too widely scattered and are thus subject to capture, or when (usually with pawns other than a rook-pawn) White can afford to give up one pawn on the kingside, blockade the remaining pawns, and win his opponent's rook.

Once his pawn is on the seventh, White must be two pawns ahead to win, and the other pawn must be able to lure the Black king out of its corner, which is why it must not be a rook-pawn or a knight-pawn.

No. 734

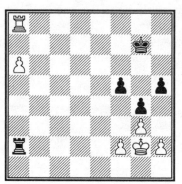

Black to play. Draw

In **No. 734**, the continuation after **1. ... Ra3** is **2. a7 Ra1 3. f4**!? (the only way to get the king out) **3. ... gxf3+! 4. Kxf3 h4! 5. Kf4** (or **5. gxh4**) **5. ... hxg3** only draws. See No. 703.

If Black has an e-pawn or d-pawn, the ending is lost. White advances his pawn to the seventh, and then marches in his king and captures Black's pawn.

No. 735: White king at f2, rook at a8, pawns at a6, e2, g2, h2; Black king at g7, rook at a2, pawns at e6, g6, h6. White wins. **1. a7 Ra3 2. e3 Ra2+ 3. Kf3 Ra4 4. e4 Ra3+ 5. Kf4 Ra5 6. Ke3 Ra4 7. Kd3 Kh7 8. Kc3 Kg7 9. Kb3 Ra1 10. Kb4 Kh7 11. Kb5 Kg7 12. Kc6 Kh7 13. Kd7 Ra4 14. e5 Ra6 15. Ke8! Kg7 15. Ke7 Ra1 16. Kxe6**, etc.

The second possibility, giving up one pawn and blockading the opponent's, occurs much less frequently because the defender will not voluntarily consent to a blockade.

No. 736

Black to play, White wins

But if the pawns are already blocked, as in **No. 736**, the win is forced as follows: **1. ... Ra3+ 2. Kd4! Rxg3 3. Rc8!** (but not 3. a7?? Ra3, =) **3. ... Ra3 4. Rc7+ Kf6** (4. ... Kf8 5. a7 and 6. Rc8+) **5. a7 Ke6** (Usually the best counterplay is to create a passed pawn. But here 5. ... g5!? 6. hxg5+! Kg6 7. Kc5 h4 8. Kb5! h3 9. Rc6+ Kg7 10. Ra6 wins) **6. Kc5 Ra1? 7. Kb6 Rb1+** (or 7. ... Kd5 8. Rc5+ Ke4 9. Ra5) **8. Kc6 Ra1 9. Kb7 Kd5** (9. ... Rb1+ 10. Kc8 is equally useless) **10. Re7! Kd6 11. Re5! Rb1+** (11. ... Rxa7+ is hopeless) **12. Ka6 Ra1+ 13. Ra5** and wins.

With the passed pawn on another file, this second winning stratagem is much less likely to succeed because the Black king is necessarily so much nearer White's passed pawn.

To sum up: If White's rook is in front of his passed pawn and Black's rook behind it, the game is drawn unless the Black pawns are exposed to attack or blockaded.

This conclusion is in accordance with our fundamental rule that *rooks belong behind pawns, not in front of them.*

If we reverse the positions of the rooks in No. 732, we get another verification of our rule, for White now wins. This case, with the White rook behind the passed pawn, and the Black rook in front of it, is seen in **No. 737.**

No. 737, Alekhine-Capablanca, 34th match game. 1927

Black to play, White wins.

This is the game with which Alekhine won the world championship. The win consists of four steps.

1. Centralizing the king. Black will eventually have to allow the king to penetrate to one side or the other, since his rook must not move (if it does, the pawn advances), while White has an inexhaustible number of tempi.

2. The Black king will go to blockade the pawn, for if it stays on the king-side White will attack and capture the rook.

3 White's king will attack the group of pawns on the kingside.

4. At the right moment the White rook will abandon the passed pawn and establish a decisive material superiority (two pawns, or rook and pawn vs. rook in a theoretical win) on the kingside.

All these steps are exemplified here. The game continued **1. ... Ra6** (1. ... Rf5 2. Ra4 is worse) **2. Ra4** (actually, two harmless and meaningless moves were interspersed here) **2. ... Kf6 3. Kf3 Ke5 4. Ke3 h5 5. Kd3 Kd5 6. Kc3 Kc5 7. Ra2!** (completing the first step: Black's king must now give way) **7. ... Kb5 8. Kd4** (again two meaningless moves intervened) **8. ... Rd6+** (to blockade the pawn with his king. On 8. ... Kb4, 9. Ra1! is simplest: 9. ... Kb3 10. Kc5 Kb2 11. Kb5! Rf6 12. Ra4! Kb3 13. Rf4! Re6 14. Rxf7 and wins) **9. Ke5 Re6+ 10. Kf4 Ka6** (second step) **11. Kg5 Re5+ 12. Kh6** (third step) **12. ... Rf5** (more accurate is 12. ... Re7) **13. f4** (Alekhine pointed out that there is a quicker win: 13. Kg7! Rf3 14. h4 Rf5 15. f4 and Black must give up the bishop-pawn) **13. ... Rd5! 14. Kg7 Rd7,** and now the shortest and most logical road to victory (again pointed out by Alekhine) is **15. Kf6.**

The variation adopted is also good enough: 15. f5 gxf5 16. Kh6 f4 17. gxf4 Rd5 18. Kg7 Rf5 19. Ra4 Kb5 20. Re4! Ka6 21. Kh6 Rxa5 22. Re5 Ra1 23. Kxh5 Rg1 24. Rg5 Rh1 25. Rf5 Kb6 26. Rxf7 Kc6 27. Re7, Black resigned.

15. ... Rc7 16. f5 gxf5 (if 16. ... Rc6+ 17. Kxf7 gxf5 18. Rf2) **17. Kxf5 Rc5+ 18. Kf6 Rc7 19. Rf2! Kxa5 20. Rf5+ Kb6 21. Rxh5 Kc6 22. Rh7 Kd6 23. Rxf7,** and the rest is simple.

A similar case with the knight-pawn is **No. 738** (Fine-Reinfeld, New York

1940): **White: king at h2, rook at b2, pawns at b4, g2, h3; Black: king at h6, rook at b7, pawns at h7, g6.** White to play wins. **1. Kg3 Kg5 2. b5 Rb6 3. Kf3 Kf5 4. Ke3 Ke5 5. Kd3 Kd5 6. Kc3 Kc5 7. h4** (first step completed) **7. ... h6 8. Rb1 h5** (king and pawn endings are always lost for Black) **9. Rb2 Kd5 10. Kb4 Rb8 11. Rd2+ Ke5** (now White wins as in rook and pawn vs. rook: the Black king is cut off) **12. Rd3 Kf5 13. Rg3 Re8 14. b6,** Black resigned.

Black has drawing chances in such positions only if his king manages to squeeze in among the enemy pawns and scare up some counterchances. This is a tactical resource for which no general rules can be laid down.

No. 739, Lasker-Levenfish, Moscow 1925

White to play can draw

In **No. 739,** Lasker could have drawn by setting up a passed rook-pawn: **1. f5!! exf5** (1. ... gxf5 2. h5 is obviously bad for Black) **2. e6!! fxe6+ 3. Kxg6 Kb5 4. Ra1 f4** (4. ... Rd7 5. h5 Rd2 6. Rh1! f4 7. h6 f3 8. h7 Rd8 9. h8=Q Rxh8 10. Rxh8 a4 11. Rh3 is likewise insufficient: Black just manages to draw) **5. h5 e5** (against 5. ... f3 there is the ingenious defense 6. Rf1! a4 7. Rxf3 a3 8. Rf1 a2 9. Ra1 Kc4 10. h6 Kb3 11. h7 Ra8 12. Re1!! Kb2 13. Re2+ Kb1 [13. ... Kc3 14. Re1] 14. Rxe6 a1=Q 15. Rg1+, =) **6. Re1!!** (this saves everything) **6. ... a4** (6. ... Re7 7. Kf6 Re8 8. Kf7) **7. Rxe5+ Kb4** (7. ... Kc6 8. Re1 a3 9. h6 a2 10. h7, =) **8. Re4+ Kb3 9. Rxf4 a3** Now both sides will enjoy the satisfaction of winning a rook for a pawn.

Lasker chose the inaccurate defense **1. Kf6?** and lost after **1. ... Kb5 2. Ra1 a4 3. f5 exf5 4. e6 fxe6 5. Kxg6 f4! 6. h5 f3! 7. h6** (if now 7. Rf1 a3! 8. Rxf3 a2 9. Rf1 a1=Q wins) **7. ... e5!! 8. Re1!!** (8. h7 Rxh7! 9. Kxh7 e4 10. Rf1 a3 11. Kg6 a2 12. Kf5 e3! 13. Ke4 e2 followed by f2) **8. ... a3 9. Rxe5+ Kc4 10. Re1 a2 11. h7 Ra8 12. Kg7** (or 12. Ra1 Kb3 13. Rf1! f2! 14. Kg7 a1=Q+! 15. Rxa1 Rxa1 16. h8=Q Rg1+!!, and Black will either promote with check or capture his opponent's new-born queen) **12. ... f2! 13. Ra1** (if 13. Rf1 a1=Q+! 14. Rxa1 Rxa1 15. h8=Q Rg1+ as above) **13. ... Kb3 14. Rf1 a1=Q+! 15. Rxa1 Rxa1,** White resigned (16. h8=Q Rg1+).

Still another application of our basic rule that rooks belong behind pawns is seen in the third type of rook position with an outside passed pawn: the pawn is defended by its rook from the side and attacked by the enemy rook from behind. While this case is more favorable than where the White rook is in front of the pawn (No. 732), it is not as favorable as the second type (No. 737) and is generally a draw unless the pawn has reached the seventh.

No. 740, Kasparov-Karpov, match 1984

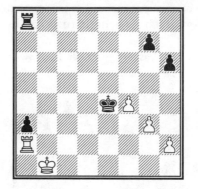

Black to play wins

1. ... Rb8+ 2. Ka1 Rb2! 3. Rxa3 Rxh2 4. Kb1 Rd2! (the plan is Rd3) **5. Ra6 Kf5 6. Ra7 g5 7. Ra6 g4! 8. Rxh6 Rg2 9. Rh5+** (if 9. Kc1 Rxg3 10. Kd2 Rf3 11. Ke2 Kxf4 wins) **9. ... Ke4 10. f5 Rf2! 11. Kc1 Kf3 12. Kd1 Kxg3 13. Ke1 Kg2 14. Rg5 g3 15. Rh5** (15. Kd1 Kh3! 16. Ke1 Kh4 wins) **15. ... Rf4 16. Ke2 Re4+ 17. Kd3 Kf3 18. Rh1 g2 19. Rh3+ Kg4 20. Rh8 Rf4 21. Ke2 Rxf5,** White resigned.

The case with the rook defending the pawn from the side is seen in **No. 741.**

No. 741, Euwe-Alekhine, 23rd match game, 1937

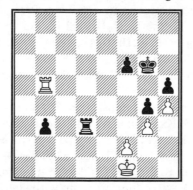

Draw. Win with pawn on the 7th

The game continued **1. Ke2 Rf3 2. Ke1!!**

The only move: White must keep the Black king out of the queenside. If, e.g., 2. Rb7 Kf5! 3. Rb5+ Ke4! 4. Rxh5 Kd4 5. Rb5 Kc3!, and the pawn reaches the seventh and costs White his rook: 6. h5 b2 7. h6 Rf5!! 8. Rb7 Re5+ 9. Kd1 Rd5+ 10. Ke2 Rd7!! 11. Rb8 Kc2 12. Rc8+ Kb1 13. Ke3 Rb7!, etc.

2. ... f5 3. Rb6+ Kf7 4. Rh6! (forcing the issue) **4. ... Rc3!**

On 4. ... f4, as played, White had the easy equalizing line 5. Rxh5 Rc3 (or 5. ... fxg3 6. fxg3 Rxg3 7. Kf2 Rf3+ 8. Kg2 Ke6 9. Rb5, =; compare No. 717) 6. Rb5 f3 7. Kd2 Rc2+ 8. Ke3 b2 9. Kf4 Rc4+ 10. Ke3 Rc2, draw.

5. Kd2! (freeing the king: 5. Rxh5? b2 6. Rh7+ Kg6 7. Rb7 Rc1+ loses) **5. ... Rc2+ 6. Ke3 b2 7. Rb6 Ke7 8. f4!!**

Not 8. f3? Kd7 9. Kf4 Kc7 10. Rb5 Kc6 11. Rb8 Re2 12. fxg4 fxg4 13. Rb3 Kc5 14. Rb8 Kc4 and wins.

8. ... Kd7 9. Kd4!! (the point: the Black king cannot get through) **9. ... Kc7 10. Rb3 Kc6 11. Rb8 Rg2 12. Rb3 Rxg3** (12. ... Rd2+ 13. Ke3!) **13. Rxb2 Rh3 14. Ke5! Rxh4 15. Kxf5,** and in view of White's strong pawn and the lack of coordination of Black's pieces, no win is possible.

With the pawn on the seventh, however, White would be doomed to passive defense and Black could win by simply marching his king to the queenside. **No. 742: White king at f1, rook at b5, pawns at f2, g3, h2; Black king at g6, rook at d2, pawns at b2, f6, g4, h5.** Black wins. **1. Kg2** (forced: on 1. Ke1 Rc2 2. Kd1 Rc1+, White can resign) **1. ... Kf7 2. Rb6 Ke7 3. Rb5 Kd7 4. Rb6 Kc7 5. Rb3 Kc6 6. Rb8 Kc5 7. Rb3 Kc4 8. Rb8 Kc3 9. Rc8+ Kb3 10. Rb8+ Kc2 11. Rc8+ Kd1 12. Rb8 Kc1 13. Rc8+ Rc2.**

When the pawn is on the seventh and the defending king is out in the open air (not confined to a dungeon as in No. 739), the win is far more difficult. Its outlines, however, remain the same as those in No. 737, where the White rook is behind the pawn: First the White king goes to the center (or near it), then the Black king must stay near the pawn or else the White king can march in and capture the rook.

But now there is the all-important difference that Black has just as many tempi as White. So the only way to win is to capture two pawns with the rook, or to capture one pawn and get to a theoretical win either by threatening to capture a second or by transposing into the equivalent of one of the rook and two pawns vs. rook and pawn wins.

No. 743 illustrates this process:

No. 743, Tartakower-Nimzovich, Bad Kissingen 1928

White wins

First White centralizes his king.
1. ... Kf6 2. Ke1 g6!
Essential, or the king will be tied down to the kingside forever, which is too long.
3. Kd1 Ke5 4. Kc1 Kd5 5. Kb1 Ra6 6. Kb2 Kc6 7. Rg7 Kc5
The problem now is how to continue. The Black king cannot be driven away from c5 and the White king can get no closer than b3 or c3. The only attempt he can make is to secure a winning advantage on the kingside. 8. Rxg6 Rxa7 9. Rg5+ Kd4 10. Rxh5 Rf7! is not good enough, since Black will have a strong passed pawn supported by both king and rook. After further preparatory moves, we find that White's only way out of his dilemma is to bring the king back to defend the f-pawn while not allowing the Black king to return.
8. h4! (first fixing the pawns) **8. ... Ra5 9. g3**
The move actually chosen was 9. g4?!, but this was based on a trap and turned out to be strategically premature: 9. g4 hxg4 10. h5! g3!! 11. fxg3 e3! 12. Rxg6 Rxa7 13. Kc2 Ra2+ 14. Kd1 Kd4 15. h6 e2+ 16. Ke1 Ke3 17. Re6+ Kf3 18. h7 Ra1+ 19. Kd2 Rd1+ 20. Kc2 Rd8, and obviously nothing can be done.
9. ... Ra6 10. Kb3 Ra1
10. ... Kd5 11. Kb4 Ra1 12. Kb5 Ke5 13. Kb6 Kf5 14. Kb7 Kg4 is hopeless.
11. Kc3!! Ra3+
Essential: if 11. ... Ra2 12. Rxg6 Ra3+ 13. Kd2 Rxa7 14. Ke3! Re7 15. Rg5+ decides, while a king move allows the White king to enter.
12. Kd2 Kd4 (12. ... Kd5 13. Rxg6 transposes to the main variation after 13. ... Rxa7 14. Rg5 Kd4 15. Rxh5) **13. Rd7+!**
White must see to it that the Black e-pawn does not become too strong. If 13. Rxg6 Ra2+! 14. Ke1 e3!! 15. Rd6+ Ke5 16. Rd8 exf2+ 17. Kf1 Rxa7 18. Rh8 Ke4 19. Kxf2 Ra5 and draws.
13. ... Kc5

On 13. ... Ke5, White wins by one vital tempo: 14. Kc2 Ke6 15. Rg7 Kd5 16. Kb2! Ra6 17. Kc3!! Kc5 18. Rxg6 Ra3+ 19. Kd2 Rxa7 20. Ke3, etc.

14. Ke2 Kc6 15. Rg7 Kc5 16. Rxg6 Rxa7 17. Ke3 Re7 18. Rg5+, and it's all over but the scoring.

If the defender's rook were in front of the pawn in any of the above examples, it is obvious that the superior side could simply walk in with his king and capture at least several extra pawns.

Finally, we must consider those positions where the pawn is blocked by the king. In that event, if the White king is nearby the win is fairly easy, but if the pawn can be defended only by the rook, Black should draw.

No. 744, Eliskases-Keres, Semmering 1937

Black to play, White wins

This is a model case, where the Black king is blocking the passed pawn. Remember that the drawing method in rook and pawn vs. rook is to keep the Black rook on the third rank until the pawn reaches the sixth and then play it to the eighth. This is good enough when there is nothing to capture but empty squares, but when there are pawns around, a king let loose among them always manages to have a satisfying repast. The winning method in such positions is:

1. The pawn is advanced as far as convenient.

2. If Black's rook leaves the third rank, White will win as in the case of rook and pawn vs. rook.

3. If Black's rook keeps the White king out, the White rook will sneak behind the Black pawns and, aided later by the king, capture at least one or two.

No. 744 illustrates the method with a bishop-pawn. Keres tried **1. ... h5**, when **2. Ra2 Kc8 3. Kb5** soon decided. The immediate threat of 4. Kc6 Rc7+ 5. Kd6 forced Black to stake everything on a counterattack; see step 2 above. **3. ... h4 4. Kb6** (simpler is 4. Kc6 Kb8 5. Kd6 but the move played is good enough) **4. ... Rf3 5. gxh4 gxh4 6. Ra8+ Kd7 7. c6+ Ke7 8. Rh8** (simpler than 8. c7 Rb3+ 9. Ka7 Ra3+ 10. Kb8 Rb3+ 11. Kc8 Rb2, but 12. Rb8 is also quite adequate) **8. ... Rb3+ 9. Kc7 Rb2 10. Rh7+ Kf6** (or 10. ... Ke8 11. Kd6 Rd2+ 12. Kxe6 Re2+ 13. Kd6 Rd2+ 14. Kc7 Rxf2 15. Rxh4, etc.) **11. Kd8 Rd2+ 12. Rd7 Rxf2 13. c7 Kg5 14. c8=Q Rf8+ 15. Kc7 Rxc8+ 16. Kxc8 e5 17. Re7,** and Black soon recognized the futility of further resistance.

The similar position with the knight-pawn is won by setting up a decisive material superiority on the other wing. **No. 745, White king at b4, rook at a2, pawns at b5, f4, g3, h2; Black king at c8, rook at e7, pawns at f7, g6, h5.** Black to play, White wins. **1. ... Kb7 2. Rd2 Kc7 3. Kc5 Kb7 4. b6 Kc8 5. Kc6 Re8 6. b7+ Kb8 7. Rd6 Rg8 8. Rf6 Rg7 9. h4 Rh7 10 Kd6** wins.

Things are not so clear with a rook-pawn because Black needn't worry about his king being chased out. Still, by concentrating the major forces on the other wing, enough material can be won to assure victory.

If the Black king is cut off from the passed pawn, White will always win. If the White pawn is on the third or fourth rank, he can always sacrifice it to capture one or two pawns on the other wing.

No. 746

White wins

No. 746, which would be drawn if there were no queenside pawns, is a fairly elementary win. The best defense is **1. ... b5** (1. ... Kf7 2. Kc4 Rc8+ 3. Kd5 Rd8+ 4. Kc5 Rc8+ 5. Kd6 Rd8+ 6. Kc7 Rxd4 7. Kxb7 a5 8. Kb6 a4 9. a3 Kf6 10. Ka5 Kf5 11. Re8 Rd2 12. Rb8 Rd4 13. Rb4 also leads to a loss) **2. Kc3 a5 3. Re5 Rb8 4. Kd3 a4 5. Ke4 Rb7 6. Kd5 Rc7** (6. ... b4 7. Kc4 a3 8. bxa3 bxa3 9. Ra5, or even 8. b3 followed by Rb5) **7. Re6+ Kf7 8. Rb6 a3 9. Rxb5,** and the two passed pawns decide.

When the Black king is cut off at some distance from the White pawn, the simplest winning method is to hold the remaining pawns with the rook, leaving the king free to support the passed pawn. For example, **No. 747** (Rabinovich-Ragosin, Tiflis 1937): **White king at f2, rook at g6, pawns at g2, h4; Black king at f4, rook at e7, pawns at a7, g7, h6.** Black wins. **1. ... Rf7 2. Kg1** (or 2. Ke2 Kf5 3. h5 a5! 4. Ra6 Kg4 5. Rxa5 Kg3, and Black wins both pawns; compare No. 746) **2. ... Kf5 3. h5 Ke4 4. Ra6** (if 4. Rd6 Ke5 5. Rd8 Ke6

6. Kh2 Rd7 7. Rc8 Kd6 8. Kh3 Rc7 9. Rb8 Kc6 10. Kg4 a5, and the Black pawn will cost White his rook; meanwhile, he can do nothing on the kingside but bite his nails in despair) **4. ... Kd5 5. Kh2 Kc5 6. Ra1 Kb6 7. Rb1+ Kc6 8. Rc1+ Kb7 9. Rb1+ Ka8! 10. Ra1 Rf5! 11. g4 Rg5 12. Kg3 a5 13. Kf3 Ka7 14. Ra4 Kb6 15. Ke3 Rd5!** (the White king is cut off again and the pawn marches triumphantly on) **16. Rf4 Rd7 17. Rf5 a4 18. g5 hxg5 19. Rxg5 a3 20. Ke4 a2 21. Rg1 Kb5 22. Ra1 Ra7 23. Kd3 Kb4 24. Kc2 Ka3 25. Rg1 Rc7+ 26. Kd3 Kb2,** White resigns.

Sometimes defending the remaining pawns is not essential, but it may be feasible to give one up and win with the passed pawn. For example, **No. 748** (Vidmar-Dus-Chotimirsky, Carlsbad 1907): **White king at e5, rook at b5, pawns at a5, g4, g6; Black king at f8, rook at a2, pawns at g7, h6.** White wins. **1. Kd6 Rd2+ 2. Kc7 Ke7 3. Rf5!** (he must keep the Black king out; letting the rook capture a pawn is not harmful since it costs Black so much time) **3. ... Rd7+ 4. Kc6 Rd6+ 5. Kb5 Rxg6 6. a6 Rd6 7. a7 Rd8 8. Kb6 g6 9. Rb5 Kf6 10. Kc7 Rh8 11. Kb7 Rh7+ 12. Ka6 Rxa7+ 13. Kxa7 g5 14. Ka6 Ke6 15. Ra5,** resigns.

Black has drawing chances when his king is cut off only when the enemy pawn structure is weakened and he can get his king in to attack the pawns.

No. 749, Alatortsev-Chekhover, Tiflis 1937

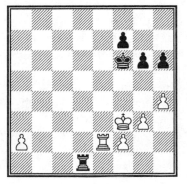

Draw. White wins with pawns at g2 and h3

To win, White must play his king to the queenside, but this leaves his kingside exposed.

The continuation was **1. Ke3** (1. Ke4 does not threaten anything, while 1. a4? Ra1 2. Re4 Ra3+ 3. Ke2 Kf5 is inferior: see No. 732) **1. ... Kf5** (the saving counteraction) **2. Rd2 Rc1 3. Kd3 Kg4! 4. Rc2 Rd1+ 5. Ke2**

A psychological retreat. If 5. Kc3 f5 6. Kb3 Rb1+ 7. Rb2 Re1 8. a4 f4! 9. gxf4 Kxh4 10. a5 Kg4 11. a6 Re8, =, since the Black h-pawn is just as dangerous as his playmate on the a-file.

5. ... Ra1 6. Ke3 Re1+ 7. Kd2

Now **7. ... Re5!** was the most direct drawing line.

In the game Black tried 7. ... Ra1 8. Kc3 g5? (8. ... f5 is better) 9. hxg5 hxg5 10. Kb2 Re1, when White evolved the problem-like finish 11. a4 f5 12. Kb3 f4 13. gxf4 gxf4 14. a5 f3 15. a6 Kh3 16. a7 Re8 17. Ra2 Ra8 18. Kc4 Kg2 19. Kc5! Rc8+ (equally inadequate is 19. ... Rxa7 20. Rxa7 Kxf2 21. Kd4) 20. Kb6 Re8 21. Kc6!! (but not now 21. a8=Q Rxa8 22. Rxa8 the White king is too far away) 21. ... Kf1 (or 21. ... Rh8 22. Kb7 Rh7+ 23. Kb6 Rh8 24. Rc2! Re8 25. Kb7 and Black will have to give up the rook for the passed pawn without getting the f-pawn, for if 25. ... Re7+ 26. Kb8! Re8+ 27. Rc8 and queens) 22. Rc2 Kg2 23. Kc7! Re7+ 24. Kb8 and wins: after 24. ... Re8+ 25. Rc8 Rxc8+ 26. Kxc8 Kxf2 27. a8=Q, Black's pawn is only on the sixth.

But after the defense given above (7. ... Re5!) Black can afford to give up his rook at the appropriate moment because he will capture a pawn on the king-side.

8. a4

Or 8. Rc4+ Kh3! 9. Rf4 f5 10. Kc3 g5 11. hxg5 hxg5 12. Rb4 Kg2 13. Rb2 f4 14. gxf4 gxf4 15. Kb4 f3 16. a4 Re2!!, etc., =.

8. ... f5 9. Ra2 Ra5 10. Kc3 f4 11. Kb4 Ra8 12. Ra3

Despite his extra pawn, White's position is no bed of roses. If, e.g., 12. gxf4 Kxh4 13. Ra3? Rf8! 14. a5 Rxf4+ 15. Kb5 Rxf2, and Black may even win.

12. ... Rb8+! 13. Kc5 Rb2 14. a5 Rxf2 15. gxf4

Essential: if 15. a6? fxg3 16. a7 Rf8 17. a8=Q Rxa8 18. Rxa8 g2 19. Ra1 Kxh4 20. Kd4 Kg3 21. Ke3 h5, the pawns are too strong and will win.

15. ... Rxf4 16. a6 Rf8! 17. a7 Ra8!

It is important to draw White's king as far as possible from the pawns.

18. Kb6 g5! (again not to lose time) **19. hxg5 hxg5 20. Kb7 Rxa7+ 21. Kxa7 Kf4 22. Kb6 g4 23. Kc5 g3,** draw.

If the pawns were not weakened, White could win because Black would have no counterplay. The White king would march over to the queenside and the advance of the pawn would be conclusive.

The important point about the weakness of the pawns is that Black must be able to capture one and then transpose into a drawn rook vs. pawn ending. Where the pawns are merely exposed but not capturable, there is no real defense.

One more example will help to make the winning method clear. **No. 750** (Marshall-Capablanca, 9th match game, 1909): **White king at g5, rook at d4, pawns at a4, e3, h3; Black king at e6, rook at f2, pawns at a5, f7**. White wins. Marshall played **1. Re4+ Kd5 2. Rf4 Rg2+ 3. Kf6 Rg3 4. e4+ Kd4 5. e5+ Kd5** (if 5. ... Ke3 6. Rf1 Rxh3 7. Kxf7 Rh4 8. e6 Rxa4 9. e7 Re4 10. Re1+)

Now the most precise win is **6. h4.**

Against 6. Rf5, as played, Capablanca succeeded in drawing after 6. ... Ke4! 7. Rh5 Rf3+ 8. Ke7 Rf4 9. Rg5 Kd4 10. Rh5 Kc3 11. Rh7 Rf5 12. Kd6 Kb3? 13. Rh4 Rf3 14. Ke7 Re3 15. Kxf7 Rxe5 16. Rg4? Rc5 17. Rf4 Rc7+ 18. Kg6 Rb7!! 19. h4 Rb4!!. If 20. Kg5 Kxa4 21. h5 Ka3! draws. White can no longer win.

6. ... Re3

Or 6. ... Rh3 7. Rf5! Ke4 8. h5 Rh1 9. e6! fxe6 10. Kxe6, and with the Black king cut off on a rank the win with the two rook-pawns is only a question of time.

7. Rf5 Ke4 (else 8. Kxf7) **8. Rf1! Ra3** (8. ... Rh3 is met in the same way) **9. Re1+ Kd5 10. Kxf7 Rf3+** (10. ... Rxa4 11. e6 Rf4+ 12. Kg6 Rf8 13. e7, or 11. ... Rxh4 12. e7 Rh8 13. Ra1 Rh7+ 14. Kf6! Rh8 15. Rxa5+ Kd6 16. Ra6+ Kd7 17. Ra7+ Kd6 18. Kf7 Rh7+ 19. Kf8 Rh8+ 20. Kg7 Re8 21. Kf7) **11. Ke7 Rf4 12. e6 Rxa4 13. Kd7 Rxh4 14. e7 Rh8 15. Ra1** and wins.

The point here is that Black could bring about exchanges but could never actually win any material, so the whole ending became a more complicated version of No. 746.

If the pawns are not otherwise balanced (e.g., three to one on one side, one to two on the other), *the winning method consists of setting up two connected passed pawns.* Of course, the enemy pawn must not be allowed to become too dangerous. The position reached will be the same structurally as the ending with rook and two pawns vs. rook and pawn – the extra pawns will make no difference. This is why it's necessary to set up connected passed pawns, for unconnected pawns often do not win (see Nos. 707-723 for the elementary cases).

No. 751, Euwe-Alekhine, 1st match game, 1937

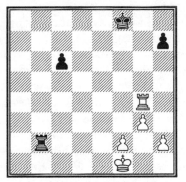

White to play wins

No. 751 is typical of such endings with three pawns vs. two. Euwe's conduct of the final phase is exemplary.

1. Rc4! (first tying the Black rook down and also hindering the advance of the pawn) **1. ... Rb6 2. Ke2 Kf7** (2. ... Ke7 3. Rh4 is hopeless) **3. Rh4 Kg6 4. Rf4 Rb3 5. Rc4 Rb6 6. Ke3!** (now the pawns will soon start rolling) **6. ... Kf5 7. g4+ Ke6** (if 7. ... Kg5 8. f3 Kh4 9. Rc5! Rb3+ 10. Ke2! Rb2+ 11. Kd1! Rb1+ 12. Kc2 Rb5 13. Rxc6 Kg5 14. Kd3 and wins).

8. f4 Kd5

Hoping to get his pawn going. The alternative 8. ... h5 loses prettily after 9. g5! Kf5 10. Rc5+ Ke6 (10. ... Kg4 11. g6 Rb8 12. Rg5+ Kh4 13. g7 Rg8 14. Rg3 followed by the march of the f-pawn) 11. f5+ Kd6 12. g6! Kxc5 13. g7 Rb8 14. f6, and the Black king is one move too late.

9. Rd4+! Ke6 (on 9. ... Kc5 10. f5 is conclusive) **10. f5+ Ke7** (10. ... Kf6 11. Kf4) **11. Re4+ Kf7 12. h4** (there are various satisfactory alternatives; the line chosen is the most direct) **12. ... Rb1 13. Kf4 Rc1** (if 13. ... h6 14. Rc4 Rf1+ 15. Kg3 h5 16. Kg2 Re1 17. g5 and the win is only a question of time) **14. Ra4 h6 15. Ra7+ Kg8 16. g5 Rc4+ 17. Ke5 Rxh4** (Alekhine resigned here) **18. g6 Rh1 19. Kf6,** and mate cannot be postponed for more than one move.

When the Black pawns are weak White is ordinarily in a position to come out two pawns ahead. For example, **No. 752** (Lasker-Bogolyubov, New York 1924): **White king at f3, rook at h7, pawns at a2, g2, h2; Black king at b5, rook at a8, pawns at f5, f4.** White wins. **1. ... Ra3+!** (the only way to hang on to his last pawn for a while; on 1. ... Rxa2 2. Rf7 he soon loses both pawns) **2. Kxf4 Rxa2 3. Rg7 Rf2+ 4. Ke3!** (the game continuation, 4. Ke5 f4!, gives Black excellent counterchances, since the sacrifice ... f3 always threatens to lead into the rook plus bishop-pawn and rook-pawn vs. rook ending) **4. ... Rf1** (or 4. ... Ra2 5. Rg5 Kc4 6. Kf3 Ra5 7. Kf4) **5. Rg5 Kc6 6. Ke2 Rf4** (6. ... Rh1 7. h3 f4 8. Rf5 Rg1 9. Kf2) **7. g3 Re4+ 8. Kf3 Re5 9. Kf4! Re2 10. h4 Rf2+ 11. Ke3 Rf1 12. Ke2 Rg1 13. Kf2,** and despite Black's stubborn defense White will capture the f-pawn and secure two connected passed pawns.

The defender can normally draw if his pawn has become a serious threat. When White does not yet have two passed pawns, a pawn on the seventh defended from the side or from behind is surely sufficient. We can see this in **No. 753**, another Alekhine-Euwe game (13th match game, 1935): **White king at e1, rook at c7, pawns at a7, h3; Black king at g7, rook at a4, pawns at f7, g6, h7.** Draw. The difficulty with Black's position is that his king cannot leave the neighborhood of the f-pawn and his pawns cannot advance quickly enough. After **1. Kd2 g5 2. Kc3 h5 3. Kb3 Ra1 4. Kc4 g4** (if 4. ... Kg6 5. Kb5! f6 6. Kb6 g4 7. hxg4 hxg4 8. Rc8 Kf5 9. a8=Q Rxa8 10. Rxa8 Ke4 is a draw.) **5. hxg4 hxg4 6. Kd4 Kg6 7. Ke3** draws (No. 714).

Again, if the pawn majority is blockaded or devalued, no wins possible. In **No. 754** (Schlechter-Janowski, Ostend 1907) the doubled pawns foretell a draw: **White king at g3, rook at a5, pawns at a4, h3; Black king at h7, rook at b2, pawns at f5, g7, g6.** Draw. **1. Ra8 g5 2. a5 Rb3+ 3. Kh2 Rb2+ 4. Kh1 Rb7 5. a6 Rb1+ 6. Kg2 Ra1 7. a7,** and now the Black king dare not expose itself to a check, while Black is unable to set up two passed pawns. Janowski tried **7. ... Kg6 8. Kh2 f4 9. Kg2 Ra2+ 10. Kh1 g4!,** but the reply **11. Rf8!** (11. hxg4 Kg5! loses, since Black gets two connected passed pawns) **11. ... Rxa7 12. Rxf4 gxh3 13. Rg4+ Kh5 14. Rg3 Kh4 15. Rg6!** made the draw plain.

To sum up: With an outside passed pawn and an otherwise balanced pawn position, White wins easily if the Black king is cut off or if White's rook is behind his pawn, but in general only draws if his rook is in front of or to the side of the pawn and the Black king is free to roam about. A weak pawn structure, however, is usually fatal for Black, while for White a weak pawn structure destroys his winning chances. If the pawn position is not balanced, White must set up two connected passed pawns as quickly as possible and then proceed in exactly the same manner as in rook and two pawns vs. rook and pawn: advance his own pawns but at the same time guard the enemy pawn.

B. Potential Outside Passed Pawn

This of course is the same as saying that White has a majority of pawns on one wing.

First we consider positions where the pawn structure is otherwise balanced. Unlike the analogous cases with minor pieces, the winning method does not involve merely setting up a passed pawn, for, as we saw in section A above, in some positions such a pawn does not win.

The superior side must not exchange before he is sure that the resulting ending is won. In general, the two most common ways to be sure are: the enemy king is cut off from the passed pawn, and his own rook is behind the passed pawn.

If the defending king is not near the potential passed pawn; i.e., it is on the side where the pawns are numerically balanced, the winning method consists of three steps:

1. Placing the king and rook on the best possible squares. This means placing the rook aggressively (with as much freedom of action as possible), while using the king to defend any weak pawns.

2. Advancing the pawns that are in the majority as far as convenient without actually setting up a passed pawn.

3. Transposing to one of the won positions with an outside passed pawn. Sometimes this may mean securing two connected passed pawns against a single passed pawn.

No. 755. Mieses-Dus-Chotimirsky, Carlsbad 1907

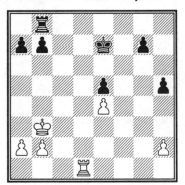

Black wins

No. 755 is a case where two connected passed pawns are set up. Black's king and rook are placed well enough (... Ke6 and ... Rd8 or ... Rg8 may be played at an opportune moment), so he starts his pawns rolling. **1. ... g5 2. Rg1 g4 3. Rc1** (if 3. h3 Rg8 leads to a win with the rook behind the passed pawn: No. 736) **3. ... Rd8 4. Rf1 Rd3+ 5. Kc2** (the game continued 5. Kc4 Rd4+ 6. Kc5 Rxe4, and with two extra pawns the rest was simple: 7. Rf5 h4 8. Rh5 g3 9. hxg3 hxg3 10. Kd5 Re2 11. Rg5 g2 12. b4 Kf6 13. Rg8 Kf5 14. Rg7 Rd2+

15. Kc4 Kf4, White resigned) **5. ... Re3!** (the most direct) **6. Rf5 Re2+!** (far better than the alternative 6. ... Rxe4 7. Rxh5) **7. Kd3 Rxh2 8. Rxe5+ Kf6 9. Rf5+ Ke6** (on 9. ... Kg6 10. Rf1 Rxb2 11. e5 the e-pawn may become dangerous) **10. b3 g3 11. Rg5 h4 12. Ke3 g2 13. Kf2 h3 14. Rg7 Rh1 15. Rg5 Rf1+,** and wins White's rook.

A three-to-one complex, where the passed pawn is supported by the king, is just as good as two connected passed pawns.

No. 756 (Opocensky-Fahrni, Baden 1914) is analogous to the above: **White king at g2, rook at c3, pawns at a4, g3, h4; Black king at f6, rook at b4, pawns at a5, b6, g6, h5.** After **1. ... Rxa4** (on 1. ... Kf5 2. Rc6 also gives White excellent drawing chances because Black has clarified the situation on the queenside too soon) **2. Rc6+ Kf5 3. Rxb6 Rb4 4. Ra6 a4 5. Kh3 Rc4 6. Ra5+ Ke4 7. Ra6 Kd3 8. Rxg6 a3 9. Ra6 Rc3 10. Ra5 Kc2 11. Rxh5 a2 12. Ra5 Kb2 13. Rxa2+ Kxa2 14. h5,** a draw was agreed.

The transposition to a won ending with an outside passed pawn may occur when the defending king is cut off, or when the superior side's rook gets behind its passed pawn, or when the pawn is on the seventh and defended from the side. Of course, special cases with other varieties of outside pawn endings may also be won.

No. 757, Teichmann-Schallopp, Nuremburg 1896

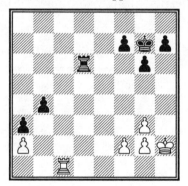

Black wins

Black exchanges when he can force his pawn to the seventh and defend it with his rook, which is also on the seventh. In **No. 757,** Schallopp wound up as follows: **1. Rc4 Rb6 2. Kg1 Kf6 3. Kf1 Ke6** (Black does not exchange until his pawn can reach the seventh) **4. Ke2 b3! 5. axb3 Rxb3 6. Ra4 Rb2+ 7. Ke3 a2,** and the rest is routine: **8. g4 Kd5 9. g5 Kc5 10. g4 Kb5 11. Ra8 Kb4,** White resigned.

The transposition with the rook behind the pawn is seen in **No. 758.**

No. 758, Breyer-Johner, 1914

Black to play wins

Black's extra pawn at g7, being doubled, makes no difference; Black is for all practical purposes only one pawn ahead. The conclusion was both simple and straightforward: **1. ... b6 2. Ra3 a5 3. Rd3 b5 4. Rd6 Kf7 5. a3 Re6 6. Rd7+ Re7 7. Rd5 Rb7 8. Ke3 b4! 9.** axb4 (9. a4 b3 is worse) **9. ... axb4 10. Kd2 b3 11. Kc1 b2+ 12. Kb1 Rb3 13. h4 Rb4 14. Rd6 Rxh4 15. Kxb2 Rc4,** and the rest is academic: **16. Kb3 Rc7 17. Rd1 g5 18. Rf1+ Kg6 19. Rg1 Kf5 20. Rf1+ Ke4 21. Rg1 Kf4** (21. ... g4! 22. Rxg4+ Kf5 23. Rg1 g5 is shorter, but the text is good enough) **22. Rf1+ Ke3 23. Rg1 Rc5 24. Kb4 Rf5 25. Kc3 Kf2 26. Rg4 Kf3 27. Rd4 g4 28. Rd3+ Kg2,** and White soon abandoned the hopeless struggle.

The most common error in this type of ending is to transpose at the wrong time, usually too early but sometimes too late. A few examples will illustrate.

No. 759 (Reggio-Przepiorka, Barmen 1905): **White king at f3, rook at d1, pawns at a2, b2, c4, f4, g3, h3; Black king at f6, rook at e8, pawns at a6, b7, e6, g6, h5.** Black to play. **1. ... Re7 2. Rd6 Rc7 3. b3 b5 4.** Rxa6 (the correct refutation is 4. Rd4 bxc4 5. Rxc4 Rd7 6. Rc6 a5 7. g4! Rd3+ 8. Ke4 Rxh3 9. g5+ Kf7 10. Rc7+ Ke8 11. Ke5, etc.) **4. ... bxc4 5. bxc4 Rxc4 6. g4 Rc3+ 7. Kg2 hxg4 8. hxg4 Rc4 9. Kf3 Rc3+ 10. Kf2,** and White tried everything but it was too late.

No. 760 (Fine-Thomas, Nottingham 1936): **White king at g2, rook at d3, pawns at a2, b3, g3, h2; Black king at e6, rook at f5, pawns at b5, g7, h6.** White to play. Draw. The continuation 1. a4! bxa4 2. bxa4 Ra5 3. Ra3 Kd5 4. Kf3 Kc4 5. h4 Kb4 6. Ra1 Kb3 7. Rb1+! Kc4 8. Rb7! g5 9. hxg5 hxg5 10. Re7 Kd5 11. Kg4 Rxa4+ 12. Kxg5 Ra8 13. g4 Rg8+ 14. Kf5 Rf8+ 15. Kg6 Rg8+ 16. Rg7 would have decided. But White delayed the advance too long and Black built up an ingenious counter-threat on the other wing **1. Rd2 Rc5 2. Kf3 Ke5 3. Rd7 g6 4. Re7+ Kf5 5. Re2 Rc3+ 6. Kf2 h5 7. Ke1 Kg4 8. Kd2 Rc5 9. Kd3 g5 10. Rc2 Rf5 11. Kc3 h4 12.** gxh4 gxh4 **13. Kb4 h3 14. a4** (ten years overdue!) **14. ... bxa4 15. Kxa4 Kf3 16. b4 Rg5 17. b5 Rg2!,** draw, for both sides will queen.

Often the defender prefers not to wait for the transposition to a won ending with an outside passed pawn, and resorts instead to some tactical sortie. In that event, more material can usually be won.

No. 762, Janowski-Rubinstein, Carlsbad 1907

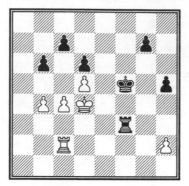

Black to play wins

No. 762 is a case in point. After 1. ... Rb3! (to fix the queenside pawns) 2. Rf2+ Kg6 3. Rg2+ Kh6 4. b5 Rf3, Black wins. Janowski reasoned that against Rubinstein it was useless to try to hold the position by passive defense, such as 5. Rc2 g5 6. Rg2 h4 7. Rc2 g4 8. Rg2 Kh5, etc., so he goes all out to do or die: 5. Ke4 Rf6 6. Ra2 g5 7. Ra7 Rf4+!! (essential: the point will soon be clear) 8. Kd3 Rf7 9. c5 dxc5 10. d6 Rd7! (now we see why the king had to be driven to the d-file) 11. Rxc7 Rxd6+ 12. Ke4 Rd4+! 13. Kf5 h4 14. Rc8 (or 14. Rc6+ Kh5 15. Rxb6 Rf4+ 16. Ke5 Rf2 17. Rc6 Rxh2 18. Rxc5 Rb2, and the two passed pawns march on) 14. ... Rf4+ 15. Ke5 c4 16. Rh8+ Kg7 17. Rc8 Kg6 18. Rg8+ Kh5 19. h3 c3 20. Rh8+ Kg6 21. Rg8+ Kh6 22. Rh8+ Kg7 23. Rc8 Rf3 24. Rc6 Rxh3 25. Rxb6 Rf3, White resigned.

Two other examples of the refutation of tactical counterattacks will further illustrate this important practical point. It is hardly possible to set up any general rules, of course, but in a position where the major pieces do not cooperate, loss of material is inevitable.

No. 763 (Rubinstein-Duras, Pistyan 1912): **White king at e2, rook at c5, pawns at a2, b3, e3, f2, g3, h2; Black king at d6, rook at b7, pawns at a6, d7, f5, g6, h7.** White to play wins. 1. Rc8 Rb6 2. Kd3 Kd5 3. h4 h6 4. Rc4 g5 5. hxg5 hxg5 6. g4! Rb5 (or 6. ... fxg4 7. Rxg4 Rg6 8. f4) 7. gxf5 Ke5 8. Ra4 a5 9. Kc4 Rd5 10. f3! d6 11. e4 Rc5+ 12. Kd3 d5 13. Rd4 dxe4+ 14. fxe4 g4 15. Rd8, and Black soon gave up.

No. 764 (Foltys-Fine, Margate 1937): **White king at e3, rook at d2, pawns at b2, c3, e4, g2; Black king at c6, rook at g4, pawns at c5, d6, e5, g7, h5.** White to play, Black wins. 1. Kf3 Rf4+ 2. Ke3 h4 3. Rd1 g5 4. g3 (giving Black a passed pawn, but against passive play the advance of the pawns on the kingside and of the king on the other wing win easily) 4. ... hxg3 5. Rg1 g4 6. Rxg3 c4! 7. Rg1 Kb5 8. Rh1 g3! 9. Rg1 Rf2! (Black has carefully calculated that he will be able to win both queenside pawns) 10. Rxg3 Rxb2 11. Rg8 Rc2 12. Rb8+ Ka6 13. Ra8+ Kb7 14. Ra3 Kc6 15. Ra6+ Kd7 16. Ra3 Ke6! 17. Kf3 Kf6 18. Kg3 Kg5 19. Kf3 Kh4 20. Ra6 Rxc3+ 21. Ke2 Rd3 22. Rc6 Rd4 23. Ke3 Kg3

24. Rc8 Rd3+ 25. Ke2 Kf4, White resigned. If 26. Rxc4 Rd4 27. Rxd4 exd4 28. Kd3 Ke5.

In all the examples above, the defending king was on the side where the pawns were balanced. When the king is on the same side as the potential passed pawn the winning method is essentially the same as that given above. The main difference is that, as a rule, the step that involves transposition to a won ending with an outside passed pawn is of minor importance because any such pawn is already blocked by the defending king. Instead, the decisive maneuver is the entry of the superior king to the other wing.

No. 765, Lawrence-Mieses, Cambridge Springs 1904

White wins

No. 765 is typical. The winning idea is simplicity itself: after adequate preparation (safeguarding the rook position and the pawns), White marches his king to the queenside and wins at least one more pawn.

The game continued **1. ... Kf6 2. f4 h6 3. Kf3 a5 4. Ke4** (this is step one in our schema on page 309; the rest is a variant of the third step) **4. ... Rd7 5. c3 Rb7 6. Kd5 Rd7+ 7. Kc4 Rd8** (or 7. ... b5+ 8. Kxb5 Rxd3 9. Rxc5 Rxh3 10. g5+ hxg5 11. fxg5 Ke6 12. Kxa5) **8. Rd5 Re8 9. f5**

Super-cautious. 9. Rd6+ Kg7 10. Rxb6 Re3 11. Rb5 Rxh3 12. Rxa5 Rf3 13. Rxc5 Rxf4+ gives Black splendid counterchances, but the simple 9. Kb5 Re3 10. g5+ Ke6 11. Re5+! Rxe5 12. fxe5 hxg5 13. d4 puts an end to all resistance.

9. ... gxf5 10. Rxf5+ Kg6 11. h4 (first safeguarding the kingside pawns) **11. ... Re3 12. h5+ Kg7 13. g5 hxg5 14. Rxg5+ Kf7 15. Rd5**

Now that Black has been deprived of his last chance on the kingside, the inroad on the other wing is conclusive.

15. ... Ke7 16. Kb5 (or, as played, 16. d4 cxd4 17. cxd4 Re6 18. Re5, resigns) **16. ... Re6 17. c4 Kf6 18. Rd7 Kg5 19. Rb7 Rd6 20. Rxb6 Rxd3 21. Kxa5 Kxh5 22. Rb5 Kg6 23. Kb6** and the rest is routine.

A simpler example is **No. 766** (Flohr-Vidmar, Nottingham 1936): **White king at e4, rook at e5, pawns at a3, b4, g3, h5; Black king at b6, rook at h7; pawns at a6, g5, h6.** Black to play, White wins. After **1. ... Kc6 2. Re6+ Kb5 3.**

Kf5 Rf7+ 4. Rf6, Black resigned because he must lose both pawns on the kingside: 4. ... Rh7 5. Kg6 Rh8 6. Kg7 Re8 7. Kxh6 Re3 8. Rf5+ Kb6 9. Rxg5 Rxa3 10. Kg7, etc.

The transposition to a won ending with an outside passed pawn is seen in **No. 767** (Levenfish-Botvinnik, 11th match game, 1937): **White king at e3, rook at d3, pawns at a3, b2, f4, h2; Black king at f6, rook at c8, pawns at a5, b5, g6.** White to play wins. The game concluded **1. Rd6+ Kf7 2. Rd5 b4 3. axb4 axb4 4. Rd4 b3 5. Rd3 Rh8 6. Ke4 Rxh2 7. Rxb3 Re2+ 8. Kd3 Rf2 9. Ke3 Rg2 10. Rb5 Rg1 11. Kd3 Rf1 12. Rb4 Rf2 13. b3 Rf3+ 14. Ke4 Rg3 15. Rb5 Rg1 16. Rb4 Rb1 17. Rb7+ Kf6 18. Rb6+ Kf7 19. b4 Re1+ 20. Kd4 Rf1 21. Ke5! Re1+ 22. Kd6 Re4 23. b5 Rxf4 24. Rc6**, resigns, for if **24. ... g5 25. b6 g4 26. b7 Rb4 27. Kc7 g3 28. b8=Q**, etc. The g-pawn is lost.

With an unbalanced pawn position, we see the same main winning possibilities: reduction to a more elementary case with an outside passed pawn, and setting up two connected passed pawns vs. one. In addition, if the pawns are weak, as they are apt to be, more material may be won.

The only one of these eventualities that differs from anything we have seen before is where both players secure sets of connected passed pawns. The superior side will then have an extra pawn somewhere else, but the speed with which the pawns can be advanced is the decisive factor. Such endings often end in hair-raising spectacles, where one player wins by a hair.

No. 768, Kostic-Grünfeld, Teplitz-Schönau 1922

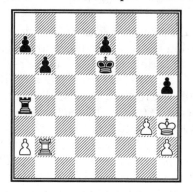

White to play, Black wins

No. 769 illustrates. Against passive defense Black wins by a judicious advance of his queenside pawns; e.g., **1. Rd2 Re4 2. Rc2 b5 3. Rd2 a5 4. Rc2 b4 5. Rd2 a4 6. Rc2 Kd5 7. Rf2 b3 8. axb3 axb3 9. Rb2 Rb4**, etc. So Kostic tried **1. Rb5**, when Grünfeld won by pushing his queenside pawns with both hands: **1. ... Rxa2 2. Rxh5 Rb2!**

Black has two advantages: 1. His king is protected from checks; 2. The White king and rook have to get out of the way of his pawns. These advantages make the ending an example of the well-known Manhattan Chess Club rule that Black pawns travel faster than White ones.

3. Rh8 a5 4. Kg4

If 4. Ra8 Kf5! is the most precise:

a) 5. g4+ Kg5 6. Rg8+ Kh6! 7. g5+ Kh5 8. g6 Rb4 and wins, for if 9. g7 Kh6 10. Re8 Kxg7 is a simple win (No. 707);

b) 5. Rf8+ Kg6 6. Rg8+ Kf7 7. Ra8 Rb4 8. g4 a4 9. Kh4 b5 10. Kg5 Rb3 11. h4 a3 12. h5 b4! 13. Kh6 (13. h6 Rh3) 13. ... Rg3 14. g5 Rg2 15. g6+ Kf6 16. Rf8+ Ke5! 17. g7 a2 18. Ra8 b3 19. Ra5+ (19. Kh7 b2) 19. ... Kf6 20. Ra6+ e6 and queens).

4. ... a4 5. Ra8 Rb4+ 6. Kf3 b5 7. h4 Kf6 8. g4 Rb3+ 9. Ke4 a3 10. Ra6+ Kg7 11. Kf5 b4 12. Ra7 Rf3+ 13. Ke4 Rf2 14. Ke3 Rb2!, White resigned, for if now **15. Rxe7+ Kf8 16. Ra7 a2 17. h5 b3 18. h6 Rh2 19. g5 b2 20. Rxa2 Rh3+! 21. K any b1=Q.**

C. The Extra Pawn Is in the Center

It makes little or no difference whether a passed pawn is on the board or is merely potential. If the pawn is not yet passed, it is usually best to exchange it and make a passed pawn as soon as possible. This contrasts with the cases with outside pawns, mainly because the drawing dangers (enemy rook behind the pawn) involved with outside pawns are much more remote here.

We again distinguish between otherwise balanced and unbalanced pawn positions. If the pawn position is balanced, it is best for the defense to have the passed pawn blockaded by the king, leaving the rook free to annoy the opponent in other quarters.

With such a setup — i.e., a balanced pawn position (except for the extra pawn) and the Black king in front of the pawn — the win consists of five steps.

1. Weakening the Black pawns by forcing them to advance and be blockaded.

2. Tying up the Black rook by attacking the weakened pawns.

3. Advancing the king and passed pawn as far as convenient, usually pawn to the fifth rank.

4. Putting Black in zugzwang by threatening to march in with the king or to capture more material.

5. Transposing to an elementary win either by winning additional material, by making an advantageous exchange, or by reducing to one of the standard positions.

It is rare, of course, to see all these steps carried out in their entirety. Black will most often resort to some tactical sortie, forcing White to discard the plan temporarily to ward off the threats. But against passive defense, which usually staves off defeat longest in such endings, the win will always conform to the pattern given.

There are two classic endings that illustrate the whole winning process beautifully. in **No. 769**, Tarrasch's handling of the ending is exemplary.

No. 769, Tarrasch-Thorold, Manhester 1890

White wins

1. Kf2 g6

Black is very obliging and advances his pawn voluntarily. But on 1. ... Kd6 2. Rg3 Rf4+ 3. Ke3 Rf7 4. Rh3 g6 5. Rf3 White would also have achieved his objective.

2. Rh3 h5 (first step completed) **3. Ke3 Rd6 4. d4**

The order in which the second and third steps are carried out is of minor importance and varies with the position.

4. ... Re6+ 5. Kd3 Re1 6. Rg3! (the rook's short-lived freedom is over. The second step is now completed.) **6. ... Re6** (6. ... Rb1? 7. Kc2 loses a pawn, while 6. ... Rd1+ 7. Kc3 Rc1+ 8. Kd2 Rc6 transposes back to the game) **7. Re3** (White makes a few useless moves here, but they do no harm 7. a4 is more direct) **7. ... Rd6 8. Re5 Rf6 9. a4** (to safeguard the pawns on the queenside and prepare the advance of the d-pawn and the king. In effect, Tarrasch is executing the fourth step, which is, as a rule, the most difficult.) **9. ... Rf2** (this rook is a kind of jack rabbit: it pops out and then goes right back) **10. Re2 Rf6 11. b4 Rf1 12. Re5 Rf2 13. Rg5!** (forcing the rook to return. Note the effect of the weakening of the Black pawns.) **13. ... Rf6 14. h3** (14. d5 at once is also possible, but the text is more methodical) **14. ... Kd6** (or 14. ... Rd6 15. d5 Rf6 16. Ke4 Kd6 17. Re5, as in the game) **15. Ke4 Re6+ 16. Re5 Rf6 17. d5!!**

Black's king is finally forced to give way. If the rook moves, 17. Re6+ wins a pawn, while if 17. ... a5 18. bxa5 bxa5 19. Kd4! Rf4+ 20. Re4 Rf6 21. Re6+!! Rxe6 22. dxe6 Kxe6 23. Kc5, with a simply won pawn ending.

17. ... Kd7 18. Rg5 (to allow the king to occupy e5. The fourth step is not yet completed.) **18. ... Kd6 19. Rg3 Ke7** (he must prevent the exchange of rooks, which White was threatening) **20. Rf3 Rd6 21. Ke5**

The second key position. The Black rook is forced to abandon the third rank and White's pawn advances to the sixth.

21. ... Rd8 22. d6+!!

A nice tactical finesse: if 22. ... Rxd6 23. Rf7+ Kxf7 24. Kxd6, and the pawn ending is hopeless for Black.

22. ... Kd7

This finally finishes the fourth step: the Black pieces have been driven back as far as possible. White can now win in a variety of ways; Tarrasch chooses to cut off the Black king from the d-pawn and capture Black's rook.

23. Rf7+ Kc8 (more merciful is 23. ... Kc6 24. Rc7+ mate) **24. Rc7+ Kb8 25. Rc2 Re8+ 26. Kf6 b5 27. d7** (anything goes) **27. ... Rh8 28. Ke7 Rh7+ 29. Kd6 Rh8 30. Re2**, resigns.

It is clear from the last example that the main problem is to force Black into zugzwang (fourth step). In this classic ending, **No. 770**, we see how this problem is solved by Rubinstein's consummate artistry.

No. 770, Rubinstein-Lasker, St. Petersburg 1909

White to play wins

The second step has already been completed: the Black rook is tied down to the defense of the exposed a-pawn. Now Rubinstein advances his king and passed pawn.

1. Ra6 (1. e4 at once is also good, but it helps to have the Black king confined.)

1. ... Kf8 2. e4 Rc7

Lasker wisely marks time. Playing the king to the queenside to free the rook would lose more quickly.

3. h4

As in the previous example, before his king goes out into the world, White wants to have his pawns insured.

3. ... Kf7 4. g4 Kf8 5. Kf4 Ke7 6. h5 h6

The crisis. Why, you might ask, does Lasker create a hole at g6 with this pawn move? The answer is that he cannot afford to let the White pawn get to g6. For instance, 6. ... Kf7 7. Kf5 Ke7 8. g5 Kf7 9. e5 Ke7 10. g6 h6 11. Re6+!! and Black faces a dilemma: should he lose beautifully or prosaically?

The beautiful variation is 11. ... Kd7 12. Rf6!! Ke8 (12. ... gxf6 13. g7 Rc8 14. exf6 and queens) 13. Rf7!! Rxf7+ 14. gxf7+ Kxf7 15. e6+ Ke7 16. Ke5 Ke8 17. Kd6 Kd8 18. e7+ Ke8 19. Ke6 a6 20. a3 a5 21. a4 g5 22. hxg6, and mates in two.

The prosaic line is 11. ... Kf8 12. Rd6 Ke7 13. Ra6 Rb7 14. Rc6 Rd7 15. Rc8 (threatening Rg8) 15. ... Rd2 16. Rc7+ Kd8 17. Rxa7 Rh2 18. Rxg7 Rxh5+ 19. Ke6, and Black can resign.

7. Kf5 Kf7

Now Black's king is in zugzwang because he cannot allow the White king to get to g6.

8. e5 Rb7 9. Rd6 Kf8 10. Rc6

If 10. Kg6 Rb4 11. Rd8+ Ke7 attacking the rook. Now White is threatening this inroad.

10. ... Kf7 11. a3!! Zugzwang! The various unpleasant alternatives are:

a) 11. ... Kf8 12. Kg6 Rb3 (note that the rook cannot go to b4) 13. Rc8+ Ke7 14. Rc7+ Ke6 15. Rxg7 Rxa3 16. Kxh6, and the two connected pawns are irresistible.

b) 11. ... Re7 12. e6+ Kg8 13. Kg6! Re8 14. e7!! Kh8 15. Rd6 Kg8 16. Rd8 and mates.

c) 11. ... Rd7 12. e6+.

There remains only the variation chosen by Lasker: he resigned.

In positions where there is no obvious target to attack, the only resource is tying down the opponent's rook and simplifying. If everything is exchanged on one side, the center pawn is in effect an outside passed pawn and should be exploited as such.

No. 771 (Schlechter-Chigorin, Hastings 1895), is a case where there is no other winning possibility: **White king at e3, rook at h3, pawns at b4, c4, c5, g4; Black king at g6, rook at g7, pawns at a6, b7, c6, e5, f6.** Black to play wins. The only winning chance is **1. ... f5 2. gxf5+ Kxf5 3. Rh5+ Ke6**, and because of the weakness of the White queenside pawns it turns out to be sufficient: **4. Rh6+ Kd7 5. b5 axb5 6. cxb5 cxb5 7. Ke4 Re7 8. Rb6 Kc7 9. Rxb5 Kc6 10. Ra5** (now Black wins a second pawn) **10. ... Re8 11. Ra7 Re6 12. Ra5 Re7 13. Ra1 Kxc5 14. Rc1+ Kd6 15. Rd1+ Kc6 16. Rc1+ Kd7 17. Rd1+ Kc8 18. Rd5** (or 18. Rc1+ Kb8 19. Rb1 Kc7 20. Rc1+ Kd6 21. Rd1+ Kc5 22. Rc1+ Kb4 23. Rb1+ Kc4!! 24. Rc1+ Kb3 25. Rc5 Kb4 26. Rc1 b5, etc.) **18. ... Kc7 19. Rc5+ Kd6 20. Rb5 Kc6 21. Rb1 b5**, and White soon resigned.

If the pawn is not yet passed, it is good to exchange it and create a passed pawn, unless exchanging it lands it on the sixth rank. It is too easily blockaded there and it will only be in the way. Instead, the constant threat of forcing a passed pawn is usually sufficient to tie up the enemy pieces and secure the required plus elsewhere.

A model ending with a potential passed pawn on the fourth rank is **No. 772** (Tartakower-Kashdan, Folkestone 1933): **White king at h1, rook at e1, pawns at a2, b3, f3, g2, h3; Black king at g7, rook at d3, pawns at a6, b4, e5, f6, g6, h7.** Black won as follows: **1. Re2 Kf7 2. Rc2 Rc3** (the White rook must not be freed: if the queenside pawns are exchanged the game would be drawn) **3. Rd2 Ke6 4. Kg1 f5 5. Kf2 g5 6. Ke2 a5 7. Kd1 e4 8. fxe4 fxe4 9. Rd8** (White prefers to take a chance with his rook out in the open. Against passive play Black wins – see the last two diagrams) **9. ... Rg3** (9. ... Rd3+ wins) **10. Ra8 Rxg2 11. Rxa5 Kf6 12. Ke1 Rh2 13. Ra4 Kf5 14. Rxb4 Rxa2 15. Rb7 h5 16.**

Rf7+ Ke5 17. b4 Rh2 18. b5 Rxh2 19. b6 Rb2, and the rest is routine (No. 707).

It often happens that the schema that we have set up is not feasible because there is no way to force Black into zugzwang. This usually occurs when the Black king and rook are near the passed pawn on the fifth or sixth rank. In such cases the game is sometimes a forced draw. Where a win is possible, the method is to transpose to some other type (outside passed pawn) by giving up the center pawn in return for one of the opponent's wing pawns. The most valuable subsidiary stratagem is getting the rook to the seventh rank, where it always plays a predominant role.

If the pawn is on the sixth, unsupported by the king, this sort of transition is much less favorable.

No. 773, Euwe-Bogolyubov, Zurich 1934

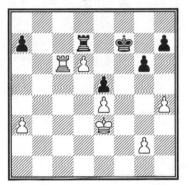

Black to play, White wins

No. 773 is a successful ending that shows some of the difficulties involved.
1. ... Ke6 2. Ra6 h5 3. a4 Rxd6 4. Rxa7 Rb6! 5. a5 Rb3+ 6. Kf2 Rb2+

Or 6. ... Rb4 7. Ke3 Rb3+ 8. Kd2 Rb2+ 9. Kc3 Rxg2 10. Ra8 and wins. In this line, if 7. ... Ra4 8. Ra8 Kf7 9. a6 Kg7. White wins by capturing the e-pawn.
7. Kg3 Rb3+ 8. Kh2 Ra3 9. a6 Kd6!

Bogolyubov now worked out a dangerous counterattack against White's e-pawn that Euwe could refute only with great ingenuity.
10. Rg7! Kc5 11. Rxg6 Kd4 12. g4! hxg4

On 12. ... Ra2+, the main winning variation is 13. Kg1 Ra1+ 14. Kf2 Ra2+ 15. Ke1 Ra1+ 16. Kd2 Ra2+ 17. Kc1 hxg4 18. Kb1! Ra5 19. h5 g3 20. h6 g2 21. Rxg2 Rxa6 22. Rh2 Ra8 23. h7 Rh8 24. Rh4, and White will eventually capture the e-pawn, since Black can only move his king.
13. h5 Kxe4 14. h6 Kf5 15. Rb6 e4 16. Kg2 Ra2+ 17. Kf1, and the White pawns get there first: **17. ... Ra1+ 18. Ke2 Ra2+ 19. Ke3 Ra3+ 20. Kd2 g3 21. h7 e3+ 22. Ke2 g2 23. h8=Q g1=N+** (a little joke) **24. Kf1 e2+ 25. Ke1,** resigns.

The difficulty in this and similar endings is that the passed pawn is so exposed that White does not have the freedom of choice that he has in the other cases.

Blocking the pawn with the rook is much less favorable for the defense. A rule that applies to all endings is that passed pawns should be blockaded by the king and not by a piece.

When the Black king is not near the pawn, a valuable new winning method (in addition to those given above) is available: cutting off the king and then continuing as in the elementary cases, disregarding the extra pawns.

No. 774, Alekhine-Euwe, Amsterdam 1936

White to play, Black wins

We see this method quite clearly in **No. 774**. The key to Black's strategy is to keep the White king away from the d-pawn. His winning plan against passive defense would then consist of playing his king to the queenside and advancing the passed d-pawn. White can offer no effective resistance to such a plan, so Alekhine decides to try to win Black's a-pawn and get enough compensation with his own passed a-pawn. But this means giving up his g-pawn, and Black's two unconnected passed pawns vs. one prove to be too much.

The game continued: **1. Kg4 Kf7 2. Rc3 a5 3. Kf3** (not 3. Ra3 directly because of 3. ... Re4+ and 4. ... a4) **3. ... Kg6** (3. ... a4 holds everything, for if 4. Ra3 Re4. But the course Black chooses is somewhat more direct) **4. Ra3 Kxg5 5. Rxa5 Kf5 6. a4 g5** (with a view to using this pawn to decoy the White king and facilitate the advance of the d-pawn) **7. Ra8 Re4 8. Rf8+!** (apparently forcing Black to go where he wants to go, but White could not prevent the entry of the king anyway, and White wants to block the d-pawn temporarily by using Black's king) **8. ... Ke5 9. Re8+ Kd4 10. Rb8** (threatening to set up a drawn position with 11. b4! and 12. a5. The Black rook would then have to return and free the White king) **10. ... c5! 11. a5** (in the game the variation 11. b4 led to a quick loss because the White pawns are easily stopped: 11. ... c4 12. a5 Re3+ 13. Kf2 Ra3 14. Rg8 c3 15. Rxg5 Ra2+ 16. Kf3 c2, White resigned) **11. ... Re1 12. a6 Ra1 13. Ra8 Kd3 14. a7 d4!** (better than 14. ... c4 15. Rd8 Rxa7 16. Rxd5+ Kc2 17. Rb5!) **15. b3** (or 15. Rc8 Rxa7 16. Rxc5 Rf7+ 17. Kg4 Rb7 18.

Rxg5 Rxb2 19. Kf3 Rb8, with a standard win; the king is on the long side of the pawn) **15. ... Rf1+! 16. Kg4 Rf7 17. Kxg5 Kc2! 18. Rc8** (18. Kg6 Rc7! and the pawn marches on) **18. ... Rxa7 19. Rxc5+ Kxb3 20. Kf5 Re7 21. Rd5 Kc4 22. Rd8 d3** and wins.

When the Black king is at some distance from the pawn, whether directly cut off or not, it is often advisable to sacrifice material in order to support the passed pawn with the king and advance it to the sixth or seventh. With the enemy king out of the way, the opponent will have to give up his rook to stop the pawn. Of course, the resulting ending with rook vs. pawns must be carefully appraised, but if the superior side retains at least one pawn he will usually win.

An example of an ending that abounds in such sacrificial possibilities is **No. 775.**

No. 775, Alekhine-Euwe, Berne 1932

Black to play. Draw

After the obvious 1. ... Rf5+, White can give up a few pawns and just manage to capture Black's rook and get back in time: 1. ... Rf5+ 2. Ke3 Rh5 3. d5! Rxh3+ 4. Kd4, etc.

Possibly inspired by this or similar variations, Euwe tried **1. ... Ra5 2. a3**

The sacrificial line 2. d5! is answered by 2. ... Rxa2 3. Ke4 Rxb2 4. Ke5 Kg7! 5. Kd6 Rxf2 6. Ra8 g5 7. Kc7 Rc2+ 8. Kd7 f5 9. Rxa7 Kf6 10. d6 g4 11. hxg4 fxg4 12. Ke8 Kg5 13. d7 Rd2 with a draw as the result.

2. ... Rb5 3. Rd7! (3. b4? a5) **3. ... Kg7** (3. ... Rxb2 4. Rxf7+ Kh6 5. Rxa7) **4. Rxa7 Rxb2 5. Re7!** (to keep the Black king cut off) **5. ... Kf6 6. Re2 Rb3+ 7. Re3 Rb2 8. h4**

The only way to make any progress is to sacrifice a pawn in order to permit the advance of the d-pawn. 8. d5 Rd2 9. Ke4 Rxf2 lets the Black king out. The most enterprising, and the most dangerous for Black, is 8. Re8! Rb3+ 9. Ke4!, but by rapidly advancing his own pawns Black can hold the game: 9. ... Rxa3 10. Kd5! Rxh3 11. Kc6 Rc3+ 12. Kxb6 Rd3 13. Kc5 Rd2 14. d5 (14. f4 Kf5) 14. ... Rxf2 15. d6 Rd2 16. Kc6 Rc2+ 17. Kb6 Rd2 18. Kc7 Rc2+ 19. Kd8 g5 20.

d7 g4 21. Re4 Kg5 22. Rd4 Ra2 23. Ke7 Ra8 24. d8=Q Rxd8 25. Rxd8 g3 26. Kxf7 Kf4, =.

8. ... Rd2! (now White does not have to sacrifice; he loses a pawn anyway) **9. Ke4 Rxf2 10. Rb3** (on 10. Kd5 Rf4 11. Rb3 Rxh4 12. Rxb6+ Kf5, the connected Black pawns are dangerous and may even win) **10. ... Re2+ 11. Kd5 Re6 12. Rc3** (threatening Rc6) **12. ... Ke7 13. Rc7+ Ke8 14. a4**, and although White still has a minimal positional advantage, he cannot win.

The worst possible position for the defense is to have his rook in front of the passed pawn and the attacking rook behind it, even when the pawn is in or near the center.

An example is **No. 776** (Maroczy-Marshall, New York 1924): **White king at g4, rook at c2, pawns at a2, b4, c5, h4; Black king at e4, rook at c6, pawns at a7, b6, g7.** White wins by reducing to an ending with rook and two pawns vs. rook and pawn. The first step is to fix the Black a-pawn with b5; next to exchange the c-pawn for Black's b-pawn; then to transfer the rook to the seventh and capture the a-pawn.

The conclusion was: **1. Rc1** (not 1. a4 Kd3 2. Rc1 Kd2 with "perpetual check" to the rook) **1. ... Ke3 2. Re1+ Kd4** (if now 2. ... Kd2 3. Re7 bxc5 4. bxc5 a5 5. Rxg7 Rxc5 6. h5 Rc4+ 7. Kg5 Rc5+ 8. Kh4! Rc4+ 9. Rg4 Rc6 10. Ra4! Ra6 11. Kg5, and wins) **3. Rd1+ Ke5 4. Rc1 Ke4 5. a4!** (by checking, White has gained the tempo necessary for this important move) **5. ... Ke3 6. b5! Rg6+** (6. ... Rxc5 7. Rxc5 bxc5 8. a5 c4 9. b6 c3 10. b7! c2 11. b8=Q c1=Q 12. Qf4+) **7. Kh3 bxc5 8. Rxc5 Rf6** (on 8. ... a6 9. Rc6 is decisive) **9. Rc3+ Kf2 10. Rc7 a6 11. Rc2+ Kf3 12. Rc6 Rf4 13. Rxa6 Rg4 14. Ra7**, and the rest is simple: **14. ... Rg3+ 15. Kh2 Rg2+ 16. Kh1 Rg4 17. b6 Rxh4+ 18. Kg1 g5 19. Rf7+ Kg3 20. b7! Rb4 21. Kf1 g4 22. a5 Kh3 23. Rh7+ Kg3 24. a6**, resigns.

Where the pawn position is otherwise unbalanced, much more attention must be paid to tactical considerations. As a rule, the winning method involves weakening the opponent's pawns, centralizing the pieces, and then either capturing material or reducing to an elementary case. But because the pawns are scattered, simplification, especially to rook and two pawns vs. rook and pawn, is always a possibility. When exchanges are unavoidable, White should always try to set up two connected passed pawns, while Black's best chance lies in a strong passed pawn defended by his king.

No. 777, Levenfish-Riumin, Moscow 1935

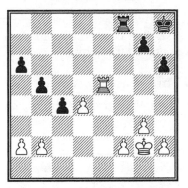

White to play wins

No. 777 is a model win. The first step is to weaken Black's queens side pawns. **1. Rc5!** (preparing 1. a4) **1. ... Kg8** (if 1. ... Rd8 2. d5 Kg8 3. Kf3 Kf7 4. Kf4 Ke7 5. Ke5 Kd7 6. d6 Re8+ 7. Kd5 Re2 8. Rc7+ Kd8 9. Rxg7 Rxb2 10. Kc6, is conclusive) **2. a4! Rd8** (2. ... bxa4 3. Rxc4 Rb8 4. Rxa4 is hopeless) **3. axb5** (not 3. d5? bxa4!) **3. ... axb5 4. d5 Rb8**

Now that the Black rook and pawns are tied up, the next step is to bring the king to the queenside. **5. Kf3 Kf7 6. Ke3 Ke7 7. Kd4 Kd7 8. Kc3 Kd6 9. Kb4.**

Next, in view of his powerful rook and king positions, White wins another pawn. **9. ... Rf8**

Or 9. ... Re8 10. Rxb5 Re2 11. Kxc4 Rxf2 12. Rb6+, and if 12. ... Ke5 to save the pawn, 13. Re6+ Kf5 14. Re3 cuts off the Black king from the d-pawn and decides quickly.

10. f4 g5 11. fxg5 hxg5 12. Rxb5 Rf2 13. Kxc4 Rxh2 14. Rb6+ Kd7 15. Rg6 Rxb2 16. Rxg5. With rook and two pawns vs. rook, the rest is routine. (No. 697).

As a rule, the extra pawn in such cases exercises a restraining influence on the opponent's pieces, and in the early stages of the ending this is frequently its main value. With the mobility of one of the enemy pieces restricted, pawn weakening and reduction to simpler cases are in order.

An example is **No. 778** (Schlechter-Teichmann, Vienna 1904): **White king at c1, rook at f1, pawns at a3, b2, c2, f3, g3; Black king at g6, rook at f8, pawns at a7, b7; c6, d5, g7, h7.** Black to play wins. The only immediate effect of the extra pawn is to allow the Black rook to get to the seventh rank, and this is sufficient here. After **1. ... Rf5 2. Kd2 Rh5 3. Re1** (3. Rf2 Rh3 4. Rg2 Kf5 5. Ke3 g5 6. Kf2 g4) **3. ... Rh2+ 4. Kd3** (4. Re2 is impossible because Black's extra pawn would win without any trouble in the pure pawn ending) **4. ... Kf7 5. b4 h5 6. Re5 g6 7. a4 Rg2 8. Rg5 Rf2 9. f4 Kf6 10. c3 h4! 11. Ke3** (11. gxh4 Rxf4 and also wins the h-pawn) **11. ... Rc2 12. Kd3 h3! 13. Rg4 Rg2 14. Kd4 Rg1!** and Black soon won; White must lose another pawn.

D. All the Pawns on One Side

We have seen that rook and two pawns vs. rook and pawn, all on one side, is drawn. The two other cases that occur most often are those where the superior side has three pawns and four pawns.

1. Rook and Three Pawns vs. Rook and Two Pawns

Unless White has an e-pawn, there are no winning chances at all.

No. 779

White to play. Draw

No. 779 is the general case. The White king cannot get through to h6, for if 1. Kh4 Rb5. If the pawn advances and gets exchanged, 1. f5 gxf5 2. gxf5, we have in effect the ending with rook and bishop-pawn vs. rook. Though Black can then again cut off the White king off, this is the best try. **1. f5 gxf5 2. gxf5 Rc6** (More dangerous, but also good if correctly continued, is 2. ... Rb4 3. f6 Rb6, etc., =. A trappy continuation here is 3. ... Rc4 4. Rg7+ Kh8? 5. Rg4 Rc6? 6. f7 Rc8, but after all these doubtful and inferior moves, 7. Re4 Kg7 8. Re8 Rc3+ still draws.) **3. Kg4 Rb6 4. Kg5 h6+ 5. Kh5 Rf6 6. Kg4 Rb6**, etc.

Another attempt is **No. 780** (Sämisch-Spielmann, Teplitz-Schönau, 1922): **White king at a1, rook at g4, pawns at a2, b3; Black king at b7, rook at e6, pawns at a7, b4, c5.** Black to play. Draw. Black has his a-pawn's eyes set on a3, but even that doesn't help: **1. ... Re1+ 2. Kb2 Re2+ 3. Kb1 Kc6 4. Rg5 Rd2 5. Ka1 a5 6. Kb1 Rd5 7. Rg8 Rh5 8. Rd8 Rh1+ 9. Kc2 Rh2+ 10. Kb1 a4 11. Rd1!** (11. bxa4 c4 creates some chances) **11. ... Kb5 12. Rd6 Rh1+ 13. Kc2 Ka5 14. Rd8 a3 15. Rd1!** (adding insult to injury: a pawn down and he dares to exchange!) **15. ... Rxd1 16. Kxd1 c4 17. Kc2 c3 18. Kc1,** and a draw was agreed.

White can win this ending only if the Black king is cut off from the pawns, as in **No. 781: White king at f3, rook at e2, Pawns at f4, g4, h2; Black king at d5, rook at a7, pawns at g7, h7.** Black to play. **1. ... Rb7 2. f5 Ra7 3. g5 Kd6** (3. ... Ra4 4. Re7) **4. h4 Ra4 5. Re4 Ra1 6. Re8 Rf1+ 7. Kg4 Rg1+** (7. ... g6 8. fxg6 hxg6 9. Rg8) **8. Kh5 Rf1** (8. ... Ra1 9. Rh8) **9. Rg8 Rxf5 10. Rxg7** and wins. A better defense is 1. ....Kd6 2. f5 Kd7!, etc.

Or **No. 782: White king at f3, rook at e3, pawns at f4, g2, h2; Black king at d5, rook at a7, pawns at g6, h5.** White wins. **1. Re5+ Kd6 2. Kg3!** (but not 2. Rg5? Ra3+ 3. Kf2 Ke6!! 4. Rxg6+ Kf5 5. Rg5+ Kxf4 6. Rxh5 Ra2+ 7. Kf1 Ra1+ 8. Ke2 Ra2+, etc., =) **2. ... Kd7 3. Rg5 Ra6 4. f5 gxf5 5. Rxf5 Rh6 6. Kh4 Rg6 7. g3** and again the last pawn goes.

When White has an e-pawn his prospects are brighter, but except for certain positions the game is a draw.

No. 783, Capablanca-Yates, Hastings 1930-31

White wins

No. 783 is one of those exceptions, played wonderfully by Capablanca despite the inaccuracies (for an earlier stage of this ending, see No. 787).

1. Rb6? (the winning line is 1. Rd6! Ra4 2. Kf3 Ra3+ 3. Ke4 Ra4+ 4. Rd4!, etc) **1. ... Re3?** (hoping to prevent the advance; if 1. ... Ra2+ 2. Kf3 Ra3+ 3. Ke4 Ra4+ 4. Kf5 Rc4, =) **2. Rb4 Rc3** (if 2. ... f6 3. Rb7+ wins a pawn) **3. Kf2? Ra3?** (3. ... h5! 4. g5 h4 5. Rb7 Kg6 6. Rb6+ Kg7 7. Rh6 h3 draws) **4. Rb7** (threatening 4. e6) **4. ... Kg8** (or 4. ... Kg6 5. f5+ Kg5 6. Rxf7 Kxg4 7. e6 and wins) **5. Rb8+ Kg7 6. f5** (the threat is 7. f6+ Kh7 8. Rf8 Kg6 9. Rg8+ Kh7 10. Rg7+) **6. ... Ra2+** (or 6. ... Kh7 7. Re8 Rb3 8. f6 Ra3 9. Rf8 Ra7 10. Ke3 and White wins, as in the game, by marching his king to c6) **7. Ke3 Ra3+ 8. Ke4 Ra4+ 9. Kd5!! Ra5+** (on 9. ... Rxg4 10. f6+ Kh7 11. Rf8 Kg6 12. Rg8+ Kh5 13. Rxg4 Kxg4 14. e6 queens) **10. Kd6 Ra6+ 11. Kc7 Kh7** (there is nothing better) **12. Kd7 Ra7+ 13. Kd6 Kg7 14. Rd8 Ra5 15. f6+ Kh7 16. Rf8 Ra7 17. Kc6! Kg6 18. Rg8+ Kh7 19. Rg7+ Kh8 20. Kb6 Rd7 21. Kc5!** (threatening 22. e6) **21. ... Rc7+ 22. Kd6 Ra7 23. e6 Ra6+ 24. Ke7 Rxe6+ 25. Kxf7 Re4 26. g5! hxg5 27. Kg6,** resigns.

Black can draw if he gets his pawn to f6 (i.e., prevents e5).

No. 784

White to play. Draw

Appearances to the contrary, not even **1. Rb7** wins. The reply is **1. ... h5! 2. f5+** (if 2. g5 fxg5 3. Rb6+ Kg7 4. fxg5 [or 4. f5 g4+ 5. Kg3 Re4 6. Kh4 Rxe3 7. Kxh5 (7. Kg5 Kf7) 7. ... Kf7 8. Kxg4 Re7, etc., draws] 4. ... Rg4 5. Rb5 Kg6 draws; or here 2. gxh5+ Kxh5 3. Rg7, hoping to get a passed e-pawn, but then 3. ... Kh6! 4. Rg2 f5! 5. Rg5 Ra5 makes the draw clear: the White king cannot get near the pawn without giving up the e-pawn) **2. ... Kh6 3. gxh5 Kxh5 4. Rg7 Rb4 5. Rg6 Rb6 6. Ke4** (6. e4 is no better; e.g., 6. ... Ra6 7. e5 Ra3+ 8. Ke4 fxe5 9. Kxe5 Ra5+ =. Note that Black's king is always on the short side of the f-pawn: No. 666) **6. ... Ra6 7. Kd5 Ra3! 8. e4 Ra6! 9. e5 Ra5+ 10. Ke6 Rxe5+ 11. Kxf6 Ra5** =, since the White king will be checked away from its dominating position: **12. Rg1 Ra6+ 13. Kg7 Ra7+ 14. Kh8 Rf7**, etc.

The other possible attempt by White is to advance his e-pawn: **1. Rb6 Ra5 2. e4 Ra3+ 3. Kf2 Kg7! 4. Rd6 Rb3 5. e5** (5. Ke2 Rg3; or 5. Rd7+ Kg8! and White can make no progress) **5. ... fxe5 6. fxe5 Rb5 7. Re6** (7. e6 Kf6) **7. ... Kf7 8. Rf6+ Ke7 9. Rf5 Ke6 10. Kg3 Rxe5**, or **10. Rh5 Rxe5 11. Rxh6+ Kf7, =**.

If the White pawn is not at g4 Black can still play his pawn to f6 and prevent the entry of the White king by deploying his rook along the fourth rank. The only real danger to Black in all variations of this ending arises from the advance of the White pawn to f6.

We have purposely chosen positions that are much more favorable for White than average positions in tournament play. In the Capablanca-Yates game, Black could have staved off defeat time and again had he realized the importance of preventing the advance of the f-pawn. Once the Black pawn is at f6 with any normally active rook position, White has no real winning chances.

For example, **No. 785** (Reshevsky-Apscheneek, Kemeri 1937): **White king at h4, rook at g8, pawns at g2, f3, e4; Black king at h6, rook at e2, pawns at f6, h7.** Draw. The game continued **1. ... Rf2 2. Kg3 Ra2 3. Kf4 Ra5!** (keeping the White king out) **4. g4** (4. Rd8 Kg6 5. Rd5 Ra2 gets White nowhere quickly) **4. ... Ra3!** (again ties down the White king) **5. Rd8 Kg7 6. Rd5 h6,** and White saw nothing better than **7. e5 fxe5+ 8. Rxe5,** when **8. ... Kf6** makes the draw obvious (No. 727).

When the defender has an e-pawn and can get his rook to the seventh rank, the game is a fairly certain draw. One example will suffice. **No. 786** (Kashdan-Alekhine, Folkestone 1933): **White king at e2, rook at h5, pawns at f2, g3, h2; Black king at e5, rook at a5, pawns at e4, f5.** Black to play draws. **1. ... Ra2+ 2. Kf1** (2. Ke3 Ra3+) **2. ... e3!** (riskier but good enough is 2. ... Ra1+ 3. Kg2 Ra2 4. g4! Kf4! 5. Rxf5+ Kxg4 6. Re5 Kf4 7. Re8 Rb2, =) **3. fxe3 Ke4 4. Kg1** (if 4. h4 Ra3! equalizes) **4. ... Re2 5. Rh4+ Ke5!** (but not 5. ... Kxe3 6. Rf4, although even here 6. ... Re1+ 7. Kg2 Re2+ 8. Kh3 Rf2! probably draws) **6. Rh8 Kf6! 7. Rf8+ Kg6 8. Re8 Kf7 9. Rc8** (9. Re5 Kf6) **9. ... Rxe3.**

2. Rook and Four Pawns vs. Rook and Three Pawns

Many writers have assumed that this ending is normally won, mainly because of two famous games of Capablanca's. Analysis of these games reveals that in both of them, Capablanca's opponents made the mistake of allowing the exchange of their g-pawn for the enemy h-pawn, thus remaining with rook, bishop-pawn, and rook-pawn vs. White's rook, king-pawn, bishop-pawn, and knight-pawn. But even after this error was committed a draw could have been held by proper handling of the sequel, for, as we have just seen, this ending is won only if the White king can reach e5 and prevent the advance of Black's f-pawn. In view of all this, it is clear that in any ordinary position, the four pawns will not win against the three.

No. 787, Capablanca-Yates, Hastings 1930-31

White to play. Draw

No. 787 is typical. The simplest drawing line is 1. ... h5! (No. 788), but as played by Yates, quite a few inaccuracies were required to drift into a loss.

The game continued **1. Ra6 Rb4 2. h3 Rc4 3. Kf3** (on 3. g4, Rc5 followed by ... h5 was still strong) **3. ... Rb4 4. Ra5! Rc4** (now the advance of the h-pawn will be prevented once and for all, but even that should not be fatal) **5. g4 h6**

If Black plays passively, White may play h4-h5, Kg3, f4, Kf3, and finally

Ra7, threatening e4-e5, f5 and f6+. In that event, ... h6 at some point would be forced.

6. Kg3 (preparing the advance of the f-pawn) **6. ... Rc1** (if 6. ... g5 7. h4 with a position similar to the game) **7. Kg2 Rc4 8. Rd5 Ra4** (on 8. ... g5 9. Kg3 and 10. h4) **9. f4 Ra2+ 10. Kg3 Re2 11. Re5 Re1 12. Kf2 Rh1 13. Kg2 Re1 14. h4 Kf6**

Better is 14. ... f6! 15. Re7+ Kf8 16. Re6 Kf7 17. f5 gxf5 18. gxf5 h5, =, or 14. ... Ra1 15. h5 gxh5 16. Rxh5 f6 17. Rb5 Kg6 18. Kf3 Ra4, =. No better for White in this line is 16. gxh5: the h-pawn will only be a target later.

15. h5 Re2+ 16. Kf3 Re1? (pointless; 16. ... Rh2 is in order) **17. Ra5 Kg7 18. hxg6 Kxg6**

If 18. ... fxg6 19. Ra7+ Kg8 (or 19. ... Kf6 20. Rh7! Rf1+ 21. Kg2 Re1 22. Kf2 Rh1 23. g5+ or even 23. Rxh6) 20. e4! Rf1+ 21. Ke3 Rg1 22. f5!! Rxg4 23. f6!! Rg1 24. e5, and White's passed pawns win because they are much nearer the eighth rank.

19. e4 (a slight tactical inaccuracy 19. Rd5 Rf1+ 20. Kg2 Re1 21. Kf2 Ra1 would have forced 22. e4 with a better king position) **19. ... Rf1+ 20. Kg3 Rg1+ 21. Kh3 Rf1 22. Rf5 Re1??**

The final, but this time decisive, blunder. 22. ... f6 would have drawn without much trouble.

23. e5! Re3+ 24. Kg2!

But not 24. Kh4? Rf3 25. Rf6+ Kg7 26. f5 Re3, or 26. g5 hxg5+ 27. Kxg5 Rf1 28. Ra6 Re1 29. Ra7 Re2, =: 30. Re7 Re1! 31. Kf5 (31. f5 Rxe5) 31. ... Ra1 32. e6 Ra5+ 33. Ke4 Kf6!, etc., =) **24. ... Ra3 25. Rf6+ Kg7** and now we have No. 783.

The simplest draw beginning from the original position (No. 787) is, as we have mentioned, to play the h-pawn to h5. The resulting ending is No. 788 (with colors reversed; Alekhine had the four pawns). It makes no difference whether White keeps his pawn at h3 or not; he can make progress only by advancing his e-pawn. The plan h3 and g4 is met by ... hxg4, when Black draws easily in the absence of weak pawns.

No. 788, Mikenas-Alekhine, Warsaw 1935

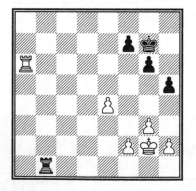

White to play. Draw

The only reasonable try is **1. f4**, since king or rook moves do not threaten anything. There followed **1. ... Rb2+ 2. Kh3 Re2! 3. e5**. Now Black can draw by shifting his rook back and forth along the seventh rank, but Mikenas found a tactical resource that soon put an end to White's winning attempts: **3. ... g5 4. fxg5** (if 4. Rf6, as played, then 4. ... g4+ 5. Kh4 Rxh2+ 6. Kg5 h4!, =) **4. ... Rxe5 5. Kh4 Re2! 6. h3 Re3!**, and with White's king bottled up, the two pawns do not win. **7. Rh6 Ra3 8. Rxh5 Ra4+ 9. g4 Ra3! 10. Rh6 Rb3 11. Rd6 Ra3 12. g6! f6!** (the simplest) and a draw was agreed.

No. 789, Kasparov-Anand, Wijk aan Zee 2000

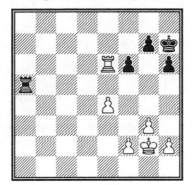

White to play. Draw

It is not possible for Black here to set up the well-known defensive formation f7-g6-h5 since the f-pawn has already moved. Yet I proved more than fifty years ago that this fact does not mean any specific disadvantage for the defender (Lilienthal-Benko, Moscow 1949).

Kaparov-Anand continued **1. Rd6 Ra4** (he doesn't fall for the trap 1. ... h5? 2. Rd5!) **2. Kf3 Ra3+ 3. Ke2 h5** (after this move Anand evaluates the position as equal) **4. Rd3 Ra2+ 5. Ke3 Kg6 6. h3 Ra4 7. f4 Rb4 8. Ra3 Rc4 9. g4 hxg4 10. hxg4 Rb4 11. Ra6 Kf7 12. Ra7+ Kg6 13. f5+** (the last try) **13. ... Kh6 14. g5+ fxg5 15. e5** (15. Kf3 Rb1) **15. ... g4 16. e6 Kg5**, draw. The defender operates with his rook from the side and cuts of the opponent's king from supporting his possible passed pawn.

Again, against careful play from a normal position White will not be able to build up any real winning threats. For example, **No. 790** (Reshevsky-Apscheneek, Kemeri 1937): **White king at g1, rook at a6, pawns at e4, f3, g2, h3; Black king at f8, rook at e8, pawns at f7, g7, h7**. Draw. The continuation was: **1. ... Rc8 2. Ra7 Rc1+ 3. Kh2 Rc2 4. h4 Rb2 5. Kh3 g6 6. h5 gxh5 7. Ra5 h4! 8. Rh5 Kg7 9. Rg5+ Kh6 10. Kxh4 f6!**, and nothing can be done. The defense ... g6 and ... h5 is also strong here.

White can win by force only if he has a passed e-pawn.

No. 791, Vidmar-Menchik, Carlsbad 1929

White wins

No. 791 is the model for this point.. There is nothing to stop White from getting his king to d6 and his rook to the c-file, and then advancing his e-pawn. Miss Menchik tried to hinder this plan by playing her king to the queenside, but then her kingside pawns proved to be irretrievably weak.

1. ... Rb7 2. Kf3 Kg7 3. Ke3

In the game, Black tried 3. ... Ra7, and the conclusion was 4. Rb3 Kf7 5. Rb4 Ke7 6. Rb5 Rd7 7. Rb6 Ra7 8. Rc6 Kd7 9. Rd6+ Ke7 10. h5! Ra3+ 11. Kd4! (but not 11. Rd3? Rxd3+ 12. Kxd3 gxh5 13. Ke3 Kf7 14. Kf3 Kg7! 15. Kg3 h6 16. Kh4 Kg6! 17. e6 hxg5+ 18. fxg5 f4, =) 11. ... Ra4+ 12. Kd5 Ra5+ 13. Kc6 Ra6+ 14. Kc5 (now 14. ... Ra5+ is answered by 15. Kb4, and Black has no more checks) 14. ... Ra4 15. hxg6 hxg6 16. Rxg6 Rxf4 17. Kd5 Ra4 18. Rg7+ Kf8 19. Rb7 Ra6 20. e6 f4 21. Ke5 f3 22. Kf6 Ra8 23. g6 f2 24. g7+ Kg8 25. Rb1 f1=Q+ 26. Rxf1 Ra2 27. Re1, resigns.

Against the best defense, **3. ... Rb4!,** the win is more difficult: **4. Rc7+ Kg8 5. Rc6! Re4+**

Or (a) 5. ... Rb3+ 6. Kd4 Rb4+ 7. Kd5 Rxf4 8. e6 Re4 9. Kd6 Rd4+ 10. Ke5 Rd8 11. e7 Re8 12. Ke6 f4 13. Rd6 f3 14. Rd8 and mates; (b) 5. ... Kf7 6. Rf6+ Ke7 7. h5 gxh5 8. Rxf5 h4 9. Rf6 Rb3+ 10. Ke4 Rb4+ 11. Kf5, and the rest is routine.

6. Kf3 Ra4 7. Rf6 Kg7

Or 7. ... Ra3+ 8. Ke2 Ra4! 9. Ke3! Re4+ 10. Kf3, etc., as in the main line. If here 7. ... Ra3+ 8. Ke2 Ra2+ 9. Kd3 Ra3+ 10. Kd4 Ra4+ 11. Kd5 Rxf4 12. e6 Re4 13. Rf7 Re1 14. Kd6 Re4 15. Ra7 f4 16. Ra8+ Kg7 17. e7 Kf7 18. Rf8+ and wins.

8. h5! Rb4 (8. ... gxh5 9. Rxf5 Ra3+ 10. Kg2 h4 11. Rf6, etc.) **9. h6+! Kg8 10. Rc6** wins.

E. Special Difficulties in Converting a Material Advantage Into a Win

1. Weak Pawns

This is the most common type of handicap for the superior side, very often nullifying the material advantage. There are two main subdivisions: isolated and doubled pawns.

Isolated pawns are a weakness peculiarly exploitable by rooks. In endings with minor pieces they make no practical difference.

No. 792, Capablanca-Alekhine, New York 1924

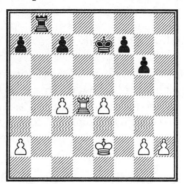

White to play. Draw

No. 792 is a splendid example of how such pawns may be pounced upon by the defense to hold a seemingly lost position.

Capablanca tried **1. Rd2 Ke6 2. Ke3 c6! 3. h4**

Not 3. c5 Rb5! 4. Rd6+ Ke5 5. Rxc6 Ra5, =. Alekhine recommends 3. h3! in order to continue with Kd4-c3 and then c5. But Black has the resource 3. ... Ke5!, for if 4. Rd7 Rb2 5. Rxf7 Rxa2 6. g4 Ra3+ he at least draws. The weakness of the White pawns makes any Black counterattack too effective:

3. ... Rh8! 4. g3 Rh5!

The point. With the rook on the fourth rank White can no longer win.

5. Rh2 (threatening 5. g4) **5. ... Ra5! 6. Kf4** (6. g4? Ke5) **6. ... f6!** (if 7. g4 g5+ 8. hxg5 fxg5+ 9. Ke3 Ke5, and White will be lucky to draw) **7. Rc2 Re5** (the threat was 8. c5) **8. c5 Rh5 9. Rc3** (with a view to 9. Ke3) **9. ... a5 10. Kf3 Ke7 11. Kg4 Kf7 12. Rc4 Kg7 13. Rd4** (a last attempt) **13. ... Rxc5 14. Rd7+ Kf8 15. Kf4 Kg8 16. Ra7 Kf8 17. a4 Kg8 18. g4 g5+ 19. hxg5 Rxg5 20. Ra6 Rc5 21. Ke3 Kf7 22. Kd4 Rg5 23. Rxc6 Rxg4 24. Rc5 Rg5,** and a draw was agreed, for if 25. Rxg5 fxg5 26. Ke5 Kg6! 27. Kd6 Kf7! (the simplest) and if now 28. Kd7 Kf6!, while if 28. e5 Ke8! 29. Kd5 Ke7 30. Kd4 Ke6 31. Ke4 g4 32. Kf4 g3 33. Kxg3 Kxe5, etc., =.

An example where two pawns are not enough to win is **No. 793** (Reti-Tartakower, Baden 1914): **White king at e2, rook at a6, pawns at a4, c3, f2, f4;**

Black king at g7, rook at h2, pawns at f6, h7. The doubled f-pawns and the isolated queenside pawns make the win impossible. The conclusion was **1. ... Rh1 2. a5 h5! 3. Ra7+ Kg6 4. a6 Ra1 5. Ra8 Kf5 6. Ke3** (if 6. Kf3 Ra3) **6. ... h4 7. a7 h3 8. c4 h2 9. Rh8 Rxa7 10. Rxh2 Re7+ 11. Kd4 Rd7+ 12. Kc5 Kxf4 13. Kc6 Rd2 14. c5 f5 15. Kc7 Kf3 16. c6 f4 17. Kb6 Rb2+,** draw. White can get his pawn to the seventh but cannot queen without removing his rook from h2. Black then captures the c-pawn, gives up his rook for the pawn, and draws by advancing his own pawn.

Note that the drawing method in both examples above is essentially the same: limit the mobility of the opponent's pawns, advance one's own passed pawn as rapidly as possible, and finally reduce to an elementary draw position.

Cases where two pawns do not win are rare exceptions, although winning may often present difficulties. Ordinarily, however, it is possible to reduce to a standard win.

For example, **No. 794** (Steinitz, 1895): **White king at e1, rook at a2, pawns at a4, f3, h2; Black king at h3, rook at b4, pawn at a5.** Although the ending is not easy, White can win in the following manner: **1. Kf2! Kxh2 2. Ra1 Rb3** (if 2. ... Rc4 3. Ke3 Kg3 4. Rg1+ Kh3 5. f4! Rxa4 6. f5 Rb4 7. f6 Rb8 8. Kf4 and wins) **3. Re1 Ra3 4. Re4 Kh3 5. Rg4 Ra2+ 6. Ke3 Ra3+ 7. Ke2 Ra2+ 8. Kd3 Ra3+ 9. Kc2 Rxf3 10. Rg5 Rf4 11. Rxa5 Kg4 12. Ra8!,** and the rest is routine.

Doubled pawns are a handicap in all types of endings, especially when two pawns are held by one. **No. 795** is an example where White's four pawns on the kingside are held by Black's two.

No. 795, Tarrasch-Johner, Teplitz-Schönau 1922

White to play. Draw

After **1. a4 h5 2. Kg2 g6 3. h3 Kf5 4. Rc7 Rb4 5. Rc6 Rb2 6. Kf1 Rb4 7. Ke2 Rb3 8. Kd2,** Black can draw by moving his rook back and forth. Instead he chose to try for more by **8. ... h4?**, which gave White a chance to undouble his weak pawns and win: **9. gxh4 Rxh3 10. Rxb6 Kxf4 11. Rf6+! Ke4 12. Rxg6**

Rxh4 13. Rg5 Kf3 14. Rf5+ Kg2 15. Rxa5 Kxf2 16. Ra8, and wins by marching the pawn on to the seventh.

If the doubled pawns are not liquidated and there is a disadvantage on the other wing, it is possible even to lose with an extra pawn. For example, **No. 796** (Belavienetz-Ebralidze, Tiflis 1937): **White king at g3, rook at d1, pawns at a2, b2, d5, f3, g4; Black king at g7, rook at e8, pawns at a7, b6, c5, f7, f6, h7.** Here Black must get rid of the doubled pawn at once by **1. ... f5 2. gxf5 Kf6,** when he will surely at least draw and may even win. Instead he played passively and lost after 1. ... c4? 2. Kf4! b5 3. Rd4 Rc8 4. d6 Kf8 5. a3 a5 6. Ke4 b4 7. axb4 axb4 8. Kd5 c3 9. bxc3 bxc3 10. d7! Rd8 11. Kd6 Ra8 12. Rc4 Ra6+ 13. Kc7 Ra7+ 14. Kc8 Ra8+ 15. Kb7 Rd8 16. Kc7, resigns.

To win, it is necessary either to exchange the doubled pawns or to transform them into a more concrete advantage. How to win by exchanging them is seen in **No. 797** (Keres-Capablanca, Semmering-Baden 1937): **White king at c3, rook at f5, pawns at a3, b2, g2, g5; Black king at g8, rook at e1, pawns at a4, b5, h7.** After **1. ... Re3+ 2. Kb4!** is necessary: 2. ... Rb3+ 3. Ka5 Rxb2 4. Rxb5 Rxg2 5. Kxa4 Kf7 6. Re5! Kg6 7. Kb5, White wins by the odd tempo.

Transforming doubled pawns into an outside passed pawn supported by the rook behind it is seen in **No. 798** (Colle-Alekhine, Scarborough 1926): **White king at h2, rook at e3, pawns at a2, b3, c4, g2, h3; Black king at f7, rook at f1, pawns at a5, b6, c7, c5, g6, h7.** Alekhine secured a clear advantage by **1. ... a4! 2. bxa4 Rc1 3. a5! Rxc4 4. Ra3 Rd4! 5. Rb3 bxa5 6. Rb5 c4! 7. Rxa5 Ke6 8. Kg3 Rd5! 9. Ra4 Rc5,** and the rest is routine: 10. Rb4 c3 11. Rb1 c2 12. Rc1 Kd5 13. Kf3 Kd4, White resigned.

Blockaded pawns are of little importance in this connection because they are so easily disposed of with rooks on the board. Nevertheless, the defender must be careful not to exchange rooks or unblock the pawns.

2. Strong Passed Pawn

An enemy passed pawn may be just as great an obstacle for the winning side as weak pawns in his own camp. It should be securely blockaded as early as possible, preferably by the king, but by the rook if there is no alternative.

The danger that a distant passed pawn may create, together with the manner of combating it, are clearly illustrated in **No. 799.**

No. 799, Euwe-Capablanca, Carlsbad 1929

Black to play, White wins

Remove Black's a-pawn and White's e-pawn and it's all over for Black. But here White is hard pressed to take care of the a-pawn. The game went **1. ... Kc5** (the threat was e5) **2. Rxh6 Kd4** (if 2. ... a5 3. e5 fxe5 4. Rxd6 Kxd6 5. Kd3, and the king is in the square of the a-pawn) **3. Kf3 a5 4. Kf4** (better than 4. e5 Kxe5 5. Rh5+ f5 6. g4 Rf6 7. Ke3 a4! 8. Kd3 Rd6+ 9. Kc4 Kf4!, =) **4. ... a4,** and now the most direct win is **5. Rh3!** (in the game, Euwe played 5. Rh5? and could only draw after 5. ... Ra6 6. Rd5+ Kc3 7. Rd1 a3 8. Kf5 a2 9. f4 a1=Q 10. Rxa1, etc: see No. 619) **5. ... Ra6** (or 5. ... Re6 6. Re3 a3 7. Rxa3 Rxe4+ 8. Kf5, etc.) **6. Ra3 Kc4** (the difference between this and the line played is that Black requires five more moves to win the White rook) **7. h4 Kb4 8. Ra1 a3 9. Kf5 a2 10. g4 Kb3 11. h5 Kb2 12. Rxa2+ Rxa2 13. Kxf6 Kc3 14. f4 Kd4 15. e5 Ra8 16. f5 Rg8 17. e6 Rxg4 18. e7 Re4 19. h6,** and the pawns are too much for the poor rook.

With the White rook behind the pawn this type of sacrifice may be more difficult, but if two or three connected passed pawns remain, it's usually a fairly simple matter to calculate whether they will be successful against the lone rook. An example is **No. 800** (Bogolyubov-Alekhine, first match game, 1934): **White king at f3, rook at c8, pawns at f4, g3, h3; Black king at d3, rook at a2, pawn at b3.** White wins. The main variations begin with **1. Rb8 b2 2. f5,** and now:

a) 2. ... Kc2 3. Ke4 Ra4+ 4. Ke5 Ra5+ 5. Ke6 Ra6+ 6. Kf7 Ra7+ 7. Kg6 Ra3! 8. Rxb2+! Kxb2 9. g4 Rxh3 10. f6 Kc3 11. f7 Rf3 12. Kg7 Kd4 13. g5! (but not 13. f8=Q? Rxf8 14. Kxf8 Ke5, =) 13. ... Ke5 14. g6 Ke6 15. f8=Q (just in time!) and wins;

b) 2. ... Kc3 3. g4 Ra1 4. g5 b1=Q 5. Rxb1 Rxb1 6. Ke4 Kc4 7. Ke5 Kc5 8. g6 Re1+ 9. Kf6 Kd6 10. g7 Rg1 11. h4, and wins by advancing the h-pawn.

A passed pawn can often save the game for Black when it is supported from behind by the rook and blockaded by the enemy rook, for then the enemy rook is stalemated and unable to come to the aid of its own pawns.

No. 801, Leonhardt-Schlechter, Nuremburg 1906

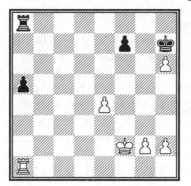

White to play wins.
Black to play draws

The essential stratagem in endings such as **No. 801** is to blockade the passed pawn as early as possible. For this reason White plays **1. Ra4!**, and after **1. ... Kxh6 2. Kf3 Kg5 3. g3 Kf6 4. Kf4 Ra6 5. e5+ Kg7 6. g4 Kg6 7. h4 Kh6 8. g5+ Kg7** (or 8. ... Kh5 9. Kf5 Ra8 10. Kf6 Ra7 11. g6! fxg6 12. e6 and wins) **9. Kf5 Kh7 10. h5 Kg7 11. h6+ Kh7** (White can afford to free his rook) **12. Rc4! a4** (or 12. ... Ra7 13. e6! fxe6+ 14. Kf6 e5 15. g6+ and mate next move) **13. Rc7 Kg8 14. Rc8+ Kh7 15. Rf8 Ra7** (15. ... a3 16. Rxf7+ Kg8 17. g6 Ra8 18. h7+ Kh8 19. Kg5 a2 20. Kh6 a1=Q 21. g7+ mate) **16. e6 a3** (16. ... fxe6+ 17. Kf6) **17. Rxf7+ Rxf7+ 18. exf7 a2 19. f8=Q a1=Q 20. g6+** mate.

Since both the main line and a number of subvariations succeed by only one tempo, it is reasonable to suppose that Black to play can draw.

This is in fact borne out by the game and analysis: **1. ... a4! 2. Ra3 Kxh6**

If White goes after the a-pawn with his king, Black will win the e-pawn and draw the resulting rook and two pawns vs. rook and pawn ending.

An application of the same idea is seen in **No. 802** (Koehnlein-Spielmann, Hamburg 1910): **White king at g2, rook at e2, pawns at b2, e4, f5, g4, h4; Black king at h7, rook at f8, pawns at a5, b4, g7, h6.** Black to play draws. **1. ... a4 2. Rc2** (if 2. e5 a3 3. bxa3 bxa3 4. e6 Ra8 5. e7 a2!, and since 6. Rxa2? Rxa2+! loses, 6. Re1 Re8 7. Ra1 Rxe7 8. Rxa2 is forced) **2. ... a3 3. bxa3 bxa3 4. Ra2 Ra8 5. g5 hxg5 6. hxg5 Kg8 7. Kf3 Kf7 8. Kg4 Ra4! 9. Kf4 Ra5 10. Ke3 g6!** (forcing the draw) **11. Kf4 gxf5 12. exf5 Ra4+ 13. Ke5 Ra5+ 14. Kf4 Ra4+**, etc., draw. The king cannot get to the a-pawn without losing both kingside pawns.

Where the pawns are advanced, it becomes less important how many there are because of the threat of promotion. For that reason, it is essential for the superior side to nip any such counterattacks in the bud by stopping the passed pawn at an early moment. In addition to the examples we've already seen, three others will clarify the technique and the kind of trap to be expected.

No. 803 (Alekhine-Euwe, fifth match game, 1937): **White king at h2, rook at e6, pawns at a5, b4, c5, e5; Black king at h8, rook at e3, pawns at a6, b7, c6, d5, e4.** Black to play.

The first consideration must be to stop the dangerous e-pawn. With that in mind, **1. ... Rf3!** seems the natural move, and in fact wins. The main variation is **2. Kg2 Rf5 3. b5! e3! 4. bxa6 bxa6 5. Rxc6 e2 6. Rh6+ Kg7 7. Rh1 d4! 8. c6 d3 9. c7 Rf8 10. Rg1!! Kh6!!** (not 10. ... d2? 11. c8=Q Rxc8 12. Kf2+) **11. Rh1+ Kg5 12. Rg1 Kf4! 13. Kf2 Kxe5+ 14. Ke1 Kd4 15. Kd2 Rf1 16. Rg4+ Kd5 17. Rg5+ Kd6 18. c8=Q e1=Q+** and either wins the White queen or mates.

Euwe chose **1. ... d4** instead, when **2. Rg6!**, threatening to advance the e-pawn, led to a draw: **2. ... Rf3** (or 2. ... Kh7 3. Rg2 d3 4. e6 Re2 5. e7, etc.), and a draw was agreed, since 3. Rg4 d3 4. Rxe4 Rf8 5. Kg3 Re8 eliminates all the passed pawns.

No. 804 (Reshevsky-Alekhine, AVRO 1938) is a perfect example of when extra material is more hindrance than help. **White king at f2, rook at h5, pawns at d4, g2, h2; Black king at f7, rook at d3, pawn at a4.** Without the d-pawn, White would surely have placed his rook behind the Black a-pawn and pushed his pawns as rapidly as possible. This would doubtless have won, since the Black king is quite far from his pawn, while if the rook gets in front of it, White could reach the favorable position in No. 707.

White can win by following the same principle: **1. Ra5! Rxd4** (1. ... a3 2. Ke2 Rb3 3. h4 Ke6 4. g4 Kd6 5. h5 is worse) **2. Ke3!** (to facilitate the advance of his pawns) **2. ... Rb4 3. Kf3 Ke7** (the only chance: if 3. ... Rb3+ 4. Kg4 Ra3 5. h4 Ra1 6. Kh5 a3 7. g4 a2 8. g5 and wins – No. 707) **4. g4 Kd7 5. h4 Kc7 6. h5 Kb6 7. Ra8 Kb7** (7. ... Kb5 8. h6 Kc4 9. h7) **8. Re8 a3 9. Re1 a2 10. Ra1 Ra4 11. h6 Kc6 12. h7 Ra8 13. Rxa2** and wins.

But instead, Reshevsky tried to hold on to his extra pawn, and this gave his ingenious opponent time to bring his king over to support his a-pawn. The game continued **1. d5 a3 2. Rh7+ Kf6 3. Ra7 Ke5 4. Ra5** (more loss of time, but now it's too late to get the pawns going) **4. ... Rd2+ 5. Kf3 Rd3+ 6. Ke2 Rb3 7. Kf2 Rb2+ 8. Kg3 Rb3+ 9. Kh4 Rb2 10. Kh3 a2 11. d6+** (to get the Black king out of the way: if 11. g4 Kf4! 12. Ra4+ Ke5, or 12. Ra3? Rb3+) **11. ... Kxd6 12. g4 Kc6!**, and now the Black king can draw by approaching the passed rook-pawn (No. 711).

No. 805 (Gilg-Mattison, Carlsbad 1929): **White king at f3, rook at f5, pawns at e3, f2, g2, h2; Black king at c6, rook at a4, pawns at a5, b6, f6.** Black to play. After the capture at f6 White will have no fewer than four passed pawns. Nevertheless, by marching his own b- and a-pawns, Black is assured of a draw. The best line is **1. ... b5! 2. Rxf6+ Kc5 3. Rf8 b4 4. Rb8** (else 4. ... b3 and ... Rb4) **4. ... Kc6! 5. g4 Kc7! 6. Rb5 Kc6!**, and White does best to take a draw. Instead, Black gilded the lily and lost after **1. ... Rc4? 2. Rxf6+ Kb5 3. Rf8 a4 4. Ra8 Kb4 5. g4! Rc5 6. h4 Ra5 7. Rxa5 bxa5 8. g5**. Both sides promoted but White won the queen and pawn ending.

Finally, positions come up where a strong passed pawn wins despite a material deficit of one or two pawns. Such a case is **No. 806** (Capablanca-Thomas, Carlsbad 1929): **White king at g3, rook at c7, pawns at e3, f2, g2, h3;**

Black king at c5, rook at b6, pawns at b4, g7, h6. Here **1. ... Kd6!** decides without much trouble because White has no time to go pawn-grabbing **2. Rc1** (2. Rxg7 b3 3. Rg8 b2 4. Rd8+ Ke7 5. Rd1 b1=Q 6. Rxb1 Rxb1, and wins because he still has one pawn) **2. ... b3 3. Rb1 b2 4. Kf4 Kd5 5. e4+ Kd4 6. e5 Kc3 7. Kf5 g6+ 8. Ke4 Kc2**, and the rest is simple. Instead, the game continued **1. ... Rc6? 2. Rxg7 b3 3. Rd7 Rd6** and a draw was agreed because White has too many pawns on the kingside.

When your pawn is close to being promoted, watch for combinations by your opponent.

No 807, P. Benko and E. Janosi, 1988

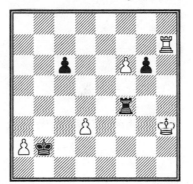

White wins

1. f7 Ka3

The a-pawn may not be taken, because 2. Kg3 g5 3. Rh2+ and 4. Rf2 wins immediately.

2. d4! g5

To survive, Black must keep the White king in captivity; away from the action. The other try is 2. ... Rf5 3. Kg3! Kb4! 4. Kg4 (4. d5? Kc5 holds) 4. ... Ka4 5. a3! Kb5 (5. ... Kxa3 permits the change 6. Rh3+ and 7. Rf3, winning) 6. Rh5!! wins.

3. Kg3 Kb4 4. d5! Kc5!

If 4. ... cxd5, again 5. Rh4!! wins.

5. dxc6 Kxc6 6. a4 Kc5!

The best defense. If 6. ... Kd6 7. a5 Ke7 8. a6 Ra4 9. a7, etc., wins. Or 6. ... Kb6 7. Rg7 Ka6 8. a5 with a win.

7. Rg7 Kb6

It seems that Black has reached his goal and has brought White into zugzwang. But as it so often happens, White can turn the tide by king triangulation.

8. Kg2!! Ka5

If 8. ... Ka6 9. Kh3 Kb6 10. Kg3 Ka6 11. a5 wins.

9. Rxg5+ Kxa4 10. Rg4!! The final sacrifice, finishing the business. **10. ... Rxg4+ 11. Kf3 Rg1 12. Kf2!** wins.

3. Strong Rook Position

This usually means a rook on the seventh or sixth rank attacking a mass of pawns. Such a rook can often save the day for the inferior side by capturing material directly or by forcing the sacrifice of material to avoid perpetual check or a mating combination.

No. 808, Nimzovich-Marshall, New York 1927

Black to play. Draw

No. 808 is typical: a strong rook working together with a strong king position. The White king is confined to the side of the board, and his connected passed pawns can advance only with the greatest difficulty. As a result, Black has excellent counterplay, which assures him of a draw.

Marshall played **1. ... a5** (necessary, to keep the White king confined) **2. Rh7** (not 2. Ka4? Kc5! 3. a3?? Ra2!! 4. b4+ [forced, to stop mate] 4. ... axb4 5. Kb3 Rxa3+ and Black might win).

Now the most exact drawing continuation is 2. ... Kc6!, for if then 3. Re7 to prepare f5, 3. ... b5! 4. b4 (necessary, to stop mate) 4. ... axb4+ 5. Kb3 Re3+ 6. Kc2 Rf3 7. Rf7 Kd5 8. Rf6 c5, the result is an exciting draw: 9. e6 c4 10. f5 b3+ 11. axb3 cxb3+ 12. Kb2 Kc4 13. e7 Rf2+ 14. Kb1! Rf1+ 15. Kb2, =, but not 15. ... Rf2+ 16. Kc1?? b2+ 17. Kb1 Kb3 and mates.

So the normal continuation is 3. Rh6+ Kd5 4. Rh7 Kc6, etc.

But the game continued **2. ... Rc2** (hoping for a mating attack) **3. Re7** (if 3. Ka4!? Rxa2+ 4. Kb5 c6+ 5. Kb6 Rb2 6. Kxa5 Rxb3 7. Re7 Kc5! 8. Ka4! Rb1 9. f5 Kc4 10. Ka3, a draw should still result) **3. ... b5 4. b4** (or 4. f5 b4+ 5. Ka4 Rxa2+ 6. Kb5 c6+ 7. Kb6 a4!, =) **4. ... a4?** (the simple 4. ... axb4+ 5. Kxb4 Rc4+ 6. Kxb5 c6+ 7. Kb6 Rxf4 draws at once) **5. f5 c5 6. f6?** (and now 6. e6 would have won: 6. ... Rc3+ 7. Kb2 cxb4 8. Rd7+ Kc6 9. Rd8 a3+ 10. Kb1 Re3 11. f6 b3 12. axb3 Re1+ 13. Ka2 b4 14. e7 Re2+ 15. Kb1 Re1+ 16. Kc2 a2 17. Ra8 Kd7 18. f7!, and queens or wins the rook) **6. ... Rc3+ 7. Kb2 cxb4**, and now a draw was agreed, for after the only try, **8. f7 a3+ 9. Kb1 Rf3 10. e6 Rf1+ 11. Kc2 Rf2+ 12. Kd3 b3 13. axb3 a2 14. Ra7 Kxe6 15. Rxa2 Rxf7**, there's too little wood for a fire.

A normal position where a well-placed rook yields perpetual check is **No.**

809 (Keres-Fine, Semmering-Baden 1937): **White king at e3, rook at b6, pawns at f4, g3, h3; Black king at f6, rook at a4, pawns at a5, f5, g6, h6.** The game was called a draw here, since the winning attempt **1. ... Kf7 2. Rb7+ Ke6 3. Rb6+ Kd5? 4. Rxg6** might win for White, but not for Black.

A rook on the seventh rank is usually sufficient compensation for a pawn. Sometimes the "pig," as Janowski used to call it, even counterbalances the loss of two pawns. A classic instance of such "piggishness" is **No. 810**.

No. 810, Tarrasch-Rubinstein, San Sebastian 1911

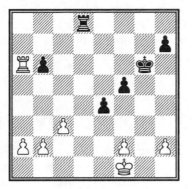

Black to play. Draw

Passive defense is hopeless: White simply sets up two passed pawns on the queenside and walks in. So Rubinstein plays *va banque*: **1. ... Rd2!! 2. Rxb6+ Kg5 3. Ke1** (or 3. a4 f4 4. a5 f3 5. Ke1 Re2+ draws, but Black can even try to win with 5. ... Rc1+ 6. Kd2 Rf1 7. Ke3 Re1+ 8. Kd4 e3!, etc.) **3. ... Rc2 4. Rb5 Kg4!** (he must not block his pawn; the threat is now f4-f3) **5. h3+** (the only chance) **5. ... Kxh3 6. Rxf5 Rxb2 7. Rf4** (or 7. a4 Ra2 8. a5 Kg4 9. Re5 Kf3, etc. If 7. Rh5+ Kg4 8. Rxh7 Rxa2) **7. ... Rxa2 8. Rxe4 h5! 9. c4 Kg2! 10. Rf4** (10. f4? h4! might well lose) **10. ... Rc2 11. Rh4 Kf3!** (Rubinstein's play is a model of precision. On 11. ... Rxf2 12. Rh2+! Kxh2 13. Kxf2 Kh1 14. c5, White wins: 14. ... h4 15. c6 h3 16. c7 h2 17. Kg3! Kg1 18. c8=Q h1=Q 19. Qc1+ mate) **12. Kd1 Rxf2 13. c5 Ke3 14. Rxh5** (or 14. c6 Rf6!!, and now 15. c7 Rc6, =, is forced, for if 15. Rc4?? Kd3!!, and Black wins the rook) **14. ... Kd4,** draw.

Against a rook in a strong position, the old adage that the best defense is a counterattack is applicable. Passive play in such cases usually yields nothing (compare the last two diagram positions).

An example of a successful counterattack is **No. 811** (Alekhine-P. Frydman, Podebrady 1936): **White king at e3, rook at a5, pawns at b2, c2, e4, f5, h2; Black king at c6, rook at g7, pawns at b7, e5, f6, h7.** White to play. Alekhine, aggressive as usual, scores in the following interesting way: **1. Ra8! Rg2 2. Rf8! Rxh2 3. Rxf6+ Kc5 4. b4+!!** (the point: Black's king is diverted and one pawn is removed from the second rank) **4. ... Kc4 5. Rd6!! Rh3+** (if 5. ... Rxc2 6. Rd5! Kxb4 7. Rxe5, and White's two connected passed pawns decide) **6.**

Ke2 Rh4 7. Kf3 h5 (if instead 7. ... Rh3+ 8. Kg4 Re3 9. f6 Rxe4+ 10. Kf5 Rf4+ 11. Kxe5 Rf2 12. Rd4+ Kc3 13. Rf4 Re2+ 14. Kd6 Re8 15. f7 Rf8 16. Ke7 and wins) 8. Re6 Rf4+ 9. Ke3 h4 10. Rxe5 h3! 11. Rd5! (not 11. Kxf4 h2! and queens) 11. ... Rh4 12. Rd4+! Kc3 13. Rd1 h2 14. Rh1 Rh3+ 15. Kf4 Rh4+ (15. ... Kd4 16. f6) 16. Ke5 Kd2 17. f6 Ke3 18. Kd6! Rxe4 (or 18. ... Kxe4 19. f7 Rf4 20. Ke7 Rf2 21. Rxh2) 19. Rxh2 Rd4+ 20. Ke5, resigns.

Always be sure to keep the rook as mobile as possible. An example where a bad (cramped) rook is fatal despite an extra pawn is **No. 812** (Sämisch-Treybal, Teplitz-Schönau 1922): **White king at e4, rook at a7, pawns at d5, f5; Black king at g7, rook at f6, pawns at b6, f7, g4.** White to play wins. **1. Ke5 Rh6 2. Ra4! Kf8 3. d6 Ke8 4. Ra8+ Kd7 5. Ra7+ Kd8** (5. ... Ke8 6. Re7+ Kf8 7. f6 and 8. d7) **6. Rxf7 Rh1 7. Rg7 Rg1 8. f6 Re1+ 9. Kd5 Rd1+ 10. Kc6 Ke8 11. d7+ Kf8 12. Re7! b5 13. Re8+ Kf7 14. d8=Q Rxd8 15. Rxd8 Kxf6 16. Kd5,** resigns.

VI. POSITIONAL ADVANTAGE

As usual, we divide the material into three subdivisions: better rook, better pawns, and better king. It is largely a theoretical task to distinguish the three groups in any given case. Pawn position and rook superiority, in particular, are practically inseparable.

A. Better Rook Position

The criterion by which we can judge whether one rook is better than another is its *degree of mobility*: its freedom of action and the number of squares it can control. It is this that justifies our basic maxim: *rooks belong behind pawns*. We find five types of superiority.

1. The Rook on the Seventh Rank

Normally, a White rook is attacking several pawns on the seventh rank. To defend them with the Black rook would be to immobilize that piece, while if there are pawns on both sides of the board, the king cannot possibly defend them all. In any event, Black is severely handicapped and must always weaken his position, often losing a pawn.

No. 813 is the simplest case where the rook captures material without any real compensation.

No. 813

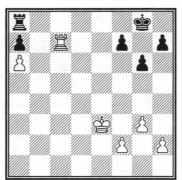

White wins

The Black king is tied down to the defense of the kingside pawns, the rook to the a-pawn. Against passive play White will march his king to b7 and capture a pawn. The best chance is **1. ... Rb8** (the defense 1. ... Re8+ 2. Kd4 Re6, which would work in the absence of so many kingside pawns, fails here after 3. Rxa7 Kg7 4. f4! Kf6 5. Kc5, for the White king gets to b5, supports the pawn, and frees the rook. Compare No. 683) **2. Rxa7 Rb3+ 3. Kd4 Ra3 4. Kc5 Ra2 5. Kb6 Rxf2 6. Rc7 Rxh2 7. a7 Rb2+ 8. Kc5! Ra2 9. Rc8+ Kg7 10. a8=Q Rxa8 11. Rxa8 h5 12. Kd4,** and with the White king so near, the win is simple. With the White pawn at a3 or a4 here, the game may likewise be won, but other complications arise (see No. 823).

A more complicated variant on the same idea is **No. 814** (Thorvaldsson-Feigin, Folkestone 1933): **White king at g1, rook at b1, pawns at a2, c3, f3, g2, h2; Black king at g8, rook at e2, pawns at a7, c7, d6, g6, h7.** Black to play wins. **1. ... Rc2!!** (best; 1. ... Rxa2 2. Rb8+ Kf7 3. Rb7 gives White a sure draw) **2. Rb3** (now 2. Rb8+ Kf7 3. Rb7 is met by 3. ... Rxc3 4. Rxa7 d5, when the two connected passed pawns decide) **2. ... Kf7 3. h4 Ke6 4. Ra3 a5! 5. Kh2 c5 6. Kh3 d5 7. Kg3 Ke5** and White resigned. This may seem a bit premature, but he has no way to prevent the decisive entry of the Black king; e.g., **8. Kh3 Kd6! 9. f4 Kc6 10. g4 Kb5! 11. f5 gxf5 12. gxf5 Rf2 13. Kg4 c4!! 14. Kg5 h5! 15. Kxh5 Rxf5+ 16. Kg4 Re5 17. h5 Re4+ 18. Kg5 Re3 19. h6 Rh3 20. Kg6 d4 21. h7 d3,** etc.

If there is a mass of pawns undefended by the king, a rook on the seventh just eats them up. One enemy passed pawn on the other wing can then be disregarded. **No. 815** is an elementary illustration of the idea.

No. 815, Euwe-Capablanca, Carlsbad 1929

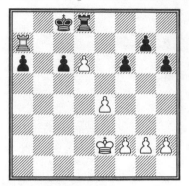

White to play wins

After **1. Rc7+ Kb8 2. Rxc6** (first getting rid of one potentially dangerous passed pawn) **2. ... Kb7 3. Rc7+ Kb6 4. Rxg7 Rxd6 5. Rg6** (the sixth rank functions here in exactly the same way as the seventh in other cases) **5. ... Kc5 6. Rxh6** should win (see No. 799).

When pawns must be lost, it is better to saddle the opponent with unconnected pawns rather than connected ones. For example, **No. 816** (Bogolyubov-Maroczy, Carlsbad 1929): **White king at c3, rook at a5, pawns at a4, f2, g2, h3; Black king at f6, rook at a1, pawns at a7, e6, g6, h6.** Black to play. **1. ... Ra2 2. Rxa7 Rxf2 3. Rh7 h5,** and White, seeing that he must lose a pawn no matter what he does, played **4. a5?** and lost. Instead, **4. g4!** draws, for if **4. ... hxg4 5. hxg4 Rf4 6. a5! Ra4** (or 6. ... Rxg4 7. a6 Ra4 8. Ra7 g5 9. Ra8 g4 10. a7 Kg7 11. Kd2 g3 12. Ke2, =) **7. Ra7 Kg5 8. a6 Kxg4 9. Ra8 g5 10. a7 Kg3 11. Kb3 Ra1 12. Kb4 g4 13. Kc5 Kg2 14. Kb6** with a simple draw, while if **4. ... Rf3+ 5. Kb4 Rxh3 6. gxh5 gxh5** (6. ... Rxh5? 7. Rxh5 gxh5 8. a5 and queens first) **7. a5 Rh1 8. Rh6+! Kf5 9. a6 e5 10. a7 Ra1 11. Rxh5+,** =. After the game continuation, 4. a5?, Maroczy ensconced his king behind his pawns and won handily: **4. ... Rxg2 5. a6 Ra2 6. a7 Kg5 7. Re7 Kh4 8. Kb3 Ra1 9. Rxe6 Rxa7 10. Rxg6 Kxh3 11. Kc2 Rd7** and we have No. 649.

To avoid such loss of material, the defender often resorts to a counterattack with his rook. Normally such tactics are far more promising than passive defense. **No. 817** (Alekhine-Euwe, 27th match game, 1935) is typical. **White king at f2, rook at d1, pawns at a2, b4, c3, f3, g2, h2; Black king at g8, rook at e8, pawns at a7, b6, e6, f7, g7, g6.** White to play. After **1. Rd7! Rc8!** (1. ... Ra8 2. Ke3 a5 3. b5 Rc8 4. Kd3 leaves him with a hopeless loss) **2. Rxa7 Rxc3 3. Ra8+ Kh7,** Black has fair counterchances. For the continuation see No. 860.

When the rook has undisputed control of the seventh rank, and the enemy king is on the eighth rank, confined there by the rook, White is said to have the "absolute seventh." In conjunction with the king and a passed pawn, the absolute seventh is murderous.

No. 818, Capablanca-Tartakower, New York, 1924

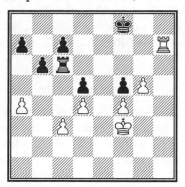

White to play wins

Witness **No. 818**, where White sacrifices two pawns to get his king to the sixth. **1. Kg3!! Rxc3+ 2. Kh4 Rf3**

This loses quickly. He could have put up much stiffer resistance with 2. ... Rc1!, for if 3. g6? Rh1+ 4. Kg5 Rxh7 5. gxh7 Kg7 6. Kxf5 c5! 7. Ke6 cxd4 8. f5, =. The most exact line after 2. ... Rc1 is 3. Kh5! c5 (or 3. ... Rh1+ 4. Kg6 Rxh7 5. Kxh7 c5 6. g6 and queens too soon) 4. Rd7! cxd4 (4. ... c4 5. Kg6) 5. Rxd5 Rd1 6. Kg6 d3 7. Kf6 Ke8 8. g6 d2 9. g7 Rg1 10. Rxd2 and wins.

3. g6! Rxf4+ 4. Kg5 Re4 (Black must be able to return to the first rank. If 4. ... Rxd4 5. Kf6 Kg8 6. Rd7 and mates, or 5. ... Ke8 6. Rh8+ Kd7 7. g7, winning the rook) **5. Kf6 Kg8 6. Rg7+ Kh8 7. Rxc7** (now White gets all his pawns back with interest) **7. ... Re8 8. Kxf5** (the simplest) **8. ... Re4 9. Kf6 Rf4+ 10. Ke5 Rg4 11. g7+ Kg8** (after 11. ... Rxg7 12. Rxg7 Kxg7 13. Kxd5, the pawn ending is hopeless) **12. Rxa7 Rg1 13. Kxd5 Rc1 14. Kd6 Rc2 15. d5 Rc1 16. Rc7 Ra1 17. Kc6 Rxa4 18. d6**, resigns.

If there is little material left, a rook on the seventh is usually much less effective, since there is less for it to capture. For instance, **No. 819** (Kashdan-Alekhine, Folkestone 1933): **White king at f1, rook at g7, pawns at f2, g3, h2; Black king at e6, rook at a5, pawns at e5, f6, h7.** Black to play. **1. ... h5 2. Rh7 e4 3. Ke2,** and now 3. ... f5 demonstrated the draw quickly (if instead 3. ... Re5? 4. Ke3 Kd5 5. h4 Ke6 6. Ra7 Kd5 7. Kf4 Ke6 8. Ra6+ Ke7 9. Ra4, and Black loses the pawns in worse circumstances) **4. Rh6+** (or 4. Rxh5 Ra2+ 5. Kf1 Ra1+ 6. Kg2 Ra2! 7. Rh8 Kf7, and the threat ... e3 equalizes) **4. ... Ke5 5. Rxh5 Ra2+ 6. Kf1 e3!**, etc.; see No. 785.

A somewhat more complicated case, though with only two pawns on each side, is **No. 820** (Chekhover-Romanovsky, Leningrad 1934): **White king at b1, rook at f7, pawns at e3, g3; Black king at c6, rook at c2, pawns at b3, e4.** Black to play. Here the seventh rank is meaningful only to the extent that the rook confines the White king. The game continued **1. ... Re2 2. Rf5?** (correct is 2. g4 Rxe3 3. g5 Rg3 4. Re7 Kd5 5. Kb2 Kd4! 6. Rg7! e3! 7. g6! e2 8. Rd7+ Ke3 9. Re7+ Kd2 10. Rd7+, and draws, for if 10. ... Rd3 11. Rxd3+ Kxd3 12. g7, and there is no mate after both sides queen) **2. ... Rxe3 3. g4 Rg3** (or 3. ... Re2 4. g5 Kd6 5. g6 e3 6. Rf3 Ke5 7. g7, =) **4. g5?** (4. Re5 Rxg4 5. Kb2 Kd6 6. Re8 Kd5 7. Kxb3 Kd4 8. Kc2 is a standard draw: No. 626) **4. ... Kd6 5. Kb2 e3 6. Rf1 Ke5! 7. Rf8 Rxg5 8. Kxb3 Ke4 9. Kc2 Rd5** and wins, for the White king is on the long side of the pawn.

2. The Open File

Unchallenged control of an open file always confers an advantage. Where there are weak pawns in the enemy camp, and the rook can penetrate to the seventh rank, material can usually be won. The method of exploiting an open file involves branching off to one of the wings at the appropriate moment.

No. 821, Marshall-Euwe, Bad Kissingen 1928

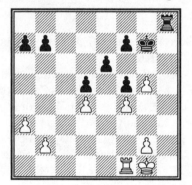

Black to play wins

No. 821 is typical. Place the White rook at c1 and Black will have to fight hard to draw. But now he can first cramp the White pieces and then secure a decisive material superiority. Euwe won as follows: **1. ... Rc8 2. Rf3!** (relatively best. If 2. Rf2 Rc1+ 3. Rf1 Rc4! 4. Rd1 Rc2 5. b4 Rc3 and wins a pawn) **2. ... Rc1+!** (driving the White king away. On 3. Rf1? Rc4! 4. Rd1 Rc2 wins a pawn) **3. Kh2 Rd1 4. Rb3 Rxd4 5. Rxb7 Rxf4 6. Rxa7 Rf2**.

Material is still even, but the White pawn at g5 is hopelessly weak. White has two connected passed pawns on the queenside, Black's are in the center. This in itself is of no great moment, but here it makes all the difference in the world because Black is in a position to support his pawns, while White is not.

7. b4 Rb2 8. Rb7 Ra2 9. Ra7 Kg6 10. b5 d4!

This advance will force the exchange of the Black d-pawn for the White b-pawn or a-pawn and leave Black with two connected passed pawns vs. one.

11. b6

White has no time to advance his pawns methodically. If 11. a4 d3 12. b6 d2, and now 13. Rd7 Rxa4 14. Rxd2 Rb4 15. Rd6 Rb2 is necessary, when Black will win as in the game. Similarly, to try to stop the Black pawns with the king would be suicidal: 11. Kg1? e5 12. Kf1? d3 13. a4 Ra1+ 14. Kf2 d2 and wins.

11. ... Rb2 12. Ra4 Rxb6 13. Rxd4 Rb3! (to be sure to get behind the passed pawn) **14. Ra4 Kxg5** (now Black only needs to rid himself of the doubled pawn, which is easily done) **15. Ra8 f4 16. a4 f3! 17. Rg8+!** (if 17. gxf3 Rxf3 18. a5. Black has time to force the crucial position of No. 707 because his pawn is still on the second rank; 18. ... Ra3 19. a6 Kf4! 20. a7 e5!, and if 21. Rf8 Rxa7 and the f-pawn is protected.) **17. ... Kh6! 18. gxf3 Rxf3 19. Rg3 Rf5 20. Rg4** (20. Ra3 Ra5 is somewhat more difficult, but the a-pawn is so far back that Black will still win) **20. ... Rc5 21. Rb4 Rc3 22. Kg2 Kg6** and wins. For the conclusion, see No. 709.

The strength of the open file lies in the fact that it can be used as a springboard to get the rook to other parts of the board. So where there is no available jumping-off place on the fifth, sixth or seventh rank, the open file will not be of much use.

No. 822 (Bogolyubov-Johner, Carlsbad 1929) is an illustration of this principle: **White king at f3, rook at c1, pawns at a2, c3, c4, d5, f4, g4, h2; Black king at g6, rook at e7, pawns at a7, b6, c7, d6, f7, f6, h6.** White to play. If 1. f5+ Kg7 (1. ... Kg5 is enterprisingly fatal: 2. h4+ Kxh4 3. Rh1+ Kg5 4. Rh5+ mate) **2. a4 a5** makes the draw definite. The open file gets Black nowhere because the rook cannot occupy any square beyond the fourth rank.

Bogolyubov played **1. a4?,** and after **1. ... f5!** realized that the threat 2. ... Re4 would cost him at least one pawn. He chose the counteroffensive **2. c5,** but after the series of peaceful exchanges **2. ... bxc5 3. Rb1 fxg4+ 4. Kxg4 Re3 5. Rb7 h5+ 6. Kh4 Rxc3 7. Rxc7 Rf3 8. a5 Rxf4+ 9. Kg3 Rg4+ 10. Kf3 Kf6 11. Rxa7 Ra4 12. Rd7 Ke5! 13. Rxf7 Rxa5 14. Rh7 Kxd5** the Black connected passed pawns carried the day.

3. White's Rook Is Attacking a Pawn or Pawns Defended by Black's Rook

Pawns should be defended by the king because only the king does not thereby lose mobility. A rook that is defending any pawn (except a strong passed pawn) is cramped and much inferior to its rival attacking those pawns. The seventh rank is but one illustration of this general fact: in No. 813 Black loses only because his rook is chained to a defensive post.

No. 823 is the usual type of position in which this advantage is seen.

No. 823, Match St. Petersburg-London 1886-88

Black to play

The game was adjourned here and was not played to a finish. Chigorin later published analysis to support his claim that White should win, but he appears to have been overoptimistic.

Two important guiding principles are displayed in this ending:

1. Purely passive play loses for Black.

2. An adequate counterattack at the proper moment will suffice to draw.

The first is illustrated in the following variations: 1. ... Ra7? 2. Ke4 Ra6 3. Kd4 Ra7 4. f4 and now:

a) 4. ... Ra6 5. Rb7+ Kd6 (5. ... Ke6 6. Kc5 Ra8 7. Rb6+ Kf7 8. Kb5) 6. f5 gxf5 7. gxf5 Ra8 8. Rb6+ Ke7 9. Kc5 Rh8 10. Rb5! Kd7 11. Rxa5 and wins.

b) 4. ... Kd6 5. Rb6+ Ke7 6. Kc5 Rc7+ 7. Kb5 Rc1 8. g5 f5 (8. ... fxg5 loses both pawns) 9. Rxg6 Rf1 10. Kxa5 Rxf4 11. Rf6! Rf1 12. Kb6 f4 13. a5 Rg1 14. Rxf4 Rxg5 15. a6 Rg1 16. a7 Ra1 17. Rf5 and wins.

Therefore, Black's only chance lies in getting his rook behind the White a-pawn. In fact, the immediate sacrifice seems to draw most effectively: **1. ... Rc6! 2. Rxa5 Rc4+ 3. Ke3** (if 3. Kg3 g5 4. Ra7+ Ke6 5. a5 Rc2 6. a6 Ra2 7. Ra8 Kf7!, =) **3. ... Kf7** (3. ... Rc3+ is dubious; it just makes the White king active. After 4. Ke4 Rc4+ 5. Kd5 Rf4 6. Ra7+ Kd8 7. Kd6!, and Black is in trouble: 7. ... Kc8 8. Rc7+ Kd8 [if 8. ... Kb8 9. Rc3 Rxa4 10. Ke6., etc.] 9. Rf7 Ke8 10. Ke6 or Ra7 wins) **4. Ra8** (if 4. Ra7+ Ke6 5. a5 Ra4 6. a6 Ke5 7. f4+ Kd5 8. Ra8 Ra3+, =) **4. ... Kg7 5. a5 Ra4 6. a6 Kh6! 7. f4 g5 8. fxg5+ fxg5 9. Kd3 Kg7 10. Kc3 Rxg4** draws.

A similar instance where an aggressive counteraction would have saved a seemingly lost ending is **No. 824.**

No. 824, Tarrasch-Janowski, Ostend 1907

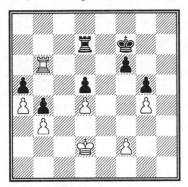

Black to play

Black must lose a pawn, for if 1. ... Ra7 2. Rd6. Janowski instead played **1. ... Rc7!** when **2. Rd6 Rc3 3. Rxd5 Rxb3 4. Rxa5 Ke6 5. Rf5 Ra3 6. a5 Ke7!** should have drawn.

The continuation was **7. Kc2 Ke6 8. Rb5 Kd6 9. Kb2 Ke6 10. Rb6+** (10. Rxb4 Rxa5 will not win, since the Black king is too close to the passed pawn) **10. ... Kd5 11. Rxf6 Kc4! 12. Rf5!**

Or 12. a6 Rb3+ 13. Kc2 Rc3+, and it is dangerous for White to try to avoid perpetual check; e.g., 14. Kd2 Rd3+ 15. Ke2 Ra3 16. Rg6 b3! 17. Rxg5 b2 18. Rc5+ Kxd4 19. Rb5 Kc3 20. f4 Rxa6 21. f5 Ra4! 22. Rxb2 Kxb2 23. Kf3 Kc3 24. f6 Kd4 25. Kf4 Kd5+ 26. Kf5 Ra1 27. g5 Rf1+ 28. Kg6 Ke6! and wins.

12. ... Rb3+ 13. Kc2 Rc3+ 14. Kd2 Rd3+ 15. Ke2 Rxd4 16. a6 Rd8 17. Rxg5 b3 18. Rg7 b2 19. Rb7 Kc3 20. f4 Ra8 21. f5 Rxa6 22. Ke3, and now **22. ... Ra1!** draws: **23. Rxb2 Kxb2 24. f6 Rf1 25. g5 Kc3 26. Ke4 Kc4 27. Ke5 Kc5 28. Ke6 Re1+ 29. Kf7** (if 29. Kd7 Rd1+ 30. Kc7 Rf1! threatening ... Rf5) **29. ... Kd6 30. g6 Rg1 31. g7 Ke5,** =: No. 589. Instead, Black played 22. ... Ra4? and lost after 23. Rxb2 Kxb2 24. f6!!: see No. 593.

An instance where passive play was fatal is **No. 825** (Dake-Campolongo, Folkestone 1933): **White king at g1, rook at a1, pawns at a4, e5, g3, h2; Black king at g8, rook at d4, pawns at a6, f7, g7, h7**. White to play can draw by **1. Rb1! g6** (the best chance) **2. Rb8+ Kg7 3. Rb7! Kf8 4. Rb8+ Ke7 5. Rb7+ Ke6 6. Rb6+**, etc. Instead, he tried 1. Kf2?, when 1. ... Re4 2. Kf3 Rxe5 cost him a pawn and the game.

The superior side should likewise play aggressively and attempt to convert his positional advantage into something decisive at the earliest possible moment. Besides the simple capture of material, the main types of superiority are connected passed pawns and an outside passed pawn supported by the king or a rook behind it.

For example, **No. 826** (Spielmann-Alekhine, New York 1927): **White king at f1, rook at e4, pawns at b4, f2, g3, h4; Black king at f6, rook at a4, pawns at b7, c5, f7, g6**. White to play. After **1. Rf4+ Ke6 2. Re4+** (or 2. bxc5 Rxf4 3.

gxf4 Kd5 4. f5! Kxc5 5. fxg6 fxg6 6. f4 Kd5! wins), and now, as Alekhine later demonstrated, he could have scored by **2. ... Kd5! 3. Re7 cxb4 4. Rxb7 Kc4 5. Rc7+ Kd3 6. Rd7+ Kc2 7. Rc7+ Kb2 8. Rxf7 b3 9. Rf6 Ka3! 10. Rb6 b2,** and now **11. Rxb2** is forced, when Black's king gets back very quickly. Instead, the passive 2. ... Kd7 3. g4! cxb4 4. h5! should have led to a draw.

The position is usually easier for White when his rook is attacking pawns on the file rather than on the rank because any counterattack such as in the above examples is necessarily less successful. **No. 827** is a classic exploitation of this type of advantage.

No. 827, Flohr-Vidmar, Nottingham 1936

White to play

White stands better for two reasons: first, because his rook is active and his opponent's is passive, and second, because the Black pawns on the queen-side are blockaded and therefore weak. But in rook endings such advantages are not permanent. Black threatens to play his king to d6 and ultimately b6, freeing his rook and obtaining counterplay.

With this in mind, White's plan consists of five steps: 1. Definite prevention of the freeing ... c5. 2. Centralization of his king. 3. Weakening the Black kingside pawns. 4. Forcing an entry with his king. 5. Capture of material.

Our main variation, given in **boldface** type, is the actual course of the game.

1. Ke2 Ke7 2. Kd3 Kd6 3. Ra5 Ra8 4. Kd4

The first two steps go together.

4. ... f5?

Played with a view to exchanging as many pawns as possible, but it voluntarily weakens his pawn structure. The principal alternatives are:

a) 4. ... Ra7 5. g4 f5! (Black must not allow the crippling of his pawn position by g5. Also bad is 5. ... f6 6. h4 Ra8 7. e4 dxe4 8. fxe4 Ra7 9. g5) 6. g5 (after 6. gxf5 gxf5 7. e4 is the last chance, but 7. ... fxe4 8. fxe4 dxe4 9. Kxe4 Ke6 should draw, since Black has exchanged so many pawns) 6. ... Ra8 7. h4 Ra7 8. e4 fxe4 9. fxe4 dxe4 10. Kxe4 Ke6 11. Kf4 Kd6 12. Kg4 Ke6 13. h5 Kd6 14. h6

Ke6 15. Kf4 Kd6 16. Ke4 Ke6 17. Re5+ Kd6 (17. ... Kf7 18. Kd4-c5) 18. Ra5 (there is no good continuation: if 18. a4 Rb7) 18. ... Ke6 19. Kd4 Kd6, and although White still has his advantage there is no forced win.

b) 4. ... Kc7? 5. Kc5 Kb7 6. Ra4 a5 (if 6. ... Re8 7. Rb4+ Kc7 8. Rb6, while if 6. ... Kc7 7. Rf4 f5 8. g4 Rf8 9. e4! dxe4 10. fxe4 Re8 11. exf5 gxf5 12. gxf5, and the extra pawn wins) 7. Rf4 f5 (7. ... Rf8 8. Rf6) 8. g4 fxg4 (or 8. ... Rf8 9. e4, as above) 9. Rf7+ Ka6 10. fxg4 Re8 (the best chance) 11. Rxh7 Rxe3 12. Kxc6 d4 13. Rh8 Ka7 14. Rd8 Re2 15. Rxd4 Rxa2 16. Ra4! Rc2+! 17. Kb5 Rxh2 18. Rxa5+ Kb7 19. Ra6 Rb2 20. b4! wins.

After the move chosen Flohr demonstrates that White wins by force. The fourth step now commences.

5. b4! (permanently preventing the liberating 5. ... c5+) **5. ... Rb8** (but now 5. ... Kc7 6. Kc5 Kb7 and Re8 could free the Black rook) **6. a3 Ra8** (6. ... Rb6 immobilizes the rook completely) **7. e4!** (forcing a favorable exchange. White's king now threatens to get to the other wing) **7. ... fxe4 8. fxe4 dxe4 9. Kxe4 Ra7**

Again, Black plays passively. Instead, 9. ... Kc7 10. Re5 Kb6 11. Re7 a5! 12. Rxh7 axb4 13. axb4 Ra4 14. Rg7 Rxb4!, and the passed c-pawn gives good counterchances. If 9. ... Ke6 10. Kf4 Kf6 11. Rc5 Rc8 12. a4 Ke6 13. Kg5 Kd6 14. Kh6 Rb8 15. Rc4 wins. The immediate entry of the White king can be stopped only at the cost of a further weakening of the pawn position.

10. Kf4 h6

Allowing the White king to get to h6 is equally fatal: 10. ... Ra8 11. Kg5 Ra7 12. Kh6 Ke6 13. g4 Kd6 14. g5 Ke6 15. a4 Rb7 16. Rxa6 Rxb4 17. Rxc6+ Kf7 18. Rc7+ Ke6 19. Rxh7 and wins.

11. h4 Ke6 (11. ... Kc7 12. Ke5 Kb6 13. Kf6 is worse) **12. Kg4 Ra8** (on 12. ... Kf7 13. h5 is equally effective) **13. h5!** (fixing the kingside pawns) **13. ... g5** (13. ... gxh5+ 14. Kxh5 Rg8 15. g4! Kd6 16. Rf5! Kc7 17. Rf4! is no better) **14. g3** (the Black pawns have been sufficiently softened up: now the king tries to get in) **14. ... Ra7 15. Kf3 Ra8 16. Ke4 Ra7 17. Re5+!!** (forcing the reluctant Black king to make up its mind) **17. ... Kd6**

The other side is no better: 17. ... Kf6 18. Rc5 Rc7 19. Ra5 Ra7 20. Kd4 Ke6 21. Kc5 Rd7 22. Rxa6 Rd3 23. Rxc6+ and b5-b6, etc.)

18. Re8! (threatening both Rh8 and Kf5) **18. ... c5** (desperation; on 18. ... Re7+ 19. Rxe7 Kxe7 20. Ke5, the win is routine) **19. Rd8+!!** (again chasing the Black king to where it does not want to go) **19. ... Kc6**

On 19. ... Kc7 or 19. ... Ke7 the answer is 20. Rh8 threatening both Rh7 and Rxh6; e.g., 19. ... Kc7 20. Rh8 cxb4 21. Rh7+! Kb6 22. Rxa7 Kxa7 23. axb4 Kb6 24. Kf5 Kb5 25. Kg6 Kxb4 26. Kxh6 a5 27. Kxg5 a4 28. h6, and queens first, preventing the opposing a-pawn from promoting.

20. Rc8+ Kb6 (or 20. ... Kb5 21. Rxc5+ Ka4 22. Ra5+ Kb3 23. Kf5) **21. Rxc5** (the rest is simple) **21. ... Rh7 22. Re5** (22. Kf5 is also strong) **22. ... Kc6 23. Re6+ Kb5 24. Kf5 Rf7+ 25. Rf6,** resigns, for he must lose both kingside pawns.

4. Rook Behind a Passed Pawn, Opposing Rook in Front of It

As we have seen, to have the rook behind the passed pawn is the strongest possible position. It is so strong that with equal material it also confers a marked and at times winning superiority. The enemy rook is then bottled up, while the enemy pawns can be taken care of by White's king.

No. 828 is the type of position where this advantage is sufficient to win.

No. 828, Lasker-Rubinstein, St.Petersburg 1914

White wins

Black's rook is tied up and his passed pawn is securely blockaded. Lasker won as follows: **1. f5 gxf5 2. gxf5 Rf6** (if 2. ... d4 3. f6 Kd5 4. f7 Ke5 5. b4! Kd5 6. Rf4! Ke5 7. Re4+!! Kf5 8. Re1! Rxf7 [the only chance] 9. Rf1+ Ke6 10. Rxf7 Kxf7 11. Kxd4 Ke6 12. Kc5 Kd7 13. Kxb5 Kc7 14. Ka6 and wins) **3. Rf4! b4** (3. ... d4 4. Ke4 Kc4 5. Ke5 Rf8 6. f6 Kd3 7. Rxd4+, etc.) **4. b3 Rf7 5. f6 Kd6 6. Kd4 Ke6 7. Rf2! Kd6** (7. ... Rxf6 8. Rxf6+ Kxf6 9. Kxd5 is also lost) **8. Ra2! Rc7 9. Ra6+ Kd7 10. Rb6,** resigns. After 10. ... Rc3 11. Rxb4 Rf3 12. Ke5 Rf1 13. Rf4 Rxf4 14. Kxf4 Ke6 15. f7 Kxf7 16. Ke5 Ke7 17. Kxd5, the win is routine.

When the enemy's pawn majority is not adequately blocked, the win is more difficult, although it is quite certain in the absence of the Black king. For example, **No. 829** (Kashdan-Steiner, Pasadena 1932): **White king at g2, rook at c2, pawns at c5, g3, h3; Black king at h7, rook at d4, pawns at a5, g7, h6.** White to play wins. **1. c6 Rd8 2. Kf3!** (2. c7? would be inaccurate: 2. ... Rc8 3. Kf3 a4 4. Ke4 a3 5. Kd5 a2, =) **2. ... a4** (or 2. ... Kg6 3. Ke4 Kf6 4. c7 Rc8 5. Kd5 Ke7 6. Kc6, etc.) **3. Ke4 a3 4. Ke5! Rd3** (4. ... Rc8 5. Kd6) **5. c7 a2 6. Rxa2 Rc3**. The rest is simple: **7. Kd6 Rd3+ 8. Kc6 Rc3+ 9. Kb7 Rb3+ 10. Ka8 Rc3 11. Ra7,** resigns. Black must give up his rook in two moves and has no counterplay on the kingside.

5. The More Active Rook

Here we consider everything not covered in the previous four sections.

The more active rook is generally the one in possession of a half-open file.

Ordinarily, such a superiority is not decisive in itself but leads to a win only if the superior side is able to blockade the enemy pawns.

A famous instance of the exploitation of enemy inaccuracies in such an ending is **No. 830**.

No. 830, Marshall-Tarrasch, match 1905

White to play

Before following the game continuation, we will first analyze the position.

Black has a slight superiority because his rook is more aggressively posted and because his center pawn exerts a bind on the White position. Against purely passive play this could be exploited as follows: advance on the queenside, exchange rooks, play the king to a4, fix the pawns on the kingside, and break on the queenside at the appropriate moment. It goes without saying that all this is by no means forced, but it does show that there are some real dangers for White. To avoid them he should play his king to the queenside and try to get his rook into the game. Followed properly, this idea should draw.

The game continued **1. Rf1+ Ke7 2. Rf4?**

This is an unnecessary loss of time 2. Kf2 Ra5 3. Ke2 Rc5 4. Kd2 would have held the position. The exchange of rooks need not be feared, for after 4. ... b5 5. b4 White blocks the queenside and can get counterplay on the kingside.

2. ... Ra5!! (preparing to weaken the queenside pawns) **3. Kf1**

Not 3. e5 Rxe5 4. Rxd4 Re2 5. Rc4 c5 6. b4 Kd6, and White's rook is tied to the defense of the c-pawn, while Black's is powerfully posted on the seventh. Still, White could play 3. Rf1 Rc5 4. Rc1 and Kf2-e2-d2.

3. ... Rc5 4. Rf2 Rb5! 5. b3 Rh5! (to gain time to blockade the Black a-pawn) **6. h3 b5! 7. b4?**

A second mistake, after which the rook must defend the a-pawn. Correct was 7. Ke2, and if then 7. ... Rh6 8. Kd2 e5 9. Kc1 Ra6 10. Kb2 Rf6 11. Re2, and, although Black retains an undeniable advantage, there is no forced win in sight.

7. ... Rh6! 8. Rf4

A better defensive opportunity was 8. e5!; e.g., 8. ... Rh5 9. Re2 b6 10. Ke1 Kd7 11. Re4 c5 12. Kd2 Kc6 13. c4! dxc3+ 14. Kxc3 Kd5 15. a4! bxa4 16. bxc5 bxc5 17. Rxa4 Rxe5 18. Ra7 Rg5 19. g4, and in view of Black's scattered pawns it is doubtful whether he can win. For instance, if 19. ... Ke5 20. Rf7 h6 21. Kc4 Kd6 22. d4 cxd4 23. Kxd4.

8. ... e5 9. Rf5 Re6 10. Ke2 g6 11. Rf1 Ra6 12. Ra1 b6 13. Kd2 Ra4 14. c3

If now 14. Kc1 Ra8! 15. Kb2 Rf8 16. Rg1 Rf2 17. Kb3 Ke6, and the White pieces are all tied up.

14. ... c5 15. cxd4

It's too late to do anything but weep. 15. bxc5 bxc5 16. Kc2 c4! leaves White just as badly pickled as ever; e.g., 17. cxd4 cxd3+ 18. Kxd3 Rxd4+ 19. Ke3 Ra4, and a pawn is lost. After 20. Rb1 Rxa3+ 21. Kf2 Ra5 22. Ke3 Kd6 23. Rd1+ Kc6 24. Rd5 Ra2; the extra pawn will decide, since Black gets passed pawns on both sides and his king is near White's passed e-pawn.

15. ... cxb4 16. dxe5 Ke6 17. d4 bxa3

"Black pawns are faster than White ones" — the Manhattan Chess Club rule applies again. The Black passed pawns are farther advanced and better protected.

18. Kc3 a2! 19. g4

Zugzwang! If 19. Kb3 Rxd4 20. Rxa2 Kxe5 21. Ra7 h5 22. Re7+ Kf4 23. Re6 g5 24. Rxb6 Rxe4 25. Rxb5 Re5 26. Rb8 Kg3 27. Rh8 h4, while if 19. Kd3 Ra3+ 20. Kc2 Rg3! 21. Rxa2 Rxg2+ 22. Kb3 Rxa2 23. Kxa2 g5 24. Kb3 h5 25. Kb4 g4 26. hxg4 hxg4 27. Kxb5 g3 28. d5+ Kxe5 29. Kc6 g2, winning easily in both cases.

19. ... g5 20. Kd3 b4 (20. ... Ra3+ is also strong) **21. Kc4 b3+ 22. Kxb3** (22. Kc3 Rxd4) **22. ... Rxd4 23. Rxa2 Rxe4 24. Ra6 Re3+ 25. Kc2 Rxh3 26. Rxb6+ Kxe5 27. Rb4 Re3 28. Kd2 Re4** and White resigned. After 29. Rb7 Kf4 30. Rxh7 Kxg4 31. Rh1 Kf3! 32. Kd3 Re8 33. Rf1+ Kg2 34. Rf5 g4, we have No. 633.

When the pawns are scattered and exposed, the aggressive rook is sure to bring in some booty, although exploiting the material won may not be so simple.

No. 831, Zukertort-Mason, Vienna 1882

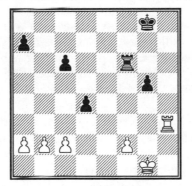

White to play wins

1. Ra3! Rf7 2. Ra5 Rg7 3. Kg2 Kh7 4. Kg3 Kh6 5. Rc5

An inaccuracy. 5. Ra6 Rc7 6. Kg4 Kg6 7. b4, threatening b5, wins a pawn by force. But even after the move played White should win.

5. ... Rg6 6. Kg4 Rf6 7. f3 Rf4+ 8. Kg3 Rf6 9. Rc4 Rd6 10. Kg4 c5!

The best way to give up the pawn. There was no way to save everything; e.g., 10. ... Rf6 11. Rxd4, or 10. ... Kg6 11. Rc5 Rd5 12. Rxc6+.

11. Rxc5 d3 12. cxd3 Rd4+! 13. Kg3 Rxd3 14. Ra5 Rd7 15. Ra6+ Kh5! 16. b4 Rf7 17. b5 Rh7 18. a4 Rd7 19. Re6!

The game continued 19. a5? Rd5 20. Rxa7 Rxb5 21. a6 Ra5, with a theoretical draw. If the pawn advances to the seventh, the king backs up to g7 and the rook holds the pawn at g5.

19. ... Rd4

Or 19. ... Rb7 20. Re4 a6! 21. bxa6 Rb6 22. a5 Rxa6 23. Re5 Rf6 24. Rb5!, and Black is in zugzwang: if 24. ... Rg6 25. Rb6.

20. Re4! Rd7 (20. ... Rd1 21. Re7 a6 22. b6! Rb1 23. Rb7! Kg6 24. Rb8 Kg7 25. Kg4 and wins) **21. Rb4 Rb7 22. a5 Rb8 23. b6 axb6 24. axb6 Rb7 25. Rb5 Kg6 26. Rb4 Kf6 27. Rb1! Kg6 28. Rb2! Kf6 29. Rb5! Rb8** (else the pawn goes with check) **30. b7**, and Black must still lose the g-pawn, after which the rest is routine.

B. Better Pawn Position

In most of the above examples the superior side had better pawns, but the decisive factor was the rook positions. Here we consider cases where the rook positions make little or no difference.

1. Better Passed Pawns

In general, the more advanced and better protected passed pawns are superior. Whenever possible, they should be supported by the king. This rule conforms to other cases noted; e.g., that a strong passed pawn supported by the king counterbalances two or even three connected passed pawns.

With one passed pawn, a pawn on the seventh will normally win against one on the third. Black will have to give up his rook for the advanced pawn and take his chances in the rook vs. pawn ending, which, with his pawn so far back, will not usually offer him much solace. With the pawns differently distributed — e.g., one on the fifth, the other on the sixth — the king positions will be decisive.

If the more advanced pawn is not yet on the seventh in such cases, there may still be time to make use of the more backward one. For example, **No. 832** (Tarrasch-Blümich, Breslau 1925): **White king at h3, rook at a5, pawn at h5; Black king at b2, rook at b4, pawn at a3.** White to play. Dr. Tarrasch resigned here, but it was later demonstrated that he could have drawn with **1. h6! Rb6** (or 1. ... Rb8 2. Kg4 a2 3. Kg5, and both sides lose their rooks) **2. Rh5! Rb8** (if 2. ... a2 3. h7 Rb8 4. Rb5+!! Rxb5 5. h8=Q+, =) **3. h7 Rh8 4. Kg4! a2 5. Rb5+ Kc3 6. Ra5 Kb3 7. Rb5+ Ka4 8. Rb7!**

As these examples show, the results of such endings often depend on tactical finesses and intermezzos. Two studies will further illustrate some of the typical traps that may arise.

In **No. 833** (Dr. Lasker 1890), a pawn on the seventh wins against another on the seventh because of an unfortunate king position. **White king at c8, rook at h7, pawn at c7; Black king at a5, rook at c2, pawn at h2.** White to play wins. **1. Kb7! Rb2+ 2. Ka7 Rc2 3. Rh5+ Ka4** (if the king ever goes to the knight file, Kb7 does not permit a check and the pawn queens) **4. Kb7 Rb2+ 5. Ka6 Rc2 6. Rh4+ Ka3 7. Kb6 Rb2+** (if instead 7. ... Kb3 8. Kb7, or 8. ... Ka2 9. Rxh2 or 8. ... Rc1 9. Rxh2) **8. Ka5 Rc2 9. Rh3+ K any 10. Rxh2** and the pawn queens.

In **No. 834** (Horwitz 1881), a pawn on the sixth wins against one on the fifth by means of mate threats. **White king at g2, rook at c1, pawn at g6; Black king at h4, rook at a3, pawn at f4.** White to play wins. After **1. Rg1!!** Black is lost. **1. ... Ra8** (on 1. ... Rg3+ 2. Kf2 the pawn marches on; or 1. ... Ra2+ or 1. ... f3+, the Black pawn is captured and the White one supported) **2. g7 Kh5 3. Kf3 Rg8 4. Kxf4 Kh6 5. Kf5 Kh7** (or 5. ... Rxg7 6. Rh1+ mate) **6. Kf6 Rf8+** (or 6. ... Ra8 7. g8=Q+ Rxg8 8. Rh1+ mate) **7. gxf8=B/N/R** and mates in a few, but not 7. gxf8=Q? stalemate.

In any normal position, two passed pawns, especially if they are connected, are far superior to one. The outcome, however, may then often be determined by other factors, mainly how far the pawns have advanced.

When both sides have two passed pawns, certain essential distinctions must be made. Other things being equal, *connected passed pawns are better than unconnected ones.* **No. 835** is an elegant demonstration of this fact with a minimum of material.

No. 835, Alekhine-Alexander, Margate 1937

White to play wins

White's superiority lies in the fact that he can both stop the opponent's pawns from advancing and facilitate the advancement of his own pawns. After **1. Ra5!** (preventing 1. ... g5 and ... Kf6) **1. ... Rb6** (loses time, but there is not much to be done; if 1. ... Kg6 2. e5 Rb6 3. Kc4 Kf7 4. d4 g5 5. Kf5 Rg6 6. d5 g4 7. e6+ Kg7 8. Rxa6 g3 9. e7 and wins) **2. d4 Rb3+** (only to go right back, but even if 2. ... Kf6 3. Kf4 Re6 4. e5+ Kf7 5. d5 decides quickly) **3. Kf4 Rb4 4. d5 Rb6 5. Rc5! Rb4** (or 5. ... Rb7 6. e5 Ra7 7. Rc8! a5 8. e6+ Kf6 9. Rf8+ Kg6 10. d6 and wins) **6. Rc7+ Kf8** (if the king goes to the third rank the rook checks and captures the a-pawn) **7. Ra7**, resigns. The conclusion might be **7. ... Ra4 8. d6 Ke8 9. Ke5 g5 10. Kd5 g4 11. e5 g3 12. e6** and queens sooner.

When the pawns are far advanced, the rule that connected passed pawns are stronger than unconnected ones may not hold, for the position may well be such that the unconnected pawns queen sooner.

No. 836 (Mattison-Rubinstein, Carlsbad 1929) is a case in point. **White king at c3, rook at e3, pawns at a4, c4, f3, g4; Black king at d7, rook at f8, pawns at a6, c5, d6, h4.** Black to play wins. **1. ... Re8!! 2. Kd2** (2. Rd3 h3 3. Rd1 Re3+ wins a pawn) **2. ... Rxe3 3. Kxe3 d5!** and White resigned because Black queens first.

No. 837 (P. Benko 1990): **White king at h1, rook at e5, pawns at b6, g2; Black king at f7, rook at f6, pawns at c6, d7.** White to play wins. **1. Kg1 c5 2. Rf5! Rxf5 3. b7** wins. If 1. ... Rf4 2. Rb5! or 1. ... Rh6 2. Re8! wins. If 1. b7 Rf1+ 2. Kh2 Rb1, etc.

Where both sides have connected passed pawns, it is often a good oldfashioned horserace – whoever gets there first wins. In such cases it is essential to cut off the enemy king whenever possible, for a rook alone cannot stop two passed pawns supported by a rook or king.

No. 838, Keres-Alekhine, AVRO 1938

White to play wins

No. 838 is typical. The simplest win is **1. c6 Ke7** (the only chance to get the king to the pawns. If 1. ... Rc2 2. b5 Rb2 3. Rc4, or 2. ... Ke7 3. Rb4! as in the main line) **2. Rd4!**

It is essential to cut off the king. The game continued 2. b5? Rb2! 3. Rc4 Kd8 4. Rc5 g4 5. Kf4 Rb4+ 6. Kg3 Kc7 7. Kh4 Kc8 8. Rh5 Kc7 9. Rh7+ Kc8! 10. Rb7 Rc4!! 11. Kg3 f5 12. Kh4 Rc5!, drawn because the White king has no time to come to the aid of the pawns.

2. ... Rc2 (if instead 2. ... Rb2 3. Kd3 threatening c7, and on 3. ... Rb1 4. Kc2 Ra1 5. c7 Ra8 6. b5, etc., queening soon) **3. b5 Rc5** (the only chance: if 3. ... Rb2 4. c7 Rc2 5. b6, or 3. ... f5 4. Rb4 Kd8 5. b6, as in the main line) **4. Rb4!** (the most precise. On 4. Rd7+ Ke8 5. Rb7 Kd8 6. Kd4 Rc1 7. Kd5, however, White also wins) **4. ... Kd8 5. b6! Kc8 6. b7+ Kb8 7. Rb6 f5** (there is no defense: 7. ... Ra5 8. c7+ Kxc7 9. b8=Q+) **8. Ra6 Kc7 9. Ra8 f4+** (spite check) **10. Ke4 Rb5 11. Rc8+ Kd6 12. b8=Q+** and wins.

With the pawns far advanced, the superior side may sometimes get caught in a mating net, but he can usually get out of it without difficulty.

For example, **No. 839** (Metger-Caro, Berlin 1897): **White king at c6, rook at h7, pawns at e3, g2, h2; Black king at c8, rook at a2, pawns at a3, b2, e4.** Black to play wins. **1. ... Kd8!** (but not 1. ... Kb8? 2. Rh8+ Ka7 3. Rh7+ Ka6 4. Rh8! Ka5 5. Kc5, and Black cannot avoid perpetual mate threat) **2. Kd6 Ke8 3. Ke6 Kf8 4. Kf6 Kg8 5. Rb7** (5. Rg7+ Kh8 6. Rb7 Ra1, and now 7. Rb8+ Kh7 8. Rb7+ is refuted by 8. ... Kh6 9. Rb8 Rf1+ 10. K any, b8=Q, while 7. Kg6 is likewise met by 7. ... b1=Q) **5. ... Ra1** and wins.

Where both sets of pawns are far advanced, tactical considerations, such as who manages to queen first, determine the outcome.

We may take as an example one of the most hair-raising encounters ever recorded.

No. 840, Walbrodt-Zinkl, Leipzig 1894

White to play wins

1. c8=Q f1=Q (if 1. ... g1=Q 2. Qxf8+! Kxf8 3. b8=Q+ Kf7 4. Qa7+ K any 5. Rxg1 fxg1=Q 6. Qxg1 — three queens do a disappearance act in six moves!) **2. Qg4+ Kh8** (or 2. ... Kf7 3. Rd7+ Kf6 4. Rd6+ Ke5 5. Re6+ Kd5 6. Qe4+, and mates in a few) **3. Qh3+ Kg7** (he must not allow the b-pawn to queen with check: 3. ... Kg8 4. Rxf1 gxf1=Q 5. Qxf1 Rxf1 6. b8=Q+. After the text move this combination does not work because Black has ... Rb1+ at the end) **4. Rd7+ Rf7** (king moves lead to mate) **5. Qg4+ Kh7** (or 5. ... Kh6 6. Rd6+ Rf6 7. Rxf6+ Qxf6 8. b8=Q, and Black has only one check) **6. Qe4+ Kg7 7. b8=Q! g1=Q 8. Qbe5+ Qf6 9. Qxf6+ Kxf6 10. Qf4+ and wins!**

Finally, where both sets of pawns are not yet beyond the middle, they must march on as quickly as possible and hope for the best. For example, **No. 841** (Treybal-Reti, Teplitz-Schönau 1922): **White king at h1, rook at h5, pawns at g2, h4; Black king at f8, rook at a2, pawns at a6, b5.** Black to play. Draw. **1. ... b4 2. Rh8+ Kg7 3. Rb8 a5 4. Kh2!** (on 4. g4 Black does best to play 4. ... Rd2 5. Rb5 a4! 6. Rxb4 a3 7. Rb7+ Kf6, etc., wins. If, e.g., 4. ... Rb2? 5. g5 a4 6. h5 a3 7. h6+ Kg6 8. Rb6+ Kh7 9. Rb7+ Kg8 10. g6 Rf2 11. Rb8+ Rf8 12. h7+ and wins) **4. ... Rb2! 5. Ra8 Ra2!**, and both sides are well advised to take the draw by repetition of moves.

Where there are more pawns on the board, it is in general impossible to stop them in any rational manner. The only thing to do is to advance as rapidly as possible.

No. 842, Perlis-Nimzovich, Carlsbad 1911

White to play. Draw

No. 842 illustrates some of the possibilities. The game continued **1. a4 h4 2. a5 Rh1 3. Ra8+ Ke7 4. Rh8**

If 4. a6 h3 5. a7 Ra1 6. Rh8 Rxa7 7. Rxh3, =. Or here 6. Rg8 h2! 7. Rh8, etc. But 4. ... g5? instead of 4. ... h3 is weak: after 5. a7 Ra1 6. Rg8! Rxa7 7. Rxg7 White has two connected passed pawns while Black's pawns are scattered and exposed.

4. ... g5 5. b4 Ra1 6. Ke4?

A fatal loss of time. Correct is 6. c4! threatening 7. b5 Rxa5 8. b6. On 6. c4 the best reply is 6. ... Kd6, when 7. c5+ Kc6 8. Kc4 Rc1+ 9. Kb3 Ra1 10. Kc4 leads to a draw by repetition.

6. ... Kd6 7. c4 (now it is too late because the Black pawns advance with tempo) **7. ... f5+ 8. Kd3** (if instead 8. Kf3 g4+ 9. Kf4 Rf1+ 10. Kg5 g3, or 9. Kf2 h3 10. c5+ Kc6 11. Rc8+ Kb7 12. Rh8 Ra4 and wins) **8. ... g4!** (a pretty combination: if 9. Rxh4 g3 costs White his rook) **9. c5+** (or 9. b5 g3! 10. b6 Kc6 11. Rc8+ Kb7 12. Rc7+ Kb8 13. c5 g2, and Black gets there first) **9. ... Kc6 10. Rc8+** (there is no defense: if 10. Ke2 h3 11. Kf2 Ra4) **10. ... Kd7 11. Rh8 g3 12. b5 g2 13. c6+ Kd6 14. Rd8+ Kc7 15. Rg8 g1=Q,** and White soon resigned.

A similar instance where dilatory tactics prove fatal is **No. 843** (Spielmann-Vidmar, Carlsbad 1907): **White king at f1, rook at c4, pawns at b2, c2, f2, g2, h2; Black king at c8, rook at a2, pawns at a7, b7, c7, d4, h7.** White to play. It is clear that White must first safeguard the pawns on the queenside (for any Black passed pawn threatens to queen with check) and then get his own majority on the kingside going. Instead, he first allows Black two passed pawns and then jockeys around trying to stop them with his king and rook and of course loses.

1. b4? (1. b3 b5 2. Rc5 b4 3. Ke2 gives Black at most one passed pawn) **1. ... b5 2. Rxd4** (weak too is: 2. Rc5 Rb2 3. Rxb5 Rxc2 4. Ke1, while none too good, is far better than the line chosen) **2. ... Rxc2 3. Rd5??** (a third mistake, after which no more are necessary. 3. f4! c5 4. bxc5 a5? 5. f5! is still good enough to draw at least) **3. ... a6 4. Rd4?** (4. f4 is still better) **4. ... c5 5. bxc5 a5 6. Ke1 a4 7. Rd2 Rc1+ 8. Rd1 Rxc5 9. Kd2 Kb7.** And now the advance comes too late.

The rest is simple **10. Rc1 Rf5 11. f3 Kb6 12. Kc3 Rc5+ 13. Kd2 Rh5 14. h3 b4 15. Kc2 Kb5 16. Re1 Rd5 17. f4 b3+ 18. Kb1 a3 19. g4 Rd4 20. Rf1 Kb4,** resigns. Against the threat of 21. ... a2+ 22. Ka1 Ka3 there is no defense.

On the basis of the above discussion we may set up four rules:

1. Passed pawns must be advanced as quickly as possible. What Nimzovich called their "lust to expand" must be satisfied.

2. Other things being equal, the more advanced pawns win.

3. Two or more connected passed pawns cannot be stopped by a king alone or by a rook alone; *both* pieces are required to stem the tide.

4. It is advisable to support passed pawns with the king rather than with the rook.

2. Exposed Pawns

This is a type of weakness that first becomes important in rook endings, largely because minor pieces, especially when working alone, cannot attack such pawns easily. The main disadvantage of these weak pawns is not so much that material is lost sooner or later – sometimes this happens only after long and complicated maneuvering – *but that defending them limits the mobility of the defending pieces.*

The simplest case is where a number of pawns are exposed and fall like ripe fruit. The only chance in such endings is a counterattack, but when several pawns behind such an attack should fail. **No. 844** is typical.

No. 844, Alekhine-Bogolyubov, 8th match game 1934

White to play. Black wins

White's position is so badly crippled that he must lose a pawn no matter what he does. For instance, 1. Kg4 Ra2 2. Rf1 Rc2, or 2. f3 Rg2+ 3. Kh3 Rd2, or, finally, 2. f4 Rg2+ 3. Kf3 Rh2.

But this is not the worst: after the first pawn is gone White's remaining pawns are still so scattered and feeble that another will probably fall before long. Accordingly, Alekhine chooses a line that may give him a passed pawn and some counterplay.

The main variation up to move 11 is the game continuation: **1. Re1! Ra4?**

This is a good chess move but a psychological blunder. The simplest is 1. ... Re7, which wins the pawn and gives White no compensation at all. For if then 2. Rxe7 Kxe7 3. Kf3 Kf6 4. Ke4 g4! 5. Kf4 (or 5. c4 Kg5 6. f6! Kxh5 7. Kf5 Kh4 8. Kf4 Kh3 9. Kf5 g3 10. fxg3 Kxg3 11. Ke4 Kg4, and the win is routine) 5. ... c4 6. Kxg4 Ke5 7. f4+ Kxd5 8. Kf3 f6 9. Ke3 Kc5 10. Ke4 d5+ 11. Ke3 d4+ 12. cxd4+ Kd5, and it's all over. Nor can White hope for anything by avoiding the exchange of rooks; e.g., 2. Ra1 Re5 3. c4 Rxf5 4. Ra6 Ke5 5. Ra8 Kd4 6. Rh8 Rf6, etc. But from a purely objective point of view the move chosen is just as good, since it should also win.

2. Re8 Rc4 (*embarras de richesse:* 2. ... Ra3, 2. ... Rh4, and 2. ... Kxf5 are all just as strong) **3. Rh8 Rxc3+ 4. Kg2** (or 4. Kg4 Rc4+ 5. Kg3 Rh4 6. Rxh6+ Ke5, etc.) **4. ... Kxf5 5. Rxh6 f6 6. Rh7 Ke5 7. h6 Ra3 8. Re7+ Kxd5 9. h7 Ra8 10. Kg3 f5 11. f4**

With his customary ingenuity Alekhine has indeed secured some counterthreats, but with accurate play Bogolyubov could still have won by the odd tempo.

11. ... g4!

The game continued 11. ... gxf4+?? 12. Kxf4 c4 13. Kxf5 c3, with a draw: 14. Rd7 Rc8 15. Rc7 Rf8+ 16. Kg6 Kd4 17. Kg7 Rb8 18. h8=Q, etc.

12. Kh4 (the best chance) **12. ... c4 13. Kg5 c3 14. Kxf5 g3 15. Kg6**

If 15. Kg4 g2 16. Re1 Kd4 17. Kg3 c2 18. Kxg2 Kd3 19. Kg3 Kd2. At any intermediate point here, ... Rh8 is also strong.

15. ... g2 16. Re1 c2 17. Kg7 Kd4 18. h8=Q Rxh8 19. Kxh8 Kd3 20. Rg1! Ke3! 21. f5 (with two knight-pawns White can continue playing hide-and-go-seek: see No. 602) **21. ... Kf2 22. f6 Kxg1 23. f7 c1=Q 24. f8=Q Qc3+ 25. Kg8 Qg3+ 26. Kh7 Kh2** and queens, since White has no good checks and cannot pin the pawn.

Endings in which the counterplay is a serious danger and does in fact assure the draw occur often. They almost always involve (as in the last example) the use of strong passed or advanced pawns. Two examples:

No. 845 (Tartakower-Bogolyubov, New York, 1924): **White king at c5, rook at b4, pawns at a3, c3, d5, g2, h3; Black king at d7, rook at b8, pawns at a7, b5, f6, g3, h4.** Black to play. Obviously, Black can't keep everything; in fact, he seems to be losing a pawn without compensation. But by making use of his strong pawn he can secure a draw.

The game continued **1. ... f5!!**

So that if now 2. Rxb5? Rxb5+ 3. Kxb5 f4 and Black wins, while if 2. Rxh4 Rc8+ 3. Kxb5 (3. Kb4? Rc4+! and again Black wins) 3. ... Rxc3 4. Rf4 Rxa3 5. Rxf5 Ra2, =.

2. a4 a6 3. Kd4 Re8! (the threat was 4. c4) **4. Kd3** (not 4. axb5? Re4+ 5. Kd3 Rxb4 6. cxb4 axb5 and Black wins) **4. ... bxa4 5. Rxa4 Re1 6. Rxa6**

Now 6. ... Rd1+ draws with no difficulty, for if 7. Kc4 Rd2 8. Kc5? Rxg2 9. Ra7+ Ke8 10. Kd6 Re2 11. c4 g2 12. Rg7 f4 13. c5 f3 14. c6 Rc2 15. Ke6 Kf8 16. Rg4 f2, and Black wins, while if 7. Ke3 Rxd5 8. Rh6 Re5+ 9. Kf3 Re4, with an even game.

Instead Bogolyubov played 6. ... Rg1? and lost after 7. Ra2! Kd6 8. c4 Kc5 9. Re2+ Kd6 10. Rc2 Kc5 11. Rd2 Rf1 12. Ke2 Rg1 13. Ke3 Kd6 14. c5+! Kxc5 15. d6 Re1+ 16. Kf4 Re8 17. d7 Rd8 18. Kxf5, resigns.

No. 846 (Thomas-Alekhine, Hastings 1922): **White king at h4, rook at e4, pawns at b3, d5, f4, h3; Black king at h7, rook at g6, pawns at c7, d6, g7, h6.** Black to play. Alekhine secured two connected passed pawns against Thomas's unconnected passed pawns, but Thomas could still have held the draw. The game went **1. ... Rg1 2. Rc4 Kg6 3. Rxc7 Kf5 4. Rd7 Kxf4 5. Rxd6 Rg3! 6. Rd8 g5+ 7. Kh5 Rxh3+ 8. Kg6 Ke5 9. d6 Ke6 10. b4 g4;** and here **11. b5!** would have drawn, for if **11. ... g3 12. Kh7!! g2 13. Rg8** and **13. ... Kxd6** is forced, since **13. ... Rh2? 14. b6 Kxd6 15. b7** loses. Instead, White played **11. d7?** and lost after **11. ... g3 12. Rg8 Kxd7 13. Kf5 h5** (see No. 708).

When the pawns are not just hanging in the air, converting the positional advantage into a win is far more complicated. In general, it involves first tying up the enemy pieces and then advancing on the side with the majority. Once more we have a classic to guide us:

No. 847, Schlechter-Rubinstein, San Sebastian 1912

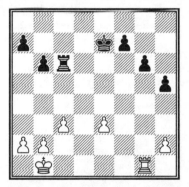

Black to play wins

Now, offhand you would not suppose that the position of **No. 847** is lost for White. The Black majority on the kingside is matched by White's on the queenside, and the two isolated pawns are easily defended. Yet it is precisely this last point that is White's problem: he has to *defend* his pawns, while Black can *attack* them. If nothing else, this assures Black of the initiative, which in chess is of central importance. Accordingly, Rubinstein's plan here may be summed up in four steps.

1. Attacking the kingside pawns to immobilize the White rook.

2. Centralizing the king.

3. Advancing his pawns on the kingside.

4. If the White king goes to the kingside, Black will capture material; if the White king stays on the queenside and assists his own potential passed pawn, Black will create a passed pawn and force White to sacrifice his rook for it.

The actual moves were: **1. ... Re6! 2. Re1** (2. Rg3 Rf6 3. Rg2 Rf3 4. Re2 loses a tempo) **2. ... Rf6 3. Re2** (the threat was 3. ... Rf2).

The first step is complete, since the White rook dare not leave either the e-pawn or the h-pawn to its fate.

3. ... Ke6 4. Kc2 Ke5 5. c4

At this early stage Schlechter is already desperate. And not without reason, for the passive line 5. Kd2 Ke4 6. Ke1 Rf3 is hopeless; e.g., 7. Kd2 g5 8. c4 g4 9. b4 h4 10. c5 bxc5 11. bxc5 Rf5, and after the loss of the pawn White is just as badly off as ever.

5. ... Ke4 6. b4 g5 7. Kc3 g4 8. c5 h4 9. Rg2 Rg6

Black will soon have a strong passed pawn with his rook behind it. The third step is complete, and now the second part of the fourth step will be carried out. The rest is simple: **10. Kc4** (10. c6 Rxc6+) **10. ... g3 11. hxg3 hxg3 12. Kb5 bxc5 13. bxc5 Kf3 14. Rg1 a6+!!**, White resigned. After **15. Kc4 g2 16. Kd5 Kf2 17. Rxg2+ Rxg2 18. c6 Kxe3,** the win is child's play.

Even when the defending side has a passed pawn, if his remaining pawns are weak he is in a bad way.

No. 848, Spielmann-Rubinstein, St. Petersburg 1909

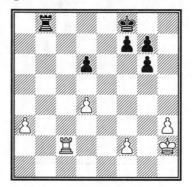

Black to play

No. 848 is a striking example. According to all the ordinary rules, White should have the better of it: he has an outside passed pawn and he can put his rook behind it, and his two pawns on the kingside hold Black's three. But the weakness of all his pawns nullifies everything else and swings the pendulum the other way.

The procedure is similar to that in the previous example: first, tie up the White pieces, then centralize. After that it will be found that White's position is so full of holes that he must lose a pawn.

The game continued. **1. ... Ra8! 2. Rc3**

The "natural" move, 2. Ra2, placing the rook behind the passed pawn, was rejected by Spielmann because it would have immobilized that piece after 2. ... Ra4!. Even so, the Black rook would itself then be none too free to move about, so 2. Ra2 was preferable on theoretical grounds. And analysis indicates that it might well have saved the game, for Black can then capture material only at the cost of allowing the White a-pawn to advance and become dangerous.

For example, 2. Ra2 Ra4 3. Kg3 Ke7 4. Kf3 Ke6 5. Ke4 d5+ 6. Kd3 Kd6 7. Kc3 Kc6 8. Kd3 Kb5 9. Kc3! Rc4+ 10. Kd3 Ka4 11. Rb2 Rc7 12. Rb6 Kxa3 13. Rd6 Kb3 14. Rxd5 Rc3+ 15. Ke2 Rxh3 16. Rd7, =. Or (instead of 5. ... d5+) 5. ... g5 6. Ra1 f6 7. Ra2 f5+ 8. Kd3 Kd5 9. Kc3 Rc4+ 10. Kb3! Rxd4 11. a4 Rd3+ 12. Kb4 Kc6 13. a5 Kb7 14. Re2 Rxh3 15. Re7+ Ka6 16. Rxg7 Rh4+ 17. Kc3 Kxa5 18. Rxg5 Rf4 19. Rg6 d5 20. Rd6, =. From here on the game is a forced win.

2. ... Ra4! 3. Rd3 (first step completed) **3. ... Ke7 4. Kg3 Ke6 5. Kf3 Kd5 6. Ke2!**

Black dare not go into a king and pawn ending with 6. ... Rxd4 because of White's outside passed pawn. That Rubinstein can still evolve a winning scheme borders on the miraculous. The key to his following maneuvers is to get to a position where White will be in zugzwang and have to move his rook, abandoning the defense of one of his pawns.

6. ... g5 (solidifying his kingside position) **7. Rb3** (a tactical intermezzo that does not affect the outcome) **7. ... f6!**

Avoiding the traps and setting one of his own! If 7. ... Rxd4 8. Rd3, and White may win, while if 7. ... Kxd4 8. Rb7, with a fairly certain draw.

8. Ke3 (if now 8. Rb7? Rxa3 9. Rxg7 Rxh3, and the d-pawn falls, so Black will be two pawns up) **8. ... Kc4 9. Rd3 d5** (now the rook has no good moves) **10. Kd2 Ra8! 11. Kc2** (on 11. Ke3 Rb8! 12. Kd2 Rb2+ 13. Ke3 Ra2 wins a pawn) **11. ... Ra7 12. Kd2 Re7!**

White is finally compelled to move his rook away. If 13. Kc2 Re2+ 14. Rd2 Rxd2+ 15. Kxd2 Kb3! 16. Ke3 Kxa3 17. Kf3 Kb3 18. Kg4 Kc4, etc., while if 13. a4 Ra7 14. Ra3 Kxd4. Or, finally, 13. Re3 Rb7!! 14. Rd3 Rb2+ 15. Ke3 Ra2.

13. Rc3+ Kxd4 14. a4 Ra7 15. Ra3 Ra5! (blockading at an early moment to prevent the pawn from becoming dangerous) **16. Ra1 Kc4 17. Ke3**

White should try 17. Rc1+ Kb4 18. Rb1+ Kxa4 19. Kd3, or 18. ... Ka3 19. Rb7 Rxa4 20. Rxg7 Rf4 21. Ke2 Kb3 22. Rc7! to lock out the Black king.

17. ... d4+ 18. Kd2 Rf5!

The beginning of the end. First, the king will replace the rook as a blockader. Once the rook is free, it will establish a decisive superiority on the kingside.

19. Ke1

To give up the f-pawn would be immediately fatal: 19. a5 Rxf2+ 20. Ke1 Rb2 21. a6 Rb8 22. a7 Ra8 23. Kd2 Kc5 24. Kd3 Kb6 25. Kxd4 Rxa7, and wins on the kingside.

19. ... Kb4 20. Ke2 Ka5! (20. ... Ra5? 21. Kd3 Rxa4 22. Rxa4+! Kxa4 23. Kxd4) **21. Ra3 Rf4 22. Ra2**

Losing a second pawn. But if 22. Kf1 Rh4 23. Kg2 Kb4 24. Ra1 d3 25. a5 d2 26. a6 Rh8 27. a7 Ra8 28. Kf3 Rxa7, and it's all over.

22. ... Rh4 23. Kd3 Rxh3+ 24. Kxd4 Rh4+ 25. Kd3 Rxa4 26. Re2

The rook cannot reach the seventh: if 26. Rc2 Rf4 27. Ke3 Kb6 28. Rc8 Ra4!, etc., transposing back into the game.

26. ... Rf4 (the rest is not difficult; Black needs only to exchange the g-pawn for the f-pawn) **27. Ke3 Kb6 28. Rc2 Kb7 29. Rc1 Ra4** (preparing to get his king over to the pawns) **30. Rh1 Kc6 31. Rh7 Ra7 32. Ke4 Kd6 33. Kf5**

Loses quickly, but on other moves the rook gets back and the steady pawn advance decides; e.g., 33. Kf3 Ke6 34. Ke4 Ra4+ 35. Kf3 g6 36. Rh6 Kf5 37. Rh1 g4+ 38. Kg3 Kg5 39. Rb1 f5 40. Rb5 Ra3+ 41. Kg2 Kh4 42. Rb4 Ra2 43. Rf4 Rb2 44. Ra4 g5 45. Ra8 g3, etc.

33. ... g6+! 34. Kxg6 Rxh7 35. Kxh7 Ke5 36. Kg6 g4, White resigned (for the pawn ending see No. 69).

If there were no weaknesses in Black's position in the above example, the win would have been much simpler, since he could afford to exchange rooks.

The speed with which material is lost in such cases is seen in the similar ending **No. 849** (Marshall-Chigorin, Barmen 1905): **White king at e3, rook at b2, pawns at a3, d4, f4, g3, h2; Black king at f7, rook at c4, pawns at a6, b5, f6, g7, h7.** Black to play.

After **1. ... Ke6!** (if 1. ... Rc3+ 2. Ke4, White's d-pawn might become dangerous) **2. Rb3 Kd5 3. Rd3 f5!** (White is already in zugzwang, for if 4. Rd2 Rc3+ 5. Rd3 Rxd3+ 6. Kxd3 a5, and the outside passed pawn is decisive.

Marshall tried **4. h3 h5 5. Ke2**, but **5. ... Rxd4 6. Rc3 Re4+ 7. Kd2 h4** left him without any real hope.

The remaining moves were 8. Rc7 hxg3 9. Rxg7 Rxf4 10. Rxg3 Ke5 11. Ke2 Rc4 12. Rg6 Ra4 13. Rg3 f4 14. Rb3 Rc4 15. Kd1 (Note the uselessness of the White h-pawn) 15. ... Ke4 16. h4 f3 17. Ke1 Kf4 18. h5 Rc1+ 19. Kf2 Rc2+ 20. Ke1 Kg3 21. h6 Re2+ 22. Kd1 Rh2 23. a4 b4 (23. ... bxa4 is also good enough) 24. Rxb4 Rh1+ 25. Kd2 f2, and White soon resigned.

No. 850 (Flohr-Petrov, Semmering-Baden 1937) illustrates a different kind of winning possibility: attacking a pawn mass with the king. Examining the position, we find that Black has two isolated and exposed pawns (a6, d5) and one exposed at h5, which weakens the kingside. If we place the Black rook at a7 or d6, the Black king at f8, we have substantially the same type of ending as in the last two examples.

No. 850, Flohr-Petrov, Semmering-Baden 1937

Black to play

But here Black's king is supporting his passed pawn and cannot come to the defense of the kingside. The winning plan that therefore suggests itself for White is to hold the a-pawn with the rook and create a passed pawn on the kingside. It is also clear that Black's only chance lies in advancing his a-pawn.

The game continued **1. ... Rb5**

The alternative 1. ... Kb6 seems to offer better drawing chances, but appearances are deceiving: 2. Rxd5 a5 3. Rd6+! Kb7! 4. Rd7+ Kb6 5. Rxf7 a4 6. d5 a3 7. Rf4 Ka5 (or 7. ... a2 8. Ra4 Rb5 9. Rxa2 Rxd5 10. Ra8 and wins) 8. Rf8 Rb6 (or 8. ... a2 9. Ra8+ Kb5 10. e4 Kb4 11. Kf4! Kb3 12. d6 Rd2 13. e5 and wins) 9. Ra8+ Ra6 10. Rc8 a2 11. Rc1 Kb4 12. Ra1 Kb3 13. e4 Kb2 14. Rxa2+ Rxa2 15. e5!!, and the pawns win: 15. ... Kc3 16. e6 Ra8 17. e7 Kd4 18. d6, etc. Or 15. ... Ra1 16. Ke4 Re1+ 17. Kf5 Kc3 18. d6 Kc4 19. d7 Rd1 20. e6, etc.

2. Ra2! (guarding the second rank and thereby freeing his king) **2. ... g6?**

This passive continuation is, however, quite inferior. Since the best that White can do at the moment is to capture the h-pawn, Black should play 2. ... a5!. and if then 3. Kf4 Kb6, with two possibilities:

a) 4. Kg5? Rb1 5. Kxh5 Kb5 6. Kg4 a4 7. Kf5 Kb4 8. Ke5 Kb3 9. Rxa4 Kxa4 10. Kxd5 Kb5 11. e4 Rb3! 12. e5 Rf3, and Black should win.

b) 4. Ke5 Kc6! (not 4. ... Rb4? 5. Kxd5 Kb5 6. Ke5+ a4 7. d5 Rb1 8. Rd2 and White's passed pawn is too strong) 5. Rc2+ Kd7! 6. Ra2 Kc6 7. f3 Kd7!, and White cannot do anything, for if 8. Rc2 a4 9. Ra2 Ra5, the Black h-pawn is too dangerous, or if 8. g4 hxg4 9. fxg4 Ke7 10. h5 f6+ 11. Kf5 Kf7 12. Rc2? Rb7 with at least a draw.

3. Kf4! f6

He must stop the entry of the king. Now White's threats are so immediate that Black has no time to nurse his pawn along.

4. g4! hxg4 5. Kxg4 (threatening 5. h5) **5. ... Rb1** (so that if 6. h5 Rg1+) **6. Ra5!** (driving the rook back again) **6. ... Rb5?**

After this mistake the game is lost 6. ... Kb6! is necessary, for if then 7. Rxd5 a5 8. Rd6+ Kb7 9. Rxf6 a4, White's rook cannot get back (10. d5 a3) and he can at best draw after giving up the rook for the pawn. Consequently, after 9. ... a4 White must take the draw by 10. Rf7+ Kb6 11. Rf6+ Kb7 (but not 11. ... Ka7? 12. Rc6 a3 13. Rc3 and wins) 12. Rf7+, etc. Nor can White take only one pawn and retain any real winning chances: 6. ... Kb6 7. Rxd5 a5 8. Rc5 a4 9. Rc2 Ka5 10. Rc8 Rd1 11. h5 Rg1+ 12. Kf4 gxh5 13. d5 a3 14. Kf5 Kb4 15. d6 Rd1 and Black cannot lose.

7. Ra1!! (the first rank must be controlled now rather than the second) **7. ... Rb2** (or 7. ... a5 8. h5 gxh5+ 9. Kxh5 Rb2 10. f4 Kb6 11. Kg6 and White wins) **8. Kf3 Rb6**

It's too late. If 8. ... Kb6 9. Rg1 a5 10. Rxg6 a4 11. Rg1! a3 12. Ra1 a2 13. h5, and Black's rook must go after the h-pawn, giving up his own a-pawn, when the resulting ending with rook and three pawns vs. rook and two pawns is lost because of the weakness of the Black pawns. If 10. ... Rb1 instead of 10. ... a4, then 11. Rg8 Kb7 12. Kf4 a4 13. f3 a3 14. Rg2 Rb2 15. Rg1 a2 16. Ra1 Kb6 17. h5 and wins as above.

9. Rg1! f5 (9. ... a5 10. Rxg6 a4 11. Rg1 a3 12. Ra1, etc., as in the last note) **10. Kf4 Re6 11. Rb1+** (11. h5 at once is also strong) **11. ... Ka7 12. h5! Re4+** (or 12. ... gxh5 13. Kxf5 Rh6 14. Kg5 Rh8 15. f4, and the advance of the f-pawn is decisive, as in the game) **13. Kg5 Rg4+**

The alternative is 13. ... gxh5 14. Kxf5 a5, but then 15. Rb5 Ka6 16. Rxd5 Rg4 17. Rd6+ Kb7 18. Rh6 a4 19. Rxh5 Rg2 20. f4 a3 21. Rh1 a2 22. e4, wins without any trouble.

14. Kf6 gxh5 15. Kxf5 Rg2 16. Ke5 Rg5+ (after 16. ... Rxf2 17. Kxd5 h4 18. e4, the two connected pawns win easily; e.g., 18. ... h3 19. e5 h2 20. e6 a5 21. e7 Re2 22. Kd6 a4 23. d5 a3 24. Kd7 a2 25. Ra1, etc.) **17. Ke6 h4 18. Rh1!** (so that if 18. ... a5 19. Rxh4 a4 20. Rh2! a3 21. f4, and it's all over) **18. ... Rh5 19. f4 Kb6 20. f5 Kc7 21. f6 Kd8** (a futile attempt to get back in time) **22. Rf1 Rh6** (there is nothing to be done. On 22. ... Ke8 23. Rb1 Kd8 24. Rb8+ Kc7 25. f7 is murder) **23. Kf7**, resigns. There is no stopping the f-pawn.

Unless they are passed, pawns that are too far advanced are weak. Even if only one pawn has stuck its neck out, that may be enough to provide the opponent with a tangible advantage. A stratagem often employed in such cases is the sacrifice of a pawn to disrupt the pawn position completely.

No. 851, Eliskases-Keres, Semmering-Baden 1937

White to play

No. 851 is typical. White has a slight advantage because of the Black pawn at b5. Nothing can be done about it at the moment because it is adequately defended. The first step, therefore, is to remove its support; i.e., exchange pawns. This is done by **1. a4! Rb7**

1. ... bxa4 2. Ra1 Ra7 3. Rxa4 a5 4. Kc4 Rc7+ 5. Kb3! Ra7 6. Rc4 is much worse for Black, since White can blockade the a-pawn with his king while Black's rook is occupying a useless post.

2. d5! (preparing to bring the king in) **2. ... e6 3. dxe6 fxe6 4. axb5 axb5**

Now that Black's pawns have been scattered, the next step is to get the king or rook in to attack them.

5. Ke4! (threatening 5. c4, which would not be good at the moment because of the check at d2) **5. ... Kf7?**

After this Black is lost. The best defense is 5. ... Rc7! 6. Rxb5 Rxc3 7. Rb7, when 7. ... Rc5!, cutting the White king off, draws without much trouble. If here 6. Kd4 Rc4+ 7. Ke5 Rxc3 8. Rxb5 Rc7! 9. Kxe6 Kf8 10. Kf6 Rf7+ is an easier theoretical draw.

6. c4 b4 7. Kd4 Ke7

There is not much he can do: on 7. ... Rd7+ 8. Kc5 Rd2 9. Kb6 Rxf2 10. c5 Rxh2 11. c6, he loses his rook and the White king gets back in time, especially since the Black pawns are so scattered.

8. c5 g5 9. Kc4 Kd8 10. Rxb4 Rf7 11. Rb2, and the rest is not difficult (No. 744).

When there is one exposed pawn and it is not adequately defended by the king, it may well cost the game.

No. 852, Capablanca-Reti, New York 1924

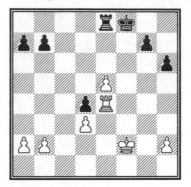

Black to play. White wins

After **1. ... Kf7 2. Kf3 Rd8** (the threat was 3. Kf4 or 3. Re1; if 2. ... g5 3. Re2 Ke6 4. Ke4 Rf8 5. Kxd4 Rf4+ 6. Kc5, White wins with ease) **3. Rg4 g5 4. h4** (he is in no hurry) **4. ... Kg6 5. hxg5 hxg5 6. Ke4,** the win is straightforward: **6. ... Kh5 7. Rg1 Kh4 8. e6 g4 9. e7 Re8** (Reti resigned here) **10. Kf5! Rxe7** (or 10. ... g3 11. Rh1+ mate) **11. Rxg4+ Kh5 12. Rxd4 Re2 13. Rb4!** (not 13. Rd7 Rf2+) **13. ... b6 14. d4 Kh6 15. d5 Kg7 16. Re4! Rxb2 17. Ke6 Rxa2 18. d6 a5 19. d7 Rd2 20. Ke7,** and wins easily because the Black pawns are still far back.

Usually some tactical finesses must be countered before the pawn can be won in similar positions. For instance, **No. 853** (Chekhover-Budo, Tiflis 1937): **White king at f3, rook at e2, pawns at a2, b2, d5, f2, g3, h2; Black king at d7, rook at b5, pawns at a7, c5, d6, f7, g7, h7.** Black to play wins.

The pawn at d5 is exposed and weak but Black must chop down a lot of wood before he can get to it. Black's play is exemplary: **1. ... Rb4 2. Rd2 Ke7 3. Ke3 Kf6 4. f4** (to prevent ... Ke5. Now Black must get rid of this pawn) **4. ... Kf5 5. Kf3 h5 6. b3**

If 6. h3 g5! 7. g4+ hxg4+ 8. hxg4+ Kf6, and the f-pawn must be exchanged, when Black wins a pawn. For instance, 9. f5 Rf4+ 10. Kg3 Ke5 11. b3 Rd4 12. Re2+ Kf6!, or 9. fxg5+ Kxg5 10. Re2 Rf4+!, etc.

6. ... a5 7. Rd3 (if 7. Re2 a4 8. bxa4 Rxa4 9. Re7 Ra3+, etc.) **7. ... a4 8. bxa4 Rxa4 9. a3 g5! 10. fxg5 Kxg5.** White now has two badly exposed pawns and Black has a strong passed pawn to boot. The rest is not difficult: **11. Ke2 Kf5 12. Kd2** (or 12. Re3 Re4 13. h4 Rd4, or 13. Rxe4 Kxe4 14. h4 f5) **12. ... Ke4 13. Kc2 c4 14. Rc3 Kxd5 15. Rf3 Kc6 16. Kb2 Ra7 17. Rf5 d5 18. Rxh5 Rb7+ 19. Kc2 Rb3 20. Rh6+ Kc5 21. Ra6 Rf3 22. h4 Rxg3 23. h5 Rh3 24. h6 f6! 25. Rxf6 Rxa3,** with a standard ending: No. 707.

Attention should be paid to the ending that results after the weak pawn has been captured. In particular, critical pawn endings must be calculated carefully.

For example, **No. 854** (Kostic-Grünfeld, Teplitz-Schönau 1922): **White king at f3, rook at e2, pawns at a2, e6, g3, h2; Black king at f5, rook at a5, pawns at a7, b6, e7, h5.** Black to play wins.

The simplest line is 1. ... Re5 2. Rxe5+ Kxe5 3. g4 hxg4+ 4. Kxg4 b5! 5. Kg5 a5 6. h4 Kxe6 (threatening to get back) 7. Kg6 b4 8. h5 a4 9. h6 b3 10. axb3 axb3 11. h7 b2 12. h8=Q b1=Q+ 13. Kg5 Qf5+ 14. Kh4 Qf6+, and after the exchange of queens Black has the opposition.

Grünfeld, in time pressure, did not have time to examine the niceties of this ending, and instead played 1. ... Ra3+ 2. Kg2 Ra5, when White tried 3. Kh3. Now 3. ... Re5? would be a blunder because after 4. Rxe5+ Kxe5 5. Kh4!, Black can at best draw: the main line is 5. ... Kxe6 6. Kxh5 Kf7 7. Kh6 Kg8 8. a4! a6 9. Kg6 b5 10. axb5 axb5 11. Kf5! Kf7! 12. h4 b4 13. Ke4 e5 14. Kd3! Ke6 15. Kc4 Kf5! 16. Kxb4 Kg4 17. Kc3 Kf3 18. Kd2 Kf2 19. Kd3 Kf3, =. Instead, 3. ... Ra4! put White in zugzwang, for if 4. Kg2 Re4 wins, while the rook is stalemated. For the ending after 4. Rb2 Kxe6 5. Rb5 Rxa2 6. Rxh5 Rb2, see No. 768.

An isolated pawn in the center is a handicap, but, as in similar endings with minor pieces, if there is no other weakness it should not lose.

This is seen in **No. 855** (Rubinstein-Cohn, Carlsbad 1907), where, despite a bad pawn on the queenside, Black can draw. **White king at e3, rook at d3, pawns at a5, b2, c3, g2, h2; Black king at e7, rook at c5, pawns at a6, b5, e5, g7, h7. Black to play.**

After **1. ... Rc4 2. b3**, now **2. ... Rc5!** should have been played, with two main variations:

a) 3. Ke4 b4! 4. cxb4 (4. c4 Rxa5 5. Rd5? Rxd5 6. Kxd5 a5 7. Kxe5 a4 8. bxa4 b3 and wins) 4. ... Rb5 5. Rc3 Rxb4+ 6. Kxe5 Rb5+ 7. Ke4 Rxa5 8. Rc7+ Kf6 9. Ra7 Ra3, =.

b) 3. b4 Rc4 4. Kd2 Rf4 5. Rd5? Rf2+ 6. Ke3 Rxg2 7. Rxe5+ Kd6 8. Rf5 Rxh2, with at least a draw.

But the game continued **2. ... Rc6**, and when Rubinstein won as follows: **3. Ke4 Ke6 4. Rh3 h6 5. Rg3 Kf6** (5. ... g5 6. Rh3) **6. Kd5 Re6 7. Rf3+ Ke7 8. g3 g6 9. Re3 Kf6 10. c4**, and White's passed pawn is far superior to Black's. The remaining moves were **10. ... bxc4 11. bxc4 Re8 12. Rf3+ Kg5 13. c5 e4 14. h4+ Kg4 15. Rf4+ Kxg3 16. Rxe4 Ra8 17. c6 g5 18. hxg5 hxg5 19. c7 Kf3 20. Re1** and Black resigned. White wins the Black rook for his c-pawn, gives up his rook for the g-pawn, captures the Black a-pawn, and then queens the last pawn.

3. Doubled Pawns

In pawn endings, doubled pawns that are qualitatively inferior — i.e., held in check by a smaller number — are a serious handicap, but even when they do not produce a passed pawn their lack of mobility is often fatal. With pieces on the board, especially rooks, any deviation from a normal pawn position is a disadvantage because it offers the enemy new targets. Besides, there is always the possibility of reducing to a pawn ending where less mobile doubled pawns are bad.

No. 856, Alekhine-Spielmann, New York 1927

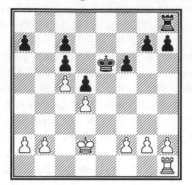

White to play wins

Black loses because he cannot afford to exchange rooks. The main line is the game continuation.

After **1. Re1+, Kd7** is necessary because the queenside pawns must be defended by the king.

On 1. ... Kf7 White has a forced win with 2. Kc3! Rb8 3. Re3 Rb7 4. a3 Rb8 5. Kc2 Re8 (else 6. Rb3 forces the exchange under less favorable circumstances) 6. Rxe8 Kxe8 7. Kb3 Kd7 8. Ka4 Kc8 9. Ka5 Kb7 10. f3! g6 11. g3 h6 12. h3 h5 13. f4! f5 14. h4 a6 (or 14. ... Kb8 15. Ka6 Ka8 16. b4 Kb8 17. b5 Ka8 [or 17. ... cxb5 18. Kxb5 Kb7 19. c6+ and wins] 18. a4 Kb8 19. a5 Ka8 20. b6 axb6 [20. ... Kb8 21. b7! g5 22. hxg5 h4 23. g6 and queens with mate] 21. axb6 cxb6 22. Kxb6 and wins) 15. b3 Ka7 16. b4 Kb7 17. a4 Ka7 18. b5 axb5 19. axb5 cxb5 20. Kxb5 Kb7 21. c6+ followed by Kc5 with a simple win.

2. Kc3 (2. Re3 at once is also strong) **2. ... Rb8 3. Re3 Rf8 4. Rg3 Rf7 5. Rh3 h6 6. Kd2!**

Now the double threat of Ra3 and R-e3-e8 can be parried only by playing the king to b7 and the rook to the king file.

6. ... Re7

Or 6. ... Kc8 7. Ra3 Kb7 8. Re3 Rd7 9. Re8 and the march of the White king to the kingside decides. Black's king is a prisoner of his pawns on the other wing.

7. Re3!

Alekhine played 7. Ra3, when 7. ... Re4! should have proved an adequate defense: 8. Ra4 Kc8 9. f3 Rh4 10. h3 Kb7 11. Ke3 f5! 12. Rb4+ Kc8 13. a4 and now 13. ... f4+ 14. Kf2 Rh5 draws.

Spielmann instead tried 13. ... g5?, bottling up his rook, when Alekhine won ingeniously: 14. a5 g4 15. hxg4 fxg4 16. a6! gxf3 17. gxf3 Rh1 18. Rb7 Re1+ 19. Kf4! Rd1 20. Ke5 Re1+ 21. Kf5 Rd1 22. Rxa7 Rxd4 23. Ra8+ Kd7 24. f4 Ra4 25. a7 h5 26. b3!! Ra1 27. Ke5 Re1+ 28. Kd4! Rd1+ 29. Kc3 Ra1 30. f5 Ke7 31. Kd4 h4 32. Ke5 Re1+ 33. Kf4 Ra1 34. Kg5 Rg1+ (or 34. ... h3 35. Rh8 Rxa7 36. Rxh3 Ra1 37. f6+ Kf7 38. Rh7+, winning easily) 35. Kxh4 Ra1 36. Kg5 Rg1+

37. Kf4 Ra1 38. Ke5 Re1+ 39. Kd4 Ra1 40. Kc3 Ra3 41. Kb2 Ra6 42. b4 Kf7 43. Kb3 Ra1 44. f6! (to stalemate the king) 44. ... Ra6 45. b5! cxb5 46. Kb4, resigns. For if 46. ... c6 47. Rh8!, or if 46. ... Ra1 47. Kxb5 d4 48. Kc4 Ra4+ 49. Kd3 c6 50. Ke4 winning the d-pawn, after which White can capture the c-pawn with his king.

7. ... Rxe3 (7. ... Rf7 8. Ra3 Re7 9. f3! is hopeless) 8. Kxe3 Ke6 9. Kf4 g6 10. g4 (White is trying to seal the kingside because he can win on the queenside) 10. ... g5+ 11. Ke3 Kd7 12. Kd3 Kc8 13. Kc3 Kb7 14. Kb4 Ka6 15. Ka4 Kb7 16. Ka5 a6 (if 16. ... Kb8 17. Ka6 and wins as in the note to Black's first move) 17. a4 Ka7 18. b3! Kb7 19. b4 Ka7 20. b5 axb5 21. axb5 Kb7! 22. b6!! (not 22. bxc6+?? Ka7!!, draw, because the position is completely blockaded) 22. ... cxb6+ (22. ... Kb8 23. Ka6 is worse) 23. cxb6 Kb8 24. Ka6! c5 (24. ... Ka8 25. b7+ Kb8 26. Kb6) 25. dxc5 d4 26. b7 d3 27. Kb6 d2 28. c6 d1=Q 29. c7+ mate.

4. A Protected Passed Pawn

Since a rook is not an effective blockader (a knight is), it stands to reason that a protected passed pawn will be quite powerful in rook endings.

In an earlier example (No. 818), such a pawn showed its strength in conjunction with a rook on the seventh. In **No. 857**, only the inferior position of the Black pieces, caused by the strong White pawn at e5, is the reason for losing.

No. 857, Capablanca, Eliskases, Moscow 1936

White to play wins

The position does not look too good for White, but Capablanca uses the temporary sacrifice **1. f5!!** to demonstrate his superiority. After **1. ... exf5** (1. ... Kf7 2. Kf4 Re8 3. Rg3 is no improvement) **2. Kf4 Re6** (the alternative is 2. ... Kf7 3. Kxf5 Re6 4. Rg3 Rh6, but on 5. Rg5 Black is in zugzwang: if his rook moves along the h-file, he allows the ruinous e6+) **3. Kxf5 Rg6** (or 3. ... Kf7 4. Rg3 as in the last note) **4. e6!** (Capablanca's winning line is simplicity itself) **4. ... Rg4 5. Ke5 Re4+ 6. Kd6 Rxd4** (spite nibble; if 6. ... Kf8 7. Kd7, and Black must lose his rook for the e-pawn regardless of how he continues) **7. Re3,** resigns. The pawn queens by force: **7. ... Re4 8. Rxe4 dxe4 9. e7 Kf7 10. Kd7,** etc.

5. Qualitative Pawn Majority

This occurs (see Chapter II) when an extra pawn on one wing is meaningless either because it is blockaded or doubled. The opponent is then in effect a pawn ahead. King and pawn endings in such cases are almost always lost, but in rook endings counterplay is often available.

a) If the pawns are doubled, there is no way (except a blunder by the opponent) to straighten them out. The only chance then is to try to reduce the severity of the disadvantage by seeking compensation elsewhere.

No. 858, Eliskases-Levenfish, Moscow 1936

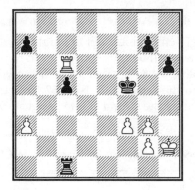

White to play

No. 858 is typical of endings where doubled pawns are a fatal handicap. For all practical purposes, White is a pawn down because his three pawns on the kingside are held by Black's two. But with his rook so well placed, White can still manage to draw with the proper continuation.

After **1. Rc7! g5!** (the best chance: if he abandons the g-pawn White will have a passed f-pawn) **2. Rxa7 c4 3. Re7!!** draws by keeping the Black king away from the pawns.

In the game, Eliskases played 3. Ra5+? and lost because he could not get his kingside pawns going in time: 3. ... Ke6! 4. Ra6+ Kd5 5. Rxh6 c3 6. Rh8 Ra1! 7. Rc8 Rxa3 8. Kh3 (the cramped pawns make progress too slow. If 8. f4 g4! 9. Kg1 Kd4 10. Kf2 Ra2+ 11. Kf1 Rd2! 12. Rd8+ Ke3 13. Re8+ Kd3 14. Rd8+ Kc2 15. Rc8 Kb2 16. Rb8+ Kc1 17. f5 c2 18. f6 Kd1 19. f7 c1=Q 20. f8=Q Kc2+, and mate) 8. ... Kd4 9. Kg4 (or 9. f4 gxf4 10. gxf4 c2+ 11. K any Rc3) 9. ... Ra5!! 10. f4 Rc5 11. Rd8+ Ke3 12. Rd1 c2 13. Rc1 gxf4 14. gxf4 Kd2 15. Ra1 c1=Q 16. Rxc1 Rxc1, and the rest is simple: 17. Kg5 (17. f5 Ke3 18. f6 Rf1 19. Kg5 Ke4 20. Kg6 Ke5 21. f7 Ke6) 17. ... Ke3 18. f5 Ke4 19. g4 Ke5 20. Kg6 Rc6+ 21. Kg7 Ra6! 22. Kf7 Kf4 23. Kg7 Kg5!!, and White resigned. If 24. Kf7 Kxg4 25. f6 Kf5, and the last pawn goes.

3. ... c3 (or 3. ... Kf6 4. Re3 c3 5. a4 c2 6. Rc3, =) **4. a4! Ra1**

If 4. ... c2 5. Rc7 Ke5 6. a5 Kd4 7. a6 Kd3 8. Rd7+, and the Black king will never be able to remain in the neighborhood of the pawn — even without the White a-pawn the game would be drawn.

5. Rc7 Ra3 6. a5 Ke5 7. a6 Kd4 8. a7 Kd3 9. f4 c2 10. Rd7+! (10. f5? Rxa7) **10. ... Ke2 11. Rc7 Kd2 12. Rd7+,** draw, since 12. ... Kc1? 13. f5! forces Black either to take the draw at once or lose.

Where the passed pawn is far advanced, or where there is no counterplay as in the previous example, the superior side wins by proceeding as though he were a pawn ahead.

For example, **No. 859.** (Rabinovich-Kan, Moscow 1935): **White king at e4, rook at d3, pawns at a3, c3, c4, c5, f4; Black king at f6, rook at h2, pawns at a6, b7, c6, f7, h3.** Black to play wins. He gives up his h-pawn in order to establish a decisive material superiority on the other wing: **1. ... Re2+ 2. Kf3 h2! 3. Rd1 Rc2 4. Kg3 Kf5 5. Re1 f6 6. Kf3 Rxc3+ 7. Kg2 Rxc4 8. Rb1 Rxc5 9. Rxb7 Kxf4** and with two clear pawns to the good the rest is simple: **10. Kxh2 f5 11. Kg2 Rc3 12. Rb4+ Ke3 13. Kg3 Rxa3 14. Rc4 a5 15. Rxc6 Ke4+ 16. Kf2 Ra2+,** etc.

When there is no clear or strongly supported passed pawn, the opponent may often have time to use the doubled pawn complex to save the game. Always keep in mind that an extra pawn very often does not win in rook endings.

No. 860 is an interesting example from a world's championship match.

No. 860, Alekhine-Euwe, 27th match game, 1935

Black to play. Draw

With the b-pawns off the board and White's a-pawn at a7, he could win by playing h4, g4, and g5 and then getting his king to e7 (see No. 735). But now Black can dictate the terms under which a queenside passed pawn will be permitted. The game continuation gives us a hint as to what these terms should be: **1. ... Rb3? 2. b5! g5 3. Ke2 e5 4. Kd2 f6 5. Kc2 Rb4 6. Kc3 Rd4 7. Ra6 Kg6 8. Rxb6 Rxa4 9. Ra6 Rd4 10. b6!,** and Black resigned. If 10. ... Rd8 11. b7 Rb8 12. Rb6 Kf7 13. Kc4 Ke7 14. Kb5 Kd7 15. Ka6 Kc7 16. Ka7, etc.

Clearly, Black's mistake lay in not mobilizing his kingside pawns soon enough. Consequently, as later analysis showed, **1. ... e5!** would have drawn: **2. b5**

The alternatives are 2. Ke2 f5 3. Kd2 Rc4 4. b5 e4! 5. fxe4 fxe4 6. Ke3 g5, and 2. g4 g5! 3. b5 g6 4. Ra6 Ra3 5. Ke2 f5 6. Kd2 e4 7. fxe4 fxe4 8. Kc2 e3, and again the Black passed pawn prevents the White king from supporting the queen-side.

2. ... f5 3. Re8 Rc4 4. Rxe5 Rxa4 5. Re6 Ra2+! 6. Kg3 (on 6. Ke3 Rxg2 7. Rxb6 Rxh2 8. Re6 Rb2 9. b6 g5 Black's passed pawn again saves the game) **6. ... g5! 7. Rxb6 Rb2** (White has won a pawn but the cramped position of his king and the strong Black rook nullify the advantage) **8. Rb8 Kg6 9. b6 Kf6 10. b7**

10. h4 gxh4+ 11. Kxh4 Kg6 12. Kg3 Rb4, =: No. 732. White's king cannot get to the pawn without sacrificing a valuable pawn on the kingside.

10. ... f4+ 11. Kg4! Kg6! (not 11. ... Rxg2+? 12. Kh3 Rb2 13. Rf8+) **12. g3** (or 12. h4 gxh4 13. Kxh4 Kh7! 14. Kh3 g6 15. Kh2 Rb1!, etc Also, 12. Rc8 Rxb7 13. Rc6+ Kh7 14. Kxg5 Rb2 is only a theoretical draw) **12. ... fxg3 13. hxg3 Rb4+ 14. f4** (14. Kh3 Rb2) **14. ... gxf4 15. gxf4 Rb1,** draw.

An analogous instance where aggressive action counterbalances the weakness of the doubled pawns. This example, incidentally, shows once more that a passed pawn in the center is not quite as strong as one on the side.

No. 861 (Spielmann-Reti, Baden 1914): **White king at d3, rook at b1, pawns at a4, c2, c4, d5, g2, h2; Black king at f7, rook at f4, pawns at a7, b6, c7, e5, g7, h7.** White to play draws. **1. a5! Ke7 2. c5!! bxc5 3. Rb7 Kd6 4. Rxa7 Rd4+ 5. Ke3 Rc4 6. a6 Rxc2 7. Ra8 Rc3+ 8. Ke4 Rc4+ 9. Kd3 Ra4 10. a7 Kd7 11. Rg8!** (the simplest; on 11. d6!? Ra3+ 12. Ke4 c4, Black retains winning chances) **11. ... Rxa7 12. Rxg7+ Kd6 13. Rxh7 Ra4 14. Rh8,** and now the Black doubled pawns are worthless, so a draw is the legitimate result.

b) If the pawns are blockaded, the opponent is likewise temporarily a pawn ahead. For practical purposes, an immobile pawn is as bad as a doubled one. As a rule, however, it is necessary to proceed with more energy here than in the previous case because a blockade is not permanent but depends on the position of the pieces.

No. 862 is a classic example of the exploitation of such a pawn blockade.

No. 862, Rubinstein-Alekhine, Carlsbad 1911

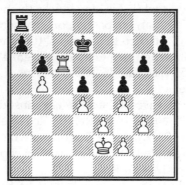

White to play wins

The White advantage is threefold:

1. The single pawn at b5 holds the two Black pawns at a7 and b6.
2. Black's pawn at d5 is isolated and his kingside pawns are weakened.
3. Black's rook is passive, White's active.

Accordingly Rubinstein formulates a winning plan consisting of four steps.

1. Preventing the liberating ... h6.
2. Tying the Black rook down permanently to the defense of a pawn.
3. Breaking through on the kingside to clear the way for the king.
4. Establishing a decisive material advantage.

Rubinstein's treatment of the ending is beyond praise.

1. f3!!

A subtle prophylactic measure. If in reply, 1. ... Rc8?? 2. Rxc8 Kxc8 3. e4!, and the pawn ending is won: 3. ... fxe4 (or 3. ... Kb7 4. exf5 gxf5 5. g4 fxg4 6. fxg4 a5 7. bxa6+ Kxa6 8. f5 and queens) 4. fxe4 dxe4 5. g4 Kd7 (5. ... h5 6. f5! gxf5 7. gxh5 and promotes first) 6. Ke3 Ke6 7. Kxe4, and since the two Black pawns on the queenside are no better than one, White is a pawn ahead and wins with his two passed pawns.

1. ... Re8

At any rate preventing e4. On the desperate 1. ... a5? 2. Rxb6 a4 3. Ra6! wins at once. If here 2. ... Kc7 3. Rc6+ Kb7 4. Kd3 a4 5. Kc2 a3 6. Kb1 Ra5 7. Re6! Rxb5+ 8. Ka2 Rb2+ 9. Kxa3 Rg2 10. g4! fxg4 11. fxg4 Rxg4 12. Kb4! h5 13. Kc5 h4 14. Kxd5 h3 15. Re7+ Kb6 16. Rh7 Rg3 17. e4, and White's connected passed pawns win.

2. Kd3 Re7 3. g4 (first and third steps – the second is being carried out indirectly) **3. ... Re6! 4. Rc1!** (to exchange rooks would be a mistake because Black is threatening to set up a passed h-pawn).

4. ... Re7 (thus the rook is tied down: the threat was 5. Ra1) **5. Rh1 Ke6 6. Rc1 Kd7** (6. ... h5 7. gxh5 gxh5 8. Rc6+ Kd7 9. Rh6 and wins a pawn) **7. Re1** (tempo moves to gain time) **7. ... Rf7**

If 7. ... h5 8. gxh5 gxh5 9. Ke2 h4 10. Kf2, and White's rook can then go around to the loose pawns while his king blocks the h-pawn. Still, this line is probably more promising than the passive one chosen.

8. Ra1 Kd6 9. Rc1 Kd7 10. Rc6 Rf8 11. Ke2! (the third step now enters its second phase: the White king threatens to reach g5) **11. ... Rf7** (11. ... Rc8 12. Rxc8 Kxc8 13. gxf5 gxf5 14. e4 Kb7 15. Kf2 and wins) **12. Kf2 Rf8 13. Kg3 Re8 14. Rc3 Re7 15. Kh4! h6**

To allow the king to enter would be fatal. The most direct win would be 15. ... Rf7 16. Kg5 Kd6 17. Kh6 Kd7 18. g5 Re7 19. Rc6 Rxe3 (the only chance) 20. Kxh7 Rxf3 21. Kxg6 Rxf4 22. Kf7 Rxd4 23. g6, and wins the rook. Now that all the pawns have been uprooted, White is bound to capture material.

16. Kg3! (threatening Kf2, Rc1, Rg1, gxf5, Rg6, and Rf6) **16. ... h5 17. Kh4! Rh7 18. Kg5!** (the simplest) **18. ... fxg4** (a trap: if 19. Kxg6 g3! 20. Kxh7 g2 21. Rc1 h4 and Black wins) **19. fxg4 hxg4 20. Kxg4 Rh1** (he has no choice; on 20. ... Re7 21. Kg5 Re6 22. Kh6!-g7-f7, and eventually Black will have to play ... Rd6, when Ra3 will decide) **21. Kg5 Rb1** (21. ... Rg1+ 22. Kf6 Kd6 23. Rc6+ Kd7 24. Ke5 is hopeless) **22. Ra3 Rxb5 23. Rxa7+ Kd6 24. Kxg6 Rb3 25. f5** (25. Rb7 Kc6 26. Re7 holds the extra pawn, but the move chosen is more forceful) **25. ... Rxe3 26. f6 Rg3+ 27. Kh7 Rf3 28. f7 Rf4** (the last chance) **29. Kg7 Rg4+ 30. Kf6!** (30. Kf8 Rxd4 31. Ra8 Rf4 32. Kg7 d4 is less clear) **30. ... Rf4+ 31. Kg5! Rf1 32. Kg6** (threatening 32. Ra8) **32. ... Rg1+ 33. Kf6 Rf1+ 34. Kg7 Rg1+ 35. Kf8 Rd1 36. Ke8 Re1+ 37. Kd8 Rf1 38. Rd7+ Kc6 39. Ke8 Rf2 40. Re7! Kb5 41. Rc7!**

Again the simplest. Black resigned. The conclusion might be 41. ... Re2+ 42. Kd7! Rf2 43. Ke6 Re2+ 44. Kxd5 Rf2 45. Ke6 Re2+ 46. Kd7 Rf2 47. Ke8 Re2+ 48. Kd8 Rf2 49. d5, etc.

When the blockade remains effective and there are no doubled pawns or other weaknesses, the superior side is in effect a pawn ahead and should proceed accordingly: centralize, advance the majority, tie up the enemy pieces, secure a decisive material advantage.

No. 863 is a perfect example.

No. 863, Naegeli-Alekhine, Zurich, 1934

Black to play wins

The game continued **1. ... Ke5** (centralization) **2. Re3 f5** (second step: advancing the pawn majority in order to tie up the enemy pieces) **3. h4**

If 3. f4+ Kd4! 4. Rb3 Rc8! 5. Re3 Rc2+ 6. Kxc2 Kxe3 7. a4 bxa4 8. b5 Kf2 9. b6 e3 10. b7 e2 11. b8=Q c1=Q 12. Qa7+ Kg2, and Black will emerge with two extra pawns on the kingside.

3. ... Kd4 4. Rb3 h6 5. Re3 (White's rook is tied down to the weak queenside pawns. If 5. Rb1 Rc3 6. Ra1 e3+ 7. fxe3+ Rxe3 8. a4 bxa4 9. Rxa4 Rxg3 and wins) **5. ... g5 6. hxg5 hxg5 7. Rb3 Rc8** (the rook has performed nobly on the c-file and now switches to the other wing) **8. Re3 Rh8 9. Re2 f4 10. gxf4 gxf4 11. Kc2** (he must give his rook some leeway) **11. ... Rh2 12. Kb3**

Desperation. After 12. Kd2 Rxf2 13. Rxf2 e3+ 14. Ke2 exf2 15. Kxf2 Kc4! 16. Kf3 Kb3 17. Kxf4 Kxa3 18. Ke3 Kxb4 the win is routine.

12. ... Rh3+

To centralize the rook. An alternative win, which had to be carefully calculated, is 12. ... f3 13. Rc2 Rxf2!! 14. Rxf2 Ke3 15. Rf1 f2 16. a4 bxa4+ 17. Kxa4 Ke2! 18. Rh1 f1=Q 19. Rxf1 Kxf1 20. b5 e3 21. b6 e2 22. b7 e1=Q 23. b8=Q Qa1+ 24. Kb5 Qb1+ and wins White's queen.

13. Kb2 Rd3 (Now the White king will not be able to stop the eventual passed e-pawn or f-pawn. The rest is simple.) **14. Rc2 f3 15. Kc1 e3 16. fxe3+ Kxe3,** resigns. After 17. Rc8 f2 White's rook is lost.

C. Better King Position

One king may be better placed than another for one of two reasons: either on general principles, i.e. one is centralized while the other is not, or on the special principle that one is closer to the vital pawns. The second category is really the basic one because a centralized king is strong only to the extent that it can switch to one side or the other and capture material or support a strong passed pawn.

1. Centralization

Examples of this in conjunction with other advantages may be found throughout the previous discussion; see Nos. 847, 851, and 857. Here we are concerned with positions where centralization alone is the decisive factor.

No. 864 is a typical instance of where such centralization is conclusive.

No. 864, Treybal-Mattison, Carlsbad 1929

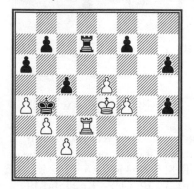

Black to play

The fact that White is a pawn down is of no consequence since the two Black h-pawns are doubled. We notice, first of all, that Black cannot afford to exchange rooks because White's king is too close to the h-pawn. After 1. ... Rxd3 2. cxd3 h3 3. Kf3 c4 4. bxc4 Kc5 5. f5 Kc6 6. d4 and wins. So **1. ... Rc7** is forced. But now White can advance his center pawns, which, in the absence of Black's king, will win a rook. The game continued **2. f5 b5 3. axb5 axb5 4. e6 fxe6 5. fxe6 c4 6. Re3!** (but not 6. Rd7? Rc8 7. e7 Re8 8. Ke5 h3 9. Kf6 h2 10. Rd1 cxb3) **6. ... Rg7 7. bxc4 bxc4 8. Kf4 Rg8 9. e7 Re8 10. Kf5 h3 11. Ke6 h2 12. Rh3**, resigns. Black's king is unable to capture the c-pawn. If the Black king were at e7 in the diagram, he would have drawn quite easily. In fact, White would then not have dared to oppose rooks, for with the king in the center Black would win the pawn ending.

A similar instance is **No. 865** (Stahlberg-Fine, 2nd match game, 1937): **White king at d5, rook at a1, pawns at b5, c6, e3, g2, h2; Black king at b8, rook at c7, pawns at a7, e4, f5, g7, h7**. White to play wins.

After **1. Rf1 Rf7** (1. ... g6 2. g4 fxg4 3. Rf8+ Rc8 4. Rxc8+ Kxc8 5. Kxe4, and White has two passed pawns to Black's one. Nevertheless, the pawn ending is won only by the odd tempo: 5. ... h5 6. Kf4 Kc7 7. e4 Kd6 8. e5+ Ke6 9. Kg5! Ke7 10. c7! Kd7 11. e6+ Kxc7 12. Kf6 h4 13. e7 g3 14. e8=Q, and Black is one move too late) **2. g4** (Black is already reduced to the desperate **2. ... f4!?**, since 2. ... g6 3. Ke6 is hopeless. The text is refuted by **3. exf4 e3 4. f5 h5 5. h3 hxg4 6. hxg4 Kc7 7. Re1 Re7 8. Re2 Kb6 9. g5 Kxb5 10. f6 gxf6 11. gxf6 Rc7** (if 11. ... Rf7 12. Rxe3 Rxf6 13. c7 Rf8 14. Rb3+ K any 15. Rb8) **12. Rxe3 a5 13. Re7**, and Black resigned. The two passed pawns are too much.

2. One King Is Closer to the Vital Pawns

The "vital" pawns may be either a strong (advanced) passed pawn or simply a mass of pawns. In the former case the pawn either queens or wins a rook; in the latter case the king or king and rook combined simply capture material.

The more important case is that where a king is closer to its passed pawn. The first typical position is **No. 866**.

No. 866, Schlechter-Perlis, Carlsbad 1911

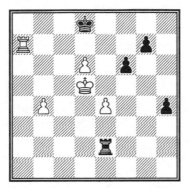

White to play wins

Obviously, if White could get his king to a6 or c6 without being checked away, he could escort his pawn to the eighth. But if at once 1. Ke6 Rxe4+ and if 1. Kc6 Rc2+. He must therefore block the files by a sacrifice:

1. e5!!, after which Black loses in all variations:

a) **1. ... fxe5 2. Ke6 Rc2** (2. ... Kc8 3. d7+ and queens at once. After 3. ... Kb8 4. d8=Q+ Kxa7 5. Qa5+ Kb7 6. Qb5+ the rook goes) **3. Ra8+ Rc8 4. Rxc8+ Kxc8 5. Ke7 h3 6. d7+ Kb7 7. d8=Q h2 8. Qd5+** and wins.

b) 1. ... Rxe5+ 2. Kc6 Ke8 3. Ra8+ Kf7 4. d7 and queens.

c) 1. ... Rd2+ 2. Ke6 Kc8 3. d7+! (the simplest) 3. ... Kb8 4. Ra6! Kc7 5. Rd6 Rxd6+ 6. exd6+ Kd8 7. b5 h3 8. b6 h2 9. b7 h1=Q 10. b8=Q+ mate!

d) 1. ... h3 2. e6 Kc8 3. d7+ Kd8 4. Ra8+ and mates.

The second typical position occurs when one rook is tied up.

No. 867 is a good example. By constant mate threats Black eventually forces the White king to abandon the immediate neighborhood of the passed pawn.

No. 867, Apscheneek-Petrov, Kemeri 1937

White to play. Black wins

Best play for both sides is **1. Kc1** (1. Ke3? c3 2. Rg8 Rxb7 3. Rxg6 c2 is hopeless) **1. ... Kc3!!** (not 1. ... c3? 2. Rg8 Rxb7 3. Rxg6 and draws) **2. Rg8** (on 2. Kd1 Rd6+ 3. Ke2 Rd7, the threat of ... Kb3 and ... c3-c2 forces White to get his rook out of the way under much less favorable circumstances) **2. ... Rxb7 3. Rxg6 Re7!** (better than 3. ... Ra7 4. Kd1 Ra1+? 5. Ke2 Kb2 6. Rb6+ Kc2 7. Rb5 c3 8. Rxf5 Kb3 9. Rxh5 c2 10. Rc5 c1=Q 11. Rxc1 Rxc1 12. Kf3, and Black is unable to win against the three passed pawns) **4. Kd1** (relatively best. On 4. Kb1 Re1+ 5. Ka2 Kc2 6. Rg5 c3 7. Rxf5 Kd3 8. Rxh5 c2 9. Rc5 c1=Q, Black wins because his king is near the pawns, while 4. Rd6 Re1+ 5. Rd1 Rxd1+ 6. Kxd1 Kb2 is immediately fatal) **4. ... Re3!!** (4. ... Kb2 5. Rb6+ gets Black nowhere) **5. Ra6** (the alternative is 5. Rg5 Kb2 6. Rxf5 Rd3+, as in the main line) **5. ... Kb2! 6. Ra5 Rd3+ 7. Ke2 Rxg3 8. Rxf5 c3 9. Rb5+ Kc1 10. Rxh5 c2 11. Rc5?** (11. Rb5! Rg2+ 12. Ke1 Rg4 13. h5 Rxf4 14. h6 it is even.) **11. ... Kb2 12. Rxc2+** (the threat was ... Rc3. On 12. Kd2 Rg2+ 13. Kd3 c1=Q 14. Rxc1 Kxc1 15. Ke4 still draw) **12. ... Kxc2 13. h5 Kc3 14. Kf2 Rh3 15. Kg2 Rxh5 16. Kf3 Kd4** and wins.

Positions where one king is nearer a set of pawns are usually pretty simple: a material advantage must soon result.

One fairly complicated example is **No. 868** (Levenfish-Lisitsin, Moscow 1935): **White king at f4, rook at c6, pawns at a4, b5, g3, h2; Black king at h7, rook at e7, pawns at a7, b6, f5, h6.** Black to play, White wins.

The game went **1. ... Rf7** (if 1. ... Re4+ 2. Kxf5 Rxa4 3. Rc7+ Kg8 4. Kg6 Kf8 5. Kxh6, and White has two connected passed pawns) **2. h4 Rg7 3. h5!** (now Black must lose the f-pawn no matter how he plays, for if 3. ... Rf7 4. Re6 Kg7 5. Re5) **3. ... Rg4+** (the only chance) **4. Kxf5 Rxa4**

If instead 4. ... Rxg3 5. Rc7+ Kg8 6. Rxa7 Rg5+ 7. Kf6 Rxh5 8. a5!! Rxb5 (or 8. ... bxa5 9. b6 Rb5 10. b7 followed by 11. Ra8+, winning the rook) 9. a6 Ra5 10. Rg7+! Kf8 11. a7 Ke8 12. Ke6 Kd8 13. Rg8+ and wins.

5. Rc7+ Kg8 6. Kg6 Rg4+ 7. Kxh6 Rxg3 8. Rxa7 Rb3 9. Rb7!! (the point: White either captures the second pawn or forces his h-pawn through) **9. ... Rxb5 10. Kg6 Kf8 11. h6 Re5 12. Rb8+,** resigns.

VII. TWO-ROOK ENDINGS

Most such endings differ in no essential respect from those with single rooks; often the exchange of one pair is unavoidable. The superior side must take care to reduce to an ending favorable for him; that is, get his rook behind a passed pawn.

If no exchange is feasible, there are several ways in which these endings may differ from those previously considered. The most important of these is when both rooks reach the seventh. Other things being equal, they will then draw with a pawn down, and will force the capture of material in even positions.

No. 869 is the typical position where two rooks on the seventh compensate for the loss of a pawn.

No. 869, Schlechter-Maroczy, Carlsbad 1907

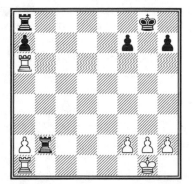

Black to play. Draw

Black gives up his a-pawn to get both rooks on the seventh: **1. ... Rd8! 2. Rxa7 Rdd2 3. Ra3** (or 3. Rf1 Rxa2) **3. ... Kf8!** (the safest; after 3. ... Rxf2 4. Rg3+ Kf8 5. a3 Black might have trouble) **4. Rf1** (now 4. Rg3 is met by 4. ... Rxa2) **4. ... Rxa2 5. Rxa2** (if he does not exchange, Black will double on a file and force it anyway) **5. ... Rxa2**, and the game was eventually drawn.

White to play in the diagram cannot improve his game in any way; e.g., **1. a3 Rd8 2. Rxa7 Rdd2 3. Rf1 Ra2 4. Ra4 Kf8 5. g3 Rd3**, etc.

A more complicated variant on the same theme is **No. 870** (Capablanca-Fine, AVRO 1938): **White king at g3, rooks at a7, h1; pawns at a3, b4, e3, f2, g2, h2; Black king at g8, rooks at d8, d2, pawns at b6, e6, e4, f7, h7.** Black to play. After **1. ... Ra2 2. Ra6 Rdd2 3. Rf1 Rdb2 4. Rxb6** (the threat was 4. ... Rxb4) **4. ... Rxa3 5. b5 Kg7 6. h4 Rab3 7. Kf4 Rxb5 8. Rxb5 Rxb5 9. g4 Rb4**, the game should be drawn, since Black can afford to give up his e-pawn.

An instance where one rook on the seventh coupled with the threat of getting the other one there suffices to tie up the enemy pieces is **No. 871** (Botvinnik-Levenfish, 6th match game, 1937): **White king at g1, rooks at a7, g3,**

pawns at a2, b3, g2, h5; Black king at g8, rooks at b8, d5, pawns at b6, e6, f7, g7, h6. White to play draws.

1. Rf3 Rf8 (after 1. ... Rf5 2. Rxf5 exf5 3. a4 Rd8 4. Rb7 Rd6 5. b4, Black is in effect only one pawn ahead on the kingside, and this is more than counterbalanced by the extra White pawn on the other wing) **2. a4 Rd4 3. Rb7 Rb4 4. Kf2** (despite the pawn minus, 4. Re7 forces the draw at once, but the move played is also good enough) **4. ... e5 5. Ke2 e4 6. Rc3 Rd8 7. g4 Rf8 8. Rbc7 f5** (or 8. ... Rd4 9. R7c4 Rfd8 10. Rxd4 Rxd4 11. Rc4! Rd3 12. Rb4 Rd6 13. Rxe4) **9. Re7 f4! 10. Rcc7 f3+ 11. Kf1 Rd8 12. g5,** and now Black can force White to take perpetual check after **12. ... e3! 13. Rxg7+ Kh8 14. Rh7+ Kg8.** Instead Black tried 12. ... Rd1+? and lost after 13. Kf2 Rd2+ 14. Ke1 Re2+ 15. Kf1 hxg5 (the threat was 16. Rc8+ and 17. g6 mate) 16. Rxg7+, resigns. If 16. ... Kf8 17. h6, and mate is forced.

Two rooks on the seventh draw only because the enemy pieces are tied down to the defense of a vital pawn. But when the enemy rooks can defend the pawn and the checks from an active position, or when counterthreats are available, the rooks on the seventh will not save the game.

No. 872 is a position where White just manages to win.

No. 872, Grob-Fine, Ostend 1937

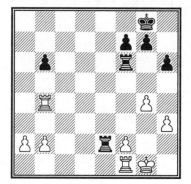

White wins

White's conduct of the ending is exemplary.

1. ... Kf8 (the combination in No. 869 does not work here: 1. ... Rd6 2. a4 Rdd2 3. Rxb6 Rxb2 4. Rxb2 Rxb2 5. Ra1 and wins) **2. Kg2 Ke8 3. Kg3** (Lifting the pin. The threat is now f3 and Rb3 followed by Rf2.) **3. ... Rd6 4. a4** (4. f3? Rdd2, threatening mate) **4. ... g5 5. Kf3 Rc2 6. Kg2 Kd7 7. Rb5 Kc6 8. Rf5!** (liberating the other rook) **8. ... Rxb2 9. Rc1+ Kb7 10. Rxf7+ Ka6 11. Rc8 Ka5 12. Rc4** (again threatens mate) **12. ... Ka6 13. Re4**

The ending now enters its second phase: White has succeeded in freeing both rooks; his next objective is to create a passed pawn on the kingside.

13. ... Ra2 14. h4! gxh4 15. Kh3 Rd1 16. Kxh4 Rh1+ (Black has no real counterplay but can only harass his opponent) **17. Kg3 h5** (better to exchange than lose it for nothing) **18. gxh5 Rxh5**

Now we have an ending that would be quite simple with only one rook apiece, but the extra pieces here produce complications.

19. Kg4 Rh1 20. f4 Rg1+ 21. Kf5 Rga1 22. Rf8! Rc1

If 22. ... Kb7 23. Re7+ Kc6 24. Rf6+ Kc5 25. Re5+ Kd4 26. Rxb6 Rxa4 27. Re4+ Kd5 28. Rxa4 Rxa4 29. Kg5, with an elementary win (No. 668), while on 22. ... Rxa4 23. Rxa4+ Rxa4 24. Ra8+ Kb5 25. Rxa4 Kxa4 26. Ke4! b5 27. f5 b4 28. f6 b3 29. Kd3! Ka3 30. f7, White queens first and wins.

23. Rfe8 Rca1 24. Rb4! Kb7 25. Re7+ Kc6 26. Rc4+ (26. Re6+ is not so clear) **26. ... Kd5 27. Rc8** (threatening mate) **27. ... Kd4 28. Rd8+ Kc3 29. Rc7+ Kb3 30. Rb8 Rxa4 31. Rxb6+.**

The rest, though routine, requires a little more care than the corresponding ending with one pair of rooks.

31. ... Ka3 32. Rc3+ Ka2 33. Re6 Rf1 34. Re4 Ra5+ 35. Ke6 Rh1 36. Re5 Rh6+ 37. Kf5 Rh5+ 38. Kf6 Ra6+ 39. Kg7 Rh1 40. f5 Rb1 41. Re2+ Ka1 42. Re6 Rg1+ 43. Kf7 Ra7+ 44. Re7 Ra6 45. Rce3, resigns. The march of the pawn cannot be halted.

A similar case that is somewhat easier for the winning side is **No. 873** (Nimzovich-Spielmann, Carlsbad 1929): **White king at g1, rooks at a1, e4, pawns at a3, b4, g2, h2; Black king at c8, rooks at d8, b3, pawns at c7, c6, h7. Black to play. White wins.**

The game continued **1. ... Rd2 2. Re7 h5 3. Rf7!** (to force the rook away from the pawn: the threat is Rf2) **3. ... Rbb2 4. Rg7 Kb7 5. h3 Rdc2 6. Rg5** (to prevent or at least postpone 6. ... c5) **6. ... Kb6 7. Rf1 c5 8. Rf4!!** c4 (8. ... cxb4 9. axb4 Rb1+ 10. Kh2 Rcb2 11. Rxh5 Rxb4 12. Rf6+ is worse) **9. h4** (to have an eventual flight square for his king; e.g., 9. Rf6+ c6 10. Rgg6 h4! 11. Rxc6+ Kb5 12. Rc8?? Rc1+ 13. Kh2 Rbb1, and mate is unavoidable) **9. ... Ra2 10. Rf6+ Kb7 11. Rb5+ Kc8 12. Rg6! Rd2 13. Rc5** (now further simplification in White's favor decides quickly) **13. ... Rac2 14. Rg7 Kb8 15. Rcxc7 Rxg2+! 16. Rxg2 Rc1+ 17. Kf2 Kxc7 18. Rg5! c3 19. Rxh5 Rh1 20. Rc5+,** and the rest is simple.

Two rooks on the seventh not only may compensate for the loss of a pawn, but also, if proper steps are not taken against them, will often win. This is especially true when there is an absolute seventh; i.e., when the king is confined to the first rank and cannot escape behind his pawns.

No. 874 is an example where overcautious defense proved fatal.

No. 874, Lasker-Eliskases, Moscow 1936

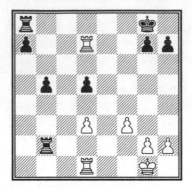

White to play

We follow the game in boldface type.
1. Rc1! (better than 1. Re1 Kh8 2. Ree7 Rg8 3. Rxa7 Rd2, =) **1. ... Kh8?**
But now this obvious move loses. The only defense is the cold-blooded 1. ... a5!! 2. Rcc7 a4 3. Rxg7+ Kh8 4. Rxh7+ Kg8 5. Rcg7+ Kf8, and White is well-advised to take perpetual check, since any winning attempt may boomerang:

a) 6. h4? a3 7. h5 a2 8. h6 a1=Q+ 9. Kh2 Rxg2+!! 10. Rxg2 Ra2 and wins.

b) 6. Ra7? Rxa7 7. Rxa7 Rb3 8. h4 a3 9. h5 b4 10. h6 Kg8 11. f4 (or 11. g4 Rb2 12. g5 a2 13. g6 Rb1+ 14. Kh2 a1=Q) 11. ... Rc3!, and White's pawns are too far back to save the game.

2. Rcc7 Rg8
Now 2. ... a5 is too late. There would follow 3. Ra7! Rc8 (3. ... Rxa7 4. Rd8+ mate) 4. h4 a4 5. Rxg7 a3! 6. Rxh7+ Kg8 7. Rab7 (holding up the advance of the pawn and preventing the Black rook at c8 from going to the seventh) 7. ... a2 8. Kh2! b4 9. h5 b3 10. Rhg7+! Kf8 11. Rh7 Kg8 12. Rbg7+ Kf8 13. h6, and mate can be postponed only by problem moves.

3. Rxa7 h6 4. h4! (not 4. Rxd5 Re8!, threatening both ... Re1 mate and doubling on the seventh) **4. ... b4 5. Rab7 b3 6. Kh2 Rd2** (else simply Rxd5 and Rdb5) **7. Rxb3 Re8 8. Rbb7!** (to reply to ... Ree2 with Rxg7) **8. ... Rxd3** (desperation: after 8. ... Rg8 9. Rxd5; he is two pawns down) **9. Rxg7 Rd8 10. Rh7+ Kg8 11. Rxh6 Re3 12. Rhh7 d4 13. Rhd7 Ree8 14. h5! d3 15. h6!** (threatening mate in four) **15. ... Rxd7 16. Rxd7 Re6 17. Rxd3**, resigns.

Against two rooks on the absolute seventh the fight is usually hopeless, especially if the king is in the center. An example is **No. 875** (Eliskases-Fine, Hastings 1936-37): **White king at e1, rooks at b6, e4, pawns at a5, e3, g3, h2; Black king at f6, rooks at a2, g2, pawns at a6, e6, g7, h7.** White to play. Black wins.

The game concluded **1. Rbxe6+** (if 1. Rexe6+ Kf7, and White has no check. After 2. Kf1 Rgc2 the only move to stop mate is 3. Rb1, which costs him a rook) **1. ... Kg5 2. R6e5+** (or 2. R4e5+ Kg4 3. Re4+ Kh5 4. R4e5+ g5) **2. ... Kh6 3. Rh4+ Kg6 4. Kf1 Rgb2** (to stop mate White must lose a rook) **5. Rg4+ Kf6**, White resigns.

White could have staved off mate in the beginning by 1. Kf1, but then 1. ... Rxh2 2. Kg1 Rhc2 3. Rb1 Rxa5 leaves him two pawns down with a hopeless position.

No. 876 is a surprising exception.

No. 876, P. Benko 1991

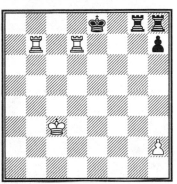

White wins, Black may still castle

1. Rd2! Rf8 2. Kc2! (the second surprise! If 2. Ra2? Rf3+ 3. Kd4 0-0!, =) **2. ... Rhg8 3. Kb2! h6 4. h3!** (mutual zugzwang; if 4. h4? h5 5. Ka2 Rf4 6. Rc2 Ra4+ and Ra8 saves the game) **4. ... h5 5. h4 Rh8** (5. ... Rf6 6. Rc2 Rd6 7. Rc8+ Rd8 8. Rxd8+ Kxd8 9. Rb8+) **6. Ka2 Rhg8 7. Ra7 Rh8 8. Rb2** wins.

When the king is in the neighborhood, there is usually no defense against a rook on the absolute seventh.

No. 877, Englisch-Gunsberg, Hamburg 1885

White to play wins

In No. 877, after **1. Rd1!**, threatening Rh1+ and Ra8 mate, Black is defenseless. **1. ... Raa2** is the only chance, but then **2. Ra8+** soon mates. **2. ... Kh7** (or 2. ... Rg8 3. Rh1+ Rh2 4. Rxh2+ mate) **3. Rd7+ Kh6 4. Rh8+** mate.

Still another type of mating possibility is with the king at h3. For instance, **No. 878** (Zukertort-Steinitz, Vienna 1882): **White king at h3, rooks at c6, e7, pawns at a4, f4, g3; Black king at g8, rooks at b2, g2, pawns at a5, f7, g6, h7.** Black to play wins. **1. ... h5 2. Kh4** (2. g4 Rh2+ 3. Kg3 h4+ 4. Kf3 Rhf2+ 5. Ke3 Rfe2+, and wins a rook) **2. ... Rb3! 3. Kg5** (or 3. Rc8+ Kg7 4. Rcc7 Rh2+ 5. Kg5 Rxg3+ mate, or 3. Rf6 Rgxg3 4. Rfxf7 Rg4+ mate) **3. ... Kg7! 4. Rxg6+ Kf8!!** and wins a rook!

Other cases where an extra pair of rooks makes a difference are of little importance. A few may be mentioned briefly.

No. 879, Rabinovich-Levenfish, Moscow 1935

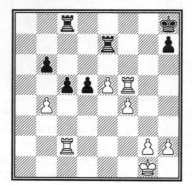

White to play wins

In **No. 879,** the advantage of having a rook behind a passed pawn is nullified. After **1. Rf6! d4** (or 1. ... Rd7 2. Rxb6 c4 3. e6 Rdd8 4. Rb7! d4 5. Ra2! Ra8 6. e7! Re8 7. Rxa8 Rxa8 8. Rd7 and wins) **2. Rd6! Rec7 3. bxc5 bxc5 4. Kf2 Rc6 5. Rd5! Kg7 6. Kf3 Kf7 7. g4 Ke7 8. f5 h6 9. h4 Rd8 10. f6+,** resigns. Notice how the two rooks completely blockaded the enemy pawns, something that one rook alone cannot do.

An example where an extra outside passed pawn is insufficient because of the extra pair of rooks is **No. 880** (from a game by Anderssen): **White king at g1, rooks at a1, h2, pawns at a2, b2, c2, g2; Black king at c8, rooks at g8, g4, pawns at a7, b7, c6.** Black to play draws. **1. ... Re4! 2. Rf1** (or 2. Kh1 Re2 3. g3 Re3) **2. ... Re2 3. Rf2** (on 3. Rc1 Kc7, White has no way to go forward) **3. ... Re1+ 4. Rf1 Re2 5. Rf2 Re1+,** etc.

No. 881, Euwe-Alekhine, 23rd match game 1937

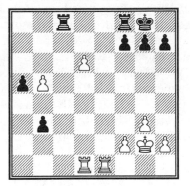

Black to play. Draw

No. 881 illustrates the play with unconnected vs. connected passed pawns. Connected pawns are normally better, but the two rooks counterbalance this slight superiority. After **1. ... Rb8 2. d7 g6** (or 2. ... Rfd8 3. Re3 a4 4. Rd4! Kf8 5. Rxa4 Rxb5 6. Rae4 Rbb8 7. Re8+ Rxe8 8. dxe8=Q+ Rxe8 9. Rxb3, =) **3. Re3!** is the simplest drawing line (the game continued 3. Ra1 Rxb5 4. Re8 Rd5! 5. Rxa5 Rxd7 6. Rxf8+ Kxf8 7. Rb5 Rd3 8. Rb7 Kg7. Black has won a pawn but the game is drawn; see No. 741) **3. ... a4 4. Rd4! b2!** (but not 4. ... Ra8? 5. b6! a3 6. b7! Rab8 7. Rxb3 a2 8. Ra4 Rfd8 9. Rxa2 Rxd7 10. Ra8 and wins) **5. Rb4 Rfd8 6. Rd3 Rb7 7. Rxb2** (the winning attempt 7. b6 Rdxd7 8. Rxd7 Rxd7 9. b7? wins for the wrong side: 9. ... Rxb7 10. Rxb7 a3, and one pawn queens) **7. ... Rdxd7 8. Rxd7 Rxd7**.

Finally, in some positions the extra pair of rooks creates winning chances that would not otherwise exist. This may occur when there are slight weaknesses on both sides of the board, which one rook alone cannot exploit. **No. 882** is a classic example.

No. 882, Kan-Capablanca, Moscow 1936

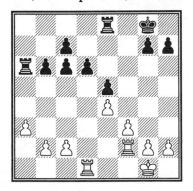

White to play

Black has an undeniable advantage because of his possession of two semi-open files (see No. 830). With only one rook on the board he could make use of only one of the files, but not both. With two rooks he can attempt to use them simultaneously.

The game continued **1. Rd3 b5 2. Rfd2** (2. f4 exf4 3. Rxf4 Ra4 4. Re3 Rc4 5. c3 d5 loses a pawn) **2. ... c5 3. Kf2 Ra4** (preparing to centralize) **4. Ke2 Kf7 5. Rd1 Ke6 6. Kd2 Rb8** (maneuvering) **7. Rc3 g5!** (to break through on the king-side: the other semi-open file) **8. h3 h5 9. Rh1 Rd4+ 10. Ke2 Rg8 11. Rd3 Ra4!** (he must not exchange yet) **12. Rhd1?** (inferior; 12. Kf2 or 12. Ke3 holds the game more easily. Now Black gets the open file.) **12. ... g4 13. hxg4 hxg4 14. Ke3** (if 14. Rh1 gxf3+ 15. gxf3 Rg2+ 16. Kd1 Rf2, and White's pieces are tied up) **14. ... Rh8! 15. Rb3** (15. fxg4 is weak: 15. ... Rg8 16. Kf3 Rf8+ 17. Ke3 Rf4, regaining the pawn with a clear advantage) **15. ... Rh2 16. Rd2 Rd4! 17. Re2** (obviously he cannot afford to exchange now) **17. ... c6 18. Rc3 g3! 19. Rd3?** (19. f4! draws: 19. ... Rh4 20. fxe5 Rdxe4+ 21. Kf3 Rhf4+ 22. Kxg3 Rg4+ 23. Kf3 Rxe2 24. Kxe2 Rxg2+ 25. Kf3 Rh2 26. Kg3 Rd2 27. exd6) **19. ... Rh1! 20. f4 Rf1! 21. f5+ Kf6,** and now White must lose a pawn: **22. c3 Rxd3+ 23. Kxd3 d5 24. b3 c4+ 25. bxc4 bxc4+ 26. Ke3 Ra1! 27. Kf3 Rxa3.**

The rest is simple: 28. Kxg3 (28. Re3 Rb3! 29. Kxg3 d4) 28. ... Rxc3+ 29. Kh4 Rc1 30. g4 Rh1+ 31. Kg3 d4 32. Ra2 d3 33. Kg2 Re1 34. Kf2 Rxe4, resigns.

Chapter VII

ROOKS AND MINOR PIECES

Although it is customary to speak of endings where each side has two rooks and two minor pieces, we shall confine ourselves to the most indispensable positions. Anything that is more complicated may usually be reduced to the simpler cases contained in this book.

I. ROOK AND KNIGHT VS. ROOK AND KNIGHT (OR BISHOP)

The only type of position where any new element is introduced is that where the rook is on the seventh or eighth and can conjure up threats of mate or perpetual check.

No. 883

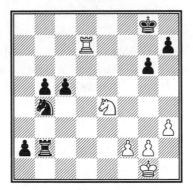

White to play draws

No. 883 is a type of position that occurs often. The draw is forced after **1. Nf6+ Kf8** (1. ... Kh8? 2. Rxh7+ mate) **2. Nxh7+ Ke8 3. Nf6+ Kf8 4. Nh7+,** etc., with perpetual check. The White rook must be at d7 here: if it were at c7 Black could get out via d8: **1. Nf6+ Kf8 2. Nxh7+ Ke8 3. Nf6+ Kd8 4. Rd7+ Kc8.** If the Black king were at h8 in the original position, Nf6 would mate even though Black can queen with check.

No. 884 is another kind of perpetual check with rook and knight:

No. 884

White to play draws. Win with White pawn at h5

1. Rc8+ Kh7 2. Nf8+ Kg8 3. Ne6+ Kh7 4. Nf8+, etc.

In **No. 885, White pawn at h5,** other pieces unchanged, this sequence leads to mate. **1. Rc8+ Kh7 2. Nf8+ Kg8 3. Ng6+ Kh7 4. Rh8+** mate. Of course, if the White knight at g6 is otherwise defended, the same mate follows.

II. BISHOPS OF OPPOSITE COLORS

A. Material Advantage

As we saw in Chapter III, a pawn ahead generally wins with bishops of opposite colors only if there is play on both sides of the board. For this reason, a simple outside or center passed pawn with no subsidiary weaknesses in the enemy camp only draws. With rooks on the board, however, the ending is much more favorable for the superior side. We shall consider only those cases that would be drawn if the rooks were off the board.

1. Outside Passed Pawn

This is a draw unless play on the other wing with rook and bishop can be obtained. That is much more often the case with two pieces than with only one, so even though the game may be a theoretical draw, the defense is far more difficult.

No. 886, Euwe-Alekhine, 8th match game 1935

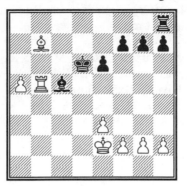

Black to play, White wins

In **No. 886**, White has two advantages in addition to the outside pawn: his pawn has only one dark square to cross before queening, and he can secure command of the open c-file. The game continued:

1. ... Ba7 (1. ... Rd8 2. a6 threatens Rxc5) **2. a6 Rd8 3. Rb2! Rd7 4. Rd2+ Ke7 5. Rc2 Rd6**

On 5. ... Kd8 6. Rc8+ Ke7 7. Bc6! forces the favorable exchange of bishops. After 7. ... Rd6 8. Rc7+ Kd8 (8. ... Kf6 9. Be8) 9. Rxa7 Rxc6 10. Rxf7 the win is routine.

6. f4! (threatening 6. e4-e5) **6. ... f5**

Black cannot allow his rook to be driven away from d6 and d8; e.g., 6. ... Rd8 7. e4 Rd4 8. g3 Rd8 9. e5 Rd4 10. Bc6 Rd8 11. Bb5 Bb6 12. Rc6 Rb8 13. Rxb6.

7. Rc7+ Rd7 8. Rc3 Rd6 9. h4!! Black is in zugzwang! On all waiting moves White has a forced win:

a) 9. ... Rd7 10. Bc8 Rd6 11. Rc7+ Kd8 12. Rxa7 Kxc8 13. Rxg7.

b) 9. ... Rd8 10. Bc8! Kd6 (or 10. ... Bb8 11. Rc6 Rd6 12. Rc7+! Kd8 13. a7 Bxa7 14. Rxa7 Kxc8 15. Rxg7) 11. Rd3+ Kc7 12. Rxd8 Kxd8 13. Bxe6, with an easy win because now there are passed pawns on both sides.

c) 9. ... Bb6 10. Rc8 Rd8 11. Rc6 Rd6 (or 11. ... Ba7 12. Bc8 as above) 12. Rxb6 Rxb6 13. a7.

Since White wins easily in all three cases, Black will be compelled, after his pawn moves are exhausted, to stake everything on a counterattack.

9. ... g6 10. Rc2 h5 11. Rc3

Simplest is 11. Rc8, for if 11. ... Rd8 12. Rxd8 Kxd8 13. e4 Ke7 14. exf5 exf5 15. Kd3, and wins, since Black must keep his king at e7 to defend the king-side pawns, whereupon the White king marches in. But the move chosen is methodical and good enough.

11. ... Rb6 12. Rc7+ Kd6 13. Rg7 Rb2+ 14. Kd3!! Ra2 15. Rxg6 Ra3+ 16. Kc4 Bxe3 17. Bd5! Bxf4 18. Rxe6+ Kc7 19. Rc6+ Kb8 20. Rg6 (if 20. Rb6+? Ka7 21. Kb5? Ra5+!! 22. Kxa5 Bc7, =) **20. ... Bc7 21. Bb7 Ka7**

There is no defense: if 21. ... Ra5 22. Kb4! Re5 23. Bf3! Ka7 24. Rg7 Kb6 25. a7 and wins. If here 22. ... f4 23. Rg8+ Ka7 24. Rg7 Bd8 25. Rd7 Bb6 26. Bf3+ Kxa6 27. Be2+ and mate next move.

22. Rg5

Winning a second pawn: if 22. ... Ra4+ 23. Kb5 Rxh4 24. Rg8 Bb8 25. Bf3, Black has to sacrifice at least a piece to avoid mate.

22. ... Bd8 23. Rxh5 Bxh4 24. Rxf5. The rest is simple: it would also be won with the rooks off the board. **24. ... Kb6 25. Rb5+ Kc7 26. Rb3 Ra5 27. Kd4 Bf2+ 28. Ke4 Kd6 29. Rd3+ Ke6 30. Bc8+ Ke7 31. Rd5 Ra4+ 32. Kf5 Bg3 33. Rd7+ Kf8 34. a7 Bf2 35. Ba6!**, resigns.

But if there are no such additional weaknesses the game should be drawn with best play.

No. 887, Keres-Fine, Zandvoort 1936

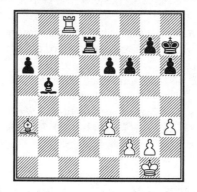

White to play. Draw

No. 887 may be taken as a model.

1. Bb4!

Preventing the advance of the a-pawn. It is futile for Black to try to get the king to the queenside, since the king cannot cross the c-file. Nor can Black attempt to advance the a-pawn by 1. ... Rd1+ and ... Ra1, for White would reply Rc7 and get up a dangerous counterattack against the Black king position. So the only chance is to secure some advantage on the kingside.

1. ... h5 2. h4! (2. ... h4! would cramp him too much) **2. ... e5 3. Kh2 Kg6 4. Kg3 Bd3 5. Rc6 Rb7 6. Bc3** (threat: 7. Bxe5) **6. ... Bb5 7. Rc8 Kf7 8. f3** (necessary to allow the king to get to the other wing if the rooks are exchanged) **8. ... Rd7 9. Kf2 Rd1 10. Rc7+ Kg8 11. g4!**

The strongest defense. If 11. Rc8+ Kh7 12. Rc7, threatening Bb4-f8, Black has a curious win with 12. ... Rc1 13. Ba5? Rf1+ 14. Kg3 Ra1 15. Bb4 Ra2!! 16. Bf8 Kg8!! 17. Bxg7 Bf1, and transposes into a won rook-and-pawn ending: 18. Rc1! Rxg2+ 19. Kh3 Rxg7+ 20. Rxf1 Ra7, etc.

11. ... Rf1+ 12. Kg2?

But this loses. 12. Kg3! is essential. If then 12. ... e4, as in the game, there is the surprising rejoinder 13. fxe4 hxg4 14. e5!! Rf3+ 15. Kxg4 Be2 16. exf6!, and Black has nothing to discover, so after 16. ... gxf6 17. Kh5!! a draw must result.

12. ... e4! 13. fxe4 (13. g5 exf3+ 14. Kg3 Be2! 15. gxf6 gxf6 16. Bxf6 Rg1+ 17. Kf2 Rg2+ 18. Ke1 Bb5 and wins) **13. ... hxg4 14. e5 Rf3!** (this mating combination is disastrous for White) **15. exf6 gxf6 16. Kg1 Bf1!**

Threatening 16. ... g3, ... Bh3 and ... Rf1 mate, so White must beat a hasty retreat. The game would still be a draw with the rooks gone, but now Black has a mating attack.

17. Rc6 Kf7 18. e4 g3 19. e5 fxe5 20. Bxe5 Bh3 21. Rc1 a5 22. Kh1 a4 23. Bd4 a3 24. Rc2 Rb3! 25. h5 Rb1+ 26. Bg1 Rb2 27. Rc7+ Ke6 28. Bd4 Rb1+ 29. Bg1 a2, resigns.

With fewer pawns the winning prospects are even more meager. **No. 888** is an example from a world championship match.

No. 888, Tarrasch-Lasker, 14th match game, 1908

Black to play. Draw

The same considerations apply here as in the previous example: White must attempt to win on the kingside, but nothing can be forced. **1. ... Kf8 2. b5 Ke7 3. Rd1 Rd8 4. Rb1 Bd5 5. Bg5+ f6 6. Bf4 Bb7 7. Re1+ Kd7 8. Rc1 Ke6 9. b6 Rd7 10. Re1+ Kd5 11. Re8 Kc6 12. Be3 Ba6 13. Ra8 Bd3 14. Rb8 Ba6 15. Kh2 Bd3 16. g4 Bg6 17. Kg3 h5 18. f4 hxg4 19. hxg4 Re7** (an inaccuracy; 19. ... f5 practically forces the draw) **20. Rc8+ Kb7 21. Rc3 Be4 22. f5 g6?** (should lose; 22. ... Bd5 is still good enough) **23. g5 Rf7** (23. ... fxg5 24. f6) **24. gxf6?** (24. Ra3 wins, for if 24. ... Kb8 25. Ra7 Rxa7 26. bxa7+ Ka8 27. gxf6, etc. Or 24. ... Bd5 25. fxg6, etc.) **24. ... Rxf6 25. Rc7+ Ka6 26. Ra7+ Kb5 27. b7 Bxb7,** and after the exchange of the last pawn, a theoretical draw results.

2. Potential Outside Passed Pawn

There is a great difference between this classification and the previous one because the superior side can not only try to create a passed pawn in a favorable position, but can also attempt to get two connected passed pawns or create an unbalanced pawn position where even the bishop alone might win.

No. 889, Keres-Fine, Warsaw 1935

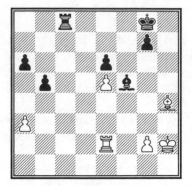

Black wins

No. 889 is a rather difficult example that illustrates this point. If we remove the two a-pawns the game is undeniably drawn. But because of the extra pawn White is always tied down to the queenside for fear of allowing two connected passed pawns. **1. ... Rc4** (1. ... Rc3 2. Be7) **2. Be7 Be4 3. Rf2 Bd5 4. Bd6 Kh7 5. Kh3 Kg6 6. g3 Be4 7. Rf4 a5 8. Rf2 Rc3 9. Rf4 Bf3 10. Be7 Bd5 11. Rg4+ Kf7 12. Bd6 Rc1!** (the following break cannot be prevented) **13. Rf4+ Kg6 14. Rg4+ Kh7 15. Rh4+ Kg8 16. Rf4 Ra1 17. Kg4!!** (the only chance is a mating attack!) **17. ... b4! 18. axb4 a4! 19. Kg5 Rg1 20. g4 a3 21. Kg6 Be4+! 22. Rxe4 a2 23. Rf4 Rxg4+! 24. Rxg4 a1=Q** and should win.

It is always wise in such endings to play aggressively and upset the balance of the pawn position whenever possible. An example is **No. 890**, (Capablanca-Tartakower, Bad Kissingen 1928): **White king at g1, rooks at a1, f1, bishop at f5, pawns at a2, b2, c4, f2, g2, h2; Black king at c7, rooks at d8, h8, bishop at f6, pawns at a7, b7, c6, h7.** White to play wins. **1. Rad1!** (1. Rab1? Rd2, or 1. Rae1? Rd2 2. Re6 Rf8!) **1. ... Bxb2 2. Rxd8 Rxd8 3. Bxh7 Rd4 4. g3! Rxc4 5. h4,** and White won by advancing his three connected passed pawns.

3. The Extra Pawn in the Center

The situation here is worse for the superior side than when he has the pawn on the wing because it is much harder to get play on two wings. The best chance is to try to get two connected passed pawns. **No. 891** is an example with a classic finish.

No. 891, Johner-Rubinstein, Carlsbad 1907

White to play. Draw

White can draw at once by **1. f4!**, for if **1. ... f6 2. fxe5 fxe5 3. h3! Bc8** (other squares are just as bad) **4. Rxe5 Rd1+ 5. Kh2 Rxc1 6. Re8+ Kf7 7. Rxc8**, while if **1. ... exf4 2. Bxf4 c6 3. b4 h6 4. Be3**, the position is too simplified to offer any real chances.

Instead, White played too passively and lost: **1. f3? Be6 2. Kf2 Rd5 3. b4 h6 4. g3 Bd7 5. Be3 f5 6. Rc1 c6 7. Rc2 Kf7 8. Ke2** (8. Rd2 Ke6!, and if White exchanges he gives Black two connected passed pawns) **8. ... g5 9. Bc5 f4 10. Ra2 Bf5 11. gxf4 Bd3+ 12. Ke1 gxf4 13. Ra7+ Kg6 14. Re7 Bb5! 15. Re6+ Kg7!! 16. Bd6 Kf7!! 17. Rxh6 Rd3!!** (the point: White gets two passed pawns in the center) **18. Kf2 Re3 19. Bc5 Re2+ 20. Kg1 Bc4 21. Rxc6 Bd5 22. Rd6 Bxf3 23. h4 e4 24. Bd4 Rd2 25. Be5 e3! 26. Bxf4 Rg2+**, White resigned, since Black queens by force.

To sum up: Material advantage is always more easily exploited with rooks on the board. In some cases, though not all, the presence of the rooks is the deciding factor.

B. Positional Advantage

With only bishops on the board, the positional advantage must be very great in order to win. But the rooks alter the situation and introduce two new elements: easier exploitation of weak pawns, and mating combinations.

1. Weak Pawns

Without rooks it is rarely possible to attack and capture enemy pawns; even if a pawn is won, a draw usually results. Weak pawns are usually fatal only if they block the action of the bishop (see No. 440). But with rooks, the situation is very different because enemy pawns can be attacked twice (bishop and rook) or even three times, (bishop, rook, and king) but defended only twice at most (rook and king).

No. 892 is an excellent illustration. Without the four rooks, Black could win two pawns starting with ... Bxf4, but the reply Bh3-c8 would give White more than enough to draw. With rooks, however, Black can also win a pawn while his position remains just as powerful.

No. 892, Alekhine-Euwe, 21st match game, 1935

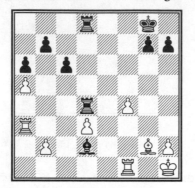

Black to play wins

The game continuation is exemplary: **1. ... Rb4!** (1. ... Bxf4 2. Rb3 gives White counterplay, or 1. ... Rxd3 2. Rxd3 Rxd3 3. Rd1) **2. Rf2** (or 2. Ra2 Rxd3 3. Rd1 Rdd4) **2. ... Rxb2 3. Bf1** (better 3. Be4 Rb1+ 4. Kg2 Be3 5. Rf3 Rb2+ 6. Kg3, though 6. ... Bg1 still wins) **3. ... Rd4 4. f5 Rf4! 5. Rxf4 Bxf4 6. h3 Bd6 7. Ra1 Kf7**. With so many weak pawns the entry of the king is conclusive. Even without rooks the win would now be only a question of time. **8. d4 Kf6 9. Re1 Bb4 10. Ra1 Rd2 11. Bc4 Rxd4 12. Be6 Rd8** (preventing Bc8), White resigned.

2. Mating Combinations

No. 893, Yates-Rubinstein, Moscow, 1925

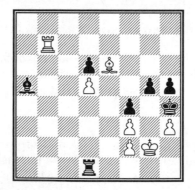

Black to play

Mating combinations occur far more often with opposite-colored bishops than with same-colored bishops because the attacking bishop cannot be opposed.

In **No. 893**, one of the more common types, Rubinstein played **1. ... Rd2??** and lost after **2. Bg4!! Bb6** (the threat was Rh7 and Rxh5 mate) **3. Rxb6 hxg4 4. hxg4** (the right continuation is 4. fxg4! f3+ 5. Kxf3 Rxd5 6. Kg2!) **4. ... Rb2?** (4. ... Rc2! 5. Rxd6 Rc6; if 5. Rc6 or 5. Kf1 Rc3 holds) **5. Rc6!!** (but not 5. Rxd6 Rb6! 6. Rd7 Rb7 7. Rd8 Rb8 8. Rd6 Rb6, etc., =. Now White has time to move his king and lift the stalemate.) **5. ... Rb1 6. Rc4!** (threatening Re4-e6) **6. ... Re1 7. Re4 Rxe4** (desperation; if 7. ... Re2 8. Re6 wins at once) **8. fxe4 Kxg4 9. e5! f3+ 10. Kg1 Kf5 11. e6**, resigns.

The correct defense would have been 1. ... Be1! 2. Rb2 Rd2, =.

A more complicated instance is **No. 894**.

No. 894, Nimzovich-Wolf, Carlsbad 1923

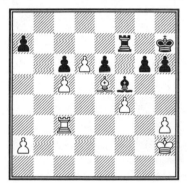

White to play wins

Nimzovitch evolved the following ingenious idea: **1. h4!** (preventing ... g5) **1. ... Kg8** (if 1. ... Rb7 2. Rb3!, and Black cannot exchange rooks) **2. Rb3 Rd7 3. Rb8+ Kf7 4. Rc8 Be4 5. Kg3 h5 6. Kf2 Bd5 7. Ke3 Bg2 8. Kd4 Bh1 9. Bh8!!** (The point of White's plan. The idea is Ke5, Bf6-g5-h6, and Rf8 mate. If Black replies ... Rb7, then Rc7+ wins. Black has no choice but to give up a pawn) **9. ... e5+ 10. Kxe5 Bd5 11. Bf6 Bf3 12. Bg5 Kg7** (now 13. Rc7 can be met by 13. ... Bg4) **13. f5!!** (the coup de grace: the immediate threat is 13. Ke6) **13. ... Bg4 14. f6+ Kh7 15. Rxc6**, resigns.

III. ROOK VS. TWO MINOR PIECES

In the ending, two pieces are approximately equivalent to a rook plus one pawn. However, the nature of the pawn configuration may force a change in this estimate. When the pawns are scattered or offer convenient targets, the pieces are superior; when the pawns are solid, a rook will usually be able to

hold its own. A great deal depends on who has the initiative; this consideration is much more prominent here than in any other ending.

If there are no pawns on the board, the game is drawn. Passing over this
trivial case, these endings fall into three groups, according to the amount of
material each side has.

A. Even Pawns

This will usually be a draw, but the two pieces win more often than the rook.
They are especially effective when the enemy pawns are exposed and cannot
be defended with other pawns. In that case, the two pieces can pile up on a
pawn, which is guarded by rook and king, and exchange both minor pieces
for rook and pawn, when they have in effect captured a pawn.

No. 895. Marco-Blackburne, Nuremburg 1896

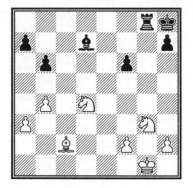

White to play wins

Sometimes the king is far away or there are too many weaknesses, and a
pawn cannot be defended at all.

No. 895 is an excellent illustration of this type of position where the two
pieces win.

One glance reveals White's considerable advantage. His pieces occupy
excellent, impregnable squares and there is no open file that is of any earthly
use to the rook. Black has a motley assortment of weak pawns and is condemned to a policy of watchful waiting.

1. f3 (releasing the pin and preparing to centralize his king) **1. ... Rc8**
(threatening ... Rc3 with some counterplay) **2. Nge2 a5?** (suicidal; the only
chance is the patient 2. ... Kg7 3. Kf2 h6, although after 4. Ke3 Kf7 5. Kd2 Ke7
6. Bb3 Kd6 7. Nf4, Black is almost completely tied up and should lose in the
long run) **3. Bd3!** (not 3. Kf2? axb4 4. axb4 Rc4! 5. b5 Bxb5, =) **3. ... axb4 4. axb4
Ra8** (another open file but it's just as useless as the others);

White now sets out to capture the b-pawn. **5. Kf2 Ra4** (this loses quickly; 5.
... Rb8 6. Ke3 Kg7 7. Nc3 also loses but it will take longer) **6. b5 Rb4 7. Ke3**

Kg7 **8. Nf4 Rb2 9. Be2 Rb1 10. Nd5! Bc8** (or 10. ... Rh1 11. Nxb6 Be8 12. Nd5 Rxh2 13. b6 Rh1 14. b7 Rb1 15. Bb5 and wins) **11. Nxb6 Bb7.**

The rest is simple: by advancing the b-pawn White will capture material. Black later gave up.

Where there are no serious weaknesses, the initiative in conjunction with the two bishops may be decisive.

No. 896, Bernstein-Alekhine, Berne 1932

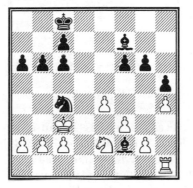

Black to play wins

Without any obvious blunders or even mistakes in judgment by his opponent, Alekhine methodically conducts the game to a successful conclusion. Black first rids himself of his doubled pawn on the queenside, then exchanges knights, and finally creates enemy targets for his king and bishops.

1. ... Ne5 2. Rf1 Be3 3. b3 c5 4. Nc1 Bd4+ 5. Kd2 c4 6. c3 Bc5 7. b4 Bf8! 8. Ne2 c5 9. a3 Kd7 10. Kc2 Nd3 11. f4 Be6 12. Nc1 Bg4! 13. Nxd3 Be2 14. Ne5+ fxe5 15. Rf2 Bd3+ 16. Kb2 cxb4 17. axb4 exf4 18. Rxf4 Bd6 (now that the position has been opened, the rest is simple. To start with, White must lose at least one pawn.) **19. Rf7+ Ke6 20. Rf3 Bxe4 21. Re3 Kd5 22. g3 a5 23. bxa5 bxa5,** White resigned.

The side with the rook can win only if he has the initiative and can convert that into material gain. As a rule, this happens when the enemy pieces are scattered and not well coordinated.

No. 897, Canal-Capablanca, Budapest 1929

Black wins

In **No. 897**, the two pieces are helpless because they do not work together. After **1. ... Rb1 2. Bd5 Rcb8 3. Kg2 R8b3! 4. Rxb3 Rxb3 5. Nd2** (5. a4 Rb4) **5. ... Rxa3**, Black's two passed pawns win. **6. Ne4 a5! 7. Nxc5 gxf6 8. Kf1 a4 9. Ke2 Ra1 10. Nd3 a3 11. c5 a2 12. Kf3 Rd1 13. Bxa2 Rxd3+ 14. Ke4 Rd2 15. Bc4 Kf8!,** and Black won. The speed with which the White position fell apart is surprising, but there does not seem to be anything that he could have done.

From this example we conclude that the rook wins with a distant passed pawn that is not adequately blockaded. This is not a very common situation, however, so we are naturally inclined to try to formulate a more general rule. One such rule is: *wherever a player has two widely separated passed pawns and the rook, the rook wins.* The reason is that two pieces can cooperate to control one given square, but not two.

However, the above rule generally applies only when the side with the rook is a pawn ahead. As we know, if the two pieces are not properly coordinated, that side will lose material.

No. 898 is another ending that helps to make this theory clearer.

No. 898, Reti-Bogolyubov, Bad Kissingen 1928

Black to play

First of all, it is clear that Black must win a pawn, mainly because of the unfortunate position of the White knight.

1. ... Rb1 2. Ne3 Rxb3 3. a5 (else he loses this pawn, too) **3. ... b5!** (he must avoid the blockading Bd8) **4. axb6 Rxb6.**

Now White's primary concern must be to blockade the a-pawn. But in addition, there is an obvious target in Black's camp – the e-pawn – that must be kept under observation. The most logical line is 5. Nc4 Rb4 (after 5. ... Rb5 6. Ke3 Rc5 7. Kd3 Kf7 8. Bd2 Ke6 9. Bc3, the game is a hopeless draw) 6. Nxe5 Rxe4 7. Nc6 Kf8 8. Be3 Ke6 9. Ke2 Kd5 10. Na5 Ra4 11. Bd2 Kc5 12. Kd3 Kb5 13. Nb7, and since the Black pawn still cannot advance, a draw must result.

Instead, White played **5. Ke2? Rb4! 6. Kf3 Kf7 7. Bh4 Rb1** (7. ... a5 at once is simpler) **8. Nc4 Ke6 9. Bg3 Rc1! 10. Na5** (not 10. Nxe5 Rc3+ and 11. ... Rxg3) **10. ... Ra1 11. Nc4 Ra4 12. Ne3 a5 13. Be1 Ra3 14. Ke2 a4 15. Nc2 Rb3 16. Bb4**

Opportunity knocks twice in this ending. The forward march of the pawn is securely stopped. Black's only chance now is to secure threats on the king-side.

16. ... h5 17. Bf8 g5 18. h3 Rb1 19. Kd2 Rf1 20. Bc5 Rf4 21. Kd3 Rf7 22. Be3 Rd7+ 23. Ke2 Rg7 24. g4??

This gives Black his long-sought chance to get play on the kingside. After 24. Bc1 or 24. Na3, the game is drawn, since 24. ... g4 25. hxg4 is meaningless.

24. ... h4!! 25. Bc1 Rc7 26. Kd3 Rb7!! 27. Bxg5 Rb3+ 28. Kc4 Rxh3, and now White must lose a piece. The remaining moves: **29. Kb4 a3!! 30. Nxa3 Rxa3! 31. Bxh4** (31. Kxa3 h3 and queens) **31. ... Re3 32. Kc4 Rxe4+ 33. Kd3 Rxg4 34. Bf2 Kf5 35. Ke3 Ra4 36. Kf3 Ra3+ 37. Be3 Rb3,** White resigned.

When all the pawns are on one side and without any weaknesses, the game is drawn. **No. 899** is the model.

No. 899, Capablanca-Lasker, St. Petersburg 1914

Draw

After **1. ... Re2 2. Bf2 f6 3. Kf1 Ra2 4. g4 Kf7 5. Ne4 h6 6. Kg2 Ra3 7. f4 Rb3 8. Ng3 Ra3 9. Nf1 Rd3 10. Ne3 Rc3 11. Kf3 Ra3 12. f5 Ra2 13. Nd5 Rb2 14. Nf4 Ra2 15. h4 Ra5 16. Ne6 Rb5 17. Ke4 Rb2 18. Bd4 Rb4 19. Kd5 Rb1**, Capablanca tried the break **20. g5**, which is the only possible winning chance but still could only draw. Lasker replied **20. ... hxg5 21. hxg5 fxg5 22. Nxg5+** (if 22. Nxg7 g4 23. Ne6 g3 24. Ng5+ Kg8 25. f6 Rb5+ 26. Bc5 Rxc5+! 27. Kxc5 g2 28. Nf3 Kf7, =) **22. ... Kg8 23. Ne6 Rd1**. White can never win the g-pawn under favorable circumstances.

B. The Player With the Two Pieces Is One or More Pawns Ahead

When there are a number of pawns on the board, two pieces plus an extra pawn always win against the rook. This is shown most simply by the fact that when there is nothing else left, two pieces plus pawn still win, unless there's a rook-pawn and wrong bishop or two knights.

The winning method is nothing more than the methodical advance of the pawns. Exceptions occur with rook-pawn and wrong-color bishop, with two knights, and in certain special positions where the two pieces are for one reason or another not working together satisfactorily.

Such a special case is **No. 900** (Fine-Appel, Lodz 1935): **White king at c5, rook at e7; Black king at f5, bishop at d5, knight at f6, pawn at e4.** White to play draws. After **1. Kd4!** the pawn cannot advance. **1. ... Kf4 2. Re5 Bb3 3. Rb5! Bc2** (if 3. ... Be6 4. Rb6 Kf5 5. Rb1) **4. Rb2 Bd1 5. Rb7!** (now 5. Rb1 Bf3 6. Rf1 Ng4 loses) **5. ... Bh5 6. Re7! Bg6** (there is no good alternative) **7. Re6 Kg5** (7. ... Kf5 8. Re5+) **8. Ke5 Ng4+ 9. Kd4 Nf2** (or 9. ... Nf6 10. Ke5) **10. Rxg6+** and a draw was agreed, since 10. ... Kxg6 11. Ke3 is routine.

While two knights plus pawn only draw vs. a rook because the rook can be sacrificed for the pawn, when there are more pawns the two knights usually win.

No. 901, Chekhover-Euwe, Leningrad 1934

White to play, Black wins

1. f4 There are no wholly satisfactory alternatives; e.g.:

a) 1. Rd1 e5 2. f4 Kd6 3. f5 Nc4! 4. Rg1 Nxa3 5. Rxg7 Ke7 6. Rh7 Nc4 7. Rxh6 Nd6 8. Rh4 Nb3 and wins the e-pawn.

b) 1. a4 Nc6! 2. Ra1 Na5 and the a-pawn is a constant headache.

1. ... Nb5 2. Rb1 Kc6 3. Rc1+ Kd6 4. Rd1+ Kc5 5. Rg1 g6 6. Rh1 h5 7. f5 (seeking salvation in exchanges, but the knights can hold everything) **7. ... gxf5 8. exf5 e5!**

With this strong passed pawn the win becomes routine. Of course, Black is careful not to allow the exchange of f-pawns.

9. Rc1+ (or 9. Rxh5 Nxa3 10. Rh7 f6 11. Rh6 Nd5) **9. ... Nc4 10. a4 Nd6 11. a5 Kb5 12. f6 Nxa5.** Now the win is straightforward: **13. Kg3 Nac4 14. Kh4 Kc5 15. Kxh5 Kd5 16. Kg5 Ke6 17. Rf1 Ne4+ 18. Kh6 Nxf6 19. Kg7 Nh5+ 20. Kf8 f5,** White resigned.

C. The Player With the Rook Is One or More Pawns Ahead

Rook plus one pawn vs. two pieces is usually a draw, though either side may have winning chances. Rook plus two pawns always win.

When there is nothing else on the board, rook plus pawn offers no winning prospects at all, since the opponent can, if he wishes, even give up one of his pieces for the pawn. With more material the game is still normally drawn, but positional considerations may weight the scale in favor of one side or the other.

No. 902, Flohr-Keres, Semmering-Baden 1937

White to play

No. 902 illustrates the chances and counterchances. White must rely first on his f-pawn, which will eventually be passed, and second on the attempt to win material by aiming at some weak point (e.g., c6). But for the time being neither of these ideas can be realized successfully. If:

a) 1. Ba4 h5! 2. Ng6! (2. Nxc6? h4 3. Kf1 h3 4. Kg1 h2+ 5. Kh1 Rf8 6. Ne7 Rxf2 7. Nxd5+ Kb7 8. Bd7 Rxa2, and Black has all the winning chances: 9. e4? Rd2, or 9. Nf6 a5 10. e4 a4 11. e5 a3 12. e6 Re2, etc.) 2. ... Rh6 3. Ne5 h4! (better than 3. ... c5 4. Nd7+ Ka5 5. Nxc5 h4 6. Bb3 h3 7. Bxd5 h2 8. Bh1, and White should win) 4. Bxc6 Rxc6 5. Nxc6 Kxc6 6. Kf3 Kb5! 7. Kg4 Kc4 8. f4! gxf4 9. exf4 Kxd4 10. Kxh4 Ke4 11. Kg5! d4 12. f5 and the resulting queen ending is drawn.

b) 1. f4?? gxf4 2. exf4 Re8. Good knight!

Therefore, White must improve his position before he can make any winning attempt. Black's prospects, on the other hand, lie first in his passed h-pawn, and second in securing a passed pawn on the queenside. The first is of more defensive than offensive value, for White can easily blockade that pawn, whereas a queenside passed pawn cannot be forced.

We must conclude, therefore, that White has the better of it and that Black may well be satisfied with a draw.

The game continued **1. Ng6 Rb8! 2. Kf3**

Hoping to stop the h-pawn and capture the c-pawn, but Black has enough counterplay on the queenside. The alternative, 2. Ne5 Kc7 3. Bb3 a5 4. Kd3 Rf8! 5. Ke2 Rb8, is no improvement, since the winning attempt 6. f4? gxf4 7. exf4 Rb4 is far too dangerous. 8. Kd3 a4 9. Bd1 a3 10. Kc3 Rb2 11. Bb3 h5, etc.

2. ... c5!

Threatening to secure another passed pawn, so White has no time for 3. Kg4-h5. For instance, 3. Kg4? c4! 4. Kh5 Kc7 5. Kxh6 Rb2 6. Bf5 Rxf2 7. Kxg5 c3 and Black wins.

3. Ne5 Rd8 4. dxc5+ Kxc5 5. Bb3!

Fastening on the new target. 5. Nf7? Rf8 6. Bg6 Kb4 7. Kg4 Ka3 8. f4 gxf4 9. exf4 a5 is much too dangerous

5. ... Re8 6. Nd3+ Kd6 7. Nb4 (leads to simplification, but 7. Kg3 a5 offers no real winning chances) **7. ... a5! 8. Nc2**

8. Nxd5 a4 9. Bxa4 Rf8+ 10. Ke4 Rxf2 11. Bb3 g4 should win for Black because his pawns are unimpeded.

8. ... Rf8+ 9. Kg2 Ra8! 10. Nd4 a4 11. Bd1 Kc5 (or 11. ... a3 12. Bb3) **12. a3 Kc4 13. Nc6 Kc3 14. Bf3.**

Here a draw was agreed. A likely conclusion is 14. ... Kb2 15. Bxd5 Kxa3 16. f4 gxf4 17. exf4 Kb2 18. Kg3 a3 19. Kh4 a2 20. Bxa2 Kxa2 21. Kh5 Kb3 22. Ne5, etc.

The rook is seen at its best when (as in Nos. 897 and 898) there are passed pawns on both sides of the board. Two rooks may be superior to rook plus bishop and knight when they have strong files at their disposal.

Rook plus two pawns vs. two minor pieces is a win, subject to the inevitable exceptions of blockade and special cases like drawn rook and pawn vs. bishop or knight endings (see Nos. 924, 926, 971, and 972).

No. 903 is the general case.

No. 903, Steinitz-Zukertort, 13th match game, 1886

Black to play. White wins

The game continuation was 1. ... Bd4?, after which White won by force: 2. Kh6 Bg7+ 3. Kh7 Bd4 4. g6+ Kf6 5. Rxe7 Kxe7 6. g7, etc.

But against the best defense, **1. ... Bg7!**, White cannot force his king through to h6 because he cannot gain a tempo with his rook. On 2. Rc7 Be5 3. Ra7 Bd4 4. Rd7 Be5! follows; if now 5. Kh6? Ke8, =.

There remains the alternative: trying to force the advance of the pawns. Though this is a long and arduous process, analysis, mainly by Berger, shows that it can be done.

After **1. ... Bg7**, the most forceful win is **2. Kg4!** (not 2. Rb5 Bd4 3. Kh6? Ng8+ 4. Kh7? Nf6+!! 5. gxf6 Be3!!, = because the White king is trapped in the corner) **2. ... Bc3** (the White king wants to reach e4; on other bishop moves, Kf3-e4 at once may follow) **3. Rb3!** (now 3. Kf3? Bd2! is useless for White) **3. ... Bg7**

The alternatives are:

a) 3. ... Nd5 4. Kf3 Ke7 5. Ke4 Kd6 6. Ra3 Kc6 7. Ra6+ Kc5 8. f6;

b) 3. ... Be5 4. Rb5 Bc3 5. Rb7! Be5 6. Kf3 Bc3 7. Ke4 Bd2 8. g6+ Kf6 (8. ... Kf8 9. Ke5) 9. Rb6+ Kg7 10. f6+!! Kxg6 11. fxe7+ Kf7 12. Re6! Ke8 13. Kf5 Bb4 14. Re4 Bxe7 15. Ke6, with a standard win: No. 913.

4. Kf4 (not 4. f6? Bxf6 5. Rf3 Ng8 6. gxf6 Kg6! 7. f7 Nh6+ and 8. ... Nxf7, =) **4. ... Bh8 5. Ke4 Bg7**

Now that the king is centralized, White can set about advancing his pawns.

6. Rb6 Bc3

If 6. ... Bh8 7. g6+ Kf8 (or 7. ... Kg7 8. Rb8 Ng8 9. Ke5 Nf6 10. Rxh8, etc.) 8. Rb8+ Kg7 9. Kf4 followed by Kg5.

7. f6 Ng6

Or 7. ... Nc8 8. Rc6, or 7. ... Bxf6 8. Rxf6+ Kg7 9. Ra6, or finally 7. ... Ng8 8. Kf5, and the sacrifices 8. ... Nxf6 9. gxf6 or 8. ... Bxf6 9. gxf6 Nh6+ 10. Kg5 are not of any use.

8. Rb7+ Ke6 (8. ... Ke8 9. Kf5 is worse) **9. Rg7! Nh4** (on other knight moves, 10. Re7+ and 11. Kf5 follow) **10. Re7+ Kd6 11. Rh7 Ng6 12. Kf5 Nf8 13. g6!,** and Black must give up both pieces for the two pawns.

If the pawns are further back, a methodical advance will get them to their goal. Unconnected pawns win even more easily because both pieces are needed to stop only one of them. The king and rook then support the advance of the other pawn. If one piece alone stops a pawn, the rook can force it to be sacrificed and then go back to the other wing. Of course, drawn positions with rook and pawn vs. bishop or knight must be avoided. When there is additional material the win is much easier because a piece sacrifice is then unavailing.

To sum up: Two pieces plus one pawn win against a rook. Rook plus one pawn vs. two pieces is normally a draw, while rook plus two pawns vs. two pieces is won. With more material on the board, positional considerations may alter these rules.

IV. THREE PIECES VS. TWO ROOKS

Though normally a draw, this favors the pieces because they have more play. With an extra pawn the pieces win. **No. 904** illustrates.

No. 904, Capablanca-Alekhine, Nottingham 1936

White to play wins

The pieces are highly effective here because Black's pawns offer so many convenient targets and because the Black rooks are so passive.

The game continued **1. Nd2!** (threatening Ne4-c3-d5, which would tie Black down to the defense of the b-pawn) **1. ... f5** (on 1. ... cxb4 2. axb4 a5 3. b5! a4 4. Nb1!, Black must defend his b-pawn and still has no real counterplay) **2. b5!** (fixing the queenside pawns) **2. ... a5** (2. ... axb5 3. cxb5 is much worse) **3. Nf1 Kf7 4. Ng3 Kg6** (on 4. ... Ke6 5. Bh3, Black's king cannot get any closer to the queenside) **5. Bf3 Re7 6. Kf1 Kf6 7. Bd2 Kg6 8. a4.**

The game was adjourned here and Alekhine resigned without resuming play. The reason is that he has no counterchances whatsoever and is defenseless against White's threats.

A likely conclusion would be 8. ... Re6 9. Bc3 Re7 10. h4 Re6 11. h5+ Kh6 12. Kg2 Re7 13. Kh3 Re6 14. Kh4 Re7 15. Bg2 Rd7 16. Bh3 Rdf7 17. Bb2. Black is in zugzwang and must lose at least a pawn and the exchange. After the further 17. ... Re7 18. Nxf5+ Rxf5 19. Bxf5 Re2 20. Bf6 Ra2 (the only chance) 21. Bg5+ Kg7 22. h6+, he must also lose the h-pawn, since 22. ... Kg8 23. Be7! Rxa4 allows mate in two: 24. Be6+ and 25. Bf6 mate. Note the helplessness of the rooks in this ending.

V. THE ADVANTAGE OF THE EXCHANGE

A. Rook vs. Bishop (No Pawns)

In the general case (pieces arbitrarily placed) this is a draw. It can be won by force only if the Black king is in the "wrong" corner or in the center with his opponent having the opposition.

The wrong corner is defined here as the one that is the same color as the bishop; the right corner is the opposite color.

It is always possible to force the king to the edge of the board by successively pinning the bishop or threatening mate. But the Black king should head for the right corner as fast as its legs will carry it, and once there nothing can happen to it. **No. 905** is the normal draw.

No. 905

White to play. Draw

The bishop may be on any square where it does not allow mate or capture. The attempt **1. Ra8+ Bg8** leads to nothing because 2. Kg6 or 2. Rb8 both stalemate.

Though No. 905 is an easy draw, there are a number of traps awaiting the unwary player, all of which arise when the bishop cannot get back to the square directly next to the king:

No. 906, Maestre 1939

White to play wins

The simplest solution is: **1. Rd4!** and Black is in zugzwang:
a) 1. ... Bg4 or 1. ... Bd7 2. Rxd7;
b) 1. ... Bf5 or 1. ... Be6 2. Kxe6;
c) 1. ... Bc8 2. Rd8+ and 3. Rxc8;
d) 1. ... Bg2 2. Rg4+ and 3. Rxg2;

e) 1. ... Bf1 2. Kg6! and either mates or if 2. ... Kf8 3. Rf4+ wins the bishop;
f) 1. ... Kf8 2. Rd8+ mate;
g) 1. ... Kh8 or 1. ... Kh7 2. Rh4+ and 3. Rxh3.
An interesting illustration of the power of the centralized rook!

No. 907

White wins

Black's king cannot escape the noose and he is limited to bishop moves. The best defense is **1. ... Ba2!** (so that White cannot threaten mate and attack the bishop simultaneously) **2. Ra3 Bb1** (2. ... Bc4 3. Ra4, or 2. ... Bd5 3. Ra5 Bf7 4. Rf5 Bg6 5. Rf6, etc.) **3. Rb3 Bc2 4. Rb2 Bf5 5. Rb5 Bg4 6. Rb6 Bh3 7. Rh6** wins.

White to play wins with the rook anywhere else on the board. However, with his rook on f1 the win is rather difficult. **No. 908** (Maestre 1939): **White king at f2, rook at f1; Black king at h2, bishop at f5.** White to play wins. **1. Rg1 Kh3** (or 1. ... Be4 2. Rg4) **2. Kf3 Kh2** (2. ... Kh4 3. Kf4 Bh3 4. Rh1) **3. Rg3 Be4+ 4. Kf2,** and we are back to No. 907.

But **No. 909,** (Maestre): **Black bishop at f7 or h5,** other pieces as in No. 908, is drawn because White cannot force the winning position; e.g., **1. Rg1 Kh3** and **2. Kf3** is impossible, so Black can get back to the right corner.

When no immediate mate is threatened, White wins only if he can transpose into No. 907.

No. 910, Maestre 1939

White to play

White wins in **No. 910** only if his rook can get to one of five different squares:

a) **1. Rb6 Bg2+ 2. Kc7**, as in No. 907.

b) **1. Rb2 B any 2. Rb6**, again No. 907.

c) **1. Ra2+ Kb8 2. Rb2+ Kc8 3. Rf2**.

d) **1. Rg3 Kb8** (or 1. ... Be2 2. Rb3! and 3. Rb6) **2. Rg7 B any 3. Rc7** followed by **4. Kb6**: No. 907.

e) **1. Rd2 Bc4** (if 1. ... Bh3 or 1. ... Kb8, then 2. Rb2 as in c) **2. Rb2 Ka6 3. Rb4** and wins.

When the king is not yet confined to the corner, the game is always drawn.

No. 911, Maestre 1939

Draw

In **No. 911** the best try is **1. Re3**, when **1. ... Bg6!** is the only reply (if 1. ... Bc2 or b1 2. Re7+ Kb8 3. Kb6 or 3. Kc6 wins because the king cannot escape) **2. Kc6 Kb8** (not 2. ... Bh5? 3. Kc7! or 2. ... Bf5 3. Re7+) **3. Kd7** (3. Re6 Bh5, =. Black always moves the bishop to where it can check the White king away from c6 and allow his own king to escape via a6 and a5) **3. ... Kb7 4. Rb3+ Ka6!,** = (but not 4. ... Ka7? 5. Kc7! and wins because 5. ... Ka6 6. Rb6+ wins the bishop).

There are some special positions here where Black is lost because he does not have enough squares for his bishop. For example, **No. 912** (Dehler 1909): **White king at g4, rook at a1; Black king at h7, bishop at b8.** White to play wins! **1. Kf5 Kg7** (the bishop has no moves; if 1. ... Bc7 2. Ra7, or if 1. ... Bg3 2. Rh1+ Kg7 3. Rg1) **2. Rb1 Bh2 3. Rb2! Bd6 4. Rb7+ Kf8** (forced, since 4. ... Kh6 5. Rb6 wins the bishop) **5. Ke6 Bc5** (or any other square: the winning combination cannot be prevented) **6. Rf7+ Kg8** (if 6. ... Ke8 7. Rc7 Bb6 8. Rc8+ Bd8 9. Ra8) **7. Kf6 Bd4+ 8. Kg6** and again we have No. 907.

With the kings in the center (f-, e-, d-, or c-files, or third to sixth ranks), White wins only if his king bars his rival's exit to the second rank (or to the knight file), so that a rook check on the eighth rank (or rook file) would be mate. **No. 913** is a model case.

No. 913, Kling and Horwitz 1851

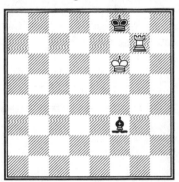

White to play wins

The idea in **No. 913** is the same as that encountered in previous instances: to gain a tempo for the mate threat by attacking the bishop. Here the solution is **1. Rg3 Be4**

The best chance. If 1. ... Bd5, Bc6, Bb7, Ba8, or 1. ... Bh1, then the reply 2. Rd3, or 2. Rc3, or 2. Rb3, or 2. Rb3!, or 2. Rh3, respectively, gets the rook to the eighth without allowing the king to move. The only variation worth mentioning is 1. ... Bc6 2. Rc3 Bd7 3. Rb3! and the bishop must move, for if 3. ... Ke8 4. Rb8+ and if 3. ... Kg8 4. Rb8+ Kh7 5. Rb7, winning the bishop in both cases).

2. Re3 Bg2! (or 2. ... Bh7 3. Rb3! and if 3. ... Kg8 4. Rb8+ mate) **3. Re2 Bf3 4. Rf2! Bc6** (his last feeble chance. On 4. ... Be4 or 4. ... Bg4 5. Ke5+ or 5. Kg5+ wins the bishop) **5. Rc2 Bd7** (5. ... Bb7 6. Rb2) **6. Rb2! Bc6** (king moves also lose the bishop) **7. Rb8+ Be8 8. Ra8 Kg8 9. Rxe8+** and mates in two.

Any rook position except g6 wins in all cases. With the rook at g6, the Black bishop at c6, c8 or a6 draws. **No. 914, White king at f6, rook at g6; Black king**

at f8, bishop at a6. Draw. **1. Rg7 Ke8 2. Ke6 Bc4+,** and the king can be confined to the eighth rank only by the combined efforts of king and rook. If the kings are at d6 and d8 we get similar variations.

When the White king is on a light square, the situation is far more difficult because only about half the possible positions win. **No. 915** (Maestre 1939): **White king at e6, rook anyplace it cannot mate or capture the bishop; Black king at e8, bishop at h5 (or f3, f1, d3, b7, b5, a6, a4).** Draw. For instance, White rook at e5, Black bishop at a6. **1. Ra5 Bc4+** or **1. Rc5 Kd8 2. Kd6 Ke8.**

The point of all these examples is that if the rook can attack the bishop *and* threaten mate and prevent a bishop check, White wins; if not, the game is a draw.

B. Rook and Pawn vs. Bishop

As you would expect, this is a win. There are, however, some special drawing positions that must be avoided, and some unforeseen difficulties may arise, especially with the rook-pawn. The investigations of Philidor, Lequesne, Centurini, Guretzky-Cornitz, Berger, and others have practically reduced this finale to a mathematical exercise.

First, **No. 916** is the general win.

No. 916, Philidor 1777

White wins

The idea in **No. 916** is to first get the king to the sixth rank, after which the pawn is advanced with a routine finish. **1. Ra1 Bg3** (or any other square) **2. Ra6+ Bd6 3. Rb6.** This is the key maneuver: whenever the bishop is pinned the rook tempos and allows the king to come forward. **3. ... Kd7 4. Kd5 Bg3 5. Rb7+ Kc8** (or 5. ... Bc7 6. Ra7) **6. Rf7 Bh2 7. Kc6 Kd8 8. d5,** etc.

With a bishop of the other color and the pawn on the d-file the win may be more difficult. **No. 917** (Berger): **White king at d3, rook at f8, pawn at d4; Black king at d6, bishop at b3.** The winning idea now is different: to sacrifice the rook at the right moment. **1. Rf6+ Kd5 2. Kc3 Bd1! 3. Rf2! Bg4 4. Rf8 Kd6**

5. Rd8+ Ke7 6. Rg8 Be6 7. Rg6 Kd6 8. Kb4 K any 9. Rxe6 Kxe6 10. Kc5 Kd7 11. Kd5. White has the opposition, so the pawn will queen.

If the pawn has been advanced to the fifth too hastily (e.g., 1. d5+ in No. 916), the ending is still won but is far more difficult. **No. 918** (Guretzky-Cornitz): **White king at e4, rook at d1, pawn at d5; Black king at d7, bishop at c7.** White wins.

The idea is this: White must get his king to e5 or c5 and then either play his rook to the seventh or advance the pawn to d6. To effect this combination he must force the bishop to a position where it cannot check the king away from one of the two vital squares. The solution is **1. Ra1** (there are various alternative sequences that are equally good) **1. ... Bg3 2. Ra7+ Kd6 3. Rg7 Be1! 4. Rg6+ Kd7 5. Kd4! Bb4 6. Rg1 Kd6 7. Rc1 Bd2 8. Rc6+ Kd7 9. Rc2 Be1 10. Kc5 Bg3 11. Rg2 Bd6+ 12. Kd4 Bf8 13. Rg3! Bb4 14. Rb3** wins.

If the pawn is still on the second or third rank, some maneuvering is needed before the pawn may advance. **No. 919** (Guretzky-Cornitz): **White king at d1, rook at b3, pawn at d2; Black king at d4, bishop at f5.** White wins. **1. Rb8 Bg4+ 2. Kc1 Bf5 3. Rd8+ Kc4 4. Kd1 Bd3 5. Ke1 Bf5 6. Kf2 Bd3 7. Ke3 Bf5 8. d4,** etc.

Once the pawn has reached the sixth ahead of the king, complications may arise. The winning stratagem then is to sacrifice the pawn at an appropriate moment.

No. 920, Guretzky-Cornitz

White wins

The solution is **1. Rg4 Ba6** (if the bishop stays on the g8-a2 diagonal, the rook goes over to the other side: 1. ... Bf7 2. Rb4 Ba2 3. Rb8+ Kd7 4. Rb7+ Kd8 5. d7 Ke7 6. Rb2! Bc4 7. Rd2, or 6. ... Be6 7. d8=Q+) **2. Rg8+ Kd7 3. Rg7+ Kd8 4. Kd5!** (the pawn must not be advanced prematurely) **4. ... Bb5** (or 4. ... Bd3 5. Rg3 Bf5 6. Ke5 Bb1 7. Rg8+ Kd7 8. Rg7+ Kd8 9. d7 Kc7 10. Ke6-e7 and wins, or here 5. ... Bb5 6. Kc5 Ba4 7. Rg4 Bd1 8. Rd4 Bf3 9. d7) **5. Kc5 Bd3 6. d7 Kc7 7. Re7!! Bf5 8. d8=Q+ Kxd8 9. Kd6 Kc8 10. Rc7+ Kb8** (10. ... Kd8 11. Rf7) **11. Kc6** and **12 Kb6,** and we have No. 907.

With a knight-pawn the same idea, forcing the bishop to unfavorable squares, is conclusive.

No. 921, Centurini

White wins

The solution is **1. Rg2 Bd3** (1. ... Bf5 2. Rd2 Bc8 3. Rd6+ Kg7 4. g6 Kh6 5. Rd8 Be6 6. Ke5-c6, or 5. ... Ba6 6. Kf5, etc.) Or here 2. ... Bh3 3. Rd3 Bf1 4. Rd6+ Kg7 5. g6 Kh6 6. Kf5, etc.) **2. Rd2 Bb1 3. Rd6+ Kg7 4. Kg4 Be4 5. Rd4 Bg2 6. Rd7+ Kg6 7. Rd6+ Kg7 8. g6 Kh6 9. Kf5 Bh3+ 10. Kf6**, etc. Note that here the king cannot get through directly but must follow the pawn. A knight-pawn on the sixth wins by sacrificing itself to force No. 907.

No. 922 (Salvio) is an example. **White king at f5, rook at b7, pawn at g6; Black king at h8, bishop at a1.** White wins. **1. g7+ Kh7 2. Rf7! Bb2** (or 2. ... Bxg7 3. Kg5) **3. g8=Q+ Kxg8 4. Kg6**, etc.

The win with the bishop-pawn on the fifth is seen in **No. 923** (Guretzky-Cornitz): **White king at f4, rook at c6, pawn at f5; Black king at f7, bishop at e1.** White wins. **1. Rc7+ Kf6 2. Rc2 Bh4!** (or 2. ... Kf7 3. Kg5, or 2. ... Bb4 3. Rc6+ Kf7 4. Ke5, or, finally, 2. ... Ba5 3. Rc6+ Kf7 4. f6 Kg6 5. Ke5 Bd8 6. Ra6, etc.) **3. Rc6+ Kf7 4. Rc1 Kf6** (again there is no good alternative. If 4. ... Bf2 5. Rc2 Bh4 6. Rh2 Be7 7. Rh7+ Kf6 8. Rh6+, whereas if 4. ... Be7 5. Rc7 Kf6 6. Rc6+ Kf7 7. Ke5) **5. Rg1 Bf2 6. Rg6+ Kf7 7. Rg2 Be1** (or 7. ... Bb6 8. Rd2 Ba5 9. Rd7+ Kf6 10. Rd6+ Kf7 11. Kg5) **8. Kg5 Ba5** (if 8. ... Bc3 9. Rc2 Bf6+ 10. Kf4 Bd8 11. Rc3 Bh4 12. Rh3 Be1 13. Ke5) **9. Rc2 Bd8+ 10. Kf4 Bh4 11. Rh2 Bd8 12. Rh7+ Kf6 13. Ra7 Bc7+ 14. Kg4! Bd8 15. Ra6+ Kf7 16. Kh5 Kg7 17. Rd6 Be7** (17. ... Ba5 18. f6+ Kf7 19. Kg5) **18. Rd7 Kf7 19. Rxe7+ Kxe7 20. Kg6** and wins. This is perhaps the most difficult case.

There are two trap positions that White must avoid. **No. 924** is the first:

No. 924, Vianna 1883

Draw

This can happen with any pawn. Obviously, if the rook leaves the sixth or if the king moves, the pawn will be captured. A tempo move does White no good, since Black has two more good squares for his Bishop.

A similar case with the bishop-pawn is **No. 925** (Vianna 1883): **White king at b7, rook at a6, pawn at c6; Black king at d6, bishop at e4.** Draw. Again, neither king nor rook has any good moves.

The second draw trap is **No. 926.** The trouble is not only that the White king cannot approach without being checked away (this was also the case in No. 920) but also that no winning position can be forced by sacrificing the pawn. Black keeps his bishop on the diagonal g8-a2, but always retains the possibility of a check if the king goes to g6.

No. 926, del Rio 1831

Draw

On **1. f7 Kg7!** followed by **2. ... Bxf7** is the proper answer, but not 1. ... Bxf7 **2. Kf6!** (No. 913). Another trap here is **1. ... Bb3 2. Rb7 Bc4 3. Rc7 Bb5?** (3. ...

Ba2 or d5 is correct) **4. f7! Kg7 5. Kf5 Ba4 6. Rb7 Bd1 7. Ke6 Bh5 8. Rc7 Bg6 9. f8=Q+! Kxf8 10. Kf6** and wins.

This struggle between the bishop and rook, **No. 927,** is worth studying.

No. 927, P. Benko 1967

White to play. Draw

The first thing to recognize are Black's real threats. White must avoid 1. ... Ra5! 2. Bd4 (Black wins on 2. Bc7 Rf5 and 3. ... Kg4) 2. ... Kg3 3. Bxf2+ Kf3.

1. Bc7!

The only move! Now after 1. ... Ra7 2. Bb6!, White attacks the pawn and rook simultaneously, leaving Black no time for ... Kg4.

1. ... Rb2 2. Bd6! Rc2 3. Be5! Rd2 (not 3. ... Rc5 4. Bd4!) **4. Bf4! (4.** ... Rb2 5. Bd6! repeats the position as above, but Black still has a dangerous threat) **4. ... Re2! 5. Bb8!!**

Again the only move. The bishop must have access to the corresponding square to avoid such problems as 5. Bc7? Ra2! Of course, Black should not play 5. Kxe2? Kg2 or 5. Bd2!? Kg3!.

5. ... Re8 6. Bg3!! (this stalemate combination saves the day) **6. ... Kg4 7. Kxf2** and draws.

The rook-pawn is an exception to the other rules. If the queening square is the same color as the bishop, the Black king is in the wrong corner and White always wins.

No. 928, Guretzky-Comitz

White to play and win

White gives up the pawn at the appropriate moment in order to transpose into one of the favorable rook vs. bishop cases. **1. Kg4 Bc1 2. Kf5 Bd2 3. Rb3! Bc1** (for ... Kxh5 at any stage, see No. 913) **4. Rb6+ Kh7 5. h6! Bd2** (5. ... Bxh6 6. Rb7+ Bg7 7. Kg5 Kg8 8. Kg6) **6. Rf6** (the point will soon be clear) **6. ... Bc3** (or 6. ... Bc3 7. Rd6 Bb4 8. Rd4 Bc3 9. Rd3 Bb2 10. Kg5 Bc1+ 11. Kh5 Bxh6 12. Rd7+ Bg7 13. Rb7 K any 14. Kg6, etc.) **7. Kg4 Bxh6 8. Kh5 Be3 9. Rf7+ Kg8 10. Kg6** and wins (No. 907). Now we see why the rook went to the f-file!

If the queening square is not the same color as the bishop, the Black king is in the correct corner and the problem is far more complicated. In general, White wins if his pawn is not beyond the fourth rank.

The main variations are seen in **No. 929.**

No. 929, Guretzky-Cornitz

Black to play. White wins

The winning idea is to chase the Black king to the f-file, but the execution of this idea is not simple. Best play for both sides is: **1. ... Bf5 2. Kg5 Bb1 3.**

Kh6 Kg8 (or 3. ... Ba2 4. Rh7+ Kg8 5. Rg7+, as in the main line) **4. Rg7+** and now there are two branches:

a) **4. ... Kh8 5. h4 Bd3 6. h5 Bb1** (now White must nudge the pawn on to h7) **7. Rb7 Ba2 8. Rb8+ Bg8 9. Kg5 Kg7 10. Rb7+ Kh8!** (10. ... Kf8 11. h6 and 12. h7) **11. Kg6 Bc4** (or Bd5 or Ba2; White's rook moves are always designed to prevent bishop checks) **12. Rh7+ Kg8 13. Rd7** (or Re7 is the bishop is on d5, or Rb7 if the bishop is on a2) **13. ... Kh8** (or 13. ... Kf8 if the rook is on e7, when 14. Kf6 Ba2 15. h6 Kg8 16. h7+ gets back to the main line) **14. h6 Ba2 15. h7 Bb1+ 16. Kh6** and wins.

b) **4. ... Kf8 5. h4 Bd3 6. Rg3 Be4 7. Rg5! Kf7!**

White is trying to get his king back to g4 via h5. If 7. ... Bd3 8. Kh5 Be2+ 9. Kg6 Kg8 10. Rd5 Kf8 11. h5 wins, and similarly for other bishop moves.

8. Rg3 Bc2 9. Kh5 (the winning idea now is to drive the Black king to the e-file) **9. ... Kf6**

Or 9. ... Bb1 10. Rg5 B any 11. Kg4 followed by Kf4 and the advance of the h-pawn to h6 and the eventual penetration of the White king. For instance, 9. ... Bb1 10. Rg5 Bc2 11. Kg4 Bg6 12. h5 Bb1 13. h6 Bg6 14. Kf4 Kf6 15. Rb5 Bd3 16. Rb7! and 17. h7. If 9. ... Bd1+ 10. Kg5! Kg7 11. Rc3+, and Black cannot get on the right diagonal: 11. ... Be2 12. h5 Bf1 13. h6+ Kh7 14. Rc7+ Kh8 15. h7 and 16. Kh6.

10. Rg5 Bd1+ (else 11. Kg4, as in the last note) **11. Kh6 Kf7 12. Rg7+ Kf6** (if 12. ... Kf8 13. Kg6 Be2 14. Kf6 followed by 15. Rg5 and then 16. h5 17. h6 18. Rg7 19. h7 decides) **13. Rg1 Be2 14. Rg2 Bd3 15. Rf2+ Bf5** (or 15. ... Ke7 16. h5 Bb1 17. Kg7 and the pawn goes on) **16. h5 Ke6 17. Rxf5** (the simplest) **17. ... Kxf5 18. Kg7** and queens.

Once the pawn is on the fifth, only a special position, such as those above, is enough to win. The draw is seen in **No. 930**.

No. 930, Berger

White play. Draw

After **1. Rb7 Bc2 2. Kg5 Bd3 3. Kh6 Kg8! 4. Rg7+ Kf8!!** (4. ... Kh8?? loses, transposing to variation (a) of the previous diagram).

White cannot win because he does not have the square h5 at his disposal. If the pawn is at h6 even this slight spark is snuffed out because White's king cannot get to h6. Black keeps his bishop on the diagonal h7-b1 and nothing can touch him.

To sum up: Rook and pawn win against bishop except in certain positions. These occur when the pawn has been advanced to the sixth too hastily (Nos. 924 and 926) or with a rook-pawn that would queen on a square a different color from that of the bishop. Such a rook-pawn generally draws if it is on the fifth or sixth but wins on the fourth. In the winning process, it is wise to remember that the pawn should not be too far in front of the king.

C. Rook vs. Bishop and Pawns

In general, a rook is equivalent to slightly less than a bishop plus two pawns. The ending with rook vs. bishop and two pawns is ordinarily a draw, but when the pawns are far advanced, the bishop wins. When there is no other material on the board, a rook draws vs. a bishop and pawn because rook vs. bishop is in general drawn. However, with three pawns the bishop will always win.

1. Rook vs. Bishop and Pawn

Since the game is generally drawn without the pawn, its presence does not change the theoretical result. But two new considerations come up:

1. If the rook vs. bishop ending is won, the extra pawn will not save the defender.

2. When the pawn is far advanced it may in certain special positions force a queen with the help of the bishop.

No. 931 is the simplest case to illustrate the first remark:

No. 931, Berger

White to play wins

After **1. Rd2 Bc5 2. Rd8+ Bf8 3. Rb8** (the pawn sacrifice still leaves Black in a mess) **3. ... b5 4. Rxb5 Bd6 5. Rd5 Be7 6. Ra5**, etc. Even if the pawn reached b4, White wins because he has so many extra tempi. For instance, **3. Ra8** (instead of 3. Rb8) **3. ... b5 4. Rb8 b4 5. Rc8 b3 6. Rb8 b2 7. Rxb2** and he still wins.

A more complicated instance is **No. 932** (Sackmann): **White king at g6, rook at f3; Black king at g8, bishop at b4, pawn at c5.** White to play and win.

Here the problem is to force the pawn to advance so that the bishop will not be defended. Accordingly, the solution is **1. Rf5! Ba3 2. Rf1!! Bb4 3. Rf3!!** (the point: now the bishop has no moves that do not permit an immediate attack) **3. ... c4 4. Rf5! Bc3** (hiding behind the pawn. If 4. ... c3 5. Rb5 c2 6. Rxb4 c1=Q 7. Rb8+ and mates) **5. Rf7!!** (now he has no less than eight squares at his disposal, but not a single one can save him) **5. ... Bd4 6. Rd7 Bc5 7. Rd8+ Bf8 8. Rc8**, etc., or **5. ... Bh8 6. Rc7 Kf8 7. Rc8+**, etc.

There are even positions where the pawn only gets in Black's way. An example is **No. 933** (Sackmann): **White king at c6, rook at c1; Black king at b8, bishop at f8, pawn at h6.** White to play and win.

White wins despite the fact that the Black king is in the right corner. The reason is that the Black bishop cannot go to h6. **1. Re1 Ka7** (or 1. ... Ba3 2. Rb1+ Kc8 3. Ra1. The only saving move would be 1. ... Bh6 if the pawn were not there) **2. Rf1,** and now the bishop is lost, for if **2. ... Bb4 3. Ra1+ Kb8 4. Rb1**.

No. 934 is the type of position in which the bishop and pawn win:

No. 934, Deutsche Schachzeitung 1887

Black to play and win

After **1. ... c2 2. Rc8 Bc3 3. Rd8+ Ke2! 4. Re8+ Kf2!!** (but not the retreat to the e- and d-files: 4. ... Kd3 5. Rd8+ Ke4 6. Re8+ Kd5? 7. Re1!! Bxe1 8. Kb2, =) **5. Rf8+ Kg2 6. Rg8+ Kh2,** White has no good checks and cannot get back to the first rank, so the pawn queens.

2. Rook vs. Bishop and Two Pawns

This is a draw unless the pawns manage to advance so far that the rook must be given up for one of them. This is usually not possible.

Connected passed pawns draw if they are on the fourth rank but win on the fifth or beyond. An exception must be made for the rook-pawn. **No. 935** is the draw.

No. 935

Black to play and draw

The most promising attempt is **1. ... Kf5.**

If 1. ... Be7 2. Rh1! and now:

a) 2. ... e4+ 3. Kd4 Bf6+ 4. Ke3 Bb2 (4. ... Kf5 5. Rh5+ Bg5+ 6. Kd4) 5. Rh4! Ke5 6. Rh5+ Kd6 7. Rh4+ Bc1+ 8. Kd4!, etc., =.

b) 2. ... e4+ 3. Kd4 Bf6+ 4. Ke3 Bd8 5. Rh6+ Ke5 6. Rh5+ Kd6 7. Rh6+ Kc5 8. Re6! Bg5+ 9. Ke2 Bf4 10. Kf2! Kd4 11. Ke2! Black cannot advance without blocking the pawns and his king cannot get back to f5.

c) 2. ... Kf5 3. Rf1+ Kg4 4. Rg1+ Kf3 5. Rf1+ Kg2 6. Rf5 Bd6 7. Rf6, etc.

2. Rh5+ Kf4 3. Rh4+ Kf3 (if 3. ... Kg5 4. Ra4 Kf5 5. Ra5, =) **4. Rh5 e4+ 5. Kc2 e3 6. Rxd5 e2 7. Rd1!,** and the rook is sacrificed for the last pawn.

With everything moved one rank down so that the pawns are on the fifth, the pawns win. **No. 936: White king at d2, rook at h3; Black king at e5, bishop at c4, pawns at d4, e4.** Black to play wins. After **1. ... Kf4 2. Rh4+ Kf3 3. Rh3+ Kf2 4. Rh4 e3+ 5. Kc2 e2** White does not have time to take the pawn. However, pawns on the fifth usually do not win if the opposing rook is on the eighth (No. 938).

Two pawns on the sixth win regardless of the rook's position.

No. 937, Handbuch

Black to play wins

White's rook is favorably placed but still cannot stem the tide. The solution is **1. Ke1 Kc5 2. Rc8+** (or 2. Re8 d2+ 3. Ke2 Bf3+; or 2. Kd1 Bb3+ 3. Ke1 Kc4 4. Rc8+ Kd4 5. Rd8+ Kc3 6. Rc8+ Bc4 as in the main line) **2. ... Kb4 3. Rb8+ Kc3 4. Rc8+ Bc4 5. Rd8 d2+ 6. Kd1 e2+** mate, or here 5. Re8 d2+ 6. Kd1 Bb3+ and queens. Having the rook on the second rank is worse, since Black plays ... Kc3 and the pawns go right on through.

If we move the position one rank up, **No. 938: White king at d2, rook at d8; Black king at d5, bishop at d6, pawns at d4, e4**, the game is drawn because the bishop cannot be sacrificed. **1. Ke2 Kc6 2. Re8 d3+** (2. ... Kd5 3. Rd8) **3. Ke3** and now 3. ... Bc5+ 4. Kxe4! d2 5. Rc8+! Kd7 6. Rxc5.

An exception to the rule that pawns on the sixth win is when the bishop is not mobile. **No. 939** (Goudjou 1881): **White king at f1, rook at a2; Black king at g3, bishop at f2, pawns at e3, f3.** Black to play. Draw.

If the king moves, Rxf2 simplifies. The best try, **1. ... Bg1!**, does not succeed, for after **2. Rb2 Bh2 3. Rf2! Bg1 4. Kxg1 e2! 5. Rg2+! Kf4 6. Rxe2 fxe2 7. Kf2,** the kings are left to do battle alone.

The rook-pawn, as usual, likes to be different. Except for certain special cases, rook-pawn plus knight-pawn never win because of a peculiar stalemate possibility.

No. 940

Black to play. Draw

In **No. 940,** which is surely the best Black can do, the rook plays along the second rank until the Black king leaves the b-pawn and then offers itself at b2: **1. ... Kc4 2. Rg2 Bd4 3. Rh2 Kd3 4. Rb2! Kc3 5. Re2!** (the brilliant 5. Ka1!!?? loses after 5. ... Be3! 6. Rh2 Bd2 7. Rh1 Kc2 8. Rc1+! Kd3! 9. Rd1 Ke2) **5. ... Bc5! 6. Rb2 Be3 7. Rh2 Bd2 8. Rh3+ Kc4 9. Rh4+ Kb5 10. Rh3,** etc.

To have the rook behind the pawn is dangerous but not fatal. **No. 941** (Handbuch): **White king at a1, rook at b8; Black king at a4, bishop at a5, pawns at a3, b3.** White to play and draw. **1. Ra8 Kb5 2. Rb8+ Kc4 3. Ra8 Kb5 4. Rb8+ Bb6 5. Ra8,** etc. The rook sticks to the a-file file whenever the pawn threatens to check.

A special draw is **No. 942.**

No. 942, P. Benko 1980

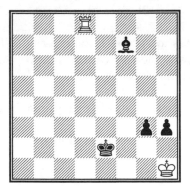

White to play and draw

White's king looks vulnerable in the corner, so it makes the "obvious" move: 1. Kg1!? h2+ 2. Kg2 Bh5 3. Rh8 h1=Q+! (following analysis by Steinitz) 4. Kxh1 Kf2 and Black wins.

Noteworthy here is an echo of the same idea: 1. Kg1?! h2+ 2. Kg2 Bh5 3. Rf8?! Bf3+ 4. Rxf3 h1=Q+ 5. Kxh1 Kxf3 and again Black wins.

One might be tempted to try 1. Kg1?! h2+ 2. Kh1!? Bh5 3. Rf8 Bf3+ 4. Rxf3 Kxf3 stalemate. But this is wrong, too. Instead of 2. ... Bh5, Black wins with 2. ... Bg6! 3. Rd4 (to protect against 3. ... Be4+ mate) 3. ... Ke3.

So where is the draw?

It's there, but you have to look for a new idea: **1. Rd4! Bh5 2. Rh4 Kf2 3. Rg4!** An amusing position. It's a stalemate after 3. ... Bxg4, and no better is 3. ... g2+ 4. Kh2 Bxg4.

When you think you've found a winning continuation, look again. These seemingly "simple" endgame positions are rarely as simple as they look.

Unconnected passed pawns win only if one of them can queen, capturing the rook, while the other is being held by the bishop. Again, this is usually not possible. **No. 943** is the drawing idea:

No. 943, Berger

Black to play. Draw

Black's only chance is to approach the e-pawn. White then must give up his rook for the pawn, and the king captures the b-pawn: **1. ... Bd3 2. Re7 Kc4 3. Re8 Kd4 4. Rxe2** (but not 4. Kxb3 Be4!).

Where one pawn is not directly attacked by the king, the defender must get his king as close to it as possible in order to make the rook sacrifice effective.

No. 944 is a position in which the rook loses.

No. 944, Stamma 1745

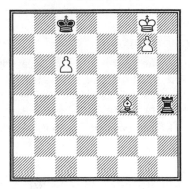

White to play and win

1. Be5 Rh1 2. c7 Rf1 3. Kh7 Rh1+ 4. Kg6 Rg1+ 5. Kf7 Rf1+ 6. Bf6! Rg1 7. Bd8 Rf1+ (or 7. ... Rg2 8. g8=Q) **8. Kg6 Rg1+ 9. Bg5!** and queens.

No. 945, P. Benko 1981

White to play and win

White seems to win easily with: 1. Kf7?! Re1 2. Be6 Rf1+ 3. Kg8 Rg1+ 4. Kh8 Rg7! 5. e8=Q Rh7+ 6. Kg8 Rh8+, and Black is stalemated after 7. Kxh8 or draws after 7. Kf7 Rxe8 8. Kxe8 Kh5. If White promotes only to a rook with 5. e8=R, then 5. ... Rf7 and White can neither take the brave rook (because of stalemate) nor protect his h-pawn.

The winning method is **1. Be6.** Now the White king threatens to begin a zigzagging maneuver with Kd7-c6-d5.

a) **1. ... Rd1.** Black decides to keep the king boxed in. **2. h5!** After 2. Kf7? Rf1+, Black can draw as above. The text move prevents the possibility of stalemate. **2. ... Kg7 3. h6+! Kh7 4. Bf5+ Kg8 5. h7+ Kg7 6. h8=Q+ Kxh8 7. Kf7 Re1 8. Be6 Rf1+ 9. Kg6** White wins by zigzagging.

b) **1. ... Kg7.** Now White's king will be able to hide behind his h-pawn. **2.**

Kd7 Rd1+ 3. Kc6 Rc1+ 4. Kd5 Rd1+ 5. Ke5 Re1+ 6. Kf5 Rf1+ 7. Kg4 Rg1+ 8. Kh5 and White wins.

3. Rook vs. Bishop and Three (or More) Pawns

This is of course a win for the pawns. The rook can be sacrificed for at most two of them while a third is left to bring home the bacon.

A rare exception is **No. 946** (Schiffers-Ascharine, 1875): **White king at h4, bishop at c5, pawns at a2, d4, e5; Black king at e6, rook at d7.** Black to play and draw. **1. ... Rd5! 2. a4 Rxe5! 3. dxe5 Kxe5 4. a5 Kd5 5. a6 Kc6 6. Kg5 Kc7 7. Ba7 Kc6!,** etc., =.

D. Rook and Pawns vs. Bishop and Pawns

The presence of extra pawns makes a vast difference. With no pawns for the exchange the rook wins easily; with one pawn for the exchange the rook wins but with difficulty; with two pawns for the exchange the game is normally a draw; finally, with three or more pawns for the exchange the bishop wins, though not always too easily.

In general, the side with the rook (usually the superior side) should bear these points in mind:

1. The central winning idea is to get the king through to a mass of pawns and thus capture material.

2. As many enemy pawns as possible should be forced onto squares the same color as the bishop.

3. A few pawn exchanges may be necessary to clear files, but *always retain pawns on both sides of the board*.

4. Try to keep the pawn position unbalanced. In particular, any passed pawn virtually confers a winning advantage immediately.

1. No Pawns for the Exchange

This is usually an easy win. With three or four pawns the king can force his way to one side or the other at once. With more pawns a few must first be exchanged. When the opportunity presents itself, giving up the rook for bishop and pawn is an effective simplification.

No. 947 is typical.

No. 947, Adams-Fine, Dallas 1940

Black to play and win

Black's four steps comprise his winning plan:

1. Centralization.

2. Advancing his pawn majority on the kingside, forcing the creation of a passed pawn.

3. Penetrating with his king or rook or both.

4. Capturing material.

After **1. ... Ke7 2. Bb5 f5 3. Ke3 Kf6 4. a4 Ke5** (first step) **5. c3 a5 6. Bc6 g5** (second step), the most difficult line is **7. h3** (the game continuation was 7. Kd2 Rd6, and White resigned, since 8. Bb5 g4 wins a pawn) **7. ... h5 8. Bf3 g4 9. hxg4 hxg4 10. Be2 f4+ 11. Kf2** (if 11. Kd2 f3 12. gxf3 g3 13. Bf1 Kf4 14. Bg2 Rh8 15. Ke2 Rh2 16. Kf1 Ke3, etc.) **11. ... Kf5 12. Bf1** (the bishop is tied down to the d-pawn) **12. ... Re8** (third step begins) **13. Be2 g3+ 14. Kf1** (if 14. Ke1 f3 15. gxf3 g2, winning the bishop) **14. ... Re3 15. Bd1! Ke5! 16. Bc2** (after 16. Be2 Kd6, White must move and lose a pawn) **16. ... f3 17. gxf3 Rxf3+ 18. Kg1 Rf2 18. B any Rxb2,** and the rest is routine – Black can capture every White pawn if he is so inclined.

Even with only one pawn apiece a win may be secured by skillful manipulation of the rook. When Black has a passed pawn on the seventh, winning may prove exceedingly difficult, but if the pawn is not supported by the king, Black loses against best play.

When there is no passed pawn, the game is won if the pawns are in the center but may be drawn with the pawns on the knight or rook files.

No. 948, Benko-Browne, El Paso 1973

Black to play. Draw

1. ... g5 2. Bc6 Rf2 3. Bb7 g4 4. Bc6 (trap: 4. Bc8? Kf3 5. Bxg4+ Kxg3) **4. ... Rf3 5. Kg2** (trap: 5. Bxf3? Kxf3 6. Kh2 Kf2 wins; the traps are too naive) **5. Kg2 Rf6 6. Bb7 Rb6 7. Ba8,** draw: White keeps the long diagonal for good.

No. 949 is the model case with pawns in the center.

No. 949

Black to play. White wins

The winning idea is to give up the rook for the bishop and pawn at a moment when the Black king cannot reach e7 (which would draw with king and pawn vs. king).

1. ... Ke6 (if 1. ... Kc5 2. Rh8! Kc6 3. Rd8! Bc5 4. Ke2 Bd4 5. Kf3 Bc5 6. Kg4, etc.) **2. Kc4 Kd6 3. Rh6+ Kd7 4. Kd5 Ke7 5. Rh7+** (but not 5. Re6+? Kd7 6. Rxe5? Bxe5 7. Kxe5 Ke7, =) **5. ... Kf6**

If 5. ... Ke8 6. Ke6 Kf8 7. Rh8+ Kg7 8. Rb8 Bc3 9. Ke7 Bd4 10. Rb1 Bc3 11. Rf1, etc., as in the main line. The idea is to get the Black king at a distance of one file from the pawn.

6. Kd6 Bc3 7. Rb7! Bd4 (or 7. ... Bd2 8. Rb8 Bf4 9. Rf8+, etc.) **8. Rb3 Kf7 9.**

Kd7 Kf6 10. Rf3+ Kg6 11. Rf5 Bc3 12. Ke6 B any 13. Rxe5, and wins, for after **13. ... Bxe5 14. Kxe5 Kf7 15. Kd6,** White has the opposition. Two rook-pawns, however, only draw because White is stalemated after the sacrifice.

A knight-pawn vs. a rook-pawn should win after the sacrifice because the resulting pawn ending is won. For instance, **No. 950: White king at a4, rook at f1, pawn at b5; Black king at b7, bishop at b6, pawn at a7.** White to play and win. **1. Rf7+ Bc7 2. Kb4 Kb6 3. Rf6+ Kb7 4. Kc5 Bb6+** and now **5. Rxb6+** is already good enough: **5. ... axb6+ 6. Kd6 Kb8 7. Kc6,** etc. If **4. ... Bd8 5. Rf7+ Bc7 6. Rh7 Kb8 7. Kc6** is conclusive. A bishop on the light squares would be worse here because the Black king would then be in the wrong corner.

Two knight-pawns draw with a bishop of the same color as the pawn on the second rank, but White may win if the bishop is of the opposite color. **No. 951: White king at b4, rook at f6, pawn at b5; Black king at a7, bishop at e3, pawn at b7.** Draw. The White king cannot get to either b5 or c5 and stay there, nor can it work its way around to c8, because the moment the king gets to the sixth rank Black's king gets to b6.

But in **No. 952, Black bishop at e2,** other pieces unchanged, White to play wins. **1. b6+ Ka6 2. Kc5** and Black is in a mating net. However, Black to play draws by **1. ... b6** because White must then guard his b-pawn and cannot move around too freely with both king and rook (see No. 948).

With rook and two pawns vs. bishop and two pawns, if the Black pawns are not on their original squares the defense is quite difficult and Black usually loses.

But not always, as Grandmaster Yuri Averbakh shows in the following two studies.

No. 953, Y. Averbakh 1962

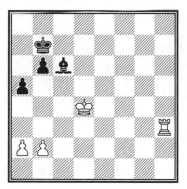

White to play. Draw

1. Ke5 Kc7 2. Rh7+ Kb8 3. Kd6 Bf3 4. a4 Be4 5. Rf7 Bg2 6. b4 axb4 7. Rf4 Kb7 8. Rxb4 Ka6 9. Kc7 Ka5, =.

No. 954 (Y. Averbakh 1962): **White king at d5, rook at g6, pawns at a2, b2; Black king at b7, bishop at e3, pawns at a6, b5.** Black to play and draw. **1. ...**

Bf2! (1. ... Ba7? 2. Rg7+ and 3. Rxa7 wins) **2. Rg2 Be3 3. Re2 Bg1**, etc., draw. The bishop only has to stay on the a7-g1 diagonal.

Any earlier weakening of the pawn position would merely hasten Black's downfall. Black has drawing chances in endings with even pawns only if he has a strong passed pawn that is not adequately blocked (i.e., by the enemy king). **No. 955** is typical.

No. 955, Vidmar-Bogolyubov, Nottingham 1936

Black to play and draw

After **1. ... Kg3 2. Ke1 b5!** draws (the game continuation, 2. ... Be4?, is below) **3. a4** (if 3. Rd2 b4!) **3. ... bxa4 4. bxa4 Bc4 5. a5 e5 6. Rc2** (or 6. e4; it makes no real difference since the rook can never leave the second rank) **6. ... Bb5 7. e4 Ba6 8. Ra2 Bc4!**, = for the attempt **9. a6?? Bxa2 10. a7 f2+!** loses for White.

In the game Bogolyubov played 2. ... Be4? which allows the White rook to get behind the f-pawn and win. 3. a4! Bc6 4. Rb2 e5 5. Rd2 Be8 6. Kf1! Bc6 (6. ... Bf7 7. Rd7 Bxb3 8. Rg7+ Kh4 9. a5, etc. as in the game) 7. Rd6! Be4 8. Rf6 (now Black can just as well resign) 8. ... Bd3+ 9. Ke1 Bc2 10. a5! Bxb3 11. Rg6+ Kh4 12. Kf2 e4 13. Rd6! Bc4 (he must lose a pawn. If 13. ... Ba4 14. Rb6 Bc6 15. a6 or 15. Rxc6) 14. Rd4 Bb5 15. Rxe4+ Kh3 16. Re7 Bc6 17. Rg7 Kh4 18. Rg3 Kh5 19. Rxf3 Kg5 20. Rf4 Bh1 21. Ke1, resigns.

2. One Pawn for the Exchange

As a rule, this is a win for the rook, but the practical difficulties are many. Again the central ideas are to gain an entry with the king or rook and to set up an unbalanced pawn position. The defense must rely mainly on blockade possibilities. An important point to remember is that with all the pawns on one side the game is drawn.

No. 956, Lasker-Ragosin, Moscow 1936

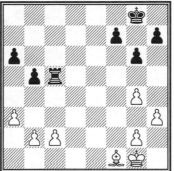

White to play. Black wins

No. 956 illustrates the play for both sides. We follow the game continuation.

1. Bd3 Kg7 2. Kf2 Kf6 3. Ke3 Ke5!

This centralization is necessary because the tempting 3. ... Kg5 leads to nothing after 4. Kd4! Rc7 5. c4 bxc4 6. Bxc4 a5 7. b4 axb4 8. axb4, and White has some winning chances!) **4. g5** (to prevent 4. ... f5-f4) **4. ... Kd6! 5. h4** (5. Kf4 Re5 6. c4) **5. ... h6?**

Now was the time to force the issue with the rook. After 5. ... Re5+ 6. Kd4 Re1 7. c4 Rd1 8. Kc3 Kc6 or 6. Kf4 Re1 7. h5 Rb1 8. b3 Ra1, Black not only wins a pawn but also creates a passed pawn.

6. gxh6 Rh5 7. g3 Rxh6 8. c4! Rh5 9. cxb5?

And now White could have drawn: 9. b4! Re5+ 10. Kf4 f5 11. cxb5 axb5 12. h5! gxh5 13. Bxf5 Re1 14. Bg6 Kd5 15. Bxh5 Ra1 16. Be8, =.

9. ... axb5 10. b3 Re5+ 11. Kf4 Rd5 12. Be4 Rd2 (wins a pawn) **13. g4** (if 13. a4 b4!) **13. ... Ra2 14. h5 Rxa3 15. b4**

If 15. h6 Rxb3 16. h7 Rh3, or if 15. hxg6 fxg6 16. Bc2 Ra2! 17. Bd3! b4! 18. Kg5 Rb2 19. Bc4 Rg2 20. Bd3 Rg3 21. Bc2 Ke7! 22. Kf4 Rc3 23. Bd1 Rc5 24. g5 Rf5+ 25. Kg4 Rf2, and black wins.

15. ... f5!!

A splendid move, which gives Black a strong passed pawn – an example of the strength of the unbalanced pawn position.

16. Bb1 (16. Bf3 Rxf3+! 17. Kxf3 fxg4+ 18. Kxg4 gxh5+ 19. Kxh5 Kd5 and wins) **16. ... gxh5 17. gxh5 Rh3 18. Kg5 Ke5 19. Kg6** (again 19. Bxf5 Rxh5+! leads to a simple win) **19. ... Rg3+ 20. Kf7 Rb3** (decisive) **21. Bc2 Rxb4 22. h6 Rh4 23. Kg6 b4 24. Bd1 f4 25. h7 Rxh7 26. Kxh7 Ke4 27. Kg6 f3 28. Kg5 Ke3**, resigns.

No. 957 is an example of the strength of the blockade as a drawing weapon.

No. 957, Blackburne-Mason, Nuremberg 1883

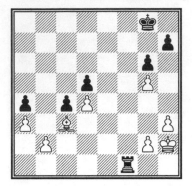

Black to play. Draw

Black tried **1. ... h5**, when White could have forced a draw by **2. gxh6 Kh7 3. g4! Kxh6 4. h4**, and there is no weak spot through which the Black king can enter. Instead, he played **2. g4?**, giving Black the needed opportunity to force his opponent into zugzwang. **2. ... Rf3 3. Kg2 Re3 4. Kh2** (if 4. gxh5 gxh5 5. Kh2 Kf7 6. Kg2 Kg6 7. h4 Kf5 8. Kh2 Re4 9. Kg3 Rg4+ 10. Kh3 Ke4, and White loses a pawn) **4. ... Re2+ 5. Kg3** (if 5. Kg1 hxg4 6. hxg4 Re4 wins) **5. ... h4+!! 6. Kxh4** (6. Kf3 Rh2) **6. ... Rg2! 7. Ba5 Rxb2**, and White loses too much material.

Black may also draw and even win by securing a strong passed pawn. **No. 958** is an interesting example of a draw.

No. 958, Alekhine-Rellstab, Kemeri 1937

Black to play and draw

The game continued **1. ... Kc6 2. Ka5?** (to activate rook, after 2. b5+ Kd5 3. Rd3+ White is better) **2. ... Kd5 3. Ka6 f4! 4. Ra3** (trying to win; the simplest draw is 4. Kxa7 Kc4) **4. ... g5 5. Kxa7 g4 6. b5 Ke4 7. b6 f3!** Now White is hard put to find a draw, but Black's bishop is not quite strong enough to win. **8. gxf3+ gxf3 9. Ra4+ Kd3** (or 9. ... Kf5 10. Ra5 f2 11. Rxe5+, etc.) **10. Ra3+ Ke2**

11. Ra5! Bf4 12. Ra2+ Ke1 13. Ra1+ Ke2 14. Ra2+, etc. Neither side can do better than accept the perpetual check.

Where the defender has an outside passed pawn and all the other pawns are on one side of the board, the game should be drawn. This is seen in **No. 959** (Ragosin-Eliskases, Moscow 1936): **White king at f1, bishop at b7, pawns at c6, f2, g3, h3; Black king at f8, rook at c5, pawns at f7, g7, h6.** White to play and draw. Black must always keep an eye on the c-pawn. The game continued **1. Ke2 Ke7 2. Ke3 Kd6 3. Kf3 Rc4 4. Ke3 g5 5. Kd3 Ra4 6. Ke3 h5 7. Kf3 h4 8. Kg2 Rc4 9. Kf3 Rb4 10. Kg2 Rd4 11. Kf3 Rc4 12. Ba8 Ke5 13. Bb7 f5 14. gxh4 Rc3+ 15. Ke2! gxh4 16. Kd2! Rc5 17. Ke3 Rc3+ 18. Kd2 Kd4 19. f4!**, etc.

Even doubled pawns and a bishop win against a rook and pawn, but only by intricate maneuvering.

No. 960, P. Benko 1975

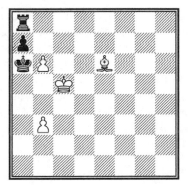

White to play and win

A wrong try is 1. b7? Kxb7! 2. Bd5+ Kb8 3. Be4 a5 4. Bxa8 a4! draws.
Solution: **1. Bc4+ Ka5 2. b7! Rf8**
The best defense. If 2. ... Rb8 3. Bb5 and b4 mates. Or 2. ... Re8 3. b4+ Ka4 4. Bb5+ or 2. ... Rh8 3. Be2! with play similar to the main line.

3. Bd3! Rg8 4. b4+ White only draws after 4. Bc2? Rg5+ and ... Rb5, or 4. Bf5 Rb8 5. Bc8 a6. **4. ... Ka4 5. Bc2+ Ka3 6. b5 Rf8 7. Bd1 Rg8 8. Bg4! Rb8** If 8. ... Ka4 9. Bc8 Rg5+ 10. Kd4 Rxb5 11. Bd7 wins.. **9. Kc6! Kb4 10. Be2 Re8 11. Kd7! Rf8 12. Kc7 Rf7+ 13. Kb8** wins.

3. Two Pawns for the Exchange

Since two pawns are usually a full equivalent for the exchange, such endings should normally be drawn. But if the side with the bishop has two passed pawns strongly supported by the king, he will generally win; conversely, if the pawns are weak and subject to attack, the rook will win.

No. 961 shows the effect of the presence of extra pawns.

No. 961, Wittek-Schwarz, Graz 1891

White to play and win

Without the queenside pawns the game would be drawn because the White pawns are too far back. But now there is the added possibility of capturing another pawn. Best play for both sides is **1. f4! Rh6+ 2. Ke5 Kd7 3. f5 Rh1** (the rook must get behind the pawns) **4. Kf6 Rh2 5. e5 Ke8 6. Ke6** (if 6. e6 Re2!) **6. ... Rh1 7. Kd5 Rh5**

A critical position. 7. ... Rf1 seems more natural but it loses after 8. f6 Rf2 9. Kc6! Re2 10. Bd6, since Black loses his last pawn; e.g., 10. ... Rb2 11. e6 Rf2 12. f7+ Rxf7 13. exf7+ Kxf7 14. Kxb5 Ke8 15. Kc6 Kd8 16. a4, etc., and the Black king cannot get to a8.

8. f6 Kf7 (if 8. ... Rg5 9. Ke6 Rg6 10. Kf5 Rg1 11. e6 and wins as in the last note) **9. Bc3 Ke8** (or 9. ... Rg5 10. Kd6) **10. Kc6 Rh3 11. Bb4 Kf7 12. Kxb5 Ke6 13. Bd6,** and the rest is simple: **13. ... Rb3+ 14. Kc4 Rb1 15. a4 Ra1 16. Kb3** (so that if 16. ... Kf7 17. Ba3) **16. ... Rb1+ 17. Ka2 Rb7 18. Ka3 Rb1 19. a5 Ra1+ 20. Kb4 Rb1+ 21. Kc5 Ra1 22. Kb6 Rb1+ 23. Kc6 Ra1 24. Bc7!**

White must not advance too hastily: after 24. Kb7 Rb1+ 25. Ka7 Ra1 26. a6 Ra2 27. Kb7 Rb2+ 28. Ka8? Ra2 29. a7 Rb2, his king can never get out and the game is drawn.

24. ... Rc1+ 25. Kb7 Kd7 26. Bb6 Ke6 27. a6 Kxe5 28. a7 Ra1 29. f7 and queens.

Similarly, if we add an extra set of pawns to No. 935 Black will win because the sacrificial drawing possibilities would disappear. If the two pawns are unconnected the win is even simpler.

When the pawns are weak or not well supported, the rook wins. **No. 962** is a typical case:

No. 962, Blackburne-Mason, Berlin 1881

White to play. Black wins

White's position is so badly riddled with holes that he cannot avoid losing several pawns. The game continued **1. g4** (if 1. Kg2 Rc2+ 2. Kg1 Kf3 3. Be5 Re2 and White must give up one pawn immediately, with more to follow) **1. ... hxg4 2. Kg2 Rd1 3. h5 Rd3 4. h6 Rh3 5. Bg7 Kf5 6. Kf2 Kg5 7. Kg2 Rxh6 8. Bxh6+ Kxh6 9. Kg3 Kg5,** and the rest is routine: **10. Kg2 Kf4 11. Kf2 Ke4 12. Kg3 Kd3** (but not, as in the game, 12. ... Kd4? 13. Kxg4 Kc4 14. Kf3 Kxb4 15. Ke3 Kb3, when 16. Kd4! draws) **13. Kxg4 Kc2 14. Kf3 Kxb2 15. Ke3 Kb3 16. Kd2 Kxb4,** etc.

Two pawns can be defended by the bishop alone only when they are both on the same color, but in that case they lose mobility.

No. 963 (Chigorin-Olland, Carlsbad 1907): **White: king at g2, rook at f1, pawns at g3, h2; Black king at g7, bishop at f7, pawns at a7, b6, g6, h7.** Black to play. The position is a draw even without the queenside pawns, after ... h5, ... g5 (see Averbakh, No. 953).

The game continued **1. ... a5** (or 1. ... a6 2. Rb1 b5 3. Ra1 Bd5+ 4. Kf2 Bb7 5. Rc1 Kg6 6. Rc7 Bd5 7. Ra7) **2. Rb1 a4 3. Rxb6 a3 4. Ra6 a2 5. Kf3,** and the rest is not difficult: White's king marches in and wins a pawn on the kingside: **5. ... Be6 6. Ke4 h5?** (6. ... g5! still draws) **7. Ke5 Bc4 8. Ra5 Kg6 9. h4 g4? 10. Ra7 Bf7 11. Ra6+ Kg7 12. Kf5 Kh7 13. Kg5 Kg7 14. Ra7 Kg8 15. Kh6 Kf8 16. Kh7! Ke8 17. Kg7 Bd5 18. Kf6! Bc4 19. Ra8+ Kd7 20. Kg6** and wins.

No. 964 is an example of two rooks vs. rook and bishop.

No. 964, Alekhine-Flohr, Nottingham 1936

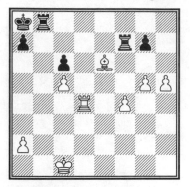

Black to play. White wins

Black is helpless against the pawns even though they are not supported by the White king. The game concluded: **1. ... Rfb7 2. Bb3 Rh8 3. h6! gxh6 4. g6 Rg7 5. f5 Rf8** (5. ... h5 6. Bc2 Rhg8 7. f6 Rxg6 8. Bxg6 Rxg6 9. f7 Rf6 10. Rd8+ and wins) **6. Bc2 h5 7. Rd6 Re7 8. f6 Re1+ 9. Kd2 Rf1 10. f7 h4 11. Rd7,** resigns.

This is another demonstration of a basic rule for all such endings: In all endings with two rooks vs. rook and minor piece, the player who is the exchange ahead should try to exchange one pair of rooks.

4. Three Pawns (or More) for the Exchange

This is usually a simple and straightforward win: the rook is unable to hold back the pawns. **No. 965** is an example where the winning side has some difficulty because his pawns are blockaded.

No. 965, Fine-Keres, AVRO 1938

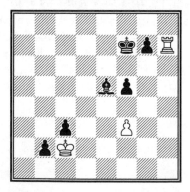

White to play. Black wins

The game continued **1. Rh1 g5 2. Re1 Kf6 3. Rg1 Kg6 4. Re1 Bf6 5. Rg1! g4!!** (the simplest) **6. fxg4 f4 7. g5 Bd4 8. Rd1 Be3! 9. Kxc3 Bc1 10. Rd6+ Kxg5 11. Rb6 f3 12. Kd3 Kf4 13. Rb8 Kg3,** White resigned. He must lose his rook for the f-pawn.

E. Rook vs. Knight (No Pawns)

This, too, is usually a draw. However, Black must stay in the center because all the won cases occur with his king at the edge.

No. 966 is the general draw.

No. 966

Black to play draws

After **1. ... Nd8+ 2. Kd6 Nb7+ 3. Kd5 Nd8,** White can do nothing. If, for instance, **4. Rh8 Kd7,** or **4. Re7 Nb7,** White can never set up a mating position or drive the king into the corner.

What happens when the king is in the corner is seen in **No. 967.**

No. 967

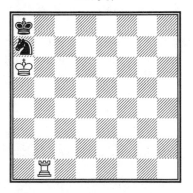

White to play wins. Black to play draws

White to play wins by **1. Kb6! Kb8** (or 1. ... Nc8+ 2. Kc7 Na7 3. Rb8+ mate) **2. Rb2!! Nc8+ 3. Kc6+ Ka8** (or 3. ... Ka7 4. Kc7) **4. Kc7,** and mate in no more than two moves.

Black to play draws by getting his knight out of the noose: **1. ... Nc8 2. Rb2** (there is nothing better: on 2. Rb7 Nd6 3. Rd7 Nc8 4. Rd8 Kb8, White is nowhere) **2. ... Ne7!!** (but not 2. ... Na7? 3. Kb6 as above, or 2. ... Nd6 3. Kb6 and if 3. ... Kb8 4. Kc6+) and if now **3. Kb6 Kb8 4. Kc5+ Kc7,** =, or **3. Re2 Nc8,** =.

To win endings with rook vs. knight, one or more of three stratagems are necessary:

1. Mating threats;
2. Pinning the knight in positions where the Black king must abandon it;
3. Freezing the knight and capturing it.

These three usually go together, but generally one is of outstanding importance.

The most complicated variations occur when the knight is in the center but can be caught because it is separated from its king. In all cases, the central idea is to drive the knight to the edge.

No. 968

White to play wins

Optimal play is **1. Rd4 Nf5 2. Re4 Kb8 3. Rb4+ Ka7 4. Kc7 Ka6 5. Re4 Ng3 6. Re5 Nh1 7. Kc6 Ka7 8. Re7+ Kb8 9. Rb7+ Kc8 10. Rh7** wins.

If the knight is on some other square on the kingside it will inevitably be caught and captured.

No. 969

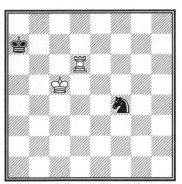

Black to play. White wins

Black's wide choice of moves still cannot save him: **1. ... Kb7 2. Kd4 Ne2+ 3. Kd3 Nf4+ 4. Ke4 Ne2 5. Rd3 Kb6 6. Re3 Nc1 7. Kd4+ Kb5 8. Kc3 Na2+ 9. Kb3 Nb4 10. Re5+** wins.

Positions with king and knight next to each other in or near the corner usually lose: if the knight stays close to the king it will be pinned and captured; if it does not it will be stalemated and captured.

No. 970 comes from the ancient war game Chaturanga, one of the antecedents of chess. It was created by al-Adli in the ninth century! These three pieces moved the same way as they do in chess.

No. 970, al-Adli, c. 800?

Black to play. White wins

This is the most favorable position White can have without winning immediately, and its variations include everything we have already considered.

1. ... Na5+ 2. Kb5 Nb7 (if 2. ... Nb3 3. Rd8! and the knight is lost) **3. Rh5! Nd8**

If 3. ... Kb8 4. Kc6 Nd8+ 5. Kd7 Nb7 6. Rb5 Ka7 7. Kc7 Ka8. Now we see why the rook is strong on the fifth rank. The stalemate trick is easily avoided: 8. Rb3 wins. For 3. ... Nd6+, see below.

4. Rd5 Ne6 5. Kc6 Kb8 6. Re5! Nf4 (6. ... Nd4+ 7. Kb6 Kc8 8. Rc5+ Kb8 9. Rd5 Ne6 10. Rd6 wins) **7. Re4 Nh5 8. Rg4 Nf6** (8. ... Ka7 9. Kc7 Ka6 10. Rg6+ Ka7 11. Rg5 is decisive) **9. Rf4 Nh5 10. Rf3 Ka7 11. Kd7** (the knight is already trapped) **11. ... Kb6 12. Ke7 Kc6 13. Kf7 Kd5?! 14. Rf5+** and wins.

An important alternative runs 3. ... Nd6+ (instead of 3. ... Nd8) **4. Kc6 Nc4!?** (4. ... Ne4 5. Rh7+ Kb8 6. Rb7+ Ka8 7. Rb4 Nf6 8. Rf4 Nh5 9. Rf5 Ng3 10. Rf3 is followed by 11. Kc7 or Kb6 with mate) **5. Rc5 Nd2 6. Ra5+** (6. Kd5? Ka6! 7. Rc3 Ka5! resists longer) **6. ... Kb8 7. Kd5! Nf3** (7. ... Kc7 8. Ra3, etc.) **8. Ke4 Nd2+ 9. Kd3 Nf3 10. Ke3 Nh2 11. Kf4 Nf1 12. Ra2 Kc7 13. Rf2** wins.

F. Rook and Pawn vs. Knight

Like the similar case with a bishop, this is a win, but there are a few positions in which the knight manages to draw.

No. 971, Handbuch

White to play. Draw

No. 971 is the simplest draw. After **1. Kg2 Ke2! 2. Rg3** (hoping to play his king to h3, g4, f4, e4, etc.) **2. ... Nf5!** forces the draw for on **3. Rh3, Nd4** repeats the position.

The most typical draw occurs when the pawn is too far advanced and cannot be supported by the king.

No. 972, Em. Lasker–Ed. Lasker, New York 1924

Black to play and draw

No. 972 (with colors reversed) is a classic case. White is helpless because his king cannot approach the pawn. **1. ... Nb7 2. Ke5 Na5 3. Kd5 Nb7 4. Rf6 Na5 5. Re6 Nb7 6. Ke5 Na5 7. Kf6 Ka6! 8. Ke5** (8. Ke7 Kb7 and 9. ... Nc4) **8. ... Kb5 9. Kd5**, etc.

With a rook-pawn the similar ending is won because of the mate possibilities.

No. 973, Lewis 1835

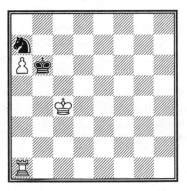

White to play and win

In **No. 973**, White wins by **1. Ra4! Nc6 2. Kd5 Na7 3. Kd6**.

The winning idea is to get the king to b8 and advance the pawn. **3. ... Nb5+ 4. Kd7 Ka7** (or 4. ... Na7 5. Kd8 Nb5 [or 5. ... Nc6+ 6. Kc8 Ka7 7. Kc7 Nb8 8. Ra5 Ka8 9. Rb5 wins] 6. Kc8 Ka7 7. Ra5 Nd6+ 8. Kc7 Nc4 9. Ra4 Nb6 10. Rd4 Na8+ 11. Kc6 Nb6 12. Rb4 Nc8 13. Kc7 Ne7 14. Rb5) **5. Kc6 Nc3 6. Rc4 Nb1** (to prevent 7. Kb5) **7. Rc1 Nd2** (7. ... Na3 8. Kc5) **8. Kb5** followed by **9. Rc7+**, etc.

Similar positions with the pawn on the 4th, 5th, or 7th are also won.

G. Rook vs. Knight and Pawns

Again the result is generally the same as with a bishop: one pawn draws but may lose; two pawns draw but may win; three pawns win.

1. Rook vs. Knight and One Pawn

This is usually a draw, of course, but there are some special positions where the rook wins.

No. 974, Salvioli 1887

White to play and win

White first captures the pawn, then transposes into a won rook vs. knight ending: **1. Kc3! h2 2. Rh4 Nc2 3. Rxh2 Ne3! 4. Kd3 Nd5** (if 4. ... Nd1 5. Rh1, or 4. ... Ng4 5. Re2, or 4. ... Nf5 5. Rh5, winning the knight in every case) **5. Rh4 Kb2 6. Rd4** and wins.

There are also special cases where the pawn may win.

No. 975 (Berger): **White king at a1, rook at b3; Black king at e1, knight at d1, pawn at c3.** Black to play and win. After **1. ... c2 2. Rb1 Kd2!** Black will queen, for if **3. Ka2 Nc3+ 4. Ka3 Nxb1+** (not 4. ... cxb1=Q or R, stalemate, or N, draw).

2. Rook vs. Knight and Two (or More) Pawns

With the White king in front of the Black pawns this is always a draw, but if the king is far away the game is untenable.

No. 976, Handbuch

White to play and draw

No. 976 is the counterpart to No. 937. There's no win for Black here because he cannot advance the pawns without blockading them. **1. Kc1 d2+** (or 1. ... Kc4 2. Rc8+ Kb3 3. Rd8! Nf4 4. Rxd3+ Nxd3+ 5. Ke2) **2. Ke2 Kc4 3. Rc8+ Kb3 4. Rd8 Nc3+** (or 4. ... Kc4 5. Rc8+ Kd4 6. Rd8) **5. Kxe3**, etc.

But if the rook were not behind the knight here White would lose. For example, **No. 977** (Berger): **White rook at a2**, other pieces as in No. 976. White to play; Black wins. **1. Kc1** (or 1. Ra4+ Kc5 2. Ra5+ Kc4 3. Ra4+ Kb3 4. Rd4 Nc3+ 5. Ke1 Kc2) **1. ... Nc3 2. Rb2 Kc4 3. Rh2 Ne4 4. Rh4 d2+ 5. Kc2 Kd5 6. Rh5+ Ke6 7. Rh6+ Kf5 8. Rh1 e2**.

Unconnected pawns are still less promising here, since the short-stepping knight cannot defend two widely separated pawns and there are quite a few positions where it cannot defend even one pawn.

However, if the White king is not near the pawns, the rook alone will not be able to hold them.

No. 978, Berger

Black to play and win

After **1. ... Kb5 2. Kf3 Nb3 3. Rh1 a3 4. Rh2 Kb4 5. Ke3 b5! 6. Rc2!** (to prevent 6. ... Kc3. If 6. Kd3 a2! 7. Rxa2 Nc1+) **6. ... Nc5 7. Kd2** (or 7. Kd4 Na4 8. Kd3 Kb3 9. Rc1 a2, etc.) **7. ... Ne4+ 8. Kc1 Nc3! 9. Rh2 Kb3** followed by ... a2.

More than two pawns usually win by straightforward advancement. Of course, there is always an exception.

No. 979, P. Benko 1991

White to play and draw

1. Rd6 Nc1 (if 1. ... Nf4 2. Kb3 h3 [2. ... Kb1 3. Rd4] 3. Rf6 h2 4. Rh6, =) **2. Ka3 h3** (if 2. ... h5 3. Rd4! h3 4. Rd5!, =, or 2. ... Kb1 3. Rd7 h3 4. Rb7+ Kc2 5. Rc7+, =) **3. Rd7 h6 4. Rd6 h5 5. Rd5 h4 6. Rd4 h2 7. Rxh4 d2 8. Rxh2 d1=Q 9. Ra2+! Kb1 10. Rb2+ Ka1 11. Ra2+ Nxa2,** stalemate.

H. Rook and Pawns vs. Knight and Pawns

The general results here are the same as those for the bishop. In the ending, the exchange is worth a little less than two pawns.

1. No Pawns for the Exchange

Rook vs. knight in such cases is normally a somewhat simpler win than rook vs. bishop. In the general case, corresponding to No. 947, the entry of either the White king or rook can never be prevented. Moreover, since the knight cannot defend anything at a distance, when there are pawns on both sides of the board Black is certain to lose material in short order. The main danger for the winning side is not (as with the bishop) Black's getting all the pawns on one side, but his blockading the pawn position so that the knight can both attack and defend at the same time.

No. 980

White to play, Black wins

No. 980, an example where the side with the knight has counterchances, illustrates how easily such endings can usually be decided by the side with the rook.

After **1. h6 Rc8 2. Kb4** (or first 2. h7 Rh8) **2. ... d4!**

Giving up two center pawns for Black's troublesome h-pawn. The noteworthy feature of this sacrifice is that White will have to lose all his pawns in the long run.

3. exd4 e3 4. h7 e2 5. Nf3 Rh8 6. Kc3 Rxh7 7. Kd2 Kc6! (7. ... Rd7 8. Ne5 is pointless) **8. Kxe2 Kd5 9. Kf2 Ra7! 10. Ng5** (desperation: if 10. Ke3 Ra3+ 11. Kf2 Ke4, the end) **10. ... Ra3! 11. Kg2 Kxd4** (see next diagram) **12. Kf2 Re3!** (White gets into zugzwang and is unable to hold his pawn) **13. Kg2 Kd3 14. Kf2 Re2+ 15. Kf3 Re1! 16. Kf2 Rd1 17. Kf3** (if the knight moves, 17. ... Ke4 decides) **17. ... Rf1+ 18. Kg3** (in the game from which this is taken, White played 18. Kg2 Rxf4 19. Ne6 Re4! and resigned) **18. ... Ke3 19. Ne6** (or 19. Nh3 Rf3+ 20. Kg2 Rxh3 21. Kxh3 Kxf4) **19. ... Rf2!** and White must give up the pawn. The last point is **20. Nc7** (20. Kh3 Rxf4) **20. ... Rf3+! 21. Kg2 Ke4 22. Ne6 Rc3 23. Kf2 Rc6**, etc.

This brings us to the question of rook and pawn vs. knight and pawn. With a passed pawn the rook of course wins quite easily, since a rook can both stop the enemy passed pawn and support its own, while a knight cannot. With no passed pawn, unlike the similar bishop ending, it makes no difference whether the pawns are in the center or on the side: the game is drawn only if the knight can both attack the pawn and prevent the entry of the enemy king. This is possible only in certain positions where the pawn is blockaded.

No. 980 showed the general win. The position after move 11 is seen in **No. 981**.

No. 981

Black wins

The case with rook-pawn vs. knight-pawn or rook-pawn is just as easy because a knight is seen at its worst at the edge of the board.

An example is **No. 982.** (Tarrasch-Reti, Bad Kissingen 1928): **White king at g2, knight at f4, pawn at h4; Black king at g7, rook at b2, pawn at h7.** White to play; Black wins. Black's king just walks in and captures the pawn. **1. Kg3 Kf6 2. Nh3 Rb3+ 3. Kg2 Kf5 4. Nf2 Kf4 5. Nh3+ Kg4 6. Nf2+ Kxh4 7. Ne4 Re3 8. Nf2 Rg3+ 9. Kh2 h6 10. Ne4 Rg4 11. Nf2 Rg7 12. Ne4 Kg4 13. Nf2+ Kf3 14. Nh3 Rg2+ 15. Kh1 Ra2,** White resigned.

The typical draw is seen in **No. 983.**

No. 983

Black to play. Draw

If Black's king leaves its d-pawn (say via b6), White moves out of the pin on his knight and threatens Nxd5. Black must then defend the pawn with his rook, only to find that his king can get nowhere because of the strongly centralized knight. For instance, **1. ... Kc6 2. Kd2 Rh5 3. Kd3 Kb6 4. Kd2** (4. Ke2 Kc6 5. Kf3? is bad: 5. ... Rh4 6. Nf5 Re4 and Black wins) **4. ... Kb5 5. Kd3 Kb4**

6. Kd2 Kb3 7. Kd3 Kb2 8. Kd2 Rh2+ 9. Kd3 Rh3 10. Kd2 Rh5 11. Kd3 Kc1 12. Kc3! Rh3 13. Kd3 Rg3 14. Ke2 Rg5 15. Kd3, etc., =.

With all the pawns on one side, the White king marches in, the Black pieces are constricted, and eventually White wins material. Few rook and pawn vs. knight and pawn endings are to be feared, since the pitfalls with the bishop do not come up and the winning technique is simpler. The main danger to be avoided is a blockade.

No. 984, P. Benko 1987

White to play and win

1. c4+

The position is drawn after 1. Rh4? Nb2! 2. Kd7 c4 3. Rh5+ (if 3. Kc7? Na4! 4. Rh3 Nxc3) 3. ... Ke4 4. Kc6 Nd1! 5. Rh4 (on 5. Rh3 Black draws with 5. ... Kf5!, but not with 5. ... Nxc3?) 5. ... Kd3 6. Rd4+ Kxc3!.

1. ... Ke5

On 1. ... Kc6 White will eventually squeeze out the Black king by 2. Rf6+ Kc7 3. Ke6 Kc6 4. Rf8.

2. Rg4!!

It's easy to go wrong with 2. Rh4?! Nb2 3. Kd7 Nxc4 4. Rxc4 Kd5 5. Rc2! c4 6. Rc1 (the Reti maneuver). But Black has a surprise defense after 2. Rh4?! Ne1!! 3. Rh1!? (or 3. Kd7 Nf3 4. Rg4 Kf5, which is easily drawn because of the threatened ... Ne5+) 3. ... Ng2!, holding the position.

2. ... Nb2 3. Rh4!

This move is the only way to win. On 3. Kd7, Black splits the point with 3. ... Kf5 4. Rh4 Kg5.

3. ... Nxc4 4. Rxc4 Kd5 5. Rc1! c4 6. Kd7 Kc5 7. Kc7! and White wins. If 7. ... Kd4 8. Kb6 or 7. ... Kb4 8. Kd6.

The obvious point in the above study is that White must lose a tempo horizontally by playing Rg4 and Rh4 rather than vertically by trying Rc2 and Rc1.

Difficulties arise in this ending mainly with two rooks vs. rook and knight. The reason is that, due to the extra material, White's king cannot penetrate the enemy defense. Accordingly, whenever possible the superior side should exchange rooks.

The technical problem is hardest when each side has only one pawn.

No. 985, Alekhine-Lasker, St. Petersburg 1914

White to play. Black wins

As long as White's rook remains on the board, there is very little that Black can do; but once the rook is exchanged, White may as well resign (No. 981). How can Black force the exchange? Mainly by using the *pin* of the knight and creating *mating threats*. With this in mind, the following moves are intelligible.

1. Rf7+ Ke5 2. Kc2 Rh6 3. Nd3+ Kd6 4. Rf5 Rb8 5. Kc3 Kc7 6. Rf7+ Kb6 7. Rd7 (the threat was 7. ... Rh3 and . ... Rd8) **7. ... Rh3 8. Rd4 Rbh8 9. Rb4+** (if 9. Rd7 R8h5 10. Rd4 c5 11. Rd6+ Kc7 12. Ra6 Rd5 and wins) **9. ... Kc7 10. Kc2 R8h4 11. Rb3 Rh2+**

Somewhat quicker is 11. ... c5! 12. Rc3 Kd6 13. Ra3 c4 14. Ra6+ Kd5 15. Nc1 Rh2+ 16. Kb1 Rh1 17. Ra3 R4h3 18. Rxh3 Rxh3, for after 19. Kc2 Kc5! 20. Na2 Kd4 21. Nb4 Rh2+ 22. Kb1 Kc5 23. Nc2 Kb5, the Black king reaches b3.

There now ensued a good deal of maneuvering (doubtless with an eye on the clock!), which was equivalent to:

12. Kc3 Rh5 13. Ra3 Rd5 14. Rb3 Rg2 15. Ra3 Kb6.

Alekhine is now virtually compelled to bring his rook around to d1, which will permit the Black king to get to b5.

16. Ra1 (if 16. Kc4 Rg4+ 17. Kc3 c5 18. Kc2 Rg2+ 19. Kc3 Rg3 20. Kc2 c4) **16. ... Rg3 17. Rd1** (Lasker has improved his position: his opponent's knight is doubly pinned) **17. ... Kb5 18. Kc2**

If 18. Rd2 Rc5+ 19. Kb3 Rcg5 forces the exchange of rooks. Here 19. Kd4 Rc4+ 20. Ke5 Re3+ 21. Kf5 Rd4 wins more quickly for Black.

18. ... Kc4 (forcing a weakening of the pawn position) **19. b3+ Kb5 20. Rd2 Rh3 21. Rd1 Rh2+ 22. Kc3 Rd8 23. Rg1 Rh3 24. Rd1 Rdh8 25. Rg1** (the threat was 25. ... Rh1 26. Rd2 R8h2, exchanging rooks) **25. ... R8h5 26. Kc2 Rd5 27. Rd1 Rg5 28. Rf1**

In the game Alekhine played 28. Rd2, whereupon 28. ... Rhg3 forced the exchange of rooks: 29. Nc1 Rg2 30. Ne2 Kb6! and White resigned; since he has no checks, the threat of 30. ... Re5 is fatal.

28. ... Rg2+ 29. Kc3 Rhh2 30. Rc1

There is nothing better: if 30. Nb4 c5, if 30. Ne1 Ra2! 31. Rg1 c5 32. Rf1 Ra1; finally, the aggressive 30. Rf5+ is refuted by 30. ... Kb6 31. Kd4 Rc2 32. b4 Rh4+ 33. Ke3 Rh3+, and 34. Rf3 Rxf3+ 35. Kxf3 is forced, when 35. ... Kb5 wins quickly.

30. ... c5 (all the White pieces except the knight are tied to their posts) **31. Nf4 Ra2! 32. Nd3** (if 32. Kd3 Rhf2 33. Ke3 Rfb2 34. Rc3 Ra3, winning a pawn) **32. ... Ra3!** (threatening 32. ... c4) **33. Rb1**

If 33. Ne5 Rh3+ 34. Nd3 c4! The exchange of rooks by 33. Rc2 would doubtless hold on longest, but the win would then be merely a question of time.

33. ... c4 34. Nc1 (the only chance) **34. ... Kc5! 35. Rb2 Rh3+ 36. Kc2 c3 37. Rb1** (or 37. Ra2 Rxa2+ 38. Nxa2 Kd4) **37. ... Ra8! 38. Nd3+** (or 38. Ne2 Ra2+ 39. Kd1 Rh1+, or 38. b4+ Kc4) **38. ... Kd4 39. Rd1** (39. Nc1 Rh2+ 40. Kd1 c2+) **39. ... Ra2+**, and wins, for if 40. Nb2+ Kc5 costs White the knight, and if 40. Kb1 c2+.

This strategy of slowly constricting the enemy forces until the exchange of rooks is unavoidable is the key to all such endings with only one or two pawns.

Another illustration is **No. 986** (Tarrasch-Reti, Bad Kissingen 1928): **White king at f3, rook at a2, knight at h3, pawn at h2; Black king at g6, rooks at e6, d5, pawn at h7.** Black to play and win. After **1. ... Rf5+ 2. Nf4+** (tit for tat!) **2. ... Kg5 3. h4+ Kh6 4. Kg4 Ref6 5. Ra4 Rb5 6. Rc4 Rfb6 7. Rc7 Rb4 8. Rf7 Rb7! 9. Rf5 Kg7 10. Kg3 R4b5 11. Ne6+ Kg6 12. Rf2 Rb3+** White can no longer postpone the exchange, for if **13. Kg4 h5+ 14. Kf4 Rf7+** wins a rook. For the ending after **13. Kg2 Rb2 14. Rxb2 Rxb2+,** see No. 982.

With more pawns on the board, the winning strategy involves restricting the mobility of the knight, weakening the pawn position, and either penetrating with the king or setting up a passed pawn.

Of course, rooks should be exchanged whenever the opportunity presents itself, for the win then involves nothing more difficult than walking the king in. An excellent example of the model procedure when no passed pawn can be set up immediately is **No. 987.**

No. 987, Alekhine-Kashdan, Pasadena 1932

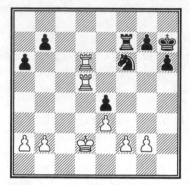

White to play and win

White's plan against passive play is to advance his b-pawn to b6 and place his rook on c5, and then to play Rc7, which would force the exchange of rooks. To prevent this, Black must undertake some desperate counteraction.

1. Rf5 Kg6 2. Rc5 Kh7 3. Ke2 (the threat was 3. ... Ng4) **3. ... g5 4. b4 Kg7 5. a4 Ng4** (his only chance: after 5. ... Kh7 6. b5 axb5 7. axb5 Kg7 8. b6 Black can give up) **6. f3 exf3+ 7. gxf3 Nh2 8. f4! gxf4 9. exf4.**

Now that a passed pawn has been created the technical problem is much simpler.

9. ... Ng4 (9. ... Rxf4 10. Rc7+ is worse: Black loses both his queenside pawns) **10. Kf3** (simpler is 10. b5) **10. ... Nf6 11. b5 Nd7** (a trap: if 12. Rc7? Ne5+!) **12. Rcd5 Nf6 13. Rf5 Kg6 14. Rc5** (now that the knight is pinned, Black is defenseless) **14. ... axb5 15. Rxb5** (15. axb5 is also good enough, but the move chosen wins a pawn) **15. ... Rc7 16. Rbb6 Rf7 17. a5 Kg7 18. Rb5 Rc7 19. Rdb6 Rc3+ 20. Ke2** (the rest is routine) **20. ... Rc4 21. Rxb7+ Kg6 22. f5+** (or 22. Rb4) **22. ... Kg5 23. a6 Ra4 24. a7 Ne4 25. Ke3,** Black resigned.

When White has a passed pawn or can create one, the win is child's play because the knight cannot both defend against the pawn and support its own pawns.

An example is **No. 988** (Tartakower-Dus-Chotimirsky, Carlsbad 1907): **White king at b2, rooks at c4, h2, pawns at a2, b3, c2, g5; Black king at g7, rook at e7, knight at f5, pawns at a7, b7, g6, h7.** White to play and win. Here he only needs to advance his queenside pawns. **1. Rc3 Ne3 2. Rd3 Ng4 3. Rh4 h5 4. gxh6+ Nxh6 5. c4 Nf5 6. Rg4 Kf6 7. c5 g5 8. b4 Kg6 9. b5 Kh5 10. Rc4 g4 11. c6 bxc6 12. bxc6 Rc7 13. Rd5 Kg5 14. Rcc5 Kh4** (14. ... Rf7 15. c7) **15. Rxf5,** and it's all over.

2. One Pawn for the Exchange

This is a win, but the technical difficulties are considerable. And, of course, there are quite a few drawn cases.

First we must note that in unbalanced pawn positions the rook will usually win. A passed pawn is created and normally cramps the opponent's game so badly that either the knight or the king becomes worthless. **No. 989** is an instance where one lone passed pawn decides.

No. 989, Em. Lasker-Ed. Lasker, New York 1924

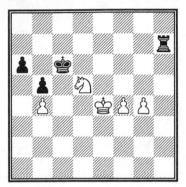

Black to play wins

White's pawns are not advanced quite far enough, giving Black time to exploit his queenside majority:

1. ... Rd7

In the game Black lost a tempo by 1. ... Rh8, after which Dr. Lasker found the justly celebrated draw with 2. Ne3 a5 3. bxa5 b4 4. a6 Kc5 5. a7 b3 6. Nd1 Ra8 7. g5 Rxa7 8. g6 Rd7 9. Nb2 Rd2 10. Kf3 Rd8 11. Ke4 Kd6 12. Kd3!! Rc8 13. g7 Ke6 14. g8=Q+! Rxg8 15. Kc4 Rg3 16. Na4, etc. See No. 972.

2. Ne3 (or 2. Nf6 Rd8 3. g5 a5 4. bxa5 b4 5. g6 b3 and queens) **2. ... a5! 3. bxa5 b4 4. g5 Kc5! 5. Nc2 b3 6. Na3 Kb4 7. Nb1 b2 8. g6 Rd1! 9. g7 Rg1 10. Kd3 Rxg7 11. Kc2 Rg2+ 12. Kd3 Kb3 13. a6 Rg6** and wins. White must lose first his pawns and then his knight.

Similarly, if the pawns are balanced but there is a sufficient number on both sides, White will normally be able to win, for the march of the king is bound to lead to the capture of material.

But with all the White pawns on one side, the game may often be drawn. By manipulating his extra pawn properly, Black should be able to divert either the rook or the king and thus guard against material loss. **No. 990** is an example of this strategy.

No. 990, Steinitz-Zukertort, match 1886

White to play. Draw

Zukertort drew by advancing his b-pawn. The game continued **1. Kg3 Ke7 2. Kf4 Ke6 3. h4 Kd5 4. g4 b5 5. Rb1 Kc5 6. Rc1+ Kd5 7. Ke3 Nc4+ 8. Ke2** (if **8. Kd3 Ne5+**) **8. ... b4 9. Rb1 Kc5 10. f4 Na3 11. Rc1+ Kd4 12. Rc7 b3 13. Rb7 Kc3** (Black still draws even though the White rook is on the seventh) **14. Rc7+ Kd4!** (but not **14. ... Kb2?** 15. Rxf7 Ka2 16. Rxg7 b2 17. Rb7 b1=Q 18. Rxb1 Kxb1 19. h5, and the pawns decide) **15. Rb7 Kc3,** and a draw was agreed.

Examining this ending carefully, we conclude that Black drew only because his knight could both attack (support the advance of the b-pawn) and defend (the kingside pawns). Therefore, if the pawns are farther apart or otherwise weakened, Black must lose.

With all the pawns on one side, one would naturally expect the game to be a draw. Yet the defender must still play with care; the slightest weakness may be fatal.

No. 991, Vidmar-Alekhine, San Remo 1930

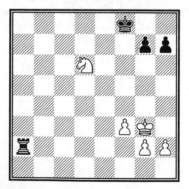

White to play, Black wins

No. 991 is instructive because it's surprising to find that such an ending is lost no matter what White does. The game continued:

1. h4

While such a move is bad on the general principle that any advance weakens the pawn structure, it apparently cannot be avoided in the long run. For example, 1. Nf5 Kf7 2. Nd6+ Ke6 3. Ne4 h6 4. Nf2 Ke5 5. Ng4+ Kd4 6. Nf2 Ke3 7. Ng4+ Ke2, and now if 8. Kf4 Kf1 9. Ne3+ Kf2 wins without much trouble: 10. Nf5 Ra7! 11. g4 Ra4+ 12. Ke5 Kxf3 13. Nxg7 Kxg4, etc. This line compels us to conclude that Dr. Vidmar's move is best, despite the violation of a basic rule.

1. ... Ke7 2. Ne4 h6 (not 2. ... Ke6? 3. Ng5+) **3. Nf2?**

White still had time to create the best defensive formation: 3. Kh3! This idea permits the vital g2-g4. With 3. ... Ke6 Black can only delay the advance of the g-pawn. If, for example 3. ... Ra3, White continues 4. Kg4 Ke6 5. Kf4 Kd5 (the pawn advance 5. ... g6 leads to an immediate 6. g4) 6. h5! Kd4 7. Nd6 Kd3 8. Nf5 Ra4+ 9. Kg3 Ra5 10. Kf4 Ra7 11. g4.

White's general strategy is to attack Black's pawns rather than give him a free hand. After 4. g4! Ke5 5. Kg3 g6, White has built his mighty fortress: 6. Nf2 Ra3 7. Nh3 Ra4, Black prevents the strong 8. Nf4 (if 8. Kf2 h5 9. gxh5 gxh5, Black would actually lose after 9. ... Rxh4 10. hxg6! Rxh3 11.g7!) 10. Kg3, Black is stymied and the position is drawn.

3. ... Ke6 4. Nd3 Kf5 5. Nf4 Ra4 6. Nd3 Rc4 7. Nf2 Rc6 8. Nh3 Ke5

A critical position. If White keeps stalling with his knight, Black's king will get to the eighth and win a pawn. For example, 9. Nf4 Rc2 10. Nh3 Rd2 11. Nf4 Ra2 12. Nh3 Kd4 13. Nf4 Ke3 14. Ne6! Ra7! (if 14. ... g6 15. Nf4 draws because now White's knight attacks g6 and defends g2 at the same time) 15. Nf4 Ra6! 16. Nh3 (if 16. Kg4 Ra4 17. g3 Rc4 wins a pawn. And 16. Nh5 threatens nothing.) 16. ... Ke2 17. Nf4+ Kf1, and White cannot hold everything; e.g., 18. h5 Ra5 19. Kh2 Kf2 20. Kh3 Rg5 21. Kh4 Ke3, or 18. Nh3 Ra2 19. Nf4 g5 20. hxg5 hxg5 21. Ne6 Rxg2+ 22. Kh3 Kf2, with an easy win in both cases.

Vidmar accordingly tried **9. h5,** but Alekhine ingeniously demonstrated a forced win.

9. ... Rc2 10. Nf4 Rd2! 11. Nh3 Kd4 12. Nf4 Ke3 13. Ne6

Relatively best. After 13. Nh3 Rb2 14. Nf4 Rb5 15. Ne6 Re5! wins a pawn, and on 13. Kg4 Rd4 14. g3 Ra4 is quite adequate: 15. Kf5 Ra5+! 16. Kg6 Rg5+ 17. Kf7 Kxf3 18. Ne6 Rxg3 19. Nxg7 Kf4 20. Kf6, and now 20. ... Rxg7 21. Kxg7 Kg5 makes the win routine.

13. ... Rd5! 14. f4!

A clever try, but it comes too late. If 14. Kg4 Re5; if 14. Kh4 Re5 15. Nxg7 Rg5 16. Ne6 Rxg2 17. f4 Ke4, and White loses all his pawns.

14. ... Rf5!

But not 14. ... Rxh5 15. Nxg7 Ra5 16. Kg4 Ke4 17. Nh5 and the game is drawn.

15. Kg4 Rf6! 16. f5 (if 16. Nxg7 Rxf4+ as in the main line) **16. ... Ke4!**

The game concluded 16. ... Rf7 17. g3 Ke4 18. Nc5+ Kd4! 19. Nb3+ Ke5, BlackWhite resigned. However, on 16. ... Rf7, 17. Nd8 makes matters more difficult.

17. Nxg7 (if 17. Nc5+ Kd5 18. Nd3 Kd4 19. Nf4 Ke4) **17. ... Rf7 18. Ne6** (best; after 18. Ne8! Ke5! 19. f6 Rf8 20. Nc7 Rxf6 the knight is lost) **18. ... Rxf5** (White is now unable to consolidate his position and must lose both remaining pawns) **19. Kh4**

If 19. g3 Re5 20. Nd8 Rg5+ 21. Kh4 Kf3 22. Nf7 Rg4+ 23. Kh3 Rxg3+ 24. Kh4 (or 24. Kh2 Kf4 25. Nxh6 Rg7! and wins as above) 24. ... Rg1 25. Nxh6 Kf4 26. Kh3 Rg3+ 27. Kh4 Rg7!! 28. Kh3 Rh7 and wins the knight.

19. ... Ke5 20. Nc5 (if 20. Nd8 Kd5! wins the knight) **20. ... Rf4+ 21. Kh3 Rd4 22. g3 Kd6! 23. Nb3** (23. Na6 Rc4) **23. ... Rd1 24. Kh4 Kd5 25. g4 Rd3 26. g5!** (the best chance: if 26. Nc1 Re3 27. g5 Re4+, etc.) **26. ... Rxb3 27. gxh6 Ke6 28. h7 Rb8 29. Kg5 Kf7** and wins.

With two rooks and a normal pawn structure, it stands to reason that some kind of impregnable position can usually be set up by the defender. However, the slightest deviation from the normal may well cost the knight and the game.

For example, **No. 992** (Pillsbury-Napier, Hanover 1902): **White king at c2, rook at e2, knight at b4, pawns at a3, b2, d4, g5; Black king at g6, rooks at f1, h3, pawns at b7, b6, d5.** Black won by a mating attack: **1. ... Rf4 2. Re6+?** (better is 2. Nxd5 Rxd4 3. Nxb6, which would probably draw) **2. ... Kxg5 3. Rxb6 Rf2+ 4. Kb1 Rb3! 5. Rxb7** (or 5. Nxd5 Rfxb2+) **5. ... Rbxb2+ 6. Kc1 Rb3 7. Rg7+ Kh6 8. Rc7 Rxa3 9. Nc2 Rb3!! 10. Rc5 Rb6!!** (White is now in zugzwang) **11. Na1 Rf1+ 12. Kc2 Ra6 13. Nb3 Rf2+,** and White resigned because his knight is lost.

3. Two (or More) Pawns for the Exchange

Roughly speaking, two pawns are somewhat more than equivalent to the exchange. Nevertheless, in endings with only one rook and one knight, the result is usually a draw, though the chances favor the side with the rook. The reason is that the knight alone is unable to defend a large number of pawns.

The helplessness of the knight in protecting widely scattered pawns is clearly demonstrated in **No. 993.** Black cannot avoid the loss of a pawn.

No. 993, Euwe-Capablanca, 8th match game 1931

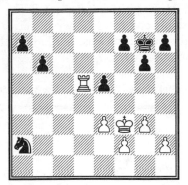

Black to play, White wins

If 1. ... Kf6 2. Rd7 and either Rxa7 or Rd6+ and Rxb6. Capablanca. tried **1. ... e4+! 2. Kf4**

2. Kg2 wins a pawn too, but after 2. ... Nc3 3. Rd7 Nb5 4. Re7 Kf6! 5. Rxe4 a5 6. Re8 Nd6 7. Rb8 b5 8. Rb6 Ke5 9. f4+ Kd5, Black's pawns are dangerous.

2. ... Nb4!

If 2. ... Nc3 3. Rd7 a5 4. Ke5!, and Black loses two and possibly three pawns.

3. Rb5

3. Rd7? Nd3+ and if 4. Kxe4 Nc5+, but 3. Rd4 gains an invaluable tempo: 3. ... Nd3+ 4. Kxe4 Nxf2+ 5. Kf3 Nh3 6. Rd7, and Black loses both queenside pawns.

3. ... Nd3+ 4. Kxe4 Nxf2+ 5. Kd4 (if 5. Kf3, Nd3 makes matters difficult) **5. ... f5**

Or 5. ... Nh3 6. Rd5 Kf6 7. Rd7 Ng5 8. h4. Black cannot reach the kind of impregnable position exemplified in No. 990.

6. Rb2 Ng4 7. h3 Nf6 8. Rc2.

Black has preserved material equality all this while, but now he can no longer hold on.

8. ... Ne4 9. g4 Kf6 10. gxf5 Kxf5

Or 10. ... gxf5 11. Rc6+ Kg5 12. Rc7 h5 13. Ke5 Nf2 14. Rg7+ Kh4 15. Rxa7 Nxh3 16. Kxf5 with an easy win.

11. Rc7 Ng5 12. Rxa7 h5.

Now **13. h4** wins most convincingly. Euwe actually played 13. Ra3 Nf3+ 14. Kd3? (14. Kd5 g5 15. Ra8 still wins), when 14. ... Ng1 15. Kd2 g5 16. Rb3 h4 led to a draw: 17. Rxb6 Nxh3 18. Ke2 g4 19. Rb5+ Ke4 20. Rb4+ Kf5 21. Kf1 Kg5 22. Rb5+ Kg6 23. Rb4 Kh5 24. Rb5+ Kg6. White's king cannot get into the game because of the strong Black passed pawns.

13. ... Nf3+ 14. Kd5 g5

Or 14. ... Nxh4 15. Rf7+ Kg4 16. e4 Ng2 17. e5 h4 18. e6 h3 19. e7 h2 20. e8=Q h1=Q 21. Qe6+ Kg5 22. Qf6+ and wins.

15. hxg5 Kxg5 (if 15. ... Nxg5 16. Ra4! b5 17. Rf4+ Kg6 18. Rb4 wins) **16. Ke4**

Nd2+ 17. Kd3 Nf3 18. Ke2 Ne5 19. Rb7 Nc4 20. Kd3 Ne5+ 21. Ke4 Ng4 22. Rxb6 h4 23. Rb5+ Kg6 24. Kf4 Nf6 25. Rg5+ Kf7 (25. ... Kh6 26. Rg1) **26. e4,** and Black will soon lose his pawn.

With the king near the passed pawns, the knight should not lose, but the winning chances are practically nil.

No. 994, Fine-Reshevsky, New York 1940

Black to play and draw

The game continued **1. ... Kd5 2. Nf4+ Kc6 3. Kc4** (a desperate winning attempt; 3. Ne2 is a routine draw) **3. ... Rxg3 4. b5+ Kd7 5. Kd5 Rg1 6. Nd3 Rd1 7. Kc4 Rb1, =.**

Nothing could be done even if the pawns got to the sixth (No. 976).

Again, however, rook plus knight and two pawns vs. two rooks (plus additional material) is usually a pretty easy win for the knight because the rook helps to defend the pawns.

No. 995, Euwe-Alekhine, 26th match game 1935

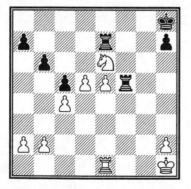

Black to play, White wins

Black's best chance is **1. ... Rxe6 2. dxe6 Kg8 3. Re3 Kf8 4. Ra3 Rxe5 5. Rxa7 Rxe6 6. b3! Re2 7. Rxh7 Rxa2 8. Rb7,** when White will barely manage to win.

Alekhine chose not to sacrifice and the pawn roller proved to be irresistible. **1. ... h6**

If 1. ... Kg8 2. Rg1+ Kh8 3. Rg5! Rxg5 4. Nxg5 Kg7 5. d6! Rxe5 6. d7 Re1+ 7. Kg2 Rd1 8. d8=Q! Rxd8 9. Ne6+. Or here 5. ... Rd7 6. Ne6+ Kf7 7. Nf4 Ke8 8. Kg2 Rg7+ 9. Kf3 Kd7 10. Ke4 Kc6 11. Nd5, followed by Ne7+, Kd5, etc.

2. Nd8! Rf2 (2. ... Rfxe5 3. Rxe5 Rxe5 4. Nf7+) **3. e6 Rd2 4. Nc6 Re8 5. e7 b5**

Desperation. Note that without the rooks Black could get his king to f7 and blockade the pawns, which would surely draw and might even win.

6. Nd8 Kg7 7. Nb7 Kf6 8. Re6+ Kg5 9. Nd6 Rxe7 10. Ne4+, resigns.

A similar instance with disconnected pawns is **No. 996** (Botvinnik-Levenfish, 2nd match game 1937): **White king at h1, rooks at b2, f3, pawns at a2, b4, h2; Black king at h8, rook at g8, knight at g4, pawns at a7, b6, c5, f4, h7. Black to play and win. 1. ... Ne5! 2. Rf1** (2. Rxf4 Nd3) **2. ... Nd3 3. Rg2** (or 3. Rd2 c4 4. b5 Rg5) **3. ... c4 4. Rc2 b5 5. a3 f3! 6. Rd2** (6. Rxf3 Ne1) **6. ... Rg2!! 7. Rxg2 fxg2+ 8. Kxg2**

Black now wins by a combination that often occurs in knight-vs.-rook endings. **8. ... c3! 9. Kf3** (if 9. Rf8+ Kg7 10. Rc8 c2!! and 11. Rxc2 Ne1+ costs White his rook) **9. ... c2 10. Ke2 c1=Q 11. Rxc1 Nxc1+ 12. Kd2 Na2 13. Kc2 Kg7 14. Kb2 Nxb4 15. axb4 Kf6,** with an easily won pawn ending.

VI. ROOK AND BISHOP VS. ROOK

For some strange reason, this ending occurs far more often than the analogous ending with the knight. It has been analyzed exhaustively ever since the days of Philidor and the general case has been definitely established as a draw. The difficulty that attaches to it, however, is due not only to the fact that there are a number of important exceptions where White wins but also to the complicated nature of the drawing variations.

No. 997, Philidor's Position

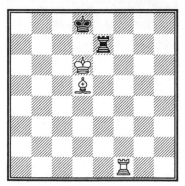

White to play and win

The general win is **No. 997**. The solution is **1. Rf8+ Re8 2. Rf7 Re2!**

Best. 2. ... Re3 or . ... Re1 transposes into the main line. If 2. ... Rh8 3. Ra7 Rh6+ 4. Be6 wins at once.

3. Rg7! (to force the Black rook to a less favorable square) **3. ... Re1** (3. ... Re3 4. Rb7 again gets into the main line) **4. Rb7 Rc1**

Forced: if 4. ... Kc8 5. Ra7! Rb1 6. Rh7! Kb8 7. Rh8+ Ka7 8. Ra8+ Kb6 9. Rb8+ and wins the rook. Or here 6. ... Rb6+ 7. Bc6 and mates soon.

5. Bb3!! (a tempo move to get the rook to the unfavorable sixth rank) **5. ... Rc3!**

Best. On 5. ... Kc8 6. Rb4, threatening mate in three beginning with Be6+, forces 6. ... Kd8 when 7. Rf4 Re1 8. Ba4 Kc8 9. Bc6 Rd1+ 10. Bd5 Kb8 11. Ra4 decides. If here 7. ... Kc8 8. Bd5 Kb8 9. Ra4, etc.

6. Be6 Rd3+ 7. Bd5 Rc3 (7. ... Kc8 8. Ra7 and wins) **8. Rd7+! Kc8**

If now 8. ... Ke8 9. Rg7 and wins because the Black rook cannot get to the f-file. This is one reason the rook had to be forced to go to the sixth.

9. Rf7 Kb8 10. Rb7+ Kc8 11. Rb4! Kd8 (or 11. ... Rd3 12. Ra4 and now the rook cannot go to the b-file) **12. Bc4!!** (the point) **12. ... Kc8** (there is no way to stop mate) **13. Be6+ Kd8 14. Rb8+ Rc8 15. Rxc8+** mate.

Philidor's position is a win with the kings on any file except the knight-file. But when the Black king is near the edge of the board the win is more difficult.

No. 998, Lolli

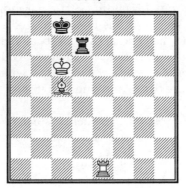

White to play and win

In **No. 998** Black has an additional defense that is not available in Philidor's Position.

1. Re8+ Rd8 2. Re7 and now:

a) **2. ... Rg8** (in Philidor's Position this led to immediate mate) **3. Ra7 Kb8 4. Rb7+ Ka8** (4. ... Kc8 5. Bd6) **5. Bd6 Rc8+** (if 5. ... Rg1 6. Rb8+ Ka7 7. Rh8 and if 7. ... Rg6 8. Rh1, and if 7. ... Rc1+ 8. Bc5+ and 9. Rh5+ mate) **6. Bc7 Rg8** (6. ... Rxc7+ 7. Rxc7) **7. Rb1 Rg6+ 8. Bd6 Rg7 9. Re1 Rh7 10. Re8+ Ka7 11. Bc5+** and mates in two. An alternative win here is **3. Re6 Rh8 4. Bd6 Kd8 5. Be5 Rf8 6.**

Bg7 Rg8 7. Bf6+ Kc8 8. Re4 Rf8 (or 8. ... Kb8 9. Be5+ Kc8 10. Rb4 Rg6+ 11. Bd6) **9. Bg7 Rg8 10. Ra4**, and either wins the rook or mates.

b) **2. ... Rd2 3. Rf7 Rd8** (if 3. ... Rd1 4. Ra7, as in No. 997, with the continuation 4. ... Rb1 5. Ba3 Kb8 6. Re7! Ka8 7. Re4 Rb7 8. Re5!! and Black is in zugzwang: 8. ... Ka7 or 8. ... Rb1, then 9. Ra5+ Kb8 10. Bd6+, and mates in two) **4. Be7 Rg8 5. Rf5 Kb8** (5. ... Rg6+ 6. Bd6 Rg8 7. Rb5) **6. Bd6+ Kc8 7. Ra5** (or Rb5) **any 8. Ra8+** mate.

With the kings on the rook-file Black has additional drawing chances due to the stalemate possibilities, but here too there is a win with best play.

No. 999, Kling and Kuiper 1846

White wins

In **No. 999**, it makes no difference whose move it is. There are two main variations:

a) **1. ... Rb2 2. Rh6 Rb1 3. Bb6 Ra1+ 4. Kb5 Kb7 5. Rh7+ Kc8 6. Kc6 Rc1+ 7. Bc5 Rd1**, and continues as in Lolli (No. 998).

b) **1. ... Re8 2. Bc7 Re6+ 3. Bb6 Re8 4. Rh6 Kb8 5. Rc6 Ka8! 6. Bd4! Rb8** (if 6. ... Kb8 7. Kb6 Re1 8. Rf6 Rb1+ 9. Kc6, etc.) **7. Re6 Rc8 8. Bc3! Rb8** (or 8. ... Kb8 9. Be5+ Ka8 10. Kb6) **9. Re2 Rd8 10. Kb6 Kb8! 11. Bb4 Kc8** (or 11. ... Ka8 12. Kc7. Or 11. ... Rg8 12. Bd6+ Kc8 13. Kc6 and 14. Ra2) **12. Kc6 Rd7 13. Re8+ Rd8 14. Re7 Rg8** and either **15. Ra7** or **15. Bd6** transposes into Lolli.

With the kings on the knight file the game is drawn because Black has just enough room to wiggle around.

No. 1000

White to play. Draw

Best play for both sides is **1. Rd8+ Rc8 2. Rd7 Rc2 3. Rf7 Rc3 4. Ba4 Rc1** (4. ... Rc4? 5. Bc6 Rb4+ 6. Bb5) **5. Bc6 Rb1+ 6. Kc5 Rb2!** (Black must stay on the knight file) **7. Bd5 Rh2** (the threat was 8. Kd6) **8. Rb7+ Kc8 9. Re7 Kb8! 10. Kc6**

Or 10. Kb6 Rc2! 11. Bb3 Rc1! 12. Rd7 Kc8! 13. Rd2 Rb1 (13. ... Kb8? 14. Bc2) 14. Rd3 Rb2 15. Kc6 Rb1 16. Be6+ Kb8 17. Rd8+ Ka7 18. Rd7+ Kb8 19. Bd5 Rc1+ 20. Kd6 Rc7!, =. Or here 16. Bd5 Rc1+ 17. Kd6 Rc7 18. Ra3 Rd7+ 19. Ke6 Rd8 20. Ra7 Kb8!, etc.

10. ... Rh6+ 11. Be6 Rh1! 12. Rb7+ Ka8 13. Rb2 (or 13. Rg7 Kb8! 14. Bf5 Rh6+ 15. Bg6 Rh8! 16. Kb6 Kc8! 17. Be4 Rh6+ 18. Bc6 Kd8, etc., =) **13. ... Rc1+ 14. Kb6 Kb8 15. Bf5 Rc4! 16. Rb5 Rh4 17. Kc6+ Ka7 18. Bd3 Rf4 19. Rb7+ Ka8 20. Rg7 Kb8!** (not 20. ... Rf6+? 21. Kc7), etc.

Other drawn positions where the Black king is on the edge of the board fall into one of the four classes typified by the following positions.

No. 1001, Szen

White to play. Draw

In **No. 1001**, the Black rook can always interpose on a check and there is no way for White to improve his position. **1. Rb8+ Rc8 2. Bf6+ Kc7 3. Be5+ Kd8 4. Rb1 Rc2**, etc.

An exception occurs only in similar positions when the Black king is at c8 or f8 and the Black rook has no effective check. For instance, **No. 1002: White king at d6, rook at a6, bishop at d5; Black king at c8, rook at b2.** Black to play, White wins. **1. ... Rb1 2. Ra8+ Rb8 3. Ra1 Rb2 4. Rh1! Kb8 5. Rh8+ Ka7 6. Ra8+ Kb6 7. Rb8+**, and wins the rook. This variation occurs repeatedly in Philidor's Position.

The other drawn cases come up when White's king is on the sixth, but there is no direct mate threat, as in **No. 1003.**

No. 1003, Kling and Kuiper

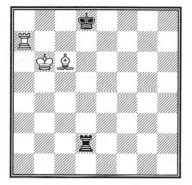

White to play. Draw

After **1. Kc5!**, Rf2 is the correct reply (but not 1. ... Rd1? 2. Bd5! and we get either Philidor's Position after 2. ... Rc1+ 3. Kd6 or the Szen position, No. 1001, after 2. ... Kc8 3. Kd6 Rb1) and now **2. Bd5 Rf6!** or **2. Rd7+ Kc8 3. Re7 Rf6 4. Kb6 Rd6.** (see No. 1005).

Exceptions occur as in the previous position, and with the rook too near the center. For instance, **No. 1004** (Berger): **White king at e6, rook at a7, bishop at d6; Black king at c8, rook at c4.** White to play and win. **1. Kd5 Rc1 2. Bc5 Kd8 3. Kc6 Ke8 4. Re7+ Kd8 5. Re2 Rc4** (5. ... Rc3 6. Rf2; and 6. ... Re3 is impossible) **6. Rd2+ Ke8** (or 6. ... Kc8) **7. Rf2** and wins.

No. 1005, Kling and Kuiper

White to play. Draw

No. 1005 is similar. If **1. Re7 Rd6 2. Re2 Rd1,** we have No. 1001.

Exceptions occur when the Black rook has fewer than three squares at its disposal. For instance, **No. 1006** (Centurini 1867): **White king at d6, rook at f7, bishop at e6; Black king at e8, rook at h6.** White to play and win. **1. Rf1 Rg6 2. Rf2! Rh6 3. Ra2 Kf8 4. Rg2 Rh8 5. Kd7! Rh7+ 6. Kd8 Rh8 7. Rg3 R any 8. Rg8+ mate.**

Finally, **No. 1007** (Cochrane): **White king at d5, rook at h7, bishop at d4; Black king at d8, rook at d1.** White to play and draw. This is perhaps the most important of all because there are no exceptions. White cannot threaten mate by **1. Kd6** because of **1. ... Rxd4+,** and other moves threaten nothing at all.

The simplest drawing rule for Black to follow is to wait until the White king has moved to one side, and then play to the other.

No. 1008, Flohr-Reshevsky, Semmering-Baden 1937

Black to play. Draw

No. 1008 illustrates the method of handling this ending. **1. ... Re2 2. Rh4**

Re1 3. Rh6+ Ke7 4. Kd4 Kd7 5. Bf4 Rd1+ 6. Kc4 Re1 7. Bd2 Rd1 8. Bb4 Rg1
9. Bc5 Rc1+ 10. Kd5 Rd1+ 11. Bd4 Kd8 (see No. 1007) 12. Rh7 Rd2 13. Ke5
Kc8! 14. Bc5 Rd7 15. Be7 Kb7 16. Ke6 Kc6 17. Rh1 Rd2 18. Rc1+ Kb5 19. Bd6
Re2+ 20. Kd7 Re4 21. Rc5+ Ka4 22. Kc6 Kb3 23. Kd5 Re8 24. Rb5+ Kc2 25.
Bc5 Kd3 26. Rb3+ Ke2 27. Bd4 Rd8+ 28. Ke4 Re8+ 29. Be5 Ke1 30. Rb2 Re7
(No. 1007 again!), and a draw was agreed.

With pawns on the board, the ending is exactly the same as bishop vs. pawns,
except that rook plus bishop and pawn win, even with rook-pawn and
bishop of the wrong color.

No. 1009, Capablanca-Tarrasch, St. Petersburg 1914

Black wins

No. 1009 is the model winning procedure. The White king will be forced
out of the corner by playing the Black king to b3 and the rook to the seventh.
1. Rc1+ Kb5 2. Rb1+ Kc5 3. Rc1+ Kd6 4. Rd1+ Bd5+ 5. Kb2 a3+ 6. Ka1 Kc5
(6. ... a2? is a mistake after which Black can only draw) **7. Rc1+ Bc4 8. Rg1
Rh2 9. Rg5+ Kb4 10. Rg1 Ra2+ 11. Kb1 Rd2!**, and White resigned, for if 12.
Re1 Kb3 13. Re3+ Bd3+, and if 14. Ka1 Ra2+ mate or 14. ... Rd1+ mate.

No. 1010, P. Benko 1982

White to play and win

1. Bg4!! Kf8

There is a trick here: 1. ... 0-0 is illegal because Black must have moved either his king or rook on the previous move. Also, 1. ... Rg8 is wrong because of 2. Ra8+ Kf7 3. Be6+. Or 1. ... Rf8 2. Bh5+ Kd8 3. Bf7, followed by Kc5 and Kd6, winning.

2. Bh5 Rg8

If 2. ... h6, White wins with 3. Kc5 Kg8 4. Kd6 Rh7 5. Ra8+ Kg7 6. Ke6 Rh8 7. Ra7+ and 8. Kf6.

3. Rf7+ Ke8 4. Kc5! Kd8

If 4. ... Rg5+, the countercheck 5. Rf5+ wins; or 4. ... Rf8, when 5. Ra7+ Kd8 6. Bf7 wins.

5. Kd6 Kc8 6. Kc6 Kd8 7. Rd7+ Kc8 8. Ra7 Kb8 9. Rb7+ Ka8

After 9. ... Kc8 10. Bf7! Rg2 11. Be6+ Kd8 12. Kd6 Rd2+ 13. Bd5, with a winning position.

10. Bf3!

a) **10. ... Rg6+ 11. Kc5!!** (11. Kb5 is bad; for instance, 11. ... Rg3! 12. Rf7+ [12. Bd5? Rb3+ is a draw] 12. ... Kb8 13. Kb6 Kc8 14. Bc6 Rd3!, and Black escapes, having reached the Szen position) **11. ... Ra6 12. Bc6! h5 13. Kd6 h4 14. Rd7+ Kb8 15. Rd8+ Ka7 16. Kc7.** Or Black can choose:

b) **10. ... Rg3 11. Be4! Re3** (or 11. ... Rg4 12. Re7 Kb8 13. Re8+ Ka7 14. Kc5 Rg5+ 15. Bd5) **12. Bd5 Rd3 13. Re7 Rc3+ 14. Kb6+ Kb8 15. Be6!** and White wins. Finally, Black may try to defend from the other side:

c) **10. ... Rf8** (if 10. ... Rc8+, then 11. Kd6! h5 12. Bc6 and White wins) **11. Bd5 Rf5** (White wins after 11. ... Rc8+ 12. Kd7! Rf8 13. Kc7!) **12. Rb4 Ka7** (or 12. ... Rf6+ 13. Kc7+ Ka7 14. Bc4) **13. Ra4+ Kb8 14. Kd6 Rf6+ 15. Kd7** and wins. Study this endgame carefully! It is a practical endgame with theoretical positions. See Philidor (No. 997) and Szen (No. 1001).

No. 1011, P. Benko 1997

White to play and draw

1. Rd8+ Kc7 2. Rg8! (2. Rd7+? Kb6!! [2. ... Kc6? 3. Rd6+ and 4. Rg6] 3. Rd6+ Rc6) **2. ... Rg2 3. Kf7 g5 4. Ke6!! g4 5. Rg7+ Kc6 6. Rg6! g3 7. Kf5+ Kd7** (7. ... Kd5? 8. Rg5!) **8. Rg5! Rf2+ 9. Kg4 g2 10. Kh3 Rf5!? 11. Rg7+ Ke6 12. Kh2 Kf6 13. Rg3** (13. Rg4/g8?? Rg5 or 13. Ra7? Rf1) **13. ... Rg5 14. Rf3+ Ke5 15. Kg1!** (15. Re3+? Kf4 16. Re1 g1=Q+ 17. Rxg1 Rh5+), and we have an unusual positional draw.

VII. ROOK AND KNIGHT VS. ROOK

This, too, is usually a draw. There are only a few won positions, however, and the defense is much easier.

There are five typical wins, in all but one of which both Black's rook and king are confined to the first rank.

No. 1012, Centurini 1850

White to play and win

No. 1012 is the simplest case. The idea is to put the king on g6 and the knight on f6, when Rh7 will be mate, or the king to h6, the knight to g6, when Rg7 mates. To do this, White must guard the sixth rank.

1. Kg6 (if 1. ... Ra6 2. Re7 Kg8 3. Kg6, transposing into the main line) **1. ... Kg8**

The alternatives are:

a) 1. ... Rg8+ 2. Kh6 Rc8 (2. ... Rg1 3. Ng5) 3. Nf4 Kg8 4. Ng6 Rc7 5. Ne7+ and wins;

b) 1. ... Rc8 2. Ra7 Rb8 3. Rc7 Ra8 4. Rc6 Re8 5. Kf7 Ra8 6. Rc5 Ra7+ 7. Nc7 and mates;

c) 1. ... Re8 2. Ng5 Rg8+ 3. Kh6 Rc8 4. Rh7+ Kg8 5. Rg7+ Kf8 6. Nh7+ Ke8 7. Nf6+ Kf8 8. Rg8+ and wins.

2. Rb6 Re8 3. Rc6 Ra8 4. Ng5 Kf8 5. Re6! Rb8 6. Nh7+ Kg8 7. Re7 Rb6+ 8. Nf6+ and mates.

No. 1013, Centurini 1850

White to play and win

No. 1013 is similar. After **1. Rc7** (it doesn't matter who moves first), there are two main variations:

a) **1. ... Rb8 2. Ra7 Rd8** (or 2. ... Kg8 3. Kg6 Kh8 4. Rh7+ Kg8 5. Rg7+ Kf8 6. Kh7 Rb7 7. Nxb7) **3. Nf5 Rb8 4. Rf7+ Kg8** (or Ke8) **5. Ne7+ Kh8 6. Ng6+ Kg8 7. Rg7+** mate.

b) **1. ... Kg8 2. Kg6 Kh8 3. Rh7+ Kg8 4. Rg7+ Kf8 5. Rf7+ Kg8 6. Ne4,** and mates in a few.

No. 1014, Centurini 1887

White to play and win

White wins in **No. 1014** even though Black seems to have a fair amount of liberty. But appearances are deceiving; in this case, it is to White's advantage that his opponent moves first.

1. Re3 Rf2 (1. ... Kf8 2. Nh7+ Kg8 3. Re8+. Or 1. ... Rf8 2. Nh7, etc.) **2. Re1 Rf4** (now forced) **3. Ra1 Rf2** (the point of forcing the Black rook to f4 is that now 3. ... Kf8 is refuted by 4. Ne6+) **4. Ne4! Rg2+ 5. Kf6 Kh8** (or 5. ... Rg4 6. Ra8+ Kh7 7. Ng5+ and mates) **6. Ra3** (tempo moves to get the Black rook to the fourth rank) **6. ... Rg1 7. Ra2 Rg4 8. Ng5 Rf4+ 9. Kg6 Kg8 10. Ne6! Rg4+ 11. Kf6 Kh8 12. Kf7! Rh4 13. Kg6 Rg4+ 14. Ng5,** and Black must give up his rook to ward off immediate mate.

The most complicated case is **No. 1015**, where the Black king is already stalemated.

No. 1015, Centurini 1878

Black to play. White wins

The solution is **1. ... Rg3+ 2. Kf7 Rg7+ 3. Ke6 Rb7** (if 3. ... Rg1 4. Rd7! Re1+ 5. Kf7 and mates) **4. Rg2** (not 4. Rh2+ Kg7 5. Rh7+ Kf8! since 6. Rxb7 is stalemate) **4. ... Rb6+ 5. Kf5 Rb5+ 6. Kg6 Rb2 7. Rg5 Rb5 8. Nd5 Rb7 9. Kf6** (the threat is now 10. Ne7 Rb6+ 11. Kf7 Kh7 12. Ra5, which is No. 1014) **9. ... Rh7**

There are three other choices:

a) 9. ... Rd7 10. Ne7 Rd6+ 11. Kf7 Kh7 12. Rg7+ Kh6 (12. ... Kh8 13. Ng6+) 13. Nf5+ and wins.

b) 9. ... Ra7 10. Rg1 Rb7 11. Ra1! Rd7 12. Ne7 Rd6+ 13. Kf7 Kh7 14. Nf5 Rd7+ 15. Kf6 Rb7 16. Rh1+ Kg8 17. Ne7+ Kf8 18. Rh8+ mate;

c) 9. ... Rg7! 10. Re5! Rd7 (10. ... Ra7 11. Re1 transposes into b) 11. Ne7 Rd6+ 12. Kf7 Kh7 13. Re1 Ra6 (13. ... Kh6 14. Nf5+) 14. Rh1+ Rh6 15. Ra1 Rh3 16. Ng8! Kh8 (it 16. ... Rh2 17. Nf6+ Kh6 18. Rg1 Rg2 19. Ng8+) 17. Nf6, and mates in two.

10. Ne7 Rh6+ (if 10. ... Rg7 11. Ra5 Rh7 12. Ra8+ mate) **11. Kf7 Rh7+ 12. Kf8 Rh3 13. Rg8+ Kh7 14. Rg7+ Kh6 15. Ng8+ Kh5 16. Nf6+** and either wins the rook or mates.

Finally, in **No. 1016**, White wins despite the relatively inoffensive placement of his pieces.

No. 1016, Centurini 1887

Black to play. White wins

The solution is **1. ... Kf8** (if 1. ... Kh8 2. Ne7! Rb8 3. Kh6 Rd8 4. Ng6+ Kg8 5. Ra7 and mates. Or 1. ... Rf8 2. Ne7+ Kh8 3. Ra1 and mates. Or 1. ... Rb8 2. Rf6 Kh8 3. Kh6 and 4. Ne7/h4 as in the main line) **2. Rf6+ Kg8 3. Nh6+ Kh8 4. Kf7! Ra8 5. Nf5 Ra7+ 6. Kg6 Ra8 7. Kh6 Re8 8. Ne7! Ra8 9. Rf7 Ra6+ 10. Ng6+** and mate in three.

Except for these five positions (and their offshoots), White can win only in problem cases or with the willing cooperation of his opponent.

The idea of the draw, generally, is to pin the knight and prevent a mating threat that forces the rook back to the first rank or the king into the corner. The pin is equally effective on either the rank or the file.

No. 1017, Centurini

White to play. Draw

In **No. 1017** Black holds the game because White's pieces are not free to move as they please. If, for example, **1. Kc6 Rb2!** (but not 1. ... Kc8? 2. Nd6+ K any 3. Re1 and wins) **2. Nd6 Rb3 3. Rc2 Rb1!**

Black must choose his rook moves carefully. If 3. ... Rb4? 4. Rh2 followed by Rh8+ and Nb5+ wins, or if 3. ... Rh3 4. Rb2+ Ka8 5. Rg2 Rh8 (5. ... Rc3+ 6. Kb6 Rb3+! 7. Nb5) 6. Rg7, which is No. 1012.

4. Nc4 Rh1 5. Rg2 Rh6+ 6. Nd6 Ka7, and again White cannot win because his knight is pinned.

No. 1018 is the second typical draw.

No. 1018, Centurini 1878

White to play. Draw

The best try is **1. Rc7+ Kb8 2. Rc6** (if 2. Rb7+ Kc8!, but not 2. ... Ka8?? 3. Re7 Rh8 4. Nd4 and wins) **2. ... Rh1 3. Nd4 Rb1+ 4. Nb5 Rb2 5. Rc1 Rb4,** etc.; see No. 1017.

A tricky position that must be handled with care is **No. 1019** (Salvioli 1887):

White king at d6, rook at f3, knight at g5, Black king at e8, rook at h4. White to play. Draw.

1. Ne6 Rh8 2. Rf6

If 2. Rf4 Rg8 3. Rf2 Rh8 4. Ng7+ Kd5 5. Rc2 Rh1! is the only saving move.

2. ... Rg8 3. Nc7+ Kd8 4. Rh6

Or 4. Rf7 Rg6+ 5. Ne6+ Kc8 6. Re7 Kb8 7. Kc6 Rh6 8. Kb6 Kc8!, etc.; see No. 1018.

4. ... Kc8 5. Kc6 Kd8!

On 5. ... Kb8, 6. Nb5! wins: 6. ... Kc8 7. Nd6+ Kd8 8. Rh7 Rg7 9. Nb7+, or here 7. ... Kb8 8. Rh7, as in No. 1012.

6. Nd5 Re8!

The only line: if 6. ... Rf8?, 7. Rh7 wins: 7. ... Kc8 8. Rc7+ Kb8 9. Kb6, followed by Nb4-c6, or 7. ... Ke8 8. Re7+ Kd8 9. Rd7+ and mates.

7. Rd6+ Kc8 8. Nb6+ Kb8 9. Nd7+ Ka7 (but not 9. ... Ka8 10. Rd1 Re6+ 11. Kc7 and wins) **10. Kc7 Re1 11. Rd5 Rc1+ 12. Nc5 Rc2 13. Kc6 Rc1 14. Rh5 Kb8! 15. Rh8+ Ka7 16. Rh3 Kb8 17. Rb3+ Kc8!**, etc., draws.

White can win this ending only in certain favorable positions where the Black king is in or near the corner.

No. 1020, Berger

White to play. Draw

The general draw where the Black king is not confined to a corner is see in **No. 1020**. The continuation might be **1. Rh6+ Ke7 2. Kd5 Rc8! 3. Ne4 Rd8+** (3. ... Rc1 4. Rh7+ Ke8 5. Ke6 Rc6+ 6. Nd6+ Kf8, = [see No. 1018] is also good) **4. Ke5 Kf7 5. Rf6+ Kg7** (or 5. ... Ke7. A trap is 5. ... Ke7 6. Nd6 Rf8 7. Nf5+ Ke8 8. Re6+ Kf7? 9. Re7+ Kg6?? 10. Rg7+ Kh5 11. Kf4 and wins) **6. Nd6 Ra8 7. Nf5+ Kg8 8. Rg6+ Kf8 9. Rb6 Kf7** (or even 9. ... Ke8 10. Ke6 Kd8 11. Rc6 Rb8) **10. Rb7+ Kg6 11. Rg7+ Kh5 12. Kf4 Ra4+**, etc. =.

With pawns, the ending is not essentially different from that with knight vs. pawns.

VIII. VARIOUS COMBINATIONS OF ROOKS AND MINOR PIECES WITHOUT PAWNS

Since these endings occur so rarely in practice, we shall confine ourselves to the general outlines of the theory and a few outstanding examples.

Rule: In general, endings without pawns can be won only if White is at least a rook or two minor pieces ahead.

Of course, if the pieces are badly placed, this could create problems. For example, **No. 1021** (P. Benko 1990): **White king at d4, rook at e7, knight at g8, bishop at h8; Black king at f8, rook at b6.** White to play wins. **1. Rg7** (1. Nf6? Rd6+, =) **1. ... Rb4+ 2. Ke5 Rh4 3. Kf6! Rxh8 4. Ra7! Ke8** (if 4. ... Kxg8 5. Kg6 wins) **5. Ke6 Kd8 6. Kd6 Kc8** (if 6. ... Ke8 7. Nf6+ Kf8 8. Ke6 and Rf7+ mate) **7. Ne7+ Kb8 8. Nc6+ Kc8 9. Rc7+** mate.

A. The Double Exchange

Two rooks always win against two minor pieces (unlike the elementary draw with only one exchange). The winning idea is to pin one piece and trap or capture the other. As you might expect, the most difficult case is with Black having two bishops.

No. 1022, Kling and Horwitz 1851

White to play wins

The win is accomplished by pinning the light-square bishop. **1. Rf2+ Kg7** (if 1. ... Ke6 2. Re1 Bh5 3. Ra2 Kf6 4. Rxe5 Kxe5 5. Ra5+, etc.) **2. Rg2 Bf4+ 3. Kb2 Be5+ 4. Kb3 Kh6** (or 4. ... Kf6 5. Rf1+ Kg7 6. Rfg1. On 5. ... Bf5 the rooks double on the f-file) **5. Rh1+ Bh5 6. Rd2 Bf4** (6. ... Kg5 7. Rxh5+ and 8. Rd5) **7. Rd5 Bg5 8. Rd6+**, winning a bishop.

With bishop and knight or two knights, the situation is even more hopeless for Black.

B. Rook and Minor Pieces vs. Two Minor Pieces

As a rule, all such positions are drawn, but there are quite a few exceptions, especially with rook and bishop vs. two knights, but it can sometimes take more than 200 moves!

No. 1023, Berger 1921

White to play wins

An unusual ending. The main line is **1. Be4!** (threatening Kf4 and Rh7) **1. ...
Bd8** (best: if 1. ... Bb3 2. Kf4 Be1 3. Rh7+ Kg1 4. Rh1+ Kf2 5. Rh2+ Kg1 6. Rg2+
Kf1 7. Rb2 Bd1 8. Ke3 followed by Rb1) **2. Kf2 Bb6+** (if 2. ... Kh3 3. Kf3 Kh4 4.
Kf4) **3. Kf3** (with the double threat of 4. Rg6 and 4. Rg2+ Kh3 5. Rg6) **3. ... Bb3
4. Rb7! Bd1+ 5. Kf4 Bc5 6. Rh7+ Kg1 7. Rh1+** and **8. Rxd1**.

C. Rook vs. Three Minor Pieces

Since a rook is approximately equivalent to a little less than two minor
pieces, these endings are theoretically drawn. Nevertheless, the three pieces
offer White many tactical possibilities, so there will be no smooth sailing for
the defending rook.

No. 1024, Rinck 1920

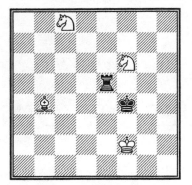

White to play wins

No. 1024 is a curious instance of a forced win. **1. Bd6?** leads to nothing after **1. ... Kf5**, since it would be madness to take the exchange! But **1. Bd2+**, leads to the capture of the rook by a knight: **1. ... Kf5 2. Nd7 Re6** (the only square where it can avoid immediate capture or a check and capture) **3. Kf3! Ra6** (on other rook or king moves, a knight check decides) **4. Ne7+ Ke6 5. Nc5+ Kxe7 6. Nxa6,** etc.

Chapter VIII

QUEEN ENDINGS

The powers of the queen are so extraordinary that these endings are unique in a number of respects. To a great extent, tactics predominate. Mating attacks and combinations to win pieces abound. It is mainly for this reason that the strategic bases of other endings are largely not applicable here. Queen endings are in a class by themselves.

I. QUEEN VS. PAWNS

A queen, unlike a rook or minor piece, can win against any number of pawns. It is not the number, however, but the *degree of advancement* and the file that the pawns are on that count. Eight pawns on the second rank will surely lose, but one pawn on the seventh may draw and two may win.

A. Queen vs. One Pawn

Obviously, Black has a chance only if his pawn is on the seventh threatening to promote, and his king is right next to it. If the White queen ever manages to get in front of the pawn and blockade it, the Black king can never drive it away; meanwhile, the White king majestically captures its booty.

When the pawn is on the seventh with the king nearby, in general rook-pawn or bishop-pawn draw, but any other pawn loses.

No. 1025

White to play wins

The general win is seen in **No. 1025**. The winning idea is to force the Black king to occupy the square in front of the pawn, which gives the White king time to approach and win it. This is done by successively checking the king and attacking the pawn. **1. Qf7+ Kg2** (1. ... Ke1 2. Kc6) **2. Qe6 Kf2 3. Qf5+ Kg2 4. Qe4+ Kf2 5. Qf4+ Kg2 6. Qe3 Kf1 7. Qf3+!** (the crucial position) **7. ... Ke1** (now forced, since 7. ... Kg1 is met by 8. Qxe2) **8. Kc6 Kd2 9. Qf2 Kd1 10. Qd4+ Kc2 11. Qe3 Kd1 12. Qd3+ Ke1 13. Kd5 Kf2 14. Qd2 Kf1 15. Qf4+ Kg2 16. Qe3 Kf1 17. Qf3+! Ke1 18. Ke4** (an alternative win is 18. Kd4 Kd2 19. Qf2 Kd1 20. Kd3 e1=Q 21. Qc2+ mate) **18. ... Kd2 19. Qd3+ Ke1 20. Kf3 Kf1 21. Qxe2+ Kg1 22. Qg2+** mate.

Exceptions occur only when the White king gets in the queen's way and bars a check. For instance, **No. 1026: White king at e5, queen at d8; Black: king at e2, pawn at d2.** Draw. White has no checks at all and cannot prevent the pawn from queening on the next move.

The zigzag maneuver seen in No. 1025 does not succeed against a bishop-pawn or rook-pawn because Black has a stalemate defense on those files.

No. 1027

White to play. Draw

After **1. Qg3+**, the reply is **1. ... Kh1!**, and since **2. Qxf2** is stalemate, White cannot gain the necessary tempo for the approach of his king.

Similarly, in **No. 1028: White king at c4, queen at f3; Black king at g1, pawn at h2.** Draw. After **1. Qg3+ Kh1!** White must release the Black king to avoid immediate stalemate.

Exceptions to these draws occur only when the White king is near the scene of action and can set up a mating position after the pawn has queened.

No. 1029

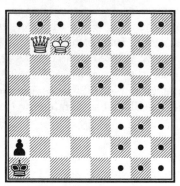

White to play wins. White king must be outside the dotted area

In **No. 1029,** first the stalemate is avoided by getting the White king in front of the queen. **1. Kb6! Kb2 2. Kc5+ Kc2** (best: if 2. ... Ka1 3. Kb4!, etc.) **3. Qe4+ Kb2 4. Qe2+ Kb1** (4. ... Kb3 5. Qe5 and 6. Qa1) **5. Kc4!! a1=Q** (any other promotion is just as bad) **6. Kb3!** (the point) **6. ... Qd4** (Black's problem is that he has no check) **7. Qe1+** and mate next.

A variant on this theme is **No. 1030: White king at e4, queen at h8; Black king at b1, pawn at a2.** White to play wins. **1. Qh1+ Kb2 2. Qg2+ Kb1** (if 2. ...

Kb3 3. Qg7 and 4. Qa1) **3. Kd3! a1=N** (or 3. ... a1=Q 4. Qc2+ mate, or 3. ... Ka1 4. Kc3 and mate next) **4. Kc3** and mate in two. For pawn endings from which these positions may come about see Nos. 51, 151, and others.

With the bishop-pawn there are similar mating positions.

No. 1031, Lolli

White to play wins. Draw with White king at f5

In **No. 1031**, the king must be prevented from getting to the queenside. **1. Qb3! Kd2 2. Qb2 Kd1 3. Kf3! Kd2** (3. ... c1=Q 4. Qe2+ mate) **4. Kf2 Kd1 5. Qd4+ Kc1 6. Qb4! Kd1 7. Qe1+** mate. With the White king at f4, White to play only draws: 1. Qb3 Kd2 2. Qa2 Kc3! (2. ... Kd1? 3. Ke4! c1=Q 4. Kd3 wins) 3. Qa1+ Kd2 4. Qb2 Kd1, etc., draw.

No. 1032 corresponds to No. 1028. **White king at a4, queen at c8; Black king at b2, pawn at c2.** White to play wins. **1. Qh8+ Ka2** (1. ... Kb1 2. Kb3 c1=Q 3. Qh7+ Ka1 4. Qa7+ Kb1 5. Qa2+ mate) **2. Qh2 Kb2 3. Qd2 Kb1** (or 3. ... Ka1 4. Kb3 or 4. Qc1+) **4. Kb3 c1=Q 5. Qa2+** mate.

A variant on this is **No. 1033: White king at d5, queen at e8; Black king at d1, pawn at c2.** White to play wins. **1. Qa4 Kd2 2. Qd4+ Ke2 3. Qc3 Kd1 4. Qd3+ Kc1 5. Kc4**, etc., as in No. 1031 (5. ... Kb2 6. Qd2 Kb1 7. Kb3).

White may also win if his king is near enough to cover the queening square. For instance, **No. 1034: White king at e3, queen at f3; Black king at b1, pawn at c2.** White to play wins. **1. Qe4 Kb2** (if 1. ... Ka1 2. Kd2! If 1. ... Kc1 2. Qb4 Kd1 3. Qd2+ mate) **2. Qb4+ Ka1** (2. ... Kc1 3. Kf2! Kd1 4. Qe1+ mate) **3. Kd2** and wins the pawn without allowing stalemate.

If the pawn is not yet on the seventh, White always wins because there is no stalemate threat. **No. 1035** is the case with the bishop-pawn.

No. 1035

Black to play. White wins

After **1. ... Kg2 2. Qg4+ Kf2 3. Kb7 Ke3**; even **4. Kc6** wins: **4. ... f2 5. Qd1 Kf4 6. Qf1**, etc. Of course, White can check the Black King, force it in front of the pawn, and use the time gained to approach with his king, exactly as in No. 1024.

The case with the rook-pawn is even simpler. **No. 1036: White king at a8, queen at a6; Black king at g2, pawn at h3.** White to play wins. **1. Qe2+**. If now **1. ... Kg1 2. Qg4+ Kh2 3. Kb7** and the pawn goes. If **1. ... Kg3 2. Qf1 Kh2** (or **2. ... h2 3. Kb7 Kh4 4. Qg2**) **3. Qf2+ Kh1 4. Kb7! h2 5. Qf1+** mate. Finally, if **1. ... Kh1 2. Qf2! h2 3. Qf1+** mate. Note that in both these and all similar endings it is possible to prevent the pawn from reaching the seventh.

Exceptions occur only when the White king is blocking a file or diagonal and preventing the queen from giving enough checks to stop the pawn from getting to the seventh. For instance, **No. 1037** (*The Chess World* 1865): **White king at g7, queen at b7; Black king at c1, pawn at c3.** White to play. Draw. After **1. Qh1+ Kb2**, White's only check that does not permit the pawn to advance is **2. Qb7+**, when **2. ... Kc1** repeats the position. With the White king elsewhere White can pin the pawn and use the time gained to approach first with his queen and then with his king.

B. Queen vs. Two Pawns

With two pawns Black is worse off than with one, for in order to have drawing chances he must have *both* pawns on the seventh.

No. 1038 is an example where the extra pawn causes Black's downfall.

No. 1038, Berger

White to play wins.
Draw with Black h7-pawn at h4 or h5

After **1. Qg4+ Kh1 2. Qh3+ Kg1 3. Qg3+ Kh1** (or 3. ... Kf1 4. Kc4 Ke1 5. Kd3 Kf1 6. Kd2 h5 7. Qh2 h4 8. Qh1+ mate) **4. Qxf2** is not stalemate now, so Black can resign.

With the Black pawn on h4 instead of h7, however, White can check at g4 but can only draw because he does not have access to the square g3.

With the pawns widely separated, White wins if he captures the one on the seventh. This usually depends on the position of his king.

No. 1039

White to play. Draw

No. 1039 is a draw because the White king is so far away. For instance, **1. Qg7+ Kh1 2. Qf6 Kg2 3. Qg5+ Kh1 4. Qf4 Kg2 5. Qg4+ Kh2 6. Qf3 Kg1 7. Qg3+ Kf1 8. Kb7 a4 9. Kc6 a3,** and draws because White must first capture the a-pawn. If the White king were at, say, d4 here, he could approach and capture the f-pawn.

No. 1040, P. Benko 1985

White to play wins

1. g7 h2 2. g8=Q Kh3 3. Qa8! Kg3 4. Kb6 a3 5. Kc5 a2 6. Kd4 a1=Q+ 7. Qxa1 Kg2 8. Qb2+ Kg1 9. Ke3 wins.

The drawing stratagem of 1039 exists only with the bishop-pawn. In the analogous case with the rook-pawn, Black gets mated. **No. 1041** (Berger): **White king at b6, queen at h8; Black king at g2, pawns at a4, h2.** White to play wins. **1. Qg8+ Kf2** (not 1. ... Kh1 2. Qg3! a3 3. Qf2 a2 4. Qf1+ mate) **2. Qh7 Kg3! 3. Qd3+**

The zigzag win of No. 1024 is not possible here because the Black king stays in the triangle g2-g3-h3. For instance, 3. Qg6+ Kh3 4. Qh5+ Kg3! 5. Qg5+ Kh3! 6. Qe3+ Kg2! 7. Qe2+ Kg3!, and Black needs only to prevent checks at either g4 or f3. Thus 4. ... Kg2?? is a fatal blunder because of 5. Qg4+ Kf2 6. Qh3 Kg1 7. Qg3+ Kh1 8. Qf2 and mate next) **3. ... Kg2 4. Qe4+ Kg3! 5. Kc5 a3 6. Kd4 a2 7. Qh1 a1=Q+ 8. Qxa1 Kg2 9. Qb2+** and wins as in No. 1028.

If Black's pawn is one square farther advanced, the game is drawn. **No. 1042: Black pawn at a3,** other pieces as in No. 1040. Draw. After the above maneuver, we get **5. Kc5 a2! 6. Qh1 a1=Q! 7. Qxa1 Kg2,** and White's king is not in the winning zone. With other pawns White decides by capturing one, since the queen-vs.-pawn ending is won.

With doubled pawns there's a peculiar situation if one pawn is on the seventh and the other on the fifth.

No. 1043, Bekey 1906

White to play. Draw. Win only with pawns on b-, c- or e-files.
Win except bishop-pawn or rook-pawns if White king is not near

White cannot win despite the proximity of his king because the square c3 is not available. On **1. Qa3+ Kc2 2. Qa2+ Kc1**; now if **3. Kd3** the pawn promotes with check.

No. 1044: White king at d4, queen at c4; Black king at d1, pawns at e4, e2. This is a win, however, because White's queen can get around to the other side. **1. Qa4+ Kd2 2. Qa5+ Kd1 3. Qh5 Kd2 4. Qg5+ Kd1 5. Qg4 Kd2 6. Qg2 Kd1 7. Kxe4 e1=Q+ 8. Kd3** and mates in a few.

The most difficult case with the White king in some other part of the board is **No. 1045** (Bekey 1906): **White king at a8, queen at b8; Black king at b3, pawns at b4, b2.** White to play wins.

The idea is to capture the pawn at b4 when the Black king is at b1, so that No. 1024 results. The solution is **1. Qg3+ Ka2** (if 1. ... Ka4 2. Qg6 and 3. Qb1; if 1. ... Kc2 2. Qf2+ Kc1 3. Qc5+, etc.) **2. Qf2 Ka1** (or 2. ... Ka3 3. Qf5 Ka2 4. Qc2 as in the main line, or 2. ... b3 3. Qd2 Ka1 4. Qa5+ Kb1 5. Qb4 Kc2 6. Qc4+, etc.) **3. Qd4 Ka2** (if 3. ... Kb1 4. Qxb4; if 3. ... b3 4. Qa4+) **4. Qd5+ Kb1**

The alternatives are

a) 4. ... Ka3 5. Qd1 Ka2 6. Qa4+;

b) 4. ... Ka1 5. Qa5+;

c) 4. ... b3 5. Qa5+ Kb1 6. Qb4, winning the back pawn in all cases.

5. Qc6 b3 (or 5. ... Ka2 6. Qa4+) **6. Qb5 Kc2 7. Qc4+ Kb1** (or 7. ... Kd2) **8. Qxb3** and we have No. 1024.

Black will often be able to draw with two unconnected pawns on the seventh, but only if he has a bishop-pawn or rook-pawn.

No. 1046

White to play wins

Where neither pawn alone can draw, the zigzag approach wins. **1. Qf7+ Ke1 2. Qg6 Kf2** (or 2. ... Kd1 3. Qd3+ Kc1! 4. Qc3+! Kd1 5. Qd4+! Kc1 6. Qg1+, etc.) **3. Qf5+ Ke1** (if 3. ... Kg3 4. Qg5+ Kf3 5. Qc1! Kf2 6. Qf4+, etc., as in the main line) **4. Qg4 Kf2** (if 4. ... Kf1 5. Qf3+ and captures one of the pawns; if 4. ... Kd1 5. Qd4+ as in the note to Black's second move) **5. Qf4+ Ke1** (or 5. ... Kg1 6. Qg3 Kh1 7. Qh4+ Kg1 8. Qe1+ Kh2 9. Qxe2) **6. Qe3 Kd1 7. Qd4+ Kc1 8. Qg1+ Kd2 9. Qxg2**, etc.

But if one of the pawns draws, Black can afford to abandon the other. **No. 1047** illustrates.

No. 1047, Kling and Horwitz

Whit to play. Draw

After **1. Qc5+ Kd1 2. Qd4+ Ke2,** White must capture the b-pawn, and then the f-pawn alone draws.

Curiously, if the Black king is not near the f-pawn the game is lost. **No. 1048** (Kling and Horwitz 1851): **Black king at a1**, other pieces as in No. 1046. White to play wins. **1. Qa3+** (not 1. Qf6? f1=Q!) **1. ... Kb1 2. Qa6! Kc2** (or 2. ...

Kc1 3. Qf1+) **3. Qe2+ Kc3** (3. ... Kc1 4. Qf1+) **4. Qf1,** and the White king approaches.

An unusual type of draw is seen in **No. 1049** (Kling and Horwitz 1851): **White king at e1, queen at h8; Black king at e3, pawns at a2, h2.** White must take perpetual check, since Black is threatening to win with 1. ... h1=Q+ and 2. ... a1=Q or vice versa. Black only has to avoid the capture of one of his pawns with check.

Two connected passed pawns on the seventh, supported by the king, draw unless the White king is nearby or one of the pawns is lost. **No. 1050** is the general case where either pawn alone would lose.

No. 1050, Berger

White to play. Draw

After **1. Qg3+ Ke4!** (not 1. ... Kd4? 2. Qf4+ Kd3 3. Qf3+) **2. Qg4+ Ke3! 3. Qe6+ Kf2! 4. Qf6+ Ke1 5. Qh4+ Kd1 6. Qg4 Kc1!**, etc., White clearly can get nowhere.

But a position such as **No. 1051** (Kling and Horwitz 1851): **White king at b1, queen at h2; Black king at e3, pawns at e2, d2** is won because the White king limits Black's moves and can help to build up an attack. The solution is **1. Qh6+ Kd3! 2. Qd6+ Kc3** (if 2. ... Ke3 3. Qc5+ Kd3 4. Qc2+! Ke3 5. Qc3+ wins. Note that the check at c2 could not be given in the previous example) **3. Qc5+ Kd3 4. Qc2+ Ke3 5. Qc3+ Kf2 6. Qxd2** and wins.

If one of the pawns alone draws, White wins only if his king is nearby. For instance, **No. 1052** (Lewis): **White king at a5, queen at d5; Black king at c2, pawns at a2, b3.** White to play wins. **1. Qg2+ Kc1** (1. ... Kc3 2. Qg7+ and 3. Qa1, or 1. ... Kd3 2. Qb2!) **2. Qf1+ Kc2 3. Qe2+ Kc1 4. Kb4! b2** (or 4. ... a1=Q 5. Qe1+ Kb2 6. Qd2+ Kb1 7. Kxb3 and wins) **5. Kc3 b1=N+ 6. Kd3! a1=N 7. Qa2** puts an end to Black's picturesque defense.

C. Queen vs. Three (or More) Pawns

As we mentioned in the introduction to this chapter, the number of pawns makes little difference. Four passed pawns on the second rank are destroyed before you can say "stalemate!" Black has chances only when his pawns are far advanced.

No. 1053, Berger 1914

White to play wins

No. 1053 is, in a sense, a critical position. The winning idea is to blockade the pawns and gain time to bring up the king.

With this in mind we begin with **1. Kb2** with the following possibilities:

a) **1. ... f3 2. Qb8 Kg5** (2. ... f2 3. Qf4, or 2. ... g3 3. Qf4+) **3. Qg3** and the king can now march in.

b) **1. ... g3 2. Qf3 Kg5** (the only hope) **3. Kc3 g2 4. Qf2 Kg4** (or 4. ... f3 5. Qg3+, and one pawn goes with check) **5. Kd3 f3 6. Ke3 h2 7. Qxf3+**, etc.

c) **1. ... h2 2. Qg2 g3 3. Qf3 h1=Q** (else the White king gets to e5 and captures every pawn) **4. Qxh1+ Kg4 5. Kc3 f3 6. Kd2 g2 7. Qh2!** and wins.

d) **1. ... Kg5** (or Kh5) **2. Qd5+ Kh4** (2. ... Kf6 3. Qe4) **3. Kc3,** and White is a tempo ahead of all of the above variations.

e) **1. ... Kg3** (threatening 1. ... f3) **2. Qh1 f3 3. Kc2 f2** (if 3. ... Kh4 4. Kd2 f2 5. Ke2 g3 6. Qe4+ Kg5 7. Kf1; or 3. ... Kf2 4. Kd2 g3 5. Qxh3 g2 6. Qh4+ Kg1 7. Ke3 Kf1 8. Qf2+ mate) **4. Kd2 h2 5. Ke2** and wins.

This example may be called critical because if the position is moved down one rank, the pawns win.

No. 1054 (Berger): **White king at a1, queen at b8; Black king at h3, pawns at f3, g3, h2.** White to play. Black wins. After **1. Qc8+ Kg2 2. Qc2+ f2 3. Qc6+ Kg1,** White has no check (except 4. Qc1+ f1=Q) and cannot prevent one of the pawns from queening.

No. 1055, Kling and Horwitz 1851

White to play wins

No. **1055** is an example of how the queen wins against four relatively advanced pawns. The main variation is **1. Qc5+ Kh2**

Or 1. ... Kf1 2. Qxc4+ Kf2 3. Qf4+, etc., or 1. ... Kh1 2. Qh5+ Kg1 3. Qh3 (3. ... c3+ must be prevented) 3. ... Kf2 (if 3. ... Kf1 4. Qf3+ Kg1 5. Qf6!, as in the main line) 4. Qh4+ Kf3 5. Qe1 Kg4 6. Qf2! Kh3 (if 6. ... c3+ 7. Ka1 Kh3 8. Qe3+ Kg4 9. Qd4+ Kf3 10. Qxc3+ and wins. Or here 8. ... Kh2 9. Qe5+ Kh1 10. Qh8+ and 11. Qxc3) 7. Ka1! c3 (7. ... Kh2 8. Qh4+, etc.) 8. Qe3+ Kg4 (8. ... Kh2 9. Qe5+ Kh1 10. Qh8+, etc.) 9. Qd4+ Kh3 (9. ... Kh5 10. Qh8+ and 11. Qg7+. If 9. ... Kf5 10. Qd5+) 10. Qxc3+ Kh2 11. Qe5+, etc., as in the main line.

2. Qe5+ Kh1 (if 2. ... Kg1 3. Qe1+ Kh2 4. Qh4+ Kg1 5. Qxc4) **3. Qh8+ Kg1 4. Qf6 Kh2 5. Qh4+ Kg1 6. Qxc4 Kf2 7. Qf4+ Kg1 8. Qg3 Kf1 9. Qf3+ Kg1 10. Qxb3** followed by the king's capture of the a-pawn, when we have No. 1024.

D. Queen and Pawns vs. Pawns

This is practically always a win, regardless of the number or position of Black's pawns. There are three ways to win: 1) sacrificing the queen for the pawn; 2) capturing the pawn and then exchanging queens after Black has promoted; 3) playing for mate. But it's good to know some exceptions.

No. 1056

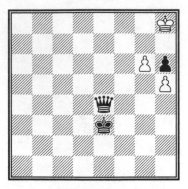

Diagram: White to play draws. Twin: Black queen at f4, Black wins

Diagram: **1. g7 Qe5 2. Kh7 Qe7 3. Kxh6! Qf6+** (if 3. … Qf7 4. g8=Q+! Qxg8 stalemate) **4. Kh7 Qf7 5. h6 Kf4 6. Kh8 Qf6 7. Kh7** (if 7. h7 Qe5! 8. Kg8 Qe8 mate) **7. … Qe7 8. Kh8 Kg5!? 9. g8=Q+ Kxh6 10. Qe6+! Qxe6** stalemate. Twin (Black queen at f4): **1. g7 Qf6 2. Kh7 Qf7 3. Kh8** (if 3. Kxh6 Qg8 wins) **3. … Kf4 4. g8=Q Qxg8+ 5. Kxg8 Kg5** wins. Of course, if the Black king is farther away, White has a sure draw even with the White pawn at h4 and the Black pawn at h5 because it is not possible to make the white king block its own pawn.

II. QUEEN AND PAWN ENDINGS

Endings where both sides have queens and pawns are notoriously difficult. One pawn ahead wins even less frequently than in rook endings, and with two pawns up the win is still not smooth sailing. *The general rule is that one pawn wins only if the White king is not exposed; two pawns always win.* This rule must be qualified, of course, by the more detailed analysis that follows.

A. Queen and Pawn vs. Queen

This is a draw unless White has a bishop-pawn or center-pawn on the seventh supported by the king. As a rule, it is best for Black to have his king as far from the pawn as possible, unless, of course, it can occupy a square in front of the pawn, in which case the game is a hopeless draw.

In general, it is impossible to advance the pawn very far. Black keeps checking until he runs out of checks and then pins the pawn. In view of the terrific number of possible positions, precise analysis can be done only by computer. In practice, however, it is usually found that the pawn can be held back.

We will consider what happens if and when the pawn reaches the seventh.

In that event, rook-pawn or knight-pawn draws, but bishop-pawn or center-pawn wins.

No. 1057

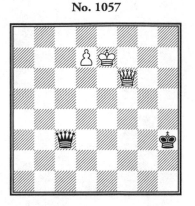

Black to play. White wins

No. 1057 is the interesting problem of the d-pawn. It makes no essential difference where the Black king is: it will always reduce the number of checks, and at h3 it is placed as well as anywhere. Here it is possible to exhaust the checks and queen the pawn. **1. ... Qc5+ 2. Kf7 Qh5+ 3. Qg6 Qf3+ 4. Kc7 Qb7** (if 4. ... Qa3+ 5. Qd6 Qa7 6. Ke8 Qe3+ 7. Qe7 wins) **5. Qd3+ Kg2 6. Qc4 Qa7 7. Qe4+ Kh3 8. Ke8** wins.

The case of the bishop-pawn is more difficult. Philidor gave **No. 1058** as a draw, but subsequent analysts have established a win.

No. 1058, Philidor 1782

Black to play. White wins

The best defense is **1. ... Qe5+ 2. Kf8 Ka4 3. Qf3 Qh8+ 4. Ke7 Qe5+ 5. Kd7 Qd4+ 6. Ke6 Qb6+ 7. Kf5 Qc5+ 8. Kg4 Qf8 9. Qf4+ Kb5 10. Kh5 Kc5 11. Qf6 Kb4 12. Kg6 Kc5 13. Kh7 Kb4 14. Qg7** wins.

White cannot win with a knight-pawn because he is exposed to perpetual check, even with two queens.

No. 1059, Lolli

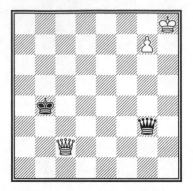

Black to play draws

No. 1059 demonstrates. **1. ... Qh4+ 2. Qh7** (if 2. Kg8 Qd8+ 3. Kf7 Qd7+ 4. Kf6 Qd4+, etc. White can do no better than the main line) **2. ... Qd8+! 3. g8=Q Qf6+ 4. Qhg7 Qh4+ 5. Q8h7 Qd8+**, etc., with perpetual check.

In this ending it is essential for Black to have his king all the way on the other side of the board since otherwise it will just get in his way and prevent him from giving perpetual check.

For example, **No. 1060** (Kling and Horwitz 1851): **White king at a8, queen at b3, pawn at b7; Black king at a6, queen at c6.** White to play wins. **1. Qb4! Qh1** (or 1. ... Qd5 2. Qa4+ Kb6 3. Qb3+!! Qxb3 4. b8=Q+ and wins. Similarly, 1. ... Qf3 or 1. ... Qg2) **2. Qa3+ Kb6** (or 2. ... Kb5 3. Qb2+ Kc4 4. Ka7 Qg1+ 5. Ka6 Qg6+ 6. Qb6) **3. Qb2+ Kc5** (3. ... Ka6 4. Qa2+ and 5. Qb1+) **4. Ka7 Qh7 5. Qb6+ Kd5 6. Ka6** and wins.

But even with the king at a distance from the pawn, there are some special winning positions. One of these, which also shows that there are other cases besides those already mentioned where queen vs. queen with no pawns may win, is **No. 1061** (Lesehalle 1887): **White king at e4, queen at a2, pawn at b4; Black king at h1, queen at d6.** White to play wins. **1. Qd5! Qg6+** (if 1. ... Qxb4+ 2. Kf3!! and Black is lost; e.g., 2. ... Kh2 3. Qh5+ Kg1 4. Qg5+ and mate in two, or 2. ... Qb2 3. Kg3+ Kg1 4. Qd1+ mate) **2. Kf4+!** (it would be a bad mistake for White to let Black out of the mating net, since he would then get to No. 1057) **2. ... Kh2 3. Qe5!! Qd3 4. b5 Qg3+ 5. Ke4 Kh1! 6. Qh5+ Kg1 7. Qd1+ Kh2 8. Qe2+ Kg1 9. Qe3+ Kh1 10. Qf3+** wins.

A rook-pawn draws just as simply as a knight-pawn: once the pawn gets to h7 and the king to h8, perpetual check is unavoidable.

In general, it is extremely difficult to determine whether a pawn will be able to reach the seventh rank by force. **No. 1062** shows that it is possible in some instances.

No. 1062, Game 1911, adjudicated by Dr. Lasker

Black wins

The first few moves are forced: **1. Kf5 Qc5+ 2. Kf6 Qd6+ 3. Kf5 c5**. The White king is still badly placed and Black can push his pawn. **4. Qg1 c4 5. Qb1+** (if 5. Qg4 Qd7+) **5. ... Kc5 6. Qg1+ Qd4**. Again there are no more checks and the pawn advances. Lasker was right, as computers have proved. It's a win in 39 moves.

To sum up: Queen and pawn vs. queen wins only with a bishop-pawn or center-pawn on the seventh. Black's king should be as far as possible from the pawn. A bad king position may cost Black the game in otherwise drawn positions.

B. Queen and Two Pawns vs. Queen

An advantage of two pawns always wins, but the ever-present danger of perpetual check makes the process tedious and complicated.

1. Connected Pawns

Black has drawing chances only if his king is in front of the pawns. Otherwise, the White king will find a haven behind the pawns and Black will never be able to give more than a few meaningless checks.

With a well-placed Black king, White's task is most difficult with a knight-pawn and rook-pawn, mainly because neither pawn alone can win. **No. 1063** is the crucial position that White should aim for.

No. 1063

Black to play. White wins

The idea is to get the king to c7, interpose the queen on a check along the rank, and then play a discovered check. The best defense is **1. ... Qe8+ 2. Kc4! Qe2+ 3. Kc5 Qe7+** (or 3. ... Qf2+ 4. Kc6 Qf6+ 5. Kc7 Qg7+ 6. Qd7, etc.) **4. Qd6 Qg5+** (4. ... Qe3+ 5. Qd4) **5. Kc6 Qg2+ 6. Kc7 Qg7+ 7. Qd7** and wins easily: **7. ... Qc3+** (on other moves, such as 7. ... Qf6, 8. Kc8+ leads to mate) **8. Kd6+ Kb8 9. Qb5+** and either **10. Qc6+** (on ... Ka8 or ... Kc8) or **10. Qc5+** (on ... Ka7) will force the exchange of queens.

The question then naturally arises whether this can be forced from any position; the answer is yes.

No. 1064

Black to play. White wins

It is immediately obvious that the proper pawn position can be secured in a few moves. **1. ... Qf7+ 2. b3 Qd7 3. Qc3+ Ka6 4. a4 Qe7 5. b4 Qe2+ 6. Ka3 Qe4 7. a5.** In all this Black has no meaningful checks and can only mark time **7. ... Qb1**

There does not seem to be anything better. If, e.g., 7. ... Qd5 8. Qc8+ Kb5 9.

Qb8+ Kc4 10. Qc7+ Kb5 11. Qb6+ Kc4 12. Qe3! Kb5 13. Qe2+ Kc6 14. Qa6+ Kc7 15. Qb6+ Kd7 16. Qc5, and now the White king will be able to find shelter at b7 or a7; or if 7. ... Qh1 8. Qd3+ Ka7 9. Ka4 Qc6+ 10. b5, and the pawn gets to g6 with check, after which White has all sorts of mating threats.

8. Qc6+ Ka7 9. Qd5 Ka6 (checks get the king to b5 and transpose into the previous example) **10. Qd6+ Ka7**

10. ... Kb5 11. Qb6+ Kc4 12. Qc6+ and wins Black's queen, which is, as a matter of fact, unimportant, for after 12. ... Kd3, 13. Ka4 also wins without any trouble.

11. Ka4 Qf1 (else Kb5) **12. Qd7+ Ka8 13. Qd4 Qe2 14. b5 Qa2+ 15. Kb4 Qb1+ 16. Kc5 Qc2+ 17. Kb6 Qg6+ 18. Kc7 Qf7+ 19. Qd7 Qf4+ 20. Kc8 Qf8+ 21. Qd8 Qf7! 22. a6!,** and a discovered check or a queen check will be fatal.

2. Unconnected Pawns

As a rule, these will win just as easily as connected pawns. The reason is the same: the extra pawn shelters the king from perpetual check. **No. 1065** is a classic case.

No. 1065, Morphy-Anderssen, Paris 1858

Black to play wins

Black's conduct of the ending is straightforward and requires little explanation. **1. ... Qd4+ 2. Kf1 a4 3. Qf5+ Kc6 4. Qc8 Kb5! 5. Ke1** (if 5. Qxc7 Qc4+ and the a-pawn queens! Similarly, if 5. Qb7+ Qb6 6. Qd5+ c5 7. Qd3+ Ka5 8. Qd2+ Ka6, and White has no checks) **5. ... c5 6. Qb7+ Kc4 7. Qf7+ Kc3 8. Qf3+ Qd3 9. Qf6+ Kb3 10. Qb6+ Kc2! 11. Qa7** (again, if 11. Qxc5+ Qc3+ wins) **11. ... Qc3+ 12. Ke2 a3 13. Qa4+ Kb2 14. Qb5+ Qb3!** (one more time! If 15. Qxc5 Qc2+) **15. Qa6 c4 16. Qf6+ c3,** and White is lost.

No. 1066 (Horwitz-Staunton, London 1851) is an example where the defender's king is at a greater distance from the pawns: **White king at d5, queen at a5, pawns at a4, e5; Black king at g3, queen at e3**. White to play wins. The conclusion was 1. Qb4 Qf3+ 2. Qe4 Qf7+ 3. e6 Qb7+ 4. Ke5 Qb8+ 5. Kf6 Qf8+ 6. Kg5! Qg7+ 7. Qg6 Qe5+ 8. Kh6+ Kh4 9. Kh7 Qc7+ 10. Kh6

Qf4+ 11. Kg7 Qc7+ 12. Qf7 Qg3+ 13. Kh7 Qd3+ 14. Qg6 Qd6 15. Qh6+ Kg4 16. e7! Qd7! (16. ... Qxe7+ 17. Qg7+) 17. Qg7+ Kh5 18. e8=Q+! Qxe8 19. Qh6+ Kg4 20. Qg6+ and wins.

3. Doubled Pawns

Although this is not a win with the Black king in front of the pawns, it is a win in all cases (except the rook-pawn) if the Black king is at a distance.

No. 1067

Black to play. White wins

No. 1067 shows the difference that the extra pawn makes (compare No. 1057). After **1. ... Qf8+** (1. ... Qf4+ 2. Ka7 Qa4+ 3. Kb6 Qf4 4. Qh7+, then 5. Qg8+ and 6. b8=Q), the quickest win is **2. Ka7 Qf2+ 3. b6 Qa2+ 4. Qa6 Qf7** (forced) **5. Qe2+ K any 6. Ka6 Qf8,** and White gets to the diagonal h2-b8 with check and queens his pawn.

More than two pawns up, as usual, win quite simply.

C. Material Advantage

Although the advantage of one pawn should usually win, there are many exceptions, and the winning process itself is most often long and intricate. *A basic rule of all queen endings is that the superior side must always be on his guard against perpetual check.*

It will be most convenient to divide these endings into three groups according to the position of the pawns and kings.

1. The Defending King Is Not Near the Opposing Pawn Majority (Outside and Potential Outside Passed Pawns)

This is the simplest case of all. White wins if his king is not exposed but only draws if it is. Consequently, the more pawns there are, the easier it is to win.

No. 1068 is the ideal type of winning position.

No. 1068

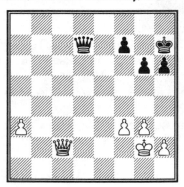

Black to play. White wins

The White queen fulfills her marital duties by defending the king from checks, and the pawn stolidly marches on. After **1. ... h5 2. b5 h4 3. b6 g5** (a desperate counterattack, else he might just as well resign) **4. Qc7+ Kg6 5. b7 g4 6. hxg4** is decisive. Clearly, with more pawns on the board, even Black's faint counterchance above disappears.

But even the slightest weakness in the White pawn structure may make it impossible for him to do any better than draw.

No. 1069, Alekhine-Reshevsky, AVRO 1938

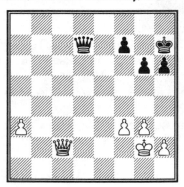

White to play. Draw

If the White pawn were at f2 instead of f3, White would win quite easily with Qe4 followed by Qa8 or a4-a5, using the same procedure as in the previous diagram. But now 1. Qe4? is answered by 1. ... Qd2+ 2. Kh3 Qd7+ 3. g4 Qd1, etc., with eventual perpetual check.

Other attempts are likewise insufficient, as the course of the game shows. **1. Qa2 Kg8 2. a4 Qc6 3. a5 Qa6!**

Again, 4. Qd5 is the "natural" move in such positions, but here it leads to nothing because of 4. ... Kg7! 5. Qe5+ Kg8 6. Qb8+ Kg7 7. Qb6 Qe2+ 8. Kh3 Qxf3, already threatening perpetual check.

4. g4 g5! 5. Kf2 (hoping to get to the queenside) **5. ... Qd6! 6. Kf1 Qa6+ 7. Kg2 Kg7 8. Qb2+ Kg8 9. Qb8+ Kg7 10. Qe5+ Kg8 11. Kf2 Qa7+ 12. Ke2 Qa6+ 13. Kd2 Qc4! 14. Qf5 Qd4+ 15. Ke2 Qb2+ 16. Kd3 Qb3+ 17. Ke2 Qb2+,** and a draw was agreed.

With an exposed king, it is often hard to win even with two extra pawns.

No. 1070, Alekhine-Euwe, Nottingham 1936

Black to play. White wins

White can always straighten out his pawns with f4, but that probably allows perpetual check. So he must postpone this advance until the right moment. The game continued:

1. ... Qe1 2. Qc5+ Kf7 3. Kg2 Qa1 (if 3. ... Qe2+ 4. Qf2) **4. Qc2**

Not 4. a5? Qa2+ 5. Kh3 Qa1, etc., =, because White's queen must defend the a-pawn. On the tempting 4. Qxg5, the reply 4. ... Qb2+ 5. Kh3 Qa1 6. Qf4+ Kg7! 7. Qc7+ Kg8 8. Kh4 Qf6+! 9. g5 Qxf3 suffices to save Black.

4. ... Kf6 5. Qb3 Ke5?

A mistake in time pressure. Now 6. Qb8+ wins at once, for if 6. ... Kf6 7. Qh8+, and if 6. ... Kd5 7. Qg8+ Kc5 8. Qxg6 Qxa4 9. Qxg5+, with an elementary win in both cases.

6. Kf2? Kf6 7. Qb6+ (if 7. f4 gxf4 8. gxf4 Qh1! 9. Qb2+ 9. ... Kf7 and White will have to lose either a pawn on the K-side or his QRP) **7. ... Kg7 8. Qb4 Qh1! 9. Qe1 Qh2+ 10. Ke3 Kh7**

If 10. ... Qa2 11. a5. The object of the Black king move is to prevent any effective check.

11. a5 Qa2 12. Qd2 Qa1 13. Ke2! Kh6

This allows f4, but there is nothing better. If 13. ... Qh1 14. Qe3! Qb1 (or 14. ... Qg2+ 15. Qf2 Qh1 16. a6 Qb1 17. Qf1!, and White will soon get out of check, so his pawn has advanced one more vital square) 15. Qxg5 Qc2+ 16. Qd2 Qc4+ 17. Kf2! and wins.

14. f4! gxf4

Or 14. ... Qa4 15. fxg5+ Kg7 16. Qc3+ Kg8 17. Qc8+ Kg7 18. Qc7+, and wins the g-pawn with check: 18. ... Kg8 19. Qd8+ Kg7 20. Qf6+ Kh7 21. Qf7+ Kh8 22. Qf8+ Kh7 23. Qh6+, etc.

15. gxf4

Now White's winning plan consists first of driving the Black king back to the first rank, and then playing his king over to the support of the a-pawn. With the Black king exposed White can escape perpetual check.

15. ... Qa4 16. Kf2

Preparing 16. g5+, which if played at once would be answered by 16. ... Kh5.

16. ... Kh7

Or 16. ... Qa1 17. Kg2 Qa4 18. g5+, and if 18. ... Kh5? 19. Qe3! concludes quickly.

17. g5 Qa3

Now the problem is to get the White king to the queenside.

18. Qd7+ Kh8 19. Qc8+ Kh7 20. Qc7+ Kh8 21. Ke2 Qa2+ 22. Ke3 Qb3+ 23. Kd4 Qb4+ 24. Kd5 Qb5+ 25. Kd4 Qa6

On 25. ... Qb4+ the quickest win is 26. Ke5 Qb5+ 27. Kd6, etc.

26. Qb6 Qc8 27. Qd6! (the ideal spot for the queen; 27. Qxg6 is also good) **27. ... Qc2 28. a6 Qd2+ 29. Ke5 Qc3+ 30. Ke6 Qc8+ 31. Ke7 Kh7 32. Qd7!** (a now familiar maneuver: he will win by giving a discovered check) **32. ... Qc3 33. Ke6+,** resigns. White can now force the exchange of queens: **33. ... Kh8 34. Qd8+ Kh7 35. Qe7+ Kg8 36. Qf7+ Kh8 37. Qf6+,** etc.

A potential passed pawn is exploited in precisely the same manner, since one passed pawn is just about as good as two in queen endings.

No. 1071, Alekhine-Maroczy, New York 1924

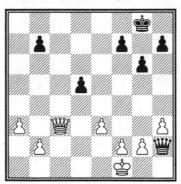

White to play wins

No. 1071 exemplifies this and also shows how beneficial additional pawns are to the superior side. Alekhine played 1. f3 and after 1. ... Qh1+ 2. Kf2 Qd1 3. Qc8+ Kg7 4. Qxb7? (4. Qc3+ Kg8 5. Qd4 is still good enough) 4. ... Qd2+ 5. Kg3 d4!! draws: 6. exd4 Qg5+, and Black has perpetual check.

The quickest win is **1. Qc8+ Kg7 2. Qxb7 Qh1+ 3. Ke2 Qxg2 4. a4 Qxh3** (if 4. ... g5 5. a5 h5 6. a6 g4 7. hxg4 hxg4 8. Qe7 Qf3+ 9. Ke1 Qh1+ 10. Kd2 Qa1 11. Qa3 and wins) **5. a5 Qg4+ 6. Kd2 Qf3 7. a6 Qxf2+ 8. Kd3 Qf1+ 9. Kd4 Qd1+ 10. Kc5 Qc1+ 11. Kd6 Qxe3 12. a7 Qg3+ 13. Kd7 Qg4+ 14. Kd8 Qh4+ 15. Qe7 Qa4 16. Qe5+ Kh6** (16. ... f6 17. Qe7+ Kh6 18. Qb7, etc.) **17. Qb8 Qa5+ 18. Ke8 Qa4+ 19. Kf8,** and Black has no checks.

A similar instructive error is seen in **No. 1072** (Maroczy-Alapin, Barmen 1905): **White king at h1, queen at d2, pawns at a2, b2, g2, h3; Black king at h7, queen at f7, pawns at a6, b5, c4, g7, h6.** Black to play wins. **1. ... Qf5 2. a3 Qd3 3. Qb4 Qb3+** (instead, Black played 3. ... Qd4, when 4. Kh2 Qf4+ 5. Kh1 Qf1+ 6. Kh2 Qc1 7. a4! bxa4 8. Qxa4 Qxb2 9. Qxc4 Qb8+ 10. Kh1 a5 11. Qd3+ only drew because Black could not both defend against perpetual check and support his pawn) **4. Qd2 a5!** wins most simply; e.g., **5. Qd7 Qxb2 6. Qf5+ g6 7. Qd7+ Qg7 8. Qxb5 Qc7 9. Qb1 c3 10. Qc2 h5 and ... Qc5-d4-d2.**

2. The Defending King Is Near the Opposing Pawn Majority (Pawns on Both Wings)

Such endings are much more complicated than the previous ones because a straightforward pawn advance (as in Nos. 1066 and 1069) simply will not do. The king is secure against perpetual check only when surrounded by pawns, so playing them out of the way merely invites a draw.

The two main winning stratagems in these cases are:
1) playing the king over to the other side of the board and
2) a mating attack.

No. 1073, Pillsbury-Burn, Vienna 1898

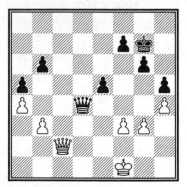

Black to play wins

No. 1073 is a splendid illustration of the difficulties ordinarily encountered and the first method of overcoming them.

Notice first of all that the natural advance **1. ... f5?** allows **2. Qc7+ Kh6 3. Qb8,** with a practically certain draw. Black must find a safe spot for his king that will not be weakened by the pawn advance; only the queenside offers

such a haven. Burn was quite well aware of this, of course, and since Pillsbury puts up the best defense we may take the game continuation as a
model.

1. ... Qd5 2. Kg2 Kf6 3. Qc3 Qc5 4. Qd3 Ke7 5. Qd2 (White's king must not
follow suit because of the danger that the queens will be exchanged) **5. ...
Qd4 6. Qe2 f5!** (now this may be played with impunity) **7. Qb5 e4! 8. fxe4
fxe4**

The advantage that the passed pawn confers is clear: the moves of the
White queen are restricted because it must not only watch the pawn but also
guard against being exchanged.

**9. Qg5+ Kf7 10. Qf4+ Ke6 11. Qg5 Qb2+ 12. Kh3 Qf6 13. Qe3 Kd5! 14.
Qd2+ Qd4 15. Qg5+ Qe5!!**

The point. 16. Qxg6 is refuted by 16. ... Qe6+ 17. Qxe6+ Kxe6 18. g4 e3!, etc.,
so Black has gained a valuable tempo.

16. Qe3 Kc6 17. Kg2 Qb2+ 18. Kh3 Qc2 19. Qg5 Qe2!!

This is Black's real object: the g-pawn makes little difference because White
cannot create a passed pawn, and meanwhile the Black e-pawn is a nasty
threat.

20. Qxg6+ Kc5 21. b4+

Desperation. If 21. g4 Qf3+, or if 21. Qf5+ Kb4 22. g4 hxg4+ 23. Qxg4
Qxg4+! 24. Kxg4 Kc3! 25. h5 e3 26. h6 e2 27. h7 e1=Q 28. h8=Q+ Kxb3 29.
Qg8+ Ka3!!, and White is out of checks (30. Qf8+ Qb4+), so he loses his last
pawn and Black has a routine win.

21. ... axb4 22. Qg5+ Kd4 23. Qf6+ Kc4 24. Qxb6 (Now White has a passed
pawn, too, but, as we know, Black pawns travel faster!) **24. ... Qf3!** (threatening mate) **25. Qe6+ Kc3 26. Qe5+ Kb3 27. Qd5+ Ka3!** (note how the pawns
protect the king from checks. 27. ... Kxa4? is a serious mistake since the pawn
is only in White's way) **28. Kh2 b3 29. Qc5+ Ka2 30. a5 b2 31. Qd5+ Qb3 32.
Qd2 Qd3 33. Qf2 e3 34. Qf7+ Qb3**, White resigned.

Sometimes the stratagem of playing the king to the other wing is used in
conjunction with a mating attack or the possibility of a queen exchange.

No. 1074, Konstantinopolsky-Budo, Tiflis 1937

White to play wins

In **No. 1074**, although White's king appears to be favorably placed, he must reorganize his pieces before he can really penetrate to the queenside. The game continued:

1. Qf8+ Kh7 2. Qf5+ Kh8 3. Qe4 Qc7+ 4. Kf5 Qd7+ 5. Ke5 Qe7+ 6. Kf5 Qf6+ 7. Kg4 Qg5+ 8. Kh3 Qh5+ 9. Qh4 Qf5+ 10. Qg4 Qc5 11. Qg6! (after this the king threatens to start going back) **11. ... Qf2!** (preventing Kg4) **12. Qe8+ Kh7 13. Qe4+ Kh8 14. f4!** (again intending 14. Kg4) **14. ... Kg8 15. Kg4 Qg1 16. Qd5+ Kh7 17. h3 Qf2 18. Kf5 Qc2+ 19. Qe4 Qc7 20. Ke6+ Kh8 21. g3!** (protecting the pawn and freeing the queen) **21. ... Qc8+ 22. Ke7 Qc7+**

If 22. ... Qxh3 23. Qe3! Qf5 24. Qxb6 Qe4+ 25. Qe6 Qxa4 26. Kf7 and wins, or here 25. ... Qb7+ 26. Kf8 Qb8+ 27. Kf7 Qc7+ 28. Kg6 Qc2+ 29. f5 and wins.

23. Ke6 Qc8+ 24. Kf7! Qg8+

Or 24. ... Qc7+ 25. Qe7 Qc4+ 26. Qe6! Qc7+ 27. Kg6 Qd8 28. f5 Qb8 29. g4 Qa8 30. f6 and wins.

25. Ke7 Qb3 26. g4! (the mating attack commences) **26. ... h5**

If 26. ... Qxh3 27. Kf7! Qb3+ 28. Qe6! Qxe6+ 29. Kxe6, with a won pawn ending: 29. ... Kg8 30. f5 Kf8 31. Kd7, etc., or 29. ... g6 30. f5 Kg7 31. Ke7!, etc.

27. gxh5 Qxh3

After 27. ... Qb4+ 28. Qxb4 axb4 29. a5, White queens with check and comes out two pawns up.

28. Qe5! Kh7 (or 28. ... Qa3+ 29. Kf7 Qb3+ 30. Qe6) **29. Qe4+ Kh8 30. Qd5!** (if now 30. ... Kh7 31. Kf7! Qc8 32. Qe4+ Kh8 33. Qe8+) **30. ... Qh4+ 31. Qg5 Qh1 32. Qe5 Kh7 33. Kf8! Qg1** (or 33. ... Qa8+ 34. Qe8 Qg2 35. f5 followed by Qg6+) **34. Qf5+ Kh8** (34. ... Kh6 35. Kg8!) **35. Qd5!** resigns. Mate cannot be prevented.

No. 1075 is an example where the mating factor is the main element (not in conjunction with playing the king to the other wing).

No. 1075, Alexander-Reshevsky, Nottingham 1936

Black to play wins

Here there is little hope of playing the king to the queenside because Black's pawns could become weak. So Reshevsky prepares to advance on the kingside.

1. ... Qg5! 2. Qe6 (if 2. Qc7+ Kh6 3. Qxa7 h4! 4. gxh4 Qf4+ 5. Kg2 Qxe4+, Black then wins the b-pawn and eventually the h-pawn, too) **2. ... Kh6 3. Qc8 Qf6+ 4. Kg2** (if 4. Ke2 g5 followed by either ... g4 or ... h4, when Black's kingside pawns decide) **4. ... h4! 5. gxh4 Kh5!** (the point) **6. Qd7 a5 7. Qd1+ Kxh4 8. Qh1+** (or 8. Qe1+ Kh5 9. Qd1+ Kh6, etc.) **8. ... Kg5 9. Qd1 Kh6 10. Qh1+ Kg7** (as soon as he has had a chance to post his queen more effectively, the king will come right back) **11. Qc1 Qd8 12. Qc2 Qg5+ 13. Kh3 Qe3+ 14. Kg4 Qf4+ 15. Kh3 Qf3+ 16. Kh2** (if 16. Kh4 Kh6!) **16. ... Kh6 17. Qc6 Qf2+ 18. Kh3 Kh5 19. Qb7 Qe3+ 20. Kg2 Qd2+ 21. Kg3 Qd3+ 22. Kf2 Qd6 23. Kg3 Kg5 24. Kf3 Qd8 25. Kg3 Qf6 26. Qd5 Qf4+ 27. Kg2 Kh4! 28. Qc6 Qg3+ 29. Kf1 Qf3+ 30. Ke1 Qe3+ 31. Kf1** (if 31. Kd1 g5) **31. ... g5 32. Kg2 Qd2+**, White resigned, for after **33. Kf1** (or Kg1) **33. ... Kg3!** he must exchange queens to avoid mate.

The direct advance of the extra pawn can win only in special positions, where the enemy king is exposed.

No. 1076, Marshall-Tarrasch, Ostend 1907

White to play. Black wins

The bad position of the White king in **No. 1076** is the only reason Black is able to win. After **1. Qg6+ Kd5 2. Qxa6 e4 3. Qb5+ Kd4 4. Qb6+ Kd3 5. Qa6+ Ke3! 6. Qxh6+ Ke2 7. Qh5+ Ke1,** White is lost despite his extra pawn. **8. g4 e3 9. Qc5** (preventing e2) **9. ... Kd1 10. Qf5** and now **10. ... e2!** wins. (Tarrasch played 10. ... Qf2 and Marshall gave perpetual check beginning with 11. Qb1+ Ke2 12. Qb5+, etc.) **11. Qb1+ Qc1 12. Qd3+ Ke1 13. Kg2 Qc6+ 14. Kg1 Qc5+ 15. Kg2 Qf2+ 16. Kh3 Kf1 17. g5 Kg1.** Now White has no checks and the pawn will queen.

The most effective *drawing device* (besides perpetual check) is an advanced passed pawn.

No. 1077

Black to play. Draw

Black is forced to take perpetual check, since any attempt such as **1. ... h5 2. a6 h4 3. a7 h3? 4. Qb7** could lose and would surely not win.

Against such a strong pawn the only recourse the superior side has is an equally strong pawn. For instance, **No. 1078** (Lasker-Capablanca, Moscow

1936): **White king at c1, queen at c3, pawn at a5; Black king at h8, queen at f2, pawns at c4, e5, f6, g7, h6.** White to play, Black wins. After **1. Qa3** (1. Qxc4 Qe1+) **1. ... Kh7 2. a6, c3!** is immediately decisive, for if **3. a7 Qd2+ 4. Kb1 c2+ 5. Kb2 c1=Q+,** or if **3. Qxc3 Qf1+ 4. K any Qxa6,** with a win in both cases.

3. All the Pawns Are on One Wing

As with other endings, if there are not pawns on both sides of the board, a win with an advantage of one pawn is rarely, if ever, possible. Two vs. one and three vs. two are both practically hopeless draws, so all we need to consider are four vs. three and five vs. four.

No. 1079, Sämisch-Maroczy, Carlsbad 1929

White to play. Draw

No. 1079 is of value because White makes every conceivable attempt to get something out of the position but without success. The game continued:

1. Qc7+ Kg8 2. f3 Qd3 3. e4 Qd2 4. Kh2 Qb2 5. Qg3 Kf7 6. f4 Qe2 7. Qb3+

If **7. e5 fxe5 8. fxe5 Qe4 9. Qg5 Ke6 10. Qf6+ Kd7 11. Kg3 Qe3+,** etc., or here **11. Qf7+ Kd8 12. e6 Qe5+,** etc., =.

7. ... Kf8 8. Qb8+ Kf7 9. Qc7+ Ke6 10. f5+ (in the game, White checked around for a while, but it led to nothing) **10. ... gxf5 11. Qc8+ Ke7 12. Qxf5 Kf7** (even now White has nothing) **13. Kh3 Qd3+ 14. Qf3 Qd7+ 15. Kh2 Qb5 16. g4 hxg4 17. Qxg4 Qb2+ 18. Kg3 Qc3+ 19. Qf3 Qc7+ 20. Kg4 Qd7+ 21. Kh5 Qe8! 22. Qf5 Qh8+ 23. Kg4 Qg8+ 24. Kf4 Qg1 25. Qd7+ Kf8 26. Qd5 Qg6 27. h5 Qh6+ 28. Kg4 Ke7 29. Qc5+ Kd7 30. Qf5+ Ke7 31. Qf4 Qg7+ 32. Kh4 Qg2 33. h6 Kf7 34. Qc7+ Kg8 35. Qd8+ Kh7! 36. Qe7+ Kxh6 37. Qxf6+ Kh7 38. Qf7+ Kh8 39. Qh5+ Kg8,** =. White has done everything in his power but the game is still drawn. If **40. Qg4+ Qxg4+ 41. Kxg4 Kf8! 42. Kf4 Ke8! 43. Kf5 Kf7,** etc.

Endings with four vs. three can be won only when the inferior side's pawns are weak and subject to attack.

No. 1080, Flohr-Keres, Kemeri 1937

Black to play. White wins

White wins in **No. 1080** because Black must lose either his g-pawn or e-pawn in the long run. After **1. ... Kh5 2. Ke1 Kg6 3. Qb5 Qa2**

This should lose, but there is little choice. For instance, if 3. ... Kf6 4. Kd2 Kg6 5. f5+! Qxf5 6. Qxf5+ Kxf5 7. Kc3, with a won pawn ending, or 4. ... Qa2+ 5. Kc3 Qxh2 6. Qe5+ Kf7 7. Qf5+ Kg7 8. Qxg4+ Kh7 9. f5 Qf2 10. Qg6+ Kh8 11. Kd4, with a simple win, since Black must lose at least one more pawn.

   4. Qe8+ Kg7 5. Qd7+! Kf6!

The best chance. If 5. ... Kf8 6. Qf5+, or 5. ... Kh8 6. Qc8+ Kh7 7. Qf5+ Kh8 8. Qxe4 Qxh2 9. Qe5+ Kh7 10. Qf5+ Kh8 11. Qxg4, and with two extra pawns the win is relatively simple.

The attempt to give perpetual check by 8. ... Qa1+ (instead of 8. ... Qxh2) fails here after 9. Kd2 Qa5+ 10. Kc2 Qa2+ 11. Kc3 Qa3+ 12. Kc4 Qa4+ 13. Kd5! Qd7+ 14. Kc5! Qa7+ 15. Kd6 Qb8+ 16. Ke7 Qc7+ 17. Kf6 Qg7+ 18. Ke6 Qg8+ 19. Kd7, and now the White queen can interpose.

   6. Qxg4 wins: 6. ... Qxh2 (6. ... Qa1+ 7. Qd1 and Black has nothing for the two lost pawns) **7. Qh4+ Qxh4 8. gxh4 Kf5 9. Kd2! Kg4 10. Kc3 Kxh4 11. Kd4 Kg3 12. Ke5! h5 13. f5 h4 14. f6 h3 15. f7 h2 16. f8=Q h1=Q 17. Qf4+ Kg2** (or 17. ... Kh3 18. Qh6+) **18. Qxe4+ Kh2 19. Qxh1+** and wins.

With five vs. four the winning chances are much greater. One would normally expect such an ending with queens to be a draw, but **No. 1079** shows that White has real winning possibilities.

No. 1081, Reshevsky-Fine, Nottingham 1936

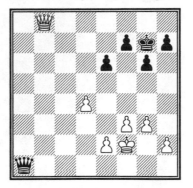

White to play

The game continued: **1. Qe5+ Kg8 2. Kg2 Qe1 3. Qb8+ Kg7 4. Qb2 Kg8 5. Qc2 Qb4 6. Qd3 Kf8 7. Kh3 Qa5 8. e4 Qh5+** (all this seems to be the best defense Black can put up) **9. Kg2 Qa5 10. d5! Ke7 11. Qd4! exd5 12. exd5 Kd6 13. Qf4+ Kxd5** (13. ... Kc7 14. Qe5+ Kd7 15. f4 is no better) **14. Qxf7+ Kd4! 15. Qd7+!** (the game continued 15. Qxh7 Qa2+ 16. Kh3 Qe6+ 17. g4 Ke3! 18. Qb7 Kf2!, and White cannot win) **15. ... Ke3 16. Qe7+ Kd3 17. h4!**, with good winning chances.

D. Positional Advantage

Queen endings are in some respects similar to those with bishops of opposite colors. In both, two or three pawns may not be enough to win (though for different reasons) and in both, positional advantages may be surprisingly overwhelming. But here the analogy stops; queen-and-pawn endings are really in a class by themselves.

1. Better Pawn Position

We consider three categories.

a) One side has a passed pawn, the other does not.

This is by far the most important, because a queen alone can escort the pawn to the eighth (see No. 1066). The passed pawn must be at some distance from the kings in order to be of any great value.

No. 1082 is an interesting example of the power of such an outside passed pawn. Black's only chance is to secure perpetual check — somehow.

No. 1082, Euwe-Reshevsky, Nottingham 1936

Black to play. White wins

With a view to this, Black should have played 1. ... Qc3!, for if then 2. a5? e4! 3. a6 Qf3+ 4. Kg1 Qd1+ 5. Kh2 e3! 6. fxe3 Qe2+ 7. Qg2 Qxa6, and White cannot win (compare No. 1067). After 1. ... Qc3 2. Qb7 e4 3. Qxe4 Qxb3 4. Qa8! e5! 5. a5 Qa2, White is one move behind the line chosen, and the game should be drawn.

Black played **1. ... Qb6?** and lost as follows: **2. a5 Qxb3 3. a6 Qa3 4. a7 e4 5. Qb8 Qf3+ 6. Kg1 Qd1+ 7. Kh2! Qe2** (7. ... Qd4 8. Kg2, a typical triangulation maneuver) **8. Qe5+**, and Black resigned. On **8. ... Kh7 9. Qf6 Qa2 10. Qxf7+ Kh6 11. Qf8+** is conclusive, and 8. ... f6 is refuted by 9. Qc7+ Kh6 10. Qf4+ Kg7 11. a8=Q.

b) Qualitatively superior passed pawn

As usual, this means that the pawns are more advanced. Queen endings are distinctive in that one strong pawn is just as good as two or three.

No. 1083, Stahlberg-Euwe, Stockholm 1937

Black to play wins

1. ... Qd4! 2. Kg3?

It's more important to advance the passed pawn; e.g., 2. Qb5 (or 2. Qc7) 2. ... Qxh4+ 3. Kg1 Qe4 4. a5 Qb1+ 5. Kh2 b3 6. Qb7 Kg7 7. a6 b2 8. a7, =.

2. ... b3 3. Qb5 b2 4. Qb3 Kg7! 5. f4 (or 5. Qc2 Qe5+ 6. f4 Qe1+ or 6. Kh3 Qf5+) **5. ... Qd2,** White resigned, since he must lose his queen.

The only defense in these cases is perpetual check. An example is **No. 1084** (Kashdan-Reshevsky, New York 1940): **White: king at e2, queen at f6, pawns at d4, f4, g5, h4; Black king at h7, queen at c7, pawns at f7, e3, d2.** White to play draws. **1. g6+! fxg6 2. h5 Qc4+ 3. Kxe3 d1=Q 4. Qe7+ Kh6 5. Qg5+ Kg7** and **6. Qe7+** is still a perpetual: **6. ... Qf7 7. h6+ Kg8 8. h7+ Qxh7 9. Qe8+ Kg7 10. Qe7+,** etc.

c) Superior pawn structure.

Quiet positional advantages, such as the opponent's slightly weaker pawn skeleton or his blockaded pawns are of little or no importance in queen endings. Surprisingly, however, there are many cases in which a minimal pawn weakness is fatal. These almost always occur in conjunction with an exposed king position.

No. 1085, Lisitsin-Capablanca, Moscow 1935

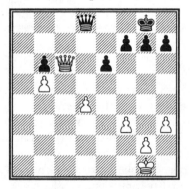

White to play. Black wins

No. 1085 is deceptively simple. The position is by no means as easy for White as it looks: he has two weak pawns to watch.

1. Qc4 h5 2. Kf1 g6 3. Kg1 Kg7 4. Kf1 Qd6 5. Kg1 Qf4! 6. Qc3 Kh7 7. Kf1 Qf5 8. Qc4 Kg7 (Black is trying to get his king to the center and prevent White from doing the same) **9. Kf2 Qg5! 10. Qe2 Kf6 11. Qb2 Qd5! 12. Ke3?** (12. Qb4 is necessary) **12. ... e5?**

12. ... Qc4! wins a pawn, for if 13. d5+ e5!, or if 13. Qb1 Ke7 14. Qb2 Kd7 15. Qb1 Kd6 16. Qb2 Kd5, and White is in zugzwang.

13. f4? (the correct reply is 13. Qb4! exd4+ 14. Qxd4+ Qxd4+ 15. Kxd4 Ke6 16. f4 f6 17. Kc4, =) **13. ... exf4+ 14. Kxf4 Ke6 15. h4 f6 16. Ke3 Qc4! 17. g3 g5 18. hxg5 fxg5.**

White is in zugzwang and must lose a pawn; e.g., 19. Ke4 g4! 20. Kf4 Kf6 21. Ke4 Qe6+ 22. Kd3 Qd5, etc.

19. Qh2 Qb3+ 20. Ke4 g4! 21. Qe2 Qxg3 22. Qc4+ Ke7 23. Qc8 Qf3+ 24. Ke5 Qf6+ 25. Kd5 Qd6+, and White resigned since his queen will be exchanged.

2. Better Queen Position

This goes hand in hand with the other categories, but it is instructive to consider it separately.

No. 1086, Maroczy-Marshall, Carlsbad 1907

White to play wins

The most common type of superiority is a more active queen than its rival. **No. 1086** is the classic ending with this theme.

Of course, the greater mobility of the White queen is due in part to the fact that the White king is safe from checks and in part to the weakness of the Black pawns.

After **1. Qh4!** one expects Black to lose a pawn soon, but Marshall manages to maintain material equality for quite a while.

1. ... Kg7 2. Qg4+ Kf7 3. Qh5+! (getting to the eighth) **3. ... Kg7 4. Qe8 Qe2**

Black now seems to have enough counterplay, but the exposed position of his king spoils everything

5. Qe7+ Kg6 6. Qf8

More solid than the spectacular 6. Qxc7 Qxg2 7. Qxb7 Qxh2 8. Qxa7 h5 9. a4 h4 10. a5 h3 11. Qb8!! Qh1 12. a6 h2 13. a7 Qxf3 14. Qg8+ Kf5 15. Qh7+ Kg4 16. Qxh2 and wins.

6. ... e5 7. Qg8+ Kh6 8. h4! Qf2 9. Qf8+ Kg6 10. h5+! (the point of White's last few moves) **10. ... Kxh5 11. Qg7! Qd2**

Relatively best. Both 11. ... h6? 12. Qg4+ mate and 11. ... Qh4 12. g4+ are not recommended.

The main alternative is 11. ... f5, but 12. Qxh7+ Kg5 13. Qg7+ wins: 13. ... Kf4 (or 13. ... Kh5 14. g4+ fxg4 15. fxg4+ Kh4 16. g5 e4 17. Qh6+ Kg3 18. g6 e3 19. g7, with an easy win) 14. Qh6+ Kg3 15. Qg5+ Kh2 16. g4 fxg4 17. fxg4 e4

18. Qh6+ Kg1 19. g5 e3 20. g6 e2 21. Qg5+ Kf1 22. g7 e1=Q 23. g8=Q Qd1 24. Qh7, and Black cannot avoid losing at least two pawns.

12. Qxh7+ Qh6 13. g4+ (simpler is 13. Qxc7) **13. ... Kg5 14. Qxc7 Kf4 15. Qxb7 Qh1 16. Qb4+!!** (excellent: he creates a passed c-pawn and exposes the Black king) **16. ... Kxf3 17. Qxd6 Kxg4 18. c4!**

In queen-and-pawn endings, one passed pawn is as good as two. The Black f-pawn is unimportant.

18. ... e4 19. c5 f5

An unavoidable loss of time. If 19. ... e3? 20. Qd4+ wins the pawn, since 20. ... Kf3?? 21. Qd5+ loses the queen.

20. c6 Qh8+

Again, if 20. ... e3 21. Qd4+ Qe4 22. Qxc4+ fxe4 23. c7 e2 24. c8=Q+ and wins.

21. c3 e3 22. Qg6+ Kf4 23. c7 e2 24. Qe6 Kf3 25. Qxf5+ Kg2 26. Qg4+ Kf2 27. Qf4+ Kg2 28. Qe3! Kf1 29. Qf3+ Ke1 30. Qf4

Good enough, but 30. Qf5 Kd2 31. c8=Q Qxc8 32. Qxc8 e1=Q 33. Qd7+ Ke3 34. Qe6+ is more direct.

30. ... Qc8 31. Qd6 Kf2 32. Qd8 e1=Q (if 32. ... Qxd8 33. cxd8=Q e1=Q 34. Qh4+) **33. Qxc8 Qd2+ 34. Ka3 Qc1+ 35. Ka4 Qf4+ 36. c4,** resigns.

Against a weak pawn formation even so slight an advantage as a centralized queen may on occasion be transferred into a win.

No. 1087, Lasker-Bird, match 1892

White to play wins

White begins by winning a pawn. **1. Qd8+ Kh7 2. Qg5 f6 3. Qxh5+ Kg7 4. Kg2.** Black's remaining pawns are just as weak as ever, so White wins by a straightforward advance on the kingside. **4. ... Qd7 5. h3 gxh3+ 6. Qxh3 Qd3 7. Qg4+ Kf7 8. Qf3 Qc4 9. Qe3 Ke6 10. f3 Kd6 11. Kf2 Qa2+ 12. Qe2 Qe6 13. Qd2+ Kc7 14. g4! Qc4 15. Qe3 Qa2+ 16. Kg3,** and the king march decides. **16. ... Qa1 17. g5 fxg5 18. Kg4 Qb2 19. Kxg5 Kd7 20. Kg4** (or 20. Kf6) **20. ... Qh2 21. Kf5 Qg3 22. Kf6! c5** (desperation: if 22. ... Kc7 23. Ke6!, or 22. ... Qh2 23. Qd3+) **23. Qg5 Qh2 24. Qf5+ Kc6 25. Qc8+ Kb5 26. Qxc5+ Ka4 27. Qxe5,** resigns.

3. Better King Position

This can mean either that one king is safe behind a wall of pawns while the other is buffeted about by unfeeling checks, or that there is a mating position. The first has been seen a number of times in previous examples (e.g., No. 1086) so it will be sufficient to give an example of the second.

No. 1088, Kling and Horwitz 1851

White to play wins

White forces the win by successive mate threats. **1. Qg2+ Kf8** (1. ... Kh8 2. Qa8+ Qg8 3. Qxg8+, and 4. d7) **2. Qa8+ Qe8 3. Qb7! Qd8** (or 3. ... Qf7 4. Qc8+! Qe8 5. d7) **4. Kg6! Qe8+ 5. Kf6! Qd8+ 6. Kxe6 Qe8+ 7. Qe7+ Qxe7+ 8. dxe7+ Ke8 9. Kd6** and wins.

III. QUEEN AND MINOR PIECE VS. QUEEN

There is a basic rule (see Chapter IX, rule 1) that, generally, in endings without pawns you must be at least a rook ahead to win. That holds here as well. Unlike the similar case with rooks, however, there are only a few exceptions to the general rule. These occur when a series of checks either leads to mate or to the capture of the enemy queen.

No. 1089, Horwitz 1872

White to play wins

No. 1089 is an interesting example with a bishop. The solution is **1. Qe3+ Kf5** (1. ... Kd5 2. Qb3+) **2. Qf3+ Ke6 3. Qb3+ Ke7** (not 3. ... Kf6 4. Bg5+) **4. Bg5+ Kf8** (again forced, for if 4. ... Ke8 5. Qb8+ Kd7 6. Qb7+, Black is either mated or loses his queen) **5. Qb8+ Qe8 6. Qd6+ Kg8** (6. ... Kf7 allows mate in two) **7. Be7!!** and Black cannot prevent mate; e.g., **7. ... Qf7 8. Qd8+**, etc.

No. 1090, Dehler 1908

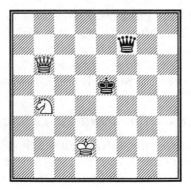

White to play wins

No. 1090 illustrates some of the possibilities with a knight. After **1. Nc6+ Kf5! 2. Qf2+ Ke4!!** offers the best chance, since **3. Qxf7** is stalemate! But **3. Qe3+** is good enough. **3. ... Kd5! 4. Qb3+ Ke4! 5. Qd3+! Kf4 6. Qe3+ Kf5 7. Qf3+**, and this time he really wins the queen (7. ... Ke6 8. Nd8+ or 7. ... Kg6 8. Ne5+).

With pawns the ending is not essentially different from endings with bishop or knight vs. pawns except that, again, queen plus bishop and pawn vs. queen wins in all cases.

IV. QUEEN VS. ROOKS AND PIECES

A. Queen vs. Two Rooks and One Piece

The advantage of the three pieces here is so great that the ending is usually won even without pawns.

No. 1091 is a rather simple example of the helplessness of the queen:

No. 1091, Kling and Horwitz 1851

White to play wins

After **1. Rc2+ Kb8 2. Rc4!**, Black must release the pin and suffer the fury of two unchained rooks. **2. ... Qf6** (if 2. ... Qb2+ 3. Kg3 Black has no checks and loses his queen. On 2. ... Qa7, 3. Kf1! is quickest: 3. ... Qa1+ 4. Rd1 Qg7 5. Rb1+, etc., or here 4. ... Qa6 5. Rd8+ and 6. Ra8+) **3. Rb4+ Kc8 4. Rdc4+ Kd8 5. Rb8+ Kd7 6. Rb7+ Kd8** (6. ... Kd6 7. Rc6+) **7. Ra4!** and wins.

B. Queen vs. Rook and Two Minor Pieces

Without pawns this is generally a draw, although there are many positions that favor the pieces. But with pawns, the queen is usually unable to defend everything against direct attack. For instance, if rook and bishop threaten an immovable pawn, it cannot be defended.

No. 1092, Zukertort-Minckwitz, Berlin 1881

White to play wins

No. 1092 illustrates the power of the pieces. After **1. Bd4!** the g-pawn must fall. The best defense is **1. ... Qb5+ 2. Kg4 Qc4** (if 2. ... Qxb4 3. Rxg7+ Kf8 4. Bc5+! Qxc5 5. Ne6+) **3. Rxg7+ Kf8 4. Bf6! Qe4** (or 4. ... Qxb4 5. Be7+ Qxe7 6. Ng6+ Kxg7 7. Nxe7 Kf6 8. Nd5+ Kc5 9. Nb4 Kd6 10. Nxa6 Kc6 11. Nb4+ and wins) **5. b5! axb5 6. a6 b4 7. a7 b3 8. Rh7!** and wins. Another possibility here is **4. ... Qc8+ 5. Kg5 Qc1 6. Rc7! Qg1+ 7. Kf5 Qb1+ 8. Ke6 Qa2+ 9. Nd5 Qe2+ 10. Be5 Qg4+ 11. Kd6 Qg6+ 12. Kc5 Qg1+ 13. Bd4** and Black is out of checks.

C. Queen vs. Rook and One Minor Piece

This is fairly common, unlike the other groups in this section.

Without pawns the ending is a draw, though naturally there will be problem positions where one side or the other may win. With pawns, however, the queen is equivalent to rook plus bishop and pawn. If the pawns are even, the queen wins (though not without difficulty); but rook plus bishop and two pawns are required to conquer the queen. When the pawns are equal, the win is easier for the queen if they are not balanced. In that case the superior side can create a passed pawn and capture one of the opponent's pieces or tie him up so badly that some other part of the board will be left defenseless.

No. 1093, Alekhine-Thomas, Hastings 1922

White to play wins

After **1. Qb5** Black must lose a pawn. **1. ... Rd6 2. g3 Rd1+ 3. Kg2 Ra1 4. Qa4** (4. Qxa5 b3 5. Qc3 is also good enough but leaves pawns only on the kingside) **4. ... Be7 5. Qxa5** (threatening Qe5, so 5. ... b3 is not possible) **5. ... Rc1 6. Qa8+ Bf8**

Now that White has done everything possible on the queenside, he must turn his attention to the other wing. The steady advance of king and pawns is bound to win there.

7. Qe4 Rc3 8. Qb1 (to prevent the exchange by 8. ... b3) **8. ... Ra3 9. Kf3 Ra6 10. e4 Rf6+** (if 10. ... Ra3+ 11. Kf4 Bd6+ 12. e5 Bf8 13. Ke4, etc., as in the game) **11. Ke2 Ra6 12. f4 g6** (12. ... Ra3 is better, but after 13. e5 White wins by the kingside advance) **13. Kd3 Rd6+ 14. Ke3 Rd7 15. Qc2 Ra7 16. e5 Ra6 17. Ke4 Rb6** (Black is reduced to complete passivity) **18. g4 Rb5 19. Kd4 Ra5 20. h4 Rb5 21. h5 gxh5 22. gxh5 Rb6** (or 22. ... Ra5 23. f5 Rb5 24. Qg2+ Kh8 25. Qa8 Kg8 26. e6 fxe6 27. fxe6 and wins) **23. f5 Kg7 24. Qc7 Rb5** (24. ... Ra6 25. e6) **25. Kc4!,** Black resigns, since **25. ... Rc5+** is forced, when **26. Qxc5** is overwhelming.

No. 1094 is the typical ending with balanced pawns.

No. 1094, Fine-Stahlberg, 3rd match game 1937

White to play wins

After **1. Qf4! a6 2. Qb8+ Bc8 3. a4!**

The game continued with the less accurate 3. b4, when 3. ... b5! could draw.
3. ... Kh7 4. b4

Black loses because he has too much to defend. White's main threat is to march his king to d8 and win the b-pawn. Black can at best only delay the execution of this plan.
4. ... f5

A further weakness, but in the long run unavoidable because of the danger of a check along the diagonal; e.g., 4. ... Rc4 5. b5 axb5 6. axb5 Rc5 7. Qd6! Rc1 8. Kg3, and the king can get through.
5. Qe5 Rf6 6. Qc7 Rc6 7. Qe7 Rg6 8. f3 Rc6 (if 8. ... b5 9. Qe8) **9. b5 axb5 10. axb5 Rc4 11. h4 Rc2 12. h5 Rc4 13. Kg3 Rc3 14. Qd6 Rc2**

All the preparations are finished and now the final assault commences.

15. Qg6+ Kh8 16. Qe8+ Kh7 17. Kf4 Rc1 18. Qg6+ Kh8 19. Ke5 Bd7 20. Qb6! Bc8 (20. ... Rb1 21. Qd8+) **21. Kd6 Kg8 22. Qe3!** resigns, for he must lose his bishop: **22. ... Rd1+ 23. Kc7 Bd7 24. Qb3+.**

No. 1095 is the type of position where rook, bishop and pawn win.

No. 1095, Shipley-Lasker, Philadelphia 1902

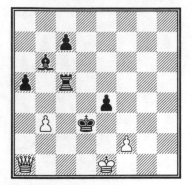

Black to play wins

After **1. ... Rc2 2. Qb1 Kc3! 3. Qa1+ Rb2 4. Qc1+ Kxb3 5. Qd1+ Kb4 6. Qg4 Bxf2+**, the Queen is unable to stop all the pawns. **7. Kd1 Bd4! 8. Qxe4 c5 9. Qe1+ Ka4 10. Kc1** (note how easily the Black king sidesteps perpetual check) **10. ... Rf2 11. Qd1+ Ka3 12. Qd3+ Kb4 13. Qa6 a4 14. Qb6+ Ka3 15. Qb5 Rb2 16. Qa6 Be3+ 17. Kd1 Rd2+ 18. Ke1 Rd4 19. Qe6 Bd2+ 20. Kd1 Kb2 21. Qg6 Bc3+ 22. Ke2 a3**, White resigned.

V. QUEEN VS. ROOK (OR ROOKS)

A. Queen vs. Two Rooks

Queen and pawn are normally equivalent to two rooks. This means that queen plus pawn vs. two rooks is drawn, but queen plus two pawns vs. two rooks is won, and with even pawns or one pawn up, the two rooks win.

Without pawns the game is most often drawn. If the enemy king is confined to the edge of the board, the rooks may win; if the rooks are not adequately defended, the queen may win.

No. 1096 is a relatively favorable situation for the rooks but still not good enough.

No. 1096, Centurini 1885

Black to play. Draw. Win with Black king at h7

After **1. ... Kh7 2. Qb1+ Rg6 3. Qf5 Rh8**, White can prevent the fatal discovered check. **4. Qf7+ Rg7 5. Qc6 Rg6 6. Qf7+ Kh6 7. Qe7 Rh7 8. Qf8+ Rhg7 9. Qf4+ Kh7 10. Qf5 Kh8 11. Qc8+ Rg8 12. Qc3+ Kh7 13. Qc7+ R6g7 14. Qc2+ Kh8 15. Qc3,** etc.

But in **No. 1097** (Centurini): **Black king at h7**, other pieces unchanged, Black to play does win. **1. ... Rh8 2. Qa2** (he must stop ... Kg8+) **2. ... Kg6+** wins the queen: **3. Kg2 Kf5+ 4. Kf3 Rh3+ 5. Ke2 Rh2+,** etc.

With pawns on the board, two rooks and one pawn always win, unless so few pawns remain that a perpetual check is possible. When there is nothing else, two rooks plus one pawn only draw; two pawns are required to win.

No. 1098, Berger

White to play, Black wins

No. 1098 illustrates the difficulties. Best play is: **1. Qh7 Rd2+ 2. Kc1 f3 3. Qh6+ Kf5 4. Qh5+ Kf4 5. Qh4+ Ke3 6. Qg5+ Ke2!** (6. ... Ke4 7. Qg4+) **7. Qxe5+ Kf1 8. Qb5+** (or 8. Qg3 Rd1+ 9. Kc2 R6d2+ 10. Kc3 f2 11. Qh3+ Ke1 12. Qh4 Rd3+ 13. Kc2 R1d2+ 14. Kc1 Rd4 15. Qe7+ Re2, etc.) **8. ... R6d3 9. Qh5 f2**

10. Qh1+ Ke2 11. Qh5+ Ke1 12. Qe5+ Re2 13. Qa5+ Rdd2 14. Qb4 Kf1 (14. ... f1=N also wins) **15. Qh4 Rc2+ 16. Kb1 Ke1 17. Qg3 Rcd2** and wins.

No. 1099 is the minimal position where two rooks plus pawn win against a queen.

No. 1099, Steinitz-Pillsbury, Nuremberg 1896

Black wins

Yet even here Black cannot advance his a-pawn by any straightforward series of moves: he must combine the possibility of advancing with a threat against White's pawns.

The game continued: **1. Qe6 Rfd8 2. Qa6 h6 3. h4 Rf8 4. Kh3** (4. g4 Rf2+ 5. Kg3 Rdf7! is worse for White) **4. ... Kh7 5. Qc6 Rd3+ 6. g3 Re3 7. Qc2+** (the threat was Rf6-g6) **7. ... Kh8 8. h5 Re5 9. Kh4 a5!** (at last!) **10. Qa4 Rb8 11. g4 Rg5 12. Qc6 Rg8** (not 12. ... Rb4 13. Qc8+ Kh7 14. Qc2+) **13. Qa6 Rd8 14. Qc6 Rgd5 15. Qa4** (if now 15. Qa6 Rf8 16. Qe6 Rd3 17. Qa6 Re3! 18. Qxa5 Rff3 and White has only one useless check) **15. ... Ra8! 16. Kh3** (or 16. Qc6 Rdd8 17. Qa4 Rd3 as in the game) **16. ... Rd3+ 17. Kh4** (better is 17. Kg2, though 17. ... Rc3! 18. Kf2 Rf8+ 19. Ke2 Rc5 will eventually win the pawns) **17. ... Re3 18. Qc6 Rf8**, White resigned, since he is defenseless against Rff3-h3 mate (if 19. g5 Rf4+ mate).

The superiority of the two rooks when the pawns are equal is seen quite clearly in **No. 1100.**

No. 1100, Chigorin-Janowski, Carlsbad 1907

Black to play wins

Here White's pawns are isolated and cannot support each other. The continuation was **1. ... Rcd6! 2. Kc4 h4 3. Kc5 Kg5! 4. d5 h3 5. Qe8 Kf4 6. Qe1 Rh6 7. Qf2+ Kg4 8. Qg1+ Kf5 9. Qf2+ Kg6!! 10. Qc2+** (if 10. Kxd6 h2 11. Qg3+ Kf7+ wins) **10. ... Kf6 11. Qb2+ Kf7 12. Qb7+ Kg8 13. a6!**

This manages to stop the h-pawn but leads to a loss with two rooks and pawn vs. queen because of the bad position of the queen.

13. ... Rxa6 14. Qb8+ Kh7 15. Qb1+ Rag6 16. d6! h2 17. d7 h1=Q 18. Qxh1 Rxh1 19. d8=Q Rg4! (forcing the king into a mating net) **20. Kb5 Rh5+ 21. Kb6 Rg6+ 22. Ka7 Rf5 23. Qd3 Rgf6**

Now the ending is won because the White queen must guard against the mate possibilities and so cannot pay attention to the pawn.

24. Kb7 g6 25. Kc7 Kg7 26. Qd4 Rf4 27. Qc3 (among other things, White has no checks) **27. ... Re4 28. Kd7 Ra4 29. Ke7 Ra6 30. Qb2 g5 31. Qc3** (if 31. Qd4 Re6+ 32. Kd7 Rd6+) **31. ... g4 32. Ke8 Rc6 33. Qg3 Rce6+ 34. Kd7 Re4! 35. Qh4 Kg6 36. Qh8 Kf5 37. Qh5+ Kf4 38. Qh2+ Kg5 39. Qd2+ Rff4** (releasing the king in order to advance the pawn) **40. Qg2 Rd4+ 41. Kc6 Rf3 42. Qe2 Rdf4**, White resigned. Once the pawn gets to the sixth the game is hopeless.

Queen and two pawns win against the rooks only when the rooks are not united, or when there are *connected passed pawns*.

No. 1101, Ed. Lasker–Fine, New York, 1940

White to play. Black wins

No. 1101 illustrates proper play with queen and rooks. **1. Kh1?**

A waste of time. The correct saving idea is to exchange one pawn on the queenside, then double rooks against Black's remaining pawn there, and finally win it. For instance, 1. Rg1 b6 2. a4 e5 3. a5! bxa5 4. Ra1 Qc3 5. Ra4 f5 6. gxf5 gxf5 7. Rda1 e4 8. Rxa5 e3 9. R5a3 Qe5+ 10. Kh1, and if 10. ... e2? 11. Re1 Qb2 12. Re3! eventually wins both pawns.

1. ... Qa3 2. Rd7

2. Rdb1 is still better. To get both rooks to the seventh is useless in these endings.

2. ... b5 3. Re1 Qxa2 4. Rexe7 a5 5. Rd8+ Kg7 6. g5 (threatening 6. Ree8) **6. ... Qc4! 7. Rdd7** (7. Ree8 Qc1+ 8. Kh2 Qxg5) **7. ... a4 8. Rc7 Qf1+ 9. Kh2 Qf4+ 10. Kg1 b4** and wins.

B. Queen vs. Rook

1. Without Pawns

This is a win, but from the general position the process is rather complicated.

In order to have drawing chances, Black must keep his rook near his king, for otherwise a check will capture the rook. *The basic winning idea is to force Black into zugzwang so that he will have to move his rook away from his king.*

No. 1102

Black to play. White wins

No. 1102 is the basic zugzwang position. Black loses his rook (or worse) very quickly in all variations.

a) 1. ... Ka6 2. Qc8.

b) 1. ... Rb8 2. Qa5+ mate.

c) 1. ... Rb4 2. Qa5+ and 3. Qxb4.

d) 1. ... Rb3 2. Qd4+ Kb8 3. Qf4+ Ka7 (3. ... Kc8 4. Qf8+ mate) 4. Qa4+ and 5. Qxb3.

e) 1. ... Rb2 2. Qd4+, etc.

f) 1. ... Rb1 2. Qd4+ Kb8 3. Qf4+ Ka8 4. Qf8+ (or 4. Kc7, leading to mate) 4. ... Ka7 5. Qf2+ Kb8 6. Qh2+ Ka7 7. Qa2+, etc.

g) 1. ... Rf7 2. Qd4+ Kb8 (or 2. ... Ka8 3. Qa1+) 3. Qb2+ Ka8 4. Qa2+.

h) 1. ... Rg7 2. Qd4+.

i) 1. ... Rh7 2. Qa5+ Kb8 3. Qb4+ Ka7 4. Qa3+ Kb8 5. Qb3+ Ka7 6. Qa2+ Kb8 7. Qg8+.

No. 1103 is the general case:

No. 1103, Berger

White to play wins

Black is forced to retreat to the edge of the board because he must keep his rook near his king, but once further retreat is cut off, zugzwang is inevitable. With optimal play it takes 32 moves to mate.

1. Kb2 Rf4 2. Kc3 Re4 3. Kd3 Rd4+ 4. Ke3 Rd5

He must let the king through. If, for example, 4. ... Rc4 5. Qh5+ Ke6 6. Qb5 Rg4 7. Qc5 Rh4 8. Kf3 Kf6 9. Qd5 Kg6, and now any move along the fourth rank costs Black his rook.

5. Qh2+ Kf5 6. Qf4+ Ke6

Or 6. ... Kg6 7. Ke4 Rg5 8. Qd6+ Kg7 9. Kf4 Rg6 10. Qe7+ Kg8 11. Kf5 Rg7 12. Qe8+ Kh7 13. Kf6 (see No. 1100; Black's best bet is to stay in the center).

7. Ke4 Rd6 8. Qf5+ Ke7 9. Ke5 Rd7?

9. ... Rc6 is best, to keep the rook on the third rank: 10. Qh7+ Kd8 11. Qf7 Ra6 12. Kd5 Rb6 13. Qf4 Kd7 14. Qa4+ Kc7 15. Qa7+ Rb7 16. Qc5+ Kb8 17. Kd6 Rg7 18. Qb4+ Rb7 19. Qe4 Rb6+ 20. Kc5 Ka7 21. Qd4 Rb7 22. Kc6+ Ka8 23. Qh8+ Ka7 24. Qd8, see No. 1100.

10. Qf6+ Ke8 11. Qh8+! (but not 11. Ke6?? Rd6+!! 12. Kxd6 stalemate) **11. ... Kf7! 12. Qh7+ Ke8 13. Qg8+ Ke7 14. Qc8!**, and now Black's rook and king must part. The various defenses are:

a) **14. ... Rd8** 15. Qe6+ Kf8 16. Kf6 and mates.

b) **14. ... Ra7** 15. Qc5+, or **14. ... Rd6** 15. Qc5.

c) **14. ... Rd3** 15. Qe6+ Kd8 16. Qg8+ Kc7 (or 16. ... Kd7 17. Qh7+) 17. Qc4+.

d) **14. ... Rd2** 15. Qc5+ Kd7 (or 15. ... Kf7 16. Qc4+ Kg7 17. Qg4+ Kh8 18. Qh5+ Kg8 19. Qg5+, or 15. ... Ke8 16. Qb5+ Kf7 17. Qc4+, etc.) 16. Qb5+ Kc8 17. Ke6! Rc2! 18. Kd6 Rh2! 19. Qe8+ Kb7 20. Qe4+ Kb6 (or 20. ... Kb8 21. Qf4! Rh7 22. Kc6+, etc., as in No. 1102, variation i) 21. Qf4 Rh5! 22. Qe3+ Ka5 23. Kc6 Kb4 24. Qf4+ Ka5 (otherwise Qf3+ decides) 25. Qd2+ and mates or wins the rook.

e) **14. ... Rd1** 15. Qc5+ Kd7 (or other moves, as in d) 16. Qb5+ Kd8 17. Qa5+ Kc8 18. Qc3+ Kd7 19. Qb4 Kc7 20. Qc4+ Kd8 21. Ke6 Re1+ 22. Kd6 Rd1+ 23. Kc6 Rd2 24. Qc5, again either mating or winning the rook.

Black's only drawing chance lies in stalemate. The long-range draw is exemplified in **No. 1104**:

No. 1104, Philidor 1782

Black to play draws

The Black rook keeps on checking on the rook- and knight-files. Since the White king cannot go to the e-file without permitting ... Re7, his only other winning chance lies in playing his king to f6, but then ... Rg6+ stalemates. Thus: **1. ... Rh7+ 2. Kg2 Rg7+ 3. Kf3 Rf7+ 4. Kg4 Rg7+ 5. Kf5 Rf7+ 6. Kg6 Rg7+ 7. Kf6 Rg6+ 8. Kxg6** stalemate. This can only arise on bishop-, knight-, and rook-files.

The analogous case on the knight and rook files is **No. 1105: White king at h6, queen at f6; Black king at g8, rook at g7.** Black to play draws because of the stalemate threat. **No. 1106: White queen at f1** (or f2, f3, f4), other pieces unchanged. Black to play draws without a stalemate threat, but has perpetual check at g7 and h7.

2. Queen vs. Rook and Pawn

This is another of the most intricate endings that can come up. In general, a knight-pawn and bishop-pawn always draw, but a center pawn and rook-pawn usually lose. The problems involved have been completely solved, and the results are outlined here.

a) Center Pawn

On the third or fourth rank this is always lost. The best defensive position for Black is shown in **No. 1107**.

No. 1107, Philidor 1782

White to play wins. Draw with pawn on second or seventh rank

White wins in 25 moves by attacking the pawn with his king. This is done by continually forcing the Black king to move.

1. Qh7+ Ke6

If 1. ... Kd8 2. Qf7 Kc8 3. Qa7 Kd8 4. Qb8+ Kd7 5. Qb7+ Kd8 6. Qc6! Ke7 7. Qc7+ Ke6 8. Qd8 Rf5+ 9. Kg4 Re5 10. Qe8+ Kd5 11. Qc8, etc., as in the main line.

2. Qc7 Rc5 3. Qd8 Re5 4. Qe8+ Kd5

Or 4. ... Kf6 5. Qd7 Re6 6. Kg4 Ke5 7. Kg5, etc. Once the White king crosses the center of the board the rest is comparatively simple.

5. Qc8 Re4+

Or 5. ... Kd4 6. Qc6 Rd5 7. Kf3 Ke5 8. Qc3+ Kf5 9. Qc4 Re5 10. Qf7+ Kg5 11. Qd7 Rd5 12. Qg7+ Kf5 13. Qf7+ Ke5 14. Qf4+ Ke6 15. Qc4! Ke5 16. Qe4+ and wins the rook.

6. Kf5 Re5+ 7. Kf6 Re4

On other rook moves the pawn falls; e.g., 7. ... Re1 8. Qb7+ Kd4 9. Qb6+, etc.

8. Qc3!

An alternative win is 8. Qf5+ Re5 9. Qd3+ Kc5 10. Qd2 Kc6 11. Qd4 Kd7 12. Qc4 Rc5 13. Qf7+ Kc6 14. Ke7! Re5+ 15. Kd8 Rc5 16. Qd7+ Kd5 17. Ke7 Rc6 18. Qf5+ Kc4 19. Kd7 Rc5 20. Qe4+, etc.

8. ... Re6+ 9. Kf7 Re5 10. Kf8 Re4 (on 10. ... Re6 11. Qb3+ Ke5 12. Kf7 wins) **11. Qd3+ Rd4**

If 11. ... Ke5 12. Ke7 d5 13. Qg3+ Kd4+ 14. Kd6 Kc4 15. Qg2 Rd4 16. Qc2+ K any 17. Qc5+, etc.

12. Qf5+ Kc4 13. Ke7 (13. Qc2+ wins faster) **13. ... d5 14. Qc2+ Kb4 15. Kd6,** and Black must abandon the pawn. A similar position with the White king on the seventh or eighth rank wins with any pawn.

White wins here only because his king can get behind the pawn. When the pawn is on the second and the rook on the third, this is impossible. **No. 1108** (Philidor 1782): **White king at d5, queen at b3; Black king at d8, rook at e6,**

pawn at d7. White to play. Draw. For instance, **1. Qb8+ Ke7 2. Qg8 Rc6 3. Ke5 Re6+,** etc. The Black king cannot be forced away from its pawn. With the pawn on the fourth rank White wins in exactly the same manner as in the previous example.

With the pawn on the fifth rank we get the critical position. **No. 1109** (Guretzky-Cornitz): **White king at f5, queen at c1; Black king at d3, rook at e3, pawn at d4.** Black to play loses.

1. ... Re2

Or 1. ... Re8 2. Qa3+ Ke2 3. Qa4 Rd8 4. Qa5 Rf8+ 5. Ke4 d3 6. Qh5+ Kd2 7. Qh6+ and wins the rook. Or 1. ... Ke2 2. Qc2+ Ke1 3. Kf4 Re2 4. Qc1+ Kf2 5. Qd1, and wins the pawn.

2. Qd1+ Ke3

There is no real defense. If, e.g., 2. ... Rd2 3. Qf3+ Kc2 4. Ke4 Kb2 5. Qf7 Kc2 6. Qc4+ Kd1 7. Kf3! Ke1 8. Qb4, and if 8. ... d3 9. Ke3, or if 8. ... Kd1 9. Qb1+ mate.

3. Ke5 d3 4. Qg1+ Kd2+ 5. Kd4 Kc2 6. Qg6 Rd2 7. Qc6+ Kd1 (or 7. ... Kb1 8. Qc3 Rd1 9. Qb3+ Kc1 10. Kc3) **8. Ke3 and wins.**

White to play wins in 14 moves: **1. Qc5 Re2 2. Qa3+ Kc2 3. Kf4 Rd2 4. Ke4 Kd1 5. Qb3+ Ke1 6. Qf3 Rd1 7. Kd5 Rd2 8. Kc5 Rd1 9. Kc4 Rd2 10. Kb3 Re2 11. Qg3+ Kd2 12. Kc4 wins.**

The pawn on the sixth usually draws. This is readily understandable, since White can only win if he has lots of leeway for his queen.

In **No. 1110** (Kling and Horwitz 1851): **White king at d1, queen at f3; Black king at d4, rook at c2, pawn at d3.** White to play, draw. The main variation is **1. Qf4+ Kd5 2. Qe3 Kc4 3. Qe4+ Kc3 4. Qd5 Rd2+ 5. Ke1 Re2+ 6. Kf1 Rc2, =.**

b) Knight-Pawn or Bishop-Pawn

For once, these two obey the same laws!

An unfavorable analogue of No. 1107 is seen in **No. 1111.**

No. 1111, v. Guretzky-Cornitz

White to play. Draw. Also with bishop-pawn. Pawn may be on any rank.

Although the defense is difficult here, Black can always hold his own because White's king cannot cross the bishop file. Berger gives the following continuation to illustrate White's attempts to win: **1. Qa2 Kb6 2. Qa3 Rc6! 3. Kd4 Rc4+4. Kd5 Rc8 5. Qd6+ Ka5 6. Qe6 Rc4 7. Qe5 Kb6 8. Kd6 Rc6+ 9. Kd7 Rc4 10. Qb8+ Ka5, =.**

But if the White king manages to attack the pawn (as a result of a favorable initial position due to prior exchanges) the game is won.

c) Rook-Pawn

The results here are rather peculiar: draw with the pawn on the third, sixth or seventh, but loss on the second, fourth or fifth.

No. 1112 is the win with the pawn on the fourth.

No. 1112, v. Guretzky-Cornitz

White to play wins

1. Qd5 Ka6

If 1. ... Rb5 2. Qd6+ Kb7 3. Kc4 Rb6 4. Qd5+, White wins the pawn, for on 4. ... Ka6 5. Qa8+ mates.

2. Qc6+ Ka7

On 2. ... Rb6 3. Qa8+ wins: 3. ... Kb5 4. Kb3 Ra6 5. Qd5+ Kb6 6. Ka4 Ra7 7. Qd6+ Kb7 8. Kb5 Kc8 9. Qf8+ Kb7 10. Qe7+ Kb8 11. Qd8+ Kb7 12. Qb6+ Ka8 13. Kc6, etc.

3. Kd3 Rb6 4. Qc7+ Ka6 5. Qc8+ Ka7 6. Kc4 Rb7 7. Qd8 Ka6 8. Qa8+ Kb6 9. Kb3 Ra7 (9. ... Kc6+ 10. Ka4) **10. Qb8+ Ka6** (or 10. ... Rb7 11. Qd6+ Kb5 12. Qd3+, and Ka4) **11. Ka4** and wins the pawn, for if **11. ... Rb7 12. Qa8+ Ra7 13. Qc6+** mate.

The win with the pawn on the fifth is achieved in the same manner.

With the pawn on the second Black will likewise soon lose his last soldier. **No. 1113: White king at c5, queen at e5; Black king at a8, rook at b6, pawn at a7.** White to play wins. 1. Qc7 Rb1 2. Qc8+ Rb8 3. Qc6+ Rb7 4. Kd6 a5 5. Qa6+ Kb8 6. Qxa5 wins.

The pawn on the third draws because there are no mate threats (as with the pawn on the second) and because White's queen cannot drive the Black king away (as with the pawn on the fourth).

No. 1114 (v. Guretzky-Cornitz): **White king at c4, queen at a3; Black king at b7, rook at b5, pawn at a6.** White to play. Draw. White might try **1. Qe7+ Kb8 2. Qe8+ Kb7 3. Qd8 Ka7 4. Qc8 Rb7 5. Qc5+ Kb8 6. Qd6+ Ka7 7. Qd4+ Ka8 8. Kc5 Ka7 9. Kc6+ Ka8 10. Qd8+**

If 10. Qf4, Ka7! is the correct reply, but not 10. ... Rb5? 11. Kc7 Rb7+ 12. Kc8 Ka7 13. Qd6 Rb5 14. Qd7+ Ka8 15. Qc7, and wins the rook.

10. ... Rb8 11. Qd5 Rb7, draw

11. ... Ka7? loses after 12. Kc7 Rb5 13. Qd4+ Ka8 14. Qd6 Ka7 15. Kc8 Rb7 16. Qd4+.

The pawn on the sixth draws as usual.

It is essential for Black to keep his king, rook, and pawn close together; any deviation usually costs the game. For example, **No. 1115** (Berger): **White king at g3, queen at a5; Black king at f7, rook at g7, pawn at g4.** White to play wins.

1. Qd5+ Kf6 2. Qc6+ Ke7

If 2. ... Kf5 3. Qc8+ Kg5 4. Qh8 Rg6 5. Qe5+ Kh6 6. Kh4 Kh7 7. Kh5! Rg8 8. Qf5+ Kh8 9. Qf6+ Rg7 10. Kh6 and mate next.

3. Qc5+ Kf7 4. Qc4+ Ke7 5. Qf1! Rg5 6. Qf2 Rg6 7. Qf4 Rg7 8. Qf5 Rg8 9. Qe5+ Kf7 10. Qd5+ Kf8 11. Qe6 Rg7 12. Kh2 g3+ 13. Kg2 Rg8 14. Qf6+ Ke8 15. Kh1 g2+ 16. Kg1 and wins the pawn.

To sum up: With queen vs. rook and pawn, Black must have his rook, king, and pawn close together to have any drawing chances at all. If White gets his king behind the pawn he will always win. When the Black rook prevents the immediate entry of the White king, any pawn on the second rank (except a rook-pawn) draws; rook-pawn, knight-pawn, and bishop-pawn on the third rank draw, but a center pawn loses; knight-pawn and bishop-pawn on the fourth rank draw, all others lose; rook-pawn on the fifth rank loses, knight-pawn and bishop-pawn draw, center pawn may lose or draw depending on whose move it is (No. 1109); and all pawns on the sixth or seventh draw.

3. Queen vs. Rook and Two or More Pawns

Two connected pawns should ordinarily draw; two unconnected or doubled pawns lose except when the position with one of the pawns is drawn.

No. 1116

Draw

No. 1116 is a typical draw. Either pawn alone would lose. Trying to apply the winning method of No. 1107, White gets nowhere because the rook and two pawns mutually defend one another, so Black has an inexhaustible supply of tempo moves.

But if the pawns are weakened, White is able to win. For example, **No. 1117** (Kling and Horwitz 1851): **White king at e3, queen at f4; Black king at f6, rook at e7, pawns at f5, e4.** White to play wins. The solution is **1. Qh4+ Ke6 2. Qg5 Rf7 3. Kf4 Rf6 4. Qg8+ Ke7 5. Ke5!** and White soon captures both pawns. Or here 2. ... Rd7 3. Qg6+ Ke5 4. Qe8+ Kd6 5. Kd4 Re7 6. Qb8+ Kd7 7. Kd5 e3 8. Qb5+ Kc7 9. Qc6+ Kb8 10. Qd6+ Rc7 11. Qe5 and again both pawns fall.

Three or more pawns usually draw, but here too there are many cases where White wins. Of course, the pawns may also win on occasion, just as three connected passed pawns may sometimes be stronger than a lone queen.

4. Queen and Pawns vs. Rook and Pawns

Barring a few unusual or problem positions, the queen will always win because the rook cannot possibly defend everything.

No. 1118, Colle-Becker, Carlsbad 1929

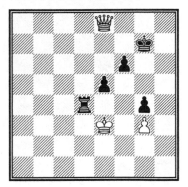

White to play wins

No. 1118 is a difficult example. Black to play loses at once because he is in zugzwang. For instance, 1. ... Rc4 2. Qd7+ Kh6 3. Qe6 Rc3+ 4. Kc4 Rxg3 5. Qxf6+ Kh5 6. Qxe5+ Kh4 7. Kf5 Rf3+ 8. Kg6, etc. So White must only lose a move. The game continued: **1. Ke2! Rd5 2. Qh5 Rd4 3. Kf2! Rb4** (if 3. ... Rd2+ 4. Ke3 Rd4 5. Qe8!) **4. Qe8! Re4** and now **5. Qd7+!** decides: **5. ... Kg6** (5. ... Kh6 6. Qf5 is hopeless) **6. Qd3 f5 7. Qd6+ Kg5 8. Qe6 f4 9. Qg8+ Kf6 10. Qxg4 fxg3+ 11. Qxg3** and wins (No. 1105).

With one pawn apiece, the only type of position that might offer any difficulty is **No. 1119** (Salvioli): **White king at a5, queen at d3, pawn at d5; Black king at b8, rook at b6, pawn at c7.** White to play wins: **1. Qf5 Kb7 2. Qf8 Ra6+ 3. Kb5 Rb6+ 4. Kc5 Ra6 5. Kd4 Rb6 6. Ke5 Ra6 7. Qe8 Rd6 8. Qe6! Rb6** (8. ... Rxe6+ 9. dxe6 Kc8 10. Kf6!) **9. Kf6 Ra6 10. Ke7 Rb6 11. Kd7 Ra6 12. Qxa6+**, etc.

VI. QUEEN VS. MINOR PIECES

A. Queen vs. One Piece

This is a simple win, regardless of the number of pawns that go with the piece. **No. 1120** is the case without pawns:

No. 1120, Berger

White to play wins

By exercising a modicum of caution, White soon forces mate. **1. Kb2 Kd5 2. Kc3 Ne4+ 3. Kd3 Nc5+ 4. Ke3 Ne6 5. Qf5+ Kd6 6. Ke4 Nc5+ 7. Kd4 Ne6+ 8. Kc4 Nc7 9. Qc5+ Kd7 10. Qb6 Ne6 11. Kd5 Nc7+ 12. Ke5 Ne8 13. Qe6+ Kd8 14. Qf7 Nc7 15. Kd6 Nb5+ 16. Kc5,** and Black must already sacrifice his knight to ward off immediate mate.

The win against the bishop is just as simple. **No. 1121** is an exception:

No. 1121, P. Benko 1983

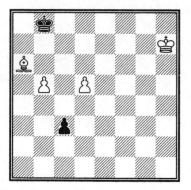

White to play. Draw

White doesn't have time to promote his own pawns. Even so, he can set up a strong defensive position to secure a draw.

1. d6 c2 2. d7 Kc7 3. Bc8! c1=Q 4. b6+ Kd8 5. b7 Qf4

The best attempt to corner the White king.

6. Kg6!

The only escape. Black wins after 6. Kg7? Qd6! 7. Kf7 Qb6 8. Kf8 Qf6+ 9. Kg8 Qg6+ 10. Kf8 Qb6 11. Kf7 Qd6 (by gaining a tempo, Black can get his king into the fight because of zugzwang) 12. Kg7 Ke7 13. Kg8 Qg6+ (or 13. ... Kf6).

6. ... Ke7 7. Kh5! Qg3 8. Kh6 Kf7 9. Kh5! Ke7 10. Kh6 Qh4+ 11. Kg6 Qg4+ 12. Kh6! draw.

It's now clear that Black can't make progress, because **12. ... Kf7 13. d8=N+!** wins the queen. It's even less dangerous for the White king elsewhere. He simply has to avoid the corners and the a-file.

B. Queen vs. Two Pieces

Without pawns this is normally a draw, but there are a number of exceptions where the queen wins, especially with the Black king on the edge of the board.

1. Two Bishops

The bishops must be set up in such a way that the White king cannot attack either of them.

No. 1122, Lolli 1763

White to play. Draw

After **1. Qd7+ Kg8!** (but not 1. ... Bf7?, when 2. Kf5 wins; e.g., 2. ... Bc3 3. Qc7 Ba1 4. Qa7 Bb2 5. Qb6! Ba3 6. Qd4+ Kf8 7. Qh8+ Ke7 8. Qe5+ Kf8 9. Kf6 Be8! 10. Qc7 Bh5 11. Qg7+ Ke8 12. Qh8+, etc.) **2. Qe6+ Kg7 3. Kf4 Bh7 4. Qd7+ Kg6 5. Qe8+ Kg7** White can make no progress; e.g., 6. Kg4 Bg6 7. Qe6 Bh7 8. Qd7+ Kg6 9. Qe8+ Kg7 10. Kh5 Bf5 11. Qc6 Bg6+, etc.

2. Two Knights

This too is a draw, because the knights can keep the White king out. For example, **No. 1123** (Handbuch): **White king at g3, queen at e2; Black king at f8, knights at f6, g6.** White to play. Draw. A plausible try is **1. Qa6 Kg7 2. Kf3,** when Nh7? is wrong. 3. Kg4? (3. Qb7+ wins) 3. ... Nhf8? (This kind of defensive setup with the knight is usually no good. 3. ... Ne7! draws) The right play is **2. ... Kf7 3. Qb7+ Ke6! 4. Qb3+ Ke7 5. Ke3 Nf8 6. Kd4 Ne6+ 7. Ke5 Nd7+ 8. Kd5 Nf6+,** etc., draw.

3. Bishop and Knight

This is the worst case for the defender. The queen wins most of the time because the pieces cannot be made to cooperate.

No. 1124, Berger

Black to play, White wins

The main variation is **1. ... Kg5** (there is nothing better, e.g., 1. ... Ne6 2. Kd5! and wins a piece) **2. Kd5** (2. Qg3+ is also good) **2. ... Bf6 3. Qg3+ Kf5 4. Qg2 Bg5! 5. Qc2+ Kf6 6. Qf2+ Kg6 7. Ke5 Bd8 8. Qg2+ Kf7 9. Qd5+ Ke7 10. Qb7+ Kf8 11. Kd6 Bf6 12. Kd7 Kf7 13. Qe4 Kf8 14. Qg6! Bh4 15. Qd6+ Kf7 16. Qd5+ Kg6** (16. ... Kf8 17. Qc5+ and 18. Qc4+) **17. Qe4+ Kh5 18. Qh7+** and wins.

No. 1125 is the typical drawn position: **White king at e8, queen at h5; Black king at g8, bishop at g7, knight at e5.** White to play. Draw. The White king cannot reach any effective square; e.g., **1. Ke7 Bh8 2. Ke6 Bg7 3. Kf5 Bh8 4. Kg5 Bg7 5. Qe8+ Kh7 6. Kh5 Bh8 7. Qe7+ Bg7 8. Qc7 Kg8,** etc.

With pawns the queen usually wins because the pieces are unable to defend everything.

C. Queen vs. Three Pieces

Without pawns this is drawn, but there are a few positions where the pieces win. For example, **No. 1126** (Berger): **White king at h2, queen at g2; Black king at d6, bishops at c8, c7, knight at h3.** Black to play wins. **1. ... Kc5+ 2. Kh1 Bf5!! 3. Qf3** (White has no checks and cannot pin the bishop) **3. ... Be4! 4. Qxe4 Nf2+,** etc.

With pawns the two forces are roughly equivalent. However, with no other material, queen and pawn vs. three pieces is drawn, but three pieces and pawn win vs. queen.

D. Queen vs. Four Pieces

Here the pieces always win: the queen is unable to prevent mate. The help-lessness of the queen is seen in **No. 1127**.

No. 1127, Kling and Horwitz 1851

White to play wins

It makes no difference whose move it is: Black cannot improve his position.

The given solution is **1. Bc5** (but 1. Bc4 is faster) **Kh7 2. Nd7 Qa1+ 3. Bd4 Qa6+ 4. Be6 Qa8 5. Kf7! Qg8+ 6. Ke7 Qa8** (or any other square) **7. Nf8+ Qxf8+ 8. Kxf8**, etc.

E. Queen and Rook v. Queen and Rook

In a fight between heavy pieces, the one who wins is usually the one who starts the attack, especially in open positions.

No. 1128, P. Benko 1999

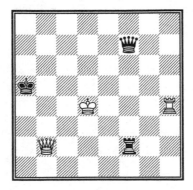

White to play wins

1. Qa1+! (the only good check) **1. ... Kb5** (if 1. ... Ra2 or Qa2 2. Qc3+ Kb6 3. Rh6+ wins because the Black rook cannot oppose) **2. Qb1+ Ka5**, or:

a) **2. ... Ka6 3. Rh6+ Rf6 4. Qf1+!** wins;

b) **2. ... Kc6 3. Qe4+ Kb6 4. Rh6+ Rf6 5. Qf5** wins.

3. Qe1+ Kb6 (if 3. ... Kb5 4. Qe5+ Kb4 5. Kd3+ wins) **4. Rh6+ Rf6 5. Qf2!** wins because if **5. ... Qd7+ 6. Kc4+** wins the helpless rook.

There can be exciting finishes even in actual play, like **No. 1129** (Kislev-Piskov, Moscow 1987): **White king at g5, queen at f6, rook at f4, pawn at g3; Black king at h7, queen at c8, rook at h2, pawns at a7, h5.** Black to play wins. **1. ... Qg8+ 2. Kf5 Re2!** (defends and attacks, with the threat Qd5+) **3. Qd6 Qf7+ 4. Kg5 Qg7+ 5. Kxh5** (if 5. Kf5 Re5+! 6. Qxe5 Qg6+ mate) **5. ... Rh2+ 6. Rh4 Rd2! 7. Qe6 Rd5+ 8. Qxd5 Qg6+** mate.

The royal personage himself seldom conducts the battle, forgetting about the danger. An exception is **No. 1130** (P. Benko 2000): **White king at e5, queen at e1, rook at h5, pawn at d5; Black king at g7, queen at d3, rook at a7, pawns at c6, g4.** White to play wins. **1. Rg5+ Kf8** (if 1. ... Kh8 2. Qh1+ Rh7 3. Qa1! Rg7 4. Rh5+ Kg8 5. Qe8+ Kf7 6. Rf5+, etc., wins) **2. Qb4+** (a wrong check is 2. Qf2+ Rf7 3. Qc5+ Re7+ 4. Kf6 Qh7, and Black is saved) **2. ... Re7+ 3. Kf6** (now if 3. ... Qh7 4. Rg8+! Kxg8 5. Qb8+ mates) **3. ... Qe4 4. Rh5!** (the queen trade is only good for a draw, but this mate threat forces Black's hand) **4. ... Qf3+ 5. Rf5 Qe4!? 6. Qb8+ Re8 7. Qc7 Re7** (the point is that if 7. ... Qe7+ 8. Kg6+ Kg8 9. Re5!! wins) **8. Qc8+ Re8 9. Kg6+ Kg8 10. Qc7! Re7** (again if 10. ... Qe7 11. Re5!! wins) **11. Qd8+ Re8 12. Qh4! Qe7** (if 12. ... Re7 13. Qf6 wins) **13. Rf8+!!!** (the final shot; Black can take the rook in three different ways, but he gets mated).

F. Queen and Piece vs. Two Rooks

This is a win for the queen and piece, but it can take some time. **No. 1131** (A. Zaremba-A. Pixton, Dallas 2002) is a rare example from actual play: **White king at a3, rooks at e2, e8; Black king at d5, queen at b1, bishop at f6.** Black to play. **1. ... Bd4 2. Rd8+ Kc4 3. Rc2+!? Kd3!** (3. ... Qxc2 4. Rc8+ Bc5+ 5. Rxc5 Kxc5 stalemate) **4. Rdc8** (4. Rcc8!?) **4. ... Qb5 5. R2c6 Bb2+ 6. Ka2 Qb4 7. Ra8 Bc3 8. Rd8+ Kc2** wins.

Chapter IX

CONCLUSION
AND SUMMARY

At the close of a book of this kind one is inevitably reminded of the story of the player who was asked by a friend how he had managed to win a position that was a "book" draw. "What good is the book," he replied, "if you don't know it and your opponent doesn't play it?"

It is of course impossible for anybody to know by heart even a small part of what is contained in this book. But the exact amount of specific knowledge is relatively unimportant; what counts is how well the principles are grasped. For this reason I have throughout tried to set up typical positions (for these are merely shorthand for general principles) and have always preferred helpful rules to mathematical exactitude. Anyone who indulges in a little practice at ordinary endings and who relies on the rules set forth will soon find that the individual positions will fall into well-recognized patterns and that a large number of the basic diagramed endings will steadily become more familiar.

There are three points that are so fundamental that they must always be borne in mind:

1. Without pawns one must be at least a rook ahead to be able to mate. The only exceptions to this, which hold in all cases, are that the double exchange wins, that two bishops defeat a knight, that a queen cannot defend successfully against four minor pieces, and that rook and bishop win against two knights.

2. With an advantage of two or more extra pawns the win is routine. By this we mean that a straightforward advance of the pawns will net considerable material gain, usually at least a piece. With a piece to the good, one can then capture more pawns, then more pieces, and finally mate.

3. The theory of the ending proper is concerned largely with the conversion of an advantage of one pawn into a win. *The basic principle is that one pawn wins only because it can be used to capture more material.* Straightforward advance will usually not do the trick (as it will with two extra pawns). The main devices to be used in the winning process are forcing an entry with the king, keeping the opponent busy on both sides (outside passed pawn), and simplification.

Chapter X

TWENTY RULES
FOR THE ENDGAME

Most of the following rules are mentioned in the body of the work. We gather them here to impress upon you the necessity of proceeding according to general principles rather than trial and error. This new list is a composite of Reuben Fine's original 15 rules (1941) and Pal Benko's additions and reordering. F: Fine; B: Benko.

1. Start thinking about the endgame in the middlegame. (B)
2. Somebody usually gets the better deal in every exchange. (B)
3. The king is a strong piece: Use it! (F)
4. If you are one or two pawns ahead, exchange pieces but not pawns. (F)
5. If you are one or two pawns behind, exchange pawns but not pieces. (F)
6. If you have an advantage, do not leave all the pawns on one side. (F)
7. A distant passed pawn is half the victory. (B)
8. Passed pawns should be advanced as rapidly as possible. (F)
9. Doubled, isolated, and blockaded pawns are weak: Avoid them! (F)
10. The easiest endings to win are pure pawn endings. (F)
11. Passed pawns should be blockaded by the king, the only piece that is not harmed by watching a pawn is the knight. (F)
12. Two bishops vs. bishop and knight constitute a tangible advantage. (F)
13. Bishops are better than knights in all except blocked pawn positions. (F)
14. Do not place your pawns on the color of your bishop. (F)
15. The easiest endings to draw are those with bishops of opposite colors. (F)
16. Rooks belong behind passed pawns. (F)
17. A rook on the seventh rank is sufficient compensation for a pawn. (F)
18. Not all rook endings are drawn! (B)
19. Perpetual check looms in all queen endings. (B)
20. Every move in the endgame is of the utmost importance because you are closer to the moment of truth. (B)

Great Titles from the McKay Chess Library

Title Information	Level of Play *
The Art of Defense in Chess by Andrew Soltis 0-679-14108-1 $15.95/C$23.95	I
The Art of Positional Play by Samuel Reshevsky 0-8129-3475-X $15.95/C$23.95	I–A
Basic Chess Endings by Reuben Fine 0-8129-3493-8 $24.95/C$37.95	All levels
Best Lessons of a Chess Coach by Sunil Weeramantry & Ed Eusebi 0-8129-2265-4 $16.95/C$24.95	B–I
Chess for Juniors by Robert M. Snyder 0-8129-1867-3 $14.95/C$22.95	B
Chess Fundamentals by J. R. Capablanca 0-679 14004-2 $14.95/C$22.95	B–I
Chess Openings the Easy Way by Nick de Firmian 0-8129-3498-9 $15.95/$23.95	B–I
How to Play Good Opening Moves by Edmar Mednis 0-8129-3474-1 $12.95/C$19.95	B–I
The Ideas Behind the Chess Openings by Reuben Fine 0-8129-1756-1 $13.95/C$21.00	B–I
The Inner Game of Chess by Andrew Soltis 0-8129-2291-3 $16.95/C$24.95	I–A
Judgment and Planning in Chess by Max Euwe 0-679-14325-4 $12.95/C$19.95	I–A
The Middlegame in Chess by Reuben Fine 0-8129-3484-9 $18.95/C$28.95	I
Modern Chess Openings, 14th ed. by Nick de Firmian 0-8129-3084-3 $29.95/C$44.95	I–A
Pawn Structure Chess by Andrew Soltis 0-8129-2529-7 $16.95/C$24.95	I–A
U.S. Chess Federation's Official Rules of Chess, 5th ed. 0-8129-3559-4 $18.95/C$28.95	All levels

* Key to levels of play: (B)=Beginner; (I)=Intermediate; (A)=Advanced

Available at your local bookseller.
To order by phone, call 1-800-733-3000.